THE
ANGLO-SAXON
CHRONICLE

*Sword-hilts from the
City of London and
Fiskerton, Lincolnshire*

THE
ANGLO-SAXON
CHRONICLE

Translated and edited by
M. J. SWANTON
University of Exeter

ROUTLEDGE

NEW YORK

Published in the United States of America in 1998 by
Routledge
29 West 35th Street
New York, NY 10001

Originally published in Great Britian in 1996 by J.M. Dent,
a division of The Orion Publishing Group,
Orion House, 5 Upper St. Martin's Lane,
London WC2H 9EA

Typeset by Deltatype Ltd., Ellesmere Port, Cheshire, Great Britian.
Printed in the United States of America on acid-free paper.

10 9 8 7 6 5 4 3 2 1

Library of Congress Cataloging-in-Publication Data

Anglo-Saxon chronicle.   English.
    The anglo-Saxon chronicle / translated and edited by M.J. Swanton.
        p.   cm.
    Includes bibliographical references and index.
    ISBN 0-415-92129-5 (alk.paper)
    1. Great Britain—History—Anglo-Saxon period, 449–1066.   2. Great
Britain—History—Norman period, 1066–1154.   3. Civilization, Medieval—
Sources. 4. Manuscripts, Medieval—England.   I. Swanton, Michael James.
DA150.A61998
942.01—dc21   98–7131
                                                                      CIP

CONTENTS

To my family and friends I am perpetually indebted. If this edition needs a dedication then it should be to the saints and demons of the word processor. It seems to be a truism of our times that while to err may be human, to really louse things up takes a computer.

LIST OF ILLUSTRATIONS

PREFACE

This book's immediate predecessor, the edition and translation of the late Professor Garmonsway published by J. M. Dent in Everyman's Library in 1953, served several generations of historians and students of literature not yet familiar with the original language but needing an entrée to this most remarkable of early texts. The last few decades have witnessed an explosion of academic interest in, books and articles published about, this particular period. The development of computer-retrievable text allows far closer, more systematic treatment than previously possible. And the steady advance of scientific archaeology, now increasingly applied to early medieval levels, massively supplements, even questions, the authority of documentary records. The expectations of the reader have changed. At the same time, the kinds of general knowledge that can be expected of the reader are different. In the large audience a book such as this must address, it cannot be assumed that, for example, the names and significance of former religious festivals, or even an intimate knowledge of British geography, can be taken for granted. As with the main text, so in annotation, it is assumed that the reader will have only limited acquaintance with ancient texts. Very little information can be conveyed in the space available. I have concentrated on historical, social and cultural details, eschewing most philological problems, assuming that those wishing to pursue such matters will prefer to follow the argument in the now very adequate editions of original texts.

Very many scholars, past and present, have worked or are working on The Anglo-Saxon Chronicle, and my indebtedness to these – not least to Norman Garmonsway – will appear on every page, and the sole acknowledgement the bibliography. Any work of scholarship is necessarily provisional. Those with specific insights will be able to help further, now or in the future, and their comments, directed to the author, will be appreciated. In the meantime, in a period of continuing pressures on our institutions, I can only plead with King Alfred:

> þæt he for hine gebidde, and him ne wite gif he hit rihtlicor
> ongite þonne he mihte, forþæmðe ælc mon sceal be his andgites
> mæðe and be his æmettan sprecan ðæt he sprecþ and don þæt þæt
> he deþ.

M. J. SWANTON

INTRODUCTION

To chart the passage of time was particularly important for the literate, that is to say, the church-educated, Anglo-Saxon, for whom the year was marked not only by the natural rhythm of the agricultural seasons: winter, seed-time and harvest, but by the regular sequence of religious festivals. The complicated business of determining the date of Easter (the most important festival in the Christian year, but a movable feast related to the lunar cycle) was exceedingly important; and disagreement as to the correct method of calculation might result in schism or even accusations of heresy.[1] And on the larger scale, the passage of year on year was no less important as the Millennium approached and the Second Coming of Christ was confidently expected.

Looking backwards, it might be convenient to remember that a particular event occurred during a certain year. In contemporary terms, 'The year 1988' might mean very little in itself, but swims into historical focus and perspective if labelled 'The year of the Lockerbie disaster' or 'The Year when Salman Rushdie published *The Satanic Verses*', or 'The year when Professor X died and Professor Y was appointed to run the Department'. This last would only be of significance to the institution concerned; but if the archive of another institution were lost or destroyed in the vicissitudes of time, and a copy of these 'annals' was made to make good the loss, such a detail, now strictly irrelevant, might well survive as a fossil embedded in an otherwise standard document.

Looking forward, booklets could be drawn up in the form of a calendar with a line or two assigned to each forthcoming year, to be filled with notes of significant events – or what might be considered significant events to the institution or locality in which the document was maintained. The illustration, pp. xii–xiii, shows part of a rare survival of a diagnostic form of document: a set of Easter tables drawn

---

[1] Cf. annals 528, 627, 716.

Part of an eleventh-century Easter Table with Annals, from British Library MS Cotton Caligula Axv, ff. 134ᵛ-135ʳ, courtesy of the British Library

Text

MLVIII	Her Benedictus papa sende Stigand þone pallium
MLXI	Her forðferde Godwine biscop and Wulfric abbod.
MLXVI	Her forðferde Edward kyng. and her com Wilhelm.
MLXVII	Her on þison geare barn Cristes cyrce.
MLXX	On þison geare com Landfranc abbod, and hine man halgode to bisceope to Cristes cyrcian.

ues pasche	Luna	Ebd	Dies			

Translation

1058   Here Pope benedict sent Stigand the pallium.

1061   Here Bishop Godwine and Abbot Wulfric passed away.

1066   Here King Edward passed away and here William came.

1067   Here in this year Christ Church burned.

1070   In this year Abbot Lanfranc came, and was consecrated as [arch]bishop for Christ Church [Canterbury].

up at Canterbury Cathedral to cover the years 988–1193.[2]

Beginning on the left with the year-number, most of the columns in the Easter-table are taken up with the complex system of lunar epacts, concurrents, dominical letters and the like,[3] but a substantial right-hand margin allowed the insertion of notes of significant events to label the years. Most of these labels or 'annals' are introduced by the word 'Here', i.e. 'at this point', reflecting the physical as much as the chronological placement of the event. Others are more explicit: 'Here, in this year', or at a later stage merely 'In this year'. It will be seen that the fact of the Norman Conquest was at first ignored until a later hand decided to add: '. . . and here William came'. In this type of document it is the year rather than the event which is of primary significance; it is not the event which needs putting in its year – but rather the year which needs a label, which might have incidental temporal significance. The fact that occasionally chroniclers refer to an event taking place on, e.g. a Tuesday or the night of a full moon, suggests that such tables were commonly to hand.

Chronicle manuscripts were books laid out specially and solely for annals. Any page layout which plotted the passage of year on year impelled the use of the concept Anno Domini (The Year of the Lord), rather than the more archaic form of suggestion that an event took place 'in King X's time',[4] or perhaps more precisely 'in the fourth year of X's reign',[5] which gave a very local, even trivializing effect, in view of the large number of kings, or those given or claiming that title in early England. Bede opens his account of the Synod of Hatfield by citing the regnal years of each of four Anglo-Saxon kings reigning at the time.[6] Among the very oldest surviving vernacular texts is an eighth-century list of Northumbrian kings which merely gives their names followed by the number of years they reigned.[7] There is constant reference throughout the Chronicle to the number of years any given king reigned in all.[8]

---

[2] British Library MS Cotton Caligula Axv, ff. 132ᵛ–39; N. R. Ker, *Catalogue of Manuscripts containing Anglo-Saxon*, 2nd edn (Oxford, 1990), p. 175. The text (to 1202) is printed by F. Liebermann, *Ungedruckte anglo-normannische Geschichtsquellen* (Strassburg, 1879), pp. 1–8.   [3] For a brief introduction to the system, see C. R. Cheney, ed., *Handbook of Dates for Students of English History*, revd edn (London, 1981), pp. 7–9, and further F. P. Pickering, *The Calendar Pages of Medieval Service Books* (Reading, 1980).   [4] Cf. annals 449, 565, 616, 675E, 787, 869   [5] Cf. annals 47, 552 F, 752, 762 E; the regnal years of Burhred remain embedded *s.a.* 874.   [6] *Historia Ecclesiastica*, IV, 17.   [7] H. Sweet, ed., *The Oldest English Texts*, Early English Text Society, Original Series LXXXIII (London, 1885), p. 148.   [8] It forms a large concern in the relatively brief *Annals of Lindisfarne*, ed. G. H. Pertz, *Monumenta Germaniae Historica, Scriptores* XIX (Hannover, 1866), pp. 503–7.

But any year-on-year system poses the question: at which point did one year succeed another? The eleventh-century homilist Ælfric says that 1 January, The Feast of the Circumcision, was frequently regarded as the beginning of the year; he can find no theological reason for this, but was aware that this was in accordance with Roman civil custom.[9] This it typically the starting point of contemporary calendars.[10] On the other hand the Old English Martyrology and the Menology (or Metrical Calendar),[11] both begin with 25 December, Christmas – the birth of Christ, and thus arguably the beginning of the Christian era. This coincided with the natural cycle's turning-point at mid-winter; the term 'mid-winter' was long retained, and apparently interchangeable with 'Christmas' or 'The Nativity' throughout the Chronicle.[12] Bede says that the English custom of beginning the year at this point was falling into disuse in his day,[13] but through much of the Chronicle it seems still to be the case that the year begins at Christmas. This is clear for example s.a. 1091 (pp. 225–7) when the annal begins with the king's Christmas Court, then goes on to his expedition to Normandy in February, and concludes with Robert and Edgar leaving the Isle of Wight two days before the next Christmas. Some entries during the eleventh century appear to be based on a year beginning with the 25 March (the Annuciation, which celebrated the archangel Gabriel's announcement to the Virgin Mary that she was pregnant with the Christ, and thus the beginning of the incarnation, Luke, i:26–38). In the Abingdon manuscript [C], 1044 ends with the marriage of Edward the Confessor to Edith on 23 January, while the death of Bishop Beorhtwald on 22 April following is assigned to 1045 (p. 164).[14] At other times annalists seem to mark the of the year in September, employing a system deriving from the Roman Indiction – a cycle of tax assessment made on 1 September every fifteenth year.[15] The indiction is explicitly referred to at the opening of the annal for 1090 (p. 225); and though not explicitly mentioned, indictional dating seems to have been used in several ninth-century annals which begin with the viking armies taking up winter-quarters,

[9] The Homilies of the Anglo-Saxon Church, ed. B. Thorpe (London, 1844–6), I, pp. 98–9. [10] F. Wormald, English Kalendars before AD 1100, Henry Bradshaw Society LXXII (London, 1934). [11] The Old English Martyrology, ed. G. Herzfeld, Early English Text Society, Original Series CXVI (1990); Swanton, Anglo-Saxon Prose, p. 70; and the Menology, ed. E. v. K. Dobbie, The Anglo-Saxon Minor Poems, p. lx et sequ, 49. [12] For example when referring to the date of the king's court, traditionally held at Easter, Whitsun and Christmas, cf. annals 1086, 1099, 1114 E H (pp. 219, 234, 244); see generally Biddle, 'Seasonal festivals and residence', pp. 51–72. [13] De Temporum Ratione, PL, XC, 356. [14] For further examples see R. L. Poole, 'The beginning of the year in the Anglo-Saxon Chronicles', English Historical Review XVI (1901), 719–21. [15] Cf. Bede De Temporum Ratione, PL, XC, 496, although, due

presumably in late autumn, before mentioning further encounters which must have taken place some time within the twelve months thereafter.[16] In the absence of any uniform system, chronological discrepancies between and even within manuscript recensions were inevitable. Clearly, events ascribed to a year beginning either in September or in March might well be dated a year too early or a year too late by modern reckoning beginning 1 January.[17] For the purposes of this edition, it seemed best to retain the scribal manuscript dating – although adjusted dates are provided in square brackets where helpful, and possible. Occasionally one year-number was omitted and that of the following year inserted instead, so that the chronology is dislocated. For example, in the Worcester manuscript [D] the figure 1044 was left out, with the result that annals numbered from 1045 to 1052 are a year in advance, and only brought into line when, with another error, the figure 1052 was duplicated (pp. 165, 176). Or the reverse might happen. The repetition of the year-number 1085 put the chronology a year in arrears up to 1089, when the correct date is restored by the scribe omitting the number 1088 altogether (pp. 216, 225). The disjunction is explicit *s.a.* 1086 [*recte* 1087], where the annalist first wrote *Millesimo lxxxvi* then went on to spell out in words: 'one thousand and eighty-seven years (p. 217). Moreover, with hand-written Roman numerals it was all too easy to add or omit a digit[18] or to mistake the two strokes of a *v* for *ii*.[19]

Those who initially laid out a manuscript with a line for each annal did not anticipate the need to provide for more than the simple entry of an event or two in simple formulaic sentences. The annalist, *strictu sensu*, is not concerned with historical perspective, and will rarely relate one event to another[20] – except that a passing comet might be believed to have some relationship with human affairs, whether prognostic or causal.[21] Of course, what may seem to us a bald dry

to a misreading of Ambrose, he thought it began on 24 September, cf. C. W. Jones, *Saints' Lives and Chronicles in Early England* (Ithaca, NY, 1947), pp. 40–41.   [16] e.g. annals 868, 870, 872, 873, 874, 875; cf. M. L. R. Beaven, 'The beginning of the year in the Alfredian Chronicle (866–87)', *English Historical Review* XXXIII (1918), 328–42; R. Vaughan, 'The chronology of the Parker Chronicle, 890–970', *English Historical Review* LXIX (1954), 64–6; and cf. W. Levison, *England and the Continent in the Eighth Century* (Oxford, 1946), p. 265ff., and references there cited.   [17] As late as 1200, the Canterbury chronicler Gervase complains that there were different practices, and consequently errors among historians as to when to begin the year, *Historical Works*, ed. W. Stubbs, Rolls Series LXXIII (London, 1879–80), I, pp. 88–9.   [18] Cf. p. 16, note 5; p. 51, note 20.   [19] Cf. p. 46, note 2; p. 51, note 19.   [20] See also Gervase of Canterbury, op. cit., I, pp. 87–8.   [21] Cf. annal 975 (p. 121, note 7); and compare annal 729 version A with E; and most famously annal 1066

statement – the name of a battle-place or location of a synod, could form the stimulus for a thousand particulars, whether remembered or read. But occasionally, and increasingly with time, those responsible for composing an entry felt that what they had to say was more important than the constraints of the space allocated by the original layout of lines, and went on to provide a whole narrative sequence more in the fashion of modern journalism. Notable is the remarkable story of the *coup d'état* at Merton (*s.a.* 755), where the scribe has incorporated what appears to be saga material complete with exchanges in direct speech;[22] this seems undoubtedly to derive from oral, perhaps poetic, transmission. The mere mention of the names Cynewulf and Cyneheard had triggered an anachronistic entry which properly belonged thirty-one years on, *s.a.* 784 (q.v.). In a handful of instances the annals take the form of genuine, probably ready-made, poems like The Battle of Brunanburh (*s.a.* 937). Other entries display poetic or highly rhetorical leanings. In two of these (*s.a.a.* 959, 975) it is possible that we can recognise the hand of a known author, the homilist Archbishop Wulfstan – or someone writing in his style.[23]

Otherwise the annalists are wholly anonymous, and usually impersonal, though in 1066 a Worcester scribe lets slip a note of enthusiasm in referring to Harold 'our king' (p. 197). The writer's attitude is rarely declared. But in speaking of the Domesday survey, the chronicler at Peterborough cannot disguise his shock at the thoroughness of a king prepared to count his assets down to the very last pig, the last yard of land (p. 216). On another page the customary laconic dryness of the annalist gives way to what may be an eye-witness account of the massacre of the monks at Glastonbury (pp. 214–15). The best of the entries are far from negligible as literature. Through the course of the Chronicle from the ninth to the twelfth century we can witness the development of a distinctive prose genre, evolving from brief marginal annotations of plain fact to vivid thumb-nail sketches of dramatic events.[24] From the 890s onwards entries are fuller, syntactically more complex, and occasionally linked one with another.[25] The style is increasingly personal and colloquial – accusa-

(p. 194, note 3). [22] C. L. Wrenn, 'A saga of the Anglo-Saxons,' *History* XXV (1940), 208–15; F. P. Magoun, 'Cynewulf, Cyneheard, and Osric', *Anglia* LVII (1933), 361–76. [23] K. Jost, 'Wulfstan und die angelsächsische Chronik', *Anglia* LXVII (1923), 105–23. [24] See generally C. Clark, 'The narrative mode of The Anglo-Saxon Chronicle before the Conquest', in *England before the Conquest: Studies presented to Dorothy Whitelock*, ed. P. Clemoes and K. Hughes (Cambridge, 1971), pp. 215–35. [25] See the backward references in annals 893 A (892 E) – 897 (pp. 84–90).

tions are 'thrown at' a traitor, whereupon words are said to 'shoot out' of him against his will (pp. 185–6), or a coward's vomiting is dismissed as pretence (p. 135). There is both rhetoric and characterisation – witness the exhortatory obituary of William in 1086 (pp. 218–21). More and more we see annalists taking sides, in describing events of which they felt part, the author of one version [E] revealing pro-Godwine and that of another [D] anti-Godwine sentiments, as Anglo-Danish and pro-Norman parties confronted each other in the England of the Confessor.[26] The final annals, describing the atrocities committed by the barons during the Anarchy (pp. 263–5), are graphic indeed.

It is probable that the Chronicle, as we know it, had its origins towards the end of the ninth century: a reflection of both the 'revival of learning' and revival of English national awareness during the reign of King Alfred.[27] The twelfth-century Anglo-Norman chronicler Gaimar said that Alfred had 'caused a book to be written in English about events and about laws and about battles in the land and about kings who made war'.[28] In fact the Chronicle may not have been directly inspired by the king himself, but by some other patron of letters; and probably in the south-west,[29] since it seems particularly knowledgeable about events in Dorset and Somerset, and may have been composed by or for men familiar with the West Country.[30] It draws on local information in describing the circumstances leading up to the murder of the reeve of Dorchester in 787 (pp. 54–5), and knows the names of places in the Somerset swamps where Alfred sheltered before defeating the Danish invaders in 878 (pp. 76–7).

But this archetype was a composite document, drawing on several sources for its information. Records of world history from the beginning of the Christian era to the year 110 probably came from one of the small encyclopaedic volumes that were in circulation, perhaps similar to that Roman 'cosmography' which Ceolfrid, abbot of Jarrow, gave to the scholarly King Aldfrith in exchange for a parcel of river-side land.[31] Other early annals were transferred from the

---

[26] Compare for example the differing accounts of the year 1052; and see Clark, op. cit., pp. 231–3.   [27] Cf. D. Whitelock, 'The prose of Alfred's reign', in *Continuations and Beginnings*, ed. E. G. Stanley (London, 1966), pp. 96–7.   [28] *L'Estoire des Engleis*, ed. A. Bell (Oxford, 1960), ll . 3445–8.   [29] Though perhaps not far from the Mercian border, cf. C. Sprockel, *The Language of the Parker Chronicle* (The Hague, 1965), I, p. xix.   [30] F. M. Stenton, 'The south-western element in the Old English Chronicle', *Essays in Medieval History presented to Thomas Frederick Tout* (Manchester, 1925), pp. 15–24 (reprinted in *Preparatory to Anglo-Saxon England* (Oxford, 1970), pp. 106–15.   [31] Bede, *Vita Sanctorum Abbatum*, PL, XCIV, 725.

chronological summary appended by Bede to his *Ecclesiastical History*.[32] Then there seem to have been a set of annals extending Bede's work into the early ninth century; lists of Northumbrian and Mercian kings together with their genealogies (cf. annals 547, 560, 626 etc.); a list of the bishops of Wessex down to 754; and a set of West Saxon annals extending from the invasions to the middle of the eighth century. It is not impossible that some entries may have incorporated oral traditions first committed to writing in the seventh century, passed on by word of mouth from men who in their youth received the information from old men who had been alive in the time of Cerdic.[33] Perhaps quasi-poetic mnemonic formulae lie behind some entries (e.g. 473, 584).[34] Some seventh-century annals have the appearance of a contemporary record – the battle Cenwalh fought at Posent's stronghold in 661 is said very precisely to have been fought 'at Easter'; and the annalist has bothered to record a 'great mortality of birds' *s.a.* 671. Later material continues to be uneven in character and is presumably drawn from diverse sources, including a Continental source for the years 880–90. From 823 to 840 the run of annals is almost consecutive; possibly the original archetype ended with this sequence; or it may have been extended as far as the annal for 855, where the substantial genealogical coda tracing the house of Alfred back to Adam would have formed an impressive and appropriate conclusion.

This compilation was obviously sufficiently authoritative at the time to be used by 'independent' historians such as the Welshman Asser, who drew on it for his Latin Life of King Alfred,[35] and Ealdorman Æthelweard who, towards the end of the tenth century deployed a substantial amount of material which clearly came from an early version of the archetype – probably part of the stem from which [A] derived.[36] At Abingdon in the first half of the twelfth century, (1120–40) the author of a Latin chronicle we now call the Annals of St Neots, apparently had access to a relatively pristine version, now lost,

---

[32] Compare for example annals 47, 167, 189, 409, 540 with *HE* V, 24.   [33] Cf. the later story about the death of the East Anglian king Edmund, which Ælfric says was passed on by word of mouth from old to young from 870 to the 980s (Swanton, *Prose*, p. 158), told to the young Dunstan by the king's former sword-bearer, now an old man, and passed on by Dunstan to the writer Abbo when Dunstan was in his 70s.   [34] Cf. H. Sweet, 'Some of the sources of the Anglo-Saxon Chronicle', *Englishche Studien* II (1879) 310–12. [35] Ed. W. H. Stevenson, revd edn. D. Whitelock (Oxford, 1959); transl. S. Keynes and M. Lapidge (Harmondsworth, 1983). Asser seems to have drawn on a supplemented or second edition which brought the text as far as 887.   [36] *The Chronicle of Æthelweard*, ed. A. Campbell (London, 1962). For the relationship

but which seems to have extended at least to AD 912.[37] At about the same time this compilation was being made, other historians were consulting various more developed versions of the Chronicle: 'Floren-ce' of Worcester a West Midland version, and Henry of Huntingdon a version similar to that kept at Peterborough, while the Peterborough historian Hugh Candidus was certainly familiar with that in his own institution.[38]

It is significant that so fundamental a cultural document of English history should have been composed in English. Alfred may not have been exaggerating when he lamented the decay of Latin scholarship in his day.[39] That English prose was considered of sufficient status to be regarded as an appropriate medium for documentary record at this time is not surprising;[40] but this is the first continuous national history of any western people in their own language; at this time no other European nation apparently felt confident enough in its own language to record its own history.

It was Anglo-Saxon practice to deposit duplicate copies of impor-tant documents with a variety of repositories for greater security, as Alfred did with his will.[41] The king needed archives in the localities as well as centrally, and cathedrals and monasteries which were under royal patronage would expect to receive copies of important works.[42] As with Alfred's translation of the *Cura Pastoralis*, copies of this first Chronicle were no doubt circulated to various regional institutions and centres of learning,[43] to be maintained and kept up to date, either from official bulletins issued from the West Saxon court, or with matters of more local interest. The given record, from whatever source

between Æthelweard and [A], see L. Whitbread, 'Æthelweard and the Anglo-Saxon Chronicle', 577–89, and more recently J. Bately, ed., *The Anglo-Saxon Chronicle: A Collaborative Edition*, 3, MS A (Cambridge, 1986), pp. lxxix-lxxxviii.   [37] *The Anglo-Saxon Chronicle: A Collaborative Edition*, 17, *The Annals of St Neots*, ed. D. Dumville and M. Lapidge (Cambridge, 1984). The precise relationship of the Annals of St Neots to the common stock of the Chronicle is difficult to establish because of the highly selective nature of the St Neots compilation, but the compiler may have had access to a copy of a northern recension of the Chronicle or a Latin derivative of that recension (pp. xxxi-xxxix, lxiv-lxv).   [38] Florence, *Chronicon ex Chronicis*, ed. B. Thorpe (London, 1848–9), transl. J. Stevenson, *The Church Historians of England* (London, 1853–68), II; cf. R. R. Darlington and P. McGurk, 'The Chronicon ex Chronicis and its uses of sources for English history before 1066', 185–96. Henry, Archdeacon of Huntingdon, *History of the English*, ed. T. Arnold, Rolls Series LXXIV (London, 1879). Hugh Candidus, *The Chronicle of a Monk of Peterborough*, ed. W. T. Mellows (Oxford, 1949).   [39] *King Alfred's West-Saxon Version of Gregory's Cura Pastoralis*, ed. H. Sweet, Early English Text Society, Original Series XLV, L (1871), pp. 2–9; Swanton, *Prose*, pp. 60–62.   [40] Swanton, *Prose*, pp. x-xxiv.   [41] Swanton, *Prose*, pp. 50–51.   [42] M. T. Clanchy, *From Memory to Written Record: England 1066–1307*, 2nd edn (Oxford, 1993), *passim*.   [43] Op. cit. in note 38.

or sources received, was then supplemented and maintained, either systematically year on year, or sometimes, as it seems from the evidence of handwriting, at intervals in sporadic bursts of activity.

Given all this, it is not surprising that what we call The Anglo-Saxon Chronicle does not consist of one uniform text, but a number of individual texts which have a similar core, but considerable local variations; each has its own intricate textual history.

THE MANUSCRIPTS[44]

The Winchester Manuscript

[A] Cambridge, Corpus Christi College MS 173, ff. 1ᵛ–32ʳ
This is the oldest surviving manuscript of the Chronicle, and the only one in which the language was not brought into conformity with the late West Saxon literary standard. In the last years of the ninth century a scribe at Old Minister, Winchester,[45] wrote out the genealogy of King Alfred and then began copying out a version of the Chronicle. He copied up to the end of the annal for 891, wrote the year-number DCCCXCII in the margin of the next line, and then stopped. Thereafter it was continued at intervals through the tenth century by a sequence of several scribes. It provides a full and contemporary account of the Danish invasions during the reigns of Alfred and his son Edward the Elder, until 924. At this point half a page is left blank, and there was bound in a copy of the Laws of Alfred and Ine.[46] Then a new scribe, beginning a new quire, embarked on a series of comparatively sparse annals covering the reigns of kings from Athelstan to Æthelred the Unready. It is curious how barren these entries are considering how eventful this period was. But there are introduced here four occasional poems in traditional Old English alliterative verse. Under 937 there is found a rousing patriotic celebration of Athelstan's victory at Brunanburh over a combined invasion-force of Scots and vikings; then three rather more routine literary exercises dealing with: the liberation by Edmund in 942 of five strongholds in Danish Mercia, the coronation of Edgar at Bath in 973, and another

---

[44] There is an excellent codicological summary of the various manuscripts in N. R. Ker, *Catalogue of Manuscripts Containing Anglo-Saxon*, 2nd edn (Oxford, 1990); and see also the introductions to the most up-to-date editions.   [45] See annals 643 A, 641 E; p. 26, note 8.   [46] This was subsequently removed and placed at the end of the final Chronicle entry, apparently some time before the Chronicle copy A² was made at the beginning of the eleventh century.

on his death two years later in 975. These poems, which also appear in some other manuscripts,[47] may perhaps have derived from bulletins issued from the West Saxon court. After this, any agreement between [A] and the other manuscripts ends. With the exception of a relatively long entry for 1001 describing the Danish raids in Hampshire and Devon, the later entries are typically scant, single-line, single-event, formulaic entries, but valuable because independent of other recensions. Now relatively neglected, this book was transferred to Canterbury, perhaps to make good the losses suffered by the Canterbury archive during the disastrous year-long viking occupation of the city in 1011.[48] At Canterbury such additional entries as were made are very brief indeed, although they made a point of recording the terms of a privilege given their institution by King Cnut (*s.a.* 1031, p. 158). The last vernacular entry was made for the year 1070, describing the institution of Lanfranc as archbishop of Canterbury, and an incident in the ongoing dispute as to whether or not the archbishopric of York was technically subordinate to that of Canterbury, settled by the pope in favour of Canterbury. Then there was added a Latin *Acta Lanfranci*, covering church events in the period from 1070–93; this is followed by a list of popes and the archbishops of Canterbury to whom they sent the pallium.

This manuscript once belonged to Matthew Parker, archbishop of Canterbury 1559–75, and is sometimes referred to simply as 'The Parker Chronicle'. A simple collotype facsimile was issued by the Early English Text Society in 1941, but lacking introduction or apparatus because of difficult war-time circumstances.[49] There is an up-to-date scholarly edition by Janet Bately.[50]

[A²] British Library MS Cotton Otho Bxi, 2
Before [A] left Winchester a copy was made. This probably happened some time between 1001, the date of the last annal copied, and 1012–13, a date suggested by the final names in the episcopal lists

---

[47] The first two poems also appear in MSS B, C and D, and the second two also in B and C but not in D.   [48] pp. 141–2, note 1. It is not impossible that it may have been taken to Canterbury when Ælfheah, bishop of Winchester, left to become archbishop of Canterbury in 1006; cf. M. B. Parkes, 'The palaeography of the Parker manuscript of the Chronicle, laws and Sedulius, and historiography at Winchester in the late ninth and tenth centuries', *Anglo-Saxon England* V (1976), 149–71 (171).   [49] R. Flower and H. Smith eds, *The Parker Chronicle and Laws*, Early English Text Society, Original Series CCVIII (London, 1941).   [50] *The Anglo-Saxon Chronicle: A Collaborative Edition*, 3, MS A (Cambridge, 1986).

appended to [A²]. This manuscript was burned in a disastrous fire in the Cotton Library in 1731 (the same fire which scorched the Beowulf manuscript) and only a few leaves remain. But before the fire, a transcript had been made by the pioneering sixteenth-century Saxonist Laurence Nowell, the antiquarian dean of Lichfield;[51] and in 1643 it was used for an edition of the Chronicle by Abraham Wheloc.[52]

[A²] is sometimes referred to as [W] after Wheloc, and sometimes as [G] following Thorpe's collective edition of 1861 which printed six other versions in parallel columns A to F.[53] A 'reconstructed' edition is printed by Angelika Lutz.[54]

The Abingdon Manuscripts

[B] *British Library MSS Cotton Tiberius Aiii, f. 178 + Avi, ff. 1–34.*
[C] *British Library MS Cotton Tiberius Bi, ff. 115ᵛ–64*

Manuscript [B] was written by a single scribe in the second half of the tenth century; it contains annals from 60 BC to 977. It began with a genealogical preface similar to that in [A], but this was subsequently detached and is now f. 178 of British Library MS Cotton Tiberius Aiii. This preface modified the Alfredian ending and continued the genealogy to Edward the Martyr, but without filling in his regnal years. This, together with the fact that the annals end in 977, points to a date of composition between 977 and 979, the year of Edward's assassination. This manuscript was evidently at Abingdon during the mid-eleventh century when it was used in the compilation of [C].[55] But shortly after this it went to Christ Church, Canterbury, where various interpolations and corrections were added, and a list of popes and the archbishops of Canterbury to whom they sent the pallium,

---

[51] British Library, Additional MS 43703, ff. 200–32; cf. R. Flower, 'Laurence Nowell and the discovery of England in Tudor times', *Proceedings of the British Academy* XXI (1936), 47–73 (54).   [52] *Historiæ Ecclesiasticæ Gentis Anglorum Libri V. a Venerabili Beda . . . aliiusque MSS. Saxonicis hinc inde excerptis . . .* (Cambridge, 1643), pp. 501–79.   [53] B. Thorpe, ed., *The Anglo-Saxon Chronicle*, Rolls Series XXIII (London, 1861).   [54] *Die Version G der angelsächsischen Chronik: Rekonstruktion und Edition* (Munich, 1981)   [55] For the relationship between [B] and [C], see S. Taylor, *The Anglo-Saxon Chronicle: A Collaborative Edition*, 4, *MS B* (Cambridge, 1983), pp. xxxiv–l.

ending with Anselm (1095). There is an up-to-date and scholarly edition by Simon Taylor.[56]

Manuscript [C] was made in the mid-eleventh century and, to judge from the incorporation of local annals, at Abingdon on the border between Wessex and Mercia. A composite volume, it began with an Old English translation of Orosius' world history,[57] followed by a metrical calendar (or menologium) and a series of verse maxims on the laws of the natural world and of humanity.[58] Then, towards the bottom of the leaf where these verses finish, the scribe went straight on to begin a copy of the Chronicle; he started with 60 BC and copied up to annal 490. At this point a second scribe took over and continued to the end of the entry for 1048. From 491 where the new scribe began, to 652 MS [C] appears to be identical with [B], but after this [C] had access to another version – possibly the exemplar of [B]. Between the annals for 915 and 934, this scribe inserted material which has become known as the 'Mercian Register' – a handful of short annals covering the years 902–24 and focusing on the activities of Æthelflæd, Lady of the Mercians. They form a discrete unit, not wholly integrated with the main text: they are out of sequence (896 of the Register following 915 of the main text), and information found in them was sometimes already present.[59] After this [C] turned back to West Saxon sources for the reigns from Athelstan to Edgar, adding occasional original entries (e.g. 971, 977), and continued at short intervals to 1066. Halfway through the description of the Battle of Stamford Bridge the manuscript was mutilated, but a century later a twelfth-century hand added a few lines to complete the account of the battle (p. 198). A text, including the calendar and maxims, was issued by Rositzke in 1940;[60] and a scholarly edition of the annals from 978 to 1017 was anthologised by Margaret Ashdown in 1930.[61] A full up-to-date edition is anticipated.[62]

---

[56] Op. cit. in previous note.   [57] Ed. J. Bately, Early English Text Society, Supplementary Series LXXXI (London, 1980).   [58] Ed. E. v. K. Dobbie, *The Anglo-Saxon Minor Poems* (New York, 1942), pp. 49–57; transl. (Maxims only) S. A. J. Bradley, *Anglo-Saxon Poetry* (London, 1982), pp. 512–15.   [59] Thus for example the death of Alfred's queen Ealhswith and the battle at Holm, already given under 905 in the running text, are now duplicated under 902.   [60] H. A. Rositzke, *The C-Text of the Old English Chronicle* (Bochum-Langrendreer, 1940).   [61] *English and Norse Documents relating to the Reign of Ethelred the Unready* (Cambridge, 1930), pp. 13–17, 38–71, 90–106.   [62] *The Anglo-Saxon Chronicle: A Collaborative Edition*, 5, MS C (Cambridge, forthcoming).

The Worcester Manuscript

[D] British Library MS Cotton Tiberius Biv, ff. 3–86

This was apparently written out in the middle of the eleventh century, and probably at Worcester to judge by the insertion of a number of local records from 1033 onwards. Five hands may be distinguished up to 1054; thereafter the hand is similar but varies from year to year in ink and slope which suggests it was written up at intervals, though the wording of some annals shows that they are not strictly contemporary.[63] The body of the text seems to have been copied from a now lost north-country exemplar, perhaps compiled at York or Ripon. These northern scribes, unlike those at Abingdon, had not merely taken up and continued the Alfredian archetype but added material from the body of Bede's *Ecclesiastical History* and from a set of eighth-century Northumbrian annals. In place of the West-Saxon genealogical preface, they set a Description of Britain taken from Bede and, instead of incorporating the Mercian Register wholesale, they attempted an amalgam, omitting some events and entering others twice.[64] Through the remainder of the tenth century this northern institution apparently continued to receive West Saxon bulletins, including the official propaganda poems on the Battle of Brunanburh and the Capture of the Five Boroughs. But instead of using those on Edgar's coronation and death, it substituted rhetorically heightened prose entries (*s.a.a.* 959 and 975) composed perhaps by the homilist Archbishop Wulfstan.[65] As we would expect, these scribes were well-informed about events in the north of England and on Anglo-Scandinavian relations in particular.[66] [D] displays an unusual interest in Scottish affairs[67] and, unlike other versions, lays emphasis on the virtues of Queen Margaret of Scotland and her English ancestry;[68] possibly it was a copy intended for the Anglicised Scottish court.[69] The arrival of a northern recension of the Chronicle in Worcester is explained by the close connection of the dioceses of York and Worcester between 972 and 1016 when the two sees were jointly held by the same incumbent.[70]

---

[63] For example, *s.a.* 1064 E (1065 D) we are told that after being ravaged, the land was 'for many years' the worse (pp. 192–3), or at the end of the annal for 1066: 'it always grew very much worse afterwards' (p. 200).   [64] For example, there are two accounts of the battle of Tettenhall, one *s.a.* 909, the other *s.a.* 910 (pp. 95, 97); the death of Æthelred of Mercia and the submission of London and Oxford to Edward the Elder are mentioned *s.a.* both 910 and 912 (p. 97).   [65] Jost, op. cit. in note 23.   [66] e.g. Jarl Hakon's depredation of York minster in 1076 and the death of his son there (pp. 211–12).   [67] e.g. detailing the reception of the ætheling Edgar at Malcolm's court in 1075 (p. 209) or the defeat of Angus, earl of Moray, *s.a.* 1080, *recte* 1130 (p. 214).   [68] *s.a.* 1076, pp. 201–2.   [69] F. M. Stenton, *Anglo-Saxon England*, 3rd edn, (Oxford, 1971), p. 681.   [70] Cf. annal 992 (pp. 126–7).

The manuscript is now incomplete. One gathering of leaves was missing by the sixteenth century, when eighteen pages were inserted containing substitute entries culled from other sources for the years 262–633.[71] A sound text of [D] was published by Classen and Harmer in 1926, and a full scholarly edition is forthcoming from Geoffrey Cubbin.[72]

The Peterborough Manuscript

[E] Oxford, Bodleian Library MS Laud 636
In 1116 the monastery at Peterborough was destroyed by fire – all but the chapter house and dormitory (p. 247) – and no doubt many if not all of its books were lost. Whether or not they lost their own copy of the Chronicle at this time, shortly afterwards they seem to have borrowed one from a Kentish library, probably that at St Augustine's, Canterbury, copied it up to date and continued it through much of the next half-century. This is the latest of the manuscripts, and the one longest maintained. It was written in one hand and at one time down to the entry for 1121. The monk Warner was still alive when his name was written down *s.a.* 1114 (a later hand altered 'is' to 'was called Warner', p. 246). In the course of his work the scribe inserted various spurious charters and other details relating to his abbey which are not found in other versions.[73] As far as the annal for 891, his, now lost, Canterbury exemplar had much in common with the northern version used by [D], but made no use of the Mercian Register and omitted the Brunanburh panegyric. After 1023, however, [E] is more original; fewer northern events are mentioned, but the scribe transcribes a handful of Latin entries from a Continental source. Towards the end the local character of the chronicle becomes marked. From 1121 to 1131 [E] was continued in the same hand, but at intervals, which suggests that this part is strictly contemporary. The scribe ended annal 1131 with a prayer to God for his community, which he is convinced is in need of Christ's help (p. 262). The manuscript was then laid aside; possibly the conditions of Stephen's reign were not conducive to historical writing. But with more settled conditions in 1154 it was brought up to date when another scribe wrote a composite account of the years 1132–54. Most of the events he records are only approxi-

[71] The handwriting is probably that of John Joscelyn, secretary to Archbishop Parker (Ker, op. cit. in note 44, p. 254).   [72] E. Classen and F. E. Harmer, eds, *An Anglo-Saxon Chronicle from British Museum, Cotton MS. Tiberius Biv* (Manchester, 1926); G. Cubbin, ed. *The Anglo-Saxon Chronicle: A Collaborative Edition, 6, MS D* (Cambridge, forthcoming).   [73] See H. H. Howorth, 'The Anglo-Saxon Chronicle, its origin and history', *Archaeological Journal* LXV (1908), 158–81.

mately datable. The long entry assigned to 1140 includes several events which are known to have occurred at different times during Stephen's reign. Only two of these annals are of any length, but include (*s.a.* 1137) a horrific description of atrocities perpetrated by the barons at a time when it was openly said that Christ and his saints slept! (pp. 263–5). The last few lines tell of the installation of a new abbot of Peterborough, with a prayer that he will do well. The end of the manuscript is mutilated and several readings are partly conjectural.[74]

Up to and including the annal for 1131 the Peterborough manuscript employed the late Old English standard literary language. But during the following hiatus, this conservative archival language (perhaps the formal medium of Old English scholarship) appears to have fallen into disuse, and the new scribe chose to use the contemporary local colloquial speech. These latest entries are among the earliest examples of Middle English, though their linguistic importance can only be judged from the original text. In the margins of the last folios of this manuscript there is written a crude rhyming chronicle in French; this was done in the later thirteenth century, by which time English had ceased to be an official medium of record in England.

Manuscript [E] is occasionally referred to as the Laud Chronicle, having once belonged to William Laud, archbishop of Canterbury 1633–45. There is a facsimile edited by Dorothy Whitelock,[75] and a good edition of the later part of the text by Cecily Clark.[76]

The Canterbury Bi-Lingual Epitome

[F] British Library MS Cotton Domitian Aviii, ff. 30–70
Although the Old English literary standard language was not used as a medium of official record after the 1070s by the king's government or by the clergy as a whole, it persisted at certain monastic centres which maintained English culture in the face of Norman newfangledness. Monastic scriptoria at Worcester or Rochester, for example, would continue to copy Anglo-Saxon texts like cartularies or legal codices for a century after the Conquest.[77] At Canterbury bi-lingual Latin/Old English documents were produced, including copies of royal

---

[74] See generally C. Clark, 'Notes on MS. Laud Misc. 636', *Medium Ævum* XXIII (1954) 71–5.   [75] *The Peterborough Chronicle*, Early English Manuscripts in Facsimile IV (Copenhagen, 1954).   [76] *The Peterborough Chronicle 1070–1154*, 2nd edn (Oxford, 1970).   [77] Clanchy, op. cit. in note 42, pp. 165–6.

charters and religious texts.[78] About 1100 a Chronicle manuscript was written at Christ Church, Canterbury, probably by one of the scribes who made notes in [A]. The text he used appears to have been an abridgement of the Canterbury chronicle which provided the exemplar for [E]. It is prefaced with the Description of Britain as in [D] and [E], and ends imperfectly in the annal for 1058. Each entry was followed by a Latin version. The same scribe, as well as others, made continual annotations and insertions between the lines, in the margins and over erasures.

There is a fascsimile presented by David Dumville;[79] the Latin text was printed by Magoun in 1945,[80] but as yet the only full vernacular text available is that in the Rolls Series.[81]

A Fragment

[H] British Library MS Cotton Domitian Aix, f. 9
This single leaf contains annals for the years 1113 and 1114; it was probably written in Winchester, in view of the expression *s.a.* 1114 'he came to Winchester' (p. 245). This scribe employed an even more conservative form of the late West Saxon literary standard language than that in use at Peterborough at this date. The text was published by Zupitza in 1878.[82]

The relationship between the different versions is extraordinarily complex;[83] witness for example the irreconcilable differences in the three accounts given by [C], [D] and [E] of the circumstances surrounding the death of Earl Beorn in 1049 (pp. 168–9). The first two are so similar in some points that they cannot be independent; but in other important details they differ. The account in [E] is independent of both.[84] Though several aspects continue to be disputed, the relationship between the main versions of the Anglo-Saxon Chronicle[85] and its dependents might be represented thus:

---

[78] Most remarkably perhaps the Eadwine Psalter, with three Latin versions of the psalms: Roman, Gallican and Hebrew, in parallel columns, and a continuous English and French gloss, M. R. James, ed., *The Canterbury Psalter* (London, 1935). [79] *The Anglo-Saxon Chronicle: A Collaborative Edition, 8, Facsimile of MS F: the Domitian Bilingual* (Cambridge, 1995). [80] F. P. Magoun, 'The Domitian bilingual of the Old English Annals: notes on the F-text', *Modern Language Quarterly* VI (1945), 371–80. [81] Ed. B. Thorpe, *The Anglo-Saxon Chronicle*, Rolls Series XXIII (London, 1861), col. 6. [82] J. Zupitza, 'Fragment einer englischen Chronik aus den Jahren 1113 und 1114', *Anglia* I (1878), 195–7. [83] See generally Janet Bately, *The Anglo-Saxon Chronicle: Texts and Textual Relationships* (Reading, 1991), and the references there cited. [84] See Earle and Plummers' edition, II, pp. 229–30, where a comparative table of incidents is printed. [85] Too little survives of [H] to be sure of its placement.

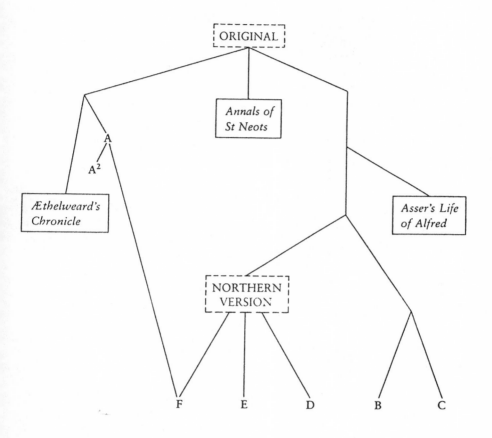

Schematic illustration of the relationship between manuscript versions of the
Anglo-Saxon Chronicle and related texts.

EDITION AND TRANSLATION

Recognising that many who use this book may need to find their way into and around the original documents, for ease of reference I have followed the layout of the comparative edition by Earle and Plummer,[86] although collating their texts with later editions. Comparative texts are printed side by side across the double page, focusing on the Winchester manuscript [A] on the left-hand page and the Peterborough manuscript [E] on the right-hand page, with extensive supplementary extracts from other manuscripts where the material enlarges on or varies from these to any great extent. Towards the end [E] stands alone, and runs consecutively through the last pages.

Ultimately translation cannot reproduce, or even adequately reflect, the style of an original without departing from its substance considerably. I have tried to supply as close a rendering as possible without being awkwardly over-literal. But I have thought it important not silently to 'improve' the original in those cases where I felt it to be at all clumsy, repetitive or obscure. To do so would be to present as unreal a picture as it would be to reduce everything to my own personal style, or to the 'colloquial Modern English' beloved of the university examiner. Given the limits of the exercise, I have presented as conservative a text as possible, for example, distinguishing between MSS *cc* and *twa hund* (respectively E '200' and D 'two hundred', p. 211), which may be significant in respect of the transmission of data. And 'two-and-a-half hundred' sounds a lot less precise than 250 *s.a.* 851 (pp. 64–5). I have aimed at internal consistency in the way particular words or expressions are rendered. Where consistency throughout is quite impossible – and it may be so with semantic development over some centuries – I have tried at least to be consistent within any immediate environment, but even that is not always possible.

One persistent difficulty lies in translating the expression *man*, as in 'Then *man* killed the king'. To render this 'one' would be hopelessly awkward, and 'somebody' impossibly vague. Modern colloquial English uses 'they' in such a position, but this is too often ambiguous in context. For example, after the vikings had burned down Kingsteign-

---

[86] *Two of the Saxon Chronicles parallel, with supplementary extracts from the others*, revd C. Plummer on the basis of an edition by J. Earle (Oxford, 1892), reissued with a note by Dorothy Whitelock, 1952.

ton in 1001, it is said: *heom man syððan þær frið wið nam*, 'afterwards *they* made peace with *them*' (p. 132), but this fails to make clear who 'they' and 'them' were. A passive construction side-steps the issue, and is generally an improvement. The only difficulty occurs where this *man* usage lies in close proximity to, or in a comparative situation with, a genuinely passive construction, so that to render a *man* construction similarly would blur an original differentiation. For example, in telling how Harold's moustachioed bishop Leofgar was killed campaigning in Wales *s.a.* 1056, the Abingdon scribe employs the construction with *man: hine man ðar ofsloh*, while the Worcester scribe uses the passive: *he wearð þær ofslagen* (pp. 186–7). Both Winchester and Peterborough versions employ alternative constructions in consecutive entries *s.a.a.* 746, 748 (pp. 46–7).

The importance of the Anglo-Saxon Chronicle as a continuous and at least nominally dated record cannot be overestimated in a period when documents of all kinds are few and difficult to date, and even relative chronologies hotly disputed for well-known literary works such as *Beowulf*. Semantic shift is an obvious consideration in the course of a work which has (or at least purports, and may possibly have) developed over centuries. Technical terminology is inevitably problematic. Some words like *thegn* simply disappeared and have no modern equivalent; the term *baroun*, which came to fill the semantic vacuum left by *thegn* during the course of the twelfth century, has a very different etymology and very different connotations. There is a clear development in the meaning of *heretoga* from 'war-leader', as used of the commanders of landless mercenaries *s.a.* 449 (p. 13) or viking raiders, *s.a.a.* 794, 993 (pp. 57, 127),[87] and as used of the feudal prince of Louvain in 1121 (p. 249, note 25).[88] A similar evolution is observable with the term *ealdorman*. Titles are in any case difficult. Where the Winchester scribe refers to Eanulf and Osric as *ealdormen* the Peterborough scribe calls them both *dux* (*s.a.* 845, pp. 64–5); perhaps the connotations of these titles were roughly equivalent;[89] the

---

[87] And cf. the proverbial use 'when the war-leader weakens, then the raiding army is hindered' *s.a.* 1003 E (p. 135).   [88] Cf. a late interpolation by the Peterborough scribe *s.a.* 656 E implying a particular status ranked between earl and thegn (p. 32).   [89] A. T. Thacker, 'Some terms for noblemen in Anglo-Saxon England', *Anglo-Saxon Studies in Archaeology and History* II (1981), pp. 205–7.

use of the separate words in consecutive annals 845, 851 (p. 65) suggests some sort of differentiation in the mind of the annalist, if only of tone; but it may be mere carelessness. The Continental title 'count' was invariably rendered 'earl' by the Chronicle, and has been retained thus in the body of the text. But Continental forms are used in the index for greater clarification.

Earlier notions of royal authority have no current counterparts. The expression *feng to rice*, 'succeeded to power' is used, for example, of a pope in 814 and an abbot in 990 (pp. 58–9, 126); but the overwhelming use of this expression is in connection with one king succeeding another. At what point *rice* 'rule' was understood to mean 'kingdom, *Reich*' is uncertain – perhaps about the time of King Alfred. But the Chronicle as we have it only came into formal existence at this time, and we are unlikely ever to know whether the compilers were assuming the former existence of present conditions, or were trying consciously to reconstruct an original set of circumstances. And at what stage is kingship considered the equivalent of kingdom? It is clear enough that 'king of the East Anglians' is not the same as 'king of East Anglia'. As with tribal names like *West Seaxe, Suð Seaxe* (West Saxons, South Saxons), the general insistence on people rather than place reflects a migration tradition.[90] Through much of the Chronicle the term *Angelcynn* 'the English race' is used in contexts where later generations would have used *England*. But when it is said that 'cattle disease came to the English *race*' (*s.a.* 986, p. 125), or that orders were given to slay all those Danes who were in the English *race*' (*s.a.* 1002, p. 135), the sense of *Angelcynn* seems recognisably to have shifted, marking a clear territorial assumption which can equate the people with a particular piece of land.[91] In parallel, *Engla land* 'land of the English', became the territory, or even by extension, the nation 'England'.[92] William the Conqueror is decidedly not king of the English, but king of England (p. 213).[93]

---

[90] Even in the case of Kent and the Isle of Wight where the inhabitants seem to have come from a mixed ethnic background, the term used is not Kent or The Isle of Wight, but *Cantwaru* or *Wihtwaru* – those dwelling in Kent or the Isle of Wight. See p. 14, note 6.   [91] For the development of national consciousness, see P. Wormald, 'Engla Lond: the making of an allegiance', *The Journal of Historical Sociology* VII (1994), 1–24.   [92] In the same way, *Franca land* 'the land of the Franks' becomes simply *France*, see C. Clark, '"France" and "French" in the Anglo-Saxon Chronicle', *Leeds Studies in English* NS III (1969), 35–45.   [93] It is the foreigner Cnut who is first to use this formula to distinguish himself as 'king of the Danes' and 'king of the

Most generic settlement names are difficult. *Tun*, for example, which originally denoted merely an enclosed homestead, may well come to mean 'village' or metaphorically 'local community' in this period, but not yet 'town'.[94] The term *burh* (later 'borough') has an exceptionally wide semantic field, covering both town and fortification; and consequently it is not always easy to tell whether by *burh-wara*, '*burh*-dwellers', it is garrison or citizenry that is intended. This is particularly so when used of London, especially after 800.[95] Thetford is then to be a *byrig s.a.* (p. 112) but there is no evidence of it ever having been fortified. In the case of Eddisbury (*s.a.* 914, p. 98) nothing other than a fort was ever meant. Then, metaphorically even a monastic enclosure could be thought of as a 'fortress'.[96]

The Old English term *minster* is no less problematic. The word was used for any kind of religious establishment with a church, whether monastery or houses of priests devoted to parochial care,[97] and apparently used indifferently of the church building as of the institution. The Chronicle uses the uniform term for a variety of institutions which we know to have been separately abbeys, cathedrals, churches; clarification is confined to footnotes and not allowed to muddy the actual quality of the record. But when we hear in 963 that St Dunstan founded many 'minsters' (p. 115), it seems clear from what follows – driving out clerks from his province and replacing them with monks – that here *minstra* was thought of as 'monasteries'. In the account of how the abbot of Glastonbury had soldiers attack his recalcitrant flock in 1083, the words, 'church' and 'minster' may denote separate parts of one building (p. 215, note 12).

The Old English word for 'army' is *fyrd*, etymologically associated with the verb *feran*, 'to set out', 'campaign'. By contrast, the usual word for an invading or raiding army is *here*, for which no modern equivalent exists. I would have liked to retain the association between

Norwegians' but 'king of England' (A. J. Robertson, ed., *The Laws of the Kings of England from Edmund to Henry I* [Cambridge, 1925], pp. 155–6). [94] A. H. Smith, *English Place-Name Elements* II, English Place-Name Society XXVI (Cambridge, 1956), pp. 188–98. [95] e.g. annals 894 (p. 86, note 4), 896, 994 E (p. 129), 1016 E (p. 147, note 10); and cf. 895 (p. 88, note 5). [96] See the name Burh given to Medeshamstede *s.a.* 963 (p. 117, note 13). [97] J. Blair, 'From minster to parish church' in J. Blair, ed., *Minsters and Parish Churches: the local church in transition, 950–1200* (Oxford, 1988), pp. 1–20; 'Minster churches in the landscape', in *Anglo-Saxon Settlements*, ed. D. Hooke (Oxford, 1988), pp. 35–58.

the noun *here* and the verb *hergian* 'to act like a raiding army', but 'to harry' is both archaic and insufficiently forceful in Modern English. The term *here* was carefully defined in Anglo-Saxon times; the laws of Ine say: 'We call up to seven men "thieves", between seven and thirty-five a gang (*hloð*), after that it is a *here*'.[98] Understandably, the term *here* is found most frequently through the Chronicle referring to the viking armies which raided the British Isles. But it was applicable to any army intended for attack rather than defence, and thus applied not merely to hostile viking armies, but English armies sent to invade Ireland in 684, Scotland in 1054 or Wales in 1056 (pp. 39, 184–5, 186). In 910 E the one word is used to describe both English and Danes when they fought at Tettenhall on the English border with Danelaw (p. 95), and were perhaps both intent on invasion.[99] A century later, when these Danes had long abandoned casual raids in favour of long-term settlement, the term *here* continued to be used of them.[100] In 1004 [E] distinguishes between Ulfcytel's local *fyrd* and Swein's intruding *here*, whereas the scribe of [F] uses *here* of both the viking raiders and the counter-attacking territorial force (pp. 134–5). Latterly *here* seems synonymous with *fyrd*; [E] uses *here* of the Conqueror's invasion force, where [D] has *fyrd*.[101] Similarly in compounds, [D] uses *scip-land-here* where [C] has *scip-land-fyrd* (pp. 194–5).

Among other words which occur repeatedly, I have been unable exclusively to distinguish between *gan* and *faran* 'go, travel', or to distinguish adequately between various compounds with *slean* 'slay, kill'. The choices, and problems, which confront the translator at every turn, are innumerable; whole books have been written about them. Only those who have subjected their translations to the scrutiny of a number of others will readily appreciate how a dozen different readers will make a dozen different demands on a translation at any one time. It is simply not possible to satisfy on every point at all times; of its nature, translation must compromise. The number of possible interpretations, not simply of substance, but of style and tone, is often

---

[98] F. L. Attenborough, ed., *The Laws of the Earliest English Kings* (Cambridge, 1922), pp. 40–41.   [99] The single word similarly appears to apply to both Danish and English armies at the battle of Sherston *s.a.* 1016, pp. 150–51.   [100] *s.a.* 906 the Peterborough scribe uses *here* of the Danes settled in East Anglia where the Winchester scribe says simply 'the East Anglians'; *s.a.* 1013 the scribe of the Canterbury bi-lingual version uses *here* in English and *the people* (*populus*) in Latin when describing Scandinavian settlers to the north of Watling Street (p. 143, note 20).   [101] Though *fyrd* is normally used of the king's defensive army in England, it is used of the Saracen army invading Greece in 982 [C].

large. And the decisions which must be taken are more often than not purely subjective. It is understood that this book will often be consulted rather than read through consecutively, but it is normally possible to footnote details of semantic interest only on their initial appearance. For all such matters, the notes and glossary of Earle and Plummer remain an indispensable beginning, supplemented by those of later scholars, and in particular the splendid collaborative edition brought together by David Dumville and Simon Keynes.[102]

M. J. SWANTON

[102] *The Anglo-Saxon Chronicle: A Collaborative Edition* (Cambridge, 1983, in progress).

NOTE ON THE TEXTS AND ABBREVIATIONS

A   Cambridge, Corpus Christi College MS 173.

A²   London, British Library MS Cotton Otho Bxi, 2.

B   London, British Library MS Cotton Tiberius Avi.

C   London, British Library MS Cotton Tiberius Bi.

D   London, British Library MS Cotton Tiberius Biv.

E   Oxford, Bodleian Library MS Laud 636.

F   London, British Library MS Cotton Domitian Aviii.

H   London, British Library MS Cotton Domitian Aix.

< >   Material wanting in any manuscript and supplied from other sources is enclosed in angular brackets.

[ ]   Square brackets are used to enclose explanatory or other necessary matter provided by the editor, including adjusted dates.

Passages in the body of the text printed in italics are translated from Latin.

Passages printed in smaller type are later insertions in that manuscript.

For the identification and location of many particular places the reader is referred to the Index.

THE ANGLO-SAXON CHRONICLE

[Preface: The Genealogy of King Alfred][1]

In the year when 494 years[2] had passed since Christ's birth, Cerdic and Cynric his son landed at Cerdic's Shore[3] with 5 ships. And that Cerdic was Elesa's offspring, Elesa Esla's offspring, Esla Gewis' offspring, Gewis Wig's offspring, Wig Freawine's offspring, Freawine Frithugar's offspring, Frithugar Brand's offspring, Brand Bældæg's offspring, Bældæg Woden's offspring.

And 6 years after they landed, they conquered the West Saxons' kingdom; and these were the first kings who conquered the West Saxons' land from the Britons. And he[4] held the kingdom 16 years, and then when he departed his son Cynric succeeded to the kingdom and held it <26 years. Then when he passed away, his son Ceawlin succeeded and held it>[5] 17 years. Then when he departed Ceol succeeded to the kingdom and held it 6 years. Then when he departed Ceolwulf his brother succeeded and he ruled 17 years; and their ancestry goes back to Cerdic. Then Cynegils, Ceolwulf's brother's son, succeeded to the kingdom and ruled 31 years, and he was the first of the West Saxons' kings to receive baptism. Then Cenwalh succeeded and held it 31 years; and that Cenwalh was Cynegils' son. And then his queen, Seaxburg, held the kingdom one year after him. Then Æscwine, whose ancestry goes back to Cerdic, succeeded to the kingdom and held it 2 years. Then Centwine, Cynegils' offspring, succeeded to the West Saxons' kingdom and ruled 7 years. Then Cædwalla, whose ancestry goes back to Cerdic, succeeded to the kingdom and held it 3 years. Then Ine, whose ancestry goes back to Cerdic, succeeded to the <West>[5] Saxons' kingdom and held it 37 [*continued on p. 4*]

---

[1] This 'official' genealogy of King Alfred is found as a separate document in several other manuscripts, which show slight variations from A, particularly in the regnal years. See Dumville, 'The West Saxon genealogical regnal list: manuscripts and texts', 1–32, and 'The West Saxon genealogical regnal list and the chronology of early Wessex', 21–36. For the incorporation of mythic and divine names, see Davis, 'Cultural assimilation in the Anglo-Saxon royal genealogies', 23–36, and generally Faulkes, 'Descent from the gods', 92–125. See also Tables pp. 288–9.   [2] MS *cccc wintra 7 xciiii uuintra*; early Germanic peoples reckoned time by nights rather than days (cf. Tacitus, *Germania*, pp. 148–9), and similarly by winters; cf. p. 27, note 18.   [3] See annal 514.   [4] i.e. Cerdic.   [5] Supplied from an appendix to B, now detached (British Library, MS Cotton Tiberius A iii, f.178).

[Topographical Preface][6]

The island of Britain is eight hundred miles long and two hundred broad; and here in this island are five languages: English and British and Welsh[7] and Scottish[8] and Pictish and Book-language.[9] The first inhabitants of this land were Britons, who came from Armorica,[10] and settled at first in the southern part of Britain. Then it happened that Picts came from the south, Scythia,[11] with long-ships (not many) and landed at first in northern Ireland, and there asked the Scots[12] if they might live there. But they would not let them, because they <said that they could not all live there together. And then>[13] the Scots said: 'We can, however, give you good advice. We know another island to the east from here where you can live if you wish, and if anyone resists you, we will help you so that you can conquer it'. Then the Picts went and took possession of the northern part of this land; and the Britons had the southern part, as we said earlier. And the Picts obtained wives from the Scots, on condition that they always chose their royal family from the female side; and they held to that for a long time afterwards. And then it happened, after the course of years, that a certain part of the Scots went from Ireland into Britain [continued on p. 5]

[6] This preface, based on Bede (*HE*, I, 1), is found also in D and F; in C, however, the Chronicle text is prefaced by two pieces of Old English verse: a liturgical calendar (Dobbie, *Minor Poems*, pp. 49–55) and Maxims (Dobbie, pp. 55–7, and Bradley, *Poetry*, pp. 512–15).   [7] *Brittisc ond Wilsc*; D *Bryt-Wylsc*; by differentiating 'British' (perhaps Cornish), from 'Welsh', E suggests six rather than five languages.   [8] Down to the time of Alfred the terms 'Scots' or 'Scottish' refer to the Irish and to Irish settlers in south-west Scotland.   [9] i.e. Latin; omitted in F.   [10] MS *Armenia*, misreading Bede's *Armoricano* 'Brittany'.   [11] i.e. north and east of the Black Sea, but it is unlikely that this was the origin of the Picts.   [12] See note 8.   [13] Supplied from D.

A *continued from p. 2*
years. Then Æthelheard, whose ancestry goes back to Cerdic, succeeded and held it 14 years. Then Cuthred, whose ancestry goes back to Cerdic, succeeded and held it 17 years. Then Sigeberht, whose ancestry goes back to Cerdic, succeeded and held it one year. Then Cynewulf, whose ancestry goes back to Cerdic, succeeded and held it 31 years. Then Beorhtric, whose ancestry goes back to Cerdic, succeeded and held it 16 years. Then Egbert succeeded to the kingdom and held it 37 years and 7 months; and then his son Æthelwulf succeeded and held it eighteen and a half years. That Æthelwulf was Egbert's offspring, Egbert Ealhmund's offspring, Ealhmund Eafa's offspring, Eafa Eoppa's offspring, Eoppa Ingeld's offspring, Ingeld Cenred's offspring, and Ine Cenred's offspring, and Cuthburg Cenred's offspring and Cwenburg Cenred's offspring, Cenred Ceolwald's offspring, Ceolwald Cuthwulf's offspring, Cuthwulf Cuthwine's offspring, Cuthwine Ceawlin's[1] offspring, Ceawlin[1] Cynric's offspring, Cynric Cerdic's offspring.

And then Æthelbald his[2] son succeeded to the kingdom and held it 5 years. Then his brother Æthelberht succeeded and held it 5 years. Then their brother Æthelred succeeded and held it 5 years. Then their brother Alfred succeeded to the kingdom; and he was then 23 years old; and it was 300 and 96 years since his ancestors had first conquered the West Saxons' land from the Britons.

* * *

60 years[3] before the Incarnation of Christ, Julius Caesar, the first emperor of the Romans, sought out the land of Britain and beat the Britons in battle and overcame them, but nevertheless could not win a kingdom there.

Year 1.[4] Octavian ruled 56 years, and in the 42nd year of his rule Christ was born.

2. The astrologers from eastern parts came in order to worship Christ; and the children in Bethlehem were killed because of Herod's persecution of Christ.

3. Here Herod died, stabbed by himself, and his son Archelaus succeeded to the kingdom. [*continued on p. 6*]

---

[1] MS *Celming Celm*, probably a misreading of the Anglian form: *Celining Celin*; cf. Dumville, 'The West Saxon genealogical regnal list: manuscripts and texts', 19, 25.   [2] i.e. Æthelwulf's.   [3] See p. 2, note 2.   [4] Each annal begins with an abbreviated form of the word *anno* followed by the year-number in Roman lettering.

E *continued from p. 3*
and conquered some part of the land;[5] and their war-leader was called Reoda, from which they are named Dál Riada.[6]

Sixty years[3] before Christ was born, Julius Caesar, emperor of the Romans, sought out Britain with eighty ships. There at first he was harassed with fierce fighting, and led a great part of his raiding-army to destruction. And then he left his raiding-army waiting with the Irish,[7] and went into Gaul and there gathered six hundred ships, with which he went back into Britain. And when they first joined battle, they killed the emperor's tribune, who was called Labienus.[8] Then the Britons went and staked all the ford of a certain river with great sharp piles[9] in the water – that river is called the Thames. When the Romans discovered that, they would not cross over that ford. Then the Britons fled to the protection of the woods.[10] And, with great trouble, the emperor conquered very many of the major strongholds, and went back into Gaul.

Year 1.[4] Octavian ruled 56 years, and in the 42nd year of his rule Christ was born.

2. The astrologers from eastern parts came in order to worship Christ; and the children in Bethlehem were killed because of Herod's persecution; and he died, stabbed by himself. And his son Archelaus succeeded to the kingdom. [*continued on p. 7*]

THE CANTERBURY MANUSCRIPT (F)

3. Here Herod passed away, and the Christ child was carried back from Egypt. [*continued overleaf*]

---

[5] The kingdom of Dál Riata, originally confined to north-eastern Ulster, had colonised the closely adjacent parts of south-western Scotland – roughly what is present-day Argyll – thus forming a bipartite kingdom on both sides of the straits; its royal family moved across so as to rule from the Scottish half of the kingdom *c.* 500. See generally Bannerman, *History of Dalriada*, pp. 1, 122–6.   [6] The etymology of Gaelic *dál Riata* and Old English *dæl Riada*, 'the division (tribe) of Riata', coincides, but may not have been known to do so. Riata (Reoda) must be assumed to have lived some time during the second century.   [7] MS *Scottum*; this statement seems to have been based on a spelling-error found in several Bede manuscripts of *Hibernia* 'Ireland' (cf. p. 3, note 7) for *hiberna* 'winter-quarters'.   [8] As also Bede (*HE*, 1, 2); *recte* Quintus Laberius Durus (cf. Caesar, *The Gallic War*, V, 15 and p. 600); Bede's source, Orosius, mistook the tribune Labenius for the more frequently spoken-of legate Laberius.   [9] D 'stakes'.   [10] D 'to the wild woodlands'.

A *continued from p. 4*

6. From the beginning of the world to this year, 5 thousand and 200 years had gone.[1]

11. Here the son of Herod Antipas succeeded to the kingdom in Judæa, and

12. Philip and Herod divided Lycia and divided Judæa into four kingdoms.[2]

16. Here Tiberius succeeded to the kingdom.

26. Here Pilate succeeded to governorship over the Jews.[3]

30. Here Christ was baptized, and Peter and Andrew converted – and James and John and Philip and the 12 apostles.

33. Here Christ was hanged, 5 thousand 200 and 26 years from the beginning of the world.[1]

34. Here Paul was converted, and *St Stephen* stoned to death.

35. Here the blessed Peter the[4] apostle occupied the bishop's seat in the city of Antioch.

39. Here Gaius[5] succeeded to the kingdom.

45. Here the blessed apostle Peter occupied the bishop's seat in Rome.

46. Here Herod died – he who killed James one year before his own death.

47 [43]. Here Claudius, the second of the Roman kings, sought out the land of Britain, and took possession of the greatest part of the island, and likewise made the Orkney islands subject to the kingship of Romans.[6] This was in the fourth year of his rule; and in this same year occurred the great famine in Syria of which Luke speaks in the book *The Acts of the Apostles*.[7] [*continued on p. 8*]

THE CANTERBURY MANUSCRIPT (F) [*continued from previous page*]

38. Here Pilate killed himself with his own hand.

39. Gaius[5] succeeded to the kingdom.

40. Matthew in Judæa began to write his gospel.

44. Here the apostle Peter occupied the bishop's seat in Rome. [*continued opposite*]

---

[1] The date of Creation was calculated by adding the intervals between Biblical events and the ages of successive patriarchs; the exact total would depend on the selection made, and various conclusions were possible. See generally Finegan, *Handbook of Biblical Chronology*, p. 184 *et passim*; and cf. *Patrologia Latina* XCIV, 1163–4.   [2] F 'four tetrarchies'. The MS (A) version represents a misreading of Luke iii:1, the tetrarch of Abilene called Lysanias being mistaken for a province called Lycia.   [3] This annal is supplied from A[2]; the original text was erased, presumably after the MS had gone to Canterbury, and repeated *s.a.* 27.   [4] 'the' erased. [5] Better known by his nickname 'Caligula'.   [6] Cf. Bede (*HE*, I 3) and Tacitus, *Agricola*, pp. 44–5.   [7] Acts, xi:28.

E *continued from p. 5*

11. From the beginning of the world to this year, 5 thousand and 200 years had gone.[1]

12. Philip and Herod divided Judæa – divided into 4 kingdoms.

16. Here Tiberius succeeded to the kingdom.

26. Here Pilate succeeded to governorship over the Jews.

30. Here Christ was baptized, and Peter and Andrew converted – and James and John and the 12 apostles.

33. Here Christ was hanged, 5 thousand 200 and 26 years from the beginning of the world.[1]

34. Here *St Paul* was converted, and *St Stephen* stoned to death.

35. Here the blessed apostle Peter occupied the bishop's seat in the city of Antioch.

39. Here Gaius[5] succeeded to the kingdom.

45. Here the blessed apostle Peter occupied the bishop's seat in Rome.

46. Here Herod died – he who killed James one year before his own death.

47 [43]. Here Claudius, king of the Romans, went with a raiding-army to Britain and conquered the island and made all the Picts and Welsh subject to the Roman kingdom. He accomplished this battle in the fourth year of his rule. Here occurred the great famine in Syria which was foretold by Agabus the prophet in *The Acts of the Apostles.*[7] Then, after Claudius, Nero succeeded to the kingdom – he who in the end lost the island of Britain because of his inactivity. [*continued on p. 9*]

THE CANTERBURY MANUSCRIPT (F) [*continued from opposite*]

45. Here James, the brother of John, was killed by Herod.

46 [43]. Here the emperor Claudius came to Britain and conquered a great part of the island; and he also reduced the island of Orkney to Roman rule.[6]

47. Mark the evangelist in Egypt begins to write the gospel. [*continued overleaf*]

A *continued from p. 6*

    62. Here James, *the brother of the Lord*, suffered martyrdom.

    63. Here Mark the evangelist passed away.

    69. Here Peter and Paul suffered martyrdom.

    70. Here Vespasian succeeded to the kingdom.

    71. Here Titus, son of Vespasian, killed 111 thousand Jews in Jerusalem.

    81. Here Titus succeeded to the kingdom – he who said that he lost the day on which he did no good.[1]

    83. Here Domitian, brother of Titus, succeeded to the kingdom.

    84. Here John the evangelist in the island of Patmos wrote the book *of Apocalypse.*

    99. Here Simon the apostle[2] was hanged, and John the evangelist fell asleep in Ephesus.

    101. Here Pope Clement passed away.[3]

    110. Here Bishop Ignatius[4] suffered martyrdom.

    155. Here Marcus Antonius and his brother Aurelius[5] succeeded to the kingdom.

    167. Here Eleutherius succeeded to the bishopric in Rome, and held it gloriously[6] for 15 years. To him Lucius, king of Britain, sent letters – asked that he might be made a Christian,[7] and he carried out what he asked;[8] and afterwards they remained in the true faith until the rule of Diocletian.

    189. Here Severus succeeded to the kingdom and ruled 17 years. The land of Britain he girt with a rampart[9] from sea to sea; and then ended[10] in York, and his son Bassianus succeeded to the kingdom. [*continued on p. 10*]

THE CANTERBURY MANUSCRIPT (F) [*continued from previous page*]

    48. In this year was a very severe famine.

    49. Here Nero began to rule.

    50. Here Paul was sent bound to Rome.

    62. Here James, the brother of Christ, suffered martyrdom.

    63. Mark the evangelist passed away.

    69. Here Peter suffered martyrdom on the cross and Paul was killed – beheaded.[11]

    116. Here the emperor Hadrian began to rule.

    137. Here Antoninus began to rule. [*continued on p. 10*]

---

[1] For this aphorism of Titus see *The Old English Orosius*, ed. Bately, pp. 139, 325.   [2] F adds 'the relative of Christ'.   [3] Annals 99 and 101 were transferred from erased entries *s.a.* 90 and 92 respectively.   [4] Bishop of Antioch.   [5] D Aurelianus.   [6] F Lat *governed vigorously.* [7] This assertion, found also in Bede (*HE*, I, 4) and the *Liber Pontificalis* (p. 6), appears to be based on the misunderstanding of a papal contact with another Lucius, king of Edessa, formerly Britio Edessenorum, hence the ascription to Britannia, see Smith, 'Lucius of Britain: alleged king and church founder', 29–36. Æthelweard (p. 5) assumes that it was the pope who took the initiative.   [8] Altered by a post-Conquest hand, after the MS had gone to Canterbury, to 'and what he asked was granted him'.

E *continued from p. 7*

62. Here James, *the brother of the Lord*, suffered martyrdom.

62.[12] Here Mark the evangelist passed away.

69. Here Peter and Paul suffered martyrdom.

70. Here Vespasian succeeded to the kingdom.

71. Here Titus, ‹son of›[13] Vespasian, killed 111 thousand Jews in Jerusalem.

81. Here Titus succeeded to the kingdom – he who said that he lost the day on which he did no good.[1]

84. Here Domitian, brother of Titus, succeeded to the kingdom.

87. Here John the evangelist in the island of Patmos wrote the book *of Apocalypse.*

100. Here Simon the apostle[2] was hanged, and John the evangelist fell asleep[14] in Ephesus.

101. Here Pope Clement passed away.

110. Here Bishop Ignatius suffered martyrdom.

114. *Here Alexander decreed that water should be blessed.*[15]

124. *Here Pope Sixtus decreed that the hymn 'Holy, Holy, Holy'*[16] *be sung in the office of the mass.*

134. *Here Pope Telesphorus decreed that the hymn of the angels 'Glory to God in the highest'*[17] *be sung on feast days.*

155. Here Marcus Antonius and his brother Aurelius[5] succeeded to the kingdom.

167. Here Eleutherius succeeded to the bishopric in Rome, and held it honourably[6] for 15 years. To him Lucius, king of the Britons, sent men and asked for baptism,[7] and he straightway sent to him, and they afterwards remained in the true faith until the rule of Diocletian.

189. Here Severus succeeded to the kingdom, and proceeded with a raiding-army into Britain, and by battle conquered a great part of the island, and then he constructed [*continued overleaf*]

---

[9] MS *dice*; Severus' reconstruction of Hadrian's Wall resulted in the assumption that he had actually built it (cf. Bede, *HE*, I, 5; Æthelweard, p. 5). For Severus and the defence of Britain see Salway, *Roman Britain*, pp. 225–30.   [10] i.e. died, ended his days.   [11] F interlines 'beheaded'; F Lat *Peter's crucifixion and Paul's beheading.*   [12] Altered by a later hand from *lxii* to *lxiii.*   [13] Supplied from D.   [14] B C add 'on that day'.   [15] The *Liber Pontificalis* (p. 4) refers to Alexander I's introduction of blessing water (other than that used for baptism) which, mixed with salt, was to protect from evil influences. Cf. the Life of St Guthlac, Swanton, *Prose*, pp. 73, 113.   [16] Revelation, iv:8.   [17] Luke, ii:14

A *continued from p. 8*
200. Two hundred years.
283. Here *St Alban*, the martyr, suffered martyrdom.
300. Three hundred years.
379. Here Gratian succeeded to the kingdom.
381. Here the emperor Maximus succeeded to the kingdom. He was born in the land of Britain[1] and then went into Gaul; and there he killed the emperor Gratian, and drove his brother, who was called Valentinian, from the country. And that Valentinian later gathered a troop and killed Maximus and succeeded to the kingdom. In those times the heresy of Pelagius arose throughout the world.
409 [410]. Here the Goths destroyed the stronghold of Rome, and afterwards the Romans never ruled in Britain;[2] that was 11 hundred and 10 years after it was built. In all they ruled in Britain for four hundred and seventy years after Julius Caesar first sought out the country.
418. Here the Romans assembled all the gold-hoards which were in Britain and hid some in the earth so that no one afterwards could find them, and took some with them into Gaul.
423. Here Theodosius the younger succeeded to the kingdom.
430. Here the bishop Palladius[3] was sent from the pope Celestine to the Scots in order to strengthen their faith. [*continued on p. 12*]

THE PETERBOROUGH MANUSCRIPT (E) 189 [*continued from previous page*]

a wall with turves and a palisade thereon, from sea to sea[4] as a protection for the Britons.[5] He ruled for 17 years and then ended[6] in York. His son Bassianus succeeded to the kingdom; his other son, who was called Geta, perished.[7]
202. *Here Pope Victor, like his predecessor Eleutherius, decreed that Easter be celebrated on a Sunday.*
254. *Here Pope Cornelius took the bodies of the apostles from the catacombs by night, and placed that of Paul on the Ostia Road where he was beheaded, but Peter's near the place where he was crucified.* [*continued opposite*]

THE CANTERBURY MANUSCRIPT (F) [*continued from p. 8*]

200. In this year the Holy Cross was discovered.[8] [*continued on p. 12*]

---

[1] He was in fact born in Spain, but rose to prominence as an army commander in Britain. The assumption that 'Maxen Wledig' was born in Britain, found also in the Old English Bede (I, 9) and Æthelweard (p. 5), is probably due to a mistranslation of Bede's: *Maximus . . . in Brittania . . . imperator creatus* (*HE*, I, 9).   [2] Cf. Procopius: *The Romans never succeeded in recovering Britain, but it remained from that time on under tyrants* (*History of the Wars*, II, pp. 20–21).   [3] A has or *Patrick* interlined by a post-Conquest hand; E says Patrick; all other MSS and Bede (*HE*, I, 13) read Palladius. For Palladius, see Charles-Edwards, 'Palladius, Prosper, and Leo the Great: mission and primatial authority', pp. 1–12; and for the confusion with Patrick, see Dumville, ' "Acta Palladii" preserved in Patrician hagiography', pp. 65–84 *et passim*.   [4] F Lat *In Britain Severus built a great dyke and the strongest of walls with regular towers, a hundred-and-twenty-two miles from sea to sea.*   [5] See p. 9, note 9.

E *continued from p. 9*

286. Here *St Alban*, the martyr, suffered martyrdom.

311. *St Silvester, the 23rd pope; in whose time the Council of Nicaea* [325] *was held, also the first at Arles,* [314] *at which Avitianus, archbishop of Rouen, was.*

379. Here Gratian succeeded to the kingdom.

379. *At this time* [381] *the Council of Constantinople, of 150 fathers, was held under Damasus against Macedonius and Eunomius.*[9]

380 [383]. Here Maximus succeeded to the kingdom. He was born in the land of Britain[1] and from there he went into the Gauls,[10] and there he killed the emperor Gratian, and drove his brother, who was called Valentinian, from the country. And that Valentinian later gathered a troop and killed Maximus and succeeded to the kingdom. In those times the heresy of Pelagius arose throughout the world.

403. *Here Pope Innocent sent a letter of decree to Victricius, archbishop of Rouen; here was established that Sunday should be a fast-day because the Lord lay in the sepulchre on that day.*

409 [410]. Here the stronghold of the Romans was destroyed by the Goths, 11 hundred and 10 years after it was built. Afterwards, beyond that, the kings of the Romans no longer ruled in Britain;[2] in all they had ruled there 4 hundred and seventy years since Julius Caesar first sought out the country.

418. Here the Romans assembled all the gold-hoards which were in Britain and hid some in the earth so that no one afterwards could find them, and took some with them into Gaul.

423. Here Theodosius the younger succeeded to the kingdom.

425. *At which time the kings of the Franks began – the first, Faramund.*[11]

430. Here Patrick[3] was sent from Pope Celestine to preach baptism to the Scots.[12]

431. *At this time the Devil, appearing to the Jews in Crete in the form of Moses, promised to lead them dry-shod through the sea to the Promised Land; and thus, after many were killed, the remainder were converted to Christ's grace.*

433. *Pope Celestine; in whose time a synod of two hundred bishops was assembled at Ephesus,* [431] *which Cyril of Alexandria led against Nestorius, bishop of Constantinopole.*

439. *Pope Leo; here he blessed the Synod of Calcedon.* [451]

[*continued on p. 13*]

---

[6] i.e. died, ended his days.   [7] Being accused of treason by Bassianus, explains Bede, *HE*, I, 5.   [8] Reputedly by St Helena, mother of the emperor Constantine; for the story see Swanton, *Prose*, pp. 114–21.   [9] In 381 a hundred and fifty bishops from Thrace, Asia Minor and Egypt met at Constantinople to discountenance the Arian party led by Macedonius the Syrian anchorite and Eunomius bishop of Cyzicus, confirming the Nicene Creed, and sending their acts to Pope Damasus the following year.   [10] MS *in Galwalas*; a rather clumsy rendering of Bede's *in Galliam* 'into Gaul' (*HE*, I, 9).   [11] The first of the 'long-haired' kings, for whom see *Liber Historiae Francorum*, pp. 244–5.   [12] Not in fact a missionary campaign, since they were already Christian by this time (cf. annal 430 A), but to combat Pelagianism; he did not complete his mission.

A *continued from p. 10*

443. Here the Britons sent to Rome and asked them for help against the Picts, but they had none there because they were campaigning against Attila, king of Huns; and then they sent to the Angles and made the same request to the princes of the Angle race.

449. Here Mauricius[1] and Valentinian succeeded to the kingdom and ruled 7 years. And in their days Hengest and Horsa,[2] invited by Vortigern,[3] king of the Britons, sought out Britain in the landing-place which is named Ebba's Creek,[4] at first to help the Britons, but later they fought against them. The king ordered them to fight against the Picts, and they did so and had victory wheresoever they came. They then sent to Angeln[5] and ordered them to send more help, and tell them of the worthlessness of the Britons and of the excellence of the land. They then sent them more help. These men came from three tribes of Germany: from the Old Saxons, from the Angles, from the Jutes. From the Jutes[6] came the Cantware[7] and the Wihtware – that is the tribe which now lives on Wight – and that race in Wessex which they still call the race of Jutes. From the Old Saxons came the East Saxons and South Saxons and West Saxons. From Angeln, which has stood waste ever since between the Jutes and the Saxons, came the East Angles, Middle Angles, Mercians, and all the Northumbrians.[8]

455. Here Hengest and Horsa fought against Vortigern the king in the place which is called Aylesford,[9] and and his brother Horsa was killed. And after that Hengest, and Æsc his son, succeeded to the kingdom.

457. Here Hengest and Æsc fought against the Britons in the place which is called Crayford,[10] and there killed 4,000 men;[11] and the Britons then abandoned the land of Kent and in great terror fled to the stronghold of London.

465. Here Hengest and Æsc fought against the Welsh[12] near Wipped's Creek,[13] and there killed 12 Welsh chieftains;[14] [*continued on p. 14*]

THE CANTERBURY MANUSCRIPT (F) [*continued from p. 10*]

444. Here *St Martin* passed away.

448. Here John the Baptist revealed his head to two monks who came from eastern parts to worship in Jerusalem, in the place which once was Herod's dwelling.[15] At that same time Martianus and Valentinian ruled; and in those times the race of Angles came to this land, invited by King Vortigern, to help him overcome his enemies. They came to this land with three longships, and their commanders[16] were Hengest and Horsa. First of all they killed the king's enemies and drove them away, and afterwards they turned against the king and against the Britons, and did for them by fire and by the edge of the sword. [*continued on p. 14*]

---

[1] A *Mauricius* corrected to *Martianus* later at Canterbury. B C read *Mauricius*, and E *Martianus*; D has no original entry between 262–93.   [2] Meaning 'stallion' and 'horse' respectively, and perhaps by-names; see Tolkein, *Finn and Hengest*, appendix C, especially pp. 173–80.   [3] For whom see H. M. and N. K. Chadwick, 'Vortigern', pp. 21–46.   [4] A *Ypwines fleot*, E *Heopwines fleot*; Ebbsfleet at the entrance to the Wantsum Channel in east Kent, opposite the Roman fort at Richborough and the later point of entry at Sandwich, see Map p. 273.   [5] The neck of land between Denmark and mainland Germany.   [6] For these people see Hawkes, 'The Jutes of Kent', pp. 91–111.   [7] Literally 'the inhabitants of Kent'; cf. the chronicler's subsequent explanation of Wihtware. See generally, Brooks, 'The creation and early structure of the kingdom of Kent', 55–74, and Yorke, 'The Jutes of Hampshire and Wight and the origins of Wessex', 84–96.

E *continued from p. 11*

443. Here the Britons sent across the sea to Rome and asked them for help against the Picts, but they had none there because they were campaigning against Attila, king of the Huns; and then they sent to the Angles and made the same request to the princes of the Angle race.

449. *In which time the Council of Calcedon of 630 bishops was held against Abbot Eutyches and Dioscorus.*[17] Here Martianus[1] and Valentinian succeeded to the kingdom and ruled 7 years. In their days Vortigern invited the Angle race here and they then came here to Britain in three ships at the place Ebba's Creek.[4] The king Vortigern gave them land in the south-east of this land on condition that they fought against the Picts. They then fought against the Picts and had victory wheresoever they came. Then they sent to Angeln,[5] ordered [them] to send more help and ordered them to tell of the worthlessness of the Britons and of the excellence of the land. They then at once sent here a larger troop to help the other. These men came from three tribes of Germany: from the Old Saxons, from the Angles, from the Jutes.[6] From the Jutes came the Cantware[7] and the Wihtware – that is the tribe which now lives on Wight – and that race in Wessex which they still call the race of Jutes. From the Old Saxons came the East Saxons and South Saxons and West Saxons. From Angeln, which has stood waste ever since between the Jutes and the Saxons, came the East Angles, Middle Angles, Mercians, and all the Northumbrians.[8] Their commanders[16] were two brothers, Hengest and Horsa, that were sons of Wihtgils. Wihtgils was Witta's offspring, Witta Wecta's offspring, Wecta Woden's offspring. From that Woden originated all our royal family, and [that] of the Southumbrians also.[8]

455. Here Hengest and Horsa fought against Vortigern the king in the place which is called Aylesford,[9] and his brother Horsa was killed. And after that Hengest, and Æsc his son, succeeded to the kingdom.

456. Here Hengest and Æsc fought against the Britons at a place which is called Crayford,[10] and there killed 4 troops; and the Britons then abandoned the land of Kent and in great terror fled to the stronghold of London.

465. Here Hengest and Æsc fought against the Welsh[12] near Wipped's Creek,[13] [*continued on p. 15*]

---

[8] This information is based on Bede (*HE*, I, 15). In E the words 'our *et sequ*', suggest a northern origin. See also Davis, op. cit. p. 2, note 1.   [9] Most MSS read *Ægælesþrep* and variants, but A[2] *Agelesford*. The ford on the River Medway in mid Kent, avoiding a defended Roman bridge to the north at Rochester.   [10] In north-west Kent, the last significant river-crossing approaching south-east London.   [11] F 'four troops of Britons'.   [12] Not 'Welsh' in the later sense, but rather 'British', see p. 14, note 1.   [13] MS *Wippedesfleot*; unidentified, cf. p. 15, note 18.   [14] A *aldor menn*, E *ealdor men*; but not, presumably, in the specific Anglo-Saxon sense.   [15] This legend is told by Marcellinus Comes *s.a.* 453 (*PL*, LI, 928–9) and repeated by Bede in his commentary on St Mark's gospel (*PL*, XCII, 192–3). The saint's head was taken first to Edessa and *c*. 1000 'discovered' anew in the church of St Jean d'Angély (MGH, *Scriptores* IV, p. 141), for which institution see below, *s.a.* 1127–8, 1130–31.   [16] MS *heretogan* 'war-leaders'.   [17] Abbot in Constantinople and patriarch of Alexandria respectively, both monophysites, denying the existence of two natures (human and divine) in Christ.

A 465 *continued from p. 12*
and one of their thegns, whose name was Wipped,[18] was killed there.

473. Here Hengest and Æsc fought against the Welsh[1] and seized countless war-loot, and the Welsh fled from the English like fire.[2]

477. Here Ælle and his 3 sons, Cymen and Wlencing and Cissa, came to the land of Britain with 3 ships at the place which is named Cymen's Shore,[3] and there killed many Welsh and drove some to flight into the wood which is named The Weald.[4]

485. Here Ælle fought against the Welsh near the margin of Mearcred's Burn.[5]

488. Here Æsc succeeded to the kingdom, and was king of the inhabitants of Kent[6] 24 years.[7]

491. Here Ælle and Cissa besieged Anderitum,[8] and killed all who lived in there; there was not even one Briton left there.

495. Here two chieftains;[9] Cerdic and Cynric his son, came to Britain with 5 ships at the place which is called Cerdic's Shore[10] and the same day fought against the Welsh.[11]

501. Here Port and his 2 sons, Bieda and Mægla,[12] came with 2 ships to Britain at the place which is called Portsmouth,[13] and killed a certain young British man – a very noble man.

508. Here Cerdic and Cynric killed a certain British king, whose name was Natanleod, and 5 thousand men with him – after whom the land as far as Charford[14] was named Netley.

514. Here the West Saxons (Stuf and Wihtgar)[15] came to Britain with 3 ships in the place which is called Cerdic's Shore,[11] and fought against the Britons and put them to flight. [*continued on p. 16*]

THE CANTERBURY MANUSCRIPT (F) [*continued from p. 12*]

482. Here the blessed abbot Benedict shone throughout this world through the glory of his mighty works, just as the blessed Gregory relates in the book of *Dialogues*.[16]

509. Here the abbot *St Benedict*, father of all monks, went to heaven. [*continued on p. 17*]

[1] 'Welsh' is used at this stage side by side, and perhaps interchangeably, with 'British'; cf. 'British-Welsh' etc., p. 3 note 7.   [2] MS *swa* [*þær* erased] *fyr*; for the construction *swa þær*, found introducing similes in Alfredian-period prose, see Bately, 'Lexical evidence for the authorship of the prose psalms in the Paris Psalter', 89, n. 131. F 'as one flies from fire'.   [3] *Cymenes ora*, probably now The Owers, sandbanks off Selsey, West Sussex (Mawer and Stenton, *The Place-Names of Sussex*, pp. 83–4).   [4] *Andredes leag*, the forest in the hinterland of the Roman fort of Anderitum (Pevensey), East Sussex, see note 8.   [5] A *Mearcrædes* (E *Mearcredes*) *burnan*; unidentified.   [6] *Cantwara*. Like the term *Wihtwara* 'inhabitants of Wight', but unlike for example *Suð Seaxe*, 'South Saxons, Sussex', or *West Seaxe*, 'West Saxons, Wessex', this expression foregrounds the territory rather than the people; the archaeological evidence suggests that Kent was settled by a people of a relatively mixed cultural, and probably therefore racial, background.   [7] E *xxxiiii*, A and other MSS *xxiiii*; but for possible re-dating of Æsc's rule see further Wheeler, 'Gildas de Excidio Britanniae, Chapter 26', 500–2.   [8] MS *Andredes cester*; the Roman coastal fort at Pevensey, Sussex, easily besieged, lying at the seaward end of a small, low-lying peninsula; not a 'city', the term *ceaster* here reflects the earlier sense of the borrowing, Lat. *castrum*, pl. *castra*, 'fort, camp'. See generally Maxfield, *The Saxon Shore*, pp. 157–60.

E 465 *continued from p. 13*
and there killed 12 Welsh chieftains;[17] and one of their thegns, whose name was Wipped,[18] was killed there.

473. Here Hengest and Æsc fought against the Welsh and seized countless war-loot, and the Welsh fled from the English very hard.

477. Here Ælle and his 3 sons, Cymen and Wlencing and Cissa, came to Britain with 3 ships at the place which is named Cymen's Shore,[3] and there killed many Welsh and drove some to flight into the wood which is named The Weald.[4]

485. Here Ælle fought against the Welsh near the margin of Mearcred's Burn.[5]

488. Here Æsc succeeded to the kingdom, and was king 34 years.[7]

490. *At this time the blessed Mamertus, bishop of Vienne, instituted the solemn litanies of the Rogations.[19]*

491. Here Ælle and Cissa beseiged Anderitum,[8] and killed all who lived in there; there was not even one Briton left there.

495. Here two chieftains,[9] Cerdic and Cynric his son, came to Britain with 5 ships at the place which is called Cerdic's Shore,[10] and on the same day fought against the Welsh.[11]

501. Here Port and his two sons, Bieda and Mægla,[12] came with 2 ships to Britain at the place which is called Portsmouth,[13] and immediately seized land and killed a certain young British man – very noble.

508. Here Cerdic and Cynric killed a certain British king, whose name was Nazaleod, and 5 thousand men with him – and after whom the land all the way to Charford[14] was named Netley.

514. Here the West Saxons came to Britain with three ships at the place which is called Cerdic's Shore,[10] and Stuf and Wihtgar[15] fought against the Britons and put them to flight. [*continued on p. 17*]

[9] A *aldormen*, E *ealdormen*; the word is presumably not yet used in the later sense of territorial jurisdiction. [10] A *Cerdices* (E *Certices*) *ora*; cf. 'Cymen's Shore', *s.a.* 477. [11] Æthelweard (p. 11) adds *and were victors in the end.* He then says [*s.a.* 500] *In the sixth year from their arrival they encircled that western part of Britain now known as Wessex*, material transferred by A to the Genealogy of King Alfred (above, p. 2). [12] Port may well derive, aetiologically, from Portsmouth Harbour, Roman *Portum Adurni*. Bieda may similarly derive from Bieda's Head (annal 675); Mægla is probably a British name, cf. Coin-mægl, Farin-mægl (*s.a.* 577), Scroc-mail (*s.a.* 605 E, 606 A). [13] Perhaps the Roman fortress of Porchester, for which there is evidence of Saxon occupation from this time onwards, see Cunliffe, *Excavations at Porchester Castle*, II, Saxon. [14] *Cerdices ford*, presumably Charford in Hampshire; Æthelweard (p. 12) says it is *on the River Avon.* [15] Cf. p. 16, note, 4. [16] Pope Gregory I ('the Great'), *Dialogues*, a collection of brief saints' lives and miracles, was translated into Old English by Bishop Wærferth of Worcester. [17] Cf. p. 13, note 14. [18] F Lat *a very rich man of Hengest's party, called Wipped.* [19] Cf. p. 83, note 18.

A *continued from p. 14*

519. Here Cerdic and Cynric succeeded to the kingdom of the West Saxons; and the same year they fought against the Britons at the place they now name Cerdic's Ford.[1] And the royal family of the West Saxons ruled from that day on.

527. Here Cerdic and Cynric fought against the Britons at the place which is called Cerdic's Wood.[2]

530. Here Cerdic and Cynric took the Isle of Wight and killed a few[3] men at Wihtgar's stronghold.[4]

534. Here Cerdic passed away, and his son Cynric continued to rule 26 years.[5] And they gave all Wight to their two nephews[6] Stuf and Wihtgar.

538. Here 14 days before 1 *March* the sun grew dark from early morning until nine a.m.[7]

540. Here on 20 *June* the sun grew dark and stars appeared for well-nigh half an hour after nine a.m.[7]

544. Here Wihtgar passed away and they buried him at Wihtgar's stronghold.

547. Here Ida, from whom originated the royal family of the Northumbrians, succeeded to the kingdom and ruled twelve years. And he built Bamburgh, which was first enclosed with a stockade and thereafter with a wall.[8] <Ida was Eoppa's offspring, Eoppa was Esa's offspring, Esa Ingui's offspring, Ingui Angenwit's offspring, Angenwit Aloc's offspring, Aloc Benoc's offspring, Benoc Brand's offspring, Brand Bældæg's offspring, Bældæg Woden's offspring, Woden Frithowulf's offspring, Frithowulf Finn's offspring, Finn Godwulf's offspring, Godwulf Geat's offspring>.[8]

552. Here Cynric fought against the Britons at the place which is named Salisbury,[9] and put the Britons to flight. Cerdic was Cynric's <father; Cerdic Elesa's offspring, Elesa Esla's offspring, Esla Gewis' offspring, Gewis Wig's offspring, Wig Freawine's offspring, Freawine Frithugar's offspring, Frithugar Brand's offspring, Brand Bældæg's offspring, Bældæg Woden's offspring.>[10]

556. Here Cynric and Ceawlin fought against the Britons at Bera's stronghold.[11] [*continued on p. 18*]

---

[1] See above, annal 508.   [2] A and most other MSS read *Cerdices leag* or *leah*, but E *Certices ford*, perhaps influenced by the very similar wording of the previous entry.   [3] Corrected, probably after the MS had gone to Canterbury, to 'many'; but B and C also read 'few'; Asser (I, 2) and Æthelweard (p. 12) *but only killed a few Britons*; Florence (I, p. 5) *a few men*.   [4] *Wihtgaræsbyrg*; this is apparently an aetiological development from the name of the supposed founder, Wihtgar (cf. annal 534); the name of the place was probably *Wihtwarabyrg*, 'the stronghold of the inhabitants of (the Isle of) Wight' (Lat *Vectis*, pronounced *Wectis*); cf. Kökeritz, *Place-Names of the Isle of Wight*, pp. xlvii–lvi. The most obvious location would be what later became Carisbrooke Castle in the centre of the island, where a cemetery of this date contained one rich male burial which is not impossibly that of 'Wihtgar' himself who died in 544 (q.v.); cf. Young, *Excavations at Carisbrooke Castle*.   [5] *xxvi*; but B, C, F and Æthelweard (p. 12) say *xxvii*.   [6] *nefa* means either grandson or nephew, but Asser (p. 68, note p. 230) refers to Cerdic as their uncle and Cynric as their cousin.   [7] *undern*, 'the third hour of the day', reckoning the day starting at six o'clock.

E *continued from p. 15*

519. Here Cerdic and Cynric succeeded to the kingdom of the West Saxons, and the same year they fought against the Britons at the place they now name Cerdic's Ford.[1] And the royal family of the West Saxons ruled from that day on.

527. Here Cerdic and Cynric fought against the Britons at the place which is called Cerdic's Ford.[2]

528. *At this time Dionysius composed the Easter Cycle*[12] *in the city of Rome. Priscian searched the depths of grammar then.*[13]

530. Here Cerdic and Cynric took Wight, and killed many men at Wihtgar's stronghold.

534. Here Cerdic passed away, and his son Cynric continued to rule 26 years; and they gave all Wight to their two nephews[6] Stuf and Wihtgar.

538. Here on *16 February* the sun grew dark from early morning until nine a.m.[7]

540. Here on *20 June* the sun grew dark and the stars appeared for well-nigh half an hour after nine a.m.[7]

544. Here Wihtgar passed away and they buried him at Wihtgar's stronghold.[4]

547. Here Ida, from whom the royal family of the Northumbrians first originated, succeeded to the kingdom and ruled 12 years. And he built Bamburgh, which was first enclosed by a stockade and thereafter by a wall.

552. Here Cynric fought against the Britons at the place which is named Salisbury,[9] and put the Britons to flight.

556. Here Cynric and Ceawlin fought against the Britons at Bera's stronghold.[11] [*continued on p. 19*]

THE CANTERBURY MANUSCRIPT (F) [*continued from p. 14*]

552. Here Cynric fought against the Britons at the place which is called Salisbury.[9] And Egelbert [Æthelberht] was born in the . . ., the son of Eormenric, and in the thirtieth[14] year of his rule he was the first of the kings in Britain to receive baptism. [*continued on p. 20*]

---

[8] After the MS went to Canterbury the original text of Ida's genealogy was erased in order to make room for the detail about Bamburgh. The genealogy is supplied from A[2]. B and C insert the name Freotholaf (for Frealaf, cf. annal 855 A) between Woden and Frithowulf. The Canterbury interpolator makes similar subsitutions at 560, 565, 603, 604, 626. At 552 and 611 the genealogy was erased, but nothing put in its place. [9] A *Searo byrg*, E *Searo byrig*; the Roman hillfort of Sorbiodunum (now Old Sarum) controlling an important cross-roads two miles above present-day Salisbury down on the Avon flood-plain (VCH, *Wiltshire* VI, pp. 51–3); the name was etymologized by invading Saxons as 'dry-' or perhaps 'tricky-fort'. F gives the post-Conquest Norman spelling *Sælesberi*; Gover, *The Place-Names of Wiltshire*, pp. 18–19. [10] Genealogy largely erased, supplemented from A[2]. [11] *Beran byrg*, now Barbury (Castle), a pre-Roman hillfort controlling the Ridgeway along the crest of the Marlborough Downs in Wiltshire. Florence says (I, p. 6): *and put them to flight.* [12] See p. 25, note 10. [13] Teaching in Constantinople, *fl.* 500, Priscianus was the author of an eighteen-book *Institutiones Grammatici.* [14] The year restored from F Lat.

A *continued from p. 16*

560. Here Ceawlin succeeded to the kingdom in Wessex, and Ælle succeeded to the kingdom of the Northumbrians, Ida having passed away;[1] and each of them ruled 30 years. <Ælle was Yffe's offspring, Yffe Uxfrea's offspring, Uxfrea Wilgisl' offspring, Wilgisl Westerfalca's offspring, Westerfalca Sæfugl's offspring, Sæfugl Sæbald's offspring, Sæbald Sigegeat's offspring, Sigegeat Swæfdæg's offspring, Swæfdæg Sigegar's offspring, Sigegar Wægdæg's offspring, Wægdæg Woden's offspring, Woden Frithowulf's offspring.

565. Here Columba the priest came from Ireland to Britain to teach the Picts, and made a monastery on the island of Iona.>[2]

Here Æthelberht succeeded to the kingdom of Kent and held it 53 years.[3] In his days Gregory sent us baptism, and the mass-priest Columba came to the Picts, and converted them to the faith of Christ – they are the dwellers among the northern moors[4] – and their king gave him the island which is named Iona, where it is said there are five hides.[5] There that Columba built a monastery, and he was abbot there 32 years, and passed away there when he was 77 years old. His heirs still have that sacred place. The South Picts had been baptized earlier by Bishop Ninian who had been educated in Rome. His minster[6] is Whithorn, consecrated in the name of St Martin; there he rests with many saints. There must always be an abbot in Iona now, and not a bishop; and all the bishops of the Scots must be subject to him, because Columba was an abbot not a bishop.[7]

568. Here Ceawlin and Cutha[8] fought against Æthelberht and drove him into Kent;[9] and they killed two ealdormen,[10] Oslaf[11] and Cnebba, on Wibba's Mount.[12]

571. Here Cuthwulf fought against the Britons at Bedcanford and took 4 settlements:[13] Limbury and Aylesbury, Benson and Eynsham;[14] and in the same year he passed away.

577. Here Cuthwine and Ceawlin fought against the Britons, and they killed 3 kings, Coinmail and Condidan and Farinmail, in the place which is called Dyrham;[15] and took 3 cities: Gloucester and Cirencester and Bath.

583. Here Mauritius succeeded to the kingdom of the Romans.[16] [*continued on p. 20*]

---

[1] This phrase, found only in MSS A (a late addition), E, F and F Lat, suggests that Ælle succeeded Ida, king of Bernicia (northern Northumbria); in fact Ælle succeeded to Deira (southern Northumbria) see Florence (I, p. 8). [2] The genealogy and subsequent annal erased, and restored from A². [3] Cf. p. 23, note 13. [4] *wærteras be norðum morum*; cf. Simeon of Durham (II, p. 124) *Werter-morum*. [5] A hide (*hid*) was originally as much land as would support one family. [6] For the minster/monastery distinction see the Introduction p. xxxiii. The late MS E distinguishes between 'church' and 'minster' (which may therefore have the sense 'monastery'), whereas in A (although a late addition to that manuscript) it is one and the same – the minster of St Martin. [7] Cf. Bede, *HE*, III, 4, and further, Anderson, *Scottish Annals from English Chroniclers*, p. 9, note 2. [8] F 'Ceawlin's brother'; cf. E *s.a.* 571. Cutha may be a nickname or shortened form. [9] This is the first acknowledgement of conflicting interests among the settlers.

E *continued from p. 17*

560. Here Ceawlin succeeded to the kingdom in Wessex, and Ælle succeeded to the kingdom of the Northumbrians, Ida having died,[1] and each of them ruled 30 years.

565. Here Æthelberht succeeded to the kingdom of Kent and held it 53 years.[3] In his days Gregory sent us baptism, and the mass-priest Columba came to the Picts and converted them to the faith of Christ – they are the dwellers among the northern moors[4] – and their king gave him the island which is named Iona, where it is said there are 5 hides.[5] There that Columba built a monastery, and he was abbot there 32 years, and passed away there when he was 77 years old. His heirs still have that sacred place. The South Picts were baptized much earlier. Ninian, who had been educated in Rome, preached baptism to them, whose church and his minster[6] is at Whithorn, consecrated in the name of Martin; there he rests with many saintly men. Now there must always be an abbot in Iona, not a bishop, and all the bishops of the Scots must be subject to him, because Columba was an abbot not a bishop.[7]

568. Here Ceawlin and Cutha[8] fought against Æthelberht and drove him into Kent;[9] and they killed 2 ealdormen,[10] Oslac[11] and Cnebba, on Wibba's Mount.[12]

571. Here Cutha fought against the Britons at Biedcanford and took four settlements:[13] Limbury and Aylesbury and Benson and Eynsham;[14] and in the same year he passed away. That Cutha was Ceawlin's brother.

577. Here Cuthwine and Ceawlin fought against the Britons and they killed 3 kings, Coinmagil and Candidan and Farinmagil, in the place which is called Dyrham;[15] and took 3 cities: Gloucester and Cirencester and Bath.

583. Here Mauritius succeeded to the kingdom of the Romans.[16] [*continued on p. 21*]

---

[10] By this date (cf. p. 15, note 9) the term *ealdorman* was used of an official of some standing, appointed by the king to govern one or more shires. From the time of Cnut, and earlier in Northumbria, the term is superseded by *eorl* 'earl', borrowing Old Norse *jarl*.   [11] A B C Oslaf, F E Oslac.   [12] *Wibbandun*; unidentified.   [13] MS *tunas*; for the evolution of the term *tun* from 'enclosure' to 'town', see Smith, *English Place-Name Elements*, II, pp. 188ff. Florence (I, p. 7): *four royal vills.*   [14] The location of the battle remains unidentified; it was an odd collection of places seized; compare Leeds, 'The West Saxon invasion and the Icknield Way', 97–109; Hughes, 'Grimsditch and Cuthwulf's expedition to the Chilterns in AD 571', 291–314; Stenton, 'The historical bearing of place-name studies: the English occupation of southern Britain', 19–21 (*Preparatory*, pp. 266–80). Three of the four settlements were in royal hands at the time of the Conquest (Sawyer, 'The royal *tun* in pre-Conquest England', 279).   [15] The most important consequence of this battle (close to where a major Roman road approached the Avon crossing at Bath), was to separate the 'North' Welsh from the 'West' Welsh and open up the Severn valley to the invaders.   [16] i.e. of the Eastern Roman Empire, Byzantium.

A *continued from p. 18*

584. Here Ceawlin and Cutha fought against the Britons at the place which is named Battle Wood,[1] and Cutha was killed; and Ceawlin took many towns and countless war-loot, and in anger he turned back to his own [territory].

588. Here King Ælle passed away, and after him Æthelric[2] ruled for 5 years.

591. Here Ceol ruled for five years.[3]

592. Here there was great slaughter at Woden's Barrow,[4] and Ceawlin was driven out. And Gregory succeeded to the papacy in Rome.

593. Here Ceawlin and Cwichelm and Crida perished, and Æthelfrith succeeded to the kingdom in Northumbria.

595. Here Pope Gregory sent Augustine to Britain[5] with very many monks who preached God's word to the English nation.[6]

597. Here Ceolwulf began to rule in Wessex, and he continually fought and strove either against the Angle race,[7] or against the Welsh, or against the Picts, or against the Scots. He was Cutha's offspring, Cutha Cynric's offspring, Cynric Cerdic's offspring, Cerdic Elesa's offspring, Elesa Esla's offspring, Esla Gewis' offspring, Gewis Wig's offspring, Wig Freawine's offspring, Freawine Frithugar's offspring, Frithugar Brand's offspring, Brand Bældæg's offspring, Bældæg Woden's offspring.

601. Here Pope Gregory sent the pallium to Archbishop Augustine in Britain, and very many religious teachers to help him, and Bishop Paulinus [who][8] turned Edwin, king of Northumbria, to baptism.

603. Here <was a battle at Egesan stan.>[9] Aedan, king of the Scots,[10] fought with Dæl Reoda[11] and against Æthelfrith, king of the Northumbrians, at Dægstan; and they killed almost all his raiding-army.

604. Here <the East Saxons received the faith and baptismal bath under King Sæberht.>[12] Augustine consecrated 2 bishops, Mellitus and Justus. He sent Mellitus to preach baptism to the East Saxons; there the king was called Sæberht, whom Æthelberht set as king – son of Ricole, Æthelberht's sister. And Æthelberht gave Mellitus a bishop's seat in London, and to Justus in Rochester which is 24 miles from Canterbury.[13] [*continued on p. 22*]

THE CANTERBURY MANUSCRIPT (F) [*continued from p. 17*]

597. Here came Augustine and his companions to England.[5] [*continued on p. 22*]

---

[1] *Fethan leag*; a lost name at Stoke Lyne, Oxfordshire; cf. Gelling, *The Place-Names of Oxfordshire*, pp. 238–9.   [2] King of Bernicia.   [3] Altered by a later Canterbury scribe to 'Ceolric . . . six years'.   [4] A tumulus now called 'Adam's Grave', at Alton Priors, Wiltshire, close to a gap in the defensive line of Wansdyke (Woden's Dyke); it was still a land-mark in the ninth century, Gover, *The Place-Names of Wiltshire*, pp. xiv, 17, 318. For the Woden cult see Ryan, 'Othin in England', 460–80.   [5] For the Augustinian mission, see Bede, *HE*, I, 23ff., and generally, Deanesly, *Augustine of Canterbury*, and Brooks, *The Early History of the Church of Canterbury*.   [6] Written over an erasure; transferred from an erased entry *s.a.* 596.   [7] *Angelcyn*. As with tribal names (see p. 14, note 6), the insistence on people rather than place reflects a migration tradition; the term *Englaland* 'England' is a later development, see the Introduction p. xxxii.

E *continued from p. 19*

584. Here Ceawlin and Cutha fought against the Britons at the place which is named Battle Wood,[1] and Cutha was killed; and Ceawlin took many towns and countless war-loot.

588. Here King Ælle passed away, and after him Æthelric[2] ruled for five years.

591. Here Ceolric[14] ruled for 6 years. *Here Pope Gregory added 'Order our days in thy peace' in the canon of the prayer.*[15]

592. Here Gregory succeeded to the papacy in Rome; and there occurred great carnage in Britain this year at Woden's Barrow,[4] and Ceawlin was driven out.

593. Here Ceawlin and Cwichelm and Crida perished; and Æthelfrith succeeded to the kingdom of the Northumbrians. He was Æthelric's offspring, Æthelric Ida's offspring.

596. *At this time the monastery of St Benedict*[16] *was destroyed by Lombards.* Here Pope Gregory sent Augustine to Britain[5] with very many monks who preached God's word to the English nation.

597. Here Ceolwulf began to rule in Wessex, and he continually fought and strove either against the Angle race,[7] or against the Welsh, or against the Picts, or against the Scots.

601. Here Pope Gregory sent the pallium to Archbishop Augustine in Britain, and very many religious teachers to help him, and Bishop Paulinus [who][8] turned Edwin, king of Northumbria, to baptism.

603. Here Aedan, king of the Scots,[10] fought with Dæl Reoda[11] and against Æthelfrith, king of the Northumbrians, at Dægsanstan; and they killed almost all his raiding-army; there Æthelfrith's brother, Theodbald, was killed, with all his troop. After that no king of the Scots dared lead a raiding-army into this nation. Hering, son of Hussa,[17] led the raiding-army there.

604. Here Augustine consecrated 2 bishops, Mellitus and Justus. He sent Mellitus to preach baptism to the East Saxons; there the king was called Sæberht,[12] whom Æthelberht set there as king – the son of Ricole, Æthelberht's [*continued on p. 23*]

---

[8] F inserts 'and among them was Paulinus'. The relative pronoun is omitted in all MSS. F Lat reads correctly: *among them was Paulinus who afterwards converted Edwin.* The conversion referred to occurred in 626 (q.v.).   [9] Passage in A erased and restored from A[2]. E and Bede (*HE* I, 34) call the site of the battle Degsastan, Bede providing the etymology *that is, Degsa's stone*; possibly Dawston in Liddesdale, but see Balir, 'The Bernicians and their northern frontier', 155–8.   [10] Aedan son of Gabrán, king of Dal Riada c. 574–608, see Bannerman, *History of Dalriada*, pp. 80–90.   [11] The reading is common to all MSS: 'Aedan fought *wið* (with) Dalriada and *wið* (against) Æthelfrith'. The repetition of *wið* is misleading; its primary and usual sense represents opposition, the later shift to association as yet rare. Bede's account of the battle (*HE*, I, 34) makes it clear that Dal Riada led by Aedan were decidedly vanquished by Æthelfrith. See also Bannerman, pp. 86–8.   [12] Passage in A erased and restored from A[2]; B C add 'and Bishop Mellitus.'   [13] *Dorwitceastre.*   [14] *Recte* Ceol, as B C and the original reading of A (see note 3). The additional syllable has apparently been read in from the following verb; *ricsode* A, *rixade* E.   [15] A prayer added by Gregory to the canon of the mass.   [16] Monte Cassino, Italy, where Benedict (c. 480–542) founded the most influential of medieval monastic orders; it was not rebuilt until 719.   [17] Hussa, king of Bernicia, is said by Nennius (*History of the British*, 63) to have reigned for seven years, but with no mention of Hering.

A *continued from p. 20*

606. Here Gregory passed away, 10 years after he had sent us baptism; and his father was called Gordianus.[1] And here Æthelfrith led his army to Chester[2] and there killed a countless number of Welsh; and thus was fulfilled Augustine's prophecy which he spoke: 'If the Welsh do not want peace with us, they shall perish at the hands of the Saxons'.[3] There were also killed 200 priests[4] who had come there in order to pray for the Welsh raiding-army. Their chieftain[5] was called Scrocmail,[6] who escaped from there as one of fifty.

607. Here Ceolwulf fought against the South Saxons.

611. Here Cynegils succeeded to the kingdom in Wessex and held it 31 years. <Cynegils was Ceol's offspring, Ceol Cutha's offspring, Cutha Cynric's offspring.>[7]

614. Here Cynegils and Cwichelm fought on Bea's Mount,[8] and killed 2 thousand and 65[9] Welsh.

616. Here Æthelberht, king of the inhabitants of Kent, passed away, and Eadbald, his son, succeeded to the kingdom. <And from the beginning of the world to that same year had passed away five thousand and 800 years.>[10] He[11] abandoned his baptism and lived by heathen custom, inasmuch as he had his father's widow as wife. Then Laurentius, who was archbishop in Kent, decided that he would [go] south across the sea[12] and abandon all, but the apostle Peter came to him at night and fiercely scourged him because he wanted to abandon God's flock, and ordered him to go to the king and preach the true faith to him. And he did so, and the king turned to the true faith. In the days of this king Archbishop Laurentius, who was in Kent after Augustine, [*continued on p. 24*]

continued from p. 20

614 . . . . Laurentius became archbishop – he whom Augustine in his holy lifetime [ordained] to be archbishop there.

616. Here Æthelberht, king of the inhabitants of Kent, passed away; he was the first of the English kings to receive baptism; and he was Eormenric's son; he ruled 53 years.[13] After him his son Eadbald succeeded to the kingdom. He abandoned his Christianity, inasmuch as he had his father's widow as wife. At that time Laurentius was archbishop, and because of the grief he had because of the king's unbelief, he had decided to abandon all this land and travel across the sea. But *St Peter* the apostle scourged him fiercely one night, because he wanted to abandon God's flock thus, and ordered him boldly to instruct the king in the true faith. And he did so, and the king turned to the truth. In the day of this same King Eadbald, this same Laurentius passed away. The holy Augustine, while alive and in health, had ordained him bishop in order that Christ's congregation, which was still new in the land of the English, should not be without an archbishop for any length of time after his passing away. After him Mellitus, who was bishop of London earlier, succeeded to the archbishop's seat; and within five years of the passing away of Laurentius, while Eadbald was ruling, Mellitus went to Christ.

619. Here Archbishop Laurentius passed away. [*continued on p. 28*]

[1] Erased and restored from A²; B and C add 'and his mother Silvia', the latter detail neither in Bede nor the *Liber Pontificalis* but in *The Earliest Life of Gregory the Great*, ed. Colgrave, p. 73, and

E 604 *continued from p. 21*

sister. And Æthelberht gave Mellitus a bishop's seat in London, and to Justus he gave Rochester, which is 24 miles from Canterbury.

605. Here Pope Gregory passed away. And here Æthelfrith led his army to Chester[2] and there killed a countless number of Welsh; and thus was fulfilled Augustine's prophecy which he spoke: 'If the Welsh do not want peace with us, they shall perish at the hands of the Saxons'.[3] There were also killed 200 priests[4] who had come there to pray for the Welsh raiding-army. Their leader[5] was called Scrocmail,[6] who escaped from there as one of fifty.

607. Here Ceolwulf fought against the South Saxons.

611. Here Cynegils succeeded to the kingdom in Wessex and held it 31 years.

614. Here Cynegils and Cwichelm fought on Bea's Mount,[8] and killed 2 thousand and 65 Welsh.

616. Here Æthelberht, king of the inhabitants of Kent, passed away; he ruled 56 years.[13] And after him his son Eadbald succeeded to the kingdom. He abandoned his baptism and lived by heathen custom, inasmuch as he had his father's widow as wife. Then Laurentius, who was archbishop in Kent, decided to [go] south across the sea[12] to Rome and abandon it all; but the apostle Peter came to him at night and fiercely scourged him because he wished to abandon God's flock thus, and ordered him to go to the king and preach the true faith to him. And he did so, and the king was converted and was baptized. In the days of this king, Archbishop Laurentius, who was in Kent after Augustine, passed away, and was buried beside Augustine on 2 *February*. Then after him Mellitus, who was bishop of London earlier, succeeded to the archbishopric. At that time the inhabitants of London, where Mellitus had been, were heathen; [*continued on p. 24*]

presumably draws on tradition.   [2] In fact the battle at Chester must actually have occurred between 613 and 616 (Bede, *HE*, II, 2); see generally N. K. Chadwick, 'The Battle of Chester: a study of sources', pp. 167–85.   [3] Cf. Bede, loc. cit. in note 2.   [4] From the monastery at Bangor, says Bede (*HE*, II, 2).   [5] A *ealdormann*, E *ealdor*.   [6] A *Scrocmail*; F Lat *Scrocmagil*; D E *Scromail*; Bede (loc. cit.) *Brocmail*.   [7] Passage erased, restored from A[2].   [8] *Beandun*; unidentified. Cf. Henry of Huntingdon p. 56.   [9] MS *lxv* over erasure; B C *xlv*, A[2] *lxvi*.   [10] Passage erased but restored from A[2], supplemented by B, C.   [11] i.e. Eadbald.   [12] *he wolde suð ofer sæ*; the expression 'to go south' is commonly used of pilgrimage, cf. the Exeter Guild Statutes, (Whitelock, *Documents*, p. 558), or the will of the reeve Abba (Harmer, *Documents*, p. 3).   [13] E reads *lvi* in agreement with Bede (*HE*, II, 5) who places his accession in 560; but in annal 565, E and the addition to A both read *liii*; F gives *liii* under both 565 and 616. For these discrepancies see further Wheeler, 'Gildas de Excidio', 501–2.

A 616 *continued from p. 22*
passed away on 2 *February*, and he was buried beside Augustine. After him Mellitus, who was bishop of London, succeeded to the archbishopric, and within five years of this Mellitus passed away. Then after him Justus succeeded to the archbishopric; he was bishop of Rochester, and consecrated Romanus bishop there.

625. Here Paulinus was ordained bishop for the Northumbrians by the archbishop Justus.

626. Here Eanflæd, daughter of King Edwin, was baptized on the holy eve of Pentecost.[1] And Penda had the kingdom for 30 years; and he was 50[2] years old when he succeeded to the kingdom. <Penda was Pybba's offspring, Pybba Cryda's offspring, Cryda Cynewald's offspring, Cynewald Cnebba's offspring, Cnebba Icel's offspring, Icel Eomer's offspring, Eomer Angeltheow's offspring, Angeltheow Offa's offspring, Offa Wermund's offspring, Wermund Wihtlæg's offspring, Wihtlæg Woden's offspring.>[3]

627. Here King Edwin, with his nation,[4] was baptized at Easter.

628. Here Cynegils and Cwichelm fought against Penda at Cirencester, and then came to an agreement.

632. Here Eorpwald[5] was baptized.

633. Here Edwin was killed, and Paulinus turned back to Kent and occupied the bishop's seat in Rochester. [*continued on p. 26*]

616 *continued from previous page*
and 5 years after, while Eadbald was ruling, Mellitus went to Christ. Then afterwards Justus succeeded to the archbishopric and he consecrated Romanus to Rochester, where earlier he [himself] had been bishop.

617. Here Æthelfrith, king of the Northumbrians, was killed by Rædwald, king of the East Anglians,[6] and Edwin, Ælle's offspring, succeeded to the kingdom, and conquered all Britain except for the inhabitants of Kent alone, and drove out the princes, the sons of Æthelfrith: that was first Eanfrith, [then] Oswald and Oswy, Oslac, Oswudu, Oslaf and Offa.[7]

624. Here Archbishop Mellitus passed away.

625. Here Archbishop Justus consecrated Paulinus bishop on 21 *July*. Here the Cycle of Dionysius,[8] consisting of five [*continued opposite*]

---

[1] 6 June, Pentecost (Whit-Sunday) being the seventh Sunday after Easter Day, cf. note 10.   [2] 'fifty years' is sometimes used in Old English to mean 'a long time', much as Hebrew historical literature uses 'forty years' of the reigns of kings and judges (cf. annal 963 E, p. 117).   [3] This genealogy is erased; restored from A[2]; cf. Dumville, 'The Anglian collection of royal genealogies and regnal lists', 23–50. For the ancient kings of Continental Angeln see generally Chadwick, *The Origin of the English Nation*, pp. 111–43.   [4] Presumably not the entire people; if literally, perhaps in the sense of his court or council. See Bede, *HE*, II, 13, for a dramatic account of Edwin's conversion.   [5] King of the East Anglians.   [6] At a battle on the Mercian border, at the River Idle, a tributary of the Trent, before 616. For Rædwald, see p. 61, note 11.   [7] They lived in exile among the Scots and Picts, where they were converted to Christianity, cf. Bede, *HE*, III, 1.   [8] The Scythian canonist Dionysius Exiguus ('the modest').   [9] MS *Ennia kaið Johannes papa kaderida*. The words 'Pope John' were perhaps incorporated accidentally from an adjacent entry.

E 625 *continued from p. 24*
nineteen-years, that is, 95 years. And it starts from 30 AD and finishes in the
year 626. This nineteen-year system, which the Greeks call kaderida,[9] *was*
instituted by the holy fathers at the Synod of Nicaea [325] *in which the 14th*
[day of the] *Paschal moon* [was fixed] *for every year without any uncer-*
tainty.[10]

626. Here Eomer came from Cwichelm, king of the West Saxons – he
wanted to stab King Edwin, but he stabbed Lilla, his thegn, and Forthhere,
and wounded the king.[11] And that same night a daughter was born to Edwin,
who was called Eanflæd. Then the king promised Paulinus that he would give
his daughter to God, if by his prayers he should obtain from God that he might
fell his enemy who had earlier sent the assassin there. And then he went into
Wessex with an army and felled 5 kings there and killed a great number of the
people. And Paulinus baptized his daughter at Pentecost, as one of twelve, and
within a 12-month the king was baptized at Easter with all his chief men;[12] that
Easter was on 12 *April*. This was done in York, where earlier he had ordered a
church to be built of wood; it was consecrated in the name of St Peter. There
the king gave Paulinus a bishop's seat, and afterwards ordered a larger church
to be built there of stone. And here Penda succeeded to the kingdom, and ruled
30 years.

627. Here King Edwin was baptized by Paulinus; and this Paulinus also
preached baptism in Lindsey,[13] where the first who believed was a certain
powerful man called Blecca with all his chief men.[14] And at this time Honorius
[I], who sent the pallium here to Paulinus, succeeded to the papacy after
Boniface [V]. And Archbishop Justus died on 10 *November*; and Honorius
was consecrated[15] by Paulinus at Lincoln; to this Honorius the pope also sent
the pallium, and he sent a letter to the Scots in order that they should adopt the
correct Easter.

628. Here Cynegils and Cwichelm fought against Penda at Cirencester, and
then came to an agreement.

632. Here Eorpwald was baptized.

633. Here King Edwin was killed by Cadwallon and Penda at Hatfield[16] on
14 *October*; and he ruled 7[17] years. And his son Osfrith also was killed with
him. And then afterwards Cadwallon and Penda went and did for the whole
land of Northumbria. When Paulinus saw that, then he took Æthelburh,
Edwin's widow, and went [*continued overleaf*]

---

[10] Cf. Bede, *HE*, V, 21. Easter was fixed on the first Sunday after the full moon that occurs on
or after the vernal equinox (21 March); its calendar date is variable since lunar and solar years do
not coincide (the solar year is longer by 10.875 days). Dionysius reconciled them by intercalating 7
lunar months every 19 years. See Harrison, *The Framework of Anglo-Saxon History*, pp.
30–51.   [11] Cf. Bede, *HE*, II, 9.   [12] *duguþ*, the older, more reliable part of the retinue, as
distinct from the younger, untried *geoguþ* 'youth'; cf. Bede, *HE*, II, 14.   [13] 'Lincoln island', a
province bounded by the River Humber, North Sea and Witham Fens, and variously under the
control of Northumbria and Mercia; see Eagles, 'Lindsey', 202–12; Stenton, 'Lindsey and its
kings', 136–50 (*Preparatory*, pp. 127–35).   [14] Bede (*HE*, II, 16) speaks of Blecca as *praefectus*
(translated 'reeve' in the Old English version) of the city of Lincoln, with all his 'household'.   [15] F adds 'as archbishop of Canterbury'.   [16] Probably Hatfield Chase, West Riding
of Yorkshire; Bede (*HE*, II, 20) says the battle was fought on 12 October.   [17] MS *vii* in error for
xvii; cf. Bede, *HE*, loc. cit.

A *continued from p. 24*

634. Here Bishop Birinus[1] preached baptism to the West Saxons.

635. Here Cynegils was baptized by Birinus, the bishop in Dorchester,[2] and Oswald received him.[3]

636. Here Cwichelm was baptized in Dorchester, and passed away the same year. And Bishop Felix preached the faith of Christ to the East Anglians.[4]

639. Here Birinus baptized Cuthred[5] at Dorchester and received him as a son.

640. Here Eadbald, king of the inhabitants of Kent, passed away; and he ruled 25 years.[6] He had two sons, Eormenræd and Eorcenberht, and this Eorcenberht ruled there after his father. And Eormenræd engendered two sons – who were afterwards martyred by Thunor.[7]

642. Here Oswald, king of Northumbria, was killed.

643. Here Cenwalh succeeded to the kingdom of the West Saxons, and held it 31 years; and that Cenwalh ordered the church at Winchester to be built.[8]

644. Here Paulinus passed away; he was archbishop in York and later at Rochester.

645. Here Cenwalh was driven out by King Penda.[9]

646. Here Cenwalh was baptized. [*continued on p. 28*]

THE PETERBOROUGH MANUSCRIPT (E) 633 *continued from previous page*

by ship to Kent, and Eadbald and Honorius received him very honourably and gave him the bishop's seat at Rochester, and he remained there until his end.

634. Here Osric, whom Paulinus had baptized earlier, succeeded to the kingdom of the Deirans (Deira); [*continued opposite*]

---

[1] Probably a Frank, consecrated bishop at Genoa by Asterius archbishop of Milan (Bede, 47HE, III, 7).   [2] Dorchester-on-Thames, Oxfordshire, see Map p. 277.   [3] As his sponsor or godfather; Bede (*HE*, III, 7) *after his new birth and dedication to God* [Cynegils] *was received by Oswald as his son*; cf. below, *s.a.* 639.   [4] F Lat says *s.a.* 633: *Here there came from the region of Burgundy a bishop who was called Felix, who preached the faith to the people of East Anglia; called here by King Sigeberht, he received a bishopric in Dunwich, in which he remained for seventeen years.* Felix's mission had begun 630/1 (Bede, *HE*, II, 15; III, 18). Cf. generally Whitelock, 'The pre-Viking age church in East Anglia', pp. 3–7.   [5] B C F 'King Cuthred'; see p. 28, note 2.   [6] So also B C; but F xviiii.   [7] Eormenræd seems in fact to have been their grandfather; for the story see Swanton, 'A fragmentary life of St Mildred', 15–27, and generally Rollason, *The Mildrith Legend*.   [8] B, C assign both the death of Oswald and succession of Cenwalh to 641, and the building of the old church at Winchester to 642; E places all under 641. F is likely to be correct in ascribing the Winchester foundation to 648, since Cenwalh was only baptised in 646. B and C speak of the 'old church' since they are writing after the foundation of the 'New Minster' (consecrated in 903). See generally Biddle, *Winchester in the Early Middle Ages*, p. 306ff.   [9] For the circumstances of Cenwalh's exile see annal 658 and Bede, *HE*, III, 7.   [10] i.e. Osric and Eanfrith in Deira and Bernicia respectively. Bede explains that *all those who compute the dates of kings have decided to abolish the memory of those perfidious kings and to assign this year to their successor Oswald, a man beloved of God* (*HE*, III, 1).

E 634 *continued from opposite*
he was the son of Ælfric, Edwin's paternal uncle; and Æthelfrith's son, Eanfrith, succeeded to Bernicia. And also here Birinus[1] first preached baptism to the West Saxons under King Cynegils. That Birinus came there by command of the pope Honorius; and he was bishop there until his life's end. And also here Oswald succeeded to the kingdom of Northumbria, and he ruled 9 years. They reckon that ninth year his on account of the heathenism practised by those who had ruled that one year between him and Edwin.[10]

635. Here Cynegils was baptized by Birinus, the bishop at Dorchester,[2] and Oswald, king of Northumbria, received him.[3]

636. Here Cwichelm was baptized at Dorchester, and the same year he passed away. And Bishop Felix preached the faith of Christ to the East Anglians.[4]

639. Here Birinus baptized Cuthred[5] at Dorchester and received him as a son.

639 [640].[11] Here Eadbald, king of the inhabitants of Kent, passed away; he was king 24 years. Then his son Eorcenberht succeeded to the kingdom; he overthrew all devil-worship[12] in his kingdom, and was the first of the English kings to establish the Easter festival. His daughter was called Eorcengota, a holy virgin and a remarkable person,[13] whose mother was Seaxburh, daughter of Anna, king of the East Anglians.[14]

641. Here Oswald, king of Northumbria, was killed by Penda the Southumbrian at Maserfeld,[15] on *5 August*, and his body was buried at Bardney. His holiness and miracles were afterwards abundantly made manifest throughout this[16] island, and his hands, undecayed, are at Bamburgh.[17] And here [643] Cenwalh succeeded to the kingdom of the West Saxons and held it 21 years. That Cenwalh ordered the church at Winchester to be built;[8] and he was Cynegils' offspring. And the same year that Oswald was killed, his brother Oswy succeeded to the Northumbrian kingdom, and he ruled 28 years.[18]

643 [644].[19] Here Archbishop Paulinus passed away in Rochester on *10 October;* he was bishop for 19 years,[18] 2 months and 21 days. And here Oswine, the son of Osric,[20] the son of Edwin's paternal uncle, succeeded to the kingdom of the Deirans, and ruled 7 years.

644 [645]. Here Cenwalh was driven from his kingdom by King Penda.

645 [646]. Here Cenwalh was baptized. [*continued overleaf*]

---

[11] The annal number is duplicated in E, thus antedating this and the next few entries by one year. [12] MS *deofelgyld*, alternatively 'devilish-idols'; Bede (*HE*, III, 8) has *idola*. [13] MS *man.* [14] For Eorcengota, saintly abbess of the fashionable nunnery at Faremoûtier-en-Brie, and Seaxburh, abbess of Ely, see Bede, *HE*, III, 7–8 and Ridyard, *Royal Saints*, pp. 56–8, 60–61 *et passim.* [15] Traditionally identified with Oswestry ('Oswald's tree [or] cross') in Shropshire, Stancliffe, 'Where was Oswald killed?', pp. 84–96; but see Gelling, *The Place-Names of Shropshire*, I, pp. 230–31. For Oswald's death and subsequent miracles see generally Bede, *HE*, III, 9–13. [16] MS *his.* [17] Cf. Thacker, 'Membra disjecta', pp. 97–127. [18] MS *twa læs xxx geara. . . an læs xx wintra*; the words 'year' and 'winter' are apparently used indiscriminately by the chroniclers. [19] From 642 to 647, E is one year behind A. Then by the omission of 647 in E harmony is restored; but A has no entry for 649 and E immediately drops a year in arrears. [20] MS *Oswines; recte Osrices*, cf. annals 634, 650.

A *continued from p. 26*

648. Here Cenwalh gave his relative Cuthred[1] '3 thousands' of land[2] by Ashdown.[3] That Cuthred was Cwichelm's offspring, Cwichelm Cynegils' offspring.

650. Here Agilbert of Gaul received the bishopric of Wessex after Birinus, the Roman bishop.[4]

651. Here King Oswine was killed and Bishop Aidan passed away.

652. Here Cenwalh fought at Bradford on Avon.[5]

653. Here the Middle Saxons[6] under Ealdorman Peada received the true faith.

654. Here King Anna was killed; and Botwulf began to build a minster at Icanho.[7]

655. Here Penda perished, and the Mercians became Christians. Then 5 thousand and 850 years had passed away from the beginning of the world. And Peada, Penda's offspring, succeeded to the kingdom of the Mercians. [*continued on p. 32*]

THE CANTERBURY MANUSCRIPT (F) *continued from p. 22*

648. Here was built the minster in Winchester which King Cenwalh had made in St Peter's name and consecrated. [*continued on p. 38*]

THE PETERBOROUGH MANUSCRIPT (E) *continued from previous page*

648. Here Cenwalh gave his relative Eadred[1] '3 thousands' of land[2] by Ashdown.[3]

649. Here Agilbert of Gaul received the bishoprics[8] of the Saxons after Birinus, the Roman bishop.

650. Here, on *20 August*, King Oswy ordered King Oswine to be killed; and 12 days[9] later Bishop Aidan passed away on *31 August*.

652. Here the Middle Angles under Ealdorman Penda[10] received the true faith.

653. Here King Anna was killed, and Botwulf began [*continued opposite*]

---

[1] A B C Cuthred, E Eadred.   [2] B C 'three thousand "hides" of land'; the word 'hide' is often omitted (cf. *Beowulf*, 2995, or the Old English translation of Bede, *HE*, IV, 13). Æthelweard (p. 19) *three thousands from his farmlands adjacent to the hills called by the commonalty Ashdown*. A large area along the line of the Berkshire Downs and possibly the origin of that county, it was perhaps given with a view to making a secure border against Mercia (cf. annal 661). Cuthred may have shared in the kingship (cf. p. 26, note 5; p. 41, note 10).   [3] Asser (37) explains that *Æscesdun in Latin means 'Ash-tree Hill'*, cf. Gelling, *The Place-Names of Berkshire*, pp. 2–4.   [4] F Here Bishop Birinus passed away and Agilbert the Frank was ordained.   [5] William of Malmesbury (*Gesta Regum*, I, p. 23) speaks of a battle against the Britons at *Wirtgernes burg* (i.e. Vortigern's stronghold) which might perhaps be identified with Bradford. Æthelweard (p. 19) uses the term *civil war*, and thus presumably thought it a battle against Saxons rather than Britons.   [6] So also BC, but properly 'Middle Angles' as in E and Bede (*HE*, V, 24).   [7] Perhaps Iken, Suffolk, see F. S. Stevenson, 'St Botolph (Botwulf) and Iken', 29–52.   [8] Plural perhaps in anticipation; the West Saxon diocese was divided in 704, see p. 40, notes 5–6.'   [9] MS *niht*; see p. 2, note 2.   [10] *Recte* Peada, as all other MSS.

E 653 *continued from opposite*
to build a minster at Icanho.[7] And here Archbishop Honorius passed away on
30 September.

654. Here Oswy killed Penda at Winwidfeld[11] and 30 royal children with
him, and some of them were kings; one of them was Æthelhere, brother of
Anna, king of the East Anglians. Then five thousand and 800 years had passed
away from the beginning of the world. And Peada, Penda's offspring,
succeeded to the kingdom of the Mercians.[12]

In his time they came together, he and Oswy, brother of King Oswald, and
declared that they wished to establish a minster in praise of Christ and in
honour of St Peter. And they did so, and gave it the name Medeshamstede,[13]
because there is a spring there called Medeswæl.[14] And then they began the
foundations and built upon them, and then entrusted it to a monk who was
called Seaxwulf. He was a great friend of God, and all people loved him, and
he was very nobly born in the world and powerful. He is now much more
powerful with Christ.

But that King Peada ruled no length of time, because he was betrayed by his
own queen at Eastertide.

655. Here Ithamar, bishop of Rochester, consecrated Deusdedit to
Canterbury on *26 March.*

656. Here Peada was killed, and Wulfhere, Penda's offspring, succeeded to
the kingdom of the Mercians.[15]

In his time the abbey of Peterborough, which his brother Peada had begun,
grew very powerful. The king greatly loved it for love of his brother Peada,
and for love of his pledged brother[16] Oswy, and for love of Seaxwulf its abbot.
He said that he wished to honour and reverence it according to the advice of
his brothers Æthelred and Merewala,[17] and according to the advice of his
sisters Cyneburh and Cyneswith, and according to the advice of the
archbishop who was called Deusdedit, and according to the advice of all his
councillors, both spiritual and temporal, who were in his kingdom. And he did
so.

Then the king sent for the abbot to come quickly to him; and he did so. Then
the king spoke to the abbot: 'Well, dear Seaxwulf, I have sent after you for my
soul's need, and I want to tell you fully as to why. My brother Peada and my
dear friend Oswy began a minster in praise of Christ and St Peter, but my
brother, as Christ willed, has passed from this life; but I wish to ask you, O
dear friend, that they [*continued overleaf*]

---

[11] Unidentified. Bede says the battle was fought near the flooded River Winwæd in which many
were drowned (*HE*, III, 24). This river may have been a tributary of the Humber.   [12] In fact
Peada ruled only the South Mercians, an area of five thousand hides, and then by Oswy's grant
(Bede, *HE*, III, 24).   [13] Subsequently 'Burh' then 'Peterborough', see below, pp. 33,
117.   [14] The element *wæl* means 'pool, spring' but the sense of *Medes* is obscure.   [15] After a
Mercian rebellion which expelled Oswy's ealdormen in 658 (Bede, *HE*, III, 24).   [16] For the
expression 'sworn brothers' see the decrees of William I (*fratres conjurati*), Robertson, *Laws*,
pp. 244–5, or Simeon (*fratres adjurati*) I, p. 129; and cf. below, *s.a.* 1016, where kings affirm
friendship 'both with pledge and with oath'.   [17] Æthelred succeeded Wulfhere in 675;
Merewala (*alias* Merewald, father of the infants martyred by Thunor, *s.a.* 640 A), is said by
Florence (I, p. 33) to have ruled in West Mercia; for his family see Finberg, *Early Charters of the
West Midlands*, pp. 217–25.

E 656 *continued from previous page*
should work with the greatest haste on the work, and I will find you gold and silver, land and goods for it, and all that is required for it'. Then the abbot travelled home and began to work. As Christ granted him, so he succeeded, so that in a few years the minster was ready. Then when the king heard tell of this, then he was very joyful; [he] ordered to send throughout all his[1] people to all his thegns, to the archbishop and to bishops, and to his earls, and to all those who loved God, that they should come to him; and he set the day when they were to consecrate the minster.

Then, when the minster was consecrated, the king Wulfhere was there, and his brother Æthelred and his sisters Cyneburh and Cyneswith; and Archbishop Deusdedit of Canterbury consecrated the minster, and the bishop of Rochester, Ithamar, and the bishop of London who was called Wine, and the bishop of the Mercians [who] was called Jaruman, and Bishop Tuda;[2] and also there was the priest Wilfrid who was bishop afterwards,[3] and there were all his thegns who were in his kingdom.

When the minster had been consecrated in the name of St Peter and St Paul and St Andrew, then the king stood up before all his thegns and said in a loud voice: 'Thanks be to the High Almighty God for this worship which is done here; and I want this day to honour Christ and St Peter, and I want that you should all approve my words:[4]

I, Wulfhere, to-day give St Peter and the abbot Seaxwulf and the monks of the minster these lands and these waters and meres and fens and weirs and all the lands that lie thereabout which belong to my kingdom, freely, so that nobody shall have any authority there except the abbot and the monks. This is the gift: from Peterborough to Northborough and so to the place they call Folies,[5] and so all the fen direct to Asendike, and from Asendike to the place which they call Fethermude, and so along the direct way 10 miles distance to Cugge dyke, and so to Rag Marsh, and from Rag Marsh 5 miles to the direct stream[6] that goes to Elm and to Wisbech, and so 3 miles about to Throckenholt, and from Throckenholt direct through all the fen to Dereworth, which is a distance of 20 miles and so to Grætecros, and from Grætecros through a clear stream called Broad Water,[7] and from there 6 miles to Paccelad, and so on through all the meres and fens[8] that lie [*continued opposite*]

---

[1] MS *hi*.   [2] Bishop of Lindisfarne, 664, see annal 664 E.   [3] Wilfred was associated in turn with York, Leicester, Lindisfarne, Hexham and Selsey.   [4] There follows a spurious charter of which a Latin version is given by Hugh Candidus (pp. 10–16); note the precocious use of the word 'earl', and various errors in the supposed attestors. For stylistic devices in such documents see generally Harmer, *Writs*, pp. 85–92.   [5] A French word, perhaps *folie* 'foolish enterprise', or *feuillie* 'leafy shelter' (Smith, *English Place-Name Elements*, I, pp. 179–80.   [6] *þe rihte æ*; Hugh Candidus (p. 11) reads *the main stream*, identifiable as the River Nene. For this and other place-names, see Reaney, *The Place-Names of Cambridgeshire*, pp. xxviii-xxix.   [7] *A beautiful water* (Hugh Candidus, loc. cit.) identifiable as the old course of the Nene on which lie Bradney Farm and Bradney House (Reaney, loc. cit. and p. 254.)   [8] *many meres and immense fens* (Hugh Candidus, loc. cit.).

E 656 *continued from opposite*

towards the market[9] of Huntingdon and these meres and lakes: Chalderbeach and Whittlesey Mere,[10] and all the others that lie thereabout, with the land and houses that are on the east side of Chalderbeach, and from there all the fens to Peterborough, and from Peterborough all the way to Wansford, and from Wansford to King's Cliffe, and from there to Easton, and from Easton to Stamford, and from Stamford just as the river runs to the foresaid Northborough.'

These are the lands and the fens which the king gave into[11] St Peter's minster. Then said the king: 'It is small, this gift, but I want that they should hold it royally and freely, so that neither tax nor rent be taken from it except for the monks alone. I want to free this minster thus, so that it be subject to Rome only, and I want all of us who cannot go to Rome to seek out St Peter here'.[12]

During these words the abbot begged that he would grant him what he wanted from him, and the king granted him it: 'I have here God-fearing monks who would like to conduct their lives in an anchorite's cell if they knew where: but here is an island that is called 'Anchorites Island',[13] and I would that we might make a minster there in praise of St Mary, so that those who wish to lead their lives in peace and in quiet may dwell there'.

Then the king answered and spoke thus: 'O dear Seaxwulf, I praise and approve not only what you want, but all those things that I know you want on our Lord's behalf, thus. And I ask you, brother Æthelred and my sisters Cyneburh and Cyneswith, for your souls' salvation, that you be witnesses and that you write it[14] with your finger. And I pray all those who come after me, be they my sons, be they my brothers, or kings that shall come after me, that our grant may stand, just as they want to be partakers of the life eternal and just as they want to escape eternal punishment. Whosoever shall diminish our grant, or other good men's grants, may the heavenly doorkeeper diminish him in the kingdom of heaven; and whosoever shall make it greater, may the heavenly doorkeeper make him greater in the kingdom of heaven'.

These are the witnesses who were there and who wrote it with their finger on the mark of Christ and agreed with their tongue. That was: first the king Wulfhere who first confirmed it by his [*continued overleaf*]

---

[9] MS *port*; see Smith, *English Place-Name Elements*, II, pp. 70–71.   [10] The largest body of fresh water then in lowland Britain; such things figure prominently in land-charters because an important resource of fish and water-fowl, see Hill, *Atlas*, pp. 10–11.   [11] For this formula cf. Swanton, *Prose*, p. 56.   [12] Although Wulfhere was undoubtedly a friend of the Church, this whole account may be largely wishful thinking by the Peterborough source.   [13] *Ancar ig*, a by-name for Thorney Island (so-called, says Hugh Candidus [p. 6], because of the abundant thorns there – as Ely for eels); Reaney, op. cit. in note 6, p. 280.   [14] i.e. the cross. The formula occurs repeatedly in this annal. In the context of witnessing or attestation, the expression 'to write with the finger' might mean either marking the sign of the cross on the parchment with a pen, or merely tracing over a cross already made by the scribe. Cf. Ordericus (VI, pp. 174–5) *confirmed, making a cross . . . ratified with the sign of the cross.*

A *continued from p. 28*

657. Here Peada passed away, and Wulfhere, Penda's offspring, succeeded to the kingdom of the Mercians.

658. Here Cenwalh fought at Penselwood[1] against the Welsh, and drove them in flight as far as the Parret.[2] This [battle] was fought after he came from East Anglia; he was there in exile for 3 years – Penda had driven him out and deprived him of the kingdom[3] because he abandoned[4] his sister.[5]

660. Here Bishop Agilbert left Cenwalh, and Wine held the bishopric for 3 years; and that Agilbert received the bishopric of Paris on the Seine in Gaul.

661. Here, at Easter, Cenwalh fought at Posent's stronghold;[6] and Wulfhere, Penda's offspring, raided as far as[7] Ashdown. And Cuthred, Cwichelm's offspring, and King Coenberht passed away in the one year. And Wulfhere, Penda's offspring, raided on Wight, and gave the inhabitants of Wight to Æthelwald,[8] king of the South Saxons, because Wulfhere had received him [as god-son][9] at baptism. And Eoppa, [*continued on p. 34*]

THE PETERBOROUGH MANUSCRIPT (E) 656 *continued from previous page*

word and afterwards wrote it with his finger on the sign of Christ and spoke thus: "I, King Wulfhere, with these kings, and with earls and with commanders and with thegns, the witnesses to my gift, I [do] confirm it before the archbishop Deusdedit with Christ's mark" +. And I, Oswy, king of Northumbria, friend of this minster and of Abbot Seaxwulf, approve it with Christ's mark +. And I, King Sigehere, grant it with Christ's mark +. And I, King Sebbi,[10] attest it with Christ's mark +. And I, Æthelred, the king's brother, grant the same with Christ's mark +. And we, the king's sisters, Cyneburh and Cyneswith, we approve it. And I, Deusdedit, archbishop of Canterbury, grant it. After that all the others who were there agreed to it with Christ's mark +. That was by name: Ithamar, bishop of Rochester, and Wine, bishop of London, and Jaruman, who was bishop of the Mercians, and Bishop Tuda, and Wilfrid the priest who was afterwards bishop,[11] and Eoppa the priest whom King Wulfhere sent to preach Christianity on Wight,[12] and Abbot Seaxwulf, and Ealdorman Immine, and Ealdorman Eadberht, and Ealdorman Herefrith, and Ealdorman Wilberht, and Ealdorman Abo, Æthelbald, Brorda, Wilberht, Ealhmund, Frithugis; these and many [*continued opposite*]

---

[1] MS *Peonnum*; Penselwood 'the head of Selwood', where lies the earthwork Keniwilkin's castle (VCH, *Somerset*, VII forthcoming); or perhaps Pinhoe on the approach to Exeter in Devon (cf. Hoskins, *The Westward Expansion of Wessex*, pp. 15–16). [2] A river running north-south through the wet-lands of Somerset, and a significant westward boundary. [3] See annal 644 E, 645 A. [4] Bede (*HE*, III, 7), says *repudiated*. [5] i.e. Penda's sister, whom Cenwalh had married. [6] A *Posentes byrg* (E *byrig*); Hoskins, *The Westward Expansion of Wessex*, p. 14 suggests Posbury, Devon. Or it may be Pontesbury, south-west of Shrewsbury. [7] A *oþ*, B C *on* E *of*; if this refers to the line of the Berkshire Downs (see p. 28, note 2); *on* need not necessarily refer to the Downs (hills) as such, since the collocation *gehergian on* is sometimes used where no sense of height is involved, cf. annal 910. [8] Bede (*HE*, IV, 13) calls him Æthelwealh. [9] The significance of the god-father god-son relationship is defined in wergild terms in the laws of Ine (Attenborough, *Laws*, pp. 60–61). [10] Sighere and Sebbi shared the rule of the East Saxons, under the Mercian hegemony of Wulfhere (Bede, *HE*, III, 30; IV, 6).

E 656 *continued from opposite*
others who were there, of the king's most thegnly men[13] all agreed to it. This charter was written 664 years after the birth of our Lord, the seventh year of King Wulfhere, the 9th year of Archbishop Deusdedit. Then they laid the curse of God and the curse of all saints and of all Christian people on any who should undo anything that was done there. So be it, say all. Amen.

Then, when this thing was done, the king sent to Rome to the pope Vitalian, as then was, and begged that he would grant with his charter and with his blessing all this aforesaid thing. And the pope then sent his charter saying thus: I, Pope Vitalian, grant to you, King Wulfhere, and to Archbishop Deusdedit and to Abbot Seaxwulf all the things which you want, and I forbid any king or any man to have any authority there but the abbot alone, and that he obey no man but the pope in Rome and the archbishop in Canterbury. If anyone breaks this in any thing, may St Peter destroy him with his sword; if anyone maintains it, may St Peter with the key of heaven open to him the kingdom of heaven. Thus was the minster at Medeshamstede begun, which afterwards was called Burh.[14]

Afterwards came another archbishop to Canterbury who was called Theodore,[15] a very good man and wise, and held his synod with his bishops and with the learned people.[16] Then Winfrith, bishop of Mercia, was put from his bishopric, and Abbot Seaxwulf was chosen as bishop there, and Cuthbald, a monk from the same minster was chosen as abbot. This synod was held six hundred and 3-and-seventy years after the birth of our Lord.

658. Here Cenwalh fought at Penselwood[1] against the Welsh, and drove them in flight as far as the Parret.[2] This [battle] was fought after he came from East Anglia, where he was for 3 years on a journey of exile. Penda had driven him out and deprived him of the kingdom[3] because he abandoned[4] his sister.[5]

660. Here Bishop Agilbert left Cenwalh,[17] and Wine held the bishopric for 3 years; and that Agilbert received the bishopric of Paris on the Seine in Gaul.

661. Here at Easter Cenwalh fought at Posent's stronghold[6] and Wulfhere, Penda's offspring, raided from[7] Ashdown. And Cuthred, Cwichelm's offspring, and King Coenberht passed away in the one year. And Wulfhere, Penda's offspring, raided on Wight, and gave the inhabitants of Wight to Æthelwald,[8] king of the South Saxons, because Wulfhere had received him [as god-son] [*continued overleaf*]

[11] For Tuda and Wilfrid, see p. 30, notes 2–3. [12] *Recte* Sussex, see p. 34, note 2. [13] MS *penost men*. [14] i.e. Peterborough, 'St Peter's *burh*'; Gover, *The Place-Names of Northamptonshire*, p. 224. See p. 117, note 13. [15] A Syrian monk sent by Pope Vitalian in 668; he had become a refugee in Rome after his native land was invaded by Arabs; see generally Brooks, *Early History of the Church of Canterbury*, pp. 71–6. [16] MS *lerede folc*, i.e. the clergy as distinct from laymen. For the Synod of Hertford see annal 673 and Bede, *HE*, IV, 5. [17] Cenwalh who spoke only English and was unable to understand the Frank Agilbert, appointed an additional, English, bishop for Wessex (Wine) with a seat at Winchester; Agilbeit was offended at not being consulted, and left in a huff (cf. Bede, *HE*, III, 7). Agilbert's difficulty with the English language was to prove an impediment when asked to put the Roman case at the Synod of Whitby four years later (*HE*, III, 25).

A 661 *continued from p. 32*
the mass-priest, at the command of Wilfrid[1] and King Wulfhere, first brought
baptism to the inhabitants of Wight.[2]

664. Here the sun grew dark. And Eorcenberht, king of the inhabitants of
Kent, passed away. And Colman with his companions went to his native
land.[3] The same year there was a great plague among men.[4] And Ceadda and
Wilfrid were ordained,[5] and the same year Deusdedit passed away.

668. Here Theodore was ordained archbishop.

669. Here King Egbert gave Reculver[6] to Bass the mass-priest in which to
build a minster.

670. Here Oswy, king of Northumbria, passed away, and Ecgfrith ruled
after him. And Hlothhere, nephew of Bishop Agilbert, succeeded to the
bishopric over the West Saxons and held it for 7 years. Bishop Theodore
consecrated him. And that Oswy was Æthelfrith's offspring, Æthelfrith
Æthelric's offspring, Æthelric Ida's offspring, Ida Eoppa's offspring.

671. Here there was the great mortality of birds.[7]

672. Here Cenwalh passed away, and Seaxburh, his queen, ruled one year
after him.

673. Here Egbert, king of the inhabitants of Kent, passed away. And that
year there was a synod at Hertford, and St Æthelthryth[8] founded the
monastery at Ely.

674. Here Æscwine succeeded to the kingdom of Wessex; he was Cenfus'
offspring, Cenfus Cenfrith's offspring, Cenfrith Cuthgils' offspring, Cuthgils
Ceolwulf's offspring, Ceolwulf Cynric's offspring, Cynric Cerdic's offspring.

675. Here Wulfhere Penda's offspring, and Æscwine, fought at Bieda's
Head;[9] and the same year Wulfhere passed away, and Æthelred succeeded to
the kingdom. [*continued on p. 36*]

THE PETERBOROUGH MANUSCRIPT (E) 661 *continued from previous page*

at baptism. And Eoppa, the priest, at the command of Wilfrid and King
Wulfhere, [was] the first of men [who] brought baptism to the inhabitants of
Wight.[2]

664. Here on 3 *May* the sun grew dark, and in this year [*continued
opposite*]

[1] Bishop of Northumbria in exile (cf. Bede, *HE*, V, 19).   [2] Eoppa's mission was in fact to the
South Saxons (Bede, *HE*, IV, 13), the conversion of the still pagan Isle of Wight being later
entrusted by Wilfrid to Beornwine and Hiddila (ibid., IV, 16).   [3] i.e. Ireland; taking with him
about thirty English monks similarly unable to accept the conclusions of the Synod of Whitby
(Bede, *HE*, III, 26; IV, 4). Apart from this oblique allusion, The Anglo-Saxon Chronicle omits all
mention of the Synod of Whitby. Interestingly, passages dealing with the synod are also omitted
from the Old English version of Bede.   [4] See Russell, 'The earlier medieval plague in the British
Isles,' 73–4.   [5] Bishops of York in succession, Cedda being appointed during Wilfred's
protracted absence abroad (Bede, *HE*, V, 19; Eddius Stephanus, *Life of Bishop Wilfrid*, pp. 30–31;
and see generally, Godfrey, *The Church in Anglo-Saxon England*, pp. 129–30).   [6] The Roman
fort of Regulbium in north-east Kent, see Maxfield, *Saxon Shore*, pp. 136–9, and Map p.
273.   [7] Æthelweard (pp. 19–20) says that in consequence there was a very foul stench over
both land and sea from the corpses of small and big birds. Such mortality is likely to have been the
result of extreme cold rather than disease, cf. annal 1046.   [8] Better known as St 'Audrey',

E 664 *continued from opposite*
came to the island of Britain a great plague among men.[4] And in that plague
passed away Bishop Tuda,[10] and he was buried at Pagele;[11] and Eorcenberht,
king of the inhabitants of Kent, passed away, and his son Egbert succeeded to
the kingdom. And Colman with his companions went to his native land.[3] And
Ceadda and Wilfrid were ordained,[5] and in the same year the archbishop
Deusdedit passed away.

667. Here Oswy and Egbert sent Wigheard the priest to Rome in order that
they should consecrate him archbishop, but he passed away as soon as
he came there.

668. Here the pope Vitalian ordained Theodore as archbishop, and sent
him to Britain.

669. Here King Egbert gave Reculver[6] to Bass the priest to build a minster.

670. Here Oswy, king of Northumbria, passed away on *15 February*, and
Ecgfrith, his son, ruled after him. And Hlothhere, nephew of Bishop Agilbert,
succeeded to the bishopric over the West Saxons and held it for 7 years. And
Bishop Theodore ordained him.

671. Here there was the great mortality of birds.[7]

672. Here Cenwalh passed away, and Seaxburh, his queen, ruled one year
after him.

673. Here Egbert, king of the inhabitants of Kent, passed away. And
Archbishop Theodore summoned a synod at Hertford, and St Æthelthryth[8]
founded the minster at Ely.

674. Here Æscwine succeeded to the kingdom in Wessex.

675. Here Wulfhere Penda's offspring, and Æscwine Cenfus' offspring,
fought at Beda's Head;[9] and the same year Wulfhere passed away, and
Æthelred succeeded to the kingdom. In his time he sent Bishop Wilfrid to
Rome[12] to the pope that then was – he was called Agatho – and made known to
him in writing and by word how his brothers, Peada and Wulfhere, and the
abbot Seaxwulf had built a minster which was called Peterborough, and that
they had freed it from all service to king and to bishop, and asked him that he
should confirm that with his charter and with his blessing. And the pope sent
his charter then to England, saying thus:[13]

'I, Agatho, Pope of Rome, greet well[14] the honourable Æthelred, king of
Mercia, and the archbishop Theodore of Canterbury [*continued overleaf*]

---

daughter of Anna, king of the East Angles, married in turn by Tondbyrht, a leader among the South
Gyrwe who lived in the Fens, and Ecgfrith of Northumbria, but remaining a virgin – in praise of
which Bede composed a hymn (*HE*, IV, 19, 20). See generally Ridyard, *Royal Saints*, pp. 53–6,
176–210 *et passim*.   [9] A C *Biedan heafde*, E G *Bedan heafde*; unidentified.   [10] Bishop of
Lindisfarne.   [11] MS *Wagele*, Bede (*HE*, III, 27) *Paegnalaech*; the letters P and W look very
similar in Anglo-Saxon script (cf. p. 55, note 11). The place is unidentified, but perhaps Whalley on
the Ribble, cf. Ekwall, *The Place-Names of Lancashire*, p. 76.   [12] Cf. Bede *HE*, V,
19.   [13] What follows is based on a late Peterborough forgery, the Latin version of which is
given by Hugh Candidus (pp. 16–21), cf. Kemble, *Codex Diplomaticus*, V, pp. 22–30, and
Haddan and Stubbs, *Councils*, III, pp. 153–60; neither Bede nor Eddius Stephanus make any
reference to it as part of Wilfrid's petition to Agatho.   [14] For this formula, see Harmer, *Writs*,
p. 61ff.

A *continued from p. 34*

676. Here Æscwine passed away, and Hedde succeeded to the bishopric,[1] [*continued on p. 38*]

[*continued on p. 38*]

THE PETERBOROUGH MANUSCRIPT (E) 675 *continued from previous page*

and Seaxwulf the Mercian bishop who was abbot[2] earlier, and all the abbots who are in England, with God's greeting and my blessing. I have heard the request of King Æthelred and of the archbishop Theodore and of the bishop Seaxwulf and of Abbot Cuthbald,[2] and I want that it shall be so in every particular just as you have said. And I command, on behalf of God and of St Peter and of all saints and of all the ordained dignitaries, that neither king nor bishop nor earl nor any man shall have neither authority there, nor rent nor tax nor campaign dues, nor shall anyone take any kind of service from the abbacy of Peterborough. I also command that the diocesan bishop[3] be not so bold that he perform either ordination or consecration within this abbacy, unless the abbot ask it of him; neither bishop's fine, nor synod nor any kind of assembly have any authority there. And I also desire that the abbot be held as legate from Rome over the whole island; and whatever abbot be chosen there by the monks that he be blessed by the archbishop of Canterbury. I desire and grant that whatsoever man may have vowed to travel to Rome and he be unable to fulfil it, whether because of sickness or his lord's need or because of lack of means or some other need he cannot come there, whether he be from England or from whatever other island he be, let him come to the minster at Peterborough and have the same forgiveness from Christ and St Peter and from the abbot and from the monks that he should have if he went to Rome.

Now I ask you, brother Theodore, that you have it proclaimed throughout all England that the synod be assembled and this charter be read and maintained. Likewise I command you, Bishop Seaxwulf, that just as you desired that the minster should be free, so, by Christ and by all his saints, I forbid you and all those bishops who come after you, that you have no authority over the minster except insofar as the abbot wishes. Now I declare with words that whoever maintains this charter and this command, may he ever dwell with God [*continued opposite*]

[*continued opposite*]

---

[1] Of Wessex.   [2] Abbot of Peterborough.   [3] *scyr-biscop*, 'bishop of the shire'.

E 675 *continued from opposite*

Almighty in the kingdom of heaven, and whoever breaks it, then may he be excommunicated and thrust down into hell with Judas and with all devils unless he make reparation. AMEN.'

The pope Agatho, and a hundred and twenty-five bishops, sent this charter to England by Archbishop[4] Wilfrid of York. This was done 680 years after the birth of our Lord, in the 6th year of King Æthelred. Then the king ordered Archbishop Theodore that he should appoint a meeting of all the councillors at the place they call Hatfield.[5] Then when they were gathered there, he had the charter read which the pope had sent there, and they all granted and fully confirmed it.

Then the king said:[6] 'All those things that my brother Peada and my brother Wulfhere and my sisters Cyneburh and Cyneswith gave and granted to St Peter and the abbot, these I wish to stand, and I wish in my day to increase it for their souls and for my soul. Now I give to St Peter today into his Peterborough minster these lands and all that belong thereto, that is:[7] Breedon,[8] Rippingale,[9] Cadney, Swineshead, Heanbyrig, Louth, Shifnal, Costesford, Stratford, Wattlesborough, the Lizard, Æthelhuniglond, Bardney. These lands I give St Peter just as freely[10] as I myself held them, and so that none of my successors take anything from there. If anyone do that, may he have the curse of the pope of Rome and the curse of all bishops and of all those who are here witness; and I confirm this with Christ's token' +.

I, Theodore, archbishop of Canterbury, am witness to this charter of Peterborough, and I confirm it with my writing, and I excommunicate all those who break it in any thing there, and I bless all those who maintain it +. I, Wilfrid, archbishop of York, I am a witness to this charter and I assent to this same curse +. I, Seaxwulf, who was first abbot and now am bishop, I give him who breaks this my curse and that of all my successors. I, Osthryth, Æthelred's queen, grant it. I, Hadrian, legate,[11] agree to it. I, Putta, bishop of Rochester, I subscribe to it. I, Waldhere, bishop of London, confirm it. I, Abbot Cuthbald, agree to it, so that whoever breaks it may he have the cursing of all bishops and of all Christian people. Amen.

676. Here Æscwine passed away, and Hedde succeeded to the bishopric,[1] [*continued overleaf*]

---

[4] The insistence on Wilfrid's status is interesting; he was deprived of York in 678, and at the time of his journey to Rome was bishop of Selsey.   [5] Hertfordshire; see annal 680.   [6] Altered from 'sent'.   [7] For the place-name identifications see generally Stenton, 'Medeshamstede and its colonies'; Hart, *The Early Charters of Eastern England*, pp. 97, 110.   [8] Breedon-on-the-Hill, cf. annal 731 E.   [9] Cf. Rumble, ' "Hrepingas" reconsidered', pp. 169–72.   [10] i.e. free from control, service dues etc.; cf. the words attributed to Wulfhere, p. 30.   [11] The North African monk sent by Pope Vitalian together with Theodore in 668 (Bede, *HE*, IV, 1; Brooks, *Early History of the Church of Canterbury*, pp. 94–7).

A 676 *continued from p. 36*
and Centwine succeeded to the kingdom. And Centwine was Cynegils'
offspring, Cynegils Ceolwulf's offspring.[1] And Æthelred, king of Mercia,
raided across the land of Kent.

678. Here the star *comet* appeared. And Bishop Wilfrid was driven out of
his bishopric by King Ecgfrith.[2]

679. Here Ælfwine[3] was killed, and St Æthelthryth passed away.[4]

680. Here Archbishop Theodore chaired a synod at Hatfield because he
wished to correct the faith of Christ.[5] And the same year Hild, abbess in
Whitby, passed away.[6]

682. In this year Centwine put the Britons to flight as far as the sea.

685. Here Cædwalla began to contend for the kingdom.[7] That Cædwalla
was Coenberht's offspring, Coenberht Cadda's offspring, Cadda Cutha's
offspring, Cutha Ceawlin's offspring, Cealwin Cynric's offspring, Cynric
Cerdic's offspring. And Mul was the brother of Cædwalla, and he was later
burned in Kent. And this same year King Ecgfrith was killed; that Ecgfrith was
Oswy's offspring, Oswy Æthelfrith's offspring, Æthelfrith Æthelric's offspring, Æthelric Ida's offspring, Ida Eoppa's offspring. And this same year
Hlothhere passed away.

686. Here Cædwalla and Mul ravaged Kent and Wight.

687. Here Mul was burned in Kent and 12 other men with him; and that
year Cædwalla again ravaged Kent. [*continued on p. 40*]

THE CANTERBURY MANUSCRIPT (F) *continued from p. 28*

685. Here in Britain there was bloody rain, and milk and butter were turned
to blood . . . [*continued on p. 42*]

THE PETERBOROUGH MANUSCRIPT (E) 676 *continued from previous page*

and Centwine succeeded to the kingdom of the West Saxons. And Æthelred,
king of Mercia, raided across the land of Kent.

678. Here the star *comet* appeared in August, and every morning for 3
months shone like a sunbeam. And Bishop Wilfrid was driven out of his
bishopric by King Ecgfrith,[2] and they [*continued opposite*]

---

[1] Described in the Genealogical Preface to A (p. 2) as Ceolwulf's brother's son.   [2] Cf. Eddius
Stephanus, *Life of Bishop Wilfrid*, pp. 48–51.   [3] Brother of King Ecgfrith of Northumbria, in a
battle against the Mercians near the River Trent, and, says Bede (*HE*, IV, 21), *much beloved in
both kingdoms.*   [4] After burial, her bones were disinterred by her sister and successor, Abbess
Seaxburh, and buried in a white marble coffin from Grantchester (Bede, *HE*, IV 19). See generally,
Ridyard, *Royal Saints*, p. 179.   [5] See Bede, *HE*, IV, 17.   [6] On 17 November. For a full
account of this remarkable woman, and for her role in the story of the poet Cædmon, see Bede, *HE*,
IV, 23–4.   [7] Of Wessex. It is interesting that Cædwalla is a Celtic name, cf. Cadwallon, *s.a.* 633
E.   [8] See above, p. 25, note 13.   [9] F Lat *fire from heaven*. Coldingham, a double monastery
in Yorkshire, Bede says was burned down through carelessness – a divine judgement on the loose-
living of the men and women there (*HE*, IV, 25).   [10] MS *Wihtum*, the Isle of Wight.

E 678 *continued from opposite*
consecrated 2 bishops in his stead, Bosa to Deira and Eata to Bernicia. And they consecrated Eadhed bishop to the inhabitants of Lindsey:[8] he was the first of the bishops in Lindsey.

679. Here Ælfwine[3] was killed beside the Trent, at the place where Ecgrifth and Æthelred fought. And here St Æthelthryth passed away; and Coldingham was consumed by a divine fire.[9]

680. Here Archbishop Theodore instituted a synod at Hatfield because he wished to correct the faith of Christ.[5] And that year Hild, abbess in Whitby, passed away.[6]

681. Here Trumberht was consecrated as bishop for Hexham, and Trumwine for the Picts,[10] because they were then subject to here.[11]

682. Here in this year Centwine put the Britons to flight as far as the sea.

684. Here in this year Ecgfrith sent a raiding-army among the Irish,[12] and his Ealdorman Beorht with it, and they wretchedly abused and burned God's churches.

685. Here King Ecgfrith commanded Cuthbert to be consecrated as bishop, and Archbishop Theodore consecrated him bishop for Hexham at York on the first day of Easter, because Trumberht had been put out of the bishopric. And the same year King Ecgfrith was killed to the north of the sea[13] on 20 *May*, and a great raiding-army with him. He was king for 15 years, and Aldfrith, his brother, succeeded him to the kingdom. And the same year Hlothhere, king of the inhabitants of Kent, passed away. And they consecrated John bishop in Hexham,[14] and he was there until Wilfrid came in.[15] John afterwards succeeded to the bishopric of the city[16] because Bishop Bosa had passed away. Then afterwards Wilfrid, his priest,[17] was consecrated bishop of the city, and John went to his minster in the Deiran Wood.[18]

686. Here Cædwalla and Mul, his brother, ravaged Kent and Wight. This Cædwalla gave Hoo, which is on an island called Avery,[19] into St Peter's minster, Peterborough. The abbot of the minster was then called Egbalth: he was the third abbot after Seaxwulf. Theodore was then archbishop in Kent.

687. Here Mul was burned in Kent, and 12 other men with him; and that year Cædwalla again ravaged Kent. [*continued on p. 41*]

[11] Bede says simply: *subject to the imperium of the English* (*HE*, IV, 12); but as the English referred to were the Northumbrians, the use of the word 'here' indicates a northern standpoint; the Canterbury MS F says 'to there'.   [12] *a harmless race that had always been most friendly to the English* says Bede (*HE*, IV, 26).   [13] i.e. the Firth of Forth, dividing Anglian from Scots territory.   [14] MS *on Agust'*, the abbreviated form of the place-name *Hagustaldesea*.
[15] Transferred from Leicester in 706. See generally Kirby, *Saint Wilfrid at Hexham*.
[16] i.e. York.   [17] Not the famous Wilfrid, but Wilfrid II of York, a pupil of abbess Hild of Hartlepool and Whitby (see Bede, *HE*, IV, 23).   [18] For the forested area of east Yorkshire, see Map p. 275. The minster was Beverley, by which place John is generally known.   [19] *Heabur-eagh*, a low-lying promontory situated between the Thames and Medway estuary in north Kent, and probably a real island at this time, see Wallenberg, *Kentish Place-Names*, pp. 19–21.

A *continued from p. 38*

688. Here Ine succeeded to the kingdom of Wessex and held [it] 37 years; and he built the minster at Glastonbury.[1]

And the same year Cædwalla went to Rome and received baptism from the pope, and the pope called him Peter, and 7 days later he passed away. This was Ine Cenred's offspring, Cenred Ceolwald's offspring; Ceolwald was the brother of Cynegils, and they were the sons of Cuthwine Ceawlin's offspring, Ceawlin Cynric's offspring, Cynric Cerdic's offspring.

690. Here Archbishop Theodore passed away, and Berhtwald succeeded to the bishopric. Earlier the bishops[2] were Roman; afterwards they were English.

694. Here the inhabitants of Kent came to terms with Ine and granted him 30,000[3] because they burned Mul earlier. And Wihtred succeeded to the kingdom of the inhabitants of Kent and held [it] 33 years: that Wihtred was Egbert's offspring, Egbert Eorcenberht's offspring, Eorcenberht Eadbald's offspring, Eadbald Æthelberht's offspring.

703. Here Bishop Hedde passed away; and he held the bishopric in Winchester 27 years.

704. Here Æthelred, Penda's offspring, king of Mercia, received a monk's orders; and [he] had held that kingdom 29 years. Then Coenred succeeded.

705. Here Aldfrith, king of Northumbria, and Bishop Seaxwulf[4] passed away.

709. Here Aldhelm passed away: he was bishop to the west of the wood.[5] And in the early days of Daniel, the land of Wessex was divided into two dioceses – and earlier it had been one; Daniel held one, Aldhelm the other.[6] After Aldhelm, Forthhere succeeded. And Ceolred succeeded to the kingdom of Mercia, and Coenred went to Rome, and Offa[7] with him. [*continued on p. 42*]

---

[1] This marginal note, made *c.* 1001–12, must refer to additional building or re-building, since Glastonbury was the site of a British monastery; here as elsewhere Ine was completing or adding to what others had begun.   [2] i.e. archbishops. In fact Deusdedit was the first native archbishop, but the continuous series of English primates begins with Berhtwald.   [3] B thirty thousand pounds; C thirty pounds; F thirty thousand pounds in friendship; F Lat *thirty thousand pounds*. A D E leave the denomination unexpressed. If it was sceattas, this would be approximately equal to a king's wergild according to the Law of the Mercians (Liebermann, *Gesetze*, I, pp. 462–3; transl. Whitelock, *Documents*, p. 433).   [4] Bishop of Mercia. He may have died earlier than this; Wilfrid was acting as bishop of the Middle Angles by 692 (Bede, *HE*, IV, 23).   [5] B 'to the west of Selwood'. Æthelweard (p. 21) says Aldhelm's diocese was vulgarly called 'Selwoodshire'. See Magoun, 'Aldhelm's diocese of Sherborne *bewestan wuda*', 103–14. It was Selwood that divided Wessex east from west; the British called it *Coir Maur* 'the great forest' (Asser, p. 84).   [6] Daniel remaining at Winchester after a new seat was made at Sherborne for Aldhelm.   [7] King of the East Saxons.   [8] F Lat *while he was still in white*; cf. Bede, *HE*, V, 7. The newly-baptised appeared with their sponsors wearing white for a week – until the 'octave', when the chrismal fillet was unloosed (cf. *s.a.* 878; and generally Alcuin's letters, *Monumenta Germaniae Historica, Epistolae*, IV, pp. 202–3, 214–5 and cf. 535–7). See also Stancliffe, 'Kings who opted out', p. 171.

E *continued from p. 39*

688. Here King Cædwalla went to Rome and received baptism from Sergius the pope, and he gave him the name Peter. And 7 days afterwards, on 20 *April*, he passed away under the clothes of Christ,[8] and he was buried within St Peter's church. And Ine succeeded to the kingdom of Wessex after him, and ruled 27[9] years; and afterwards departed to Rome, and remained there until his last day.

690. Here Archbishop Theodore passed away: he was bishop 22 years, and he was buried within Canterbury.

692. Here Berhtwald was chosen as archbishop on *1 July*: earlier he was abbot in Reculver. Before this time the bishops[2] were Roman, and afterwards they were English. There were then 2 kings in Kent: Wihtred and Wæbheard.[10]

693. Here Berhtwald was consecrated as archbishop by Godun, a bishop of Gaul, on *3 July*. Meanwhile Bishop Gifemund passed away, and Berthwald consecrated Tobias in his stead; and Berhthelm was led out of life.[11]

694. Here the inhabitants of Kent came to terms with Ine and granted him '30 thousands'[3] because they had burned Mul earlier. And Wihtred succeeded to the kingdom of the inhabitants of Kent[12] and held it three and twenty years.

697. Here the Southumbrians[13] killed Osthryth, Æthelred's queen, Ecgfrith's sister.

699. Here the Picts killed Ealdorman Beorht.[14]

702. Here Coenred succeeded to the Southumbrian kingdom.[15]

703. Here Bishop Hedde passed away; and he held the bishopric in Winchester 27 years.

704. Here Æthelred, Penda's offspring, king of Mercia, received a monk's orders; and had held that kingdom 29 years. Then Coenred succeeded.

705. Here Aldfrith, king of Northumbria, passed away on *14 December* in Driffield;[16] then Osred, his son, succeeded to the kingdom.

709. Here Bishop Aldhelm passed away: he was bishop to the west of the wood.[5] And in the early days of Daniel, the land of Wessex was divided into 2 dioceses – earlier it was one; Daniel held one, Bishop Aldhelm the other.[6] After Aldhelm, Forthhere succeeded. And Ceolred succeeded to the kingdom of Mercia, and Coenred went to Rome, and Offa[7] with him; and Coenred was there until his life's end. And the same year Bishop Wilfrid passed away at Oundle, and his body was carried to Ripon. He was bishop 45 years – whom King Ecgfrith had earlier exiled to Rome. [*continued on p. 43*]

---

[9] *xxvii*, recte *xxxvii*, as A and annal 726 E, 728 A.   [10] E *Nihtred ond Wæbheard*, F *Wihtred ond Webheard*; Bede (*HE*, V, 8) Wihtred (*Uictred*) and Swæfheard (*Suaebhard*). Such joint rule was not uncommon, but the territorial division of Kent was long-standing, east and west having their own bishops from earliest times; see generally Yorke, 'Joint kingship in Kent', 1–19.   [11] A monk of Melrose, whom D and Bede (*HE*, V, 12) call Dryhthelm. Such 'out of the body' experiences, conventionally describing a tour of heaven and hell, were not uncommon among early ascetics; cf. Swanton, *Prose*, pp. 37–42, 97.   [12] i.e. as sole ruler; cf. note 10.   [13] Here and *s.a.* 702 Southumbria presumably refers to Mercia, although used more generally *s.a.* 449 E. The reference perhaps indicates the northern origin of the annal.   [14] Cf. annal 684 E.   [15] This is apparently at odds with annal 704 (the date according to Bede's *Epitome*); possibly Coenred ruled jointly with Æthelred from 702.   [16] Great Driffield, East Yorkshire.

A *continued from p. 40*

710. Here Ealdorman Beorhtfrith fought against the Picts; and Ine and Nunna, his relative, fought against Geraint, king of the Welsh.[1]

714. Here Guthlac the saint passed away.[2]

715. Here Ine and Ceolred fought at Woden's Barrow.[3]

716. Here Osred, king of Northumbria, was killed;[4] he had the kingdom for 7[5] years after Aldfrith. Then Coenred succeeded to the kingdom, and held it 2 years; then Osric, and [he] held it 11 years. And in that same year Ceolred,[6] king of Mercia, passed away; and his body rests in Lichfield, and Æthelred Penda's offspring's in Bardney. And then Æthelbald succeeded to the kingdom of Mercia, and held it 41 years. Æthelbald was Alweo's offspring, Alweo Eawa's offspring, Eawa Pybba's offspring, whose ancestry is written down above.[7] And that revered man Egbert correctly converted the monks on the island of Iona so that they held Easter correctly[8] and the church-style tonsure.[9]

718. Here Ingeld, Ine's brother, passed away; and their sisters were Cwenburh and Cuthburh; and that Cuthburh founded 'the life'[10] at Wimborne; and she had been given to Aldfrith, king of Northumbria, and they separated during their lifetime.

721. Here Daniel[11] travelled to Rome. And the same year Ine killed Cynewulf.

722. Here Queen Æthelburh threw down Taunton, which Ine built earlier;[12] and the exile Ealdberht departed into Surrey and the South Saxons, and Ine fought against the South Saxons.

725. Here Wihtred, king of the inhabitants of Kent, whose ancestry is above[13] passed away; and Eadberht succeeded to the kingdom of Kent. And Ine fought against the South Saxons, and there killed Ealdberht.

728. Here Ine travelled to Rome and there gave up his life; and Æthelheard succeeded to the kingdom of Wessex and held it 14 years. And that year Æthelheard and the ætheling[14] Oswald fought; and that Oswald was Æthelbald's offspring, Æthelbald Cynebald's offspring, Cynebald Cuthwine's offspring, Cuthwine Ceawlin's offspring. [*continued on p. 44*]

THE CANTERBURY MANUSCRIPT (F) 714 *continued from p. 38*

714. Here Guthlac the saint[2] and *King Pippin*[15] passed away.

715. Here the king Dagobert[15] passed away. [*continued on p. 44*]

---

[1] i.e. the 'West Welsh' of Devon and Cornwall; this is the Gerontius to whom Aldhelm addressed a revealing tract on differences in British and Roman church practice (MGH, *Auctorum Antiquissimi*, XV, pp. 480–86). The entry in A was inserted by the tenth-century scribe responsible for annals 924–55. [2] For a Latin Life of Guthlac by Felix, a monk at Crowland, see Swanton, *Prose*, pp. 88–113, and for two Old English Guthlac poems, one focusing on his death, see Bradley, *Poetry*, pp. 248–83. [3] For this location see p. 20, note 4. William of Malmesbury suggests that Ceolred was the victor, calling him *virtute contra Inam mirabilis* (*Gesta Regum* I, p. 79). [4] He is said by Bede (*HE*, V, 18) to have come to the throne about the age of 8 and to have ruled for 11 years. William of Malmesbury (*Gesta Regum* I, pp. 58) suggests that Coenred who succeeded him may have been implicated. [5] D eight. [6] B C Ceolwald. [7] s.a. 626. [8] i.e. at the correct time: calculating its date according to the fashion of the Continental Roman church (see p. 25, note 10), adopted, together with the form of tonsure, by

E *continued from p. 41*

710. Here Acca, Wilfrid's priest, succeeded to the bishopric which he [Wilfrid] held earlier; and the same year Ealdorman Beorhtfrith fought between The Avon and The Carron against the Picts.[16] And Ine and Nunna, his relative, fought against Geraint, king of the Welsh,[1] and that same year Hygebald was killed.[17]

714. Here Guthlac the saint passed away.[2]

715. Here Ine and Ceolred fought at Woden's Barrow.[3]

716. Here Osred, king of Northumbria, was killed to the south of the border:[18] he had [the kingdom] for 7 years after Aldfrith. Then Coenred succeeded to the kingdom and held it 2 years. And then Osric, and [he] held it 11 years. And also that same year Ceolred, king of Mercia passed away; and his body rests in Lichfield, and Æthelred Penda's offspring's in Bardney. And then Æthelbald succeeded to the kingdom in Mercia and held it 41 years. And that revered man Egbert <converted>[19] the Iona community to the correct Easter[8] and to St Peter's tonsure.[9]

718. Here Ingeld, Ine's brother, passed away; and their sisters were Cwenburh and Cuthburh; and that Cuthburh founded 'the life'[10] at Wimborne; and she had been given to Aldfrith, king of Northumbria, and they separated during their lifetime.

721. Here Daniel[11] went to Rome. And the same year they killed the ætheling[14] Cynewulf. And here passed away the saint Bishop John; he was bishop 33 years and 8 months and 13 days; and his body rests in Beverley.[20]

722. Here Queen Æthelburh threw down Taunton, which Ine built earlier;[12] and the exile Ealdberht departed into Surrey and the South Saxons.

725. Here Wihtred, king of the inhabitants of Kent,[21] passed away on 23 *April*; he ruled for 34 years. And Ine fought against the South Saxons, and there killed the ætheling[14] Ealdberht whom he had earlier driven out.

726. Here Ine went to Rome,[22] and Æthelheard, his relative, succeeded to the kingdom of Wessex and held it 14 years.

727. Here passed away Tobias, bishop in Rochester, and in his stead Archbishop Berhtwald consecrated Ealdwulf as bishop. [*continued on p. 45*]

decision of the Synod of Whitby (see p. 34, note 3). For Egbert, a Northumbrian monk and friend of Bede, *pilgrim for Christ* in Ireland, see Bede, *HE*, III, 4, 27; V, 22.   [9] For styles of monastic tonsure see Colgrave, ed. Eddius Stephanus' *Life of Wilfrid*, p. 154; Plummer, ed. Bede's *Historia Ecclesiastica*, II, pp. 353-4.   [10] i.e. the monastic life of the community, cf. *munuc-lif*, p. 121, note 9. Wimborne was a double monastery under an abbess, see RCHM, *Dorset*, V, pp. 78-80.   [11] Bishop of Winchester.   [12] The stronghold built to contain the West-British was now apparently a factor in West Saxon politics; Henry of Huntingdon (p. 112) explains that the young dissident Ealdberht had sought refuge at Taunton, whereupon the queen destroyed the fort and obliged him to flee eastwards. William of Malmesbury (*Gesta Regum*, I, p. 35) calls the queen *a woman of royal breed and spirited*.   [13] *s.a.* 694.   [14] For the use of this term see Dumville, 'The ætheling', 1-33.   [15] These references to the Austrasian King Pippin II (of Héristal) and Dagobert III were apparently introduced from a Frankish chronicle. See the Introduction p. xxvi.   [16] These rivers flow together into the south bank of the Forth some twenty miles west of Edinburgh, and thus at or near the Anglian frontier.   [17] *Recte* Sigbald, as D and Gaimar (1631).   [18] i.e. the border between Northumbria and Mercia.   [19] Supplied from D.   [20] See p. 39, note 18.   [21] F Lat *Wihtredi gloriost regis Cantiæ* (note the hybrid Latin-Old English adjective); F adds 'and Eadberht reigned after him in Kent'.   [22] F Here King Ine passed away.

A *continued from p. 42*

729. Here the star *comet* showed itself; and St Egbert[1] passed away.

730. Here the ætheling Oswald passed away.

731. Here Osric, king of Northumbria, was killed, and Ceolwulf succeeded to the kingdom and held it 8 years.[2] And that Ceolwulf was Cutha's offspring, Cutha Cuthwine's offspring, Cuthwine Leodwald's offspring, Leodwald Ecgwald's offspring, Ecgwald Aldhelm's offspring, Aldhelm Ocga's offspring, Ocga Ida's offspring, Ida Eoppa's offspring.[3] And Archbishop Berhtwald departed, and the same year Tatwine was consecrated as archbishop.

733. Here Æthelbald captured Somerton;[4] and the sun grew dark.[5]

734. Here the moon was as if it were suffused with blood;[6] and Tatwine and Bede passed away.[7]

736. Here Archbishop Nothhelm obtained the pallium from the bishop of the Romans.[8]

737. Here Bishop Forthhere and Queen Frithugyth travelled to Rome.[9]

738. Here Eadberht Eata's offspring – Eata Leodwald's offspring – succeeded to the Northumbrian kingdom, and held it 21 years. And his brother was Archbishop Egbert, Eata's offspring; and they both rest in York city in the one side-chapel.[10]

741. Here King Æthelheard passed away; and Cuthred succeeded to the kingdom of Wessex and held it 16[11] years, and boldly made war against King Æthelbald. And Cuthbert was consecrated as archbishop, and Dunn bishop for Rochester. [*continued on p. 46*]

THE CANTERBURY MANUSCRIPT (F) *continued from p. 42*

742. Here there was a great synod assembled at Cloveshou,[12] and Æthelbald, king of Mercia, and Archbishop Cuthbert and many other learned men were there. [*continued on p. 46*]

[1] The 'revered man' of annal 716, see p. 42, note 8. For the portentous comet, see Bede, *HE*, V, 23.   [2] D places the death of Osric and accession of Ceolwulf correctly under 729 (as E and F), and then again under 731 (as A B C). Ceolwulf was the Northumbrian king who read and criticized Bede's *Ecclesiastical History* in draft (*HE* Prefatory Letter).   [3] Cf. Dumville, 'The Anglian collection of royal genealogies and regnal lists', 23–50.   [4] Æthelweard (p. 21) calls it a royal vill.   [5] F and all the circle of the sun became like a black shield; F Lat (following the Continuator of Bede, *HE*, cont. s.a. 733) *and the whole orb of the sun seemed to be covered with a black and terrifying shield about nine o'clock in the morning.*   [6] There was a lunar eclipse on 24 January; the redness was perhaps caused by refraction of light in a vaporous atmosphere.   [7] Bede's death is assigned to various dates in early sources, cf. Plummer, ed. *Venerabilis Baedae, Opera Historica* I, pp. lxxi–lxxii, n.3. Alcuin speaks of Bede's relics working miraculous cures (*The Bishops, Kings, and Saints of York*, pp. 102–5).   [8] *and held it five years* adds F Lat, although placing Nothhelm's death in 740. Bede acknowledges Nothhelm's assistance in searching out documents in the Roman archives (*HE*, Preface).   [9] The bishop of Sherborne and the wife of Æthelheard of Wessex.   [10] *porticus*, chapel; in 658 the Council of Nantes (Mansi, XVIII, 168) had confined burial in church to atrium or porticus, outside the main body of the church. Cf. *HE*, II, 3; Hope, 'Recent discoveries in the abbey church of St Austin at Canterbury', especially 390–99.   [11] xxvi B C.   [12] Unidentified; in 673 the Synod at Hertford had unanimously decided that: *we should meet once a year on 1 August at the place known as Clovæshoh* (Bede, *HE*, IV, 5).

E *continued from p. 43*

729. Here two *comets* appeared; and the same year Osric passed away, who had been king 11 years; and Egbert the saint[1] passed away in Iona. Then Ceolwulf succeeded to the kingdom and held it 8 years.[2]

730. Here the ætheling Oswald passed away.

731. Here Archbishop Berhtwald passed away on *13 January*; he was bishop 37 years and six months and 14 days. And the same year they consecrated Tatwine as archbishop; he was earlier priest in Breedon, in Mercia. Daniel, bishop of Winchester and Ingwald, bishop of London, and Ealdwine, bishop of Lichfield, and Ealdwulf, bishop of Rochester, consecrated him on *10 June*.[13]

733. Here Æthelbald captured Somerton;[4] and the sun grew dark;[5] and Acca was driven from the bishopric.[14]

734. Here the moon was as if it were suffused with blood,[6] and Archbishop Tatwine passed away, and also Bede;[7] and Egbert was consecrated as bishop.

735. Here Bishop Egbert obtained the pallium from Rome.

736. Here Archbishop Nothhelm obtained the pallium from the bishop of the Romans.[8]

737. Here Bishop Forthhere and Queen Frithugyth travelled to Rome.[9] And King Ceolwulf received Peter's tonsure;[15] and granted his kingdom to Eadberht, the son of his paternal uncle; he ruled 21 years.[16] And Bishop Æthelwold and Acca passed away,[17] and Cynewulf was consecrated as bishop. And the same year Æthelbald[18] raided the land of Northumbria.

738. Here Eadberht Eata's offspring – Eata Leodwald's offspring – succeeded to the Northumbrian kingdom, and he held it 21 years. And his brother was Archbishop Egbert, Eata's offspring; and they both rest in York city in the one side-chapel.[10]

740. Here King Æthelheard passed away; and Cuthred, his relative,[19] succeeded to the kingdom of Wessex and held it 16 years,[11] and boldly made war against Æthelbald, king of Mercia. And Cuthbert[20] was consecrated as archbishop, and Dunn bishop for Rochester.

741. Here York burned down.[21] [*continued on p. 47*]

---

[13] F adds 'He had the archbishopric three years'. [14] The reason for this is unknown, but his patron Ceolwulf of Northumbria was deposed the same year. [15] For this expression see annal 716 E. F reads 'and entered clerical orders'. [16] Like D, E gives the accession of Eadberht correctly under 737, then again under 738, as all other MSS. His ancestry is given under A 731 and 738. [17] Bishop of Lindisfarne and the deposed bishop of Hexham respectively. It was Æthelwold who had bound the Lindisfarne Gospels with a cover of gold and jewels (Simeon, I, p. 68); see generally *Codex Lindisfarnensis*, I, pp. 18–20, 84–5. [18] MS *Æthelwald*, a reading presumably influenced by the name of the bishop in the previous sentence. [19] Simeon (I, p. 32) and the Annals of Lindisfarne (p. 505) say they were brothers. [20] MS *Eadberht*, a reading presumably influenced by Eadberht just above *s.a.* 738. [21] Perhaps not helped by the *great drought in the land* mentioned in the Continuation of Bede (*HE*, Cont. *s.a.* 741).

45

A *continued from p. 44*

743. Here Æthelbald and Cuthred fought against the Welsh.

744. Here Daniel retired[1] in Winchester, and Hunferth succeeded to the bishopric.

745. Here Daniel passed away; 43[2] years had then passed since he succeeded to the bishopric.

746. Here they killed King Selred.[3]

748. Here Cynric, ætheling of Wessex, was killed, and Eadberht, king of the inhabitants of Kent, passed away, and Æthelberht, son of King Wihtred, succeeded to the kingdom.

750. Here King Cuthred fought against Æthelhun, the arrogant ealdorman.

752. Here, in the 12th[4] year of his rule, Cuthred fought against Æthelbald at Beorgford.[5]

753. Here Cuthred fought against the Welsh.

754[6] [756]. Here Cuthred passed away; and Cyneheard succeeded to the bishopric in Winchester after Hunferth; and that year Canterbury burned down, and Sigeberht succeeded to the kingdom of Wessex and held it one year.

755 [757]. Here Cynewulf[7] and the councillors of Wessex deprived Sigeberht of his kingdom because of unlawful actions – except for Hampshire; and he had that until he killed the ealdorman who stayed with him longest. And Cynewulf then drove him away into The Weald,[8] and he stayed there until a herdsman stabbed him by the stream at Privett – and he [thus] avenged the ealdorman Cumbra. And that Cynewulf often fought great battles against the Britons; and 31[9] years after he took the kingdom,[10] he wanted to drive out a certain ætheling who was called Cyneheard; and that Cyneheard was that Sigeberht's brother. And then he [Cyneheard] learned that the king, with a small troop, was in the company of woman[11] at Merton;[12] and he rode after him there, and surrounded the chamber[13] before the men who were with the king became aware of him. (*continued on p. 48*]

THE CANTERBURY MANUSCRIPT (F) *continued from p. 44*

755 [757]. Here Cynewulf[7] deprived King Sigeberht of his kingdom, and Sigeberht's brother, called Cyneheard, killed Cynewulf at Merton;[12] and he had ruled 31 years. And this same year Æthelbald, king of Mercia, was killed at Repton.[14] And Offa seized the kingdom of Mercia, having put Beornred to flight.[15] [*continued on p. 50*]

---

[1] MSS *gesæt*, 'sat down, resided'; possibly confusing *recedit* for *resedit* in a Latin source; the same confusion seems to have occurred also in the reference to Cynewulf's resignation *s.a.* 779 D E F.   [2] A C D *xliii*, E *xlvi*.   [3] King of the East Saxons.   [4] A C D *xii*, E *xxii*.   [5] 'Hill-' or 'barrow-ford'; Florence (I, p. 55) *Beorhtford*; unidentified.   [6] From here down to 845 there is a chronological dislocation in all extant manuscripts; down to 828 the majority of events are dated two years too early.   [7] For whom see Whitelock, *Documents*, p. 23, and White, 'The story of Cynewulf and Cyneheard', 1–18.   [8] For the character of the Wealden forest, see Brandon, 'The South Saxon Andredesweald', pp. 138–59.   [9] A B C *xxxi*, D *xxi*, E *xvi*; cf. annal 784, where this narrative properly belongs.   [10] The events now described actually took place in 786 (q.v.).   [11] *on wifecyþþe*; Æthelweard (p. 23) says: *with a certain whore*.

46

E *continued from p. 45*

743. Here Æthelbald, king of Mercia, and Cuthred, king of Wessex, fought against the Welsh.

744. Here Daniel retired[1] in Winchester, and Unferth[16] succeeded to the bishopric. And there were many shooting stars. And Wilfrid the Young,[17] who was bishop in York, passed away on 29 *April*: he was bishop 30 years.

745. Here Daniel passed away; 46[2] years had then passed since he succeeded to the bishopric.

746. Here they killed King Selred.[3]

748. Here Cynric, ætheling of Wessex, was killed, and Eadberht, king of the inhabitants of Kent, passed away.

750. Here Cuthred, king of Wessex, fought against Æthelhun, the arrogant ealdorman.

752. Here, in the 22nd[4] year of his rule, Cuthred, king of Wessex, fought at Beorhford[5] against Æthelbald, king of Mercia, and put him to flight.

753. Here Cuthred, king of Wessex, fought against the Welsh.

754[18] [756]. Here Cuthred, king of Wessex, passed away, and Cyneheard succeeded to the bishopric in Winchester after Hunferth; and that year Canterbury burned down and Sigeberht, his [Cuthred's] relative, succeeded to the kingdom of Wessex and held it 1 year.

755 [757]. Here Cynewulf[7] and the councillors of Wessex deprived Sigeberht, his relative, of his kingdom because of unlawful actions – except for Hampshire; and he had that until he killed the ealdorman who stayed with him longest. And Cynewulf then drove him away into The Weald,[8] and he stayed there until a herdsman stabbed him by the stream at Privett – which herdsman avenged the ealdorman Cumbra. And that Cynewulf often fought great battles against the Britons; and after ruling 16[9] years he wanted to drive out a certain ætheling called Cyneheard – which Cyneheard was Sigeberht's brother. And then he [Cyneheard] learned that the king, with a small troop, was in the company of a woman[11] at Merton;[12] and he rode after him there, and surrounded the chamber [*continued on p. 49*]

---

[12] There is no way of knowing which of the many Mertons is meant.   [13] B C read *burh* 'stronghold', which would refer to the entire site, surrounded by wall or stockade; A A[2] D E read *bur*, which might be one of a number of outbuildings – here the 'bower' where the lord or lady of the manor will typically have sought rest away from the communal hall (cf. *Beowulf*, 139–40, 662–5). For the layout of such a manor see, for example, Rahtz, *The Saxon and Medieval Palaces at Cheddar*, especially figs. 11, 14.   [14] See p. 49, note 9.   [15] F Lat *fugato Bernredo rege herede Adelb[aldi]*.   [16] *Recte* Hunferth as A and annal 754, but an interesting slip; cf. Unferth 'Mar-peace', Beowulf's notoriously troublesome opponent.   [17] i.e. Wilfrid II, appointed *c.* 714, cf. annal 685 E.   [18] See note 6, and for chronological discrepancies generally the Introduction p. xvi.

A 755 [757] *continued from p. 46*
And then the king perceived this, and he went to the door and then defended himself in no disgraceful way until he caught sight of the ætheling, and then rushed out on him and greatly wounded him; and they were all fighting against the king until they had killed him. And then from the woman's cries the king's thegns became aware of the disturbance, and whoever then was ready and quickest[1] ran there; and the ætheling offered each of them money and life, and not any of them wanted to accept it; but they were fighting continuously until they all lay [dead] except for one British[2] hostage, and he was very wounded. When in the morning the king's thegns whom he had left behind heard that the king was killed, they rode there – and his ealdorman Osric and Wigfrith his thegn and the men whom he left behind earlier – and found the ætheling in the stronghold where the king lay killed, and they had locked the gates against them;[3] and then they went there. And then he [the ætheling] offered them their own choice of money and land if they would grant him the kingdom, and told[4] them that relatives of theirs were with him who did not want to leave him;[5] and then they said that no relative was dearer to them than their lord, and they would never follow his slayer; and then they offered their relatives that they might go away unharmed. And they said that the same had been offered to their companions who were with the king earlier; then they said they themselves did not pay attention to this 'any more than your companions who were killed with the king'.[6] And they were fighting around the gates until they forced their way in[7] and killed the ætheling and the men who were with him, all except for one who was the ealdorman's godson, and he saved his life, although he was often wounded.

And that Cynewulf ruled 31 years, and his body lies at Winchester, and the ætheling's at Axminster;[8] and their direct paternal ancestry goes back to Cerdic. And the same year Æthelbald, king of Mercia, was killed[9] at Seckington, and his body lies in Repton.[10] And Beornred succeeded to the kingdom, and held it a little while [*continued on p. 50*]

---

[1] A *gearo wearþ ond radost*, E *gearo wearð hraðost*.   [2] A *Bryttisc*, E *Brytwylisc*; see p. 3, note 7; p. 14, note 1.   [3] or 'locked the gates upon themselves'; Æthelweard (p. 23) translates as *against them*.   [4] In A the verb is plural although no pronoun is given, i.e. [they] told; and consequently later in the sentence 'him' might mean 'them' (the form of the pronoun being ambiguous in Old English).   [5] or 'relatives of theirs were with them who did not want to leave them'.   [6] The use of direct speech in A (A[2]) and C suggests that this dramatic annal may derive from poetic oral or saga tradition. See also Magoun, 'Cynewulf, Cyneheard, and Osric', 361–76; Towers, 'Thematic unity in the story of Cynewulf and Cyneheard', 310–16; Waterhouse, 'The theme and structure of 755 Anglo-Saxon Chronicle', 630–40.   [7] A C D *fulgon*. E reads *flugon*, which if not a mistake for *fulgon*, could mean that they left the gates and fell back to a new defensive position inside the residence; the change of grammatical subject in what follows is of frequent occurrence in the annal.

E 755 [757] *continued from p. 47*
before the men who were with the king became aware of him. And then the king perceived this, and he went to the door, and then defended himself in no disgraceful way until he caught sight of the ætheling, and then rushed out on him and greatly wounded him; and they were all fighting against the king until they had killed him. And then from the woman's cries the king's thegns became aware of the disturbance, and whoever then was ready the quickest[1] ran there; and the ætheling offered each of them money and life, and not any of them wanted to accept, but they were fighting continuously until they were all killed, except for one British[2] hostage, and he was very wounded. When in the morning the king's thegns who were left behind heard that the king was killed, [they] rode there – and his ealdorman Osric and Wigfrith his thegn and the men whom he left behind earlier – and found the ætheling in the stronghold where the king lay killed, and they had locked the gates against them;[3] and then they went there. And then he offered them their own choice of money and land if they would grant him the kingdom, and told them that relatives of theirs were with him who did not want to leave him; and then they said that no relative was dearer to them than their lord, and they would never follow his slayer; and then they offered their relatives that they might go away from them unharmed. And they said that the same had been offered to their companions who were with the king earlier. Then they said this, that they would not pay attention to that any more than their companions who were killed with the king. Then they were fighting around the gates until they fled inside,[7] and [they] killed the ætheling and the men who were with him, all except for one who was the ealdorman's godson, and he saved his life, and he was often wounded.

And that Cynewulf ruled 31 years, and his body lies in Winchester, and the ætheling's in Axminster;[8] and their direct paternal ancestry goes back to Cerdic. And the same year Æthelbald, king of Mercia, was killed[9] at Seckington, and his body rests at Repton;[10] and he ruled 41 years. And then Beornred succeeded to the kingdom, and held it a little while [*continued overleaf*]

[8] The minster by the river Axe in East Devon, probably an ancient foundation on what was from early times a possession of the West Saxon royal house (Harmer, *Writs*, pp. 530–31). [9] *Treacherously murdered at night by his own bodyguards*, says the continuator of Bede, *s.a.* 757. [10] F says he was killed at Repton. Seckington, close to the Mercian royal centres at Lichfield and Tamworth, may have been a royal manor at this time, but was not so by the time of the Domesday survey. Æthelweard (p. 24) speaks of him as being buried in *a monastery called Repton*. For the royal mausoleum there, see Taylor, 'Repton reconsidered', pp. 382–5, fig. 23.

A 755 [757] *continued from p. 48*
and unhappily; and the same year Offa succeeded to the kingdom and held it 39 years; and his son Ecgfrith held it 141 days.[1] That Offa was Thingfrith's offspring, Thingfrith Eanwulf's offspring, Eanwulf Osmod's offspring, Osmod Eawa's offspring, Eawa Pybba's offspring, Pybba Creoda's offspring, Creoda Cynewald's offspring, Cynewald Cnebba's offspring, Cnebba Icel's offspring, Icel Eomer's offspring, Eomer Angeltheow's offspring, Angeltheow Offa's offspring, Offa Wermund's offspring, Wermund Wihtlæg's offspring, Wihtlæg Woden's offspring.

758 [760]. Here Archbishop Cuthbert passed away.[2]

759 [761]. Here Bregowine was ordained as archbishop at Michaelmas.[3]

760 [762]. Here Æthelberht, king of the inhabitants of Kent,[4] passed away; who was King Wihtred's son.

761 [763–4]. Here was the big winter.

763 [765]. Here[5] Jænberht was ordained as archbishop on the fortieth day after midwinter.[6]

764 [766]. Here Archbishop Jænberht obtained the pallium.

768. Here Eadberht, Eata's offspring, passed away.[4]

772 [774]. Here Bishop Milred[7] passed away.

773 [776]. Here a red sign of Christ appeared in the heavens after the sun's setting.[8] And that year the Mercians and the inhabitants of Kent fought at Otford; and snakes[9] were seen extraordinarily in the land of the South Saxons.

777 [779]. Here Cynewulf and Offa fought around Benson,[10] and Offa took the settlement [*continued on p. 52*]

THE PETERBOROUGH MANUSCRIPT (E) 755 [757] *continued from p. 49*

and unhappily; and that same year Offa put Beornred to flight and succeeded to the kingdom, and held it 39 years; and his son Ecgfrith held it 141 days.[1] That Offa was Thingfrith's offspring. [*continued opposite*]

THE CANTERBURY MANUSCRIPT (F) *continued from p. 48*

777. Here Æthelberht was consecrated in York as bishop for Whithorn. [*continued on p. 52*]

---

[1] MS *xli daga 7 c daga.*   [2] A late addition to F reads: and he held the archbishopric eighteen years.   [3] In F a later hand has erased 'Michaelmas' and added: 'and he held it four years'.   [4] F inserts in a later hand: 'King Wihtred's son'.   [5] An insertion in F adds: Archbishop Bregowine passed away.   [6] i.e. Christmas (see the Introduction p. xv), the fortieth 'day being Candlemas, 2 February', the festival of the purification of the Virgin Mary (or presentation of Christ in the Temple), celebrated with a great display of candles. An insertion in F adds: and held it twenty-six years.   [7] A *Milred,* E *Mildred* etc., bishop of Worcester.   [8] Presumably some kind of aurora borealis.   [9] MSS *nædran;* the word is not yet confined to the species 'adder'. Why their appearance should have been remarkable (*wundorlice* all MSS except A *wunderleca*) is unclear, unless they were unseasonal.   [10] MS *Bensington;* perhaps the place captured by the West Saxons in 571, cf. Gelling, *The Place-Names of Oxfordshire,* pp. 116, 119.

E *continued from opposite page*

757. Here Eadberht, king of Northumbria, received the tonsure,[11] and Oswulf, his son, succeeded to the kingdom and ruled 1 year; and his household killed him on *24 July*.

758 [760]. Here Archbishop Cuthbert passed away.

759 [761]. Here Bregowine was consecrated as archbishop at Michaelmas; and [759][12] Æthelwald Moll[13] succeeded to the kingdom in Northumbria and ruled 6 years, and then abandoned it.

[762]. Here Æthelberht, king of the inhabitants of Kent, passed away, and [764] Ceolwulf[14] also passed away.

761 [763–4]. Here was the big winter; and [761] Moll, the Northumbrian king, killed Oswine at Edwin's Cliff[15] on *6 August*.

762 [765]. Here Jænberht was ordained as archbishop on the 40th day after midwinter;[6] and [763] Bishop Frithuwald at Whithorn passed away on *7 May*; he was consecrated in the city[16] on *15 August* in the 6th year of Ceolwulf's rule; and he was bishop 29 years; then they consecrated Peohtwine as bishop for Whithorn at Elvet[17] on *17 July*.

765. Here Alhred succeeded to the kingdom of Northumbria and ruled eight[18] years.

766. Here Archbishop Egbert passed away in York on *10 November*: he was bishop 36[19] years; and Frithuberht in Hexham: he was bishop 34 years. And [767] they consecrated Æthelberht for York and Ealhmund for Hexham.

768. Here Eadberht, Eata's offspring, passed away on *19 August*.[20]

769. *The beginning of the rule of King Charles*.[21]

772 [774]. Here Bishop Mildred[7] passed away.

774. Here the Northumbrians drove out their king Alhred from York at Eastertide, and took Æthelred, son of Moll, as their lord, and he ruled 4 years. And [776] men saw a red sign of Christ in the heavens after the sun's setting.[8] In that year the Mercians and the inhabitants of Kent fought at Otford; and snakes[9] were seen extraordinarily in the land of the South Saxons.

776. Here Bishop Peohtwine passed away on *19 September*: he was bishop 14 years.

777 [779]. Here Cynewulf and Offa contended around Benson,[22] and Offa took the settlement. And the same year [777] on *15 June* in York they consecrated Æthelberht bishop for Whithorn. [*continued overleaf*]

---

[11] [erasure] *scære*, 'shaving'; F Lat *clerical 'crown'*; cf. p. 43, note 9. See generally, Stancliffe, 'Kings who opted out', p. 156. [12] Some entries peculiar to the northern recension derive from a source unaffected by the chronological dislocation of the main texts (see p. 47, note 18). [13] A Northumbrian *patrician*, cf. Thacker, 'Some terms for noblemen', 216. [14] The king of Northumbria who had abdicated in 737. [15] *Ædwines clif*, unidentified; Simeon of Durham (II, p. 41) says the battle took place at Eldunum, probably the Eildon Hills, Roxburghshire. [16] i.e. of York. [17] On the river Wear opposite Durham, but before the establishment of the cathedral there (VCH, *Durham*, III, p. 167). [18] MS *eahta*, D *viii*. [19] *xxxvi*, perhaps for *xxxiii*, cf. annal 734 E. [20] E *xiiii kl Septembris*, D *xiii kl Septembris*. [21] Charles the Great (Charlemagne). [22] E *geflyton ymb*; possibly 'about, with reference to' Benson. See also note 10.

A *continued from p. 50*

780 [782]. Here the Old Saxons and the Franks fought.[1]

784 [786]. Here Cyneheard killed King Cynewulf, and he [too] was killed there and 84 men with him;[2] and then Beorhtric succeeded to the kingdom of Wessex, and he ruled 16 years, and his body lies at Wareham; and his direct paternal ancestry goes back to Cerdic. At this time King Ealhmund ruled in Kent.

785 [787]. Here there was a contentious synod at Chelsea,[3] and Archbishop Jænberht relinquished some part of his bishopric,[4] and [*continued on p. 54*]

THE CANTERBURY MANUSCRIPT (F) 778 [779] *continued from p. 50*

778 [779]. Here Ælfwald succeeded to the kingdom[5] and ruled 10 years.

779 [780]. Here Archbishop Æthelberht passed away, and Eanbald was consecrated [778][6] in his place. And Cynebald retired[7] in Lindisfarne island.

780 [782]. Here Ealhmund, bishop in Hexham, passed away; and Tilberht was chosen for there, and Hygebald for Lindisfarne island;[8] and King Ælfwald sent to Rome for the pallium for the use of Archbishop Eanbald.

782. Here Cynewulf, bishop of Lindisfarne, passed away; and there was a synod at Aclea.[9]

784. *At this time King Ealhmund was in Kent*: this King Ealhmund was Egbert's father, Egbert was Æthelwulf's father.[10]

785 [787]. Here a full synod sat at Chelsea,[3] and Archbishop Jænberht relinquished some part of his bishopric,[4] and Hygeberht was chosen by King Offa, and Ecgfrith consecrated as king.[11] And at this time messengers [*continued on p. 54*]

THE PETERBOROUGH MANUSCRIPT (E) 777 [779] *continued from previous page*

In this King Offa's day there was an abbot in Peterborough called Beonna. This same Beonna, on the advice of all the monks of the minster, then leased[12] to Ealdorman Cuthbert 10 holdings[13] at Swineshead, with pasture and with meadow and all that lay there, on condition that this Cuthbert gave the abbot 50 pounds for it, and each year one day's provisions or 30 shillings in money; and on condition also that after his day the land should go back to the minster. At this witnessing was the king Offa, and the king Ecgfrith, and the archbishop Hygeberht, and Bishop Ceolwulf, [*continued opposite*]

---

[1] The Saxons slaughtered Frankish invaders east of the Teutoburgerwald, and in retaliation Charlemagne carried out a large-scale massacre at Verdun.　[2] For a full circumstantial account see annal 755 [757].　[3] A piece of dry land on the north bank of the Thames upstream from London, and the venue of a dozen councils, royal or ecclesiastical, from 785 to 815.　[4] i.e. dividing the province of Canterbury when Offa created an archbishopric for Mercia at Lichfield, which lasted until Hygeberht's death c. 803.　[5] Of Northumbria.　[6] D says correctly 'earlier consecrated'; Æthelberht had retired two years before his death.　[7] *Recte* Cynewulf, as D, and cf. annal 737 E; for the verb 'retired' see p. 46, note 1.　[8] It was to Hygebald that Alcuin wrote in 797 censuring the monks of Lindisfarne for their interest in secular stories: 'What has Ingeld to do with Christ!' (MGH, *Epistolae* IV, pp. 181–4).　[9] Unidentified.　[10] The genealogical note was added in the margin by a third hand.　[11] Offa's son, consecrated in his father's lifetime. This is the first reference to the consecration of a king in England; see Swanton, *Crisis and Development in Germanic Society*, pp. 55–60 *et passim*.

E 777 [779] *continued from opposite*
and Bishop Unwona, and Abbot Beonna, and many other bishops and abbots, and many other powerful men. In this same Offa's day there was an ealdorman called Brorda[14] who requested the king that, for love of him, he should free a certain minster of his called Woking, because he wanted to give it into Peterborough and St Peter and the abbot that then was – he was called Pusa. That Pusa succeeded Beonna, and the king loved him well. And the king then freed the church of Woking from king and from bishop and from earl and from all men, so that no one had any authority there, except St Peter and the abbot. This was done in the king's town called Freoricburna.[9]

778. Here on 22 *March* Æthelbald and Heardberht killed 3 high-reeves:[15] Ealdwulf, Bosa's offspring, at Coniscliffe[16] and Cynewulf and Ecga at Helathyrne.[9] And then Ælfwald succeeded to the kingdom and drove Æthelred into the country; and he ruled for 10 years. *Charles[17] entered Spain. Charles came to Saxony. Charles destroyed the cities of Pamplona and Saragossa, joined his army, and having received hostages and subjected the Saracens, returned to the Franks through Narbonne in Gascony.[18]*

779 [782]. Here the Old Saxons and the Franks fought. And [780] on 24 *December* the Northumbrian high-reeves[15] burned Ealdorman Beorn in Seletun.[19] And Archbishop Æthelberht passed away in the city [York], and Eanbald was consecrated [778][6] in his stead. And Bishop Cynebald[7] in Lindisfarne island retired.

780. Here Ealhmund, bishop in Hexham, passed away on 8 *September*, and they consecrated Tilberht in his stead on 2 *October*. And they consecrated Hygebald bishop for Lindisfarne island at Sockburn;[20] and King Æthelwald[21] sent a man[22] to Rome for the pallium, and made Eanbald archbishop.

782. Here passed away Wærburh, Ceolred's queen, and Cynewulf, bishop in Lindisfarne island; and there was a synod at Aclea.[9]

784 [786]. Here Cyneheard killed King Cynewulf, and he [too] was killed and 84 men with him;[2] and then Beorhtric, king of the West Saxons, succeeded to the kingdom, and he ruled 16 years; and his body lies at Wareham, and his direct paternal ancestry goes back to Cerdic.

785. Here passed away Botwine, abbot in Ripon; and here [787] there was a contentious synod at Chelsea[3] and Archbishop Jænberht relinquished some part [*continued on p. 55*]

---

[12] See Stenton, 'Medeshamstede and its colonies', 313–14 (*Preparatory*, p. 191). [13] *bonde land*, land held by a husbandman (*bonda*) as tenant. [14] Offa's *prefectus*, cf. Thacker, 'Some terms for noblemen', 218–19. [15] The 'high-reeve' was probably an official responsible for the administration of a royal estate or large district, probably not very different in status from the ealdorman; the term is not found in the south of England until later in the period (Chadwick, *Anglo-Saxon Institutions*, pp. 231–2, 237–8). [16] *Cininges clife*, 'the king's cliff', County Durham. [17] Charlemagne. [18] It was the rearguard action fought at Roncesvalles on this occasion that provided the setting for the Frankish epic poem *The Song of Roland*. [19] Perhaps Silton, North Yorkshire. [20] On the Tees in County Durham; it appears to have been an ecclesiastical centre at this date, to judge by the remains of early stone crosses, see Cramp, *Corpus*, I, pp. 135–44. [21] *Recte* Ælfwald, as F. [22] In fact Alcuin of York, the foremost scholar of his time, who was used as messenger several times.

A 785 [787] *continued from p. 52*
Hygeberht was chosen by King Offa, and Ecgfrith consecrated as king.[1]

787 [789]. Here Beorhtric took[2] King Offa's daughter Eadburh. And in his days[3] there came for the first time 3 ships;[4] and then the reeve rode there[5] and wanted to compel them to go to the king's town, because he did not know what they were; and they killed him.[7] Those were the first ships of the Danish men which sought out the land of the English race.

790 [792]. Here Archbishop Jænberht passed away, and the same year Abbot Æthelheard[8] was chosen as bishop.

792 [794]. Here Offa, king of the Mercians, ordered King Æthelberht's head to be struck off.[9] [*continued on p. 56*]

[*continued on p. 56*]

THE CANTERBURY MANUSCRIPT (F) 785 [787] *continued from p. 52*

were sent by Pope Hadrian to England to renew the faith which *St Gregory* sent us; and they were received with honour.[10]

787 [789]. Here Beorhtric took as wife King Offa's daughter Eadburh; and in his days[3] there came for the first time 3 ships of Northmen from Hordaland:[4] these were the first ships of the Danish men which sought out the land of the English race.

788 [787]. Here a synod was assembled at Pincanhalh[11] in the land of Northumbria.

789 [788]. Here Ælfwald, king of Northumbria, was killed, and a heavenly light was frequently seen where he was killed. And Osred, Alhred's son, succeeded to the kingdom, because he was Ælfwald's nephew. And there was a great synod at Aclea.

790 [792]. Here Archbishop Jænberht passed away, and the same year Abbot Æthelheard[8] *of the monastery of Louth* was chosen as archbishop. [790] And Osred, king of Northumbria, was made to flee from the kingdom, and Æthelred, Æthelwald's son, again succeeded to the kingdom.

791. Here Baldwulf was consecrated as bishop for Whithorn by Archbishop Eanbald and by Bishop Æthelberht.

792 [794]. Here King Offa ordered King Æthelberht's head to be struck off.[9]

793. Here terrible portents came about in the land of Northumbria, and miserably afflicted the people: these were immense flashes of lightning, and fiery dragons were seen flying in the air,[6] and there immediately followed [*continued on p. 56*]

[*continued on p. 56*]

---

[1] See p. 52, note 11.   [2] i.e. took as wife, married.   [3] i.e. between 784 [786] and 800 [802]. For this kind of general ascription of events to a reign, cf. annal 449.   [4] The author of A feels no need to mention their origin; B C D E F say they were Northmen, E F specifying that they came from Hordaland, the district around Hardanger Fjord in West Norway. F Lat and Æthelweard (p. 26) say they were *Danes*; *Annals of St Neots* (p. 39) *Northmen, that is, Danes*. The terms 'Northmen' and 'Danes' are apparently used synonymously in The Chronicle.   [5] *The Annals of St Neots* (p. 39) says they *landed in the island which is called Portland.*   [6] Perhaps these might be interpreted as the long-tailed comets which were regarded as portents of disaster, see p. 83, note 20; p. 121, note 7.

E 785 *continued from p. 53*
of his bishopric,[12] and Hygeberht was chosen by King Offa, and Ecgfrith
consecrated as king.[1] And at this time messengers were sent from Rome by
Pope Hadrian to England to renew the faith and the peace which St Gregory
sent to us through bishop Augustine; and they were received with honour.[10]

787 [789]. Here Beorhtric took[2] King Offa's daughter Eadburh. And in his
days[3] came first 3 ships of Northmen from Hordaland:[4] and then the reeve
rode there[5] and wanted to compel them to go to the king's town because he did
not know what they were; and then they killed him.[7] These were the first ships
of the Danish men which sought out the land of the English race.

788 [787]. Here on 2 *September* a synod was assembled at Pincanhalh[11] in
the land of Northumbria, and Abbot Aldberht passed away.[13] *Charles*[14] *came
through Germany to the borders of Bavaria.*

789 [788]. Here on 23 *September* Ælfwald, king of Northumbria, was
killed by Sicga, and a heavenly light was frequently seen where he was killed;
and he was buried in Hexham inside the church.[15] And a synod was assembled
at Aclea. And Osred, Alhred's son, succeeded to the kingdom after him – he
was his nephew.[16]

790 [792]. Here Archbishop Jænberht passed away, and the same year
Abbot Æthelheard[8] was chosen as archbishop. [790] And Osred, king of
Northumbria, was betrayed and driven from the kingdom; and Æthelred,
Æthelwald's son, again succceeded to the kingdom.

791. Here on 17 *July* Baldwulf was consecrated as bishop for Whithorn by
Archbishop Eanbald and by Bishop Æthelberht.

792 [794]. Here Offa, king of Mercia, ordered Æthelberht's head to be
struck off.[9] And Osred, who had been king of Northumbria, after coming
home from a period of exile was seized and killed on 14 *September*; and his
body lies at Tynemouth. And on 29 *September* King Æthelred took a new wife
who was called Ælflæd.

793. Here terrible portents came about over the land of Northumbria, and
miserably frightened the people: these were immense flashes of lightning,[17]
and fiery dragons were seen flying in the air.[6] [*continued on p. 57*]

---

[7] Æthelweard (p. 27) says the reeve was called Beaduheard; being in the town of Dorchester
[the closest royal estate to Portland] he went to the harbour with a few men, assuming the arrivals
to be merchants rather than marauders, and spoke to them haughtily, whereupon they killed both
him and his companions on the spot. The laws of King Alfred decreed that traders should bring to
the king's reeve, publicly, the men they are taking up into the country, and declare how many there
are (Attenborough, *Laws*, pp. 78–9).   [8] Abbot of Louth, Lincolnshire; a Mercian amenable to
Offa, see Brooks, *The Early History of the Church of Canterbury*, pp. 120–32, 179–80.   [9] See
James, 'Two Lives of St Ethelbert, King and Martyr', 214–44, and Wright, *The Cultivation of
Saga*, pp. 95–106. For his relics, see below p. 186, note 3.   [10] D adds 'and sent back with
agreement'. See generally Haddan and Stubbs, *Councils*, III, pp. 447–62, transl. Whitelock,
Documents, pp., 836–40.   [11] D *Wincanheale*; EF *Pincanheale*, the Anglo-Saxon letter-forms
W and P are very similar and were presumably mistaken in an exemplar (cf. p. 35, note 11). The
place is unidentified.   [12] See p. 52, note 4.   [13] D 'in Ripon'.   [14] Charlemage.   [15] A
particularly elaborate structure, Taylor, *Architecture*, pp. 297–312.   [16] i.e. Ælfwold's
nephew, see F.   [17] D 'whirlwinds and flashes of lightning'. For the association of bad weather
and bad news, cf. p. 121, note 7.

A *continued from p. 54*

794 [796]. Here Pope Hadrian and King Offa passed away.[1] Æthelred, king of Northumbria, was killed by his own nation; and Bishop Ceolwulf and Bishop Eadbald[2] left the country. And Ecgfrith succeeded to the Mercian kingdom, and passed away the same year. And Eadberht, who was by another name named Præn,[3] succeeded to the kingdom in Kent.

796 [798]. Here Ceolwulf,[4] king of Mercia, ravaged over the inhabitants of Kent as far as the Marsh,[5] and [they] captured Præn, their king, and led him bound into Mercia.

797 [799]. Here the Romans cut out the tongue of the pope Leo and put out his eyes, and made him flee from his seat; and then immediately afterwards, by God's help, he could see and speak, and was pope again as he was before. [*continued on p. 58*]

THE CANTERBURY MANUSCRIPT (F) 793 *continued from p. 54*

a great famine, and after that in the same year the raiding of the heathen miserably devastated God's church in Lindisfarne island by looting and slaughter.[6]

794 [796]. Here Pope Hadrian and King Offa passed away;[1] and Æthelred, king of Northumbria, was killed. And Bishop Ceolwulf and Bishop Eadbald[2] left the country. And Ecgfrith succeded to the Mercian kingdom, and passed away in that year. And Eadberht Præn[3] succeeded to the kingdom in Kent.

795 [796]. Here the moon grew dark between cock-crow and dawn.[7] And Eardwulf succeeded to the Northumbrian kingdom, and was blessed as king by Archbishop Eanbald and Bishop Æthelberht and Hygebald and Bishop Baldwulf.[8]

796 [798]. Here Ceolwulf,[4] king of Mercia, ravaged over Kent[5] and captured Eadberht Præn, their king, and led him bound into Mercia and had his eyes put out and his hands cut off. And Æthelheard, archbishop of Canterbury, arranged a synod, and, by command of Pope Leo,[9] strengthened and confirmed all the things concerning God's minsters which were established in Wihtgar's day[10] and in other kings' days.

798. [As 797 E] . . . and Bishop Æthelberht passed away. And Bishop Ælfhun passed away at Sudbury;[11] and he was buried in Dunwich,[12] and Tidfrith was chosen after him. And Sigeric, king of Essex, travelled to Rome. Here in this same year the body of Wihtburh[13] was found wholly sound and undecayed at Dereham,[14] fifty-five years after she departed this life. [*continued on p. 58*]

---

[1] Hadrian I on 25 December 795, and Offa 29 July 796.   [2] Bishops of Lindsey and of London respectively.   [3] A one-time priest, intent on freeing Kent from the Mercian hegemony, Brooks, *History of the Early Church of Canterbury*, pp. 114, 121–5; the origin of his surname is unclear, cf. Tengvik, *Old English Bynames*, p. 394.   [4] A A² C E F *Ceolwulf*; *recte* Coenwulf, as B C (*Cynulf*), and cf. annal 819. The error may be due to confusion with the name of the next Mercian king, cf. annal 819.   [5] i.e. Romney Marsh. F reads merely 'Kent', E and all other MSS, have 'the inhabitants of Kent and the inhabitants of the Marsh'; Æthelweard (p. 27) *Kent and the district which is called 'Merscwari'* (inhabitants of the Marsh).   [6] F Lat adds: *Translation of the martyr St Alban.*   [7] F Lat *vi Kalendas Iunii* (27 May).   [8] Bishops of Hexham, Lindisfarne and Whithorn respectively.   [9] Leo III.   [10] Presumably an error for Wihtred, king of Kent, c. 694 to 725, in the early part of whose reign a legal code favourable to the Church was enacted, see Swanton, *Prose*, pp. 3–6.

E 793 *continued from p. 55*

A great famine immediately followed these signs; and a little after that in the same year on *8 January*[15] the raiding of heathen men miserably devastated God's church in Lindisfarne island by looting and slaughter. And Sicga passed away on *22 February*.

794 [796]. Here Pope Hadrian and King Offa passed away. And Æthelred, king of Northumbria, was killed by his own nation on *19 April*. And Bishop Ceolwulf and Bishop Eadbald[2] left the country. And Ecgfrith succeeded to the Mercian kingdom, and passed away the same year. And Eadberht, who was by another name named Præn,[3] succeeded to the kingdom in Kent. And [794] Ealdorman Æthelheard passed away on *1 August*. And the heathen raided in Northumbria and looted Ecgfrith's minster at the Don mouth;[16] and there one of their commanders was killed, and also some of their ships were broken up by bad weather, and many of them drowned there; and some came to shore alive, and then were immediately killed at the river mouth.

795 [796]. Here the moon grew dark between cock-crow and dawn on *28 March*. And Eardwulf succeeded to the kingship in Northumbria on *14 May*; and he was afterwards blessed and raised to his kingly seat on *26 May* in York by Archbishop Eanbald and Æthelberht and Hygebald and Baldwulf.[8]

796. Here Offa, king of Mercia, passed away on *10 August*;[17] he ruled 40 years; and Archbishop Eanbald on *10 August* the same year, and his body lies in York; and this same year passed away Bishop Ceolwulf, and they consecrated a second Eanbald in the other's stead on *14 August*. And the same year [798] Ceolwulf,[4] king of Mercia, ravaged over the inhabitants of Kent and the inhabitants of the Marsh,[5] and captured Præn, their king, and led him bound into Mercia.

797 [799]. Here the Romans cut out the tongue of the pope Leo and put out his eyes and made him flee from his seat; and immediately afterwards by God's help he could see and speak, and was pope again as he was before. And [797] Eanbald obtained the pallium on *8 September*; and Bishop Æthelberht[18] passed away on *<16 October*, and they consecrated Heardred bishop in his stead on>[19] *30 October*.

798. Here in the Spring, on *2 April*, there was a big battle at Whalley[20] in Northumbria, and there they killed Alric, Heardberht's son, and many others with him. [*continued on p. 59*]

---

[11] Presumably an episcopal manor at this time.   [12] The seat of the East Anglian bishops since the time of Felix, see p. 26, note 4.   [13] Sister of St Æthelthryth of Ely (see pp. 34–5, note 8); cf. Ridyard, *Royal Saints*, p. 50 *et passim*.   [14] East Dereham, Norfolk (Ridyard, p. 57, fn. 192).   [15] *vi id Ianr*, presumably (as in annal 802E) an error for *vi id Iun* (8 June) which is the date given by the *Annals of Lindisfarne* (p. 505), when better sailing weather would favour coastal raids.   [16] i.e. Jarrow, at the confluence of the Don with the Tyne estuary, cf. Simeon (I, p. 51).   [17] MS *iiii idus* (mistakenly for *kalendas*) *Augusti*; D gives the date, correctly, as 29 July. This is the second notice of Offa's death in E (cf. annal 794 in all MSS).   [18] Bishop of Hexham.   [19] From D; the hiatus in E is presumably due to the recurrence of the words *on . . . kal. Nov.*   [20] On the River Ribble in Lancashire.

A *continued from p. 56*

799 [801]. Here Archbishop Æthelheard and Cyneberht, bishop of Wessex, went to Rome.

800 [802]. Here King Beorhtric and Ealdorman Worr passed away. And Egbert succeeded to the kingdom of Wessex: and the same day Ealdorman Æthelmund rode from the Hwicce[1] across at Kempsford;[2] then Ealdorman Weohstan met him with the Wiltshire men. There was a big battle, and both ealdormen were killed there, and the Wiltshire men took the victory.

802 [804]. Here Beornmod was ordained bishop for Rochester.

803 [805]. Here Archbishop Æthelheard passed away, and Wulfred was ordained as archbishop,[3] and Abbot Forthred[4] passed away.

804 [806]. Here Archbishop Wulfred obtained the pallium.

805 [807]. Here King Cuthred passed away among the inhabitants of Kent – and Abbess Ceolburh[5] and Ealdorman Heahberht.[6]

812 [814]. Here King Charles passed away; and he ruled 45 years. And Archbishop Wulfred and Wigberht, bishop of Wessex, both went to Rome.

813 [815]. Here Archbishop Wulfred turned back to his own bishopric, with the blessing of the pope Leo; and that year King Egbert raided in Cornwall[7] from east to west.

814 [816]. Here Leo the noble pope, and the holy, passed away, and after him Stephen succeeded to the rule.[8] [*continued on p. 60*]

THE CANTERBURY MANUSCRIPT (F) *continued from p. 56*

806. [As E] . . . . Also in this same year, on *4 June*, the sign of the cross appeared in the moon one Wednesday at the dawning; and again in this year, on *30 August*, an amazing ring appeared around the sun.

809. Here the sun grew dark at the beginning of the fifth hour of the day, on *16 July, on Tuesday, the 29th day of the moon.*[9] [*continued on p. 63*]

---

[1] A group of people occupying the south-west midlands, north of Ashdown (see p. 28, note 2) with their bishop's seat at Worcester; their name survives in the area called Wychwood Forest. See generally Smith, 'The Hwicce', pp. 56–65; Hooke, *Kingdom of the Hwicce*.   [2] i.e. across the upper Thames from Gloucestershire into Wiltshire.   [3] i.e. archbishop of Canterbury.
[4] Probably a Mercian abbot, since he was counted at the Synod of Clofesho among clergy of the see of Leicester.   [5] Abbess of Berkeley, Gloucestershire, says Florence (I, p. 64).   [6] A *Heabryht*; B C *Heabriht*; D *Heardbryht*.   [7] MSS *on West Walas*.   [8] MSS *feng to rice*; see the Introduction p. xxxii.   [9] F Lat *on Sunday, the twelfth day of the moon, at the fourth hour*.

E continued from p. 57

799 [801]. Here Archbishop Æthelred[10] and Cyneberht, bishop of Wessex, went to Rome.

800. Here the moon grew dark at the second hour of the night on *16 January*. And [802] King Beorhtric and Ealdorman Worr passed away. And Egbert succeeded to the kingdom of Wessex: and the same day Ealdorman Æthelmund rode from the Hwicce[1] across at Kempsford;[2] then Ealdorman Weohstan met him with the Wiltshire men; and there was a big battle, and both ealdormen were killed there and the Wiltshire men took the victory. [800] *King Charles*[11] *was made emperor, and called Augustus by the Romans, and condemned to death those who had dishonoured Pope Leo, but at the entreaties of the pope, banished them, reducing death to exile. This Pope Leo in fact consecrated him as emperor.*[12]

802. Here the moon grew dark at dawn on *20 December*.[13] And [804] Beornmod was consecrated as bishop for Rochester the same year.

803. Here Hygebald, bishop of Lindisfarne, passed away on *24 June*; and they consecrated Egbert in his stead on *11 June*. And [805] Archbishop Æthelheard passed away in Kent, and Wulfred was consecrated as archbishop.[14]

804 [806]. Here Archbishop Wulfred obtained the pallium.

805 [807]. Here King Cuthred passed away among the inhabitants of Kent – and Abbess Ceolburh[5] and Heardberht.[6]

806. Here the moon grew dark on *1 September*. And Eardwulf, king of Northumbria, was driven from his kingdom, and Eanberht, bishop of Hexham, passed away.

810. *Charles*[11] *made peace with Nicephorus, emperor of Constantinopole.*

812 [814]. Here King Charles passed away; and he ruled 45 years. And Archbishop Wulfred and Wigberht, bishop of Wessex, went to Rome. *Cireneius*[15] *sent his legates with an offer of peace to the emperor Charles. The emperor Charles died.*

813 [815]. Here Archbishop Wulfred turned back to his own bishopric, with the blessing of the pope Leo; and that year King Egbert raided in Cornwall[7] from east to west.

814 [816]. Here Leo the noble pope, and the holy, passed away, and Stephen succeeded to the rule[8] after him. [*continued on p. 61*]

---

[10] *recte* Æthelheard, as A C D.   [11] Charlemagne.   [12] In effect the foundation of the Holy Roman Empire.   [13] *recte* 21 May; presumably (as in annal 793E) the scribe has mistaken *xiii kal. Jun.* for *xiii kal. Jan.*   [14] F reads Wulfred was chosen in his place.   [15] *Recte* Nicephorus, cf. previous annal.

A *continued from p. 58*

816 [817]. Here Pope Stephen passed away, and after him Paschal was ordained as pope. And the same year the 'English Quarter'[1] burned down.

819 [821]. Here Coenwulf, king of Mercia, passed away, and Ceolwulf succeeded to the kingdom, and Ealdorman Eadberht passed away.

821 [823]. Here Ceolwulf was deprived of his kingdom.

822 [824]. Here two ealdorman, Burhhelm and Muca, were killed; and there was a synod at Clofesho.[2]

823 [825]. Here there was a battle of Britons[3] and of Devon-men[4] at the Tax Ford.[5] And the same year King Egbert and King Beornwulf fought at Ellendun,[6] and Egbert took the victory; and a great slaughter was made there.[7] Then he sent his son Æthelwulf from the army,[8] and Ealhstan, his bishop, and Wulfheard, his ealdorman, to Kent with a great troop, and they drove Baldred the king north over the Thames; and the inhabitants of Kent turned to him – and the Surrey men and South Saxons and East Saxons – because earlier they were wrongly forced away from his relatives. And, for fear of the Mercians, the same year the king and the nation of the East Angles sought King Egbert as their guardian and protector; and that year the East Angles killed Beornwulf, king of the Mercians.

825 [827]. Here Ludeca, king of Mercia, was killed, and his 5 ealdormen with him, and Wiglaf succeeded to the kingdom.

827 [829]. Here [828] the moon grew dark on Christmas night.[9] And the same year King Egbert conquered the kingdom of Mercia and all that was south of the Humber, and he was the eighth king to be 'Controller of Britain';[10] the first who had so great a rule was Ælle, king of the South Saxons; the one after was Ceawlin, king of the West Saxons; the third was Æthelberht, king of the inhabitants of Kent; the fourth was Rædwald,[11] king of East Anglia; fifth was Edwin, king of Northumbria; sixth was Oswald who ruled after him; seventh was Oswy, Oswald's brother; eighth was Egbert, king of West Saxons. And this Egbert led an army to Dore[12] against the Northumbrians; and there they offered him submission and concord; and on that they parted.

[*continued on p. 62*]

---

[1] MS *Ongolcynnes scolu*, (E *Angel-*), literally 'school of the English race'. This was an area near St Peter's, with hostel and church, inhabited by a colony of English – ecclesiastics, pilgrims and others whose business took them to Rome, and referred to by them as their 'burh' (now the Borgo), cf. Levison, *England and the Continent in the Eighth Century*, pp. 40–41; Moore, *Saxon Pilgrims to Rome and the Schola Saxonum*, pp. 90–125. [2] See p. 44, note 12. [3] *Wala*, here the Britons of Cornwall and the South-West. [4] A *Defna*, E *Defena*. [5] *Gafol-ford*, 'tax-ford', now Galford, on the River Lew in west Devon. [6] Probably 'Elder-bush Down' near Wroughton, cf. Gover, *The Place-Names of Wiltshire*, p. 279. [7] Æthelweard (p. 29) adds: *and Hun 'dux' of Somerset was killed there, and he rests now in the city of Winchester*. [8] The primary sense of *fyrd* is 'a going, expedition', hence 'military service', on which see Stenton, *Anglo-Saxon England*, pp. 287–8; and generally Hollister, *Anglo-Saxon Military Institutions, passim*; and see the Introduction pp. xxxiii–xxxiv. [9] The eclipse was at 2 a.m. on 25 December 828, and opens the annal for 829, beginning the year in September; see the Introduction p. xv.

E *continued from p. 59*

815 [817]. Here Pope Stephen passed away, and after him Paschal was ordained as pope. And the same year the 'English Quarter'[1] burned down.

819 [821]. Here Coenwulf, king of Mercia, passed away, and Ceolwulf succeeded to the kingdom, and Ealdorman Eadberht passed away.

821 [823]. Here Ceolwulf was deprived of his kingdom.

822 [824]. Here two ealdorman, Burhhelm and Muca, were killed; and there was a synod at Clofesho.[2]

823 [825]. Here there was a battle of Britons[3] and of Devon-men[4] at the Tax Ford.[5] And the same year Egbert, king of the West Saxons, and Beornwulf, king of Mercians, fought at Ellendun,[6] and Egbert took the victory, and a great slaughter was made there.[7] Then he sent his son Æthelwulf from the army,[8] and Ealhstan his bishop, and Wulfheard his ealdorman, to Kent with a great troop, and they drove Baldred the king north over the Thames, and the inhabitants of Kent turned to him – and the Surrey men and South Saxons and East Saxons – because earlier they were wrongly forced away from his relatives. And, for fear of the Mercians, the same year the king and the nation of the East Angles sought King Egbert as their protector and guardian; and the same year the East Angles killed Beornwulf, king of the Mercians.

825 [827]. Here Ludeca, king of Mercia, was killed, and his 5 ealdormen with him, and Wiglaf succeeded to the kingdom.

827 [829]. Here [828] the moon grew dark on Christmas night.[9] And that year King Egbert conquered the kingdom of Mercia and all that was south of the Humber; and he was the eighth king who was 'Wide Ruler';[10] and the first who had so great a [rule] was Ælle, king of Sussex; second was Ceawlin, king of West Saxons; third Æthelberht, king of the inhabitants of Kent; fourth Rædwald,[11] king of East Anglia; fifth Edwin, king of Northumbria; sixth was Oswald who ruled after him; seventh was Oswy, Oswald's brother; eighth was Egbert, king of West Saxons. And this Egbert led an army to Dore[12] against the Northumbrians; and there they offered him submission and concord; and on that they parted. [*continued on p. 63*]

[10] *Bretwalda* A; other MSS have *Brytenwalda* 'Wide Ruler' and variants, perhaps a poetic rather than political assertion, cf. Stenton, *Anglo-Saxon England*, pp. 34–5; Yorke, 'The vocabulary of Anglo-Saxon overlordship', 171–200; Wormald, 'Bede, the Bretwaldas and the origins of the gens Anglorum', pp. 99–129; Higham, *An English Empire*, pp. 183–217 *et passim.*   [11] *Rædwald is generally believed to have been the ruler buried in the ship-grave at Sutton Hoo, Suffolk, see Bruce-Mitford, The Sutton Hoo Ship Burial;* but see Pearson, 'Three men and a boat', 27–50.   [12] South of Sheffield, and cited in the poem on The Capture of the Five Boroughs, *s.a.* 942, as the frontier of Mercia.

A *continued from p. 60*

828 [830]. Here Wiglaf obtained the kingdom of Mercia again; and Bishop Æthelwald passed away; and the same year King Egbert led the army among the Welsh,[1] and he reduced them to humble submission.

829 [832]. Here Archbishop Wulfred passed away.

830 [833]. Here Ceolnoth was chosen as bishop and ordained; and Abbot Feologild[2] passed away.

831 [834]. Here Archbishop Ceolnoth obtained the pallium.

832 [835]. Here heathen men raided across Sheppey.[3]

833 [836]. Here King Egbert fought against 35[4] ship-loads at Carhampton;[5] and great slaughter was made there, and the Danish had possession of the place of slaughter.[6] And Hereferth and Wigthegn,[7] two bishops,[8] passed away; and Dudda and Osmod, two ealdormen, passed away.

835 [838]. Here a great raiding ship-army came to Cornwall,[9] and they[10] turned into one, and were fighting against Egbert, king of Wessex. Then he heard this and travelled with the army and fought against them at Hingston,[11] and there put to flight both the Britons and the Danish.

836 [839]. Here Egbert passed away; and earlier, before he was king, Offa, king of Mercia, and Beorhtric, king of Wessex, put him to flight from the land of the English to the land of the Franks for 3 years;[12] and Beorhtric helped Offa because he had his daughter as his queen. And that Egbert ruled 37 years and 7 months; and Æthelwulf, Egbert's offspring, succeeded to the kingdom of Wessex, and he granted his son Athelstan[13] the kingdom of the inhabitants of Kent and the East Saxons and Surrey and South Saxons.

837 [840]. Here Ealdorman Wulfheard fought at Southampton against 33 ship-loads, and made great slaughter there and took the victory; and that year Wulfheard passed away.[14] And the same year Ealdorman Æthelhelm fought against a Danish raiding-army on Portland with the Dorset men, and for a good while they put the raiding-army to flight – and the Danish had possession of the place of slaughter and killed the ealdorman.[15]

838 [841]. Here Ealdorman Hereberht[16] was killed by heathen men and many with him among the inhabitants of the Marsh;[17] and [*continued on p. 64*]

---

[1] The 'North Welsh' as distinct from the 'West Welsh' (Cornish), see annal 835, note 9.   [2] Abbot of Christ Church, Canterbury.   [3] A large island in the Thames estuary off north Kent.   [4] A B C *xxxv*, D E F *xxv*.   [5] *æt carrum* 'at the rocks', a royal estate in Somerset (see Alfred's will, Swanton, *Prose*, p. 49) on the Bristol Channel in an area regularly attacked by Danes (cf. annals 840, 845, 915 D, 918 A etc.).   [6] A recurrent phrase, employed where the Danes are defeated as well as where victorious; it probably means that whatever the outcome, they stood their ground and were not put to flight.   [7] A C *Wigðen*, but erroneously *Wigferð* in D E, probably influenced by the form of the preceding name.   [8] Both of Winchester; the former never attesting without the latter, and perhaps a suffragan.   [9] *West Walas*.   [10] i.e. the Danes together with the Britons of Cornwall.   [11] A *Hengest* (E *Hengestes*) *dune*, 'Hengest's' or 'Stallion's Hill', Hingston Down, just across the Tamar into Cornwall.   [12] In fact thirteen years (787–800), presumably *iii* written for *xiii*; but this error is common to all MSS. See generally William of Malmesbury, *Gesta Regum*, I, pp. 105–6.

E *continued from p. 61*

828 [830]. Here Wiglaf obtained again the kingdom of Mercia; and Bishop Æthelbald[18] passed away; and the same year King Egbert led the army among the Welsh,[1] and he entirely reduced them to humble submission.

829 [832].[19] Here Archbishop Wulfred passed away.

830 [833]. Here Ceolnoth was chosen as [arch]bishop and ordained; and [832] Abbot Feologild[2] passed away.

831 [834]. Here Archbishop Ceolnoth obtained the pallium.

832 [835]. Here heathen men raided across Sheppey.[3]

833 [836]. Here King Egbert fought against 25[4] ship-loads at Carhampton;[5] and great slaughter was made there, and the Danish had possession of the place of slaughter.[6] And Hereferth and Wigferth,[7] 2 bishops,[8] passed away; and Dudda and Osmod, 2 ealdormen, passed away.

835 [838]. Here a great raiding ship-army came to Cornwall,[9] and they[10] turned into one and were fighting[20] against Egbert, king of Wessex. Then he campaigned against them and fought with them at Hingston,[11] and there put to flight both the Britons and the Danish.

836 [839]. Here King Egbert passed away; and earlier, before he was king, Offa, king of Mercia, and Beorhtric, king of Wessex, put him to flight from the land of the English to the land of the Franks for 3 years.[12] And that Egbert ruled 37 years and 7 months; and his son Æthelwulf succeeded to the kingdom of Wessex, and his second son, Athelstan,[13] succeeded to the kingdom of the inhabitants of Kent and to Surrey and to the kingdom of Sussex.

837 [840]. Here Ealdorman Wulfheard fought at Southampton against 33 ship-loads, and made great slaughter there and took the victory; and that year Wulfheard passed away.[15] And Ealdorman Æthelhelm fought against the Danish on Portland with the Dorset men, and the ealdorman was killed,[16] and the Danish had possession of the place of slaughter. [*continued on p. 65*]

THE CANTERBURY MANUSCRIPT (F) 829 [832] *continued from p. 58*

829 [832]. Here Archbishop Wulfred passed away and Abbot Feologild[2] was chosen after him for the archbishop's seat on *25 April*. And he was consecrated on *9 June*, a Sunday, and he was dead on *30 August* [*continued on p. 67*]

---

[13] Athelstan was son of Æthelwulf not of Egbert, as the reading in E (D and F) makes clear. [14] Æthelweard (p. 30) adds that he afterwards died peacefully. [15] Æthelweard (p. 30) adds *and his companions with him*. [16] An ealdorman of this name witnesses Kentish charters in 838–9 (*Cartularium Saxonicum*, I, pp. 585–86). [17] i.e. Romney Marsh, on the coast of south Kent. [18] *recte* Æthelwald, as A C. [19] The next eleven entries appear to be antedated by three, or sometimes four, years, but few of the events can be dated with any certainty. [20] D E *wuniende*, 'dwelling', written in mistake for *winnende*, as A C.

A 838 [841] *continued from p. 62*
the same year, again in Lindsey and in East Anglia and among the inhabitants of Kent, many men were killed by the raiding-army.

839 [842]. Here there was a great slaughter in London,[1] and in Quentovic,[2] and in Rochester.

840 [843]. Here King Æthelwulf fought at Carhampton[3] against 35 ship-loads, and the Danish had possession of the place of slaughter.[4]

845 [848]. Here Ealdorman Eanwulf with the Somerset men, and Bishop Ealhstan and Ealdorman Osric with the Dorset men, fought against a Danish raiding-army at the mouth of the Parret, and made a great slaughter there and took the victory.

851 [850]. Here Ealdorman Ceorl with Devonshire fought against the heathen men at Wicga's stronghold,[5] and made a great slaughter there and took the victory. And the same year King Athelstan and *Dux*[6] Ealhhere struck a great raiding-army at Sandwich in Kent, and captured 9 ships, and put the others to flight. And for the first time the heathen men stayed over the winter.[7] And the same year [851] three-and-a-half hundred ships came into the mouth of the Thames, and stormed Canterbury and London, and put to flight Beorhtwulf king of Mercia with his army, and then went south over the Thames into Surrey; and King Æthelwulf and his son Æthelbald with the West Saxon army fought against them at Oak Field,[8] and there made the greatest slaughter of a heathen raiding-army that we have heard tell of up to this present day, and there took the victory.

853. Here Burhred, king of Mercia, and his councillors asked King Æthelwulf that he would help them to subject the Welsh. He then did so, and with the army went through Mercia into Wales, and they made them all subject to them. And the same year King Æthelwulf sent his son Alfred to Rome. *Dom* Leo[9] was pope in Rome then, and he consecrated him as king,[10] and took him as son at confirmation.[11] Then that same year Ealhhere with the inhabitants of Kent and Huda with the men of Surrey fought in Thanet against a heathen raiding-army, and [*continued on p. 66*]

---

[1] Large coin-hoards were buried in the city at this date, see Horsman, *Saxo-Norman London*, II, pp. 286–7.   [2] Thus most MSS, Æthelweard and the *Annals of St Neots*, although C reads Canterbury. Before this disaster the port of Quentovic carried the bulk of trade and perhaps a monopoly of passenger traffic with England; its site at the mouth of the Canche (see Map p. 282) is known only from excavations (Grierson, 'The relations between England and Flanders', 80–81).   [3] See annal 833 and note.   [4] F adds 'and the emperor Louis passed away'.   [5] *Wicganbeorg*, unidentified; possibly Wigborough, in south Somerset, though Wicga is a common enough name.   [6] B C call him ealdorman; perhaps these titles are roughly equivalent; annal 845 calls Eanwulf ealdorman in A and *dux* in E.   [7] B C D E and Æthelweard (p. 31) add 'on Thanet'; Asser (3) and Florence (I, p. 72) have 'Sheppey', which both point out means 'Island of Sheep'.   [8] *Aclea*; unidentified; cf. Asser (5) who gives the etymology of the place-name.   [9] Pope Leo IV.

E *continued from p. 63*

839 [842]. Here there was a great slaughter in London,[1] and in Quentovic,[2] and in Rochester.

840 [843]. Here King Æthelwulf fought at Carhampton[3] against 35 ship-loads, and the Danish had possession of the place of slaughter.[4]

845 [848]. Here *Dux* Earnwulf[12] with the Somerset men, and Bishop Ealhstan and Ealdorman Osric with the Dorset men, fought against a Danish raiding-army at the mouth of the Parret, and made a great slaughter there and took the victory.

851 [850]. Here Ealdorman Ceorl with Devonshire fought against the heathen men at Wicga's stronghold,[5] and made a great slaughter there and took the victory. And the heathen men stayed in Thanet[7] over the winter. And the same year [851] three-and-a-half hundred ships came into the mouth of the Thames, and stormed Canterbury, and put to flight Beorhtwulf, king of Mercia, with his army, and then went south over the Thames into Surrey; and King Æthelwulf and his son Æthelbald, with the army of Wessex, fought against them at Oak Field,[8] and there made the greatest slaughter of a heathen raiding-army that we have ever heard tell of, and there took the victory. And the same year King Athelstan, and *Dux*[6] Ealhhere fought in ships, and struck a great raiding-army at Sandwich, and captured 9 ships and put the others to flight.

852. Here[13] at this time Ceolred, abbot of Peterborough, and the monks leased to Wulfred the land at Sempringham, on condition that after his day that land should go into the minster, and Wulfred should give the land at Sleaford into Peterborough, and he should give every year to the minster sixty wagon-loads of wood and twelve wagon-loads of brushwood and six wagon-loads of faggots, and two casks-full of clear ale and two cattle for slaughter and six hundred loaves and ten measures of Welsh ale, and each year a horse and thirty shillings and one day's provisions. Party to this was the king Burhred and Archbishop Ceolred[14] and Bishop Tunberht[15] and Bishop Cenred[16] and Bishop Ealhhun and Bishop Beorhtred[17] and Abbot Wihtred and Abbot Werheard, Ealdorman Æthelheard, Ealdorman Hunberht and many others.

852 [853]. Here Burhred, king of Mercia, subjected the Welsh to him with the help of King Æthelwulf. And the same year Ealhhere with the inhabitants of Kent, and Huda with the Surrey men, fought [*continued on p. 67*]

---

[10] Presumably in confirmation of baptism (cf. annal 855 F) since Alfred still had two older brothers living, although it was later represented as having dynastic significance, see Nelson, 'The problem of King Alfred's royal anointing', 145–63.   [11] MS *to biscep suna*.   [12] D E *Earnulf, recte* Eanwulf, as A C; see also note 6.   [13] A fuller version of this Peterborough insertion is printed by Robertson, *Charters*, pp. 12–13, with notes (pp. 271–4) on *foþer* ('wagon-load'), *mitta* ('measure'), and Welsh ale (frequently recommended for medicinal purposes, cf. Swanton, *Prose*, p. 259).   [14] *recte* Ceolnoth, archbishop of Canterbury.   [15] Bishop of Lichfield.   [16] *recte* Ceolred, bishop of Leicester.   [17] Bishops of Worcester and Lindsey respectively.

A 853 *continued from p. 64*
at first took the victory, and many were killed and drowned there on either side. And then after Easter, King Æthelwulf gave his daughter to King Burhred, from Wessex to Mercia.

855. Here the heathen men for the first time settled in Sheppey over winter. And the same year King Æthelwulf conveyed by charter[1] the tenth part of his land over all his kingdom to the praise of God and his own eternal salvation. And the same year he travelled to Rome in great state, living there 12 months, and then went towards home. And Charles, king of the Franks, gave him his daughter as queen, and after that he came to his people and they were glad of it. And 2 years after he came from the Franks he died, and his body lies at Winchester; and he ruled eighteen and a half years. And that Æthelwulf was Egbert's offspring, Egbert Ealhmund's offspring, Ealhmund Eafa's offspring, Eafa Eoppa's offspring, Eoppa Ingeld's offspring; Ingeld was the brother of Ine, king of Wessex, who afterwards travelled to St Peter's and afterwards gave up his life there; and they were the sons of Cenred; Cenred was Ceolwald's offspring, Ceolwald Cutha's offspring, Cutha Cuthwine's offspring, Cuthwine Ceawlin's offspring, Ceawlin Cynric's offspring, Cynric Cerdic's offspring,[2] Cerdic Elesa's offspring, Elesa Esla's offspring, Esla Gewis' offspring, Gewis Wig's offspring, Wig Freawine's offspring, Freawine Frithugar's offspring, Frithugar Brand's offspring, Brand Bældæg's offspring, Bældæg Woden's offspring, Woden Frithuwald's offspring, Frithuwald Freawine's offspring, Freawine Frealaf's offspring,[3] Frealaf Frithuwulf's offspring, Frithuwulf Finn's offspring, Finn Godwulf's offspring, Godwulf Geat's offspring, Geat Tætwa's offspring, Tætwa Beaw's offspring, Beaw Sceldwa's offspring, Sceldwa Heremod's offspring, Heremond Itermon's offspring, Itermon Hrathra's offspring – he[4] was born in the ark: Noah, Lamech, Methuselah, Enoch, Jared, Mahalaleel, Cainan, Enos, Seth, Adam *the first man, and our father who is Christ. Amen.*

And then Æthelwulf's two sons succeeded to the kingdom:[5] Æthelbald to the kingdom of Wessex, and Æthelberht to the kingdom of the inhabitants of Kent and to the kingdom of Essex and to Surrey and to the kingdom of Sussex; and then Æthelbald ruled 5 years.

860. Here King Æthelbald passed away, and his body lies at Sherborne; and Æthelberht, his brother, succeeded to the entire kingdom, and [*continued on p. 68*]

---

[1] For the text of one of these charters, see Robertson, *Charters*, pp. 14–15; cf. Stenton, *Anglo-Saxon England*, pp. 304–5.   [2] B C D insert an additional generation (Creoda) between Cynric and Cerdic.   [3] Cf. 547 A; here additional names are inserted between Frithowulf and Woden.   [4] The original reading is probably represented in B C; the person born in the ark is Scef. On King Æthelwulf's mythical ancestors, see Chadwick, *Origin of the English Nation*, pp. 252–83. Æthelweard (p. 33) runs Tætwa, Beo, Scyld, Scef, and stops there; like the *Beowulf*-poet (cf. Bradley, *Poetry*, p. 411), he makes Scef the son of Scyld. Perhaps this version derives from an alternative, more primitive, tradition to that contained in the Chronicle. The descent from Adam, which occurs in all existing Chronicle MSS, was presumably introduced after the genealogy had

E 852 [853] *continued from p. 65*
in Thanet against a heathen raiding-army; and many were killed and drowned there on either side, and the ealdormen both dead. And Burhred, king of Mercia, received[6] the daughter of Æthelwulf, king of Wessex.

855. Here the heathen men for the first time settled in Sheppey over winter. And the same year King Æthelwulf conveyed by charter[1] the tenth part of his land over all his kingdom, to the praise of God and his own eternal salvation. And the same year he travelled to Rome in great state, and lived there 12 months. And he received[6] the daughter of Charles,[7] king of the Franks, when he was on the way home, and came home in good health, and then 2 years afterwards passed away, and his body lies in Winchester; and he ruled 9 years. He was Egbert's offspring. And then his two sons succeeded to the kingdom,[5] Æthelbald to the kingdom of Wessex and to Surrey, and he ruled 5 years.

860. Here King Æthelbald passed away, and his body lies at Sherborne. And Æthelberht, his brother, succeeded to the entire kingdom. And in his day a great raiding ship-army[8] came up and destroyed Winchester. And against the raiding-army fought Ealdorman Osric with Hampshire and Ealdorman Æthelwulf with Berkshire, and put the raiding-army [*continued on p. 69*]

THE ABINGDON MANUSCRIPTS (B) AND (C)

855 [As A] . . . . Itermon Hathra's offspring, Hrathra Hwala's offspring, Hwala Bedwig's offspring, Bedwig Scef's offspring, *that is the son of Noah*: he was born in Noah's Ark; Lamech, Methuselah, Enoch, Jared, Mahalaleel, Cainan, Enos, Seth, Adam *the first man, and our father who is Christ*.

THE CANTERBURY MANUSCRIPT (F) *continued from p. 63*

855 [As A] . . . . to Sussex. Alfred his third son he [Æthelwulf] had sent to Rome, and when the pope Leo[9] heard tell he had passed away, then he blessed Alfred as king, and stood sponsor for him at confirmation,[10] just as his father Æthelwulf had asked when he sent him there. [*continued on p. 69*]

passed into monastic hands. Hill, 'The myth of the Ark-born son of Noe and the West-Saxon royal genealogical tables', 379–83. For the genealogies in general see also p. 2, note 1.   [5] A and F give the division of the kingdom in greatest detail – apparently rehearsing that made when Æthelwulf left the country for Rome, accompanied by his third son, Alfred, cf. annal 853. Alfred alludes to some such division in the beginning of his will (Swanton, *Prose*, pp. 47–8). For the relationship between Æthelwulf and his sons see generally, Kirby, *The Earliest English Kings*, pp. 198–204. D has apparently collated two sources, giving the Peterborough (E) version before the genealogy and the Winchester (A) version after it.   [6] i.e. in marriage.   [7] An insertion in F adds 'she was called Judith'.   [8] See p. 68, note 1.   [9] Leo IV.   [10] MS *heold hine to biscopes handa*.

A 860 *continued from p. 66*
he ruled it in good concord and in great tranquillity. And in his day a great raiding ship-army[1] came up and destroyed Winchester; and against the raiding-army[2] fought Ealdorman Osric with Hampshire and Ealdorman Æthelwulf with Berkshire, and put the raiding-army to flight and had possession of the place of slaughter. And that Æthelberht ruled 5 years, and his body lies at Sherborne.

865. Here a heathen raiding-army stayed in Thanet, and made peace with the inhabitants of Kent; and the inhabitants of Kent promised them money in return for that peace. And under cover of that peace and that promise of money, the raiding-army stole away by night and raided across all eastern Kent.[3]

866 [865].[4] Here Æthelred, brother of Æthelberht, succeeded to the kingdom of Wessex. And the same year a great raiding-army came to the land of the English and took winter-quarters in East Anglia and were provided with horses there, and they made peace with them.[5]

867 [866]. Here the raiding-army went from East Anglia over the mouth of the Humber to York city in Northumbria; and there was great discord of the nation among themselves;[6] and they had thrown down their king Osberht and accepted Ælla, an unnatural[7] king; and it was late in the year when they turned to making war against the raiding-army, nevertheless they gathered a great army and sought out the raiding-army at York city and broke into the city,[8] and some of them got inside;[9] and an immense slaughter was made of the Northumbrians there, some inside, some outside, and both the kings were killed, and the survivors made peace with the raiding-army. And the same year[10] Bishop Ealhstan died, and he had the bishopric at Sherborne 50 years;[11] and his body lies there in the town.[12]

868 [867]. Here the same raiding-army went into Mercia to Nottingham, and took winter-quarters there. And Burhred, king of Mercia, and his councillors asked Æthelred, king of Wessex, and his brother Alfred to help them fight against the raiding-army; and then [868] they travelled with the West Saxon army into Mercia as far as Nottingham, and met the raiding-army there in [*continued on p. 70*]

---

[1] The ninth-century Frankish *Annals of St-Bertin* (p. 92) says they were Danes stationed on the Somme.　[2] Asser (18) adds *when they were returning to the ships with immense booty.*　[3] Asser (20) adds *for they knew they would obtain more money by secret plunder than by peace.*　[4] Here the chronology is based on a year which probably began on 24 September before midwinter, see Beaven, 'The beginning of the year in the Alfredian Chronicle (866–87)', 328–42.　[5] Æthelweard (p. 35) names the Danish leader as Igwar (i.e. Ivar, one of the sons of Ragnar Lothbrok).　[6] Asser (27) comments: *as always happens to a people which has incurred the wrath of God.*　[7] A *ungecyndne*, E *ungecynde*; Asser (p. 27) says *not belonging to the royal family.*　[8] On 21 March according to Simeon (I, p. 55); the *History of St Cuthbert* (Simeon, I, p. 202) says Palm Sunday (23 March).

E 860 *continued from p. 67*
to flight and had possession of the place of slaughter. And that Æthelberht ruled 5 years, and his body lies at Sherborne.

865. Here the heathen raiding-army stayed in Thanet, and made peace with the inhabitants of Kent; and the inhabitants of Kent promised them money in return for that peace. And under cover of the promise of money, the raiding-army stole away by night and raided across all eastern Kent.[3]

866 [865].[4] Here Æthelred, brother of Æthelberht, succeeded to the kingdom of Wessex. And the same year a great heathen raiding-army came to the land of the English and took winter-quarters from the East Anglians, and were provided with horses there, and they made peace with them.[5]

867 [866]. Here the raiding-army went from East Anglia over the mouth of the Humber to York city in Northumbria; and there was great discord of the nation among themselves;[6] and they had thrown down their king Osberht and accepted Ælla, an unnatural king;[7] and it was late in the year when they turned to making war against the raiding-army, nevertheless they gathered a great army and sought out the raiding-army at York city and broke into the city,[8] and some of them got inside;[9] and an immense slaughter was made of the Northumbrians there, some inside, some outside, and both the kings were killed, and the survivors made peace with the raiding-army. And the same year[10] Bishop Ealhstan died, and he had the bishopric at Sherborne 50 years;[11] and his body lies there in the town.[12]

868 [867]. Here the same raiding-army went into Mercia to Nottingham, and took winter-quarters there. And Burhred, king of Mercia, and his councillors asked Æthelred, king of Wessex, and his brother Alfred to help them fight against the raiding-army; and then they travelled with the West Saxon army into Mercia as far as Nottingham, [*continued on p. 71*]

THE CANTERBURY MANUSCRIPT (F) 861 *continued from p. 67*

861. Here St Swithin the bishop passed away – and King Æthelbald, and he lies in Sherborne. And Æthelbert his brother succeeded to the entire kingdom. And in his day a great raiding ship-army came and broke down Winchester; and Hampshire and Berkshire fought against that raiding-army, and put the raiding-army to flight. And this Æthelberht ruled 5 years, and his body lies at Sherborne. [*continued on p. 74*]

---

[9] Asser (27) explains: *because in those times that city had not as yet firm and secure walls.* [10] Æthelweard (p. 36) adds: *Eanwulf 'dux' of the province of Somerset passed away.* [11] Perhaps a round figure, see p. 24, note 2. [12] MS *on tune*; the emphasis might be taken to mean that the bishop was buried not in his church, but in the surrounding enclosure, cf. Stenton, 'The south-western element', p. 18 (*Preparatory*, p. 109). Æthelweard (p. 36) adds *and that of the 'dux' just mentioned* [Eanwulf] *in the monastery which is called Glastonbury.*

A 868 [867] *continued from p. 68*
the fortification, and no heavy fight occured there, and the Mercians made peace with the raiding-army.[1]

869. Here the raiding-army went back to York city, and stayed there 1 year.

870. Here the raiding-army rode across Mercia into East Anglia, and took winter-quarters at Thetford; and that winter King Edmund fought against them, and the Danish took the victory, and killed the king[2] and conquered all that land. And that year [870] Archbishop Ceolnoth died;[3] and Æthelred, bishop of Wiltshire, was chosen as archbishop for Canterbury.

871 [870]. Here the raiding-army came to Reading in Wessex, and 3 days[4] afterwards 2 jarls[5] rode up-country;[6] then Ealdorman Æthelwulf met them on Englefield[7] and fought against them and took the victory.[8] Then 4 days[9] later [871] King Æthelred and Alfred, his brother, led a great army there to Reading, and fought against the raiding-army; and a great slaughter was made there on either side, and Ealdorman Æthelwulf was killed, and the Danish had possession of the place of slaughter.[10] And 4 days later King Æthelred and Alfred, his brother, fought on Ashdown[11] against the whole raiding-army; and they were in two bands: in the one were Bagsecg and Halfdan, the heathen kings, and in the other were the jarls. And then the king Æthelred fought against the kings' force, and there the king Bagsecg was killed; and Alfred, his brother, [fought] against the jarls' force, and there Jarl Sidroc the Old was killed and Jarl Sidroc the Young and Jarl Osbern and Jarl Fræna and Jarl Harald, and both the raiding-armies were put to flight, and there were many thousands of killed;[12] and fighting went on till night. And 14 days[13] later King Æthelred and Alfred, his brother, fought against a raiding-army at Basing,[14] and there the Danish took the victory.[15] And 2 months later King Æthelred and Alfred, his brother, fought against the raiding-army at Merton;[15] and they [*continued on p. 72*]

---

[1] Asser (30) explains: *Since the pagans, protected by the defences of the fortress, refused to give battle, and the Christians could not break the wall, peace was made between the Mercians and the pagans, and the two brothers, Æthelred and Alfred, returned home with their forces.* [2] An insertion in F adds that the names of the head men who slew the king were Ingware (Ivar) and Ubba. Æthelweard (p. 36) adds: *and his body lies entombed in the place which is called Beadoriceswyrthe* (Bury St Edmunds), and that Ivar died the same year. For the cult of St Edmund, see Ridyard, *Royal Saints*, pp. 211–33. [3] D reads 'went to Rome'. [4] *ymb iii niht*; see p. 2, note 2. [5] MS *eorlas*; Old English texts regularly Anglicize the Scandinavian title *jarl*; its status was roughly that of the Anglo-Saxon ealdorman, and not yet 'earl'. [6] Asser (35) says *the remainder made a rampart between the two rivers, Thames and Kennet, on the right hand* (south) *side of this same royal manor* (Reading). [7] Ten miles west of Reading, Berkshire; Asser (35) supplies the etymology 'Plain of the Angles', cf. Gelling, *The Place-Names of Berkshire*, I, p. 211. [8] BCDE all add that one of the jarls, whose name was Sidroc, was slain there. [9] See Beaven, 'The beginning of the year in the Alfredian Chronicle (866–87)', for the sequence of events on this annal.

E 868 [867] *continued from p. 69*
and met the raiding-army there in the fortification, and besieged it in there, and no heavy fight occurred, and the Mercians made peace with the raiding-army.[1]

869. Here the raiding-army went back to York city and stayed there one year.

870 [869]. Here the raiding-army went across Mercia into East Anglia, and took winter-quarters at Thetford; and in that year St Edmund the king fought against them, and the Danish took the victory, and killed the king[2] and conquered all that land, and did for all the monasteries to which they came. At the same time they came to Peterborough: burned and demolished, killed abbot and monks and all that they found there, brought it about so that what was earlier very rich was as it were nothing.[16] And that year Archbishop Ceolnoth died.[3]

871 [870]. Here the raiding-army rode to Reading in Wessex, and 3 days[4] afterwards two jarls[5] rode up-country;[6] then Ealdorman Æthelwulf met them on Englefield[7] and fought against them there and took the victory; and one of the jarls, whose name was Sidroc, was killed there. Then 4 days[9] later [871] King Æthelred and Alfred, his brother, led a great army there to Reading, and fought against the raiding-army; and great slaughter was made there on either side, and Ealdorman Æthelwulf was killed, and the Danish had possession of the place of slaughter.[10] And 4 days later King Æthelred and Alfred, his brother, fought against the whole raiding-army on Ashdown;[11] and they were in two bands: in the one were Bagsecg and Halfdan, the heathen kings, and in the other were the jarls. And then the king Æthelred fought against the kings' force, and there the king Bagsecg was killed; and Alfred, his brother, [fought] against the jarls' force, and there Jarl Sidroc the Old was killed and Sidroc the Young and Jarl Osbern and Jarl Fræna and Jarl Harald; and both raiding-armies were put to flight, and there were many thousands of killed;[12] and fighting went on till night. And 14 days[13] later King Æthelred and Alfred, his brother, fought against the raiding-army at Basing,[14] and there the Danish took the victory. And two months later Æthelred and Alfred, his brother, fought against the raiding-army at Merton;[15] and they were [*continued on p. 73*]

[*continued on p. 73*]

[10] Æthelweard (p. 37) adds: *In fact the body of the 'dux' mentioned above was carried away secretly and taken into Mercia to the place called Northworthig, but 'Derby' in the Danish tongue.* Berkshire retained its Mercian ealdorman after it finally passed into West Saxon hands *c.* 853.   [11] F adds 'and the Danes were overcome; and they had two heathen kings, Bacseg and Halfdan, and many jarls'. Asser (p. 37) says that Alfred had to begin the battle alone, since his brother was hearing mass and refused to leave until the priest had finished; and (p. 39) that the Danes had the higher ground and that the battle raged round a small thorn tree – which he himself had seen.   [12] Æthelweard (p. 37) comments: *all the nobler youth of the barbarians fell there, so that neither before nor after has such a slaughter been heard of since the race of Saxons won Britain in war.*   [13] MSS *xiiii niht*, 'a fortnight'.   [14] F Lat *but because of* [their] *sins the Danes captured the field.*   [15] E *Mæredune*, D *Meredune*, A A[2] C *Meretune*, B and Æthelweard (p. 38) *Merantune*; the identity of this place is unclear.   [16] This was the work of Ubba's Danes according to the Chronicle of John of Peterborough (p. 19).

A 871 [870] *continued from p. 70*
were in two bands, and they put both to flight and for long in the day had the victory; and there was great slaughter on either side, and the Danish had possession of the place of slaughter; and Bishop Heahmund[1] was killed there and many good men. And after this fight a great summer-fleet[2] came. And afterwards, after Easter, King Æthelred died, and he ruled 5 years; and his body lies at Wimborne.

Then his brother Alfred, Æthelwulf's offspring, succeeded to the kingdom of Wessex. And one month later King Alfred with a small troop fought at Wilton[3] against the whole raiding-army, and for long time in the day put them to flight, and the Danish had possession of the place of slaughter. And that year there were 9 national fights[4] fought against the raiding-army in the kingdom to the south of the Thames, besides those forays which Alfred, the king's brother, and a single ealdorman and king's thegns often rode on, which were never counted. And that year were killed 9 jarls and one king;[5] and that year the West Saxons made peace with the raiding-army.

872 [871]. Here the raiding-army went from Reading to London town, and took winter-quarters there, and then the Mercians made peace with the raiding-army.[6]

873 [872]. Here the raiding-army went into Northumbria, and it took winter-quarters at Torksey in Lindsey, and the Mercians made peace with the raiding-army.

874 [873]. Here the raiding-army went from Lindsey to Repton and took winter-quarters there,[7] and [874] drove the king Burhred across the sea 22 years after he had the kingdom; and conquered all that land. And he went to Rome and settled there, and his body lies in St Mary's church in the English Quarter.[8] And the same year they granted the kingdom of Mercia to be held by a foolish king's thegn,[9] and he swore them oaths and granted hostages, that it should be ready for them whichever day they might want it, and he himself should be ready with all who would follow him, at the service of the raiding-army.

875 [874]. Here the raiding-army went from Repton, and Halfdan went with some of the raiding-army into Northumbria, and took winter-quarters [*continued on p. 74*]

---

[1] Bishop of Sherborne.   [2] i.e. one not over-wintering here, but returning to its overseas base in autumn.   [3] A royal manor on the River Wylye in Wiltshire, cf. Sawyer, 'The royal *tun* in pre-Conquest England', p. 283. Alfred is said to have founded a nunnery there, cf. VCH, *Wiltshire*, III, pp. 231–2.   [4] *folcgefeoht*.   [5] Not all those referred to as 'jarls' or 'kings' would necessarily have been recognised as such in Scandinavia; titles accorded to leaders in exile by their followers are not a reliable guide to status; cf. B. and P. Sawyer, *Medieval Scandinavia*, p. 86.   [6] At this date the fate of London was a Mercian rather than a West Saxon concern, Beaven, 'The beginning of the year', 341.   [7] For evidence of a Viking mass grave, a possible dry-dock and other remains attributable to this occupation, see Biddle and Kjolbye-Biddle, 'Repton 1985', 1–5.

E 871 [870] *continued from p. 71*

in two bands, and they put both to flight and for long in the day had the victory; and there was great slaughter on either side, and the Danish had possession of the place of slaughter; and Bishop Heahmund[1] was killed there and many good men. And after this fight a great summer-fleet[2] came to Reading. And afterwards, after Easter, King Æthelred died, and he ruled 5 years; and his body lies at Wimborne minster.[10]

Then his brother Alfred, Æthelwulf's offspring, succeeded to the kingdom of Wessex. And 1 month later King Alfred with a small troop fought at Wilton[3] against the whole raiding-army, and for long in the day put them to flight, and the Danish had possession of the place of slaughter. And that year there were 9 national fights[4] fought against the raiding-army in the kingdom to the south of the Thames, besides those forays which Alfred, the king's brother, and ealdormen and king's thegns, often rode on, which were never counted. And that year were killed 9 jarls and one king;[5] and that year the West Saxons made peace with the raiding-army.

872 [871]. Here the raiding-army went from Reading to London town, and took winter-quarters there, and then the Mercians made peace with the raiding-army.[6]

873 [872]. Here the raiding-army took winter-quarters at Torksey.

874 [873]. Here the raiding-army went from Lindsey to Repton,[7] and there took winter-quarters, and drove the king Burhred across the sea 22 years after he had the kingdom; and conquered all that land. And he went to Rome and settled there, and his body lies in St Mary's church in the English Quarter.[8] And the same year they granted the kingdom of Mercia to be held by Ceolwulf, a foolish king's thegn,[9] and he swore them oaths and granted hostages, that it should be ready for them whichever day they might want it, and he himself should be ready with all who would follow him, at the service of the raiding-army.

875 [874]. Here the raiding-army went from Repton, and Halfdan went with some of the raiding-army into Northumbria, and took winter- [*continued on p. 75*]

---

[8] See p. 60, note 1.   [9] All other MSS and Asser (46) give his name as Ceolwulf; and Æthelweard (p. 41) as Ceolf. See below, *s.a.* 877 A.   [10] So also B D, but C says at Sherborne minster.

A 875 [874] *continued from p. 72*
on the River Tyne; and the raiding-army conquered that land, and often raided among the Picts and among the Strathclyde Britons; and Guthrum and Oscytel and Anund, the 3 kings, went from Repton to Cambridge with a great raiding-army, and settled there for a year. And that summer [875] King Alfred went out to sea with a raiding ship-army[1] and fought against 7 ship-loads, and captured one of them and put the others to flight.

876 [875]. Here the raiding-army stole away from the West Saxon army into Wareham.[2] And [876] the king made peace with the raiding-army, and they swore him oaths on the sacred ring,[3] which earlier they would not do to any nation, that they would quickly go from his kingdom; and then under cover of that, they stole away from the army by night – the mounted raiding-army into Exeter. And that year Halfdan divided up the land of Northumbria; and they were ploughing and providing for themselves.

877 [876]. Here the raiding-army came from Wareham into Exeter,[4] and the raiding ship-army sailed around west, and then they met a great storm[5] at sea, and 120 ships were lost there at Swanage. And Alfred the king rode after the mounted raiding-army with the army as far as Exeter, and could not overtake them before they were in the fortress where they could not be got at. And there they granted him prime hostages,[6] as many as he wanted to have, and swore great oaths and then held to a good peace. And then in harvest-time[7] [877] the raiding-army went into the land of Mercia,[8] and some of it they divided up and some they granted to Ceolwulf.

878. Here the raiding-army stole away in midwinter after Twelfth Night to Chippenham,[9] and over-rode and occupied the land of Wessex, and drove many of the people across the sea, and the greatest part of the others they over-rode – and they turned to them[10] – except for Alfred the king, and he with a small troop went with difficulty through woods and into swamp-fastnesses.[11] And that same winter a brother[12] of Ivar and Halfdan was in Wessex in [*continued on p. 76*]

THE CANTERBURY MANUSCRIPT (F) 876 *continued from p. 69*

876. Here Rollo went through Normandy with his raiding-army and he ruled fifty years.[13] [*continued on p. 93*]

---

[1] MS *sciphere*; for the use of this word in an English context see also annals 885, 933 A, 934 D E F, 972 E, etc.   [2] In Dorset at one head of Poole harbour, an Alfredian-period fort (RCHM, 'Wareham west walls', 120–38) later listed in the Burghal Hidage (Swanton, *Prose*, p. 13), and a cross-channel port; see generally RCHM, *Dorset*, II, pp. 304–12, 322–4. Æthelweard (p. 41) says that the Danish army which had been in Cambridge now *encamped in the same position as the West Saxon army, a thing which they had not previously done, near the town called Wareham.*   [3] F Lat *sacrum armillum*. Cf. *Eyrbyggja Saga*, p. 29: '[on the altar in the temple] lay a solid ring weighing twenty ounces, upon which people had to swear all their oaths. It was the business of the temple priest to wear this ring on his arm at every public meeting'; cf. Magoun, 'On the Old-Germanic altar- or oath-ring', 277–93; Chaney, *Cult of Kingship*, pp. 148–9.   [4] A fort of the Burghal Hidage (Swanton, *Prose*, p. 13): the walled Roman city of Isca, ten miles up the Exe estuary in south Devon, where ships might join them.

E 875 [874] *continued from p. 73*
quarters on the River Tyne; and the raiding-army conquered that land, and often raided among the Picts and among the Strathclyde Britons; and Guthrum and Oscytel and Anund, the three kings, went from Repton to Cambridge with a great raiding-army, and settled there for a year. And that summer [875] King Alfred went out to sea with a raiding ship-army,[1] and fought against 7 ship-loads, and captured one of them and put the others to flight.

876 [875]. Here the raiding-army stole away from the West Saxon army into Wareham.[2] And afterwards [876] the king made peace with the raiding-army, and they granted him as hostages the most distinguished men who were next to the king in the raiding-army, and they swore him oaths on the sacred ring,[3] which earlier they would not do to any nation, that they would quickly go from his kingdom; and then under cover of that, they stole away from the army by night – the mounted raiding-army into Exeter. And that year Halfdan divided up the land of Northumbria; and they were ploughing[14] and were providing for themselves. *Rollo and his* [men] *invaded Normandy and ruled 53 years.*

877 [876]. Here the raiding-army came from Wareham to Exeter,[4] and the raiding ship-army sailed around west, and then they met a great storm[5] at sea, and 120 ships were lost there at Swanage. And Alfred the king rode after the mounted raiding-army with the army as far as Exeter, and could not overtake them before they were in the fortress where they could not be got at. And there they granted him prime hostages,[6] as many as he wanted to have, and swore great oaths, and then held to a good peace. And then in harvest-time[7] [877] the raiding-army went into the land of Mercia,[8] and some of it they divided up and some they granted to Ceolwulf.

878. Here the raiding-army stole away in midwinter after Twelfth Night to Chippenham,[9] and over-rode and occupied the land of Wessex, and drove many of the people across the sea, and the greatest part of the others they over-rode – except Alfred the king with a small troop went with difficulty through woods and into swamp-fastnesses.[11] And that same winter a brother[12] of Ivar and Halfdan was in Wessex [*continued on p. 77*]

[5] A A[2] B E *yst* 'storm'; C D *myst* 'mist, fog'.   [6] MS *foregislas*; perhaps 'preliminary hostages', but Asser (56) says chosen hostages, which implies eminence.   [7] *The Annals of St Neots* (p. 75) say it was *in the month of August*, but see Asser, ed. Keynes and Lapidge, p. 246, note 94.   [8] Where, says Æthelweard (p. 42), they erected huts or tents (*ategias figunt*) in the town called Gloucester.   [9] Asser (52) says this was a *royal vill*, and that the Danes wintered there.   [10] B 'and the people submitted to them'.   [11] Asser (53) locates this refuge in Somerset; and Æthelweard (p. 42) adds that *Æthelnoth also, dux of the province of Somerset, stayed with a small force in a certain wood.*   [12] Gaimar (3141–7) says that this was Ubba, that he was killed in Pen Wood (*bois de Pen*), and that his grave-mound in Devonshire was called *Ubelaue* (Ubba's Barrow). It was Ubba who killed St Edmund (see p. 70, note 2).   [13] In fact Rollo ruled for fifty-three years, as the Latin numbering in E specifies; but see p. 24, note 2.   [14] MS *hergende* 'harrying' in mistake for *ergende* – an ironic slip.

A 878 *continued from p. 74*
Devonshire with 23 ships,[1] and he was killed there and 800 men with him and 40 men of his war-band.[2] And the Easter after, King Alfred with a small troop built a fortification at Athelney,[3] and from that fortification, with that part of Somerset-men nearest to it, was making war against the raiding-army. Then in the seventh week after Easter he rode to Egbert's Stone to the east of Selwood,[4] and there came to join him all Somerset and Wiltshire and that part of Hampshire which was on this side of the sea[5] – and were glad of him. And one day later he went from those camps to Island Wood,[6] and one [day] later to Edington,[7] and there fought against the whole raiding-army, and put it to flight, and rode after it as far as the fortification,[8] and stayed there 14 days; and then the raiding-army granted him prime hostages and great oaths that they would leave his kingdom, and also promised him that their king would receive baptism; and they fulfilled it thus. And 3 weeks later the king Guthrum came to him, one of thirty of the most honourable men who were in the raiding-army, at Aller – and that is near Athelney – and there the king received him at baptism; and his chrism-loosing[9] was at Wedmore; and he was 12 days with the king, and he greatly honoured him and his companions with riches.

879 [878]. Here the raiding-army went from Chippenham to Cirencester, and settled there for a year. And that year a gang of vikings gathered and settled at Fulham on the Thames. And the same year the sun grew dark for one hour of the day.[10]

880 [879]. Here the raiding-army went from Cirencester into East Anglia, and settled that land, and divided it up. And the same year the raiding-army[11] which had earlier settled at Fulham went across the sea to Ghent in the land of the Franks, and settled there for a year.

881. Here the raiding-army went further into the land of the Franks, and the Franks fought against them,[12] and there the raiding-army was provided with horses after the fight.

882 [881]. Here the raiding-army went up along the Meuse far into the land of the Franks, and settled there for a year.[13] And the same year [882] King Alfred went out to sea with ships and fought against four ship- [*continued on p. 78*]

---

[1] Æthelweard (p. 43) says *the brother of Ivar and Healfdane arrived with thirty ships and beseiged Odda, dux of Devon, in a certain fortress.* Asser (54) identifies the fort as Cynwit (Countisbury), *altogether unfortified, except for ramparts thrown up in our* [Welsh] *fashion*; this is on the north Devon coast, and he says that the Danes had previously ravaged Dyfed in South Wales.   [2] All MSS read *heres*; this presumably refers to a more select band of his personal retinue, and it may be a mistake for *hiredes*.   [3] A defensible island in the swamps of Somerset, reached by a bridge or causeway fortified at either end. Asser (p. 103) describes the defence at the western (land-ward) end as *a formidable fortress of elegant workmanship*. Cf. VCH, *Somerset*, VI, p. 53; Hill, 'The Burghal Hidage – Lyng', 64–6.   [4] A *be eastan Sealwyda*, E *be easton Wealwudu*; Egbert's Stone is unidentified; Asser (55) says it was in the eastern part of Selwood.   [5] Asser (55) says: *those men from Hampshire who had not sailed overseas for fear of the pagans.* Probably the 'sea' referred to is not the English Channel but the Solent or Southampton Water.   [6] 'Island Wood' (Iley Oak) was the traditional meeting-place of the Warminster and Heytesbury hundreds, see Gover, *The Place-Names of Wiltshire*, pp. 154–5.   [7] Half a dozen miles north-east of Iley, a royal manor in Wiltshire bequeathed by Alfred to Queen Ealhswith (Swanton, *Prose*, p. 50).

E 878 *continued from p. 75*
in Devonshire, and he was killed there, and 800 men with him and 40 men of his war-band;[2] and there the banner which they called 'Raven'[14] was taken. And the Easter after, King Alfred with a small troop built a fortification at Athelney,[3] and from that fortification, with the men of that part of Somerset nearest to it, was making war against the raiding-army. Then in the seventh week after Easter he rode to Egbert's Stone to the east of Selwood,[4] and there came to join him all Somerset and Wiltshire and that part of Hampshire which was on this side of the sea[5] – and were glad of him. And one day later he went from those camps to Island Wood,[6] and one day later to Edington,[7] and there fought against the whole raiding-army, and put it to flight, and rode after it as far as the fortification,[8] and settled there 14 days; and then the raiding-army granted him hostages and great oaths that they would leave his kingdom, and also promised him that their king would receive baptism; and they fulfilled it. And 3 weeks later the king Guthrum came to him, one of thirty of the most honourable men who were in the raiding-army, at Aller – and that is near Athelney – and there the king received him at baptism; and his chrism-loosing[9] was at Wedmore; and he was 12 days with the king, and he greatly honoured him and his companions with riches.

879 [878]. Here the raiding-army went from Chippenham to Cirencester, and settled there for the winter. In that year a gang of vikings gathered and settled at Fulham on the Thames. And the same year the sun grew dark for one hour of the day.[10]

880 [879]. Here the raiding-army went from Cirencester into East Anglia, and settled that land, and divided it up. And the same year the raiding-army[11] which had settled at Fulham went across the sea to Ghent in the land of the Franks, and settled there for a year.

881. Here the raiding-army went further into the land of the Franks, and the Franks fought against them,[12] and there the raiding-army was provided with horses after the fight.

882 (881). Here the raiding-army went up along the Meuse further into the land of the Franks, and settled there for a year.[13] And the same year [882] King Alfred went out to sea with ships and fought against 4 ship-loads of Danish [*continued on p. 79*]

---

[8] Perhaps Chippenham. Asser (56) says Alfred *seized everything he found outside the fort – men, whom he killed immediately, horses and cattle.* In the end the Danes surrendered *in desperation, from hunger, cold and terror.*   [9] At baptism a white fillet was bound round the head after anointing with oil (chrism), to be removed at a ceremony a week later (see p. 40, note 8). His baptismal name was Athelstan (see annal 890). Æthelweard (p. 43) says Æthelnoth, ealdorman of Somerset, *also purified him after baptism.*   [10] Asser (59): *between nones and vespers, but nearer to nones.*   [11] F Lat *pirates.*   [12] The battle of Saucourt on the Somme, 3 August 881, which is the subject of the Old High German poem *Ludwigslied* and the Old French *Gormond et Isembard.*   [13] Æthelweard (p. 44) says they *laid out a camp* at Elsloo (on the River Maas).   [14] As an intimate of the war-god Othin, the raven was an appropriate battle-symbol, carried by many Scandinavian leaders including Cnut (cf. Campbell, *Encomium Emmae*, pp. 24, 96–7). See generally Chaney, *Cult of Kingship*, pp. 132–3. *The Annals of St Neots* (p. 78) say that this particular banner was woven by three sisters of Ubba and Ivar and that the outcome of a battle was portended by whether it flapped or hung lifeless.

A 882 [881] *continued from p. 76*
loads of Danish men, and took two of the ships, and the men who were on them were killed; and two ship-loads surrendered to him,[1] and they were badly cut about and wounded before they surrendered.

883 [882]. Here the raiding-army went up the Scheldt to Condé,[2] and settled there for a year.

884 [883]. Here the raiding-army went up the Somme to Amiens,[3] and settled there for a year.

885 [884]. Here the aforementioned raiding-army divided into two, one part to the east[4] and the other part to Rochester, and besieged the city and built another fortress around themselves; and they [the inhabitants], however, defended the city until [885] Alfred came from outside with an army. Then the raiding-army went to their ships and abandoned that fortification, and they were there deprived of their horses,[5] and immediately the same summer departed across the sea.[6] And the same year King Alfred sent a raiding ship-army into East Anglia. Immediately they came to the mouth of the Stour,[7] then they met 16 ships of vikings and fought against them, and got at all the ships, and killed the men. Then when they were on their way home with the war-booty, they met a great raiding ship-army of vikings, and then fought against them the same day, and the Danish had the victory. The same year [884], before midwinter, Carl,[8] king of the Franks, passed away – and a wild boar killed him; and one year earlier his brother passed away; he also had that West Kingdom[9] and they were both sons of Louis;[10] he also had that West Kingdom and passed away the year [879] in which the sun grew dark;[11] he was the son of Charles whose daughter Æthelwulf, king of Wessex, had as his queen.[12] And the same year a great raiding ship-army gathered among the Old Saxons, and great battles occurred there, twice in the year,[13] and the Saxons had the victory, and there were Frisians with them. The same year Charles[14] succeeded to the West Kingdom, and to all the West Kingdom on this side of the Mediterranean[15] and beyond this sea,[16] just as his great-grandfather had it, except for Brittany;[17] that [*continued on p. 80*]

---

[1] F two escaped; F Lat *two fled.*   [2] France (dép. Nord), a convent of nuns, says Asser (65).   [3] France (dép. Somme).   [4] Æthelweard (p. 44) says they beseiged Louvain.
[5] Asser (66) says: *the pagans then left their fortifications and abandoned all the horses which they had brought with them from Frankia, and also left the greater part of their prisoners in the fort, and fled instantly to their ships, because the king had come there suddenly.*   [6] Æthelweard (p. 44) says that some of the raiders stayed behind and came to terms with Alfred, but deceitfully twice raided south of the Thames, aided by Danes from East Anglia, who moved to Benfleet in Essex. This would account for Alfred's immediate attack on East Anglia, see Stenton, 'The south-western element in the Old English Chronicle', pp. 20–21 (*Preparatory*, pp. 111–12).   [7] D E and Asser (67) *Sture*; A A[2] B C and Æthelweard (p. 45) *Stufe*.   [8] So all MSS and Æthelweard (p. 45), but better Carloman, as Asser (68).   [9] For the division of Frankish Europe into 'Western', 'Middle' and 'Eastern Kingdoms', see generally McKitterick, *The Frankish Kingdoms under the Carolingians*, 751–987.

E 882 [881] *continued from p. 77*

men and took two of the ships, and killed the men; and two surrendered to him,[1] and the men were badly knocked about and wounded before they surrendered.

883 [882]. Here the raiding-army went up to the Scheldt to Condé,[2] and settled there for a year. And Pope Marinus sent the *wood of the Lord*[18] to King Alfred; and the same year Sigehelm and Athelstan took to Rome – and also to St Thomas in India[19] and to St Bartholomew – the alms which King Alfred had vowed to send there when they besieged the raiding-army at London;[20] and there, by the grace of God, they were very successful in obtaining their prayers in accordance with those vows.

884 [883]. Here the raiding-army went up the Somme to Amiens,[3] and settled there for a year.

885 [884]. Here the aforementioned raiding-army divided into two, one to the east[4] and the other part to Rochester, and besieged the city, and built another fortification around themselves; and they [the inhabitants], however, defended the city until [885] Alfred came from outside with an army. Then the raiding-army went to their ships and abandoned that fortification and were there deprived of their horses,[5] and immediately the same summer departed across the sea again.[6] The same year King Alfred sent a raiding ship-army from Kent into East Anglia. Immediately they came to the mouth of the Stour,[7] then they met 16 ships of vikings and fought against them, and got at all the ships, and killed the men. Then when they were on their way home with the war-booty, they met a great raiding ship-army of vikings, and fought against them the same day, and the Danish had the victory. And the same year [884], before midwinter, Carl,[8] king of the Franks, passed away – and a wild boar killed him; and one year earlier his brother[10] passed away; he also had that West Kingdom; he passed away the year [879] in which the sun grew dark;[11] he was the son of Charles whose daughter Æthelwulf, king of Wessex, had as queen.[12] The same year [884] passed away the good pope [*continued on p. 81*]

---

[10] Louis 'the Stammerer', see McKitterick, *The Frankish Kingdoms, passim.*   [11] The eclipse was on 29 October 878 (cf. p. 77, note 10); Louis died on 10 April 879 – both dates within the same annalistic year beginning 24 September.   [12] i.e. Judith, see annal 855, and Table p. 289.   [13] i.e. within the year beginning 24 September 884; probably at Norden in Frisia (December 884), and in Saxony (May 885).   [14] Charles 'the Fat'.   [15] MS *Wendel sæ*, 'Vandal Sea', a name dating from its domination by Vandals in the fifth century.   [16] Probably the English Channel. Asser (70) has: *the arm of the sea that lies between the Old Saxons and the Gauls.* But possibly it refers back to the Mediterranean, the lands beyond being in Italy.   [17] C D *Lidwiccium*; an Anglicism apparently incorporating the British name for Amorica: Llydaw.   [18] See p. 80, note 5.   [19] D E F *Indea*; B C *Judea.*   [20] Alfred's vow is not mentioned in A, Asser or Æthelweard; the only clear association of Alfred with London is in 886, and probably this allusion belongs to that date, the author perhaps mistaking *vi* for *iii* (cf. Beaven, 'The beginning of the year', 341–2).

A 885 [884] *continued from p. 78*

Charles was the son of Louis, who was the brother of Charles, who was the father of Judith whom King Æthelwulf had; and they were sons of Louis, which Louis was son of Charles the Old,[1] which Charles was the son of Pippin.[2] And the same year passed away the good pope Marinus who freed[3] the English Quarter[4] at the request of Alfred, king of Wessex; and he sent him great gifts and part of the Cross on which Christ suffered.[5] And the same year the raiding-army in East Anglia broke the peace with King Alfred.

886 [885]. Here the raiding-army, which earlier to this had arrived in the east,[6] went west again, and then up the Seine and took winter-quarters there.[7] The same year [886] King Alfred occupied London fort[8] and all the English race turned to him, except what was in captivity to Danish men; and he then entrusted the fort to Ealdorman Æthelred[9] to hold.

887 [886-7]. Here the raiding-army went up through the bridge at Paris, and then up along the Seine as far as the Marne, as far as Chézy[10] and then settled there and on the Yonne, two winters in those two places. And the same year [888] Charles,[11] king of the Franks, passed away; and Arnulf, his brother's son, dispossessed him of the kingdom 6 weeks before he passed away. And then the kingdom was divided into 5, and 5 kings were consecrated to it; that, however, was done with the consent of Arnulf; and they said they should hold it from his hands because none of them was born on the paternal side, except him alone. Arnulf then lived in the land to the east of the Rhine, and then Rudolf succeeded to the Middle Kingdom and Odo to the western part,[12] and Berengar and Guido[13] to the land of the Lombards and to the lands on that side of the mountains;[14] and held that in great discord, and fought two national fights,[15] and over and again ravaged that land, and each regularly drove out the other. And the same year in which the raiding-army went out up over the bridge at Paris, Ealdorman Æthelhelm[16] took the alms of the West Saxons and of King Alfred to Rome.[17]

888. Here Ealdorman Beocca[18] took the alms of the West Saxons [*continued on p. 82*]

---

[1] *MS þæs aldan Carles*, Charles 'the Great', Charlemagne.   [2] For this dynasty see McKitterick, *The Frankish Kingdoms*, pp. 352-3.   [3] i.e. freed from dues; Asser (71) says: *from all tribute and tax*.   [4] See p. 60, note 1.   [5] F 'many gifts of relics'; F Lat *many gifts, that is from the cross of God and relics of saints*. Possibly this cross relic is to be identified with that surviving at the church of SS Michael and Gudule, Brussels (see Swanton, *The Dream of the Rood*, pp. 48-9).   [6] At Louvain, see p. 78, note 4.   [7] Asser (82) says: *they pitched their camp on both sides of the river near the bridge* [at Paris], *to prevent the citizens from crossing the bridge, (for that city is situated on a small island in the middle of the river), and beseiged the city all that year. But because God mercifully favoured them and the citizens defended themselves vigorously*, [the vikings] *could not break through the fortification*.   [8] Between the sixth and ninth centuries the main urban settlement at London lay to the west of the Roman walled enclosure, the intra-mural area lying empty and fallow, and the bridge in disrepair, until *c.* 900 when viking raids brought people back inside (see Horsman, *Saxo-Norman London*, I, p. 7, II-III, *passim*).

E 885 [884] *continued from p. 79*
Marinus, who freed[3] the English Quarter[4] at the request of Alfred, king of Wessex; and he sent him great gifts and part of the Cross on which Christ suffered.[5] And the same year the raiding-army went to East Anglia, and broke the peace with King Alfred.

886 [885]. Here the raiding-army, which earlier to this had arrived in the east,[6] went west again, and then up the Seine and there took winter-quarters in the town of Paris.[7] The same year [886] King Alfred occupied London fort,[8] and all the English race turned to him, except what was in capitivity to Danish men; and he then entrusted the fort to Ealdorman Æthelred[9] to hold.

887 [886–7]. Here the raiding-army went up through the bridge at Paris, and then up along the Seine, as far as the Marne, and then up the Marne as far as Chézy;[10] and then settled there [and] on the Yonne, two winters in those two places. And the same year [888] Charles,[11] king of the Franks passed away; and Arnulf, his brother's son, dispossessed him of the kingdom 6 weeks before his death. And then the kingdom was divided into 5, and five kings were consecrated to it; that, however, was done with the consent of Arnulf; and they said they should to hold it from his hands because none of them was born on the paternal side, except him alone. Arnulf lived in the land to the east of the Rhine, and then Rudolf succeeded to the Middle Kingdom, and Odo to the western part,[12] and Berengar and Guido[13] to the land of the Lombards and to the lands on that side of the mountains;[14] and held that in great discord, and fought two national fights,[15] and over and again ravaged that land, and each frequently drove out the other. And the same year in which the raiding-army went out up over the bridge at Paris, Ealdorman Æthelhelm[16] took the alms of the West Saxons and of King Alfred to Rome.[17]

888. Here Ealdorman Beocca[18] [continued on p. 83]

[9] The lord of the Mercians, Alfred's son-in-law, under whom Mercia preserved its autonomy, see annals 910 D E, 912 A. [10] D E F *Caziei*; A B C *Cariei*. [11] Charles 'the Fat'. [12] See p. 78, note 9. [13] Margrave of Friuli and Duke of Spoleto respectively. [14] i.e. the Alps. [15] For this expression cf. annal 871 (pp. 72–3, note 4). [16] Of Wiltshire. [17] Possibly the origin of the tribute later referred to as 'Peter's Pence', *s.a.* 888, 889, 890. See generally, Lunt, *Financial Relations of the Papacy with England to 1327*, pp. 3–30. This payment may have been made with coins specially minted for the purpose, cf. Dolley, 'The so-called piedforts of Alfred the Great', pp. 76–92. [18] Otherwise unknown, although perhaps the witness to a grant by Alfred of land in Somerset in 882 (*Cartularium Saxonicum*, II, p. 172).

A 888 *continued from p. 80*
and of King Alfred to Rome. And Queen Æthelswith,[1] who was King Alfred's
sister, passed away,[2] and her body lies at Pavia. And the same year
Archbishop Æthelred and Ealdorman Æthelwald[3] passed away in the one
month.[4]

889. In this year there was none who travelled to Rome, except for two
runners King Alfred sent with letters.

890. Here Abbot Beornhelm[5] took the alms of the West Saxons and of King
Alfred to Rome. And Guthrum, the northern king, whose baptismal name was
Athelstan,[6] passed away;[7] he was King Alfred's godson, and he lived in East
Anglia and was the first to settle that land.[8] And the same year [889] the
raiding-army went from the Seine to St Lô,[9] which is between the Bretons and
the Franks; and [890] the Bretons fought against them and had the victory,
and drove them out into a river and drowned many. In this year Plegmund was
chosen[10] by God and by all his saints.

891. Here the raiding-army went east; and King Arnulf with the East Franks
and Saxons and Bavarians fought against the mounted raiding-army before
the ships came, and put it to flight.[11] And three Scots came to King Alfred in a
boat without any oars,[12] from Ireland, from where they had stolen away
because they wanted for the love of God to be abroad – they did not care
where.[13] The boat in which they set out was made of two-and-a-half skins, and
they took with them food for seven days; and after 7 days they came to land in
Cornwall, and immediately went to King Alfred.[14] They were named thus:
Dubhkillede and Macbeathadh and Maelinmhain.[15] And Suibhne, who was
the best teacher among the Scots, died.[16]

892.[17] And the same year after Easter, during the Rogation Days[18] or earlier,
appeared the star which in Latin is called *cometa*; some[19] men say in English
that it is a 'haired star',[20] because a long ray stands out from it, sometimes on
one side, sometimes on every side. [*continued on p. 84*]

---

[1] Wife of Burhred of Mercia. For a gold finger-ring, inscribed + EAÐELSUIÐ REGNA found at
Sherburn, Yorkshire, see Wilson, *Anglo-Saxon Ornamental Metalwork 700–1100*, pp.
117–18.   [2] F 'on the way to Rome'; she may well have accompanied her husband into exile in
874 (q.v.).   [3] Æthelweard (p. 47), who gives the name as Æthelbald, calls him ealdorman of
Kent.   [4] Archbishop Æthelred died 30 June 888.   [5] Abbot of St Augustine's, Canterbury.
[6] Cf. annal 878; he issued coins in East Anglia using this name, see North, *English
Hammered Coinage*, I, p. 78, pl. VI.   [7] The Annals of St Neots (p. 95) say he was entombed at
the royal *vill* called Hadleigh in East Anglia (Suffolk).   [8] i.e. the first of the Danes, cf Asser (56);
for the peace-treaty which settled Danelaw, see Swanton, *Prose*, pp. 6–7.   [9] France, dép.
Manche. A *Sant Laudan*; A[2] *Sand Laudan*; B *Sand Loðan*; C *Sant Loðdan*; D *Scan Leoðan*; E F
Scandlaudan.   [10] F specifies: chosen by God and by all people to the archbishopric in
Canterbury.   [11] The battle at Leuvan on the River Dijle in Brabant, Belgium.

E 888 *continued from p. 81*
and Queen Æthelswith,[1] who was King Alfred's sister, took the alms of the West Saxons and of King Alfred to Rome; and she passed away,[2] and her body lies at Pavia. And the same year Archbishop Æthelred and Ealdorman Æthelwald[3] passed away in the one month.[4]

889. In this year there was none who travelled to Rome, except for two runners King Alfred sent with letters.

890. Here Abbot Beornhelm[5] took the alms of the West Saxons and of King Alfred to Rome. And Guthrum, the northern king, whose baptismal name was Athelstan,[6] passed away;[7] he was King Alfred's godson, and he lived in East Anglia, and was the first to settle that land[8]. And the same year [889] the raiding-army went from the Seine to St Lô,[9] which is between the Bretons and the Franks; and [890] the Bretons fought against them and had the victory, and drove them out into a river, and drowned many. *Here Archbishop Plegmund was elected*[10] *by God and all the people.* [*continued on p. 85*]

---

[12] F Lat *lacking all human steering.* Æthelweard (p. 48) TF0046: *their boat had been brought not by tackle nor by ample shoulders, but rather by the nod of him who sees all things.* [13] On such *peregrini pro amore Dei* see Whitelock, 'The interpretation of The Seafarer', pp. 267–72. [14] Æthelweard (p. 48) says they then went towards Rome, intending to go on to Jerusalem – the one dying, one returning home. [15] D Dublasne, F Lat Dubslana; B Maccnethath, C D Machbethu, F Maccbetu; B Maelinmuin, C Maelinmumin, D Maelmumin, F Maelinmum. [16] F Lat *Then died their fourth companion, who was called Sulfneh, the very greatest scholar.* The Annals of Ulster (I, p. 409) record the death in 890 of: *Suibne, son of Maelmumai, anchorite and excellent scribe of Clonmacnois.* [17] The handwriting of the first scribe of A finishes here near the foot of folio 16[r]. The rest of the annal was added on folio 16[v] by the second scribe, who omitted to cross out the numeral 892. A later scribe, misled by this into thinking that the appearance of the comet was in 892, proceeded to add 1 to the following numerals, making the 892 into 893 (p. 84 top), and so on with each annal to 929. [18] The Monday to Wednesday before Ascension Day (the fortieth day after Easter Day); this year 10–12 May. F Lat *around the Ascension of the Lord.* MS *gang dagas*, 'walking days', marked by ecclesiastical perambulations during which prayers of supplication were offered. [19] A *same*, 'likewise'; B C D *sume*, 'some men'. [20] The same description is used in annals 995 F, 1066 CD. The expression *s.a.* 1066: 'which some men call . . .' suggests their knowledge of Classical etymology: Greek *cometes*, Latin *crinitas* 'long-haired', referring to the shooting star's developing multiple 'tails', Pliny, *Natural History*, II, 22; Isidore, *Etymologiae*, III, 71.

A *continued from previous page*

893 [892]. Here in this year the great raiding-army about which we formerly spoke went again from the East Kingdom[1] westward to Boulogne, and were provided with ships there so that they moved themselves over in a single journey, horses and all, and then came up into the mouth of the Lympne[2] with 250[3] ships. That river-mouth is in eastern Kent, at the east end of the great wood which we call Andred.[4] That wood is a hundred-and-twenty miles long or longer from east to west, and thirty miles broad. The river about which we spoke earlier flows out from that forest; they pulled their ships up on the river as far as the forest, 4 miles from the mouth of the estuary, and there destroyed a fortification; inside that fortress[5] sat a few peasant men, and it was half-made.[6]

Then immediately after that, Hæsten[7] came with 80 ships into the mouth of the Thames, and made himself a fortification at Milton;[8] and the other raiding-army [was] at Appledore.

894 [893]. In this year, that was twelve months from the time that they had made the fortification in the East Kingdom,[9] the Northumbrians and East Anglians had granted oaths to King Alfred, and the East Anglians 6 prime hostages, and yet, contrary to the pledge, as often as the other raiding-armies went out in full force,[10] then they went either with them or alone on their own behalf.[11] Then King Alfred gathered his army and went so that he camped between the two raiding-armies, at a convenient distance from the fortress in the wood and the fortress on the water,[12] so that he could get at either if they wanted to seek any open country. Then afterwards they went through the forest in gangs and mounted groups, on whichever edge was without an army; and almost every day they were sought by other groups[13] both from the army and also from the strongholds, <either by day>[14] or by night. The king had separated his army into two, so that there was always half at home and half out,[15] except for those men who had to hold the fortresses. The raiding-army did not come out in full from those positions more than twice; on the one occasion when they first came to land, before the army were assembled, the other [*continued opposite*]

---

[1] See p. 78, note 9.   [2] The former name of the River Rother (Kent, Sussex).   [3] A *ccl hunde*; E F *þridde healfhund*; B *twam hund*; C *cc*; D *cc hund*; Annals of St Neots (p. 95) *cccl*.   [4] i.e. the Weald, see p. 14, note 4.   [5] A F *fenne*, E *fænne*; but B C D *fæsten(n)e*. The latter reading avoids the introduction of a redundant preposition 'on' and the awkward construction 'a fortification in on the fen'. Any fen in question would be part of Romney Marsh between Rye and Appledore, but Æthelweard (pp. 48–9) and Florence (I, p. 109) imply that this fort was *at* Appledore.   [6] Asser (91) had spoken pointedly about the uselessness of such half-prepared defences.   [7] A viking leader active on the Continent for many years prior to appearing in England, and in 891–2 at Amiens before being driven out by famine. See generally Amory, 'The viking Hasting in Franco-Scandinavian legend', pp. 265–86 (especially p. 271).

E continued from p. 83

892. Here the great raiding-army about which we formerly spoke earlier, went again from the East Kingdom[1] westward to Boulogne, and were provided with ships there so that they moved themselves over in a single journey, horses and all, and then came up into the mouth of the Lympne[2] with two-and-a-half-hundred[3] ships. That river-mouth is in eastern Kent, at the east end of the great wood which we call Andred.[4] That wood is a hundred-and-twenty miles long or longer from east to west, and 30 miles broad. The river about which we spoke earlier flows out from that forest; they pulled their ships up on the river as far as the forest, 4 miles from the mouth of the estuary, and there destroyed a fortification; inside that fortress[5] sat a few peasant men, and it was half-made.[6]

Then immediately after that Hæsten[7] came with 80 ships into the mouth of the Thames, and made himself a fortification at Milton,[8] and the other raiding-army [was] at Appledore. *Here Wulfhere, archbishop of Northumbria, died.* [*continued on p. 91*]

continued from opposite page

occasion when they wanted to leave those positions.[16] They had then captured a great war-booty and then wanted to carry that northwards over the Thames into Essex to meet the ships. Then the army[17] rode in front of them and fought against them at Farnham, and put the raiding-army to flight and recovered the war-booty; and they fled across the Thames without any ford, then up by the Colne on to an islet.[18] Then the army besieged them there for as long as they had food; but they had [*continued overleaf*]

---

[8] Milton Regis, near Sittingbourne on the Swale 'estuary' in north Kent.   [9] A winter-camp made at Leuven (Brabant) 891-2 after their defeat by Arnulf, cf. p. 82, note 11.   [10] *mid ealle herige.*   [11] C adds: 'or on the other side'.   [12] i.e. respectively those at Appledore, protected by the Wealden forest, and at Milton, on the Swale, a creek of the Thames. There was presumably access through the Wealden forest; for alternative views of forest cover at this time, see Hill, *Atlas*, pp. 16-17.   [13] A *floccum* 'groups'; B C D *folcum* 'peoples'.   [14] Omitted by A B, supplied from C D.   [15] Cf. Orosius' account of the Amazon army: *divided into two parts, one to go out to fight, the other to defend their homes* (I, 15), although there is no evidence that Alfred knew Orosius, see *The Old English Orosius*, ed. Bately, pp. 30, 220.   [16] Æthelweard (p. 49), says that at Easter they went through the Weald towards Wessex, devastating Hampshire and Berkshire. See also Shippey, 'A missing army: some doubts about the Alfredian Chronicle', 41-55.   [17] Led by King Alfred's son Edward, according to Æthelweard (loc. cit.).   [18] Named as Thorney by Æthelweard (loc. cit.); perhaps at Iver, Buckinghamshire (Stenton, 'The Danes at Thorney Island in 893', 512-3; *Preparatory*, pp. 14-15).

A 894 [893] *continued from previous page*
completed their call-up,[1] and had used up their food, and the king was on his way there [to relieve them] with the division which was campaigning with him. Then, when he was on his way there and the other army were on their way home – and the Danish stayed behind there because their king had been wounded in the fight, so that they could not move him.[2] Then those who dwelt in Northumbria and East Anglia gathered some hundred ships and went around south, and some forty ships around north, and besieged a fortification in Devonshire on the Bristol Channel;[3] and those which went around south besieged Exeter. When the king heard that, he turned west towards Exeter with all the army, except for a very inconsiderable part of the people eastwards.

Then they went on until they came to London town, and then with the inhabitants of the town[4] and the help which came to them from the west, went east to Benfleet. Hæsten had come there with his raiding-army, which earlier settled at Milton; and also the great raiding-army had come there, which earlier settled at Appledore on the mouth of the Lympne. Hæsten had made that fortification at Benfleet earlier, and was then off on a raid, and the great raiding-army was in occupation.[5] Then they [the English] went up and put that raiding-army to flight, broke down the fortification, and seized all that was inside it, both money and women and also children, and brought all into London town; and all the ships they either broke up or burned[6] or brought to London town or to Rochester. And they brought Hæsten's wife and his two sons to the king, and he gave them back to him, because one of them was his godson, the other Ealdorman Æthelred's.[7] They had received them before Hæsten came to Benfleet,[8] and he had granted him hostages and oaths, and the king had also granted him much money, and did also when he returned the boy and the woman. But immediately they came to Benfleet and the fortification was made, [*continued opposite*]

---

[1] *stemn*, lit. 'summons', to tour of duty or term of service.   [2] We next hear of these survivors in Essex with Hæsten at Benfleet. Æthelweard (pp. 49–50) says that, having given hostages and agreed to leave the kingdom, they set out for East Anglia where they were met by their ships which sailed rapidly from the Lympne.   [3] *be þære norþ sæ*.   [4] MS *Lundenbyrg . . . burgwarum*; possibly by this stage the chronicler might mean: 'the stronghold of London . . . garrison'.   [5] *æt ham*.   [6] The charred remains of many ships, surrounded by human skeletons, were found in 1890 (Spurrell, 'Hæsten's camps at Shoebury and Benfleet, Essex', 153).   [7] Ealdorman of Mercia and King Alfred's son-in-law, see p. 81, note 9.   [8] It seems as if Alfred has been in negotiations with Hæsten at some prior stage, perhaps when stationed strategically between the two enemy bases (p. 84). Although there is no mention of Hæsten leading the army in England that year, it is said he had made that Benfleet fort earlier. This may have been when based at Milton, since Benfleet was merely on the opposite (Essex) side of the Thames from Milton, the 'water fort'.

A 894 [893] *continued from opposite page*
he [Hæsten] raided his [Alfred's] kingdom – that very quarter which his son's
godfather Æthelred had to hold; and again a second time he was engaged
raiding in that same kingdom when his fortification was broken down.

Then, as I said earlier, the king turned west with the army towards Exeter,
and the raiding-army had besieged the town; then when he had arrived there,
they went to their ships.

Then, when he was busy against the raiding-army there in the west, and
both the [other] raiding-armies gathered at Shoebury in Essex, and there they
made a fortification [and] went together up along the Thames, there joined
them great reinforcements both from East Anglia and from Northumbria.
Then they went up along the Thames until they reached the Severn, then up
along the Severn. Then there gathered Ealdorman Æthelred[7] and Ealdorman
Æthelhelm[9] and Ealdorman Æthelnoth,[10] and the king's thegns who were
occupying the fortifications, from every stronghold east of the Parret, both
west and east of Selwood, and also north of the Thames and west of the
Severn,[11] and also a certain part of the Welsh race.[12] Then, when they were
all gathered, they overtook the raiding-army from behind at Buttington on
Severn shore,[13] and besieged them on every side in a fortification. Then when
they had settled for many weeks on the two sides of the river, and the king was
west in Devon against the raiding ship-army, they were weighed down with
lack of food, and had devoured the greater part of their horses, and the others
were perishing with hunger; then they went out to the men camped on the east
side of the river and fought against them, and the Christians had the victory.
And Ordheah, the king's thegn,[14] was killed there, and also many other king's
thegns killed, <and very great slaughter was made there of the Danish>,[15] and
the part that came away there were [*continued overleaf*]

[9] Ealdorman of Wiltshire, who took the alms of Alfred and Wessex to Rome in 887
(q.v.).   [10] Ealdorman of Somerset, who had supported Alfred in most dire straits in the swamps
of Somerset, and afterwards took part in Guthrum's baptism, see p. 75, note, 11; p. 77, note
9.   [11] Fortifications presumably under Mercian jurisdiction and therefore not mentioned in
the West Saxon *Burghal Hidage*.   [12] *sum dæl þæs Norð Weal cynnes*; according to Asser (8)
South Wales already belonged to Alfred, other princes submitted to him out of fear of Æthelred of
Mercia, and eventually Anarawd ap Rhodri of Gwynedd would abandon his fruitless alliance with
the Northumbrians in favour of Alfred (Lloyd, *History*, p. 328).   [13] Perhaps Buttington
Tump, on the valuable royal estate of Tiddenham in Gloucestershire (see Swanton, *Prose*, pp.
16–19), at the confluence of the Wye and Severn estuary, at the southernmost end of Offa's Dyke,
near where the Roman road crosses into South Wales. But it is said the vikings had gone *up* the
Severn. Further north there is another Buttington at a Severn crossing west of Shrewsbury, and this
site might make more sense of Alfred's forces camping both sides of the river. There are remains of
an earthwork, where some evidence of a war-grave was excavated in the nineteenth century
(RCHM, *Montgomery*, p. 28).   [14] Otherwise unknown.   [15] Supplied from B C D.

A 894 [893] *continued from previous page*
saved by flight. When they came to their fortification[1] and to their ships in Essex, the remnant again gathered together a great raiding-army from East Anglia and from Northumbria before winter; and secured their women and their ships and their money in East Anglia, and went at one stretch by day and night, until they arrived at a certain deserted city in Wirral, which is called Chester.[2] The army could not overtake them from behind before they got inside the fortification; however they besieged that fortification some two days, and took all the cattle that was outside there, and killed all the men they could ride down outside the fort; and burned up all the corn, and with their horses ate up all the neighbourhood.[3] And that was twelve months after they earlier came across the sea here.[4]

895 [894]. And immediately after that in this year, the raiding-army went from Wirral into Wales since they could not stay there; that was because they were deprived of both the cattle and the corn which they had ravaged. Then when they turned back from Wales with the war-booty they had taken there, they went across the land of Northumbria and East Anglia so that the army could not get at them, until they came east of the land of Essex, on an island which is out in the sea that is called Mersea. And then when the raiding-army which had besieged Exeter turned back homewards, they raided up in Sussex near Chichester, and the garrison[5] put them to flight and killed many hundred of them, and took some of their ships.

Then the same year before winter, the Danish who settled on Mersea pulled their ships up the Thames and then up [*continued opposite*]

---

[1] The Benfleet fort, (see p. 86, note 8) apparently slighted by local people, and in need of repair (The Annals of St Neots, p. 97). [2] *Legaceaster*; the ancient Roman legionary fort where a great battle had taken place between Mercians and Welsh in the early seventh century (*s.a.* 605 A, 606 E). Bede (*HE*, II, 2) supplies the etymology: 'The city of the legions', giving the British name Caerlegion (Welsh Caerlleon); the defining prefix *Lega-* is only lost from the mid-eleventh century, see Dodgson, *The Place-Names of Cheshire*, V, pp. 2–7. There was at least one church within the walls, so the place cannot have been completely deserted, but perhaps (as at London, see p. 80, note 8) the principal occupation lay outside the walls (Ward, *Saxon Occupation within the Roman Fortress*, pp. 115–28). What was 'restored' in 907 (q.v. C) was presumably the perimeter wall. [3] This 'scorched earth' strategy is apparently carried out by the English forces. [4] Æthelweard (p. 50) does not mention the seige of Chester, but says that Sigeferth, *piraticus*, came from Northumbria with a large fleet and ravaged the coast twice in a single expedition before sailing home. [5] *burgware*; Chichester is one of the forts listed in the Burghal Hidage (Swanton, *Prose*, p. 13). [6] Æthelweard (pp. 50–51) says: *Then when two years were complete from when a huge fleet arrived from the fortress of Boulogne bound for Lympne, a town of the English, Ealdoman Æthelnoth set out from Wessex. In the city of York he contacted the enemy, who were plundering large territories in the kingdom of the Mercians, on the western side of the place called Stamford. This is to say, between the streams of the river Welland and the thickets of the wood commonly called Kesteven* (an area corresponding with latterday Rutland). The raid may well be connected with the raids of the pirate Sigeferth (see note 4). See Stenton, 'Æthelweard's account of the last years of King Alfred's reign', 82–3 (*Preparatory*, pp. 10–11).

A 895 [894] *continued from opposite*
the Lea. That was two years after they came here from across the sea.[6]

896 [895]. In the same year the aforesaid raiding-army made a fortification by the Lea, 20 miles above London stronghold.[7] Then later in the summer, a great part of the garrison, and likewise other peoples, went so that they arrived at the Danish fortification, and were put to flight there, and some four king's thegns killed. Then later in harvest-time the king camped in the vicinity of the stronghold while they reaped the corn, so that the Danish could not keep them from the reaping. Then one day the king rode up along the river and looked to see where the river might be obstructed so that they could not bring out their ships. And then they did so: made two fortifications on the two sides of the river.[8] Then when they had just begun that work and had camped by there, the raiding-army realized that they could not bring out the ships. Then they abandoned them and went overland so that they arrived at Bridgnorth[9] on the Severn, and there made a fortification. Then the army rode west after the raiding-army, and the men of London town fetched the ships, and all that they could not take away, broke up, and those that were serviceable brought into London town. And the Danish had secured their women in East Anglia before they went out from that fortification. They settled at Bridgnorth for the winter. That was three years after they had come here across the sea into the mouth of the Lympne.[10]

897 [896]. Then the summer after in this year, the raiding-army went off, some to East Anglia, some to Northumbria, and those who were without money[11] got themselves ships there, and went south across the sea to the Seine.[12]

The raiding-army, by the grace of God, had not altogether utterly crushed the English race; but they were a great deal more crushed in [*continued overleaf*]

---

[7] Twenty miles would site this fortification in or near Hertford, where English fortifications would be built in 913 (q.v.).   [8] This kind of blockading fortification had been used on the Marne against the vikings by Charles the Bald in 862 (Hassall and Hill, 'Pont del'Arche: Frankish influence on the West Saxon burh?', 188–95 (p. 191); similar tactics are found later at Buckingham 918, Bedford 919, Stamford 922 and Nottingham 924.   [9] A *Cwatbrycge*; D *Brygce*; B C *Bricge*.   [10] Æthelweard (p. 51) says that in this year Guthfrith, king of the Northumbrians, died and was entombed in the 'high church' at York.   [11] MS *feoh*, 'fee', but the word is sometimes used in the sense of 'property', as in annal 893, where it seems more likely to refer to moveable goods (to be made safe together with women and ships).   [12] *The Annals of St-Vaast* (p. 78) record that Vikings from England led by Hun(c)deus came with five large ships and camped at Christmas at Choisy on the Oise. Hundeus may have gone back to Northumbria, see Lyon and Stewart, 'Northumbrian viking coins', pp. 117–18.

A 897 [896] *continued from previous page*
those three years with pestilence among cattle and men, most of all by the fact
that many of the best of the king's thegns there were in the land passed away in
those three years; of these, one was Swithwulf, bishop in Rochester, and
Ceolmund, ealdorman in Kent, and Beorhtwulf, ealdorman in Essex,[1] and
Wulfred, ealdorman in Hampshire, and Ealhheard, bishop at Dorchester, and
Eadwulf, the king's thegn in Sussex, and Beornwulf, town-reeve in Winchester,[2] and Ecgwulf, the king's horse-thegn,[3] and many in addition to them,
though I have named the most distinguished.

The same year the raiding-armies in East Anglia and Northumbria greatly
harassed Wessex along the south coast with predatory bands, most of all with
the 'askrs'[4] they had built many years before. Then King Alfred ordered
long-ships to be built to oppose the 'askrs'; they were well-nigh twice as long
as the others, some had 60 oars, some more; they were both swifter and
steadier, and also more responsive[5] than the others; they were neither of
Frisian design nor of Danish, but as it seemed to himself that they might be
most useful.[6] Then on a certain occasion the same year there came six ships
to Wight and did great harm there, both in Devon and everywhere along the
sea-coast. Then the king ordered nine of the new ships to go there, and they got
in front of them at the river-mouth towards the open sea. Then they [the
Danes] went out with three ships against them [the English], and three [ships]
stood on dry land at the upper end of the river-mouth[7] – and the men were
gone off up inland. Then they [the English] captured two of the three ships at
the entrance to the river-mouth, and killed the men; and the one escaped: on
that also the men were killed, except for five; that got away because the ships
of the others were aground: they were very awkwardly [*continued opposite*]

---

[1] Essex had been ceded to the Danes by the terms of the treaty between Alfred and Guthrum
in 878 (Swanton, *Prose*, p. 6, and see Map p. 279) but apparently reabsorbed with London in 886
(q.v.); and in any case 'East Saxons' extended as far west as Hertfordshire, and needed
administration.   [2] A thegn called Beornwulf witnessed a land-charter of Æthelwulf in 880
(*Cartularium Saxonicum*, II, p. 168); perhaps it was his son who was described as a relative of the
bishop of Winchester in 902 (ibid, p. 252; Harmer, *Documents*, pp. 112–14).   [3] This may be
the Ecgwulf specified in Alfred's will as the one to whom the king had entrusted some private
property (Swanton, *Prose*, p. 49). As *hors-þegn* he would have been responsbile for mounted
provision, and possibly transport-arrangements in general (cf. Frankish *marescalcus*,
'marshal').   [4] MS *æsc*, borrowing the Viking word *askr*, 'warship'; it is used of Danish ships,
much as WWII English understood *Dornier* or *Messerschmidt* of enemy aircraft.   [5] MS
hierran, possibly 'higher', but see Swanton forthcoming.   [6] For types of ship-construction at
this date, see Crumlin-Pederson, 'The vikings and the Hanseatic merchants', pp. 181–204; 'Viking
shipbuilding and seamanship', pp. 271–86, and Binns, 'The ships of the vikings, were they "viking
ships"?', pp. 287–94. See also Lebecq, 'On the use of the word "Frisian" in the 6th–10th centuries',
85–90.   [7] There are a variety of possible locales for this incident, e.g. the Exe estuary in
Devon, or Poole Harbour in Dorset; but the nature of such terrain is notoriously inconstant and the
present-day disposition of shore-line, sand-banks and channels is not necessarily that of the past.
See Magoun, 'King Alfred's naval and beach battle with the Danes', 409–14; Binns, 'The
navigation of viking ships', pp. 105–10.

E *continued from p. 85*

901 [899]. Here King Alfred departed on 26 October;[8] and he held [*continued on p. 93*]

THE WORCESTER MANUSCRIPT (D) 901 [899]

901 [899]. Here King Alfred departed on 26 October;[8] and [he] held the [*continued on p. 93*]

THE WINCHESTER MANUSCRIPT (A) 897 [896] *continued from opposite page*

aground. Three were aground on the side of the channel where the Danish ships were aground, and the others all on the other side, so that none of them could get at the others. But, when the water had ebbed many furlongs from the ships, the Danish went from the three [remaining] ships to the other three which were stranded on their side, and then they[9] fought there. There were killed Lucumon, the king's reeve, and Wulfheard the Frisian, and Æbbe the Frisian, and Æthelhere the Frisian, and Æthelfrith the king's geneat,[10] and of all men, Frisian[11] and English, 62, and 120 of the Danish. However, then the tide came first to the Danish ships, before the Christians could shove out theirs,[12] and therefore they rowed away out [to sea]. They were then so damaged that they could not row past the land of Sussex, but there the sea cast two of them up onto land; and the men were led to Winchester to the king, and he ordered them to be hanged there. And the men who were on the one ship came to East Anglia very much wounded. The same summer no less than 20 ships perished, with men and all, along the south coast. The same year Wulfric, the king's horse-thegn, passed away; he was also the Welsh reeve.[13]

898 [897]. Here in this year died Æthelhelm, ealdorman of Wiltshire, nine days before midsummer; and here passed away Heahstan,[14] who was bishop in London.

901 [899]. Here died Alfred, Æthelwulf's offspring, six days before the Feast of All Hallows.[8] He was king over all the English race except that part which was under Danish control, and he held that kingdom [*continued overleaf*]

---

[8] On the year of Alfred's death see Beaven, 'The regnal dates of Alfred, Edward the Elder, and Athelstan', 526–31. All Hallows Day (A) is 1 November.   [9] They interlined, perhaps by a later hand.   [10] The word *geneat* originally meant 'companion', and the *cynges geneat* was a member of the royal household with the same *wergild* as that of the king's thegn (cf. Chadwick, *Anglo-Saxon Institutions*, p. 136f.; Thacker, 'Some terms for noblemen in Anglo-Saxon England', 210–13).   [11] Asser (76) lists people from a variety of races, including Franks, Frisians, Gauls, Vikings, Welshmen, Irishmen and Bretons, serving Alfred. These Frisian mercenaries were perhaps refugees from Viking depredations in their homelands; see also Lebecq cited in note 6.   [12] Since the English ships grounded after the viking ships, the returning tide ought to have reached them first. But the Danish boats having been deliberately beached, it is likely that they used rollers, cf. Binns, 'The navigation of viking ships . . .', pp. 109–10.   [13] A *Wealhgefera*, B C D *Wealhgerefa*. This term does not occur elsewhere; such a post may have required bi- or even tri-lingual abilities if administering taxes among the Welsh or Cornish (cf. Attenborough, *Laws*, pp. 42–7). See also Faull, 'The semantic development of Old English *wealh*', 20–44 (pp. 28–9).   [14] All other MSS call him Ealhstan.

A 901 [899] *continued from previous page*
twenty-eight-and-a-half years.[1] Then Edward, his son, succeeded to the kingdom.[2]

Then Æthelwold, his father's brother's son, rode and seized the manor at Wimborne[3] and at Twinham[4] without leave of the king[5] and his councillors. Then the king rode with an army until he camped at Badbury,[6] near Wimborne, and Æthelwold stayed inside that manor with the men who had given him their allegiance, and had barricaded all the gates against him, and said that he would either live there or die there.[7] Then under cover of that he stole away by night and sought out the raiding-army in Northumbria. And the king ordered him to be ridden after, and he could not be overtaken then. Then they rode after the woman whom he had earlier taken without the king's leave, and against the command of the bishops, because she was earlier consecrated a nun.[8] And in this same year Æthelred, [who] was ealdorman in Devon, passed away four weeks before King Alfred.

903 [902]. Here Ealdorman Æthelwulf, the brother of Ealhswith, died; and Abbot Virgilius among the Scots, and mass-priest Grimbald on *8 July*.

904 [903]. Here Æthelwold[9] came across the sea here to Essex with the fleet with which he was.

905 [904]. Here Æthelwold enticed the raiding-army in East Anglia into hostility, so that they raided across the land of Mercia until they came to Cricklade and there went over the Thames, and took all that they could grab, both in Braydon[10] and round about there, and then turned back homewards. Then King Edward went [*continued on p. 94*]

---

[1] A *healfum læs þe xxx wintra*, D E *xxviii wintra 7 healf gear.*   [2] He was crowned at Kingston according to Diceto, see p. 104, note 10.   [3] Wimborne, Dorset, was a royal estate by the time of Edward the Confessor (DB, *Dorset*, 1, 3), and perhaps much earlier. The minster there had been founded by the ex-queen Cuthburh, sister of Ine, in the early eighth century (see *s.a* 718), and Alfred's brother King Æthelred was buried there (see *s.a.* 871).   [4] A *Tweoxn eam*, D *Tweoxnam* 'between the waters' (i.e. the Stour, Avon and sea); now Christchurch, Hampshire. Naturally defensible it would be listed among the forts of the Burghal Hidage (Swanton, *Prose*, p. 13), and remained in royal hands (DB, *Hampshire*, 1, 28).   [5] A *butan ðaes cyninges leafe*, BCD *þæs cynges unþances*. As the son of King Æthelred, Alfred's elder brother, Æthelwold may well have felt disappointed by the terms of Alfred's will (Swanton, *Prose*, pp. 47–51).   [6] Badbury Rings, Dorset, a prehistoric fort commanding wide views (RCHM, *Dorset*, V, pp. 61–3); it was in royal hands at the time of the Conquest (DB, *Dorset* I, 3 *in loco* Shapwick).   [7] The Old English phrase *oðer oððe þær licgan* has a fine rhetorical flourish, cf. p. 178, note 8. For *licgan* 'to lie dead', see above, *s.a.* 755, where a similar confrontation occurred.   [8] To take a nun from a nunnery without the permission of the king or bishop was a criminal offence incurring a fine of 120 shillings in Alfred's time (Attenborough, *Laws*, pp. 68–9).   [9] Described by the Annals of St Neots as *king of the Danes* and *king of the pagans*, *s.a.* 903, 904.   [10] A pre-English name, its etymology is obscure, see Gover, *The Place-Names of Wiltshire*, p. 11.

E 901 [899] *continued from p. 91*
that kingdom 28-and-a-half years.[1] And then Edward, his son, succeeded to the kingdom.[2] [*continued on p. 95*]

THE CANTERBURY MANUSCRIPT (F) *continued from p. 74*

903. Here Grimbald the *priest* passed away; and this same year the New Minster[11] in Winchester was consecrated, and St Judoc's arrival.[12] [*continued on p. 105*]

THE WORCESTER MANUSCRIPT (D) 901 [899] *continued from p. 91*)

kingdom 28-and-a-half years.[1] And then Edward, his son, succeeded to the kingdom.[2] And then the ætheling Æthelwold, his father's brother's son, rode and seized the manor at Wimborne[3] and at Twinham[4] against the will of the king[5] and his councillors. Then the king rode with an army until he camped at Badbury,[6] near Wimborne, and Æthelwold stayed inside that manor with the men who had given him their allegiance, and had barricaded all the gates against him, and said that he would either live there or die there.[7] Then under cover of that the ætheling rode away by night and sought out the raiding-army in Northumbria and they received him as king and submitted to him. Then they rode after the woman whom he had earlier taken without the king's leave and against the command of the bishops, because she was earlier consecrated a nun.[8] And in this same year Æthelred, [who] was ealdorman in Devon, passed away 4 weeks before King Alfred.

903. Here departed Ealdorman Æthelwulf, the brother of Ealhswith the mother of King Edward; and Abbot Virgilius among the Scots, and mass-priest Grimbald.

904. Here Æthelwold[9] came across the sea here with all the fleet he could get and submission was made to him in Essex.

905. Here a *comet* appeared on 20 October. Here Æthelwold led the raiding-army in East Anglia into hostility, so that they raided across all the land of Mercia until they came to Cricklade and there went over the Thames, and took all that they could grab, both in Braydon[10] and thereabouts, and then turned east homewards. Then King Edward went after them as quickly as he could [*continued on p. 95*]

THE ABINGDON MANUSCRIPT (C) 902 *continued from p. 67*

902.[13] Here Ealhswith passed away, and the same year was the fight at the Holm[14] of the inhabitants of Kent and the Danish.

904. Here the moon grew dark.

905. Here a *comet* appeared. [*continued overleaf*]

---

[11] Biddle, *Winchester in the Early Middle Ages*, pp. 313–21.   [12] i.e. the acquisition of the relics of this seventh-century Breton saint, for whom see Farmer, *The Oxford Dictionary of Saints*, pp. 225–6.   [13] B and C here incorporate a brief 'Mercian Register' covering about twenty years (902–24). See the Introduction p. xxiv.   [14] Presumably in Kent, but not certainly identified. For the probable sense of *holm* here see p. 156, note 8.

A 905 [904] *continued from p. 92*
after them as quickly as he could gather his army, and raided across all their territory between the Dykes[1] and the Wissey,[2] all as far north as the Fens. Then when he wanted to go back out from there, he ordered it to be announced through all the army that they all go out together; then the Kentish remained behind there against his command, and he had sent out seven messengers to them. Then they were surrounded there by the raiding-army, and they fought there. And there were killed Ealdorman Sigewulf, and Ealdorman Sigehelm,[3] and Eadwold the king's thegn, and Abbot Cenwulf, and Sigeberht, son of Sigewulf, and Eadwold, son of Acca, and many others in addition to them though I have named the most distinguished. And on the Danish side were killed their king Eohric[4] and the ætheling Æthelwold,[5] who had incited him to that hostility, and Beorhtsige, son of the ætheling Beornoth,[6] and Hold[7] Ysopa and Hold Oscytel, and very many others in addition to them whom we cannot name now; and on either hand there was great slaughter made, and there were more of the Danish killed there although they had possession of the place of slaughter. And Ealhswith departed the same year.

906 [905]. Here in this year departed Alfred, [who] was reeve at Bath; and in the same year they confirmed the peace at Tiddingford,[8] just as King Edward determined, both with East Anglians and with Northumbrians.

909 [908]. Here departed Denewulf, who was bishop in Winchester.[9]

910 [909]. Here Frithustan[10] succeeded to the bishopric in Winchester, and after that Asser, who was bishop at Sherborne, departed. And the same year King Edward sent an army both from Wessex and from Mercia, and it raided the north raiding-army very greatly, both men [continued on p. 96]

THE ABINGDON MANUSCRIPT (C) 907 *continued from previous page*

907. Here Chester was restored.

909. Here St Oswald's body was brought from Bardney into Mercia.[11]

910. In this year English and Danes fought at Tettenhall,[12] and the English took the victory. And the same year Æthelflæd built the stronghold at Bremesbyrig.[13] [continued on p. 96]

---

[1] The Devil's Dyke and Fleam Dyke boundary earthworks (RCHM, *Cambridge*, II, pp. 139–47).   [2] *Wusan*; or possibly the Ouse, see Reaney, *The Place-Names of Cambridgeshire*, pp. 12–14.   [3] King Edward would later marry his daughter.   [4] King of East Anglia.   [5] See p. 92, note 9.   [6] More correctly perhaps, Beorhtnoth, as C D.   [7] The hold (Old Norse *holdr*) was a Scandinavian hereditary landowner ranking below the jarl. In the 'Law of the North people' the hold had the same wergild as a king's high reeve and double that of a thegn (Lieberman, *Gesetze*, I, p. 460, transl. Whitelock, *Documents*, p. 469).   [8] *Teotanheale*, a ford across the Ouzel at Linslade, see Mawer and Stenton, *The Place-Names of Buckinghamshire*, p. 81.   [9] Æthelweard (p. 52) records here the dedication by Archbishop Plegmund of *a very high tower in the city of Winchester. Its foundations had been laid a little before that time in honour of Mary, mother of God. In the course of the same year the bishop just mentioned conveyed alms to Rome for the nation and also for King Edward.*   [10] In A the opening of this entry was later framed in red and marked with a cross. Frithustan's embroidered vestments survive; they were commissioned by Queen Ælfflæd and later presented by Athelstan to St Cuthbert's shrine (Battiscombe, *Relics*, pp. 375–432).   [11] To Gloucester, cf. annal 641 E.

E *continued from p. 93*

906. Here King Edward, from necessity, confirmed peace both with the raiding-army from East Anglia and with the Northumbrians.

910. Here the English raiding-army and the Danes fought at Tettenhall,[12] and Æthelred, leader[14] of the Mercians, passed away, and King Edward succeeded to London town and to Oxford,[15] and all the lands which pertained thereto. And a great raiding ship-army came here from the south, from Brittany, and raided along the Severn a lot, but they mostly all afterwards perished there. [*continued on p. 103*].

THE WORCESTER MANUSCRIPT (D) 905 *continued from p. 93*

gather his army, and raided across all their land between the Dykes[1] and the Wissey,[2] all as far north as the Fens. Then when he wanted to go back out from there, he ordered it to be announced through all the army that they all go out together; then the Kentish remained behind there against his command, and he had sent out 7 messengers to them. Then they were surrounded there by the raiding-army, and they fought there. And there were killed Ealdorman Sigewulf, and Ealdorman Sigehelm,[3] and Eadwold the king's thegn, and Abbot Cenwulf, and Sigeberht, son of Sigewulf, and Eadwold, son of Acca, and many others in addition to them though I have named the most distinguished. And on the Danish side were killed King Eohric[4] and the ætheling Æthelwold,[5] whom they had chosen as their king, and Beorhtsige, son of the ætheling Beorthnoth, and Hold[7] Ysopa and Hold Oscytel, and very many others in addition to them whom we cannot name now; and on either hand there was great slaughter made, and there were more of the Danish killed although they had possession of the place of slaughter. And Ealhswith departed the same year.

906. Here St Oswald's body was brought from Bardney.[11] Here in this year departed Alfred, [who] was town-reeve at Bath; and in the same year they confirmed the peace at Tiddingford,[8] just as King Edward determined, both with East Anglians and with Northumbrians.

909. Here the Mercians and West Saxons fought against the raiding-army near Tettenhall on *6 August* and had the victory.[12] And the same year Æthelflæd built Bremesburh.[13] Here Denewulf, who was bishop in Winchester, departed.

910. Here Frithustan[10] succeeded to the bishopric in Winchester, and after that Asser, who was bishop at Sherborne, departed. And the same year King Edward sent an army both from [*continued on p. 97*]

---

[12] Æthelweard (pp. 52–3) says: *After a year the barbarians broke the peace with King Edward, and no less with Æthelred, who then ruled the Northumbrian and Mercian areas.* They harried through Mercia and over the Severn into the west country; but, when, *rejoicing in rich spoil,* they were in the process of crossing back over the Severn bridge at Bridgnorth (*Cwatbricge*) they were attacked by squadrons of both Mercians and West Saxons, which on 5 August gained a great victory on Woden's field (Wednesfield) killing three viking kings, Halfdan (*Healfdene*), Eowils (*Eywysl*), and Ivar (*Inwær*) who with other jarls and noblemen *hastened to the hall of the infernal one.*   [13] Possibly Bromesberrow near Ledbury, but see Smith, *The Place-Names of Gloucestershire*, III, p. 167.   [14] A E *ealdor*; in A 912 he is called *ealdorman* and in C 911 *hlaford*, 'lord'.   [15] For this link, supported by evidence of trade, see Horsman, *Saxo-Norman London*, II, p. 433.

A 910 [909] *continued from p. 94*
and every kind of property, and killed many men of those Danish, and were inside there for five weeks.

911 [910]. Here the raiding-army in Northumbria broke the peace, and scorned every peace which King Edward and his councillors offered them, and raided across the land of Mercia. And the king had gathered some hundred ships, and was then in Kent; and the ships went east along the south coast towards him. Then the raiding-army imagined that the most part of his reinforcement was on these ships, and that they might go unfought wherever they wanted. Then when the king learned that they had gone out on a raid, he sent his army both from Wessex and from Mercia, and they got in front of the raiding-army from behind when it was on its way home, and then fought with them and put the raiding-army to flight, and killed many thousands of it; and King Eowils[1] was killed there.

912 [911]. Here Æthelred, ealdorman in Mercia, departed,[2] and King Edward succeeded to London and to Oxford and to all the lands which belonged thereto.

913 [912]. Here, around Martinmas in this year, King Edward ordered to be built the more northerly stronghold at Hertford,[3] between the Maran and the Beane and the Lea. And then after that, the summer after, between Rogation days and midsummer,[4] King Edward went with some of his reinforcements to Maldon in Essex, and camped there while they made and built the stronghold at Witham; and a good part of the people who were earlier under the control of Danish men submitted to him. And meanwhile some of his reinforcements made the stronghold at Hertford on the south side of the Lea.[5] [*continued on p. 98*]

THE ABINGDON MANUSCRIPT (C) *continued from p. 94*

911. Then in this, the next year, Æthelred, lord of the Mercians, departed.[2]

912. Here, on the holy eve of the *Invention of the Holy Cross*,[6] Æthelflæd, Lady of the Mercians,[7] came to Scergeat[8] and built a stronghold there, and the same year that at Bridgnorth.[9]

913. Here, God helping, Æthelflæd, Lady of the Mercians, went with all the Mercians to Tamworth, and then built the stronghold there early in the summer, and afterwards before Lammas[10] that at Stafford. [*continued on p. 98*]

---

[1] A *Ecwils*, B C *Eowils*, D *Eowilisc*.   [2] Æthelweard (p. 53) says *he was buried in peace in the fortress called Gloucester*.   [3] i.e. on the north bank of the Lea, as the end of the annal makes clear.   [4] The Annals of St Neots say it was *about the Feast of St John the Baptist*, i.e. the Nativity, 24 June.   [5] Æthelweard (p. 53) records here the death of Eadwulf, reeve of Bamburgh.   [6] 2 May; see annal 200 F and Swanton, *Prose*, pp. 81, 114–21.   [7] Perhaps a title accorded only after the ealdorman's death. See generally Wainwright, 'Æthelflæd Lady of the Mercians'.   [8] Literally 'boundary gap'; as yet unidentified.   [9] Where the Danes had taken winter quarters in 896 (q.v.).   [10] 1 August.

D 910 *continued from p. 95*

Wessex and from Mercia, and it raided the raiding-army in the north very greatly, both men and every kind of property, and killed many men of those Danish, and were inside there for 5 weeks.

Here the English and the Danes fought at Tettenhall,[11] and Æthelred, leader[12] of the Mercians, passed away, and King Edward succeeded to London town and to Oxford, and all the lands which belonged thereto. And a great raiding ship-army came here from the south, from Brittany, and raided along the Severn a lot, but they mostly all afterwards perished there.

911 [910]. Here the raiding-army in Northumbria broke the peace, and scorned every privilege which King Edward and his councillors offered them, and raided across the land of Mercia. And the king had gathered some hundred ships, and was then in Kent; and the ships went east along the south coast towards him. Then the raiding-army imagined that the most part of his reinforcement was on these ships, and that they might go unfought wherever they wanted. Then when the king learned that they had gone on a raid, he sent his army both from Wessex and from Mercia, and they got in front of the raiding-army from behind when it was on its way home, and then fought with them and put the raiding-army to flight, and killed many of it. And there was killed King Eowils and King Halfdan,[13] and Jarl Ohtor, and Jarl Scurfa, and Hold Athulf[14] and Hold Agmund.

912 [911]. Here Æthelred, ealdorman in Mercia, departed,[2] and King Edward succeeded to London and to Oxford and to all the lands which belonged thereto.

913. Here Æthelflæd built Tamworth and also Stafford stronghold. Here, around Martinmas in this year, King Edward ordered to be built the more northerly stronghold at Hertford,[3] between the Maran and the Beane and the Lea. And then after that, the summer after, between Rogation days and midsummer,[4] King Edward went with some of his reinforcements to Maldon in Essex, and camped there while they made and strengthened the stronghold at Witham; and a good part of the people who were earlier under the control of Danish men submitted to him. And some of his reinforcements made the stronghold at Hertford on the south side of the Lea.[5] [*continued on p. 99*]

---

[11] D has already referred to this battle once *s.a.* 909 (incorporated from the Mercian Register, cf. the Introduction p. xxv), and now, like other MSS, twice more *s.a.* 910. Æthelweard (pp. 52–3) also ascribes it to 909.   [12] See p. 95, note 14.   [13] Cf. Æthelweard's account, p. 95, note 12; Florence (I, 121) calls them *brothers of King Ivar* (Hinguar).   [14] B C 'and Hold Benesing, and Olaf the Black, and Hold Thurferth, and Osferth Hlytte, and Hold Guthferth, and Hold Agmund, and Guthferth'; *The Annals of St Neots* (p. 106) add also the name of Eagellus. Hlytte should probably be rendered 'Soothsayer', cf. Tengivk, *Old English Bynames*, p. 347.

A *continued from p. 96*

917 [916]. Here in this year after Easter the raiding-army rode out from Northampton and from Leicester and broke the peace, and killed many men at Hook Norton and thereabouts; and then very quickly after that, as these first came home, they found another mounted band that rode out against Luton. And then the people of the land became aware of it, and fought against them and brought them to full flight, and recovered all that they had taken and also a great part of their horses and of their weapons.

918 [917]. Here in this year a great raiding ship-army came over here from the south from Brittany, and with them two jarls, Ohtor and Hroald, and went around west until they got into the mouth of the Severn, and raided in Wales everywhere by the sea, where it suited them, and took Cameleac, bishop in Archenfield,[1] and led him with them to the ships; and then King Edward ransomed him back for 40 pounds. Then after that the whole raiding-army went up and wanted to go on a raid against Archenfield; then they were met by the men from Hereford and from Gloucester and from the nearest strongholds, and fought against them and put them to flight, and killed the jarl Hroald and the other Jarl Ohtor's brother and a great part of the raiding-army, and drove them into an enclosure[2] and besieged them there until they gave them hostages, that they would leave King Edward's domain. And the king had arranged that there should be positions on the southern side of the Severn mouth from Cornwall in the west, eastwards as far as Avonmouth, so that they dared seek land nowhere on that side. However, they then stole up by night on two certain occasions: on the one occasion east of Watchet, and on another occasion at Porlock;[3] then on each occasion they were hit, so that few came away, except only those who swam out to the ships. And then they settled out on the island at Flatholme[4] until the time came that they were very short of food, and many men perished with hunger, because they could not [*continued on p. 100*]

THE ABINGDON MANUSCRIPT (C) *continued from p. 96*

914. Then in this, the next year, [was made] that [stronghold] at Eddisbury[5] in early summer; and later in the same year, late in harvest-time, that at Warwick. [*continued opposite*]

---

[1] *Ircinga felda*, 'the plain of those who live in the district of Ariconium' (an old Roman station in the Wye valley, Herefordshire; Smith, *English Place-Name Elements*, I, p. 283). The name survives as that of a deanery, but there is no strong evidence for a bishopric here, and the text may alternatively read 'Bishop Cameleac (Welsh Cyfeiliog) was taken in Archenfield'.   [2] *pearroc*, cf. Smith, *English Place-Name Elements*, II, pp. 60–61.   [3] Both on the north coast of Somerset; for Watchet, see p. 125, note 14.   [4] A *Bradan Relice*, B C D *Steapan Reolice*; both are islets in the mouth of the Severn estuary.   [5] Refurbishing a pre-Roman hillfort (VCH, *Chester*, I, pp. 110–11, 250, 252), which the Anglo-Saxons called Ead's stronghold (Dodgson, *The Place-Names of Cheshire*, III, p. 213).

D *continued from p. 97*

914. Here in [this] year after Easter the raiding-army rode out from Northampton and from Leicester and broke the peace, and killed many men at Hook Norton and thereabouts; and then very quickly after that, as these first came home, they found another mounted band that rode out against Luton. And then the local people became aware of it, and fought against them and brought them to full flight, and recovered all that they had taken and also a great part of their horses and of their weapons.[6]

915. Here in this year Warwick was built, and a great raiding ship-army came over here from the south from Brittany, and with them 2 jarls, Ohtor and Hroald, and then went around west until they got into the mouth of the Severn, and raided in Wales everywhere along the banks where it suited them, and took Cameleac, bishop in Archenfield,[1] and led him to ship with them; and then King Edward ransomed him back for 40 pounds. Then after that the whole raiding-army went up and wanted to go on a raid against Archenfield; then they were met by [the men] from Hereford and from Gloucester and from the nearest strongholds, and fought against them and put them to flight, and killed the jarl Hroald and the other jarl Ohtor's brother and a great part of the raiding-army, and drove them into an enclosure[2] and besieged them there until they gave them hostages, that they would leave the king's domain. And the king had arranged that there should be positions on the southern side of the Severn mouth from Cornwall in the west, eastwards as far as Avonmouth, so that they dared seek land nowhere on that side. However, they then stole up by night on two certain occasions: on the one occasion east of Watchet, and on another occasion at Porlock;[3] then on each occasion they were hit, so that few came away, except only those who could swim out to the ships. And then they settled out on the island at Steepholme[4] until the time came that they were very short of food, and many men perished with hunger, because they could not get any food; then they went [*continued overleaf*]

THE ABINGDON MANUSCRIPT (C) *continued from opposite page*

915. Then in this, the next year after mid-winter, [was built] that stronghold at Chirbury,[7] and then that at Weardbyrig;[8] and in the same year before mid-winter that at Runcorn[9]. [*continued overleaf*]

---

[6] Æthelweard (p. 53) says that, the greater part of a viking fleet in the Severn having returned to Ireland, the winter of 914 was more tranquil than anyone could remember, before or since.   [7] Shropshire; little now remains, VCH, *Shropshire*, I, pp. 378–9. For these and the Æthelflæd forts, see Dodgson, 'The background of Brunanburh', 303–16.   [8] Perhaps Warburton on the south bank of the River Mersey, Cheshire.   [9] *æt Rum cofan*, 'at the roomy cover'; Runcorn is situated on a rocky promontory on the southern bank of the River Mersey, commanding entry to a wide lagoon and beyond it the upper reaches of the river (Dodgson, *The Place-Names of Cheshire*, II, pp. 176–7). The remains of a fort were destroyed in the 1860s to improve the navigation of the Mersey (VCH, *Chester*, I, pp. 250, 252, 291).

A 918 [917] *continued from p. 98*

get any food. Then they went from there to Dyfed[1] and then out to Ireland, and this was in harvest-time. And then after that, in the same year before Martinmas,[2] King Edward went to Buckingham with his army and stayed there four weeks, and before he went from there made both of the strongholds each side of the river. And Jarl Thurcytel sought him out as lord, and all the holds,[3] and almost all the principal men who belonged to Bedford, and also many of those who belonged to Northampton.[4]

919 [918]. Here in this year, before Martinmas,[2] King Edward went with his army to Bedford and took possession of the stronghold, and almost all the garrison who had earlier dwelt there turned to him. And he stayed there four weeks, and before he went from there he ordered the stronghold on the south bank of the river to be built.

920 [919]. Here in this year, before midsummer,[5] King Edward went to Maldon and built the stronghold and established it before he went from there. And the same year, with the peace and help of King Edward, Jarl Thurcytel went across the sea to the land of the Franks with those men who wanted to follow him. [*continued opposite*]

THE WORCESTER MANUSCRIPT (D) 915 *continued from previous page*

from there to Dyfed[1] and then to Ireland, and this was in harvest-time. And then after that, in the same year before Martinmas,[2] King Edward went to Buckingham with his army and stayed there four weeks, and before he went from there made both of the strongholds each side of the river. And Jarl Thurcytel sought him out as lord, and all the jarls, and almost all the principal men who belonged to Bedford, and also many of those who belonged to Northampton.[4] [*continued on p. 105*]

THE ABINGDON MANUSCRIPT (C) *continued from previous page*

916. Here before midsummer, on *16 June*, Abbot Ecgberht,[6] guiltless, was killed with his companions. The same day it was the festival of St Cyricus the martyr.[7] And three days later Æthelflæd sent an army into Wales and broke down Brecon Mere,[8] and there took the wife of the king as one of thirty-four.[9] [*continued opposite*]

---

[1] South Wales; see Map p. 274.   [2] 11 November.   [3] See p. 94, note 7.   [4] See generally, Williams, *Middle Saxon Palaces at Northampton.*   [5] 24 June.   [6] Otherwise unknown.   [7] A child-saint, martyred *c.* 304, who is said to have appeared in a dream to Charlemagne, saving him from death by a wild boar; see Farmer, *The Oxford Dictionary of Saints*, p. 99.   [8] *Brecenan mere*, presumably a structure at or near what is now Llangorse Lake, where there was a cross-ridge dyke controlling traffic (RCHM Wales, *Brecknock*, II, p. 95).   [9] This figure seems very precise; contrast 'one of fifty' *s.a.* 605 E, 606 A; 'one of twelve', *s.a.* 626 E; 'one of thirty', *s.a.*. 878. Perhaps the earlier usage was now archaic; it is rarely found after this point in the Chronicle.

A *continued from opposite*

921 [920]. Here in this year before Easter King Edward ordered them to go and build the stronghold at Towcester;[10] and then after that, at Rogationtide in the same year, he ordered them to build the stronghold at Wigingamere.[11]

The same summer, between Lammas and midsummer,[12] the raiding-army from Northampton and from Leicester and north of there, broke the peace and went to Towcester and fought against the stronghold all day, and thought that they would be able to break it down. However, the people who were inside there defended it until more help came to them; and then they[13] left the stronghold and went away. And then again very soon after that, they went out again by night with predatory bands, and came on men unprepared, and seized not a little, both in men and in property, between Bern Wood and Aylesbury.[14]

At the same time the raiding-army went from Huntingdon and from East Anglia and made that fortress at Tempsford,[15] and lived in and constructed it, and abandoned the other at Huntingdon, and thought that from there they would reach[16] more of the land again with war and with hostility; and went so that they got at Bedford, and the men who were inside there went out to meet them, and fought against them and put them to flight, and killed a good part of them.

Then yet again after that, a great raiding-army gathered from East Anglia[17] and from the land of Mercia, and went to the stronghold at Wigingamere[11] and besieged it, and fought it long into the day, and seized the cattle round about; nevertheless, the men [*continued overleaf*]

THE ABINGDON MANUSCRIPT (C) *continued from opposite*

917. Here before Lammas,[18] God helping, Æthelflæd, Lady of the Mercians, took possession of the stronghold which is called Derby, together with all that belonged to it; also four of her thegns, who were dear to her, were killed there inside the gates. [*continued on p. 105*]

---

[10] *Tofeceastre*, 'the Roman fortress on the River Tove', Roman Lactodurum. It may have been an ancient defence, since the second element of the Roman name is akin to the British word for fortress (Gover, *The Place-Names of Northamptonshire*, pp. 64–5).   [11] Possibly Wigmore, Herefordshire, on the Roman road close to Offa's Dyke and the frontier with Wales.   [12] Lammas is 1 August and midsummer 24 June; thus curiously in reverse of customary order.   [13] i.e. the Danes.   [14] Bern Wood was a great forest stretching through Buckinghamshire into Oxfordshire, perhaps with one edge at the River Thame, only a mile or two from Aylesbury (Mawer and Stenton, *The Place-Names of Buckinghamshire*, pp. 132–3; VCH, *Buckinghamshire*, II, pp. 132–3). The area raided was small, but both forest and town apparently belonged to the king.   [15] Controlling the confluence of Ivel and Ouse; whether this should be identified with the remains of earthworks here (VCH, *Bedfordshire*, I, pp. 281–2) is uncertain. It seems likely that 'Thames' was an early name for the Ouse hereabouts (Mawer and Stenton, *The Place-Names of Bedfordshire*, p. 111).   [16] Florence (I, p. 126) has *recover*.   [17] Florence (I, p. 126) adds *and Essex*.   [18] 1 August.

A 921 [920] *continued from previous page*
who were inside there, defended the stronghold, and then they [the Danes] left the stronghold and went away.

Then after that, the same summer, a great tribe gathered together in King Edward's domain, from the nearest strongholds who could travel to it, and went to Tempsford[1] and besieged the stronghold, and fought against it until they broke it down, and killed the king, and Jarl Toglos, and his son, Jarl Manna, and his brother, and all who were inside there and wished to defend themselves,[2] and seized the others and all that was inside there.

Then very quickly after that a great tribe gathered together in harvest-time, both from Kent and from Surrey and from Essex, and from the nearest strongholds everywhere, and went to Colchester and besieged the stronghold and fought against it until they captured it; and they killed all the people and took all that was inside there, except for the men who fled away over the wall.[3]

Then yet again after that, the same harvest-time, a great raiding-army gathered together from East Anglia, both from the raiding-army in occupation and from those vikings whom they had enticed to help them, and thought that they would avenge their injuries, and went to Maldon,[4] and besieged the stronghold, and fought against it until more help to assist the garrison came from outside; and the raiding-army left the stronghold and went away. And then the men from the stronghold went out after it, and also those who came from outside to help them, and put the raiding-army to flight and killed many hundreds of them, both of askr-men[5] and of others.

Then very quickly after this the same harvest-time, King Edward went with a West Saxon army to Passenham,[6] and stayed there while they made the stronghold at Towcester with a stone wall.[7] And Jarl Thurferth and the holds turned to him, together with all the raiding-army [*continued opposite*]

---

[1] The recently-built Danish stronghold, see p. 101, note 15.   [2] i.e. they killed anyone who put up a resistance.   [3] The ancient Roman fortress-city of Camulodunum or Colonia on the coast of Essex, retained impressive walls (cf. Crummy, *Anglo-Saxon and Norman Colchester*, pp. 24–6 *et passim*).   [4] At the head of the Blackwater estuary, a dozen miles south-west of Colchester.   [5] *æsc-manna*, those manning, or borne by, the ships called *æscas*, for which term see p. 90, note 4.   [6] 'Passa's Manor', controlling the point where the Roman road out of Towcester fords the River Tove; a royal manor by the time of Domesday Book (*Northamptonshire*, I 30); there is no evidence of structural remains, but plentiful human remains which might belong to this date (RCHM, *Northamptonshire*, IV, pp. 109–10).   [7] It seems that the previous building at Towcester, put in hand before Easter and stormed by the Danes the following summer (p. 101) was now reinforced. The verb used earlier is *timbrian* 'to build', and now *wyrcan* 'to work'. Perhaps previously the garrison relied on what remained of the Roman defences, but archaeological evidence is lacking (RCHM, *Northamptonshire*, IV, p. 149ff.). The Roman fort at Manchester was to be 'improved' two years later (*s.a.* 923 A).

E *continued from p. 95*

918. Here Æthelflæd, Lady of the Mercians, passed away.

921. Here King Sihtric killed Niall, his brother.[8] [*continued on p. 105*]

THE WINCHESTER MANUSCRIPT (A) 921 [920] *continued from opposite*

which belonged to Northampton, as far north as the Welland, and sought him as their lord and protector.

And then when the called-up army went home, the other went out and got to the stronghold at Huntingdon, and at King Edward's command they improved the stronghold and restored it where it was broken down earlier; and the whole tribe of local people that there was left submitted to King Edward, and sought his peace and protection.

Then still after that, before Martinmas[9] the same year, King Edward went with a West Saxon army to Colchester, and improved the stronghold and restored it where it was broken down earlier.[3] And a great tribe, both in East Anglia and in Essex, that was earlier under the control of the Danes,[10] turned to him; and all the raiding-army in East Anglia swore union with him: that they wanted all that he wanted, and would keep peace with all with whom the king wanted to keep peace, both on sea and on land. And the raiding-army that belonged to Cambridge individually chose him as their lord and protector, and confirmed that with oaths just as he determined.

922 [921]. Here in this year, between the Rogation Days and midsummer,[11] King Edward went with the army to Stamford,[12] and ordered the stronghold to be made on the south side of the river; and all the people who belonged to the more northerly stronghold submitted to him and sought him as their lord. And then when he was settled in the seat there, his sister Æthelflæd at Tamworth departed 12 days before midsummer; and then he rode and took the stronghold at Tamworth, and all the nation of the land of Mercia which was earlier subject to Æthelflæd turned to him, and the kings of Wales: Hywel and Clydog and Idwal,[13] [*continued overleaf*]

---

[8] This statement confuses two separate events. Sihtric and Niall were not related; but Sihtric killed his brother Sigefrith in 888, and Niall Glundubh, king of Ireland, in 919 (see *Annals of Ulster*, I, pp. 407, 439).   [9] 11 November.   [10] Florence (I, p. 127) says that this had been *almost thirty years*.   [11] i.e. between 11 May and 24 June.   [12] On the River Nene at the meeting point of Rutland, Northamptonshire and Lincolnshire, the location of a royal mint and perhaps an important administrative centre, see RCHM, *Stamford*, pp. xxxvii-xl.   [13] Hywel Dda and Clydog, sons of Cadell ap Rhodri, ruled in South Wales, and Idwal ap Anarawd in Gwynedd (see Table and Map pp. 274, 301).

A 922 [921] *continued from previous page*
and all the race of the Welsh, sought him as their lord. Then from there he went to Nottingham and captured the stronghold, and ordered it to be improved and occupied,[1] both with Englishmen and with Danish; and all the people that was settled in the land of Mercia, both Danish and English, turned to him.

923 [922]. Here in this year, in late harvest-time, King Edward went with an army to Thelwall,[2] and ordered the stronghold to be made, and occupied and manned. And while he stayed there he ordered another army, also from the nation of Mercians, to go to Manchester in Northumbria, and to improve[3] and to man it. Here Archbishop Plegmund passed away.

924 [923]. Here in this year, before midsummer, King Edward went to Nottingham with an army, and ordered a stronghold to be made opposite the other on the south side of the river, and the bridge over the Trent between the two strongholds; and from there went to Bakewell in the Peak District, and ordered a stronghold to be made in the neighbourhood and manned. And then the king of Scots[4] and all the nation of Scots chose him as father and lord; and [so also did] Rægnald and Eadwulf's sons and all those who live in Northumbria, both English and Danish and Norwegians and others; and also the king of the Strathclyde Britons[5] and all the Strathclyde Britons.

925 [924]. Here King Edward passed away, and Athelstan, his son, succeeded to the kingdom, and *St* Dunstan was born,[6] and Wulfhelm succeeded[7] to the archbishopric in Canterbury. [*continued on p. 106*]

---

[1] i.e. improving an earlier Danish fort (see annual 868); there is evidence for the encirclement of the site with a large-scale ditch and rampart at this further stage.   [2] A site controlling the Mersey crossing at Latchford, cf. Dodgson, *The Place-Names of Cheshire*, II, p. 138.   [3] Perhaps, as at Towcester, the walls needed repair by this date, but archaeological evidence is lacking, cf. Morris, *Medieval Manchester*, p. 15.   [4] i.e. Constantine, see 926 D.   [5] Probably Ywain, see Macquarie, 'The kings of Strathclyde, *c.* 400–1018', p. 14.   [6] For discussion of arguments for an earlier date (909 or 910) see Ramsay, *St Dunstan*, pp. 3–5.   [7] Transferred to Canterbury from Wells, where he had been made bishop *c.* 924.   [8] This annal was deleted by a later hand, probably because of a duplicating reference to Edward's death in the following entry.   [9] C *Fearn dune*, D *Farn dune*, 'Fern Hill' (Farndon-on-Dee), see Dodgson, *The Place-Names of Cheshire*, IV, pp. 73–5.   [10] Kingston-upon-Thames, Surrey, said to be the traditional crowning-place for West Saxon kings; Kingston was an important royal holding, the first bridging-point on the Thames upstream from London Bridge. The site of a council in 838 between Egbert and Archbishop Ceolnoth, respecting the administration of southern England (*Cartularium Saxonicum*, I, pp. 587–94); Æthelred would be crowned there (*s.a.* 978/9) and Ralph de Diceto, twelfth-century dean of St Paul's, London, says the same of Edward 902, Edmund 940, Eadred 946 and Edwig 950 (I, pp. 140, 144, 146–7; II, pp. 235, 237). See also generally Sawyer, 'The royal *tun* in pre-Conquest England', pp. 273–99.   [11] MS *ofsæ*, recte *ofer sæ*.   [12] For the marriage of Edith (Eadgyth) to Otto, and Anglo-German relations in general at this time see Table p. 289, and Stenton, *Anglo-Saxon England*, p. 342.   [13] *porticus*, see p. 44, note 10.   [14] *Cledemuþan*; possibly at Rhuddlan, Flintshire, closing the valley of the Clwyd and controlling the coastline

E *continued from p. 103*

923. Here King Rægnald won York.

924. In this year King Edward passed away and Athelstan, his son, succeeded to the kingdom.[8]

925. Here Bishop Wulfhelm was consecrated[7] and the same year King Edward passed away. *[continued on p. 107]*

THE CANTERBURY MANUSCRIPT (F) *continued from p. 93*

924. Here King Edward was chosen as father and lord by the king of Scots,[4] and by the Scots, and by King Rægnald, and by all the Northumbrians, and also by the king of the Strathclyde Britons[5] and by all the Strathclyde Britons.

925 [924]. Here King Edward passed away and Athelstan his son succeeded to the kingdom; and Wulfhelm was ordained archbishop for Canterbury,[7] and *St Dunstan* was born.[6] *[continued on p. 107]*

THE WORCESTER MANUSCRIPT (D) *continued from p. 100*

923. Here King Rægnald won York.

924. Here King Edward died at Farndon[9] in Mercia; and very soon, 16 days after, his son Ælfweard died at Oxford; and their bodies lie at Winchester. And Athelstan was chosen as king by the Mercians and consecrated at Kingston;[10] and he gave his sister across the sea[11] to the son of the king of the Old Saxons.[12]

925. Here King Athelstan and Sihtric, king of Northumbria, assembled at Tamworth on *30 January*, and Athelstan gave him his sister. *[continued on p. 107]*

THE ABINGDON MANUSCRIPT (C) 918 *continued from p. 101*

918. Here in the early part of this year, with God's help, she peaceably got in her control the stronghold at Leicester, and the most part of the raiding-armies that belonged to it were subjected. And also the York-folk had promised her – and some of them granted so by pledge, some confirmed with oaths – that they would be at her disposition. But very quickly after they had done that, she departed, 12 days before midsummer, inside Tamworth, the eighth year that she held control of Mercia with rightful lordship; and her body lies inside Gloucester in the east side-chapel[13] of St Peter's Church.

919. Here also the daughter of Æthelred, lord of the Mercians, was deprived of all control in Mercia, and was led into Wessex three weeks before Christmas; she was called Ælfwynn.

921. Here King Edward built the stronghold at the mouth of the Clwyd.[14]

924. Here King Edward died at Farndon[9] in Mercia, and very soon after that his son Ælfweard died at Oxford; and their bodies lie at Winchester. And Athelstan was chosen as king by the Mercians, and consecrated at Kingston;[10] and he gave his sister*[15] *[continued on p. 113]*

between the Dee and Conway, see Wainwright, 'Cledemutha', 203–12.   [15] An asterisk in the manuscript perhaps marks an acknowledged lacuna, the content of which may be restored from D. It is at this point that the 'Mercian Register' ends, see the Introduction p. xxiv.

A *continued from p. 104*

931. Here, on 29 *May*, Byrnstan was ordained bishop for Winchester, and he held the bishopric two and a half years.

932. Here Bishop Frithustan passed away.

933. Here King Athelstan went into Scotland with both a raiding land-army and with a raiding ship-army and raided across much of it.[1] And Bishop Byrnstan passed away in Winchester on *All Saints' Day*.[2]

934. Here Bishop Ælfheah succeeded to the bishopric.[3]

937. [THE BATTLE OF BRUNANBURH][4]

Here King Athelstan, leader of warriors,
ring-giver of men, and also his brother,
the ætheling Edmund, struck life-long glory
in strife round Brunanburh,[5] clove the shield-wall,
hacked the war-lime,[6] with hammers' leavings,[7]
Edward's offspring, as was natural to them
by ancestry,[8] that in frequent conflict
they defend land, treasures and homes
against every foe. The antagonists succumbed,
the nation of Scots and sea-men
fell doomed. The field darkened
with soldiers' blood,[9] after in the morning-time
the sun, that glorious star,
bright candle of God, the Lord Eternal,
glided over the depths, until the noble creature
sank to rest. There lay many a soldier
of the men of the North, shot over shield,
taken by spears; likewise Scottish also, [*continued on p. 108*]

---

[1] Florence (I, p. 132) adds that the Scots king Constantine was forced to give his son to Athelstan as a hostage, together with suitable gifts.   [2] 1 November.   [3] Ælfheah I of Winchester; Florence (I, p. 132) calls him *Ælfheah surnamed 'the Bald', a monk and relation of the blessed Dunstan.*   [4] This annal is written in traditional alliterative verse. See generally Bradley, *Poetry*, pp. 515–18, Dobbie, *Minor Poems*, pp. 16–20, and Campbell, *The Battle of Brunanburh*. It is found in all MSS except for the late versions E and F, and F leaves half a page blank at this point before entering a brief prose account. There are other verse entries *s.a.* 942, 973, 975, 1036, 1065, 1075, 1086.   [5] Æthelweard (p. 54), who calls the place *Brunandun*, remarks that it is still called *the great battle* by the common people (F Lat *that great and famous battle*). Its location is still unidentified (Smith, 'The site of the Battle of Brunanburh', pp. 43–80; Smyth, *Scandinavian York and Dublin*, II, pp. 31–88). Florence (I, p. 132) says that Olaf entered the mouth of the Humber, but we might expect a combination of Irish, Scots and Strathclyde Britons to enter from the west coast. This seems to have been the battle fought between Athelstan and Olaf the Red described in the Old Norse *Egils Saga* (52–5).

E *continued from p. 105*

927. Here Athelstan drove out King Guthfrith; and here Archbishop Wulfhelm went to Rome.

928. *William succeeded to the kingdom,*[10] *and reigned 15 years.*

933. Here the ætheling Edwin drowned at sea.[11]

934. Here King Athelstan went to Scotland with both a raiding land-army and with a raiding ship-army and raided across much of it.[1]

937. Here King Athelstan led an army to Brunanburh.[5] [*continued on p. 111*]

THE CANTERBURY MANUSCRIPT (F) *continued from p. 105*

927. Here King Athelstan drove out King Guthfrith; and here Archbishop Wulfhelm travelled to Rome.[12]

928. William[13] succeeded to Normandy, and held it 15 years.

931. Here Frithustan, bishop of Winchester, passed away, and Beornstan was blessed in his place.

934. Here King Athelstan went to Scotland with both a raiding land-army and with a raiding ship-army and raided across much of it.[1]

935. Here Ælfheah succeeded to the bishop's seat in Winchester.

937. Here King Athelstan and Edmund, his brother, led an army to Brunanburh,[5] and there fought against Olaf,[14] and, Christ helping, had the victory and there killed five kings and eight jarls. [*continued on p. 125*]

THE WORCESTER MANUSCRIPT (D) *continued from p. 105*

926. Here fiery rays appeared in the northern part of the sky. And Sihtric perished and King Athelstan succeeded to the kingdom of Northumbria; and he governed all the kings who were in this island: first Hywel, king of the West Welsh, and Constantine, king of Scots, and Owain, king of Gwent,[15] and Ealdred, Ealdwulf's offspring, from Bamburgh. And they confirmed peace with pledges and with oaths in a place which is named Rivers' Meeting[16] on 12 *July*; and they forbade all devil-worship and then parted in concord.

934. Here King Athelstan went to Scotland with both a raiding land-army and with a raiding ship-army and raided across much of it.[1] [*continued on p. 111*]

---

[6] i.e. lime-wood shields.　　[7] i.e. weapons.　　[8] MS *cneo-mægum*, perhaps 'at the knee of kinsmen'.　　[9] A *secgas hwate*, 'bold warriors'; B C D *secga swate*, 'blood of warriors'.　　[10] Of Normandy.　　[11] His body was washed up in Flanders and buried at St Bertins by his cousin Adelulf (Grierson, 'The relations between England and Flanders', 88, fn. 2). This entry is peculiar to E. Simeon (II, pp. 93, 124) and Henry of Huntingdon (p. 159) say he was drowned on the orders of his brother Athelstan; William of Malmesbury (*Gesta Regum*, pp. 156–7) gives a more romantic account, in which Edwin drowned himself, having been cast adrift in an open boat.　　[12] *for the pallium* adds F Lat.　　[13] William Longsword.　　[14] Olaf Guthfrithson.　　[15] South Wales, see Map p. 274.　　[16] *æt Ea motum*, Eamont Bridge, Westmorland, at the confluence of Lowther and Eamont rivers. In view of the location of the meeting, Owain of Strathclyde-Cumbria may also have been present (cf. William of Malmesbury, *Gesta Regum*, p. 147).

A 937 *continued from p.* 106
        sated, weary of war. All day long
        the West Saxons with elite cavalry[1]
        pressed in the tracks of the hateful nation,
        with mill-sharp blades severely hacked from behind
        those who fled battle. The Mercians refused
        hard hand-play to none of the heroes
        who with Olaf,[2] over the mingling of waves,
        doomed in fight, sought out land
        in the bosom of a ship. Five young
        kings lay on the battle-field,
        put to sleep by swords; likewise also seven
        of Olaf's jarls, countless of the raiding-army
        of Seamen and Scots. There the ruler of
        Northmen, compelled by necessity,
        was put to flight, to ship's prow,
        with a small troop. The boat
        was pushed afloat; the king withdrew,
        saved life, over the fallow flood.
        There also likewise, the aged[3] Constantine
        came north to his kith by flight.
        The hoary man of war had no cause to exult
        in the clash of blades;[4] he was shorn of his kinsmen,
        deprived of friends, on the meeting-place of peoples,
        cut off[5] in strife, and left his son[6] [*continued opposite*]

---

[1] A *eorodcistum*, B C D *eoredcystum* (*eored* 'mounted troop', from *eoh* 'war-horse'); but perhaps here, less specifically, it means 'elite troops'. For the vexed question of whether or not the Anglo-Saxon used cavalry, compare Glover, 'English warfare in 1066', 1–18 and Brown, *Origins of English Feudalism*, pp. 34–42; and cf. Hollister, *Anglo-Saxon Military Institutions*, pp. 134–40. [2] Olaf Guthfrithson, for whom see generally Smyth, *Scandinavian York and Dublin*, II, pp. 31–106. [3] MS *frod*; the semantic field of the term is wide, shifting from 'old' to (because old) 'wise, prudent'. The same word is used of Edward the Confessor at his death *s.a.* 1065. [4] A *mæcan gemanan*, B *mecea*, C *meca*. D reads *mecga*, 'clash of men'. See Campbell, *Brunanburh*, pp. 110–11. [5] A A[2] *beslagen*; C *beslegen*; D *beslægen*. B reads *forslegen* 'worsted'. [6] Possibly the son earlier given as a hostage (see p. 106, note 1).

A 937 *continued from opposite*

on the place of slaughter, mangled by wounds,
young in battle. The grey-haired warrior,
old crafty one, had no cause to boast
in that clash of blades – no more had Olaf –
cause to laugh, with the remnants of their raiding-army,
that they were better in works of war
on the battle-field, in the conflict of standards,
the meeting of spears, the mixing of weapons,
the encounter of men, when they played
against Edward's sons on the field of slaughter.

Then the Northmen, bloody[7] survivors of darts,
disgraced in spirit, departed on Ding's Mere,[8]
in nailed boats[9] over deep water,
to seek out Dublin[10] and their [own] land again.[11]
Likewise the brothers both together,
king and ætheling, exultant in war,
sought kith, the land of Wessex.

They left behind to divide the corpses,
to enjoy the carrion, the dusky-coated,
horny-beaked black raven,
and the grey-coated eagle, white-rumped,
greedy war-hawk, and the wolf,
grey beast in the forest. Never yet in this island
was there a greater slaughter [*continued overleaf*]

---

[7] *dreorig*; alternatively, 'sad, dreary'.   [8] A C *Dingesmere;* B *Dyngesmere;* D *Dynigesmere;* A[2] *Dinnesmere*. This perhaps refers to some part of the Irish Sea, although Campbell (*Brunanburh*, p. 64) followed by Smyth (*Scandinavian York and Dublin*, II, p. 45), assumed an unidentified English lake or estuary.   [9] MS *nægled cnearrum*, i.e. riveted boats. The reading in D *dæg gled garum* is confused.   [10] The centre of a Norse colony, cf. Logan, *The Vikings in History*, p. 43ff., and Smyth, *Scandinavian York and Dublin*   [11] A *hira land,* A[2] *heora land;* other MSS read 'Ireland': B *ira land,* C D *Yraland*.

A 937 *continued from previous page*
> of people felled by the sword's edges,
> before this, as books tell us,
> old authorities, since Angles and Saxons
> came here from the east,
> sought out Britain over the broad ocean,
> warriors eager for fame, proud war-smiths,
> overcame the Welsh, seized the country.

941. Here King Athelstan passed away[1] on 27 *October*, 40 years all but a day after King Alfred passed away. And the ætheling Edmund succeeded to the kingdom; and he was then 18 years old. King Athelstan ruled 14 years and 10 weeks. Wulfhelm was then archbishop in Canterbury.

942. [THE CAPTURE OF THE FIVE BOROUGHS][2]

> Here King Edmund, lord of the English,
> guardian of kinsmen,[3] beloved instigator of deeds,
> conquered Mercia, bounded by The Dore,[4]
> Whitwell Gap and Humber river,
> broad ocean-stream; five boroughs:
> Leicester and Lincoln,
> and Nottingham, likewise Stamford also
> and Derby. Earlier the Danes were
> under Northmen, subjected by force
> in heathens' captive fetters,
> for a long time until they were ransomed again,
> to the honour of Edward's son,
> protector of warriors, King Edmund.

[5][King Edmund] received King Olaf at baptism, and the same year, after a fairly long while,[6] he received King Rægnald at the bishop's hands. <Here King Edmund entrusted Glas>tonbury to St Dunstan, where he afterwards became first abbot.[7]

944. Here King Edmund brought all Northumbria into his domain, and caused to flee away two kings, Olaf Sihtricson and Rægnald Guthfrithson.[8]

945. Here King Edmund raided across all the land of Cumbria[9] and ceded it to Malcolm, king of Scots, on the condition that he would be his co-operator both on sea and on land. [*continued on p. 112*]

---

[1] D 'in Gloucester'.   [2] This annal is written in traditional alliterative verse, see Dobbie, *Minor Poems*, pp. 20–21; Mawer, 'The Redemption of the Five Boroughs', 551–7. Like the poem on the battle of Brunanburh (*s.a.* 937), this is found in all MSS except for the late versions E and F. For other verse annals see p. 106, note 4.   [3] A A[2] *maga* 'relatives'; B *mæcgea*, C *mecga* 'men'; the reading in D *mægþa* is ambiguously 'kindred, tribe' or 'maidens'.   [4] Cf. annal 827.   [5] These prose lines should probably have been put under 943, which was left blank in A. The text of A (and A[2]) runs the verse part of this annal straight on to the prose conclusion. B and C appear to start a new entry beginning 'Here King Edmund . . .', but with no year number.

E *continued from p. 107*

940. Here King Athelstan passed away, and Edmund, his brother, succeeded to the kingdom.

942. Here King Olaf passed away. *And Richard the Elder succeeded to the kingdom,*[10] *and reigned 52 years.*

944. Here King Edmund conquered all Northumbria, and caused to flee away two royally-born men, Olaf and Rægnald.[8]

945. Here King Edmund raided across all the land of Cumbria.[9] [*continued on p. 113*]

THE WORCESTER MANUSCRIPT (D) *continued from p. 107*

941. Here the Northumbrians belied their pledges, and chose Olaf[11] from Ireland as their king.

942. [as A]

943.[12] Here Olaf broke down Tamworth and a great slaughter fell on either side, and the Danes had the victory and led much war-booty away with them. Wulfrun[13] was seized there in the raid. Here King Edmund besieged King Olaf and Archbishop Wulfstan in Leicester, and he might have controlled them had they not escaped from the stronghold in the night. And after that Olaf obtained King Edmund's friendship; and then the king Edmund received the king Olaf at baptism, and gave to him royally. And the same year, after a fairly long interval,[6] he received King Rægnald at the bishop's hands. [*continued overleaf*]

---

[6] A *ymb tela micel fæc,* D *ymbe tæla mycelne fyrst,* B *fyrst,* C *ferst.*   [7] The first part erased but restored from F. Dunstan was the first abbot in a reformed order at the ancient monastic site of Glastonbury, see Ramsay, *St Dunstan,* pp. 1ff., 25ff.   [8] Æthelweard (p. 54) says that *Bishop Wulfstan and the ealdorman of the Mercians expelled certain 'deserters', that is to say, Rægnald and Olaf, from the city of York, and reduced them to submission to the aforesaid king* (Edmund).   [9] Including at this date Strathclyde; see generally Kirby, 'Strathclyde and Cumbria', 77–94 (p. 86).   [10] Of Normandy.   [11] Olaf Sihtricson, for whom see Smyth, *Scandinavian York and Dublin,* II, pp. 107–21.   [12] D inserts here events of 940 which had preceded the capture of the Five Boroughs, apparently confusing the recently-arrived Olaf (Sihtricson) with Olaf (Guthfrithson) who had contended for the Five Boroughs in 940 (cf. Campbell, *Brunanburh,* p. 50).   [13] A high-ranking Mercian lady, founder of the minster of St Mary's Wolverhampton ('Wulfrun's chief settlement'), see Table p. 295 and Sawyer, *Charters of Burton Abbey,* p. xl.

A *continued from p. 110*

946. Here King Edmund passed away on St Augustine's Day;[1] and he had the kingdom six and a half years. And then his brother the ætheling Eadred succeeded to the kingdom, and reduced all the land of Northumbria to his control; and the Scots granted him oaths that they would do all that he wanted.

951. Here Ælfheah, bishop of Winchester, passed away on St Gregory's Day.[2]

955. Here King Eadred passed away in Frome[3] on St Clement's Day;[4] and he ruled nine and a half years; and then Eadwig, the son of King Edmund, succeeded to the kingdom,

956. and put St Dunstan to flight out of the country.

958. Here King Eadwig passed away on 1 *October*, and Edgar, his brother, succeeded to the kingdom.

959. Here he sent for St Dunstan and gave him the bishopric in Worcester, and after that the bishopric in London. [*continued on p. 114*]

THE WORCESTER MANUSCRIPT (D) *continued from previous page*

946. Here King Edmund passed away on St Augustine's Day.[1] It was widely known how he ended his days, that Liofa stabbed him at Pucklechurch.[5] And Æthelflæd of Damerham, daughter of Ealdorman Ælfgar, was then his queen. And he had the kingdom six and a half years; and then after him his brother, the ætheling Eadred, succeeded to the kingdom, and reduced all the land of Northumbria to his control; and the Scots granted him oaths that they would do all that he wanted.

947. Here King Eadred came to Tanshelf, and there Archbishop Wulfstan and all the councillors of Northumbria pledged themselves to the king, and within a short while they belied both pledge and oaths also.

948. Here King Eadred raided across all the land of Northumbria, because they had taken Eric[6] for their king; and on the raid then the famous minster at Ripon, which St Wilfrid built,[7] was burned. And then when the king was on his way home, the raiding-army [which] was within York overtook the king's army from behind at Castleford,[8] and a great slaughter was made there. Then the king became so angry that he wanted to invade again and completely do for the country. Then when the council of the Northumbrians heard that, they abandoned Eric and compensated King Eadred for the act.

952. Here King Eadred ordered Wulfstan[9] to be brought into Jedburgh,[10] into the fort, because he was frequently accused to the king.[11] And also in this year the king ordered a great slaughter to be made in the town of Thetford, in vengeance of the death of Abbot Eadhelm[12] whom they killed earlier. [*continued opposite*]

---

[1] St Augustine of Canterbury, 26 May.   [2] 12 March.   [3] A Somerset manor still in royal hands at the Conquest (DB, 1, 8).   [4] 23 November.   [5] A royal manor in Gloucestershire. Florence (I, p. 134) says that Edmund was killed in trying to rescue his steward from the *atrocious robber* Liofa.   [6] Eric 'Bloodaxe', son of Harald Fine-hair, king of Norway; he had apparently been given charge of Northumbria by Athelstan (*Egils Saga*, 59).   [7] Bede, *HE*, III, 25; V, 19.   [8] *Ceaster forda*, 'the ford at the fort', i.e. the Roman station of Legeolio, where Ermine Street crosses the Aire (Smith, *Place-Names of the West Riding*, II, pp. xi, 69).   [9] Wulfstan I, archbishop of York.

E *continued from p. 111*

948 [946]. Here King Edmund was stabbed,[5] and Eadred, his brother, succeeded to the kingdom, and he immediately reduced all the land of Northumbria to his control; and the Scots granted him oaths that they would do all that he wanted.

949. Here Olaf Cuaran[13] came to the land of Northumbria.

952. Here the Northumbrians drove out King Olaf and accepted Eric, son of Harald.

954. Here the Northumbrians drove out Eric,[14] and Eadred succeeded to the kingdom of Northumbria.

955. Here King Eadred passed away, and Eadwig, son of Edmund, succeeded to the kingdom.

956. Here Archbishop Wulfstan passed away.

959. [15] Here King Eadwig passed away, and Edgar, his brother, succeeded to the kingdom. [*continued overleaf*]

THE WORCESTER MANUSCRIPT (D) *continued from opposite*

954. Here the Northumbrians drove out Eric,[15] and Eadred succeeded to the kingdom of Northumbria. Here Archbishop Wulfstan received back the bishopric in Dorchester.[16]

955. Here King Eadred passed away, and he rests in the Old Minster.[17] And Eadwig succeeded to the kingdom of Wessex, and his brother Edgar succeeded to the kingdom of Mercia;[18] and they were sons of King Edmund and *St Ælfgifu*.[19]

957. Here Archbishop Wulfstan passed away on *16 December*, and he was buried in Oundle; and in the same year Abbot Dunstan was driven across the sea.

958. Here in this year Archbishop Oda divorced King Eadwig and Ælfgifu because they were related. [*continued on p. 119*]

THE ABINGDON MANUSCRIPTS (B) AND (C) *continued from p. 105*

956. Here King Eadred passed away, and Eadwig succeeded to the kingdom.

957. Here the ætheling Edgar succeeded to the kingdom of Mercia.

959. Here King Eadwig passed away, and Edgar, his brother, succeeded to the kingdom both in Wessex and in Mercia and in Northumbria; and he was then 16 years old. [*continued on p. 119*]

---

[10] In Roxburghshire, a manor of the bishops of Lindisfarne (Simeon, I, p. 201).   [11] His sympathies were clear (cf. annal 941; he was released only after the expulsion of Eric in 954 q.v.).   [12] Perhaps Eadhelm abbot of St Augustine's Canterbury.   [13] A by-name for Olaf Sihtricson (Old Irish *cuaran* 'sandal').   [14] Roger of Wendover (I, pp. 402–3) says he was killed by a certain Earl Maccus *in a lonely place called Stainmore* (unidentified).   [15] This annal is marked by poetic rhetoric, and is in the style of Archbishop Wulfstan II of York, cf. Jost, 'Wulfstan und die angelsächsische Chronik', 105–23. For similarly heightened annals see p. 123, note 16.   [16] i.e. received back the archbishopric of York at a ceremony or decision made at Dorchester-on-Thames.   [17] The older of the two foundations at Winchester, see p. 26, note 8.   [18] Florence (I, p. 137) says: *the River Thames formed the boundary between the two kingdoms.*   [19] Sanctified as a result of miracles taking place at her tomb in Shaftesbury (Æthelweard, p. 54).

A *continued from p. 112*

961. Here Archbishop Oda departed, and St Dunstan succeeded to the archbishopric.

962. Here Ælfgar, the king's relative, passed away in Devonshire and his body rests in Wilton.[1] And King Sigferth[2] fell upon himself,[3] and his body lies at Wimborne.[4] And then during the year there was a very great pestilence among men, and there was the great fatal fire[5] in London, and Paul's minster burned down; and it was founded again the same year.

In this same year Æthelmod the mass-priest went to Rome, and passed away there on *15 August*.

963. Here Wulfstan the deacon passed away on Holy Innocents' Day,[6] and after that Gyric the mass-priest passed away.

In this same year Abbot Æthelwold[7] succeeded to the bishopric for Winchester; and he was consecrated *on the vigil of St Andrew;*[8] the day was a Sunday. [*continued on p. 116*]

THE PETERBOROUGH MANUSCRIPT (E) 959 *continued from previous page*

In his days things prospered readily, in that he dwelled in peace for as long as he lived. And he readily merited this – did as was his duty. Far and wide he exalted God's praise and loved God's law, and improved the people's security much more than those kings who were before him within the memory of men. And God helped him too, so that kings and earls readily submitted to him, and were subjected to that which he wanted. And without battle he controlled all that he himself wanted. [*continued opposite*]

---

[1] See p. 72, note 3.   [2] The identity of this Sigferth is uncertain; the name is not uncommon among Danish princes of Northumbria (Searle, *Onomasticon*, pp. 418–19); in 955 a man of this name attests a charter of King Eadred (Robertson, *Charters*, pp. 56, 313) together with the Welsh sub-king Morgan and others, and such a man may have been in attendance on Edgar at the time of his death (cf. Earle and Plummer, II, p. 154).   [3] MS *hine offeoll*, i.e. committed suicide.   [4] A royal foundation in Dorset, see annal 718.   [5] MS *man byrne*.   [6] MS on *Cilda mæsse dæge*, 28 December.   [7] Abbot of Abingdon, and one of the leaders of monastic reform, see Yorke, *Bishop Æthelwold, his Career and Influence*.   [8] 29 November.

E 959 *continued from opposite page*

He became greatly honoured wide throughout the land of the nation, for he readily honoured God's name, and deliberated God's law over and again, and promoted God's praise far and wide, and counselled all his nation wisely, very often, always continuously, for God and for the world.

One ill deed, however, he did too much, in that he loved bad, foreign habits, and brought heathen customs too fast into this land and attracted the alien here, and introduced a damaging people to this country. But God grant him that his good deeds may be greater than his ill deeds, to shield his soul on the longsome journey.

963. Here St Æthelwold[7] was chosen by King Edgar for the bishopric in Winchester; and the archbishop of Canterbury, St Dunstan, consecrated him as bishop on the first Sunday of Advent, which was on 29 *November*.

In the next year after he was consecrated he founded many monasteries,[9] and drove the clerks out of the bishopric because they would not observe any rule, and set monks there. He founded there two abbacies, one of monks the other of nuns – that was all inside Winchester.[10] Then afterwards he came to the king Edgar [and] asked him that he would give him all the monasteries the heathen men had broken up earlier, because he wanted to restore it;[11] and the king happily granted it. And the bishop then came first to Ely, where St Æthelthryth lies,[12] and had the monastery made, then gave it to one of his monks who was called Byrhtnoth, then consecrated him abbot and set monks to serve God there, where formerly there were nuns; then he bought many estates from the king and made it very rich.

Afterwards the bishop Æthelwold came to the monastery which was called Peterborough, which was formerly done for by heathen people,[13] [and] found nothing there but old walls and wild woods; then found, hidden in the old walls, writings that Abbot Hedde [*continued overleaf*]

---

[9] *minstra*; from what follows it is clear that here the term should be rendered 'monastery', see the Introduction p. xxxiii.   [10] i.e. New Minster (see annal 903 F) and Nunna minster, see generally Biddle, *Winchester in the Early Middle Ages*, pp. 313–23.   [11] i.e. the monastic life.   [12] See p. 34, note 8.   [13] See annal 870 E.

A *continued from p. 114*

964. Here King Edgar drove out the priests[1] in the city[2] from the Old Minster and from the New Minster, and from Chertsey and from Milton,[3] and set monks in them; and he set Abbot Æthelgar [*continued on p. 118*]

had earlier written,[4] as to how King Wulfhere and Æthelred, his brother, had constructed it, and how they freed it from king, and from bishop, and from all worldly service; and how the pope Agatho confirmed it with his writ – and the archbishop Deusdedit. Then he had the monastery constructed[5] and set there an abbot who was called Ealdwulf, and made monks there where earlier there was nothing; then came to the king and had him look at the writings which were found earlier; and the king then answered and said:[6]

'I, Edgar, before God and before the archbishop Dunstan, today grant freedom from king and from bishop to St Peter's monastery, Peterborough, and to all the villages which pertain to it, that is, Eastfield and Dogsthorpe and Eye and Paston; and I free it thus, that no bishop have any authority there, except the abbot of the monastery. And I give the town which they call Oundle with everything that pertains thereto, that is, what they call the Eight Hundreds, and market and toll freely, so that neither king nor bishop nor earl nor sheriff have any authority there, nor any man except the abbot alone, and those he sets thereto. And at the request of the bishop Æthelwold, I give Christ and St Peter these lands, that is: Barrow, Warmington, Ashton, Kettering, Castor, Ailsworth, Walton, Werrington, Eye, Longthorpe, and a moneyer in Stamford.[7] These lands and all the others which pertain to the monastery I declare clear, that is with 'sake and soke, toll and team, and infangenetheof'.[8] To Christ and St Peter I give these rights and all others I declare free. And I give two parts[9] of Whittlesey Mere, with waters and with weirs and fens,[10] and so through Merelad straight on to the water that they call Nene, and so eastward to King's Delph. And I desire that a market should be in the same town, and that there be no other between Stamford and Huntingdon. And I desire that [the right of] toll be given thus: first from Whittlesey Mere all up to the king's toll [*continued opposite*]

---

[1] F 'the canons'.   [2] i.e. Winchester. The will of King Eadred (*c.* 955) similarly refers to Winchester as merely 'the city' (Whitelock, *Documents*, p. 511).   [3] Chertsey Abbey, Surrey, and Milton Abbas, Dorset.   [4] See the Story of Abbot Hedde incorporated in Hugh Candidus' Chronicle (p. 59ff.), but unlikely to be older than the early twelfth century, and with no authority for the pre-Danish period (cf. Stenton, 'Medeshamstede and its colonies', p. 325, note 1; *Preparatory*, p. 190, note 4).   [5] For a list of Æthelwold's gifts to Peterborough, see Robertson, *Charters*, pp. 72–5.   [6] What follows is given, somewhat expanded in detail, by Hugh Candidus (p. 18ff.).   [7] Who seems to have struck coins specifically for the monastry, see Dolley, 'A new Anglo-Saxon mint – Medeshamstede', 263–5.   [8] For this technical formula, denoting judicial and financial rights, see Harmer, *Writs*, pp. 73–8.   [9] Hugh Candidus (p. 35) calls this a *half part*, and says that it was acquired through Bishop Æthelwold.   [10] Such rhetorical formulae are common in land-charters, cf. Swanton, *Prose*, p. 44.   [11] For this formula, see p. 31, note 14.   [12] *messe hacel*, or perhaps 'cope', cf. the list *s.a.* 1070 (p. 205) and annal 1122.

E 963 *continued from opposite page*

of Norman Cross Hundreds, and backwards again from Whittlesey Mere through Merelad straight on to the Nene, and thus as that water runs to Crowland, and from Crowland to the Muscat, and from the Muscat to King's Delph and to Whittlesey Mere. And I desire that all the freedom and all the exemption that my predecessors granted, that it stand. And I write[11] and confirm it with the sign of Christ's cross +.'

Then the archbishop Dunstan of Canterbury answered and said: 'I ratify all the things which here are given and mentioned, and all those things that your predecessors and mine have granted. I want that it shall stand: and whosoever breaks it, I give him the curse of God and of all saints and of all ordained heads – and mine – unless he make reparation. And in acknowledgment, I give St Peter my chasuble[12] and my stole and my robe for the service of Christ'.

'I, Oswald, Archbishop of York, agree to all these words, by the holy cross on which Christ was made to suffer. +'

'I, Æthelwold, bishop, bless all who observe this, and I excommunicate all who break this, unless he make reparation'.

Here was: Bishop Ælfstan, Bishop Æthelwulf, and Abbot Æscwig, and Abbot Osgar, and Abbot Æthelgar, and Ealdorman Ælfhere, Ealdorman Æthelwine, Byrhtnoth, Ealdorman Oslac, and many other powerful men; and all ratified it, and all signed it with Christ's token +. This was done 972 years after our Lord's birth, and in the king's 16th year.

Then the abbot Ealdwulf bought many estates, and altogether richly endowed that monastery, and was there then until Archbishop Oswald of York had passed away, and then he was chosen for archbishop. And there was immediately chosen another abbot from the same monastery, [who] was called Cenwulf; he was afterwards bishop in Winchester; and he first made the wall around the monastery, then gave that which was earlier called Medeshamstede, the name 'Stronghold'.[13] [He] was there until they set him as bishop in Winchester. Then they chose another abbot from the same monastery, who was called Ælfsige; this Ælfsige was abbot afterwards for fifty years.[14] He took up[15] *St* Cyneburh and *St* Cyneswith, who lay at Castor, and *St* Tibba, who lay at Ryhall, and brought them to Peterborough and offered them all to *St* Peter on the one day, and kept [their relics] during the time he was there.[16]

964. *Here the canons were expelled from the Old Minster.* [continued on p. 119]

---

[13] *Burch.* The provision of a wall would certainly have been a practical defence at such times; a nunnery at Condé may have been occupied by vikings in 882 (cf. p. 78, note 2). For the notion of the monastic community as 'stronghold of God', see Swanton, *Literature Before Chaucer*, p. 142 *et passim*. The name Burch is hereafter rendered Peterborough.   [14] A notional number (cf. p. 24, note 2); he ruled 1006/7–1042.   [15] i.e. exhumed for the purposes of 'translation'.   [16] Cyneburh and Cyneswith were daughters of the Peterborough founder Wulfhere (cf. annals 656 E, 675 E; Ridyard, *Royal Saints*, pp. 242–3) and Tibba their friend and relative. Castor had been founded by Cyneburh on an old Roman site (Gover, *The Place-Names of Northamptonshire*, p. 232) but was destroyed by the Danes in 870 (Hugh Candidus, p. 50).

A 964 *continued from p. 116*
as abbot for New Minster, and Ordberht for Chertsey, and Cyneweard for Milton.

971.[1] Here the ætheling Edmund passed away, and his body lies at Romsey.[2]

973. [THE CORONATION OF EDGAR][3]

Here, Edgar, ruler of the English,
was consecrated as king[4] in a great assembly
in the ancient town of Ache-man's city[5] –
the warriors dwelling in the island also call it
by the other term Baths.[6] There was great rejoicing
come to all on that blessed day,
which children of men name and call
Pentecost Day. There was gathered,
as I have heard, a pile of priests,
a great multitude of monks,
of learned men. By then had passed,
reckoned by number, ten hundred years,
from the time of birth of the illustrious King,
Shepherd of Lights[7] – except there remained
twenty-seven of the number of years,
as the writings say. Thus nigh on a thousand years
of the Lord of Victories had run on when this befell;
and Edmund's offspring, bold in deeds of conflict,
was nine-and-20 years in the world when this came about,
and then in the 30th was consecrated prince.

975. [THE DEATH OF EDGAR]

Here Edgar, king of the English,
ended earthly pleasures; he chose another light,
radiant and happy, and abandoned this poor,
this transitory, life. The children of nations, [*continued on p. 120*]

---

[1] This annal is largely erased in A, and restored from A[2].   [2] Recently refounded by Edgar, Taylor, *Architecture*, pp. 520–22.   [3] The next two annals are written in traditional alliterative verse, see Dobbie, *Minor Poems*, pp. 21–4. The first is found only in A, B and C; and replaced by a prose paraphrase in D, E and F. The second is found in A, B and C, with abbreviated versions in D and E, while F says simply: 'Here King Edgar passed away'. For other verse annals, see p. 106, note 4.   [4] An account of the ceremony is given in an anonymous Life of Oswald, archbishop of York, one of the participants (*Historians of York*, I, pp. 436–8).   [5] A B C *Acemannes-ceastre*, F *-beri*, F Lat *-byri*. Possibly this by-name for the town reflects its Roman name Aquae Sulis (cf. *civitate Achamanni, civitate Aquemania, Cartularium Saxonicum*, III, pp. 448, 600); but if the curative properties of the Bath waters were already known, or remembered, then 'Aching-man's city' would not be inappropriate. The Roman road from Cirencester to Bath was known in the twelfth century as *Accemannestrete* (Mawer and Stenton, *The Place-Names of Bedfordshire*, pp. 1–2).   [6] A *Baðan* 'Baths', E *Hatabaðum* 'Hot baths', named after the warm springs there, developed by the Romans into a spa town. It was a fort by the time of the Burghal Hidage (Swanton, *Prose*, p. 14).   [7] i.e. stars, sun and moon.

E *continued from p. 117*

966. Here Thored, son of Gunnar, ravaged Westmorland; and the same year Oslac succeeded to the earldom.[8]

969. Here in this year King Edgar ordered all the land of Thanet to be raided across.[9]

970. Here the ætheling Edmund passed away.

972. Here the ætheling Edgar was consecrated as king on the Feast of Pentecost on 11 *May*[10] at the Hot Baths,[6] in the 13th year after he succeeded to the kingdom; and he was then 29 years old. And immediately after that the king led his whole raiding ship-army to Chester, and there 6 kings[11] came to meet him, and all pledged that they would be allies on sea and on land.

975.[12] Here departed Edgar, governor of the English, friend of the West Saxons, and protector of the Mercians. [*continued on p. 121*]

THE WORCESTER MANUSCRIPT (D) *continued from p. 113*

965. Here, in this year, King Edgar took Ælfthryth for his queen; she was the daughter of Ealdorman Ordgar. [*continued on p. 121*]

THE ABINGDON MANUSCRIPT (B) *continued from p. 113*

971. Here passed away Archbishop Oscytel, who was first consecrated diocesan bishop[13] for Dorchester; and afterwards it was by consent of King Eadred and of all his councillors that he was consecrated as archbishop for York city. He was bishop 22 years and he passed away at Thame[14] on the night of All Saints' Day, 10 days before Martinmas.[15] And Abbot Thurcytel, his relative, carried the bishop's body to Bedford, because he was abbot there in those days. [*continued on p. 122*]

---

[8] Of Northumbria. See p. 120, note 3.   [9] To avenge the ill-treatment of York merchants, says Roger of Wendover (I, pp. 414–15, s.a. 974), transl. Whitelock, *Documents*, p. 257.   [10] Pentecost (Whit Sunday) fell on 11 May in 973, the date given in A; C gives 974 and D 972.   [11] Florence (I, pp. 142–3) says: *his eight under-kings, that is: Kenneth king of the Scots, Malcolm king of the Cumbrians, Maccus king of many islands, and five others, Dufnal* (Dunmail) *Siferth, Hywel, Jacob* (Iago) *Juchil, met him, as he commanded, and swore that they would be faithful to him and be his allies by land and sea. On a certain day he went on board a boat with them, and, with them at the oars, he took the helm himself and steered it skilfully on the course of the River Dee, proceeding from the palace to the monastery of St John the Baptist, attended by all the company of ealdormen and nobles also by boat. Having prayed there, he returned to the palace with the same pomp. As he was entering, he is reported to have said to his nobles that any of his successors could well pride himelf on being king of the English, when he might have the pomp of such honours, with so many kings subservient to him.*   [12] This annal is heightened by poetic rhetoric. For others see p. 123, note 16.   [13] *leod-bisceope*.   [14] Oxfordshire; registered as an episcopal manor in Domesday Book, and perhaps already so.   [15] 1 and 11 November respectively.

A 975 *continued from p. 118*
>men on the earth everywhere in this native turf,
>those who have been rightly trained in the art of reckoning,
>name the month that the young Edgar,
>ring-giver of warriors, departed from life,
>the month of July, on its eighth day;
>and his son afterwards succeeded
>to the royal kingdom, an ungrown child,
>leader of earls, whose name was Edward.
>And ten days before, there departed from Britain
>the glorious hero, good from native virtue,
>the bishop whose name was Cyneweard.[1]
>Then, as I have heard, praise of the Ruler
>was felled to the ground, widely and everywhere
>in Mercia; many of the wise
>servants of God were scattered.[2] That was great grief
>to those in whose breasts bore in heart
>a burning love of the Creator. Then was the Author of glories,
>Ruler of victories, Counsellor of heavens,
>too much scorned, when His law was broken.
>And then also the bold-hearted hero Oslac[3]
>was driven from the country, over the rolling waves,
>over the gannet's bath, grey-haired hero,
>wise and eloquent,[4]
>over the tumult of waters,
>over the whale's country, bereft of homes.
>And then up in the heavens appeared
>a star in the firmament which heroes, firm in spirit,
>prudent in mind, men learned in science,
>wise soothsayers,[5] widely call
>by the name of *comet*. The Ruler's vengeance
>was widely known, famine over the earth
>throughout the nation of men. Afterwards the Keeper of heavens,
>[*continued on p. 122*]

---

[1] Bishop of Wells.   [2] See Fisher, 'The anti-monastic reaction in the reign of Edward the Martyr', 254–70.   [3] His fame proved evanescent; Oslac (Old Norse Aslakr) was appointed ealdorman by Eadgar in 963 and a leading figure in Northumbria (cf. annal 966 E), but banished, after the death of Edgar, for unknown reasons; see Whitelock, 'The dealings of the kings of England with Northumbria in the tenth and eleventh centuries', pp. 77–9. For a suggestion that this refers to Oslac's death rather than banishment, see Isaacs, 'The death of Edgar, and others', 91–3.   [4] *word-snottor*, 'wise, prudent in word, speech'.   [5] A *soðboran* 'truth-bearers'; B C *woðboran* 'song-' or 'speech-bearers', i.e. prophets, seers.

E 975 *continued from p. 119*
It was widely known throughout many nations over the gannet's bath, that kings honoured Edmund's offspring, far and wide submitted to the king, as was natural to him. There was no fleet so proud, nor raiding-army so strong, that fetched itself carrion among the English race,[6] while the noble king governed the royal seat.

And here Edward, Edgar's son, succeeded to the kingdom; and then immediately in harvest-time in that same year, the star *comet* appeared, and then in the following year came a very great famine and very manifold disturbances throughout the English race.[7] And Ealdorman Ælfhere[8] ordered very many monastic institutions[9] to be overthrown[2] which King Edgar [*continued overleaf*]

THE WORCESTER MANUSCRIPT (D) *continued from p. 119*

975. *8 July.*[10] Here departed Edgar, ruler of the English, friend of the West Saxons, and protector of the Mercians. That was widely known throughout many nations over the gannet's bath, that kings greatly honoured Edmund's offspring, widely submitted to the king, as was natural to him. There was no fleet so proud, nor raiding-army so strong, that fetched itself carrion among the English race, while the noble king governed the royal seat.

Here Edward, Edgar's son, succeeded to the kingdom, and then immediately in harvest-time in that same year, the star *comet* appeared. And then in the following year came a very great famine and very manifold disturbances throughout the English race.

In his days, because of his youth, God's adversaries, Ealdorman Ælfhere[8] and many others, broke God's law, and impeded the monastic rule, and dissolved monasteries, and drove away monks, and put to flight God's servants,[2] whom earlier King Edgar ordered the holy bishop Æthelwold to establish. And over and again widows were robbed, and many wrongs and injustices arose up thereafter, and after that it always got much worse.[11]

And at that time also Oslac,[3] the famous earl, was banished from the English race. [*continued on p. 147*]

---

[6] *Angelcynn*; for the transition to 'England', see Wormald, 'Engla Lond: the making of an allegiance', 10–14.   [7] Bede, perhaps following the seventh-century encyclopaedist Isidore (*Etymologiae*, III, 71) said the appearance of a comet might portend pestilence, famine, war or change of king, *De Natura Rerum* (PL XC, 243–4), and cf. *De Tonitruis* (ibid., 609–14), Byrhtferth, *Manual*, pp. 132–3.   [8] See generally, Williams, '*Princeps Merciorum gentis*: the family, career and connections of Ælfhere, ealdorman of Mercia, 956–983', 143–72.   [9] MS *munuc-lif*; cf. 'the life', *s.a.* 718.   [10] The beginning of this annal is identical with E.   [11] This paragraph, peculiar to D, is in the style of Archbishop Wulfstan (cf. p. 113, note 15).

A 975 *continued from p. 120*
> Governor of angels, improved it, gave back bliss to each
> of the island dwellers through the fruits of the earth.

978. Here King Edward was killed. In this same year his brother, the ætheling Æthelred, succeeded to the kingdom. [*continued on p. 124*]

THE PETERBOROUGH MANUSCRIPT (E) 975 *continued from previous page*

earlier ordered the holy bishop Æthelwold to establish. And at that time also Oslac, the famous earl,[1] was banished from the English race. [*continued opposite*]

THE ABINGDON MANUSCRIPT (C) *continued from p. 119*

976. Here in this year was the great famine in the English race.

977. Here was the great assembly at Kirtlington[2] after Easter, and there Bishop Sideman passed away in a sudden death on *30 April*; he was bishop of Devonshire, and he wanted that his burial[3] should be at at Crediton – at his bishop's seat. Then King Edward and Archbishop Dunstan ordered that they carry him to St Mary's minster, that is[4] at Abingdon – and so it was done thus. And also he is honourably buried on the north side in the side-chapel[5] of *St Paul*.

978. Here in this year King Edward was martyred, and his brother, the ætheling Æthelred, succeeded to the kingdom; and he was consecrated as king the same year. In that year passed away Ælfwold, who was bishop of Dorset, and his body lies in the minster at Sherborne.[6]

979. In this year Æthelred was consecrated as king on the Sunday, fourteen days after Easter, at Kingston;[7] and there were at his consecration two archbishops and ten diocesan bishops. The same year a bloody cloud was seen, many times in the likeness of fire; and it appeared most of all at midnight; and it was formed thus of various beams; then when it became day[8] it glided away.

980. Here in this year, on *2 May*, Abbot Æthelgar was consecrated as bishop for the bishop's seat at Selsey,[9] and [*continued on p. 124*]

---

[1] See p. 120, note 3.   [2] 'Cyrtla's Farm', a royal manor in Oxfordshire (VCH, *Oxford*, p. 221).   [3] MS *lic-ræst*, lit. 'corpse-rest'.   [4] *þæt his*.   [5] *porticus*, see p. 44, note 10.   [6] Formerly the ecclesiastical centre of the church west of Selwood (cf. annal 709), but now serving Dorset alone (cf. O'Donovan, *Charters of Sherborne*; Taylor, *Architecture*, pp. 540–43; RCHM, *Dorset*, I, 1952, pp. xlvii-l, Addendum, 1975, pp. li-lvii).   [7] Kingston-upon-Thames, Surrey, a possible coronation-centre, see p. 104, note 10.   [8] *dagian wolde*.   [9] The ancient centre of the diocese of the South Saxons founded by Wilfred; see Bede (*HE*, IV, 13), who supplies the etymology *sea-calf* (seal) *island*.

E *continued from opposite page.*

978. Here in this year all the foremost councillors of the English race fell down from an upper floor[10] at Calne,[11] but the holy archbishop Dunstan alone was left standing up on a beam;[12] and some were very injured there, and some did not escape it with their life.[13]

979 [978]. Here King Edward was killed in the evening-time on *18 March* at Corfe 'passage';[14] and they buried him at Wareham[15] without any royal honours.

No[16] worse deed for the English race was done than this was, since they first sought out the land of Britain. Men murdered him, but God exalted him. In life he was an earthly king; after death he is now a heavenly saint. His earthly relatives would not avenge him, but his Heavenly Father has much avenged him. Those earthly slayers wanted to destroy his memory upon earth, but the sublime Avenger has spread abroad his memory in the heavens and on the earth. Those who earlier would not bow to his living body, those now humbly bow the knees to his dead bones. Now we can perceive that the wisdom and deliberations of men, and their counsels, are worthless against God's purpose.

And here Æthelred succeeded to the kingdom,[17] and very quickly after that, with great rejoicing of the councillors of the English race, was consecrated as king at Kingston.[7]

980. Here in this year Ealdorman Ælfhere[18] fetched the [*continued on* *p. 125*]

---

[10] D E F *anre upfloran,* F Lat *uno solario.*   [11] A royal manor in Wiltshire; land here was willed by King Eadred to Old Minster, Winchester (Whitelock, *Documents,* p. 511), but the manor remained in royal hands (DB, *Wiltshire,* 1.1).   [12] F Lat *de laquearibus* 'ceiling-strut'.   [13] F 'Some paid for it with their lives'.   [14] E *æt Corfes geate;* F Lat *in loco qui dicitur Porta Corf; corf* 'cutting', *geat* 'gap' (Mills, *The Place-Names of Dorset,* pp. 5–6). See also the anonymous Life of St Oswald (*Historians of York,* I, pp. 449–50, transl., Whitelock, *Documents,* pp. 839–42). Presumably the attack took place at or near the royal residence there (Sawyer, 'The royal *tun* in pre-Conquest England', p. 276).   [15] Dorset; a minster was said to have been founded here by Aldhelm *c.* 600 (William of Malmesbury, *Gesta Pontificum,* pp. 363–4); it was the burial-place of the West Saxon king Beorhtric in 784. By this time there was a handsome church, with side-chapels (*porticus*) appropriate for burial (Taylor, *Architecture,* pp. 634–6).   [16] This paragraph is marked by poetic rhetoric (cf. also annals 959, 975, 1011, 1057, 1067, 1075, 1086, 1104).   [17] F Lat *Æthelred succeeded his brother to the kingdom. In his time armies came too much into England and afterwards always crowded in the more.*   [18] F Lat *with the blessed Dunstan;* F (St Dunstan) and Ælfhere.

A *continued from p. 122*
983. Here Ealdorman Ælfhere passed away.
984. Here the kindly bishop Æthelwold passed away; and the consecration of the following bishop, Ælfheah, who was called by another name, Godwine, was on *19 October*; and he occupied the bishop's seat in Winchester on the Day of the two apostles Simon and Jude.[1] [*continued on p. 126*]

THE ABINGDON MANUSCRIPT (C) 980 *continued from p. 122*

in the same year Southampton was ravaged by a raiding ship-army and most of the town-dwellers killed or[2] taken prisoner. And the same year the land of Thanet was raided; and the same year Cheshire was raided by a northern raiding ship-army.
981. Here in this year Padstow[3] was raided; and the same year great harm was done everywhere along the sea-coast, both in Devon and in Cornwall. And in the same year Ælfstan, bishop in Wiltshire, passed away; and his body lies in the monastery at Abingdon;[4] and Wulfgar succeeded to the bishopric. And in the same year Womar, abbot in Ghent, passed away.[5]
982. Here in this year 3 ships of vikings came up in Dorset and raided in Portland. The same year London town burned; and in the same year two ealdormen passed away, Æthelmær in Hampshire and Edwin in Sussex; and Æthelmær's body rests in the New Minster in Winchester, and Edwin's in the monastery at Abingdon. The same year two abbesses in Dorset passed away: Herelufu in Shaftesbury[6] and Wulfwynn in Wareham. And the same year Otto,[7] emperor of the Romans, went to the land of the Greeks,[8] and then met a great army of the Saracens coming up from the sea [who] wanted to make a raid on the Christian people. And then the emperor fought against them, and there was great slaughter on either side, and the emperor had possession of the place of slaughter; and yet he was greatly harrassed there before he turned back from there. And then, as he went home, his brother's son, who was called Otto, passed away; and he was the son of the ætheling Liudolf, and this Liudolf was son of Otto the Elder and King Edward's daughter.[9]
983. Here Ealdorman Ælfhere passed away, and Ælfric succeeded to the same ealdormanship; and Pope Benedict[10] passed away.
984. Here Bishop Æthelwold passed away on *1 August*.
985. Here Ealdorman Ælfric was driven out of the country, and in the same year Edwin was consecrated as abbot for the monastery at Abingdon. [*continued on opposite page*]

[1] 28 October.   [2] MS *and*.   [3] *Sancte Petroces stow*, 'St Petrock's place, holy-place'; either Bodmin or Padstow might be meant, but the latter is more accessible on the North Cornwall coast, cf. Hoskins and Finberg, *Devonshire Studies*, p. 29, note 2.   [4] Where he was formerly abbot.   [5] For Womar, who died at New Minster, Winchester, having resigned his abbacy, see Vanderkindere, 'L'abbé Womar', 296–304; *Liber Vitae of New Minster*, p. 24.   [6] An Alfredian foundation in Dorset, cf. Kelley, ed., *Charters of Shaftesbury Abbey*.   [7] Otto II.   [8] An expression which might refer to any part of the Byzantine Empire, but this expedition was to southern Italy.   [9] Otto I had married Edith (Eadgyth) in 924, see p. 104, note 12.   [10] Benedict VII.

E 980 *continued from p. 123*

holy king's body[11] from Wareham, and carried it with great honour to Shaftesbury.[4]

981. Here first came 7 ships and raided Southampton.

983. Here Ealdorman Ælfhere passed away, and Ælfric succeeded to the same ealdormanship.

984. Here the holy bishop Æthelwold, father of monks,[12] passed away; and here Edwin was consecrated as abbot for Abingdon.

985. Here Ealdorman Ælfric was driven out.

986. Here the king did for the bishopric at Rochester;[16] and here the great pestilence among cattle first came to England.[13]

987. Here Watchet[14] was raided.

988. Here Goda, the Devonshire thane, was killed – and a great slaughter with him.[15] And here the holy archbishop Dunstan left this life and travelled to the heavenly. And Bishop Æthelgar succeeded to the archbishop's seat after him; and he lived for a short time after that – no more than a year and 3 months.

989. Here Abbot Edwin passed away, and Wulfgar succeeded; and here Sigeric was ordained as archbishop. [*continued on p. 127*]

THE ABINGDON MANUSCRIPT (C) *continued from previous page*

986. Here the king did for the bishopric at Rochester;[16] and here the great pestilence among cattle first came to England.[13]

988. Here Watchet[12] was raided, and Goda, the Devonshire thane, killed and a great slaughter with him. Here Archbishop Dunstan died, and Bishop Æthelgar succeeded to the arch-seat[17] after him; and he lived for a short time after that – no more than 1 year and 3 months. [*continued overleaf*]

THE CANTERBURY MANUSCRIPT (F) 989 *continued from p. 107*

989 [990]. Here Sigeric was ordained as archbishop [and] here afterwards travelled to Rome[18] for his pallium. [*continued overleaf*]

---

[11] An interlinear gloss in F specifies 'Edward's'; see annal 979 E.   [12] *muneca fæder*; used conventionally – cf. annals 509 F, 1089 E, but perhaps a reference to his sponsorship of the Benedictine Rule.   [13] MS *on Angelcyn*, but the sense is clearly shifting towards territory rather than race in this context, cf. p. 121, note 6, and Introduction p. xxxii.   [14] On the Somerset coast, and therefore vulnerable to raids from the sea (cf. annal 915 D, 918 A); Watchet was the site of a royal mint, and an estate, including a vineyard, recently given by King Edgar to Abingdon Abbey (*Chronicon de Abingdon*, I, p. 321);   [15] Florence (I, p. 148): *but more of them* (the Danes) *were killed, and the English had possession of the place of slaughter* (*funeribus*).   [16] Æthelred later said he acted *not so much in cruelty as ignorance*, having been prompted by a certain Æthelsige (Campbell, *Charters of Rochester*, pp. 42–4). Not for nothing was Æthelred known as the 'Unready' (*unræd*, 'ill-advised').   [17] MS *arcestole*; cf. p. 130, note 3.   [18] See Magoun, 'The Rome of two northern pilgrims', 268–77; 'An English pilgrim-diary of the year 990', 231–52. On the dates of his consecration and death see Sisam, 'MSS Bodley 340 and 342', 15–16.

A *continued from p. 124*

993[1] [991]. Here in this year Olaf[2] came with ninety-three ships to Folkestone, and raided round about it, and then went from there to Sandwich, and so from there to Ipswich, and overran all that, and so to Maldon. And Ealdorman Byrhtnoth came against them there with his army and fought with them;[3] and they killed the ealdorman there and had possession of the place of slaughter. And [994] afterwards they made peace with them and the king received him [Olaf] at the bishop's hands[4] by the advice of Sigeric, bishop of the inhabitants of Kent, and Ælfheah, bishop of Winchester.

994. Here Archbishop Sigeric passed away, and Ælfric, bishop of Wiltshire, succeeded to the archbishopric. [*continued on p. 132*]

THE ABINGDON MANUSCRIPT (C) *continued from previous page*

990. Here Sigeric was consecrated as archbishop; and Abbot Edwin[5] passed away, and Abbot Wulfgar succeeded to the rule. [*continued on previous page*]

THE CANTERBURY MANUSCRIPT (F) *continued from previous page*

991. Here Ealdorman Byrhtnoth was killed at Maldon,[3] and in the same year it was first decided that tax be paid to the Danish men because of the enormities[6] which they wrought along the sea coast. That was at first ten thousand pounds. Archbishop Sigeric decided on the decision.

992. Here the blessed Archbishop Oswald passed away,[7] and Abbot Ealdwulf succeeded to York and to Worcester. And here the king and all his councillors decided that all the ships that were worth anything should be gathered to London town, in order that it should be attempted to entrap the raiding-army somewhere outside.[8] But Ealdorman Ælfric,[9] one of those in whom the king had most trust, ordered the raiding-army to be warned; and on the night before the morning on which they should have come together,[10] this same Ælfric scurried away from the army,[11] and then the raiding-army escaped.

993. Here Bamburgh was broken down, and much war-booty taken there. And after that the raiding-army came to the Humber mouth and wrought great harm there. Then a great army was gathered; and then when they should have gone together[10] the commanders were the first to set the example of flight: that was Fræna and Godwine and Frithugist.[12]

994. Here Olaf[2] and Swein[13] came to London with ninety-four ships, and determinedly attacked the town, and they [*continued on p. 128*]

[1] By erasing the year-numbers laid out in anticipation of single-line entries, then crowding his words and writing in the margin, the scribe makes room for the entry which follows. See the Introduction p. xvi.   [2] i.e. Olaf Tryggvason, later king of Norway.   [3] 10 or 11 August. For the famous poem on the battle see Bradley, *Poetry*, pp. 518–28, and the separate edition by Scragg. See also Bately, 'The Anglo-Saxon Chronicle', pp. 37–50.   [4] i.e. as godfather or sponsor at baptism.   [5] Abbot of Abingdon.   [6] *wundræn*, 'wonders, marvels'.   [7] On 29 February according to Florence (I, p. 149), who says that he *rests at Worcester in St Mary's church, which he had built from the foundations*. For various Lives of Oswald see *The Historians of York*, I, pp. 399–475, II, pp. 1–97.

E *continued from p. 125*

991. Here Ipswich was raided, and very soon after that Ealdorman Byrhtnoth was killed at Maldon;[3] and in that year it was first decided tax be paid to the Danish men because of the great terror which they wrought along the sea coast. That was at first 10 thousand pounds. Archbishop Sigeric decided on the decision.

992. Here the blessed Archbishop Oswald left this life and travelled to the heavenly,[7] and Ealdorman Æthelwine[14] departed in the same year. Then the king and all his councillors decided that those ships that were worth anything should be gathered to London town; and the king entrusted the army to Ealdorman Ælfric[9] and Earl Thored[15] and Bishop Ælfstan[16] and Bishop Æscwig[17] to lead, that they should try if they could to entrap the raiding-army somewhere outside.[8] Then Ealdorman Ælfric sent and commanded the raiding-army to be warned; and then on the night before the day on which they should have come together,[10] he scurried away from the army by night, to his own great disgrace,[12] and the raiding-army then escaped, except for one ship which was struck there. And the raiding-army met ships from East Anglia and from London, and they made great slaughter there, and captured the ship, all armed and equipped, on which the ealdorman was.[18] And then after Archbishop Oswald's passing away, Abbot Ealdwulf of Peterborough succeeded to the York seat and to Worcester, and Cenwulf to the abbacy at Peterborough.

993. Here in this year Bamburgh was broken down, and much war-booty taken there; and after that the raiding-army came to the Humber mouth and wrought great harm there, both in Lindsey and in Northumbria. Then a very great army was gathered; and then when they should have gone together[10] the commanders were the first to set the example of flight: that was Fræna and Godwine and Frithugist.[12] In the same year the king ordered Ælfgar, son of Ealdorman Ælfric, to be blinded.[19]

994. Here in this year on the *Nativity of St Mary*[20] Olaf[2] and Swein[13] came t   o London town with 4-and-ninety ships, and then they were determinedly attacking the town, and they also [*continued on p. 129*]

---

[8] i.e. in the estuary or at sea.   [9] Ealdorman of Hampshire.   [10] i.e. 'joined battle'.   [11] Florence (I, p. 150) says that on the night before the English determined to fight the Danes, Ælfric and his men went over to the Danish side, *a singular example of infamy.*   [12] *Because*, says Florence (I, p. 151) *they were Danes on the father's side*; certainly Frani and Frithugist (but not Godwine) are Scandinavian names and men of this name were Peterborough benefactors (cf. Hart, *Early Charters of Eastern England*, p. 244; *Early Charters of the North Midlands*, pp. 335–7).   [13] Swein 'Forkbeard', king of Denmark, son of Harold 'Bluetooth' and father of Cnut.   [14] Ealdorman of East Anglia, a close friend of Archbishop Oswald and co-founder of Ramsey, see Hart, 'Æthelstan 'Half-king' and his family', 133–8.   [15] Of Northumbria.   [16] There were bishops of this name at both London and Rochester at the time.   [17] Bishop of Dorchester.   [18] Florence (I, p. 150) says that Ælfric himself had just fled from it.   [19] For examples of blinding as a punishment, see Robertson, *Laws*, pp. 190–91; and cf. annals 1006, 1075 E (1076 D), 1086 (p. 221).   [20] 8 September.

F 994 *continued from p. 126*
also wanted to set it on fire. But there, thank God, they fared worse than they ever imagined; and then travelled away from there, and wrought as much harm as any raiding-army ever could, in all things wherever they travelled. Then the king and his councillors decided that a tax should be promised them; and it was done so,[1] and they accepted it, and also provisions given to them from all the kingdom of Wessex; and they were paid 16 thousand pounds. Then the king sent Bishop Ælfheah[2] and Ealdorman Æthelweard[3] after King Olaf, and meanwhile sent hostages to the ships; and King Olaf was led with great honour to Andover.[4] And the king Æthelred received him at the bishop's hands,[5] and gave to him royally; and then Olaf promised him – and kept to it too – that he would never come back to the English race in hostility.

995. Here the star *comet*, that is the 'haired',[6] appeared; and Archbishop Sigeric passed away, and Ælfric, bishop of Wiltshire, was chosen on Easter Day[7] at Amesbury[8] by King Æthelred and by all his councillors.[9] This Ælfric was a very [wise] man – there was no more prudent man in England. Then Ælfric went to his arch-seat, and when he came there he was received by men of that order which was most distasteful of all to him, that was clerks.[10] And [he] immediately sent[11] everywhere for the wisest men he knew, and especially for knowledgeable men who knew how to give the truest account about the state of things in this land in the days of their elders, in addition to what he himself had learned in books and from wise men. Then very old men, both ordained and lay, told him that their elders had told them how it was decreed immediately after *St Augustine* came to this land:

'Then when *Augustine* had received the bishop's seat in the town which was the chief town of all this kingdom of King Æthelberht, as it is to be read in the *History of the English*[12] . . . he made a seat, with the king's help . . . they initiated in an old Roman defence[13] . . . began to flourish. The foremost of that company were: Mellitus, Justus, Paulinus, Rufianus. The blessed Pope sent the pallium[14] by these, and letters with it, and indications how he should consecrate bishops and in which places in Britain they should be set. And he also sent letters and many worldly gifts of various things to the king Æthelberht; and the church which had been got ready for him he ordered [to be consecrated] in the name of the Lord Saviour *Christ* and *St Mary*; and he [should] set there a dwelling place for himself, and for all his successors; and that he should set therein men of the same order as he [*continued opposite*]

---

[1] See Stenton, *Anglo-Saxon England*, p. 372, note 1.   [2] Bishop of Winchester.   [3] Cultured ealdorman of the Western Provinces, patron of letters and himself author of a Latin translation of The Anglo-Saxon Chronicle, see the Introduction p. xix.   [4] Land at Andover was willed by King Eadred to New Minster, Winchester (Whitelock, *Documents*, p. 511), but the manor remained in royal hands (DB, *Hampshire*, 1.41).   [5] i.e. as his godfather or sponsor at baptism.   [6] See p. 83, note 20.   [7] 21 April.   [8] A royal manor that had belonged to Alfred and Eadred in turn, see Swanton, *Prose*, p. 49; Whitelock, *Documents*, p. 511.   [9] The following lengthy, and *parti pris*, addition is written in a small hand on the margin and on an inserted leaf; it is in places illegible, but the (fuller) version in F Lat allows confident reconstruction.   [10] i.e. secular clergy as distinct from monks.   [11] MS *s..de*.

E 994 *continued from p. 127*
wanted to set it on fire, but there they suffered more harm and injury than they ever imagined that any town-dwellers[15] would do to them. But on that [day][16] the holy Mother of God manifested her kind-heartedness to the town-dwellers and rescued them from their enemies.[17] And they travelled from there and wrought the greatest harm which any raiding-army could ever do, in burning and raiding and slaughter of men, both along the sea coast in Essex and in the land of Kent and in Sussex and in Hampshire. And finally they took themselves horses, and rode widely as they wanted, and were wreaking indescribable harm. Then the king and his councillors decided to send to them, and offer tax and provisions if they would leave off their raiding, and they undertook [to do] that, and all the raiding-army came to Southampton, and there took up winter-quarters, and there they were fed from throughout all the kingdom of Wessex; and they were paid[18] 16 thousand pounds. Then the king sent Bishop Ælfheah[2] and Ealdorman Æthelweard[3] after King Olaf, and meanwhile sent hostages to the ships; and they led King Olaf with great honour to Andover.[4] And the king Æthelred received him at the bishop's hands,[5] and gave to him royally; and then Olaf promised him – as he kept to it too – that he would never come back to the English race in hostility. *Here Richard the Elder died, and Richard his son succeeded to the rule[19] and ruled 31 years.*

995. Here in this year the star *comet* appeared; and Archbishop Sigeric passed away. [*continued on p. 131*]

[*continued on p. 131*]

THE CANTERBURY MANUSCRIPT (F) 995 *continued from opposite page*

himself was, and whom he sent here to the land, and also that every other bishop who sat in the archbishop's seat in Canterbury should be a man in monk's orders; and that should be held to for ever, by the leave and blessing of God and of St Peter and of all who came after him. When this message came back to King Æthelberht and Augustine, they were very happy because of such instructions. And the archbishop then consecrated the minster in Christ's name and St Mary's, on the day which is known as the festival of the two martyrs, *Primus and Felicianus,*[20] and lodged monks inside there, just as *St Gregory* commanded; and they performed God's service in purity. And from those same monks bishops were taken for every place, as you can read in the *History of the English'.*[12]

Then Archbishop Ælfric was very happy that he had so many witnesses [amongst those] who [*continued overleaf*]

---

[12] i.e. Bede's *Ecclesiastical History of the English People*, I, 33.   [13] *wearde*; cf. Smith, *English Place-Name Elements*, II, p. 247. For the Canterbury defences, see Maxfield, *Saxon Shore*, p. 118ff. Bede does not mention the defences but says the church itself was of ancient Roman work (Old English version I, 17, *ealde Romanisce weorce*).   [14] *þæt is erce* interlined; see p. 130, note 3.   [15] *burhwaru*.   [16] C D 'on this day'.   [17] For a similar reference to the divine protection of London, see annal 1016 (pp. 150–51).   [18] C D 'paid in money'.   [19] Of Normandy.   [20] 9 June.

F 995 continued from previous page

at that time were most influential with the king. Further, those same councillors who were with the archbishop declared: 'Thus, just as we have stated, monks continued to dwell in Christ Church in Augustine's days, and in Laurentius's, Mellitus's, Justus's, Honorius's, Deusdedit's, Theodore's, Berhtwald's, Tatwine's, Notthelm's, Cuthbert's, Bregowine's, Jænberht's, Æthelheard's, Wulfred's, Feologild's. But in the year when Ceolnoth came to the archbishopric, there was such a pestilence among men that no more than five monks were left there in Christ Church[1] . . . Moreover in his time there was strife and sorrow in this land, so that no one could think about anything else but . . . Now, thank God, it is in the king's control, and in yours, whether they[2] might be within there any longer, because they could never be brought out better than they could now, if it is the king's will, and yours'.

Then without any delay the archbishop with all the wise men, travelled straight to the king and made everything known to him just as we have told here above. Then the king was very glad at this news and said to the archbishop and to the others: 'I think it advisable that first of all you travel to Rome for your pallium,[3] and you make all this known to the pope, and afterwards act according to his advice'. And they all answered that that was the best advice. When the [priests] heard this, they decided that they would take two of them and send to the pope, and offer him great treasure and silver, on condition he give them the pallium;[3] but then when they came to Rome the pope refused to do that, for they brought no letter, neither from the king nor from the people, and ordered them to go – wherever they wanted. As soon as the priests had turned away from there, the archbishop Ælfric came to Rome, and the pope received him with great honour, and ordered him to celebrate mass in the morning at the altar of St Peter, and the pope himself put on [him] his own pallium[3] and greatly honoured him. When this was done, the archbishop began to tell the pope all about the clerks, how it had come about, and how they were in the minster at his archbishopric. And in return the pope described how the priests had come to him and offered great treasure so that he should give them the pallium.[3] 'But,' said the pope, 'now travel back to England, with God's blessing and St Peter's and mine, and when you come home put into your minster the men of the same order the *blessed Gregory* commanded into the land with Augustine – by God's command and St Peter's and mine'. Then with this the archbishop turned to England. As soon as he came home he occupied his archbishop's seat, and afterwards travelled to the king. And the king and all his nation thanked God for his [*continued opposite*]

---

[1] MS *Xpes cyrican*; the name Christ is in the genitive case since the church was dedicated to him; the case-ending was later elided, hence the modern form of the name. [2] i.e. the secular clergy. [3] Pallium; the first two instances use the word *ærce, erce*, the second two *pallium*. Previously in this MS the word *pallium* is explained in an interlinear gloss: 'that is, *erce*' (p. 129, note 14); vice-versa annal 997 reads *arce* with *pallium* interlined as if a gloss. Cf. 'arch-seat' earlier in the same annal and 988 C, or 'arch-authority' in 1051 D (p. 170).

E *continued from p. 129*

996. Here in this year Ælfric was consecrated as archbishop for Christ Church.[4]

997. Here in this year the raiding-army travelled round Devonshire into the mouth of the Severn, and there raided, both in Cornwall and in Wales and in Devon; then they went up at Watchet,[5] and wrought great harm there by burning and by slaughtering of men, and after that turned back round Penwith Tail[6] to the south side, and then turned into the mouth of the Tamar, and then went up until they came to Lydford,[7] and burned and killed everything that they met, and burned down Ordwulf's monastery at Tavistock,[8] and brought indescribable war-booty with them to the ships.

998. Here the raiding-army turned eastward again, into the mouth of the Frome, and went up as widely as they wanted into Dorset. And an army was often gathered against them, but then as soon as they should have come together something always started a retreat, and they[9] always had the victory in the end. And then another time they lay in the Isle of Wight,[10] and meanwhile ate out of Hampshire and of Sussex.

999. Here the raiding-army again came round into the Thames, and then turned up along the Medway to Rochester.[11] And then the Kentish army came against them, and there they determinedly joined battle; but alas![12] they too quickly submitted and fled, because they did not have the help they should have had;[13] then the Danish had possession of the place of slaughter, [*continued on p. 133*]

THE CANTERBURY MANUSCRIPT (F) 995 *continued from previous page*

return, and that he performed his errand to the greatest satisfaction of all. He then turned back to Canterbury and drove the clerks out of the minster and set monks inside there, just as the pope commanded him.

996. Here Wulfstan[14] was ordained as bishop for London.

997. Here Archbishop Ælfric travelled to Rome for his pallium.[3] [*continued on p. 134*]

---

[4] i.e. Canterbury. [5] See p. 125, note 14. [6] E *Penwiht steort*, D *Penwæð steort*; i.e. Land's End, Cornwall. See Smith, *English Place-Name Elements*, II, p. 151. [7] In west Devon, a fort mentioned in the Burghal Hidage (Swanton, *Prose*, p. 13). [8] Six miles south of Lydford; founded *c.* 974 under the supervision of the king's brother-in-law Ordwulf, a major benefactor; see generally Finberg, *Tavistock Abbey*, pp. 1–3, 278–82. [9] i.e. the raiders. [10] *Wihtlande*. [11] Which Florence (I, p. 154) says they beseiged *for a few days*. [12] D 'woe, alas!' [13] This rueful comment on lack of support is peculiar to E. [14] Wulfstan II, the famous homilist who became archbishop of York in 1002, see Whitelock, 'A note on the career of Wulfstan the homilist', 460–66; 'Archbishop Wulfstan, homilist and statesman', 42–60.

A *continued from p. 126*

1001. Here in this year there was great hostility in the land of the English race through the raiding ship-army; and they raided and burned almost everywhere, so that in a single journey they moved up until they came to Æthelings' Valley.[1] And then Hampshire came against them there and fought with them. And there Æthelweard, the king's high-reeve, was killed, and Leofric of [2] Whitchurch and Leofwine, the king's high-reeve, and Wulfhere, the bishop's thegn, and Godwine of [2] Worthy, the son of Bishop Ælfsige,[3] and eighty-one men in all.[4] And there were many more of the Danish killed, though they had possession of the place of slaughter.

And then they went west from from there until they came to Devon, and there Pallig[5] joined them with those ships he could gather, because he had deserted King Æthelred, contrary to all the pledges which he had granted him – and the king had also made good gifts to him, in manors[6] and in gold and silver. And they burned down Kingsteignton,[7] and also many other good manors which we cannot name, and afterwards they made peace with them. And they went from from there to the mouth of the Exe, so that they moved up in a single journey until they came to Pinhoe; and there Kola, the king's high-reeve, and Eadsige, the king's reeve, [came] against them with such an army as they could gather, and they were put to flight there, and there were many of them killed – and the Danish had possession of the place of slaughter. And in the morning they burned down the manors at Pinhoe and at Clyst,[8] and also many good manors which we cannot name. And then they went back east again until they came to Wight; and in the morning they burned down the manor at Waltham[9] and many other estates.[10] And quickly after that they came to terms with them, and they made peace.[11] [*continued on p. 134*]

---

[1] *Æthelingadene*, East or West Dean, on or near the Hampshire boundary in Sussex, see Mawer and Stenton, *The Place-Names of Sussex*, p. xlv.   [2] MS *æt*; i.e. who lived at.   [3] Ælfsige I of Winchester.   [4] A Winchester calendar remembers, under 23 May, *Æthelweard and many others . . . Wulfnoth and Æthelwine, brothers, and many others slain with them* (Dickins, 'The day of the Battle of Æthelingadene', 25–7).   [5] Brother-in-law of King Swein, and apparently killed together with his wife and child in the massacre of St Brice's Day, 1002 (see below, p. 135, note 9; William of Malmesbury, *Gesta Regum*, I, p. 213).   [6] OE *ham* 'homestead, residence', might also mean village or estate, cf. Smith, *English Place-Name Elements*, I, pp. 226–9. In what follows, the places mentioned by name must have been of sufficient importance to receive notice – perhaps royal or ecclesiastical holdings.   [7] A valuable estate on the River Teign in Devon; in royal hands by the time of Domesday Book, and perhaps earlier.   [8] Both in Devon, the latter probably Broad Clyst, although there are several settlements called '-Clyst' along the river of this name.   [9] Bishops Waltham, Hampshire; a Winchester holding close to Southampton Water.

E 999 *continued from p. 131*

and took horses and rode as widely as they themselves wanted, and did for and raided well nigh all the West Kentish.[12] Then the king with his councillors decided that they should be confronted with a ship-army and also with a land-army; but when the ships were ready, there was delay[13] from day to day, which distressed the wretched people who lay on the ships. And always whenever matters should have been advanced, the slower it was from one hour to the next, and they always let their enemies' strength increase; and always the sea was retreated from, and they[14] always moved up after. And then in the end the ship-army achieved nothing, except the people's labour, and wasting money, and the emboldening of their enemies.

1000. Here in this year the king travelled into the land of Cumbria[15] and ravaged very nearly all of it. And his ships turned out round Chester, and should have come to join him, but they could not; then they raided the Isle of Man. And that summer the hostile fleet had gone to Richard's kingdom.[16]

1001. Here the raiding-army came to the mouth of the Exe and then went up to the stronghold,[17] and were determinedly fighting there, but they very determinedly withstood them, and resolutely. Then they turned through the countryside, and did just as they were accustomed: killed and burned. Then there was gathered an immense army from the Devon people and Somerseters,[18] and then they came together at Pinhoe; and then as soon as they joined battle the English army gave way and they made great slaughter there, and then rode over the countryside; and each succeeding occasion was always worse than the last; and they brought much war-booty with them to the ships, and turned from there into the Isle of Wight,[19] and there travelled about just as they themselves wanted, and nothing withstood them. No raiding ship-army on sea nor land-army dared approach them, however far inland they went. In every way it was a heavy time, because they never left off their evil.

1002. Here in this year the king and his councillors decided that they should pay tax to the fleet and make peace with them, on condition they should leave off from their evil deeds. Then the king sent Ealdorman Leofsige[20] to the fleet and then he, at the command of the king and his councillors, arranged a truce with them, and that they should receive provisions and tax. And they undertook that, and they were paid 24 thousand pounds. Then in the middle of this [*continued overleaf*]

---

[10] *cotlifa*; at this period the word seems to be used in the sense of 'manor' (*Anglo-Saxon Dictionary*, Supplement, *sub* cotlif, II); here applied to something that could be burned down.   [11] At this point the eleventh-century copy A² ends. The few subsequent annals in A are Canterbury additions (see the Introduction p. xxii).   [12] MS *Weast Centingas*.   [13] C 'the judges delayed'.   [14] i.e. the enemy.   [15] MS *Cumerland*; cf. p. 111, note 9.   [16] i.e. Normandy.   [17] Exeter, ten miles from the open sea.   [18] *Defenisces folces and Sumorsætisces*.   [19] *Wihtland*.   [20] Made ealdorman of Essex after the death of Byrhtnoth in 991 (q.v.), see Hart, 'The ealdordom of Essex', 76–7; Stenton, *Latin Charters*, pp. 76–80.

A *continued from p. 132*

1005. Here Archbishop Ælfric passed away.

1006. Here Ælfheah was consecrated as archbishop. [*continued on p. 154*]

THE PETERBOROUGH MANUSCRIPT (E) 1002 *continued from previous page*

Ealdorman Leofsige killed Æfic, the king's high-reeve, and the king then banished him from the country. And in the same spring the Lady,[1] Richard's daughter,[2] came here to the land. In the same summer Archbishop Ealdwulf [3] passed away, and in that year the king [*continued opposite*]

THE CANTERBURY MANUSCRIPT (F) 1003 *continued from p. 131*

1003. Here Exeter was destroyed because of the business[4] of a French churl[5] called Hugh, whom the Lady[1] had set as reeve;[6] and the raiding-army completely did for the town. Then a great army was gathered; and then Ealdorman Ælfric should have led the army, but he took to his old tricks; as soon as they were so close at hand that each of them looked on the other, then he pretended to vomit, and said that he was ill, and thus betrayed the people. Then when Swein saw that they were not resolute, he led his raiding-army into Wilton, and burned down the settlement, and then went to Salisbury and from there back to the sea.

1004. Here Swein came with his fleet to Norwich, and completely ravaged and burned down the town. Then Ulfcytel[7] with the councillors in East Anglia decided that they should make peace with the raiding-army, because they came unexpectedly [and] he had not had time in which he could gather his army. But under cover of the truce, the raiding-army stole up from the ships and went to Hertford,[8] and Ulfcytel gathered his raiding-army [*continued on p. 136*]

---

[1] *Hlæfdige* is used as a title of a king's wife or other ruling lady; used of Æthelflæd of Mercia *s.a.* 917 C, 919 E, of Ælfgyfu Emma *s.a.* 1023, 1035, 1043, 1051 – in the sense of dowager 1048 E, 1052, 1067 D, 1076 1003, 1013 E etc.   [2] Emma, who adopted (or was given) the name Ælfgyfu when she came to England; F regularly gives her name in both French and English forms: Ymma Ælfgiva, cf. p. 155, note 20; p. 158, note 5. See generally *Encomium Emmae*, ed. Campbell, pp. xl-l, 55ff. *et passim*; Campbell, 'Queen Emma and Ælfgifu of Northampton', 66–79.   [3] Of York.   [4] MS *ðingan*.   [5] *ceorl*; perhaps this is a very early use of the word in a disparaging sense; but Hugh is called a count (*comitis*) by Florence (I, p. 156) and *vicecomes* by Henry of Huntingdon (p. 174), terms which are regularly used as the equivalent of OE *eorl*, so *ceorl* may represent an error in transmission.   [6] Florence (I, p. 156) is more explicit: *Swein, king of the Danes, through the bad counsel, carelessness and treachery of the Norman count Hugh, whom Queen Emma had put over Devon, broke into and plundered the city of Exeter, and destroyed the wall from the east to the west gate.*   [7] Florence (I, p. 157) calls him *dux* of the East Angles.   [8] So also F Lat, but C D E say Thetford, a more likely location in view of its proximity to Norwich.

E 1002 *continued from opposite page*
ordered all the Danish men who were among the English race to be killed on
Brice's Day,[9] because it was made known to the king that they wanted to
ensnare his life – and afterwards all his councillors – and have his kingdom
afterwards.[10]

1003. Here Exeter was broken down through the French churl[5] Hugh
whom the Lady had set as her reeve;[6] and the raiding-army completely did for
the town and took great war-booty there.[11] Then a very great army was
gathered from Wiltshire and from Hampshire, and were very resolutely going
towards the raiding-army; then Ealdorman Ælfric should have led the army,
but he took to his old tricks: as soon as they were so close at hand that each
of them looked on the other, then he pretended to be ill, and began to retch so
as to vomit, and said that he was taken ill, and thus deceived[12] the people that
he should have led. As the saying goes: 'When the commander weakens then
the whole raiding army is greatly hindered'.[13] Then when Swein saw that they
were not resolute, and all dispersed, he led his raiding-army into Wilton and
raided and burned down the town, and then went to Salisbury and from there
back to the sea, travelled to where he knew his 'wave-stallions'[14] were.

1004. Here Swein came with his fleet to Norwich, and completely raided
and burned down the town. Then Ulfcytel[7] with the councillors in East Anglia
decided that it would be better that they buy peace from the enemy before they
did too much harm in the country, because they came unexpectedly and he
had not had time in which he could gather his army. Then under cover of the
truce which should have been between them, the raiding-army stole up from
the ships and turned their course to Thetford.[8] Then when Ulfcytel realised
that, he sent that they should chop up the ships – but those he thought of failed;
and then he secretly gathered his army as quickly as he could. And the raiding-
army then came to Thetford, within 3 weeks of their earlier raiding Norwich,
and were inside there one night, and raided and burned down the town. Then
in the morning, when they wanted to go to the ships, then Ulfcytel came up
with his troop[15] and they determinedly joined battle there, and a great
slaughter fell on either side. There the chief men of the East Anglian people
were killed, but if they had been up to full strength [*continued overleaf*]

---

[9] 13 November. A dramatic glimpse of the events of this day is given in a charter of Æthelred
promulgated two years later, making restitution to St Frideswide's minster in Oxford: *it will be
well known that a decree was sent out by me with the counsel of my leading men and magnates, to
the effect that all the Danes who had sprung up in this island, sprouting like weeds amongst the
wheat, were to be destroyed by a most just extermination.* The Danes of Oxford had broken into St
Frideswide's church, seeking sanctuary, whereupon the populace burned it down with them in
inside (*The Cartulary of St Frideswide*, I, pp. 2–3, transl. Whitelock, *Documents*, p. 591). For
Brice, fifth-century bishop of Tours, see Farmer, *Dictionary of Saints*, p. 55.   [10] F adds 'without
any opposition'.   [11] C and D add 'in the same year the enemy went up into Wiltshire'.   [12] E
beswac; C D *becyrde* 'betrayed'.   [13] There is no known proverb corresponding to this, but
compare Alcuin urging Archbishop Eanbald not to desert his church: *If the standard-bearer flees,
what does the army do; if the trumpet is silent in the camp, who prepares himself for battle* (cf. 1
Corinthians xiv:8); *if the leader is afraid, how shall the soldier be saved?* (MGH, *Epistolae Karolini
Aevi*, IV, p. 377; transl. Whitelock, *Documents*, p. 796).   [14] *yðhengestas*, a poetic formula for
'ships', perhaps translating Old Norse *uð-hestr* (Cleasby and Vigfusson, *Dictionary*, p. 655, sub
unnr.   [15] C adds 'so that they were compelled to give battle'.

E 1004 *continued from previous page*
they would never have got back to their ships, as they themselves said.[1]

1005. Here in this year there was the great famine throughout the English race, such that no-one ever remembered one so grim before; and this year the [enemy] fleet turned from this country to Denmark – and let little time elapse before it came back.

1006. Here Archbishop Ælfric passed away, and Bishop Ælfheah succeeded him to the arch-seat. And Bishop Beorhtwold succeeded to the authority[2] in Wiltshire;[3] and Wulfgeat[4] was deprived of all his territory;[5] and Wulfheah and Ufegeat were blinded, and Ealdorman Ælfhelm was killed;[6] and Bishop Cenwulf[7] passed away. And then after midsummer[8] the Danish fleet[9] came to Sandwich, and did all just as they were accustomed: raided and burned and killed as they travelled.[10] Then the king ordered the whole nation from Wessex and from Mercia to be called out, and all harvest-time they lay away on a campaign against the raiding-army, but it did not achieve any more than it often did before. Despite all this, the raiding-army travelled just where it wanted, and the campaign caused the local people every kind of harm, so that neither the native raiding-army nor the foreign raiding-army[11] did them any good!

Then when it drew near to winter, the army travelled home, and after Martinmas[12] the raiding-army came to its secure base[13] in the Isle of Wight,[14] and there provided themselves everywhere whatever they needed. And then towards midwinter they took themselves to their prepared depots,[15] out through [*continued opposite*]

THE CANTERBURY MANUSCRIPT (F) 1004 *continued from p. 134*

and went after [them], and they joined battle determinedly there; there many of the chief men of the East Anglian[16] people were killed.

1005. Here in this year there was the great famine throughout the English race, such that no-one ever remembered one so grim before; and this year the [enemy] fleet turned from this country to Denmark, and soon returned again. [*continued on p. 146*]

---

[1] C D 'they themselves admitted that they had never met with harder hand-play in England than Ulfcytel gave them'. [2] E *rice*; F *bishopstole* 'bishop's seat'. [3] F Lat *the bishopric in Salisbury*. [4] Leofeca's son, whom Florence (I, p. 158) says Æthelred *had loved almost more than anyone*, adding that this forfeiture was because of *unjust judgements and arrogant deeds*. [5] MS *ar*, originally 'honour'; see *Anglo-Saxon Dictionary* for the semantic link between rank (*ar* I) and estates (*ar* II). There is a parallel development in Latin *honor*, cf. Florence, II, p. 54. [6] Ælfhelm, son of Wulfrun, was ealdorman of southern Northumbria (cf. *s.a.* 1036); Wulfheah and Ufegeat were his sons and Ælfgyfu of Northampton his daughter (for this family see Table p. 295). Florence (I, p. 158) says that *the crafty and perfidious* Eadric Streona bribed the hangman of Shrewsbury, Godwin Porthund (*which means 'dog of the town'*), to ambush *the noble Ælfhelm* while hunting nearby, adding that the blinding was at the king's command and took place at Cookham, where he was staying. [7] Bishop of Winchester. [8] Florence (I, p. 158) says it was in the month of July. [9] C D 'the great fleet'. [10] Florence (I, p. 159) says *sometimes in Kent, sometimes in Sussex*. [11] MS *ne innhere ne uthere*. [12] 11 November. [13] MS *fryðstole* 'peaceful seat'. [14] *Wihtland*. [15] MS *garwan feorme*, 'provision dumps'. [16] F Lat *the East Saxons*.

E 1006 *continued from opposite*
Hampshire into Berkshire at Reading; and they did, in their custom, ignited their beacons[17] as they travelled; and travelled then to Wallingford and scorched it all up;[18] and then turned along Ashdown[19] to <Cwichelm's Barrow,[20] and there awaited the boasted threats,[21] because it had often been said that if they>[22] sought out Cwichelm's Barrow they would never get to the sea. Then they turned homewards by another route. Then the army were assembled there at the Kennet, and there they joined battle; and [the Danes] soon brought that troop to flight, and afterwards carried their war-booty to the sea. There the people of Winchester could see the raiding-army, proud and not timid, when they went by their gates to the sea, and fetched themselves provisions and treasures from over 50 miles from the sea.

The king had then gone over the Thames, into Shropshire, and took his entertainment[23] there in the midwinter season.[24] Then there arose so great a terror of the raiding-army that no-one could think or plan how they should be got out of the country, or this country guarded against them, because they had severely marked every shire in Wessex with burning and with raiding. The king began to plan earnestly with his councillors as to what they all thought most advisable as to how this country might be protected before it was entirely done for. Then the king and his councillors decided that, though it were hateful to them all, tax must needs be paid to the ‹raiding-army›[25] for the good of the entire nation. Then the king sent to the raiding-army and ordered it to be made known to them that he wished there to be a truce between them, and that they should be granted tax and provisions; and they all accepted that, and they were provisioned throughout the English race. [*continued overleaf*]

---

[17] C D 'their war-signals'.   [18] E *forspeldon*, C D *forswældon*; the Anglo-Saxon graphs P and W are commonly confused (cf. p. 35, note 11; p. 55, note 11); but F *forbernde*, F Lat *combusserunt*. C D add: 'and spent one night at Cholsey'.   [19] The Berkshire Downs – see p. 28, notes 2–3.   [20] *Cwicchelmes hlæwe*, now Cuckhamsley Knob; perhaps believed to be the burial-place of one of the West Saxon notables who died in 593 or 636 (q.q.v.), and later the meeting-place of the shire assembly (Gelling, *The Place-Names of Berkshire*, pp. 481–2).   [21] MS *beotra gylpa*.   [22] The phrase in brackets, supplied from C D, was omitted in E, probably because of the repetition of the place-name.   [23] MS *feorme*, 'food-rents, provisions'.   [24] i.e. over Christmas; and probably in Shrewsbury itself, for which see Bassett, 'Anglo-Saxon Shrewsbury', 1–23.   [25] Supplied from D.

E *continued from previous page*

1007. Here in this year the tax that was paid to the hostile raiding-army was 30[1] thousand pounds. And in this year also Eadric[2] was set as ealdorman in the kingdom of the Mercians.[3]

1008. Here the king ordered that they should determinedly build ships all over England: that is, one warship[4] from three hundred and 10 hides,[5] and from 8 hides a helmet and mailcoat.[6]

1009. Here in this year the ships about which we spoke earlier were ready, and from what books tell us, there were more of them than there had ever earlier been in England in the days of any king. And they brought them all together to Sandwich, and should lie there and guard this country against every foreign raiding-army. But as yet we had neither the luck nor the honour that the ship-army were useful to this country, any more than it often was before. Then at this same time or a little before, it happened that Beorhtric, the brother of the ealdorman Eadric, accused Prince Wulfnoth[7] the South Saxon, to the king, and he then turned away and enticed ships to him until he had 20, and he then raided everywhere along the south coast, and wrought every kind of harm. Then it was made known to the ship-army that they[8] could easily be surrounded if one wanted to set about it. Then that Beorhtric took with him eighty ships, and thought that he would make a great reputation for himself in that he would get Wulfnoth dead or alive. But then when they were on their way there, such a wind came against them as no man remembered earlier, and battered and thrashed to pieces and cast ashore all the ships. And that Wulfnoth came [*continued opposite*]

---

[1] E F *xxx*, C D *xxxvi*.   [2] Eadric 'Streona' (i.e. 'the Acquisitive'), for whom see p. 136, note 6.   [3] E *on Myrcena rice*; C D 'throughout'; F 'over all'. The office had been vacant since Ælfric was driven out in 985 (q.v.). D adds 'in this year Bishop Ælfheah went to Rome for the pallium'.   [4] MS *scegð*; F Lat: *a large ship, which in English is called 'scegð*. *Circa* 1000 Bishop Ælfwold of Crediton prepares a *scegð* of 64 oars for the king (Swanton, *Prose*, p. 55).   [5] 310 is a curious unit, but it is common to all MSS except D, which is apparently corrupt at this point (*of þrym hund scipum and x be tynum anne scægð*). See Harmer, *Writs*, pp. 266–7.   [6] Perhaps helmets and mailcoats intended for the crew.   [7] F amplifies: 'Wulfnoth the South Saxon, father of Earl Godwine'; F Lat says: *the noble man Wulfnoth*. The title *cild* 'child, youth' is used in the later Anglo-Saxon period to denote high rank. It is used of Edgar ætheling *s.a.* 1067 and, possibly in error, of Eadric *s.a.* 1067 D.   [8] i.e. Wulfnoth's ships.

E 1009 *continued from opposite page*
immediately and burned the ships. When this was known to the other ships where the king was, how the others had fared, then it was as if everything was in confusion, and the king took himself home – and the ealdorman and the chief councillors – and thus lightly abandoned the ships. And then the people who were on the ships conveyed the ships back to London, and thus lightly let the whole nation's labour waste; and the deterrent[9] in which the whole English race had confidence, was no better [than that]. Then when this ship-army had finished thus, there came to Sandwich[10] immediately after Lammas[11] the immense hostile raiding-army,[12] and immediately turned their course to Canterbury and would quickly have taken the town if they had not the more quickly begged them for peace; and all the East Kentish made peace with the raiding-army, and granted them 3 thousand pounds. And then immediately after that the raiding-army turned about until they came to the Isle of Wight,[13] and raided and burned, as their custom was,[14] everywhere in Sussex and in Hampshire and also in Berkshire. Then the king ordered the whole nation[15] to be called out, in order to guard against them on all sides, but nevertheless they travelled just where they wanted. Then on one occasion the king got in front of them with all the army when they wanted [to get to] the ships, and everybody was ready to attack them;[16] but it was Ealdorman Eadric who hindered it, as it always was. Then, after the Feast of *St Martin*[17] they travelled back towards Kent, and took for themselves winter-quarters on the Thames, and lived off Essex and off the shires which were nearest on both sides of the Thames. And they often attacked London town, but praise be to God that it still stands sound, and they always fared badly there. Then, after midwinter, they took a route up out through the Chilterns, and so to Oxford, and burned down the town, and then carried on[18] along both sides of the Thames towards [*continued overleaf*]

---

[9] E *ege*, 'awe, terror' (to the Danes); C D *sige*, 'the victory' (over the Danes). [10] Florence (I, pp. 160–61) gives details: *The Danish jarl Thurkil came with his fleet to England; then, in the month of August, another immense fleet of Danes, in which Heming and Eilaf were leaders, came to the island of Thanet and without delay joined the aforesaid fleet.* For Eilaf see *Encomium Emmae*, ed. Campbell, pp. 86–7. [11] 1 August. [12] C adds 'which we call Thurkil's raiding-army'. This was Thurkil 'the Tall', one of the notorious gang of Jómsborg vikings (cf. Snorri Sturluson, *Heimskringla: The Olaf Sagas*, pp. 35, 122, 148, 343; *The Saga of the Jomsvikings*, p. 28 *et passim*). [13] *to Wihtlande*. [14] C D 'as their custom is', the present tense suggesting currency. [15] *ealne þeodscipe*: either an exceptionally large army, or one drawn from all parts, which Florence (I, p. 161) says *he placed throughout the coastal districts against their attacks*. [16] Florence (ibid.) adds: *and because he had the whole army with him, was ready to conquer or die.* [17] Martinmas, 11 November. [18] MS *namon it*, 'took it'.

E 1009 *continued from previous page*
the ships. Then when they were warned that there was an army against them at London, they turned over at Staines;[1] and thus travelled the whole winter, and that spring [1010] they were in Kent, repairing their ships.

1010. Here after Easter in this year the aforesaid raiding-army came to East Anglia, and turned up at Ipswich, and went straight to where they had heard that Ulfcytel was with his army.[2] This was on the *first* day *of The Ascension of the Lord*.[3] And then the East Anglians immediately fled; then Cambridgeshire firmly stood against [them].[4] There was killed Athelstan, the king's son-in-law,[5] and Oswy[6] and his son, and Wulfric, Leofwine's son, and Eadwig, Æfic's brother, and many other good thegns and countless people. It was Thurcytel 'Mare's Head'[7] that first started the flight, and the Danes had possession of the place of slaughter, and then were horsed and thereafter had possession of East Anglia, and for 3 months raided and burned that country; they even travelled into the wild fens, and they killed men and cattle, and burned throughout the fens, and burned down Thetford and Cambridge, and afterwards turned south again onto the Thames; and the horsed men rode towards the ships, and afterwards quickly turned westwards into Oxfordshire, and from there into Buckinghamshire, and so along the Ouse until they came to Bedford, and so on until Tempsford; and always burned as they travelled. Then they turned back to the ships with their war-booty; and when they were dispersing[8] to the ships, then the army should have been back out, in case they wanted to go inland. The army was travelling home then; and when they [the enemy] were in the east, then the army was kept in the west: and when they were in the south, then our army was in the north. Then all the councillors were ordered to the king, and it had then to be decided how this country should be defended. But whatever was then decided, it did not stand for even one month. In the end there was no head [*continued opposite*]

---

[1] i.e. crossing the Thames some two dozen miles up-stream. [2] Simeon (II, p. 141) and Florence (I, p. 162) call the place Ringmere, and Snorri Sturluson (*Heimskringla: The Olaf Sagas*, p. 125) Ringmere-Heath. This may be either Ringmere, 4 miles north-west of Thetford, Norfolk, or Rymer, 4 miles south. [3] Ascension Day that year was 18 May, but Florence (p. 162) says the battle took place on 5 May, confirmed by Oswig's *obit* recorded at Ely (Dickins, 'The day of Byrhtnoth's death and other obits', 17). [4] F 'but Cambridge alone stood firm'. [5] Or brother-in-law; MS *aðum* can mean either (cf. annals 1091, 1096). He might have been the brother of Æthelred's first wife; his eldest son was called Athelstan (cf. Swanton, *Prose*, pp. 56–9) but this was a very common name in the West Saxon royal house. [6] Son-in-law of Ealdorman Byrhtnoth, the English leader at the battle of Maldon in 991 (q.v.), see Dickins, 'The day of Byrhtnoth's death and other obits', 15–17. [7] MS *Myran heafod*. The by-name 'Horse-head' (*heshofði*) occurs in various Old Norse sources (cf. *Origines Islandicae*, II, pp. 605, 617). An interlinear gloss to Florence (I, p. 162, note 6) understands it thus (*equæ caput*), though Henry of Huntingdon (p. 178) renders it *caput formicæ* (ant's head). [8] C D 'were travelling'.

E 1010 *continued from opposite page*
man who wanted to gather an army, but each fled as best as he could; nor even in the end would one shire help another. Then before the Feast of *St Andrew*,[9] the raiding-army came to Northampton and immediately burned down the market-town[10] and round about there seized for themselves as much as they wanted, and from there turned over the Thames into Wessex, and so on towards Cannings Marsh,[11] and burned it all. Then, when they had gone as far as they wanted, they came at midwinter to the ships.

1011. Here in this year the king and his councillors sent to the raiding-army, and begged peace, and promised them tax and provisions on condition that they leave off their raiding.

They had then overrun: (i) East Anglia and (ii) Essex and (iii) Middlesex and (iv) Oxfordshire and (v) Cambridgeshire and (vi) Hertfordshire and (vii) Buckinghamshire and (viii) Bedfordshire and (x)[12] half Huntingdonshire, and to the south of the Thames all the Kentish and South Saxons and the Hastings district[13] and Surrey and Berkshire and Hampshire and much in Wiltshire.

All these misfortunes befell us through lack of decision, in that they were not offered tax[14] in time; but when they had done great evil, then a truce and peace was made with them. And nonetheless for all this truce and peace and tax, they travelled about everywhere in bands[15] and raided and roped up and killed our wretched people. And in this year, between *the Nativity of St Mary* and Michaelmas[16] they besieged Canterbury,[17] and got inside through treachery, because Ælfmær, whose life Archbishop Ælfheah[18] had earlier saved, betrayed Canterbury to them. And there they seized the archbishop Ælfheah, and Ælfweard the king's reeve, and Abbot Leofwine,[19] and Bishop Godwine[20] – and they let Abbot Ælfmær[21] go free. And they seized all ordained people, both men and women,[22] in there – and it is impossible for any man to say how much of the people that was – and [*continued overleaf*]

[9] 30 November. [10] MS *port* perhaps has the special sense of 'market-town', Smith, *English Place-Name Elements*, II, pp. 70–71. [11] Gover, *The Place-Names of Wiltshire*, pp. 249–50. [12] So E; C reads: 'and (ix) half Huntingdonshire, and much (x) in Northamptonshire'; and D: 'and half Huntingdonshire (ix), and much in Northamptonshire (x)'. [13] *Centingas and Suð Seaxe and Hæstingas.* [14] C adds 'nor fight against them'. [15] E *folc mælum*; C D recte *flocmælum*. [16] 8 and 29 September respectively. [17] Florence (I, p. 164), says that *after the twentieth day of the seige they set fire to part of the city.* [18] Later called St Alphege; there is a Life by the twelfth-century Canterbury monk Osbern, *Patrologia Latina*, CXLIX, cols. 371–94. [19] So E F; whereas C and D read, correctly, 'Abbess Leofrun' (of Minster in Thanet, for the legendary foundation of which, see references cited p. 26, note 7). [20] Of Rochester. [21] Of St Augustine's, Canterbury. Presumably not the same person as the traitor, whom Florence (loc. cit.) previously calls *archdeacon.* [22] *gehadode menn, and weras and wif.*

E 1011 *continued from previous page*
afterwards were in the town as long as they wanted;[1] and when they had throughly searched it, then they turned to the ships, and led the archbishop with them.

[2] Then he who was earlier the head of the English race and of Christendom was a roped thing.[3] There wretchedness might be seen where earlier was seen bliss, in that wretched town from where there first came to us Christendom and bliss before God and before the world.

And they kept the archbishop with them up until the time when they martyred him.

1012. Here in this year, there came to London town Ealdorman Eadric and all the foremost councillors of the English race, ordained and lay, before Easter – that Easter Day was on the[4] 13 *April*. And they were there until after Easter, until all the tax was paid – that was 8 thousand[5] pounds. Then on the Saturday the raiding-army became much stirred up against the bishop, because he did not want to offer them any money, and forbade that anything might be granted in return for him.[6] Also they were very drunk, because there was wine brought from the south.[7] Then they seized the bishop, led him to their 'hustings'[8] on the Saturday in *the octave of Easter*,[9] and then pelted him there with bones and the heads of cattle;[10] and one of them struck him on the head with the butt of an axe,[11] so that with the blow he sank down and his holy blood fell on the earth, and sent forth his holy soul to God's kingdom.[12] And in the morning the bishops Eadnoth and Ælfhun[13] and the [*continued opposite*]

---

[1] Florence (I, pp. 164–5) adds: *Then Christ Church was plundered and burned*. He describes atrocities inflicted on the civilian population, with nine out of ten killed – many thrown from the walls or hung up by their genitals, women thrown into the fire, infants tossed on spear-points. He goes on to say that in about seven months God sent a sickness on the Danes in vengeance, laying low more than two thousand, ten or twenty at a time, with *an excruciating internal disorder*. This was presumably cholera or typhoid; the Danish had overwintered in the city, grossly inflating its normal population, and with the return of warmer weather the water supplies were inevitably polluted.   [2] The following short paragraph is marked by poetic rhetoric.   [3] MS *ræwling*, recte *ræpling*; cf. p. 137, note 18.   [4] E *on twam*; recte: C *þam*, D *þæm*.   [5] So E F; but C D say forty-eight thousand.   [6] Florence (I, p. 165) says that a ransom of three thousand pounds was asked.   [7] E *sudan*, C D *suðan*.   [8] An Old Norse word, *hús-þing*, 'house-assembly, -council'; for the possibility that the bishop's death may have been a judicial execution, see McDougal, 'Serious entertainments', 201–25.   [9] 19 April; C adds 'and shamefully murdered him'.   [10] E *mid hryðera heafdum*; D *mid hryþera neata heafedum*; this seems to have been a Scandinavian habit, cf. Garmonsway and Simpson, *Beowulf and its Analogues*, pp. 102–4.   [11] MS *yr*, the blunt end of an axe-head, commonly used to crush bones (e.g. *Leechdoms*, ed. Cockayne, III, pp. 14–15), and cf. Magoun, 'The Domitian Bilingual', 378–80.

E 1012 *continued from opposite page*

inhabitants of the town took up the holy body, and carried it to London with all honour and buried it in *St Paul's* minster, and there now[14] God reveals the holy martyr's powers.[15] Then when that tax was paid, and oaths of peace sworn, the raiding-army dispersed as widely as it had been gathered earlier. Then 45 ships[16] from the raiding-army submitted to the king, and promised him that they would guard this country, and he would[17] feed and clothe them.

1013. In the year after the archbishop was martyred, the king set Bishop Lyfing in the arch-seat of Canterbury; and in the same year, before the month of August, King Swein came with his fleet to Sandwich, and very quickly turned round East Anglia into the mouth of the Humber, and so upwards along the Trent until he came to Gainsborough. And then Earl Uhtred and all Northumbria immediately submitted to him, and all the people in Lindsey, and afterwards the people of the Five Boroughs,[18] and quickly after, all the raiding-army[19] to the north of Watling Street;[20] and he was granted hostages from every shire. Then after he recognised that all the people had submitted to him, he ordered that his raiding-army should be provisioned and horsed; then he turned southward[21] with his whole army, and entrusted his ships and the hostages to Cnut, his son. And after he came over Watling Street,[20] they wrought the greatest evil that any raiding-army could do, then turned to Oxford, and the inhabitants of the town immediately submitted and gave hostages – and from there to Winchester, and they did the same; then from there they turned eastwards to London, and a great part of his people was drowned in the Thames, because they did not look out for any bridge. Then when he came to the town, the inhabitants of the town would not submit, but held out against them with full battle because King Æthelred was inside, and Thurkil with him. Then King Swein turned [*continued overleaf*]

[12] Florence (I, p. 165) says the man responsible for this act of *impious compassion* was Thrum, whom the archbishop had confirmed the previous day. [13] Bishops of Dorchester and London respectively. [14] Clearly a contemporaneous note, since Ælfheah's relics were removed to Canterbury in 1023 (q.v.). [15] *mihta*; i.e. posthumous miracles. [16] Commanded by Jarl Thurkil, for whom see *Encomium Emmae*, ed. Campbell, pp. 73–6; Lund, 'The armies of Swein Forkbeard and Cnut', 105–18. [17] i.e. on condition that. [18] See annal 942. [19] The term *here* is apparently here used of the whole organised settlers in the area. F Lat. *the people* (*populus*) *of East Anglia*. [20] *Wætlinga stræte*; the Roman road running from London to Chester via St Albans (*Wæclinga-ceaster*, Gover, *The Place-Names of Hertfordshire*, pp. 86–7; Mawer and Stenton, *The Place-Names of Bedfordshire*, pp. 1–2, 5–7) the middle third of which formed the boundary of Danelaw by the peace-treaty of 878 between Alfred and Guthrum; see Swanton, *Prose*, p. 6. [21] *against the South Mercians* says Florence (I, p. 166).

E 1013 *continued from previous page*
from there to Wallingford, and so over the Thames westward to Bath, and settled there with his army. And Ealdorman Æthelmær[1] came there and the western thegns with him, and all submitted to Swein and gave hostages. Then when he had travelled thus far, he turned northward to his ships, and the whole nation had him as full king.[2] And after that the town inhabitants in London submitted and gave hostages, because they were afraid he would do for them. Then Swein demanded full payment and provisions for his raiding-army for the winter, and Thurkil demanded the same for the raiding-army that lay at Greenwich; and despite that, they raided as often as they wanted. Then nothing did this nation any good, neither in the south nor in the north. Then for some time the king[3] was with the fleet in the Thames, and the Lady[4] then turned across the sea to her brother Richard,[5] and Ælfsige, abbot of Peterborough, with her. And the king sent Bishop Ælfhun across the sea with the æthelings Edward and Alfred in order that he should look after them. And then at midwinter the king turned from the fleet to the Isle of Wight, and was there for the season; and after the season turned across the sea to Richard, and was there with him until the happy event of Swein's death occurred.

[6] And during the time the Lady was beyond the sea with her brother, Ælfsige, abbot of Peterborough, who was with her there, went to the monastery which is called Bonneval,[7] where the body of St Florentine[8] lay, [and] found there a wretched place, wretched abbot and wretched monks, because they had been ravaged; then bought from the abbot and from the monks there St Florentine's body – all but the head – for 5 hundred pounds;[9] and then when he came back offered it to Christ and St Peter.

1014. Here in this year Swein ended his days[10] at Candlemas, 2 *February*;[11] and the fleet[12] all chose Cnut for [*continued opposite*]

---

[1] Of the Western Provinces; *comes of Devon* says Florence (I, p. 167).   [2] This expression (and compare that used of Harold *s.a.* 1036 E) probably implies kingly power *de facto*, without perfect constitutional standing *de jure*, cf. *Encomium Emmae*, ed. Campbell, pp. liii, lxiii, note 3.   [3] Æthelred.   [4] F amplifies: 'the king sent his queen, Ælfgifu Emma, across the sea to her brother Richard'.   [5] Richard II, duke of Normandy.   [6] This paragraph is found only in E.   [7] Dép. Eure-et-Loire.   [8] Perhaps Florentinus of Sedun, martyred in the Vandal persecution.   [9] Together with its shrine, according to the expanded account given by Hugh Candidus (p. 49); later recognised by visiting monks from Bonneval to have been a poor bargain on their part.   [10] Both Gaimar (4157–62) and Simeon (II, p. 146) say that Swein died at Gainsborough and was buried at York; Gaimar adding that ten years later Cnut took his father's remains to Denmark.   [11] MS *iii Nonas* for *iiii Nonas*. D adds: 'And this same year Ælfwig was ordained bishop for London at York on the Feast of St Juliana' (16 February).   [12] F Lat *Here King Swein died; however, the king's chief men and those who had come with him to England elected Cnut to kingship.*

E 1014 *continued from opposite page*
king. Then all the councillors,[13] both ordained and lay, advised that King Æthelred should be sent for, and declared that no lord was dearer to them than their natural lord – if he would govern them more justly than he did before. Then the king sent his son Edward here with his messengers, and ordered [them] to greet[14] all his nation, and said that he would be a gracious lord to them, and would improve each of the things which they all hated, and each of those things that were done or declared against him should be forgiven, on condition that they all resolutely and without treachery turned to him. And full friendship was secured with word and pledge on either side, and [they] declared every Danish king outlawed from England for ever. Then during that spring King Æthelred came home to his own people, and he was gladly received by them all. And then, after Swein was dead, Cnut settled with his raiding-army in Gainsborough until Easter, and the people in Lindsey came to an agreement with him that they should provide him with horses and afterwards all go together and raid. Then, before they were ready, King Æthelred came there with the whole army into Lindsey, and then all human kind that could be got at were raided and burned and killed. Cnut himself went out with his fleet – and thus the wretched people were betrayed through him – and then turned southwards until he came to Sandwich, and there put ashore the hostages which were granted to his father, and cut off their hands and their noses.[15] And besides all these evils, the king ordered the raiding-army that lay at Greenwich to be paid 21 thousand pounds.[16] And in this year on St Michael's Eve,[17] that great sea-flood came widely throughout this country, and ran further inland than it ever did before, and drowned many settlements and a countless number of human beings.

1015. In this year was the great assembly at Oxford, and there Ealdorman Eadric betrayed Siferth and Morcar,[18] [*continued overleaf*]

---

[13] C adds: 'all those who were in England'.   [14] *het gretan*; this formula suggests that King Æthelred communicated with his subjects by writ in this negotiation (Harmer, *Writs*, pp. 61–2, 541–2).   [15] C D 'hands and ears and noses'. After this says Florence (I, p. 170) *he set out for Denmark, returning the following year.*   [16] Florence (I, p. 170) gives the figure as thirty thousand.   [17] 28 September.   [18] Florence (I, p. 170) identifies these as sons of Earngrim; both are mentioned in the will of King Æthelred's son Athelstan (Swanton, *Prose*, p. 57).

E 1015 *continued from previous page*
the foremost thegns in the Seven Boroughs:[1] lured them into his chamber,[2] and in there they were killed dishonourably. And the king then seized all their property, and ordered Siferth's widow[3] to be seized and brought inside Malmesbury.[4] Then after a short while, the ætheling Edmund travelled and took the woman against the king's will, and had her for wife. Then, before *the Nativity of St Mary,*[5] the ætheling travelled from the west, north into the Five Boroughs, and immediately rode into all Siferth's territory, and Morcar's, and all that people submitted to him. And then at the same time King Cnut came to Sandwich, and immediately turned around the land of Kent into Wessex, until he came to the mouth of the Frome, and then raided in Dorset and in Wiltshire and in Somerset. The king then lay sick at Cosham.[6] Then Ealdorman Eadric gathered an army – and the ætheling Edmund in the north; then when they came together, the ealdorman wanted to betray the ætheling, and therefore they parted without a fight, and retreated from their enemies. And then Ealdorman Eadric enticed 40 ships[7] from the king,[8] and then submitted to Cnut. And the West Saxons submitted and gave hostages, and provided the raiding-army with horses, and it was there until midwinter.

1016. Here in this year King Cnut came with his raiding-army of 160 ships, and Ealdorman Eadric with him, over the Thames into Mercia at Cricklade, and then turned into Warwickshire, during the midwinter festival,[9] and raided and burned and killed all [*continued opposite*]

THE CANTURBURY MANUSCRIPT (F) *continued from p. 136*

1016. Here Cnut came with 160 sixty ships, and Ealdorman Eadric with him, over the Thames into Mercia at Cricklade, and then turned into Warwickshire, in which they burned and killed all that they came to. And [*continued on p. 148*]

---

[1] Stenton, *Anglo-Saxon England*, p. 383, note 1, suggests that this phrase, which does not occur again, includes the five Danish boroughs of Lincoln, Stamford, Leicester, Nottingham and Derby (cf. annals 942, 1013) with, in addition, Torksey (Lincolnshire), and probably York. [2] E *his bure*, F Lat *camera sua*; cf. p. 47, note 13. [3] *lafe*; Florence (I, p. 170) names her Ealdgyth. [4] E *Mealdelmes byrig*, a monastery in Wiltshire founded by the Irish scholar Mailduin; the alternative name used in C D, *Ealdelmes byrig*, introduced the name of its most illustrious abbot Aldhelm, whose fame soon eclipsed that of the founder (cf. Bede, *HE*, V, 18). [5] 8 September; Florence (I, p. 170) says it was between the Feasts of the Assumption and the Nativity of St Mary, i.e. 15 August – 8 September. [6] At the head of Portsmouth Harbour in Hampshire; a royal estate by the time of Domesday Book (DB *Hampshire*, sub Wymering), and perhaps already so. [7] *manned by Danish soldiers* says Florence (I, p. 171). [8] i.e. from their allegiance to the king. [9] *Before Epiphany* (6 January) says Florence (I, p. 171).

E 1016 *continued from opposite page*

that they came to. Then the ætheling Edmund began to gather an army; then when the army was assembled, nothing would suit them but that the king were there and that they have the help of the garrison[10] from London. Then they left off the campaign and each man took himself home.[11] Then after the festival,[12] the army was ordered again, on full penalty,[13] that each man who was fit should go forth; then the king in London was sent to, and asked that he come to join the army with the help which he could gather. Then when they all came together, it did not achieve any more than it often did before.[14] Then when it was made known to the king that one who should have been of help to him wanted to betray him, [he] left the army and turned back to London.

Then the ætheling Edmund rode to Northumbria to Earl Uhtred, and everybody supposed that they wanted to assemble an army against King Cnut; then they travelled into Staffordshire and into Shrewsbury and to Chester and they raided on their [own] side[15] [*continued overleaf*]

THE WORCESTER MANUSCRIPT (D) *continued from p. 121*

1016. Here in this year Cnut came with his raiding-army, and Ealdorman Eadric with him, over the Thames into Mercia at Cricklade, and then turned to Warwickshire during the midwinter season, and raided and burned and killed all that they came to. Then the ætheling Edmund began to gather an army; then when the army were assembled, nothing would suit them about it but that the king were there with them and that they have the help of the garrison in London.[10] Then they left off the campaign and each man took himself home.[11] Then after the festival,[12] the army was ordered again, on full penalty,[13] that each man who was fit should go forth; then the king in London was sent to and asked that he come to join the army with the help which he could gather. Then when they all came together, it did not achieve any more than it often did before.[14] Then when it was made known to the king that one who should have been of help to him wanted to betray him, [he] left the army and turned back to London.

Then the ætheling Edmund rode to Northumbria to Earl Uhtred, and everybody supposed that they wanted to assemble an army against King Cnut; then they travelled into Staffordshire and into Shrewsbury and to Chester and they raided on their [own] side,[15] and [*continued on p. 149*]

---

[10] MS *burhware*, inhabitants of either town or stronghold; in this context the latter makes better sense. [11] Florence (I, p. 171) says explicitly: *the Mercians refused to engage the West Saxons and Danes unless Æthelred and the Londoners joined in.* [12] i.e. after Epiphany, see Florence loc. cit. [13] *wite* – penalties for failing to report for duty. Under Æthelred's laws army-deserters were fined 120 shillings or, if the king were present, might forfeit life and property (Swanton, *Prose*, p. 11). [14] MS *þa ne beheold hit naht* (D *beheold nan þinc*) *þe ma þe hit oftor ær did.* [15] *Because*, says Florence (I, p. 172), *they did not want to go out to fight the Danish army.*

E 1016 *continued from previous page*
and Cnut on his; and turned himself then out through Buckinghamshire into Bedfordshire, and from there to Huntingdonshire, along the fen to Stamford, and then into Lincolnshire, from there to Nottinghamshire, and so to Northumbria towards York. Then when Uhtred learned this, he left off his raiding and hastened northwards, and then of necessity submitted, and all the Northumbrians with him; and he gave hostages – and nevertheless he was killed,[1] and Thurcytel, Nafena's son, with him. And then after that, King Cnut[2] set Eric[3] as earl in Northumbria just as Uhtred was, and afterwards turned himself southwards another way, wholly to the west. And all the raiding-army then came to the ships before Easter, and the ætheling Edmund turned to London to his father; and then, after Easter, the king Cnut turned towards London with all his ships.

Then it happened that, before the ships came, the king Æthelred passed away. He ended his days on *St* George's Day,[4] after great toil and difficulties in his life.[5] And then, after his end, all the councillors who were in London, and the garrison [*continued opposite*]

THE CANTERBURY MANUSCRIPT (F) 1016 *continued from p. 146*

the ætheling Edmund turned to London to his father, and Cnut travelled towards London with all his ships. But the king Æthelred passed away earlier, before the ships came. He passed away on *St* George's Day,[4] after great toil and difficulties in his life.[5] And after his end, all the councillors of the English race chose Edmund for king, and he resolutely defended his kingdom in his time.

Then at the Rogation Days[6] the [Danish] ships came to Greenwich, and immediately turned to London, and dug a ditch on the south side and dragged their ships to the west side of the bridge, and then afterwards bedyked[7] the town around so that no one could get in or out, and often attacked the town, and they resolutely withstood them. [*continued on p. 150*]

---

[1] C adds: 'on the advice of Ealdorman Eadric'.   [2] E 'King Cnut', C D 'the king'.   [3] Eric, son of Hakon earl of Hlathir, see *Encomium Emmae*, ed. Campbell, pp. 66–73.   [4] 23 April. [5] Florence (I, p. 175) adds that: *his body was buried with great honour in the church of St Paul the Apostle; after his death, the bishops, abbots, ealdormen and all the more noble men of England assembled together and unanimously elected Cnut as their lord and king; and coming to him at Southampton and repudiating and renouncing in his presence all the race of King Æthelred, they concluded a peace with him, and swore loyalty to him; and he also swore to them that he would be a loyal lord to them, before God and the world.*   [6] 7–9 May that year.   [7] MSS *bedicodon*; i.e. constructed a rampart – presumably of ditch-and-bank type.

E 1016 *continued from opposite page*
chose Edmund for king, and he resolutely defended his kingdom for as long as
his time was.

Then at the Rogation Days[6] the [Danish] ships came to Greenwich, and
within a little while turned to London; and then dug a great ditch on the south
side and dragged their ships to the west side of the bridge, and afterwards
bedyked[7] the town around so that no one could get in or out, and regularly
attacked the town, but they resolutely withstood them. King Edmund had
gone out then before that, and then rode into[8] Wessex, and all the people
submitted to him;[9] and quickly after that he fought against the raiding-army at
Penselwood near Gillingham,[10] and he fought another [*continued overleaf*]

THE WORCESTER MANUSCRIPT (D) 1016 *continued from p. 147*

Cnut on his; turned himself then out through Buckinghamshire into
Bedfordshire, and from there to Huntingdonshire, and so into Northamptonshire, along the fen to Stamford, and then into Lincolnshire, from there to
Nottinghamshire, and so to Northumbria towards York. Then when Uhtred
learned this, he abandoned his raiding and hastened northwards, and then of
necessity submitted, and all the Northumbrians with him; and he gave
hostages – and nevertheless he was killed,[1] and Thurcytel, Nafena's son, with
him. And then after that, the king[2] set Eric[3] as earl in Northumbria just as
Uhtred was, and afterwards turned himself southwards another way, wholly
to the west. And all the raiding-army then came to the ships before Easter, and
the ætheling Edmund turned to London to his father; and then, after Easter,
the king Cnut turned towards London with all his ships.

Then it happened that, before the ships came, the king Æthelred passed
away. He ended his days on St George's Day,[4] after great toil and difficulties
in his life. And then, after his end, all the councillors who were in London, and
the garrison chose Edmund for king; and he resolutely defended his kingdom
for as long as his time was.

Then at the Rogation Days[6] the [Danish] ships came to Greenwich, and
within a little while turned to London, and then dug a great ditch on the south
side and dragged their ships to the west side of the bridge, and then afterwards
bedyked[7] the town around so that no one could get in or out, and regularly
attacked the town, but they resolutely withstood them. King Edmund had
then gone out before that, and then rode into[8] Wessex, and all that people
submitted to him;[9] and quickly after that he fought against the raiding-army at
Penselwood near Gillingham,[10] and [*continued on p. 151*]

---

[8] i.e. conquered, took possession of.   [9] Florence (I, p. 174) says *with great joy*.   [10] Florence (I, p. 174): *Therefore, lifting the siege for a time, and leaving part of the army to guard the
ships, they went away, hastening to Wessex, and gave no time for King Edmund Ironside to raise
his army; however, he met them bravely in Dorset with the army which he had been able to collect
in so short a time, supported by God's help, and engaging them at a place called Penselwood near
Gillingham he conquered and put them to flight.* Gillingham was a royal manor by the time of
Edward the Confessor (DB *Dorset*, I.4) and perhaps already so.

E 1016 *continued from previous page*
fight after midsummer at Sherston,[1] and there a great slaughter fell on either side, and the raiding-armies themselves broke off the fight.[2] And Ealdorman Eadric and Ælfmær Darling[3] were helping the raiding-army against King Edmund. And then for the 3rd time he gathered an army, and travelled to London[4] and rescued the garrison and drove the raiding-army to the ships. And then it was two days[5] later that the king turned over at Brentford, and fought against the raiding-army and put them to flight; and there many of the English people were drowned through their own carelessness when they travelled in front of the army and wanted to seize loot. And after that the king turned to Wessex and assembled his army. Then the raiding-army immediately turned to London and besieged the town, and attacked it strongly both by water and by land, but the Almighty God rescued it.

After that the raiding-army turned away from London with their ships into the Orwell, and there went inland and travelled into Mercia, and killed and burned whatsoever they came across, as was their custom, and provided themselves with supplies, and they drove both the ships and their herds to[6] the Medway.[7] Then for the 4th time King Edmund assembled the entire English nation and travelled over the Thames at[8] [*continued opposite*]

THE CANTERBURY MANUSCRIPT (F) 1016 *continued from p. 148*

After that the raiding-army turned away from London, with their ships into the Orwell, and there went up into Mercia, and killed and burned whatsoever they came across, as was[9] their custom. Then for the fourth time King Edmund gathered the entire English nation and travelled into Kent, and the raiding-army fled with horses into Sheppey, and the king killed as many as he could overtake. And Ealdorman Eadric turned to join the king at Aylesford.[10] There was no more unwise decision[11] than this was.[12]

The raiding-army travelled back into Mercia. The king heard that; then for the fifth time he gathered the entire the English nation and travelled after the raiding-army and overtook [*continued on p. 153*]

---

[1] Perhaps Sherston, Wiltshire. But Florence who gives a dramatic account of the battle at Sherston (I, pp. 174–5), locates it *in Hwiccia*. The Old Norse poem *Knútsdrápa* says that Cnut commanded the Danes in person (Ashdown, *English and Norse Documents*, p. 138).   [2] At the end of each of two days fighting, being too weary to continue; after which Canute's men left the field and returned to the siege of London (Florence, loc. cit.). Here the word *heres* (pl.) is used of both armies, English and Danish, see the Introduction p. xxxiv.   [3] Florence (I, p. 175) adds: *and Ælfgar, son of Meaw* (perhaps 'the Seagull's son', cf. Tengvik, *Old English Bynames*, p. 191).   [4] C adds 'keeping north of the Thames, and coming out through Clay Hanger' ('clayey wooded slopes', near Tottenham), see Gover, *The Place-Names of Middlesex*, p. 79.   [5] *twa niht*; see p. 2, note 2.   [6] MS *into*.   [7] This sounds like a roundabout journey of some four or five hundred miles, although only the cardinal points of the itinerary are mentioned. Florence (I, p. 176) says that the infantry were taken in ships to the Medway, but mounted forces kept the whole country in alarm by their raids.   [8] E *to*, D *æt*; river-crossings at this point are elsewhere invariably said to be 'at' Brentford; the settlement now so called was on the north bank of the river, and since Edmund's journey went on into Kent, perhaps 'at Brentford' would be a more reasonable rendering here also.

E 1016 *continued from opposite*
Brentford, and travelled into Kent,[13] and the raiding-army fled before him with their horses into Sheppey, and the king killed as many of them as he could overtake. And Ealdorman Eadric then turned to join the king at Aylesford.[10] There was no more unwise decision[11] than this was.[12]

The raiding-army turned back up into Essex and travelled into Mercia and did for all that it travelled over. Then, when the king learned that the raiding-army was inland, he assembled the entire the English nation for the 5th time and travelled behind them and overtook them in [*continued overleaf*]

THE WORCESTER MANUSCRIPT (D) 1016 *continued from p. 149*

he fought another fight after midsummer at Sherston,[1] and there a great slaughter fell on either side, and the raiding-armies themselves broke off the fight.[2] And Ealdorman Eadric and Ælfmær Darling[3] were helping the raiding-army against King Edmund. And then for the third time he gathered an army, and travelled to London[4] and rescued the garrison and drove the raiding-army to ship. And then two days[5] afterwards the king turned over at Brentford, and fought against the raiding-army and put them to flight; and there many of the English people were drowned through their own carelessness, when they travelled in front of the army and wanted to seize loot. And after that the king turned to Wessex and assembled his army. Then the raiding-army turned to London and besieged the town, and attacked it fiercely both by water and by land, but the Almighty God rescued it.

Then, after that, the raiding-army turned away from London with their ships into the Orwell, and there went up and travelled into Mercia, and killed and burned whatsoever they came across, as their custom is,[9] and provided themselves with supplies, and they drove both the ships and their herds to[6] the Medway.[7] Then for the fourth time King Edmund assembled the entire English nation and travelled over the Thames at[8] Brentford, and travelled into Kent,[13] and the raiding-army fled before him with their horses into Sheppey, and the king killed as many of them as he could overtake. And Ealdorman Eadric then turned to join the king at Aylesford.[10] There was no more unwise decision[11] than this was.[12]

The raiding-army turned back up into Essex and travelled into Mercia and did for all that it travelled over. Then, when the king learned that the raiding-army was inland, he assembled the entire English nation for the fifth time and travelled behind them and overtook them in Essex at [*continued overleaf*]

---

[9] E *wæs*, C D *is*, the latter giving a greater sense of currency.   [10] The lowest crossing point on the Medway, see p. 13, note 9.   [11] *unræd geræd*.   [12] i.e. for the king to take Eadric back into favour. F Lat says: *But when the king came to Aylesford, Dux Eadric by a trick made the English army turn back.*   [13] Where, adds Florence (I, p. 177), he fought against the Danes near Otford.

E 1016 *continued from previous page*
Essex at the hill which is called Ashingdon,[1] and there resolutely joined battle.[2] Then Ealdorman Eadric did as he so often did before, first started the flight – with the Magonsæte[3] – and thus betrayed his royal lord and the whole nation. There Cnut had the victory and won himself[4] all England.[5] There was killed Eadnoth,[6] and Abbot Wulfsige,[7] and Ealdorman Ælfric,[8] and Ealdorman Godwine,[9] Ulfcytel from East Anglia, and Æthelweard, son of Ealdorman Æthelsige,[10] and all the chief men[11] in the English race.[12]

Then after this fight King Cnut turned inland with his raiding-army to Gloucestershire, where he heard tell that Edmund the king was. Then Ealdorman Eadric and the [*continued opposite*]

THE WORCESTER MANUSCRIPT (D) 1016 *continued from previous page*

the hill which is called Ashingdon,[1] and there resolutely joined battle.[2] Then Ealdorman Eadric did just as he so often did before, first started the flight – with the Magonsæte[3] – and thus betrayed his royal lord and the whole nation of the English race. There Cnut possessed the victory and won himself[4] all the nation of the English. There was then killed Bishop Eadnoth,[6] and Abbot Wulfsige,[7] and Ealdorman Ælfric,[8] and Ealdorman Godwine,[9] Ulfcytel from East Anglia, and Æthelweard, son of Ealdorman Æthelsige,[10] and all the chief men[11] of the nation of the English race.[12]

Then after this fight King Cnut turned inland with his raiding-army to Gloucestershire, where he learned that Edmund the king was. Then Ealdorman Eadric and the councillors who were gathered there advised that the kings form a pact between them, and the kings came together at Ola's Island near Deerhurst,[13] and became partners and pledged-brothers,[14] and affirmed both with pledge and also with oaths, and set the payment for the raiding-army; and afterwards they parted, and then King Edmund succeeded to Wessex and Cnut to the north part.

Then the raiding-army turned to the ships with what they had seized, and the inhabitants of London made a truce with the raiding-army and bought peace from them; and they brought their ships to London, and had winter-quarters there. Then, on *St Andrew's Day*,[15] King Edmund passed away,[16] and is buried with his grandfather Edgar in Glastonbury. [*continued on p. 154*]

---

[1] High ground between the Thames and the Crouch estuary in south-east Essex. Florence (I, p. 177) gives the etymology 'Ass's Hill', and the *Encomium Emmae* (pp. 24–5) 'Ash-tree Hill'.   [2] On 18 October, cf. Dickins, 'The day of Byrhtnoth's death and other obits', 20–21.   [3] The name of a group of people along the Welsh borders in Herefordshire and south Shropshire, see Pretty, 'Defining the Magonsæte', 171–83.   [4] MSS *gefeaht him*.   [5] 'or nation' interlined.   [6] Bishop of Dorchester.   [7] Abbot of Ramsey.   [8] Ealdorman of Hampshire.   [9] C says 'ealdorman in Lindsey'.   [10] D *Ælfwine*, but C correctly *Æþelwine*, i.e. Æthelwine of East Anglia; cf. Hart, 'Æthelstan 'Half-king' and his family', 117, 143.   [11] MS *duguð*, 'best part, flower', see p. 25, note 12.   [12] C 'were done for there'.

E 1016 *continued from opposite*

councillors who were there advised that the kings make a pact between them; and they granted hostages between them, and the kings came together at Ola's Island,[13] and there affirmed their friendship, both with pledge and with oath, and set the payment for the raiding-army; and with this pact they parted, and King Edmund succeeded to Wessex and Cnut to Mercia.

Then the raiding-army turned to the ships with the things they had seized, and the inhabitants of London made a truce with the raiding-army and bought peace from them; and the raiding-army brought their ships to London, and took winter-quarters for themselves in there.

Then, on *St Andrew's Day*,[15] Edmund the king passed away,[16] and is buried with his grandfather Edgar in Glastonbury. And that same year Wulfgar, abbot in Abingdon, passed away and Æthelsige[17] succeeded. [*continued on p. 155*]

THE CANTERBURY MANUSCRIPT (F) 1016 *continued from p. 150*

it at Ashingdon,[1] and there determinedly joined battle.[2] Then Ealdorman Eadric did as he often did before, first started the flight – with the Magonsæte[3] – and thus betrayed his royal lord and the whole nation. There Cnut had the victory and won himself[4] all England. There was killed Eadnoth,[6] and Abbot Wulfsige,[7] and Ealdorman Ælfric,[8] and Ulfcytel from East Anglia, and Æthelweard, son of Ealdorman Æthelsige,[10] and all the chief men[11] in the English race.[12]

Then after this fight King Cnut turned inland with his raiding-army to Gloucestershire, where he heard tell that Edmund the king was. Then Ealdorman Eadric and the councillors who were there advised that the kings make a pact between them; and they granted hostages between them, and the kings came together at Ola's Island,[13] and there affirmed their friendship, both with pledge and with oath, and set the payment for the raiding-army; and with this pact they parted, and King Edmund succeeded to Wessex and Cnut to Mercia.

Then, on *St Andrew's Day*,[15] Edmund the king passed away,[16] and is buried with his grandfather Edgar in Glastonbury. [*continued on p. 177*]

---

[13] F Lat *and held a conference at 'Ola's Island'*. Florence (I, p. 178) says that this was an island in the middle of the River Severn (and thus presumably a secure meeting-place) which both kings approached by fishing-boat. It is probably to be identified with the piece of land near Deerhurst now called 'Naight Brook', rather than with Alney seven miles away, see Smith, *The Place-Names of Gloucestershire*, II, p. 79; III, p. 161. A viking tradition, no doubt familiar to eleventh-century England, speaks commonly of the *hólm-ganga* ('island-going') as a locale for single combat. The *Encomium Emmae* (pp. 24–5) and William of Malmesbury (*Gesta Regum*, p. 217) say that Edmund proposed single combat with Cnut about this time; see generally Ashdown, 'The single combat in certain cycles of English and Scandinavian traditional romance', 113–30.   [14] See p. 29, note 16.   [15] 30 November.   [16] *in London* says Florence (I, p. 179).   [17] See Knowles, *The Heads of Religious Houses*, p. 24.

A *continued from p. 134*
1017. Here Cnut was chosen for king. [*continued on p. 156*]

THE WORCESTER MANUSCRIPT (D) *continued from p. 152*

1017. Here in this year King Cnut succeeded to the whole kingdom of England,[1] and divided it in four: Wessex for himself, and East Anglia for Thurkil, and Mercia for Eadric, and Northumbria for Eric. In this year also, Ealdorman Eadric was killed,[2] and Northman,[3] son of Ealdorman Leofwine, and Æthelweard, son of Æthelmær Stout,[4] and Beorhtric, son of Ælfheah in Devonshire. And King Cnut put to flight the ætheling Eadwig,[5] and Eadwig, 'the ceorls' king'.[6] And then before *1 August* the king ordered the widow of the former[7] king Æthelred, Richard's daughter, to be fetched to him as wife.

1018. In this year the tax was rendered over all England: that was in all seventy-two thousand pounds, without that which the townspeople in London paid: ten-and-a-half thousand pounds. And then some of the raiding-army travelled to Denmark, and 40 ships were left with the king Cnut. And at Oxford Danes and English were agreed on Edgar's law.[8]

1019 [1020]. Here King Cnut turned to Denmark with 9 ships, and dwelt there all winter. And here passed away Archbishop Ælfstan, who was named Lyfing; and he was a man firm in counsel both before God and before the world.

1020. Here King Cnut came back to England; and then at Easter there was a great assembly at Cirencester; then Ealdorman Æthelweard was outlawed. And in this year the king went to Ashingdon, and Earl Thurkil and Archbishop Wulfstan and other bishops and also abbots and many monks, and consecrated the minster at Ashingdon.[9] And in that same year on *13 November* Æthelnoth,[10] a monk who was *dean* at Christ Church,[11] was consecrated bishop for Christ Church.[12]

1021. Here in this year at Martinmas,[13] King Cnut outlawed Earl Thurkil;[14] and the charitable Bishop Ælfgar[15] passed away in the early morning[16] on Christmas Day.[17]

1022. Here King Cnut went out with his ships to the Isle of Wight. And Bishop Æthelnoth went to Rome, and was received there with great honour by the very reverend pope Benedict;[18] and he put the pallium on him with his own hands, and [*continued on p. 156*]

---

[1] Florence (I, p. 179) says that the English nobles, seeking favour themselves, falsely told Cnut that Edmund wanted Cnut to succeed him in order to act as guardian to his sons.   [2] 'in London, very justly', comments F bitterly. Florence (I, p. 182) says that Cnut ordered Eadric to be killed in the palace and his corpse thrown over the city wall and left unburied.   [3] Florence (loc. cit.) adds that his brother Leofric was made *dux* in his place.   [4] Ealdorman of the Western Provinces.   [5] C adds 'and had him killed'. The ætheling was son of King Æthelred.   [6] This curious appellation remains unexplained. His expulsion is placed by C under the year 1020. Florence (I, p. 181) attributes it to Eadric's advice and says that he was later reconciled with the king.   [7] MS *oðres*, 'other'.

E continued from p. 153

1017. Here in this year King Cnut succeeded to the whole kingdom of the English race,[1] and divided it in four: Wessex for himself, and East Anglia for Thurkil, and Mercia for Eadric, and Northumbria for Eric. And in this year also, Ealdorman Eadric was killed,[2] and Northman,[3] son of Ealdorman Leofwine, and Æthelweard, son of Æthelmær the Stout,[4] and Beorhtric, son of Ælfheah[19] in Devonshire. And King Cnut put to flight the ætheling Eadwig,[5] and Eadwig, 'the ceorls' king'.[6] And then before *1 August* the king ordered the widow of the former king Æthelred, Richard's daughter, to be fetched to him as queen.[20]

1018. In this year the tax was rendered over all England: that was in all 72 thousand pounds, without that which the townspeople in London paid: 11 thousand pounds. And then some of the raiding-army travelled to Denmark, and 40 ships were left with the king Cnut. And at Oxford Danes and English were agreed.[8] And here Abbot Æthelsige passed away in Abingdon, and Æthelwine succeeded.[21]

1019 [1020]. Here King Cnut turned to Denmark, and dwelt there all winter.

1020. Here King Cnut came to England; and then at Easter there was a great assembly in Cirencester; then Ealdorman Æthelweard was outlawed. And in this year the king went to Ashingdon;[9] and Archbishop Lyfing passed away; and in that same year Æthelnoth,[10] a monk and *dean* at Christ Church,[11] was there ordained as bishop.[12]

1021. Here in this year, at *Martinmas*,[13] King Cnut outlawed Earl Thurkil.[14]

1022. Here King Cnut went out with his ships to Wight. And Bishop Æthelnoth went to Rome, and was received there with great honour by the pope Benedict,[18] and [he] put his pallium on him with his own hands, and reverently [*continued on p. 157*]

---

[8] For the agreement on this occasion, which 'took place as soon as King Cnut with the advice of his councillors completely established peace and friendship between Danes and English', see Whitelock, 'Wulfstan and the laws of Cnut', 440; *Documents*, p. 452.   [9] F adds: 'and had a minster built there of stone and mortar for the souls of those men who had been slain there, and gave it to his own priest, whose name was Stigand'.   [10] Florence (I, p. 183) adds: *who was called 'the Good', son of the nobleman Æthelmær*. See generally Brooks, *The Early History of the Church of Canterbury*, pp. 255–78, 287–96.   [11] Canterbury.   [12] F 'by Archbishop Wulfstan'; F Lat *by Wulfstan, archbishop of York*.   [13] 11 November.   [14] *with his wife Edith* says Florence (I, p. 183).   [15] Bishop of Elmham.   [16] MS *uhtan*, sometimes used to refer to 'nocturns', the earliest service of the day.   [17] Florence (loc. cit.) adds that Ælfwine succeeded him.   [18] Pope Benedict VIII.   [19] E *Ælfgetes*, D *Ælfeges*, C correctly *Ælfehes*.   [20] F adds 'she was called Ælfgifu in English, and Emma in French'; see p. 134, note 2.   [21] See Knowles, *The Heads of Religious Houses*, p. 24.

A *continued from p. 154*
1031. Here Cnut came back to England. As soon as [*continued on p. 158*]

THE WORCESTER MANUSCRIPT (D) 1022 *continued from p. 154*

very reverently consecrated and blessed [him] as archbishop on 7 *October*, and therewith the archbishop straightway sang mass on that same day, and then thereafter honourably feasted with the pope himself; and also himself took the pallium on St Peter's altar, and afterwards happily travelled home to his country.

1023. Here, in St Paul's minster inside London, King Cnut granted full leave to Archbishop Æthelnoth and Bishop Beorhtwine,[1] and all God's servants who were with them, that they might take up the archbishop St Ælfheah from the burial-place; and they did so on 8 *June*. And the illustrious king, and the archbishop, and diocesan bishops, and earls, and very many, ordained and lay, conveyed his holy body by ship over Thames to Southwark, and there entrusted the holy martyr to the archbishop and his companions; and then with an honourable company and joyous pleasure they conveyed him to Rochester. Then on the third day came Emma the Lady with her royal child Harthacnut, and then with great pomp and rejoicing and hymns of praise they all conveyed the holy archbishop into Canterbury, and honourably thus brought [him] on 11 *June* into Christ Church. Again afterwards on the eighth day, on 15 *June*, Archbishop Æthelnoth, and Bishop Ælfsige,[2] and Bishop Beorhtwine, and all those who were with them, lodged St Ælfheah's holy body on the north side of Christ's altar to the praise of God, and to the honour of the holy archbishop, and to the eternal salvation of all those who daily seek out his holy body there with devout heart and with all humility. God Almighty have mercy on all Christian men through the intercessions of the holy St Ælfheah.

1026. Here Bishop Ælfric[3] went to Rome, and received the pallium from Pope John[4] on 12 *November*.

1028–30 [as E, with minor variants].

1031 [1027]. Here King Cnut went to Rome, and as soon as he came home [*continued on p. 159*]

[1] Bishop of Wells.   [2] Bishop of Winchester.   [3] Archbishop of York.   [4] Pope John XIX.   [5] Florence (I, pp. 183–4) says he died at York on 28 May but was carried to Ely and there buried.   [6] F adds 'Archbishop Æthelnoth consecrated him in Canterbury'. Florence (I, p. 184) gives Ælfric the surname Puttoc ('Kite', cf. the name of the bishop of London 'Sparrowhawk'). For Ælfric Puttoc see Cooper, *The Last Four Anglo-Saxon Archbishops of York*, pp. 14–18.   [7] Of Normandy.   [8] *to þam holme*; the primary sense of *holm* was 'wave, sea', but this meaning is borrowed from Old Norse *hólmr* 'an island, especially in a river or creek', and thus suitable for confrontation, oral (cf. p. 153, note 13) or physical (cf. annal 902 C).   [9] In Skåne, southern Sweden. On this battle, see Snorri Sturluson, *Olaf Sagas*, pp. 307–12.   [10] Sons of Thorgils Sprakaleg, see generally *Encomium Emmae*, ed. Campbell, pp. 82–7. Snorri Sturluson (loc. cit.) says that Jarl Ulf Sprakalegsson, protector of Denmark on behalf of Cnut, and frustrated at the king's absence in England, proposed to make Harthacnut king.   [11] On Cnut's return, says Snorri Sturluson (op. cit., pp. 305–6), Kings Olaf of Norway and Onund of Sweden raided Skåne, where Cnut confronted them.

E 1022 *continued from p. 155*
consecrated him as archbishop. And afterwards, with the pallium, he celebrated mass there as the pope directed him, and after that feasted with the pope; and afterwards with full blessing turned home. And Abbot Leofwine, who had been unjustly driven from Ely, was his companion; and there, as the pope instructed him, cleared himself of everything said against him, on witness of the archbishop and all the company that was with him.

1023. Here Archbishop Wulfstan passed away,[5] and Ælfric succeeded;[6] and the same year Archbishop Æthelnoth conveyed *the relics* of St Ælfheah, the archbishop, to Canterbury from London.

1024. *Here Richard the Second*[7] *died. Richard, his son, reigned about one year, and after him Robert, his brother, reigned 8 years.*

1025. Here King Cnut went to Denmark with ships to the battle-place[8] at the Holy River,[9] and Ulf and Eilaf[10] came against [him] and a very great raiding-army, both a land raiding-army and a ship raiding-army from the Swedish nation,[11] and there many men perished on King Cnut's side, both of Danish men and of English;[12] the Swedes had possession of the place of slaughter.

1028. Here King Cnut went from England to Norway with fifty ships,[13] and drove King Olaf from the land, and appropriated that land for himself.[14]

1029. Here King Cnut came back home to England.[15]

1030. Here King Olaf came back into Norway, and that people gathered against him and fought with him, and he was killed there.[16]

1031 [1027].[17] Here Cnut went to Rome; and in the same year he went to Scotland, and Malcolm, the king of Scots, submitted to him – and [*continued on p. 159*]

THE ABINGDON MANUSCRIPT (C) *continued on p. 159*

1023. Here King Cnut came back to England, and Thurkil and he were agreed. And he entrusted Denmark and his son to Thurkil to guard, and the king took Thurkil's son with him to England. And afterwards he had *the relics* of St Ælfheah conveyed from London to Canterbury.

1028. Here King Cnut went to Norway with 50 ships.

1030. Here King Olaf was killed in Norway by his own people and was afterwards canonized.[16] And before that this year, Hákon, the doughty jarl, perished at sea.[18] [*continued overleaf*]

[12] Many of Cnut's men died when overtaken by floodwaters from a deliberately burst dam, says Snorri (loc. cit.), or from an overloaded bridge, says Saxo (*Gesta Danorum*, X, 13).   [13] F 'ships of English thegns'; F Lat *of English noblemen*.   [14] See Snorri (op. cit.), pp. 323–8.   [15] Florence (I, pp. 184–5) adds that Cnut sent Jarl Hákon and his wife Gunnhild, daughter of Cnut's sister and Wyrtgeorn, king of the Wends, into exile under pretence of an embassy, for fear of being killed or deposed by the jarl.   [16] The battle of Stiklestad, near Trondheim Fiord, Norway (cf. Snorri, op. cit., p. 361ff.). For the reference in C to Olaf as a saint, see Dickins, 'The Cult of S. Olave in the British Isles', 53–80.   [17] Perhaps the chronicler knew that Cnut's journey followed a great battle, and placed it after Stiklestad 1030 instead of Holy River 1026.   [18] Florence (I, p. 185): *but some say he was killed in the island of Orkney.*

A 1031 *continued from p. 156*

he arrived in England, he gave into[1] Christ Church in Canterbury the harbour at Sandwich, and all the rights that arise there from either side of the harbour, so that whenever the tide is at its very highest and the very fullest, [and] a ship is floating as close to the land as it might closest be, and a man stands on that ship and has a 'tapor-axe'[2] in his hand . . .[3] [*continued on p. 160*]

THE ABINGDON MANUSCRIPT (C) *continued from p. 157*

1034. Here Bishop Æthelric,[4] departed, and he lies in Ramsey.

1035. Here King Cnut passed away on 12 *November* at Shaftesbury; and he was conveyed from there to Winchester and buried there. And the Lady Ælfgifu Emma[5] then settled inside there.[6] And Harold, who said that he was son of Cnut and the other Ælfgifu[7] – although it was not true[8] – he sent and had taken from her all the best treasures which King Cnut had, which she could not withhold; nevertheless she stayed on inside there as long as she could.

1036. Here Alfred, the blameless ætheling, son of King Æthelred, came in here,[9] and wanted to visit his mother who was staying in Winchester; but Earl Godwine would not allow him to – nor also would other men who wielded great power – because the murmur was very much in Harold's favour, although it was unjust.

[THE DEATH OF ALFRED][10]

But then Godwine stopped him, and set him in captivity,
and drove off his companions, and some variously killed;
some of them were sold for money, some cruelly destroyed,
some of them were fettered, some of them were blinded,
some maimed, some scalped.
No more horrible deed was done in this country
since the Danes came and made peace here.
Now we must trust to the dear God
that they who, without blame, were so wretchedly destroyed
rejoice happily with Christ. [*continued on p. 160*]

[1] An expression commonly found in making payment to a religious foundation, anticipating 'soul dues' for burial, cf. Swanton, *Prose*, p. 56. [2] A pleonastic Viking composite: Russo-English 'axe-axe'. [3] An attempt was made to erase the remainder of this charter (cf. Batley ed., *The Anglo-Saxon Chronicle: MS A*, pp. 81–2). Christ Church was to exercise rights as far inland as the axe could be thrown from the ship, see Swanton, *Prose*, pp. 202–4. [4] Bishop of Dorchester; C and E call him Æthelric and D, incorrectly, Ælfric. [5] The French name Imme is interlined, as though to make the distinction between queen and consort quite clear; cf. p. 134, note 2. [6] Her house there was remembered at the time of the Domesday survey, cf. Biddle, *Winchester in the Early Middle Ages*, pp. 46, 342. [7] This was Ælfgifu of Northampton, daughter of Ealdorman Ælfhelm and Wulfrun (see Table p. 295, and Campbell, 'Queen Emma and Ælfgifu of Northampton', 66–79). [8] Florence (I, p. 190) says that her sons Harold and Swein (reputedly the offspring of a shoemaker and a priest respectively) were thought by Cnut to be his. [9] Crossing from Boulogne, or perhaps Wissant (*Encomium Emmae*, pp. 42–3). [10] This part of the annal is written in alliterative verse, heavily imbued with internal rhyme: Dobbie, *Minor Poems*, pp. 24–5. [11] F 'And Robert, earl of Normandy, travelled to Jerusalem, and died there; William, who was afterwards king in England, succeeded to Normandy, although he was a child'. [12] The pro-Godwinist Peterborough chronicler omits the account of

E 1031 [1027] *continued from p. 157*
two other kings, Mælbeth and Iehmarc. *Count Robert died on a pilgrimage, and King William succeeded as a child.*[11]

1032. Here in this year appeared that wild-fire such as no man remembered before, and also it did damage everywhere in many places. In the same year Ælfsige, bishop in Winchester, passed away, and Ælfwine, the king's priest, succeeded to it.

1033. Here in this year Merehwit, bishop in Somerset, passed away, and he is buried in Glastonbury.

1034. Here Bishop Æthelric[4] passed away.

1036[12] [1035]. Here Cnut passed away at Shaftesbury, and he is buried in Winchester in the Old Minster. And he was king over all England for very nearly 20 years. And soon after his passing, there was a meeting of all the councillors at Oxford, and Earl Leofric and almost all the thegns north of the Thames, and the men of the fleet[13] in London, chose Harold as regent[14] of all England, for himself and his brother Harthacnut who was in Denmark. And Earl Godwine and all the foremost men in Wessex opposed it[15] [*continued on p. 161*]

then he went to Scotland; and the king of Scots surrendered to him[16] and became his man, but he only held to that for a little while.

1033. Here Bishop Leofsige passed away,[17] and his body rests in Worcester; and Beorhtheah was raised to his seat.

1034. Here Bishop Ælfric[4] passed away, and he lies in Ramsey; and the same year passed away Malcolm, king in Scotland.

1035. Here King Cnut passed away, and his son Harold succeeded to the kingdom. He departed at Shaftesbury on 12 *November*, and he was conveyed to Winchester, and there buried. And Ælfgifu, the Lady, settled inside there.[6] And Harold said that he was son of Cnut and the Northampton Ælfgifu[7] – although it was not true.[8] He sent and had taken from her all the best treasures which King Cnut possessed; nevertheless she stayed on inside there as long as she could.

1036. Here Alfred, the blameless ætheling, son of King Æthelred, came in here,[9] and wanted to visit his mother who was staying in Winchester; but those who wielded great power in this land would not allow that – because the murmur was very much for Harold, although it was unjust. Then he[18] had him set in captivity, and he also drove off his companions, and some . . .[19] [*continued on p. 161*]

Godwine's ill-treatment of Alfred Ætheling and his followers found *s.a.* 1036 in C and D. [13] *þa liðsmen.* Presumably the men of the fleet played as significant a political role as the Kronstadt sailors in 1917 St Petersburg. [14] *to healdes.* Florence (I, pp. 190–91) says *he began to reign as if the legitimate heir – not however as powerfully as Cnut, because the more rightful heir, Harthacnut, was expected. Hence after a short time the kingdom of England was divided by lot, and the north part fell to Harold, the south to Harthacnut.* [15] *lagon ongean.* [16] *eode him on hand*; cf. the hand-clasp as a sign of comittment to a bargain or promise *s.a.* 1064 E, 1065 D (pp. 192–3). [17] Bishop of Worcester; *of the Hwicce* says Florence (I, p. 189), adding that he died at an episcopal manor at Kempsey on 19 August. [18] i.e. Godwine. [19] D continues with the poem as in C, but with small variations.

A *continued from p. 158*

1040. Here Archbishop Eadsige went to Rome, and King Harold passed away. [*continued on p. 162*]

THE ABINGDON MANUSCRIPT (C) 1036 *continued from p. 158*

> The ætheling still lived; he was threatened with every evil;
> until it was decided that he be led
> to Ely town, fettered thus.
> As soon as he came on ship he was blinded,
> and blind thus brought to the monks.
> And there he dwelt as long as he lived.
> Afterwards he was buried, as well befitted him,
> full honourably, as he was entitled,
> at the west end, very near at hand to the steeple,
> in the south side-chapel. His soul is with *Christ*.[1]

1037. Here Harold was everywhere chosen as king, and Harthacnut forsaken because he was too long in Denmark; and his mother, Queen Ælfgifu, was driven out without any mercy to face the raging winter; and she then came beyond the sea to Bruges, and there Earl Baldwin[2] received her well, and kept her there as long as she had need. And earlier this year Æfic, the noble *dean* in Evesham, departed.

1038. Here the good Archbishop Æthelnoth departed, and Æthelric, bishop in Sussex, and Ælfric, bishop in East Anglia, and on 20 *December* Beorhtheah, bishop in Worcestershire.

1039. Here came the great gale; and Bishop Beorhtmær died in Lichfield.[3] And the Welsh killed Eadwine, brother of Earl Leofric, and Thurkil and Ælfgeat,[4] and very many other good men with them. And here also Harthacnut came to Bruges, where his mother was.

1040. Here King Harold died. Then they sent to Bruges for Harthacnut – it was supposed that they did well – and then before midsummer he came here with 60 ships,[5] and then started a very severe tax that was endured with difficulty: that was 8 marks a rowlock;[6] and all who had hankered for him before, were then disloyal to him. And also he never accomplished [*continued on p. 162*]

---

[1] Alfred's obit was celebrated at Ely on 5 Feburary (Dickins, 'The day of Byrhtnoth's death and other obits', 18–19). Florence (I, pp. 191–2) says the massacre took place at Guildford and 600 men were killed, adding that Alfred's brother Edward came to England with him, but was sent back by his mother when she heard of Alfred's fate; cf. *Encomium Emmae*, pp. 48–9.   [2] Baldwin V, count of Flanders.   [3] Florence (I, p. 193) *and Wulfsige* (Wlsius) *succeeded him*.   [4] Florence (loc. cit.) *son of Eadsige*.   [5] Florence (I, p. 194) *and manned them with Danish troops*.   [6] C *æt ha*, D *æt hamelan*; i.e. for every rower; Florence (I, p. 194) adds *and twelve to each steersman*. The entry in E makes it clear that this represented payment for the crews. See generally Lawson, 'The collection of Danegeld and Heregeld', 737–8.

E 1036 [1035] *continued from p. 159*

just as long as they could, but they could not contrive anything against it.[7] And then it was decided that Ælfgifu, Harthacnut's mother, should settle in Winchester[8] with the king her son's housecarls,[9] and hold all Wessex in hand for him; and Earl Godwine was their most loyal man. Some men said of Harold that he was son of King Cnut and Ælfgifu, daughter of Ealdorman Ælfhelm, but to many men it seemed quite unbelievable;[10] nevertheless he was full king[11] over all England.

1037. Here Ælfgifu, King Cnut's widow, was driven out; she was King Harthacnut's mother.[12] And she sought refuge of Baldwin[2] by the south sea,[13] and he gave her a dwelling in Bruges, and he protected and kept her[14] for as long as she was there.

1038. Here, on *1 November*, Archbishop Æthelnoth passed away, and shortly afterwards Æthelric, bishop in Sussex, and then before Christmas Beorhtheah, bishop in Worcestershire, and quickly afterwards Ælfric, bishop in East Anglia. And then Bishop Eadsige[15] succeeded to the archbishopric, and Grimcytel to that in Sussex, and Bishop Lyfing to Worcestershire and to Gloucestershire.

1039 [1040].[16] Here King Harold passed away in Oxford[17] on *17 March*, and he was buried at Westminster; and he ruled England for 4 years and 16 weeks.[18] And in his days 16 ships were paid at 8 marks each rowlock, just was earlier done in King Cnut's days. And in this same year King Harthacnut came to Sandwich, 7 days before midsummer,[19] and he was immediately received by both English and by Danes, though afterwards his advocates severely paid for it when it was decided that [his] 62 ships be paid at 8 marks each rowlock.[6] And in this same year the sester[20] of wheat went to 55 pence and even further.

1040 [1041]. Here the raider-money was paid: that was 21 thousand [*continued on p. 163*]

THE WORCESTER MANUSCRIPT (D) [*continued from p. 159*]

1038. Here the good archbishop Æthelnoth passed away, and Æthelric, bishop in Sussex, who desired of God that he should not let him to live any time after his dear father Æthelnoth; and within seven days he also departed – and Beorhtheah, bishop in Worcester, on *20 December*. [*continued on p. 163*]

---

[7] F 'Earl Godwine and all the best men in Wessex opposed it, but they did not succeed'. [8] See p. 158, note 6. [9] *Huscarl* is borrowed from Old Norse *húskarl* (literally 'house-man'), high-ranking bodyguards or household troops; see generally Larson, *The King's Household*, pp. 152–71. [10] See p. 158, note 7. [11] See p. 144, note 2. [12] F 'Cnut's widow, and Edward's mother and Harthacnut's'. [13] i.e. the Channel; F 'in Flanders'. [14] F 'and kept her honourably'. [15] F 'the king's priest'. [16] E failed to leave annal 1039 blank, and remains a year in arrears until 1044 when, by repeating the number 1043, it falls two years in arrears. [17] Florence (I, p. 193) puts Harold's death in London. [18] This dating, if accurate, would reckon Harold's succession from a fortnight after Cnut's death on 12 November 1035. [19] i.e. 17 June. [20] On the capacity of the sester see Harmer, *Documents*, pp. 79–80.

A *continued from p. 160*
> 1042. Here King Harthacnut passed away.
> 1043. Here Edward was consecrated as king. [*continued on p. 170*]

THE ABINGDON MANUSCRIPT (C) 1040 *continued from p. 160*

anything kingly for as long as he ruled. He had the dead Harold dragged up and flung into a fen.[1]

1041. Here Harthacnut had all Worcestershire raided on account of his two housecarls[2] who were collecting the formidable tax when that people killed them within the market-town, inside the minster. And soon in that year came from beyond the sea Edward, his brother on the mother's side – King Æthelred's son, who had been driven from his country many years earlier, and yet was sworn in as king;[3] and then he dwelled thus in his brother's court as long as he lived. And also in this year Harthacnut betrayed Earl Eadwulf[4] under his safe-conduct – and then he was a pledge-breaker.

1042. Here Harthacnut died as he stood at his drink, and he suddenly fell to the earth with an awful convulsion; and those who were close by took hold of him, and he spoke no word afterwards, and he passed away on *8 June*. And all the people then received Edward as king,[5] as was his natural right.

1043. Here Edward was consecrated as king in Winchester on the first day of Easter with great honour: and Easter was then on *3 April*. Archbishop Eadsige[6] consecrated him, and fully instructed him before all the people, and fully admonished him as to his own need and that of the people.[7] And Stigand the priest was blessed as bishop for East Anglia. And quickly afterwards the king had brought into his hands[8] all the lands which his mother owned, and took from her all she owned in gold and in silver and in untold things, because earlier she had kept it from him too firmly.[9] And quickly after, Stigand was put out of his bishopric and all that he owned was taken into the king's hands, because he was his mother's closest advisor and because she did just as he advised her – so men supposed.

1044. Here Archbishop Eadsige left that bishopric because of his infirmity [*continued on p. 164*]

[1] Florence (I, p. 194) says that the king sent to London dignitaries including Ælfric, archbishop of York, Earl Godwine, Stir the major domo, Eadric his steward and Thrond his torturer, with orders that Harold's body be disinterred, then thrown into a fen and afterwards into the Thames; and that it was recovered by a fisherman and buried honourably by the Danes in their cemetery in London. [2] Florence (I, pp. 195–6) names them as Feader and Thurstan, and says they were killed on 4 May when hiding in an upper room of a tower in the monastery at Worcester. [3] Harthacnut asked Edward to come and hold the kingdom with him, according to the *Encomium Emmae* (pp. 52–3). Harthacnut died a few months later. [4] Earl of Northumbria, in revolt against Harthacnut and killed by Siward of York, see Kapelle, *The Norman Conquest of the North*, pp. 24–6. [5] D 'chose Edward and received him as king'. Florence (I, pp. 196–7) adds *chiefly by the exertions of Earl Godwine and Lyfing, bishop of Worcester*. [6] Of Canterbury; Florence (I, p. 197) adds: *and Ælfric of York*. [7] F 'his own need, and to the welfare of all the people'; F Lat *with regard to his honour and the benefit of people subject to him*. [8] MSS *let geridan ealle þa land ... him to handa*. [9] The Translation of St Mildred (Hardy, *Catalogue of Materials*, I, pp. 380–81) suggests that she had promised her treasure to Magnus, king of Norway, if he were to invade the country. [10] *Wealland* (i.e. *wealh-land*),

E 1040 [1041] *continued from p. 161*
and 99 pounds; and then 11 thousand and 48 pounds was paid to 32 ships.
And in this same year Edward, King Æthelred's son, came here to this land
from a foreign country.[10] He was the brother of King Harthacnut; they were
both sons of Ælfgifu, who was the daughter of Earl Richard.[11]

1041 [1042]. Here King Harthacnut passed away at Lambeth[12] on *8 June*;
and he was king over all England for two years, all but 10 days;[13] and he is
buried in the Old Minster in Winchester with King Cnut, his father. And
before he was buried, all the people chose Edward as king in London – may he
hold it as long as God grants him! And all that year was a very heavy time in
many and various ways: both in bad weather and crops of the earth; and
during this year more cattle died than anyone remembered before, both
through various diseases and through bad weather. In this same time passed
away Ælfsige, abbot of Peterborough, and Earnwig the monk was chosen as
abbot because he was a very good man and very sincere.

1042 [1043]. Here Edward was consecrated as king in Winchester on
Easter Day with great honour: and Easter was then on *3 April*. Archbishop
Eadsige[6] consecrated him, and fully instructed him before all the people, and
fully admonished him as to his own need and that of the people.[7] And Stigand
the priest was blessed as bishop for East Anglia. And quickly afterwards the
king had brought into his hands[8] all the lands which his mother owned, and
took from her all she owned in gold and in silver and in untold things, because
earlier she had kept it from him too firmly.[9]

1043 [1044]. Here Archbishop Eadsige left that bishopric because of his
infirmity [*continued overleaf*]

THE WORCESTER MANUSCRIPT (D) *continued from p. 161*

1041. [As C, but adding:] And here [1042] Æthelric was ordained bishop
at[14] York on *11 January*.
1042. [As C, with minor variants, and see note 5.]
1043. Here Edward was consecrated as king at Winchester on the first day
of Easter. And that year, 14 days before St Andrew's Day,[15] the king was so
counselled that he – and Earl Leofric and Earl Godwine and Earl Siward and
their band – rode from Gloucester to Winchester, on the Lady by surprise, and
robbed her of all the treasures which she owned, which were untold, because
earlier she was very hard on the king her son, in that she did less for him than
he wanted before he became king, and also afterwards;[9] and they let her stay
there inside afterwards. [*continued on p. 165*]

here specifically France; cf. Old Norse *Valland*, Cleasby and Vigfusson, *Icelandic Dictionary, sv*,
possibly borrowed from English. See also Magoun, 'The Domitian Bilingual', 378.   [11] Richard
I, duke of Normandy.   [12] A royal manor across the River Thames from Westminster; it may
already have belonged to his half-sister Countess Goda (DB, *Surrey*, 15, 1). Florence (I, p. 196) says
he collapsed there while celebrating the wedding of Gytha, daughter of Osgod Clapa, to the Dane
Tofi the Proud.   [13] F adds: 'and he lies at Winchester in Old Minster; and for his soul's sake his
mother gave into New Minster the head of St Valentine, the martyr'. F Lat, however, reads: *gave
the head of St Valentine to the same church* (i.e. Old Minster).   [14] MS *to*, the sense of which is
normally 'for' in this context; but Æthelric was made bishop of Durham, presumably *at*
York.   [15] i.e. mid-November, since St Andrew's Day is 30 November.

E 1043 [1044] *continued from previous page*
and blessed Siward, abbot of Abingdon, as bishop to it[1] by leave and counsel
of the king and Earl Godwine. Otherwise it was known to few men before it
was done because the archbishop thought that, if more men knew about it,
şome other man whom he trusted and favoured less would ask or buy it. And
in this [year] was a very great famine over the land of the English, and corn as
dear as anyone remembered before, so that the [*continued opposite*]

THE ABINGDON MANUSCRIPT (C) 1044 *continued from p. 162*

and blessed Siward, abbot of Abingdon, as bishop to it[1] by leave and counsel
of the king and Earl Godwine. Otherwise it was known to few men before it
was done because the archbishop thought that, if more men knew about it,
some other man whom he trusted and favoured less would ask or buy it. And
in this year was a very great famine over all the land of the English, and corn as
dear as any man remembered before, so that the sester of wheat went to 60
pence and even further. And the same year the king went out to Sandwich with
35 ships; and Athelstan, the sacristan, succeeded to the abbacy at Abingdon.
And in the same year [1045] King Edward took Edith, the daughter of Earl
Godwine, as his wife 10 days before Candlemas.[2]

1045. Here in this year Bishop Beorhtwold passed away on 22 *April*, and
King Edward gave his priest Hereman that bishopric.[3] And in the same
summer King Edward went out with his ships to Sandwich; and there was
gathered so great a raiding-army that no-one had ever seen a greater raiding
ship-army in this land. And in this same year [1046] Bishop Lyfing passed
away on 20 *March*, and the king gave his priest Leofric that bishopric.[4]

1046. Here Earl Swein[5] went into Wales, and Gruffydd, the northern
king,[6] together with him, and he was granted hostages. Then, when he was
on his way home, he commanded the abbess in Leominster[7] to be fetched to
him, and kept her as long as it suited him, and afterwards let her travel home.
And in this same year Osgod Clapa[8] was outlawed before midwinter. And
after Candlemas[9] in this same year [1047] came the severe winter with frost
and with snow and with all bad weather, such that there was no man alive
who could remember so severe a winter as that was, both through the
mortality of men and mortality of cattle; both birds and fish perished through
the great cold and hunger.

1047. Here in this year Bishop Grimcytel passed away: he was [*continued
on p. 166*]

---

[1] Not as archbishop of Canterbury, but bishop of St Martin's (cf. p. 191, note 12) and suffragan to
Eadsige.   [2] i.e. on 23 January.   [3] i.e. Ramsey and Sherborne both; he later removed the
joint see to Old Sarum. Hereman was a Lotharingian whom Edward had brought with him on his
return, see Barlow, *The Life of King Edward*, pp. xlvii-xlviii.   [4] The bishopric of Devon and
Cornwall, with its seat at Crediton, transferred to Exeter in 1050. Another Lotharingian, and the
king's chancellor, Leofric is perhaps best known as donor of The Exeter Book of Old English
poetry to Exeter Cathedral, see generally Barlow, *Leofric of Exeter*, pp. 1-16.   [5] Swein, the
eldest son of Earl Godwine, had been given an earldom bordering on South Wales, in
1043.   [6] Gruffydd ap Llewelyn, king of Gwynedd and Powys; joining in an attack on South
Wales.   [7] Named by Florence (I, pp. 201-2) as Eadgyfu.   [8] For Osgod Clapa (Old Norse
klápr, 'coarse, rough') the Staller, see generally Nightingale, 'The origin of the Court of
Hustings', 564-6; and for the office of 'staller', Larson, *The King's Household*,

E 1043 [1044] *continued from opposite page*
sester of wheat went to 60 pence and even further. And the same year the king went out to Sandwich with 35 ships; and Athelstan, the sacristan, succeeded to the abbacy at Abingdon; and Stigand succeeded to his bishopric.[10]

1043 [1045]. Here King Edward took the daughter of Earl Godwine as his queen. And in this same year passed away Bishop Beorhtwold; and he held the bishopric[11] for 38 years,[12] and the king's priest Hereman succeeded to the bishopric.[3] And in this year, at Christmas on St Stephen's Day,[13] Wulfric was consecrated as abbot of St Augustine's[14] by leave of the king and Abbot Ælfstan – because of his great infirmity.

1044 [1046]. Here passed away Lyfing, bishop in Devonshire, and Leofric, who was the king's priest, succeeded to it.[4] In this same year, on *5 July*, Abbot Ælfstan passed away at St Augustine's. And in this same year Osgod Clapa[8] was put to flight.

1045 [1047]. Here Grimcytel, bishop in Sussex, passed away, and the king's priest Heca succeeded to it. And in this year passed away [*continued overleaf*]

THE WORCESTER MANUSCRIPT (D) *continued from p. 163*

1045 [1044]. Here, on *25 July*, died Ælfweard, bishop in London. He was abbot in Evesham first, and had much advanced that monastery while he was there; then turned to Ramsey,[15] and there gave up his life. And Manni was chosen as abbot and ordained on *10 August*. And the same year the noble woman Gunnhild, King Cnut's relative,[16] was driven out, and afterwards she stayed at Bruges for a long time, and afterwards went to Denmark.

1046 [1045]. Here died Beorhtwold, bishop in Wiltshire, and Hereman was set in his seat. In that year King Edward gathered a great ship-army in Sandwich because of the threat of Magnus in Norway, but his and Swein's war[17] in Denmark prevented his coming here.

1047 [1046]. Here, on *23 March*, the eloquent Bishop Lyfing[18] passed away; and he had three bishoprics: one in Devonshire, and in Cornwall and in Worcester. Then Leofric succeeded to Devonshire and to Cornwall,[4] and Bishop Aldred[19] to Worcester. And here Osgod the staller[8] was outlawed, and Magnus won Denmark.

1048 [1047]. Here was the severe winter, and in that year passed away Ælfwine, [*continued on p. 167*]

---

pp. 146–52.   [9] 2 February.   [10] Of East Anglia; he was promptly deprived, cf. annal 1043 C.   [11] Of Ramsbury.   [12] F 'that was the bishopric of Sherborne'.   [13] F 'the second day of Christmas'.   [14] Canterbury; for Wulfric's radical changes to the monastic buildings there, see Taylor, *Architecture*, I, pp. 137, 141–2.   [15] The monks at Evesham turned away their former abbot who now had leprosy (*Chronicon Abbatiae Rameseiensis*, pp. 157–8).   [16] See p. 157, note 15. According to Florence (I, p. 199) she married Jarls Hákon and Harald, and her sons Hemming and Thurkil were exiled with her.   [17] Magnus' war with Swein Estrithson, king of Denmark and nephew of Cnut.   [18] Cf. Barlow, *The English Church 1000–1066*, pp. 73–4 *et passim*.   [19] Florence (I, p. 199) says Aldred was first a monk at Winchester and then abbot at Tavistock.

E 1045 [1047] *continued from previous page*
Ælfwine, bishop in Winchester, on 29 *August*, and Stigand, bishop in the north,[1] succeeded to it. And in the same year Earl Swein[2] travelled out to Baldwin's land[3] to Bruges, and lived there all winter, and then towards summer went out.[4]

1046 [1047]. *Battle at Val-ès-Dunes*.[5] Here [1048] passed away Athelstan, abbot in Abingdon, and Sparrowhawk, a monk from Bury St Edmund's, succeeded. And in this same year Bishop Siward[6] passed away, and Archbishop Eadsige again succeeded to all the bishopric. And in this same year Lothen and Yrling came to Sandwich with 25 ships, and there took untold war-booty, in men and in gold and in silver, such that no-one knew what it all was. And then [they] turned around Thanet, and wanted to do the same there, but the local people resolutely withstood and kept them both from landing and from water, and completely put them to flight from there. And they turned from there to Essex, and raided there and took men and whatever they could find, and then turned [*continued opposite*]

THE ABINGDON MANUSCRIPT (C) 1047 *continued from p. 164*

bishop in Sussex; and he lies in Christ Church in Canterbury; and King Edward gave that bishopric to Heca, his priest. And in this same year, on 29 *August*, passed away Bishop Ælfwine, and King Edward gave Bishop Stigand that bishopric.[7] And Athelstan, abbot in Abingdon, passed away in the same year [1048] on 29 *March*; Easter Day was then on 3 *April*. And there was a very great pestilence among men over all England in this same year.

1048. Here in this year was a great earth-tremor widely in England. And in the same year Sandwich and Wight were raided, and the best men that were there were killed; and King Edward and the earls went out after them in their ships. And in the same year Bishop Siward resigned the bishopric because of his infirmity, and went to Abingdon,[8] and Archbishop Eadsige again succeeded to the bishopric; and within 8 weeks of this he [Siward] passed away on 23 *October*.

1049. Here in this year the emperor[9] gathered a countless army against Baldwin of Bruges, because he had broken down the palace at Nijmegen, and also caused him many other offences. The army which he had gathered was untold; there was: Leo, the pope from Rome,[10] and numerous famous men from many nations. He also sent to King Edward, and asked him for support with ships so that he would not allow his[11] escape by water. And then he [Edward] went to Sandwich, and lay there with a great raiding ship-army until the emperor had all that he wanted from Baldwin. [*continued on p. 168*]

---

[1] This might suggest a southern standpoint; Stigand was in fact bishop of Elmham, East Anglia; but see p. 170, note 9.   [2] Son of Godwine.   [3] i.e. Flanders, currently ruled by Count Baldwin V.   [4] i.e. out to sea again.   [5] dép. Calvados, western Normandy, where William crushed a rebellion (Le Patourel, *Norman Empire*, p. 284).   [6] Suffragan bishop at Canterbury, see p. 164, note 1.   [7] i.e. of Winchester.   [8] i.e. St Mary's Abbey, where he had been abbot.

E 1046 [1048] *continued from opposite page*
east to Baldwin's land, and sold there what they had looted, and afterwards travelled east from where they came earlier.

1046[12] [1049]. Here in this year was the great synod at Rheims; there was there: the pope Leo, and the archbishop of Burgundy, and the archbishop of Besançon, and the archbishop of Trèves, and the archbishop of Rheims, and many men thereto, both ordained and lay. And King Edward sent there Bishop Duduc[13] and Wulfric, abbot of St Augustine's, and Abbot Ælfwine,[14] that they should report to the king what was decided there for Christendom. And in this same year King Edward travelled [*continued overleaf*]

THE WORCESTER MANUSCRIPT (D) 1048 [1047] *continued from p. 165*

bishop in Winchester, and Bishop Stigand was raised to his seat. And before that, in the same year, Grimcytel, bishop in Sussex, passed away, and Heca, the priest, succeeded to the bishopric. And also Swein[15] sent here, [and] asked for help against Magnus, the king of Norway, that 50 ships should be sent to his assistance; but it seemed unwise to everybody, and then it was hindered because Magnus had a great power in ships.[16] And he then expelled Swein, and with a great slaughter of men won that land, and the Danes paid him much money and accepted him as king; and Magnus passed away the same year.[17]

1049 [1048]. Here Swein[15] came back to Denmark; and Harald,[18] the paternal uncle of Magnus, went to Norway after Magnus was dead, and the Norwegians accepted him; and he sent here to this land about peace. And also Swein sent from Denmark, and asked King Edward for support with ships that would be at least 50 ships, but all the people opposed it. And here also, on 1 May, was an earth-tremor in many places: in Worcester, and in Droitwich, and in Derby and elsewhere. And there was also a very great pestilence among men and pestilence among cattle; and also the wild-fire in Derbyshire and elsewhere did great damage.

1050 [1049]. In this year the emperor[9] gathered a countless army against Baldwin of Bruges, because he had broken down the palace at Nijmegen, and also caused him many other offences. The army which he had gathered was countless; there was: the pope himself[10] and the patriarch and numerous other famous men from every nation.[19] He also sent to King Edward, and asked him for support with ships so that he would not allow his[11] escape by water. And then he [Edward] went to Sandwich, and there lay with a great raiding ship-army until the emperor had all that he wanted from Baldwin. [*continued on p. 169*]

---

[9] Henry III.   [10] Leo IX. The name is interlined in C.   [11] i.e. Baldwin's escape; Bruges was surrounded by water at this date, see Map p. 282.   [12] The year number is repeated by mistake.   [13] Bishop of Wells.   [14] Abbot of Ramsey.   [15] Swein Estrithson, king of Denmark, Cnut's nephew, see above, *s.a.* 1046 D.   [16] Florence (I, p. 200) says that Earl Godwine was in favour of sending ships, but Earl Leofric and all the people were against helping.   [17] On 25 October 1047.   [18] Harald Hardrada (i.e. 'the Ruthless').   [19] Florence (I, p. 201) says that Swein Estrithson, king of the Danes, was also there at the emperor's bidding, with his fleet, *and swore fealty for that occasion to the emperor*.

E 1046 [1049] *continued from previous page*
out to Sandwich with a great raiding ship-army. And Earl Swein[1] came into Bosham with 7 ships and made peace with the king, and he was promised that he would be entitled to all those things which he formerly possessed. Then Earl Harold,[2] his brother, and Earl Beorn[3] objected that he should not be entitled to any of the things which the king had granted them; but he was set 4 days safe-conduct back to his ships.[4] Then during that, it happened that word came to the king that hostile ships lay to the west and were raiding. Then Earl Godwine turned around west with 2 of the king's ships (Harold commanded[5] the one and Tostig his brother,[6] the other) and 42 ships of local men.[7] Then Earl Beorn[8] took over the king's ship which Earl Harold earlier commanded; then they turned west to Pevensey and lay there weather-bound. Then within 2 days Earl Swein came there and spoke with his father and with Earl Beorn, and asked Beorn that he should go with him to Sandwich, [*continued opposite*]

THE ABINGDON MANUSCRIPT (C) 1049 *continued from p. 166*

There Earl Swein[1] came back again to King Edward, and begged him for land so that he could maintain himself on it; but Harold his brother, and Earl Beorn opposed it, in that they did not want to give him back anything of what the king had given to them. He came here with guile, said that he wanted to be his [the king's] man, and asked Earl Beorn that he should be of help to him, but the king refused him everything. Then Swein turned to Bosham to his ships, and Earl Godwine went from Sandwich with 42 ships to Pevensey, and Earl Beorn along with him. Then the king allowed all the Mercians[9] to go home, and they did so. Then when the king was informed that Osgod lay in Wulpe[10] with 29 ships, the king sent after the ships he could send for, which lay within the North Mouth.[11] But Osgod set his wife in Bruges, and turned back again with 6 ships, and the others went to Eadulf's Ness in Essex[12] and did harm there and turned back to the ships. Earl Godwine and Earl Beorn then lay at Pevensey with their ships. Then Earl Swein came with treachery and asked Earl Beorn that he should be his companion to Sandwich to the king – said that he wanted to swear him oaths and be loyal to him. Then, because of their kinship, Beorn imagined that he would not betray him, then took 3 companions with him, and then rode (just as if they were to go to Sandwich) to Bosham,[13] where Swein's ships lay. And he was immediately bound and led on ship, and then conveyed to Dartmouth, and there killed and buried deep. But Harold, his relative, fetched him from there and led [him] to Winchester, and there buried [him] with King Cnut, his uncle. [*continued on p. 171*]

---

[1] Son of Godwine.   [2] Harold Godwinson, later to be Harold II, last Anglo-Saxon king of England.   [3] Swein's cousin, who held an earldom among the Middle Angles (cf. Freeman, *Norman Conquest*, I, pp. 555–60).   [4] F Lat *such that if after a three-day period he were found in England, he should be put in custody*.   [5] Literally 'steered'.   [6] For whom in general see Kapelle, *The Norman Conquest of the North*, pp. 86–104.   [7] *landes manna*.

E 1046 [1049] *continued from opposite page*
to the king, and help him to the king's friendship, and he agreed to this. They
then turned as though they meant to go to the king; then as they rode, Swein
asked him that he should travel with him to his ships – told how his sailors
would turn from him unless he came there very quickly. Then they both turned
to where his ships lay. Then when they came there, Earl Swein asked him that
he should go on ship with him. He firmly refused for long until his sailors
seized him and threw him into the boat, and bound him and rowed to the ship
and put him thereon, hoisted their sail and ran west to Axmouth; and kept him
with them until they killed him, and took the body and buried it in a certain
church.[14] And then his friends and men of the fleet came from London and
took him up, and conveyed him to Winchester to [*continued on p. 171*]

THE WORCESTER MANUSCRIPT (D) 1050 [1049] *continued from p. 167*

There also came Earl Swein,[1] who earlier went from this land to Denmark[15]
and there ruined himself with the Danes. He came here with guile, said that he
would again submit to the king, and Earl Beorn promised him that he would
be of help to him. Then after there was the pact between the emperor and
Baldwin, many ships went home, and the king remained behind at Sandwich
with a few ships, and Earl Godwine also went with 42 ships from Sandwich to
Pevensey, and Earl Beorn went with him. Then the king was informed that
Osgod lay in Wulpe[10] with 39 ships, and the king then sent after those ships he
could send for, which turned home earlier. And Osgod set his wife in Bruges,
and turned back again with 6 ships, and the others went to Eadulf's Ness in
Sussex[12] and did harm there and turned back to the ships. And then a strong
wind came upon them so that they were all lost, except four[16] which were
destroyed beyond the sea. While Earl Godwine and Earl Beorn lay in
Pevensey, then Earl Swein came with treachery, asked Earl Beorn, who was
his uncle's son,[17] that he should be his companion to Sandwich to the king, and
improve his relations with him. Then because of their kinship he [Beorn] went
with him, with three companions; and he led him then towards Bosham where
his ships lay, and then he was bound and led on ship, [and] then turned from
there with him to Dartmouth [*continued overleaf*]

[8] MS Harold, *recte* Beorn.   [9] i.e. the Mercian contingent in the fleet.   [10] An island north
of Bruges, see Map p. 282.   [11] The mouth of the Wantsum Channel in East Kent, see Map
p. 273.   [12] The Naze, on the Essex coast. D *on Suð Sexe*, C correctly *on East Seaxon*.
[13] This meant going fifty miles back along the coast in the opposite direction from Sandwich.
Perhaps it was intended to skirt around the Weald, then to Sandwich via Canterbury along the
Pilgrims Way route.   [14] F Lat *a little church*.   [15] Florence (I, pp. 201–2) says that this was
because he was not able to marry Abbess Eadgyfu whom he had abducted (see annal 1046 C);
perhaps he had been outlawed, since this was a criminal offence (cf. p. 92, note 8). Florence says
that he now returned with eight ships.   [16] Florence (I, p. 202): *except two, which were captured
overseas and all in them were killed*.   [17] See note 3.

A *continued from p. 162*

1050. Here Archbishop Eadsige passed away, and Robert succeeded to the archbishopric. [*continued on p. 182*]

THE WORCESTER MANUSCRIPT (D) 1050 [1049] *continued from previous page*

and ordered him to be killed there and buried deep. He was found again and conveyed to Winchester and interred with King Cnut, his uncle. A little before that,[1] the men from Hastings city[2] and thereabout captured with their ships two of his ships and killed all the men, and brought the ships to Sandwich to the king. He[3] had eight ships before he betrayed Beorn; afterwards all abandoned him except two.[4]

In the same year[5] 36 ships came from Ireland up the Welsh Usk, and did harm thereabout, with the help of Gruffydd, the Welsh king.[6] People were gathered against them; there was also Bishop Aldred with them, but they had too little help,[7] and they came on them by suprise in the very early morning and killed many good men there, and the others escaped along with the bishop. This was done on *29 July*.

This year Oswy, abbot in Thorney, passed away in Oxfordshire, and Wulfnoth, abbot in Westminster. And Ulf, the priest,[8] was set as pastor of the bishopric which Eadnoth had,[9] but he was afterwards driven out because he accomplished nothing bishoply in it, such that it shames us to tell more now. And Bishop Siward, who lies in Abingdon, departed.

And here the great minster at Rheims was consecrated. The pope Leo was there, and the emperor; and there had a great synod about God's service. *Pope St Leo* chaired[10] the synod. It is difficult to know which bishops came there, and abbots even; and from this land two were sent: from St Augustine's and from Ramsey.

1051 [1050]. In this year Eadsige, archbishop in Canterbury, departed, and the king granted that arch-authority to Robert the Frenchman who was earlier bishop in London. And Sparrowhawk, abbot of Abingdon, succeeded to the bishopric in London, and it was taken back from him[11] before he was ordained. And Bishop Hereman and Bishop Aldred went to Rome. [*continued on p. 173*]

---

[1] *A little after that* says Florence (I, p. 203).   [2] *ceastre*, a curious word to use of Hastings which was never more than a small town, but D is a Midland version.   [3] i.e. Swein.
[4] Florence (I, pp. 202–3) says that Swein fled to Flanders with his two ships and stayed there until Aldred, bishop of Worcester, brought him back and made peace with the king.   [5] In the month of August, says Florence (I, p. 203).   [6] Gruffydd ap Rhydderch. Florence (I, p. 203) says they crossed the Wye and burned *Dymedham* (possibly Tidenham, a valuable manor belonging to Bath Abbey, cf. Swanton, *Prose*, pp. 16–19), slaying all whom they found there.   [7] Florence (I, p. 203) says that the Welsh who were there had secretly sent asking help from Gruffydd.   [8] Florence (I, p. 203) says Ulf was *the king's chaplain, born a Norman*.   [9] F Lat *bishop for the North Saxons*. The see of Dorchester-on-Thames at this time extended as far as the Humber (see Map p. 277). Cf. the term 'bishop in the north' used of Elmham s.a. 1046 E.   [10] MS *foresæt*. Florence (I, p. 204) says the synod was held over six days.   [11] Florence (I, p. 204) says: *ejected by King Edward*.

E 1046 [1049] *continued from p. 169*
the Old Minster, and he is buried there with King Cnut, his uncle. And Swein then turned east to Baldwin's land, and stayed there all winter in Bruges under his complete protection.[4]

And in the same year passed away Eadnoth, bishop in the north,[9] and Ulf was set as bishop.

1047 [1050]. Here in this year was a great meeting in London at mid-Lent,[12] and 9 of the fleet-men's ships were dismissed[13] and five were left behind.

And in this same year Jarl Swein came into England.

And in this same year was the great synod in Rome, and King Edward sent there Bishop Hereman and Bishop Aldred, and they came there on Easter Eve.[14] And the pope had a synod again in Vercelli; and Bishop Ulf came to that, and if he had not given very costly gifts they were well near to breaking his staff[15] because he did not know how to do his duties as well as he should. And in this year Archbishop Eadsige passed away on 29 *October*.

1048 [1051]. Here in this year in spring King Edward set Robert,[16] in London, as archbishop for Canterbury; and the same spring he went to Rome for his pallium, and the king [*continued overleaf*]

THE ABINGDON MANUSCRIPT (C) 1049 *continued from p. 168*

And the king and all the raiding-army then declared Swein to be a 'nithing'.[17] He had 8 ships before he murdered Beorn; afterwards all abandoned him except 2. And then he turned to Bruges, and lived there with Baldwin.[4]

And in this year passed away Eadnoth, the good bishop in Oxfordshire,[9] and Oswy, abbot in Thorney, and Wulfnoth, abbot in Westminster. And King Edward gave that bishopric to Ulf, his priest, and bestowed it badly.

And in this same year [1050] King Edward ended the contract[13] of 9 ships, and they went away with ships and everything; and 5 of the ships were left behind, and the king promised them 12 months' pay.

And in the same year Bishop Hereman and Bishop Aldred travelled to Rome to the pope, on a mission for the king.[18]

1050. Here in this year the bishops came home from Rome, and Earl Swein was reinstated. And on 29 *October* in this same year, Archbishop Eadsige passed away, and also on 22 *January* in this same year [1051] Ælfric, archbishop in York, and his body lies in Peterborough. Then at mid-Lent [1051] King Edward had a council-meeting in London, and set Robert[16] as archbishop for Canterbury and Abbot Sparrowhawk bishop for London, and gave Bishop Rudolph,[19] his relative, [*continued overleaf*]

---

[12] C *midlencten*, mid-Lent; E *midfestene*, 'middle of the fast'.   [13] E *sette ut*, C 1049 *scylode* . . . *of male*, C 1050 (p. 172) *sette* . . . *of male*; cf. the Old Norse expression *skilja áf mal*.   [14] F Lat *Holy Saturday*.   [15] i.e. his pastoral staff, or crosier, of office.   [16] F Lat *who was abbot of Jumièges*.   [17] A Scandinavian legal term of abuse, cf. Keyser and Munch, *Norges Gamle Love*, II, p. 472.   [18] The twelfth-century Aelred of Rievaulx says that this was to ask the pope to release Edward from a vow to go on pilgrimage (*Vita Edwardi*, 749–52).   [19] Formerly bishop of Nidaros, Norway.

E 1048 [1051] *continued from previous page*
gave Sparrowhawk, abbot of Abingdon that bishopric in London; and the king gave Bishop Rudolf, his relative, that abbacy. Then the archbishop came from Rome one day before the eve of St Peter's Day, and occupied his archbishop's seat[1] at Christ Church on St Peter's Day,[2] and immediately turned to the king. Then Abbot Sparrowhawk came to him on the way with the king's writ and seal[3] to the effect that he would ordain him as bishop for London. Then the archbishop refused and said that the pope had forbidden it him. Then the abbot turned back to the archbishop again about it, and begged for this ordination as bishop, and the archbishop resolutely kept it from him, and said that the pope had forbidden it him. Then the abbot turned to London, and all that summer and that autumn occupied the bishopric which the king had earlier granted him with his full consent.

And then Eustace[4] came from beyond the sea[5] soon after the bishop, and turned to the king and spoke with him about what he wanted, and then turned homeward. When he came east to Canterbury, he and his men had a meal there and turned to Dover. Then when he was some miles or more this side of Dover, he put on his mailcoat, and all his companions, and went to Dover. Then when they came there they wanted to take quarters where they themselves liked; then one of his men came and wanted to lodge at the home of a certain householder against his will, and wounded the householder, and the householder killed the other.[6] Then Eustace got up on his horse, and [*continued opposite*]

THE ABINGDON MANUSCRIPT (C) 1050 *continued from previous page*

that abbacy in Abingdon. And in this same year he laid off[7] all his fleet-men.

1051. Here in this year Archbishop Robert came across the sea here with his pallium; and in this same year Earl Godwine and all his sons were put to flight from England, and he turned to Bruges, and his wife and his three sons: Swein and Tostig and Gyrth. And Harold and Leofwine turned to Ireland, and lived there for the winter. And in this same year [1052] on *14 March*[8] passed away the Old Lady,[9] mother of King Edward and Harthacnut, called Emma.[10] And her body lies in the Old Minster with King Cnut. [*continued on p. 178*]

---

[1] F Lat *enthroned in his archiepiscopal cathedra.*   [2] 29 June.   [3] For the sealing of writs from Edward the Confessor, see Harmer, *Writs*, pp. 92–105.   [4] For Eustace 'aux Grenons' (i.e. 'with moustaches'), count of Boulogne, see generally Andressohn, *The Ancestry and Life of Godfrey of Bouillon.*   [5] William of Malmesbury (p. 241) says *crossing from Wissant to Dover* (the narrowest crossing).   [6] F 'he wounded the householder, and the householder killed the man'; Florence (I, p. 205) *his soldiers . . . killed one of the citizens; one of his fellow-citizens, seeing this, avenged him by killing one soldier.*   [7] See p. 171, note 13.   [8] C *ii ides* perhaps in mistake for *ii nones* as D (p. 176).   [9] Perhaps in the sense of 'dowager', see p. 134, note 1.   [10] The name is written over an erasure.

E 1048 [1051] *continued from opposite page*
his companions upon theirs, and travelled to the householder and killed him upon his own hearth, and then turned up towards the town and both inside and outside killed more than 20 men; and the townsmen killed 19 men on the other side and wounded they knew not how many.[11] And Eustace escaped with a few men, and turned back to the king and gave a one-sided account of how they had fared;[12] and the king became very angry with the townsmen; and the king sent for Earl Godwine and ordered him to go into Kent with hostility to Dover, because Eustace had informed the king that it must be more the townsmen's fault than his; but it was not so. And the earl would not agree to the incursion because it was abhorrent to him to injure his own province.[13]

Then the king sent for all his council, and ordered them to come to Gloucester around the second Festival of *St Mary*.[14] The foreigners[15] had then built a castle in Herefordshire, [*continued overleaf*]

THE WORCESTER MANUSCRIPT *continued from p. 170*

1052 [1051]. Here Ælfric, archbishop in York,[16] passed away, a very reverend man and wise. And in the same year King Edward abolished that raider-tax which King Æthelred had earlier established; that was in the thirty-ninth[17] year since he had begun it. That tax oppressed the whole English nation for as long a period as it is here written above; it always came before[18] other taxes which were variously paid, and oppressed men in manifold ways.

In the same year Eustace, who had King Edward's sister as wife,[19] came in at Dover.[20] His men then travelled looking for quarters foolishly, and killed a certain man from the market-town; and another man from the market-town [killed] their companions, so that there lay dead 7 of his [*continued on p. 175*]

---

[11] Ordericus (II, pp. 204–7) tells how in 1067 the Kentishmen, in revolt against the Conqueror, would ask this same Eustace to cross from Boulogne and take Dover by surprise. The expedition was a disaster, and Eustace himself only escaped by the speed of his horse, his knowledge of the path and a ship ready to weigh anchor. [12] F 'told the king it was worse than it was'. [13] MS *folgað*. F Lat *ordered Godwine count of Kent to gather an army and invade Kent, despoiling all of it and especially Dover; but Godwine, not wishing to destroy his province, concealed his anger*. [14] The Nativity of St Mary, 8 September. [15] i.e. the French, specified in 1052 D (p. 175). [16] Florence (I, p. 204) adds that he died in Southwell and was buried at Peterborough, and was succeeded by Kynsige. [17] MS *þam nigon and þrittigoðan*; Florence (I, p. 204) *the thirty-eighth*. [18] i.e. took precedence over. [19] He had married Edward the Confessor's sister Goda (Godgifu), widow of Dreux, count of the French Vexin. [20] Florence (I, p. 204) says it was *in the month of September*.

E 1048 [1051] *continued from previous page*
in Earl Swein's province,[1] and inflicted every injury and insult they could upon the king's men thereabouts. Then Earl Godwine, Earl Swein, and Earl Harold came together at Beverstone,[2] and many men with them, to the end that they should travel to their royal lord and the whole council which was gathered with him, so that they have the king's advice and his help, and of all the council, as to how they might avenge the insult to the king and the whole nation. Then the foreign men[3] got to the king first,[4] and accused the earls so that they could not come into his sight,[5] because they said that they wanted to come there for treachery to the king. Earl Siward and Earl Leofric and many people with them from the north had come there to the king, and Earl Godwine and his sons were informed that the king and the men who were with him would take measures against them; and they firmly arrayed themselves in opposition, though it was abhorrent to them that they must stand against their royal lord. Then the council advised both sides that they should leave off all wrong-doing; and the king gave the peace of God[6] and his complete friendship to both sides.

Then the king and his council decided[7] that there should be another full council-meeting in London at the autumn equinox,[8] and the king ordered a raiding-army to be called out, both south and north of the Thames, quite the best that ever was. Then Earl Swein was declared an outlaw, and Earl Godwine and Earl Harold were summoned to the meeting as quickly as they could make it. Then when they came out there they were summoned to the meeting. Then he [Godwine] asked for safe-conduct and hostages that he might come into the meeting and go out of the meeting without treachery. Then the king asked for all those thegns that the earls formerly had, and they resigned them all into his hands.[9] Then the king sent again to them and ordered them that they [*continued opposite*]

---

[1] The Norman colony established in Herefordshire under Earl Ralph 'the Timid'.   [2] Beverstone (E) three miles away from Longtree (D), and formerly in Longtree hundred, was perhaps the formal meeting-place of the hundred.   [3] MS *þa wælisce men*; F Lat *the Normans*.   [4] MS *tæt foran* corrected to *æt foran*; F *æror* 'earlier'.   [5] MS *eagon gesihðe*, 'eye-sight'; F 'near the king'; F Lat *the king banned them from his presence*.   [6] F 'the king gave the earls his complete friendship'.   [7] F 'Then the king ordered'.   [8] 24 September.   [9] Either the earl's followers were merely placed under the king's protection or formally transferred their allegiance to him (cf. annal 921 A, p. 103).   [10] Florence (I, p. 205) says *The earl and his men . . . killed many men and women with their weapons and trampled babies and children under their horses' feet. But when they saw the citizens coming out to oppose them, they began to flee in a cowardly manner: seven of them were killed.*   [11] Florence (I, p. 205) specifies, Godwine's consisting of Kent, Sussex and Wessex; Swein's of Oxfordshire, Gloucestershire, Herefordshire, Somerset and Berkshire; and Harold's of Essex, East Anglia, Huntingdonshire and Cambridgeshire.   [12] Perhaps in Herefordshire, but Florence (I, pp. 205–6) says the castle in question was on Dover cliff, held by Normans and men of Boulogne. He adds that the king was at first alarmed, but refused to comply when he found that the army of Earls Leofric, Siward and Ralph was approaching.   [13] i.e. the Nativity, 8 September; Florence (loc. cit.) says it was *after* this festival.   [14] Ralph 'the Timid', son of King Edward's sister Goda by her first marriage (cf. p. 173, note 19).

E 1048 [1051] *continued from opposite page*
come with 12 men into the king's council. Then the earl again asked for safe-conduct and hostages, so that he might clear himself of each of the things with which he was charged. Then he was refused the [*continued overleaf*]

THE WORCESTER MANUSCRIPT (D) 1052 [1051] *continued from p. 173*

companions; and great harm was done there on either side with horse and also with weapons,[10] until the people gathered, and then they fled away until they came to Gloucester to the king, and he granted them safe-conduct. Then Earl Godwine was very indignant that such things should happen in his earldom, then began to gather people over all his earldom, and Earl Swein, his son, over his, and Harold, his second son, over his earldom;[11] and they all gathered in Gloucestershire at Longtree,[2] a great and countless army all ready for war against the king unless Eustace and his men were given into their hands – and also the French who were in the castle.[12] This was done 7 days before the later Feast of *St Mary*.[13] King Edward was then staying in Gloucester, then sent for Earl Leofric and north for Earl Siward and asked for their troops; and they came to him at first with moderate support, but after they knew how it was there in the south, then they sent north over all their earldoms and had a great army called out for the support of their lord, and Earl Ralph[14] also over his earldom; and then all came to Gloucestershire to the king's assistance, though it was late. Then all were so resolutely with the king that they were willing to attack Godwine's army if the king wanted that. Then some of them considered it would be very unwise if they joined battle, because there was in those two companies most of the finest that was in England, and considered they would be leaving the land open to our enemies, and great ruin among ourselves. Then they advised that hostages be exchanged, and a summons issued to London, and the people ordered out there over all this northern part,[15] in Siward's earldom, and in Leofric's, and also elsewhere; and Earl Godwine and his sons were to come there to make their counter-plea. Then they came to Southwark,[16] and with them a great multitude from Wessex, but his troop dwindled more and more as time went on. And all the thegns that were his son Earl Harold's were bound over to the king; then his other son, Earl Swein, was outlawed. Then it did not suit him to come to make a counter-plea against the king and against the raiding-army that was with him. Then he went away by night, and the following morning the king had a council-meeting and with all the raiding-army declared him outlaw – him and all his sons. And he turned south to Thorney,[17] and his wife and Swein his son, and Tostig and his wife, a relative of Baldwin at Bruges,[18] and his son Gyrth. And Earl Harold and Leofwine went to Bristol on the ship which Earl Swein [*continued overleaf*]

[15] Florence (I, p. 206) says that, having exchanged hostages, Godwine went to Wessex while Edward assembled a larger army from all Mercia and Northumbria, and took it with him to London.   [16] The south side of London Bridge.   [17] Thorney Island, in Chichester Harbour, Sussex, where, says Florence (I, p. 206), a ship was ready for them, which they rapidly loaded with as much gold and silver and other treasures as it could carry.   [18] Florence (loc. cit.) names her as Baldwin's daughter Judith.

E 1048 [1051] *continued from previous page*
hostages, and he was granted 5 days' protection to travel out of the country.[1]
And then Earl Godwine and Earl Swein turned to Bosham, and pushed out
their ships and turned beyond the sea and sought the protection of Baldwin,
and lived there all winter. And Earl Harold turned west to Ireland, and was
there all winter under the king's protection.[2] And then soon after this
happened the king abandoned the Lady who was consecrated his queen,[3] and
had taken from her all that she owned, in land and in gold and in silver and in
everything, and committed her[4] to his sister at Wherwell.[5]

And Abbot Sparrowhawk was then driven out of the bishopric [*continued
opposite*]

THE WORCESTER MANUSCRIPT (D) 1052 [1051] *continued from previous page*

had got ready for himself earlier and provisioned. And the king sent Aldred,
bishop of London, with a force; and they were to ride in front of him before he
came to ship; but they could not, or they would not. And he then turned out
from the mouth of the Avon[6] and met such severe weather that he got away
[only] with difficulty, and many of them perished there.[7] Then when the
weather came to him, he turned out to Ireland; and Godwine and those who
were with him turned from Thorney to Bruges, to Baldwin's land, in one ship
with as much treasure as they could stow away there for each man. It would
have seemed remarkable to everyone who was in England, if anyone earlier
told them that it should turn out thus, because he was formerly so very much
raised up, as if he ruled the king and all England; and his sons were earls and
the king's favourites;[8] and his daughter was married and espoused to the
king – then she was brought to Wherwell[5] and they committed her to the
abbess.

Then soon Earl[9] William came from beyond the sea with a great troop of
French men, and the king received him and as many of his companions as
suited him, and let him go again.[10] This same year William the priest was
granted the bishopric in London which was earlier granted to Sparrowhawk.

1052.[11] Here on *6 March* passed away the Lady Ælfgifu, widow of King
Æthelred and King Cnut.[12]

In the same year Gruffydd, the Welsh king,[13] raided in Herefordshire, so
that he came very near to Leominster; and men gathered against him, both
local men and French men from the castle. And there were killed very many
good men of the English, and also from among the French. That was the same
day on which Edwin was killed with his companions, thirteen years before.
[*continued on p. 179*]

---

[1] F 'and he was ordered out within five days, and he went across the sea to Baldwins's
land'. [2] Diarmaid mac Mael na m-Bo, king of Leinster and Dublin (*The Life of King Edward*,
p. 25). [3] Edith, daughter of Earl Godwine. [4] Florence (I, p. 207) says: *repudiating her
because of his anger against her father* (Godwine) *and sending her without honour, with one
female attendant on foot* (pedissequa). [5] A nunnery in Hampshire, VCH, *Hampshire*, II,
p. 132. [6] Into the Bristol Channel, Somerset. [7] Or perhaps 'and he suffered great losses
there'. [8] *dyrlingas*.

E 1048 [1051] *continued from opposite page*
in London, and William, the king's priest, was ordained to it.[14] And then
Odda was set as earl over Devonshire, and over Somerset, and over Dorset,
and over Cornwall; and there was set into the hand of Ælfgar, Earl Leofric's
son, the earldom which Harold earlier owned.[15]

1052.[16] Here in this year passed away Ælfgifu Emma, mother of King
Edward and of King Harthacnut. And in the same year the king and his
council decided that ships should be despatched out to Sandwich, and set Earl
Ralph[17] and Earl Odda as commanders[18] thereto. Then Earl Godwine turned
out from Bruges with his ships to the Yser, and set out the day before the Feast
of midsummer eve[19] so that he came to Ness which is to the south of
Romney.[20] This then came to the knowledge of the earls out at Sandwich, and
they turned out after the other ships, and a land-army was ordered out against
the ships. Then meanwhile Earl Godwine was warned and he then made his
way into Pevensey; and the weather became so very severe that the earls could
not find out what had happened to Earl Godwine. And then Earl Godwine
turned out again until he came back to Bruges; and the other ships made their
way back again to Sandwich. And then it was decided that these ships should
turn back again to London, and that other earls and other oarsmen[21] should
be set for the ships. Then it was delayed so long that the ship-campaign was
wholly abandoned and they all made their way home. Then Earl Godwine
learnt that and then hoisted sail – he and his fleet – and then made their way
west, [*continued overleaf*]

THE CANTERBURY MANUSCRIPT (F) *continued from p. 153*

1051. Here passed away Ælfgifu Emma, the mother of King Edward. And
Earl Godwine travelled out from Bruges with his ships to the Yser, and so to
England, and came up at Ness to the south of Romney,[20] and travelled thus to
Wight, and there seized all the ships which could be of value, [*continued on
p. 179*]

---

[9] Continental titles such as duke and count are not used in the Chronicle.   [10] This visit is
mentioned only in D; whether or not it actually took place is a moot point, cf. Douglas, 'Edward
the Confessor, Duke William of Normandy, and the English succession', 526–45; Oleson,
'Edward the Confessor's promise of the throne to Duke William of Normandy', 221–8.   [11] D
repeats the number 1052 and so restores the chronology.   [12] Florence (I, p. 207) adds that she
died at Winchester and was buried there.   [13] Gruffydd ap Llewelyn, king of Gwynedd and
Powys.   [14] F Lat *by Archbishop Robert*. Godwine being out of the country, Robert of
Jumièges took the opportunity of refusing the Anglo-Danish Sparrowhawk in favour of his fellow-
Norman. The two fled on Godwine's return in 1052 (q.v., p. 182).   [15] i.e. East
Anglia.   [16] E omits 1049, 1050, 1051 and so restores the chronology.   [17] Ralph 'the
Timid', see p. 174, note 14.   [18] *heafodmannum*, 'head-men'.   [19] *midsumeres mæsse
æfene*, 23 June; the use of the word *mæss* suggests this is a by-name for the Feast of the Nativity of
St John the Baptist, which coincides with midsummer's day, 24 June.   [20] i.e. Dungeness, the
southernmost point of Kent.   [21] *hasæton*, Old Norse *há seti* 'one who sits by a rowlock'.

E 1052 *continued from previous page*
direct to Wight, and went up there and raided so long that the local people paid as much as they charged them; and then made their way westward until they came to Portland, and went up there and did whatsoever harm they could.[1]

Harold was then coming out of Ireland with nine ships, and then came up at Porlock; and there many people gathered to oppose him, but he did not hesitate to provide himself with food, went inland, and there killed a great part of the people and seized for himself whatever came his way in cattle, and in men, and in property; and then made his way eastward to his father, and both made their way eastward until they came to Wight, and there seized what was left behind earlier, and then made their way from there to Pevensey, and caught up along with them as many of the ships there as were fit, and [*continued opposite*]

THE ABINGDON MANUSCRIPT (C) *continued from p. 172*

1052. Here Earl Harold[2] came from Ireland with ships into the mouth of the Severn near the borders of Somerset and Devonshire, and raided there a lot; and the local people, both from Somerset and from Devonshire, gathered to oppose him, and he put them to flight and killed there more than 30 good thegns besides other people, and immediately after this went around Penwith Tail.[3] And then King Edward had 40 cutters[4] embarked which lay at Sandwich for many weeks. They were to waylay Earl Godwine, who was in Bruges that winter; however, he came here to the country first before they knew about it,[5] and during the time he was here in the land he enticed to him all the Kentish and all the boatmen from Hastings[6] and everywhere there along the sea-coast, and all the east part, and Sussex and Surrey[7] and much else in addition. Then they all declared that they would live and die[8] with him. Then when the fleet which lay in Sandwich learnt about Godwine's expedition, they set out after him, and he escaped them and defended himself wherever he could, and that fleet turned back to Sandwich and so homeward to London town. Then when Godwine learnt that the fleet which lay at Sandwich had turned home, then he went back to Wight, and lay thereabouts along the sea-coast until they came together – his son, Earl Harold, and he. And they did no great harm after they came together, except that they seized provisions; but they enticed to them all the local people along the sea-coast and also up inland. And they went towards Sandwich, and kept on collecting to them all the boatmen that they met, and then came to Sandwich with a streaming raiding-army. When King Edward learnt that, [*continued on p. 180*]

---

[1] Perhaps because the island of Portland was a prime royal estate – held by Edward the Confessor and William the Conqueror in turn (DB, *Dorset*, 1.1).   [2] Florence (I, p. 208) adds: *and his brother Leofwine*.   [3] i.e. Land's End, Cornwall.   [4] *snacca*, Old Norse *snekkja*, a fast longship (Cleasby and Vigfusson, *Icelandic Dictionary*, p. 574).   [5] Florence (I, p. 208): *with a few ships*.   [6] i.e. the district around Hastings, cf. annal 1011 E.   [7] C 'all the east part and Sussex and Surrey'; D 'all Essex and Surrey'.   [8] *licgan and lybban*, literally 'lie and live', cf. p. 92, note 7.

E 1052 continued from opposite page

thus on until he came to Ness,[9] and caught up all the ships that were in Romney and in Hythe and in Folkestone; and turned then east to Dover and went up there, and seized as many ships and hostages there as they wanted, and so travelled to Sandwich, and did exactly the same; and everywhere they were given hostages and provisions wherever they asked. And then they made their way to the North Mouth,[10] and so towards London. And some of the ships [*continued overleaf*]

THE WORCESTER MANUSCRIPT (D) 1052 *continued from p. 176*

And soon Earl Harold[2] came from Ireland with his ships to the mouth of the Severn near the borders of Somerset and Devonshire, and raided there a lot; and the local people, both from Somerset and from Devonshire, gathered to oppose him, and he put them to flight and killed there more than 30 good thegns besides other people, and immediately after this went around Penwith Tail.[3] And then King Edward had 40 cutters[4] embarked which lay at Sandwich. They were to look out for Earl Godwine, who was in Bruges that winter; however, he came here to the country first before they knew about it,[5] and while he was here in the land he enticed to him all the Kentish and all the boatmen from Hastings[6] and everywhere around along the sea-coast, and all Essex and Surrey[7] and much else in addition. Then they all declared that they would live and die[8] with him. Then when the fleet which lay in Sandwich learnt about Godwine's expedition, they set out after him, and he escaped them, and that fleet turned back to Sandwich and so homeward to London town. Then when Godwine learnt that the fleet which lay at Sandwich had turned home, then he went back to Wight, and lay thereabouts along the sea-coast until they came together – his son, Earl Harold [and he]. And they did no great harm after, except that they seized provisions; but they enticed to them all the local people along the sea-coast and also up inland. And they went towards Sandwich, and kept on collecting to them all the boatmen that they met, and then came to Sandwich with a streaming raiding-army. Then when Edward learnt that, he sent [*continued on p. 181*]

THE CANTERBURY MANUSCRIPT (F) 1051 *continued from p. 177*

and hostages, and so turned himself eastward. And Harold had come up at Porlock with 9 ships, and there killed many of the people, and seized cattle and men and property; and made his way eastward to his father, and they both travelled to Romney, to Hythe, to Folkestone, to Dover, to Sandwich, and kept on seizing all those ships they found which could be of value, and hostages – travelled just so, and turned [*continued on p. 181*]

---

[9] See p. 177, note 20.　　[10] Of the Wantsum Channel in east Kent, and thus into the Thames estuary, see Map p. 273.

E 1052 *continued from previous page*
turned into Sheppey and did great harm there, and made their way to the
king's Middle-town[1] and burnt it all down, and took their way towards
London after the earls. When they came to London the king and the earls all
lay against them with 50 ships. Then the earls sent to the king and asked him
that they might be entitled to[2] all the things which had unjustly been taken
from them. However the king objected some while, so long that the people
who were with the earl became very stirred up against the king and against his
people, so that the earl himself with difficulty calmed that people. Then
Bishop Stigand travelled [*continued opposite*]

THE ABINGDON MANUSCRIPT (C) 1052 *continued from p. 178*

then he sent up for more help, but they came very late, and Godwine kept
moving towards London with his fleet, so that he came to Southwark, and
there waited for a while until the tide came up. In that time he also settled with
the town inhabitants so that they wanted almost all that he wanted.[3] Then
when he had arranged his passage, the tide came and then they immediately
pulled up their anchors and held on through the bridge[4] along the south bank;
and the land-army came down and arrayed themselves along the shore.
And then they veered with the ships towards the north bank as if they wanted
to circle around the king's ships. The king also had a great land-army on his
side in addition to his shipmen, but it was abhorrent to almost all of them that
they should fight against men of their own race, because there was little else[5] of
any great value except English men on either side; and also they did not want
that this country should be the more greatly laid open to foreign nations,
should they themselves destroy each other. It was decided then that wise men
should be sent between them and arrange peace on either side;[6] and Godwine
landed, and Harold his son, and as many of their fleet as they thought, and
then there was a meeting of the council; and Godwine was clean granted his
earldom as fully and as completely as he ever owned it,[7] and his sons[8] all just
what they earlier owned, and his wife and his daughter as fully and as
completely as they earlier owned; and they affirmed complete friendship
between them, and promised good law for all the people; and then outlawed
all the French men who earlier [*continued on p. 182*]

---

[1] Milton Regis, opposite Sheppey, close to the ancient Roman road from East Kent to London;
here lay the 'water-fort' of annal 892/3. [2] For the formulaic expression 'worthy of' see
Harmer, *Writs*, pp. 64, 444. [3] Florence (I, p. 209) says that he had previously enticed them
with various promises. [4] Florence (I, p. 209) says: *meeting no opposition at the bridge*. The
bridge was presumably fortified during Alfred's 'occupation' of 886; Southwark (the southern
bridge-head) is mentioned in the Burghal Hidage (Swanton, *Prose*, p. 14), although there is a
curious lack of archaeological evidence for this (cf. Horsman, *Saxo-Norman London*, III,
p. 135). [5] i.e. no men of any significance. [6] Florence (I, p. 209): *They ordered the army to
put aside their arms.* [7] For this formula see Harmer, *Writs*, p. 63. [8] *except Swein*, says
Florence (I, pp. 209–10), who puts here the information given by C below about Swein's
pilgrimage from Flanders to Jerusalem, adding that he went barefoot in penance for his murder of
Beorn, and died in Lycia from illness through the extreme cold. [9] The word 'castle' is
introduced from Norman-French. Osbern Pentecost's castle at Ewyas Harold, Herefordshire,
was restored (*refirmaverat*) after the Conquest (DB, *Herefordshire*, 19.1); see

E 1052 *continued from opposite*
there, with God's help, and the wise men both inside the town and outside, and advised that hostages should be fixed on either side, and so it was done. When Archbishop Robert and the French men learnt that, they seized their horses, and some turned west to Pentecost's castle,[9] some north to Robert's castle, and Archbishop Robert and Bishop Ulf and their companions turned out at East Gate,[10] and killed and otherwise injured many young men, and made their way direct to Eadulf's Ness,[11] and there he [Robert] got [*continued on p. 183*]

THE WORCESTER MANUSCRIPT (D) 1052 *continued from p. 179*

up for more support, but they came very late, and Godwine kept moving towards London with his fleet, so that he came to Southwark, and there waited for a while until the tide came up. In that time, and also earlier,[3] he settled with the town inhabitants so that they wanted almost all that he wanted. Then when he had arranged his passage, then the tide came and they immediately pulled up their anchors and held on through the bridge[4] keeping along the south bank; and and the land-army came down and arrayed themselves along the shore. And then they veered with the ships as if they wanted to circle around the king's ships. The king also had a great land-army on his side in addition to his shipmen, but it was abhorrent to almost all to fight against men of their own race, because there was little else[5] of any great value except English on either side; and also they did not want that this country should be the more greatly laid open to foreign men, should they themselves destroy each other. It was decided then that wise men should be sent between them and arrange peace on either side;[6] and Godwine landed, and Harold, and as many of their fleet as they thought, and then there was a council-meeting; and Godwine was clean granted his earldom as fully and as completely as he ever owned it,[7] and all his sons[8] all what they earlier owned, and his wife and his daughter as fully and as completely as they owned; and they affirmed complete friendship between them, and promised complete law for all the people; and then outlawed all the French men who earlier [*continued overleaf*]

THE CANTERBURY MANUSCRIPT (F) 1051 *continued from p. 179*

then to London. Then when they came to London the king and his earls all lay against them with 50 ships. Then the earls sent to the king and asked from him that they might be entitled to[2] all the property and estate which had unjustly been taken from them. Then the king objected some while, but Stigand, who was the king's advisor and chaplain,[12] and the other wise men . . .[13] advised that hostages be fixed on either side, and that thus the friendship should be confirmed. Then when Archbishop Robert learnt that, he seized his horse and he travelled to Eadulf's Ness,[10] and there got on an unsteady [*continued on p. 183*]

---

generally Stenton, *Anglo-Saxon England*, p. 554, note; Higham and Barker, *Timber Castles*, pp. 43–5.   [10] Of London, in the direction of Essex.   [11] The Naze, on the Essex coast.   [12] *þes cinges rædgifa and his handprest.*   [13] An erasure of perhaps five and two graphs.

A *continued from p. 170*

1053. Here Earl Godwine passed away. [*continued on p. 194*]

THE ABINGDON MANUSCRIPT (C) 1052 *continued from p. 180*

promoted illegality and passed unjust judgments and counselled bad counsel in this country, except for as many as they decided that the king liked to have about him, who were faithful to him and all his people.[1] And Bishop Robert and Bishop William and Bishop Ulf escaped with difficulty with the French men who were with them, and thus came away across the sea.[2] And Earl Godwine and Harold and the queen retained their estate.[3] Swein had earlier gone from Bruges to Jerusalem, and died while on his way home at Constantinople on Michaelmas Day.[4] It was on the Monday after the Feast of *St Mary*[6] that Godwine came to Southwark with his ships, and the next morning on the Tuesday they became reconciled, as it stands above. Then soon after he landed Godwine was taken ill, and afterwards recovered but he made all too little reparation for God's property which he had from many holy places. In the same year came the strong wind on the eve of the Feast of St Thomas[7] and did great harm everywhere.[8] Also Rhys, brother of the Welsh king, was killed.[9]

1053. In this year the king was in Winchester at Easter, and with him Earl Godwine, and Earl Harold, his son, and Tostig. Then when on the second day of Easter he sat at dinner with the king, he suddenly sank down against the footstool, deprived of speech and of all his strength; he was carried[10] into the king's chamber and it was thought it would pass over, but it was not so; but he remained thus, unspeaking and helpless, through until the Thursday, and then gave up his life. And he lies there in the Old Minster; and his son Harold succeeded to his earldom, and left that he earlier had,[11] and Ælfgar succeeded to that.

This same year departed Wulfsige, bishop in Lichfield, and Leofwine, [*continued on p. 184*]

THE WORCESTER MANUSCRIPT (D) 1052 *continued from previous page*

promoted illegality and passed unjust judgments and counselled bad counsel in this country, except for as many as they decided that the king liked to have about him, who were faithful to him and all his people.[1] And Archishop Robert and Bishop William and Bishop Ulf escaped with difficulty with the French men who were with them, and thus came across the sea.[2]

1053. Here [1052] was the great wind on the eve of the Feast of St Thomas,[7] and the great wind was also all midwinter.[8] And it was decided that Rhys, the brother of the Welsh king,[9] should be killed because he did harmful things, and his head was brought to Gloucester[5] on Twelfth Night.[12] And this same year, before All Saints' Day,[13] Wulfsige, bishop at Lichfield, passed away, and Godwine, abbot in Winchcombe, and Æthelweard, abbot in [*continued on p. 185*]

---

[1] Florence (I, p. 210) mentions by name: Robert the deacon and his son-in-law Richard son of Scrob, Alfred the king's marshal, and Anfrid nicknamed 'Ceocesfot' (obscure, cf. Tengvik, *Old English Bynames*, p. 300).   [2] Florence (I, p. 210) continues: *But William, being a good-natured man, was recalled after a short time and received his bishopric. Osbern, nicknamed 'Pentecost'*,

E 1052 *continued from p. 181*

on an unsteady ship and travelled right on across the sea, and abandoned his pallium and all Christendom here in the land, just as God wanted it, because he had earlier obtained the honour just as God did not want it.[14] Then a great meeting was declared outside London, and all the earls and the best men who were in this land were in the meeting. There Earl Godwine set out his case, and cleared himself there before King Edward his lord, and before all the people of the land, that he was guiltless of what he was charged with – and Harold his son, and all his children. And the king restored to the earl and his children his whole friendship, and whole earldom and all that he earlier owned, and to all those men who were with him. And the king gave the Lady[15] all that she earlier owned. And Archbishop Robert – and all the French men – were declared wholly outlaw because they were most responsible for that discord between Earl Godwine and the king. And Bishop Stigand succeeded to the archbishopric in Canterbury. And at this time Earnwig, abbot of Peterborough, resigned the abbacy, while alive and in health, and gave it to Leofric the monk, by the king's leave and by the monks'; and the abbot Earnwig lived for 8 years afterwards. And the abbot Leofric then endowed[16] that monastery, such that it was then called 'Golden Borough', when it grew greatly in land and in gold and in silver.

1053. Here, in this year, Earl Godwine passed away on *15 April*; and he is buried in Winchester in the Old Minster; and Earl Harold, his son, succeeded to the earldom and to all that [*continued overleaf*]

ship and travelled right on across the sea, and abandoned his pallium. Then a great meeting was declared outside London, and the best men who were in this land were in the meeting. There Earl Godwine set out his case, and cleared himself there before King Edward of all those things that he and all his children were charged with. And Archbishop Robert and all the [French][17] men were declared outlaw, because they were the cause of the wrath there was between him and the king. And Bishop Stigand succeeded to the archbishopric in Canterbury. [*continued on p. 188*]

and his companion Hugh, gave up their castles, and with the permission of Earl Leofric they passed through his earldom and went into Scotland, where they were received by Macbeth, king of the Scots. ³ For the sense of *ar* in a feudal context see p. 136, note 5. ⁴ MS *to Michaheles mæsse*; 29 September. See p. 180, note 8. ⁵ Where the king was (Florence, I, p. 211). ⁶ This must refer to the Nativity of the Virgin since Florence (I, p. 209) gives the day as the Exalatation of the Cross, i.e. 14 September. ⁷ MSS *on Thomes mæsse niht*, 21 December. ⁸ Florence (I, pp. 210–11) says: *the wind was so violent it broke down many churches and houses and shattered or uprooted innumerable trees.* ⁹ According to Florence (I, p. 211), Rhys, brother of Gruffydd king of South Wales, was killed in a place called Bulendun, by order of King Edward. ¹⁰ Florence (I, p. 211) says *by his sons Harold, Tosti and Gyrth.* ¹¹ i.e. East Anglia. ¹² MS *twelftan æfen*; the last day of Christmas, 6 January. ¹³ 1 November. ¹⁴ William of Malmesbury (p. 244) says that he took his case to Rome and later died at Jumièges. ¹⁵ King Edward's wife Edith, daughter of Earl Godwine. ¹⁶ MS . . . *dede*; a few graphs lost, trimmed from the margin; the most likely restoration is *godede* 'endowed', though *gildede* 'gilded' is possible, anticipating what follows. Hugh Candidus (pp. 38, 66), simply uses the words *ditaverunt, ditatus* 'enriched' in this context. See also, p. 198, note 7. ¹⁷ Erased, but visible under ultra-violet light.

E 1053 *continued from previous page*
which his father owned, and Earl Ælfgar succeeded to the earldom which
Harold earlier owned.[1]

1054. *Battle at Mortemer.*[2] Here in this year [*continued opposite*]

THE ABINGDON MANUSCRIPT (C) 1053 *continued from p. 182*

abbot in Coventry, succeeded to the bishopric, and Æthelweard, abbot in
Glastonbury, departed, and Godwine, abbot in Winchcombe.

Also the Welsh men killed a great part of the English people of the
guard near Westbury.[3]

In this year there was no archbishop in this land, except Bishop Stigand held
the bishopric in Canterbury in Christ Church; and Cynesige in York and
Leofwine and Wulfwig went across the sea and had themselves ordained
bishop there.[4] That Wulfwig succeeded to the bishopric which Ulf had while
he was living and driven out.[5]

1054. Here Earl Siward went with a great raiding-army into Scotland, and
made great slaughter of Scots and put them to flight; and the king escaped.
Also many fell on his side, both Danish and English, and also his own son. This
same year the minster in Evesham was consecrated on 10 October. In the same
year Bishop Aldred travelled south across the sea into Saxony, and was
received there with great honour.[6] The same year Osgod Clapa departed
suddenly as he lay in his bed.

[1055]. In this year Earl Siward passed away in York, and his body lies
within the minster at Galmanho,[7] which he himself earlier built to the glory of
God and all His Saints. Then within a short while after this there was a
council-meeting in London, and then Earl Ælfgar, son of Earl Leofric, was
outlawed without any fault; and then he turned to Ireland, and there got
himself a fleet, which was 18 ships apart from his own, and then turned to
Wales to King Gruffydd[8] with that troop; and he received him under his safe-
conduct. And then they gathered a great army with the Irish men and with the
Welsh race, and Earl Ralph gathered a great army [*continued on p. 186*]

---

[1] i.e. East Anglia.   [2] In Normandy (dép. Seine Maritime), where vassals of Duke William
defeated invading troops of the French king, Henry I.   [3] Westbury (i.e. 'western fort'):
probably the Westbury at the head of the tidal Severn on the 'Welsh' side of the river where the
Roman road passes into South Wales; cf. Smith, *The Place-Names of Gloucestershire*, III,
p. 201.   [4] Stigand's authority in such matters being in dispute.   [5] i.e. Dorchester.   [6] By
the emperor Henry III and Heriman archbishop of Cologne says Florence; he adds that on the
king's behalf Aldred prompted the emperor to send messengers to Hungary to bring back Edward,
son of Edmund Ironside, whom he had determined should succeed him (I, pp. 212, 215). Edward
died in London shortly after his return in 1057 (q.v.).   [7] Now lost, but close to Bootham Bar
[gate] in York, (Smith, *The Place-Names of the East Riding of Yorkshire and York*, pp. lx,
288).   [8] Gruffydd ap Llewelyn, king of Gwynedd and Powys.   [9] Pope Leo IX.   [10] Pope
Victor II.   [11] i.e. 19 March.   [12] Florence (I, p. 211): *until Godric, son of the king's chaplain
Godman, was appointed abbot*. For Winchcombe see VCH, *Gloucestershire*, II, p. 66.   [13] Florence (I, p. 211) says he died 22 December. The chapel at Deerhurst was built by Odda for his

E 1054 *continued from opposite*
Leo,[9] the holy pope in Rome, passed away; and in this year there was as great a pestilence among cattle than man could remember for many years previous; and Victor[10] was chosen as pope.

1055. Here in this year Earl Siward passed away; and a full council-meeting was ordered 7 days before mid-Lent,[11] and Earl Ælfgar was outlawed because it was thrown at him that he was traitor to the king and all the people of the land. And he admitted this [*continued overleaf*]

THE WORCESTER MANUSCRIPT (D) 1053 *continued from p. 182*

Glastonbury, all within one month. And Leofwine succeeded to the bishopric at Lichfield, and Bishop Aldred succeeeded to the abbacy in Winchcombe,[12] and Æthelnoth succeeded to the abbacy in Glastonbury. And this same year passed away Ælfric, brother of Odda of Deerhurst,[13] and his body rests in Pershore. And this same year Earl Godwine passed away; and he became ill where he sat with the king in Winchester. And Harold his son, succeeded to the earldom which his father earlier had, and Earl Ælfgar succeeded to the earldom which Harold earlier had.[14]

1054. Here Earl Siward[15] travelled forth with a great raiding-army into Scotland, both with raiding ship-army and with raiding land-army, and fought against the Scots, and put to flight the king Macbeth,[16] and killed all that was best there in the land,[17] and led away from there such a great war-booty as no man had ever got before; but his son, Osbern, and his sister's son, Siward, and some of his housecarls and also the king's, were killed there on the Day of the *Seven Sleepers*.[18] This same year Bishop Aldred went across the sea to Cologne with a message from the king, and was there received with great honour by the emperor;[6] and he lived there well-nigh a year, and both the bishop in Cologne and the emperor entertained him; and he allowed Bishop Leofwine to consecrate the minster at Evesham on 10 *October*. And in this year Osgod departed suddenly in his bed. And here *St Leo*,[9] the pope, passed away, and Victor[10] was chosen as pope in his stead.

1055. In this year passed away Earl Siward in York, and he lies at Galmaho[7] in the minster which he himself had built and consecrated in the name of God and Olaf;[19] and Tostig succeeded to the earldom which he had.[20] And Archbishop Cynesige fetched his pallium from Pope Victor.

And soon after that, Earl Ælfgar, son of Earl Leofric, was outlawed well-nigh without fault; but he turned to Ireland and Wales and there got himself a great band, and travelled thus to Hereford; but there Earl Ralph came against him with a great raiding-army, and with a little [*continued on p. 187*]

brother's soul, cf. Taylor, *Architecture*, I, p. 209.   [14] i.e. East Anglia.   [15] Florence (I, p. 212) says: *by command of the king*. Gaimar (5037–54) says that Siward had been to Scotland in an unsuccessful attempt to make peace with Macbeth.   [16] Ruler in Moray, see generally Duncan, *Scotland: the Making of the Kingdom*, pp. 99–100.   [17] Florence (I, p. 212) says that all the Normans he had mentioned (see p. 182, note 2) were killed; and adds that by the king's orders Siward made Malcolm, son of the king of the Cumbrians, king. (Malcolm finally defeated and killed Macbeth in 1057).   [18] 27 July.   [19] A dedication reflecting Scandinavian sentiment, see p. 157, note 16.   [20] i.e. Northumbria.

E 1055 *continued from previous page*
before all the men who were gathered there, although the words shot out against his will.

And the king gave Tostig, son of Earl Godwine, the earldom [*continued opposite*]

THE ABINGDON MANUSCRIPT (C) 1055 *continued from p. 184*

against them at Hereford market-town, and they sought them out there;[1] but before there was any spear thrown, the English people already fled, because they were on horse;[2] and a great slaughter was made – about four hundred men, or five – and they none in return; and they then turned to the market-town and burned it down; and the famous minster which the reverend bishop Athelstan had built earlier, that they stripped and robbed of holy things,[3] and of robes and of everything, and killed the people, and some led away. Then an army was gathered throughout all neighbouring England; and they came to Gloucester and turned a little way out into Wales, and lay there for some time;[4] and in that time Earl Harold had a dyke built round the town.[5] Meanwhile peace was spoken about, and Earl Harold and those who were with him came to Billingsley,[6] and there affirmed peace and friendship between them. And then Earl Ælfgar was reinstated and given back all that was earlier taken from him. And the fleet of ships turned to Chester, and there waited for their pay which Ælfgar had promised them. The massacre was on 24 October. In the same year, soon after the raid, Tremerig, the Welsh bishop, passed away; he was Bishop Athelstan's deputy after he was unwell.[7]

[1056]. Here departed the reverend bishop Athelstan on *10 February*,[8] and his body lies in Hereford market-town, and Leofgar, who was Earl Harold's mass-priest, was set as bishop; he wore his moustaches[9] during his priesthood until he was bishop.[10] He abandoned his chrism and his cross, his spiritual weapons, after his ordination as bishop, and took up his spear and his sword, and went thus to the campaign against Gruffydd, the Welsh king, and they killed him there,[11] and his priests with him, and the sheriff Ælfnoth, and many good men with them, and the others fled away. This was 8 days before midsummer. It is difficult to describe the hardship, and all the travelling and the campaigning, and that labour and loss of men, and also horses, which all the raiding-army of the English suffered, until Earl Leofric and Earl Harold and Bishop Aldred arrived and made reconciliation between them there, so that Gruffydd swore oaths that he would be a loyal and undeceiving under-king to King Edward. And Bishop Aldred succeeded to the bishopric[12] which Leofgar earlier had for 11 weeks and 4 days. In the same year departed the emperor Cona.[13] This year departed Earl Odda, and his body lies in Pershore; and he was ordained a monk before his end. He departed on *31 August*.[14]

[*continued on p. 190*]

---

[1] Florence (I, p. 213) says the encounter took place two miles from the city of Hereford on 24 October.   [2] Florence (I, p. 213) says that Earl Ralph ordered the English to fight on horseback *contrary to their custom;* but then the earl with his Frenchmen and Normans fled, *seeing which the English with their commander also fled.*   [3] Florence (I, p. 213) says that relics of St Æthelbert (cf. annal 793) and other saints were burned with the minster.   [4] Florence (I, p. 213) says they *pitched camp beyond Straddle* (seven miles south-west of Hereford).   [5] MS *let dician ða dic.* Florence (I, p. 214) says that Hereford was now *surrounded with a wide and high bank and*

E 1055 *continued from opposite*
which Earl Siward owned before. And Earl Ælfgar sought the protection of Gruffydd[15] in Wales; and in this year Gruffyd and Ælfgar burned down St Æthelberht's minster[3] and all the town of Hereford.

1056. *Here Henry, emperor of the Romans, died, whom his son Henry succeeded.*[13]

1057. Here in this year came the ætheling Edward, [*continued overleaf*]

THE WORCESTER MANUSCRIPT (D) 1055 *continued from p. 185*

struggle they were brought to flight, and many people killed in that flight, and then turned into Hereford market-town and raided it, burned down the famous minster which Bishop Athelstan built, and killed the priests inside the minster,[16] and many others as well, and seized all the treasures in there and led them away with them. And then when they had done most harm, it was decided to reinstate Earl Ælfgar, and give him back his earldom and all that was taken from him. This raid was made on 24 *October*. In the same year, soon after the raid, Tremerig, the Welsh bishop, passed away; and he was Bishop Athelstan's deputy after he was unwell.[7]

1056. Here Bishop Æthelric resigned his bishopric at Durham and travelled to Peterborough to St Peter's minster,[17] and his brother Æthelwine succeeded to it. And also here Bishop Athelstan passed away on *10 February*, and his body lies in Hereford, and Leofgar, who was Earl Harold's mass-priest, was set as bishop; and he had his moustaches[9] during his priesthood until he was bishop.[10] He abandoned his chrism and his cross, and his spiritual weapons, and took up his spear and his sword, and went thus to the campaign against Gruffydd, the Welsh king, and there he was killed,[11] and his priests with him, and the sheriff Ælfnoth, and many other good men, and the others fled away. This was eight days before midsummer. And Bishop Aldred succeeded to the bishopric which Leofgar had for 11 weeks and 4 days. This year Earl Odda passed away, and he lies in Pershore; he was ordained a monk before his end, a good man, and pure and very noble;[14] and he departed on *31 August*. And the emperor Cona[13] passed away.

1057.[18] Here the ætheling Edward came to England; he was son of King Edward's brother, King Edmund, [who] was called 'Ironside' for his bravery. [*continued overleaf*]

---

fortified with gates and bars. Harold seems to have been renewing or supplementing earlier defences which had fallen into disuse, cf. Shoesmith, *Hereford City Excavations*, II, p. 74.   [6] Probably Billingsley in Holme Lacy, a manor held by Harold (DB, *Herefordshire*, 2, 12).   [7] Florence (I, p. 214) explains that Athelstan had been blind for thirteen years.   [8] Florence (I, p. 214): *in the episcopal manor called Bosbury.*   [9] *kenepas*, see Oxford English Dictionary, *sub* kemp, *sb.²*, plural, a cat's whiskers.   [10] Against canon law, see Thorpe, *Laws and Institutes*, II, pp. 254–5, 294–5.   [11] Florence (I, p. 215) says this was at *a place called Clastbury.*   [12] i.e. Hereford.   [13] Henry III (Cona); succeeded by his five-year-old son Henry.   [14] Florence (I, p. 215), who gives him the alternative name Æthelwine, says he died at Deerhurst (cf. p. 184, note 13), was made a monk by Bishop Aldred of Worcester, and was *a lover of churches, restorer of the poor, defender of widows and orphans, helper of the oppressed, guardian of chastity.*   [15] Gruffydd ap Llewelyn, king of Gwynedd.   [16] Florence (I, p. 213) specifies: *seven canons who guarded the doors of the principal church.*   [17] The monk-bishop, expelled by the secular clerks of Durham, was returning whence he came (Simeon, I, pp. 91–2).   [18] The first part of this annal is marked by poetic rhetoric.

E 1057 *continued from previous page*
King Edmund's son, here to the land, and soon afterwards departed; and his body is buried in *St Paul's* minster in London. And Pope Victor passed away and Stephen was chosen as pope;[1] he was abbot in Monte Cassino. And Earl Leofric passed away,[2] and Ælfgar, his son, succeeded to the earldom which the father earlier had.[3]

1058. Here in this year Pope Stephen passed away, and Benedict was consecrated as pope;[4] the same sent the pallium to Archbishop Stigand here to the land. And in this year passed away Heca, [*continued opposite*]

THE WORCESTER MANUSCRIPT (D) 1057 *continued from previous page*

King Cnut had sent this ætheling away into Hungary to betray, but he there grew to be a great man, as God granted him and became him well, so that he won the emperor's relative for wife, and by her bred a fine family; she was called Agatha. We do not know for what cause it was arranged that he might not see his relative King Edward's [face]. Alas! that was a cruel fate, and harmful to all this nation, that he so quickly ended his life after he came to England, to the misfortune of this wretched nation.

In the same year, Earl Leofric passed away on *30 October*.[2] He was very wise, before God and before the world, in what availed all this nation. He lies at Coventry,[5] and his son Ælfgar succeeded to his authority.[3] And in that year, Earl Ralph[6] passed away on *21 December*, and lies in Peterborough. Also departed Heca, bishop in Sussex, and Æthelric[7] was raised in his seat. And here Pope Victor passed away, and Stephen was chosen as pope.[1]

1058. Here Earl Ælfgar was expelled, but he soon came back again, with violence, through the help of Gruffydd. And here came a raiding ship-army from Norway;[8] [*continued opposite*]

THE CANTERBURY MANUSCRIPT (F) *continued from p. 183*

1058. . . . Here Pope Stephen passed away, and Benedict was blessed to it;[4] the same sent the pallium to Archbishop Stigand, here to the land. And Bishop Heca passed away, and Archbishop Stigand ordained Æthelric in Christ Church[9] as bishop for Sussex, and Abbot Siward as bishop for Rochester.

[Manuscript F ends here.]

---

[1] Victor II and Stephen IX respectively.   [2] D gives the date *ii kal Oct*, and Florence (I, pp. 215–16) *ii kal Sept* (31 August), saying that this *man of excellent memory died at a good old age, in his own manor called Bromley, and was buried with honour in Coventry, which monastery he had founded and well endowed* (cf. note 5).   [3] i.e. the earldom of Mercia.   [4] Stephen IX and Benedict X respectively.   [5] Cf. Hunt, 'Piety, prestige or politics? The house of Leofric and the foundation and patronage of Coventry priory', pp. 97–117.   [6] Ralph 'the Timid'.   [7] Florence (I, p. 216) calls him *a monk of Christ Church, Canterbury*.   [8] According to Florence (I, p. 217) this force also came in support of Earl Ælfgar. The *Annales Cambriae* (p. 25) suggest a large-scale invasion led by Magnus, son of Harald Hardrada, with the help of Gruffydd ap Llewelyn.   [9] Canterbury.

[plate 1] Dragon prow- or stern-post from a Migration-period ship, dredged from the River Scheldt at Appels, near Termonde, Belgium. Carved oak, 4ft 9" high. (British Museum, 1938 2–2 1)

[plate 2] Bastions flanking the west gate of the Roman fortress of Anderitum (Pevensey), Sussex; besieged by the Saxons in 491, slaughtering all its inhabitants (see pp. 14–15)

[plate 3] West Stow, Suffolk, reconstruction of Anglo-Saxon village; excavated 1965–72

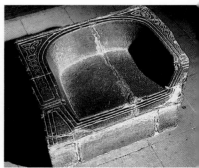

[plates 4a & b] Stone ceremonial seat of bishop or abbot, c. 700, Hexham Abbey, Northumberland

[plate 5]

[plate 6]

[plate 7]

[plate 8]

[plate 9]

[plate 10]

[plate 5] Silver *sceat*, probably Kentish, early eighth century, with Roman-derived designs of bird pecking at fruit, and wolf with twins; from a hoard at Woodham Waltham, Essex (British Museum, 1994 4–24 98)

[plate 6] Silver penny of Queen Cynethryth of Mercia, struck by Eoba, one of Offa's moneyers c. 787–92 (British Museum, BMC 60)

[plate 7] Silver penny of King Alfred c. 880; reverse with London monogram and the name of the moneyer Tilewine (British Museum, 1896 4-4 61).

[plate 8] Silver penny of Olaf Guthfrithson c. 940, obverse with raven symbol instead of head; struck at York by Æthelferth (British Museum, 1862 9-30 1)

[plate 9] Silver penny of William I, struck at Hastings by Dunning (British Museum, BMC 20)

[plate 10] Silver penny of Robert Earl of Gloucester, mid 1140s, struck at Trowbridge by Salide; hoard at Box, Wiltshire (British Museum, 1994 7-19 53)

Gold finger-rings: [plate 11, left] belonging to King Æthelwulf of Wessex, 839–58 (the father of Alfred the Great), inscribed + ETHELVVLF RX; found in a cart-rut at Laverstock, Wiltshire in 1780 (British Museum, 1829 11–14 1; [plate 12, below] belonging to Queen Æthelswith, daughter of King Æthelwulf and married to King Burgred of Mercia in 853/4, inscribed on the inside + EAÐELSVIÐ REGNA; ploughed up near Sherburn, Yorkshire in 1870 (British Museum, AF 458)

[plate 13] Two panels from embroidered vestments commissioned by Queen Ælfflæd, second wife of Edward the Elder (909–16) for Bishop Frithestan of Winchester (909–31); coloured silk and gold-thread. These panels depict the Deacon Laurence and the Prophet Jonas. Square panels from the reverse bear the running inscription: ÆLFLÆD FIERI PRECEPIT PIO EPISCOPO FRIÐESTANO, *Ælfflæd ordered to be made for the pious bishop Frithestan* (Durham Cathedral Library). After Frithestan's death given to the shrine of St Cuthbert by Ælfflæd's stepson King Athelstan

[plate 14] Detail from the stem of an altar candlestick from Gloucester Cathedral, presented in the time of Abbot Peter (1107–13); cast copper alloy, gilded, with glass bead animal eyes; the inscription running down the stem reads: + ABBATIS PETRI GREGIS ET DEVOTIO MITIS + ME DEDIT ECCLESIE SCI PETRI GLOECESTRE, *The gentle devotion of Abbot Peter and his flock gave me to St Peter's church at Gloucester*; later looted and sent to Normandy (Victoria & Albert Museum, 7649/1861). See p. 244, note 7

[plate 15] Mercian royal mausoleum beneath the chancel of St Wystan's church, Repton, Derbyshire, eighth–ninth century; sixteen feet square, four monolithic columns supporting a domical vault ten feet high

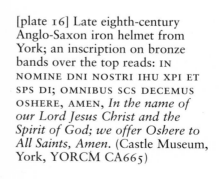

[plate 16] Late eighth-century Anglo-Saxon iron helmet from York; an inscription on bronze bands over the top reads: IN NOMINE DNI NOSTRI IHU XPI ET SPS DI; OMNIBUS SCS DECEMUS OSHERE, AMEN, *In the name of our Lord Jesus Christ and the Spirit of God; we offer Oshere to All Saints, Amen.* (Castle Museum, York, YORCM CA665)

[plate 17] Section through rampart of Anglo-Saxon *burh* at Wareham, Dorset, showing stone foundation; excavated 1954. See p. 74, note 2

[plate 18] Gate-house to William the Conqueror's Rougemont castle at Exeter; from the ditch (gateway blocked), showing evidence of Anglo-Saxon workmanship in its masonry and design

E 1058 *continued from opposite*
bishop in Sussex; and Archbishop Stigand ordained Æthelric, *monk at Christ Church*,[9] as bishop for Sussex, and Abbot Siward[10] as bishop for Rochester.

1059. Here in this year Nicholas was chosen as pope; he was bishop at the town of Florence; and Benedict, who was pope earlier, was driven out,

1060. *Here Henry, king of the French, died, whom his son Philip succeeded.*[11] In this year passed away Cynesige, archbishop in York, on 22 *December*, and Bishop Aldred succeeded to it; and Walter succeeded to the bishopric in Hereford.

1061. Here in this year passed away Duduc, bishop in Somerset, and Giso succeeded. And in the same year passed away Godwine, bishop at St Martin's,[12] on 9 *March*. And in the [*continued overleaf*]

THE WORCESTER MANUSCRIPT (D) 1058 *continued from opposite*

it is tedious to tell how it all happened. In the same year Bishop Aldred consecrated the minster in Gloucester which he himself completed in praise of God and of St Peter, and so travelled to Jerusalem, with greater honour than any other did before him,[13] and there commended himself to God, and also offered a worthy gift to our Lord's Sepulchre – that was a golden chalice worth five marks, and of very wonderful workmanship. In the same year Pope Stephen passed away, and Benedict was set as pope.[4] He sent the pallium to Bishop Stigand. And Æthelric was ordained as bishop for Sussex and Abbot Siward[10] as bishop for Rochester.

1059. Here in this year Nicholas was chosen as pope; he was bishop at the town of Florence earlier, and Benedict, who was pope earlier, was driven out. And in this year, the steeple at Peterborough was consecrated on 17 *October*.

1060. In this year on the *Translation of St Martin*,[14] was a great earthquake. And Henry[15] the king passed away in France. And Cynesige archbishop in York departed on 22 *December*, and he lies in Peterborough, and Bishop Aldred succeeded to that authority; and Walter succeeded to the bishopric in Herefordshire; and Bishop Duduc, who was bishop in Somerset, also passed away, and Giso, the priest, was set in his place.[16]

1061. Here Bishop Aldred went to Rome for his pallium, and he received it from the pope Nicholas.[17] And the earl Tostig, and his wife also,[18] went to Rome, and the bishop and the earl suffered great [*continued on p. 191*]

---

[10] Abbot of Chertsey. [11] Henry I and Philip I respectively. [12] Suffragan at Canterbury, cf. p. 164, note 1. [13] Florence (I, p. 217) says that he made Wulfstan, whom he had ordained as a monk at Worcester, abbot of Gloucester, then gave up the bishopric of Wiltshire, which he had administered during Hereman's 3-year self-imposed exile, and went to Jerusalem via Hungary, *a thing which no English archbishop or bishop was known to have done before.* [14] 4 July. [15] Henry I. [16] Florence (I, p. 218) says that Walter (Queen Edith's chaplain), Duduc, and Gisa (the king's chaplain) were all three Lotharingians. [17] William of Malmesbury (*Vita Wulfstani*, p. 16) says that at first the pope refused it him unless he surrendered Worcester, but the events of his homeward journey (see p. 191, note 1) softened the papal rigour. [18] Judith, sister of Baldwin V of Flanders and sister-in-law of William of Normandy.

E 1061 *continued from previous page*
self-same year Wulfric, abbot at St Augustine's[1], passed away in Easter week on *18 April*.[2] Then when word came to the king that the abbot Wulfric had passed away, he chose for it Æthelsige, a monk from Old Minster,[3] and thus followed [the wish of] Archbishop Stigand; and [he] became consecrated as abbot at Windsor on *St Augustine's* Day.[4]

1062. *This year Maine was subjected by William, count of Normandy.*

1063. Here Earl Harold and his brother Earl Tostig went into Wales both with land-army and with raiding ship-army, and conquered that land; and that people gave hostages and submitted to them, and afterwards went to and killed their king Gruffydd, and brought Harold his head, and he set another king for it.[5]

1064 [1063]. Here in this year the Northumbrians went together and outlawed their earl Tostig, and killed all the men of his court they could come at, both English and Danish, and seized all his weapons in York, and gold and silver, and all his monies which they could find out about anywhere there; and sent for Morcar, son of Earl Ælfgar,[6] and chose him as their earl. And he went south with all the shire, and with Nottinghamshire and Derbyshire and Lincolnshire, until he came to Northampton; and his brother Edwin came to meet him with the men who were in his earldom; and also many Welshmen came with him. There came Earl Harold to meet them, and they charged him with a message [*continued opposite*]

THE ABINGDON MANUSCRIPT (C) *continued from p. 186*

1065. Here in this year before Lammas,[7] Earl Harold ordered construction in Wales at Portskewett[8] now that he had won it, and there he gathered many goods, and thought to have the king Edward there for the sake of the hunting. And then when it was almost gathered, Caradog, Gruffydd's son,[9] came up with all those whom he could get, and killed almost all the people who built there, and seized the goods which were gathered there. And the massacre was on *St Bartholomew's* Day.[10] And then, after Michaelmas, all the thegns in Yorkshire went to York, and there killed all Earl Tostig's housecarls whom they could find out about, and seized his treasures. [*continued on p. 192*]

---

[1] Canterbury.   [2] E *xiiii kal. Mai*, D *iiii.x kal. Aprilis*.   [3] Winchester.   [4] 26 May if Augustine of Canterbury, or 28 August if Augustine of Hippo.   [5] Gruffydd ap Llewelyn, king of Gwynedd; Florence (I, p. 221) says that, because of Gruffydd's frequent attacks on the English borders, Harold went at Edward's instruction with a small mounted force, and burned the Welsh king's fleet and residence at Rhuddlan; he later sailed round Wales from Bristol, and was joined by Tostig, whereupon the Welsh gave hostages and repudiated Gruffydd.   [6] Of Mercia.   [7] 1 August.   [8] An estate on the Severn estuary on the opposite bank of the Wye from Tiddenham, see p. 87, note 13.   [9] i.e. son of Gruffydd ap Rhydderch, killed by Gruffydd ap Llewelyn, see note 5, and Table p. 301.   [10] 24 August.

E 1064 [1065] *continued from opposite*
to the king Edward, and also sent messengers with him, and [*continued overleaf*]

THE WORCESTER MANUSCRIPT (D) 1061 *continued from p. 189*

difficulties when they travelled homeward.[11] And here Godwine, bishop at St Martin's,[12] passed away, and Wulfric, abbot at St Augustine's,[1] on *19 March*,[2] and Pope Nicholas passed away, and Alexander, who was bishop at Lucca, was chosen as pope.[13]

1063. In this year [1062] Earl Harold went after midwinter from Gloucester[14] to Rhuddlan, which was Gruffydd's, and burnt down the manor, and his ships and all the equipment which belonged to them, and brought him to flight.[5] And then, towards the Rogation Days,[15] Harold went with ships from Bristol, round Wales, and that people made peace and gave hostages; and Tostig went against them with a land-army, and overran that land. But here in this same year, at harvest, on *fifth August*, King Gruffydd was killed by his own men, because of the struggle he was waging with Earl Harold. He was king over all the Welsh race,[16] and his head was brought to Earl Harold, and Harold brought it to the king – and his ship's figure-head and the embellishment[17] with it. And the king Edward entrusted that land to his two brothers, Bleddyn and Rhiwallon;[18] and they swore oaths and gave hostages to the king and to the earl that they would be undeceiving to him in all things, and everywhere ready [to serve] him on water and on land, and likewise to pay from that land what was formerly done before to the other king.

1065. Here in this year before Lammas,[7] Earl Harold ordered construction in Wales at Portskewett[8] now that he had won it, and there he gathered together many goods, and thought to have the king Edward there for the sake of the hunting. But then when it was all ready, Caradog, Gruffydd's son,[9] went with all the band he could get, and killed almost all the people who built there; and the goods which had been got ready were seized. We do not know who first advised this folly. This was done on *St Bartholomew's Day*.[10] And soon after this all the thegns of Yorkshire and Northumberland gathered together and outlawed their earl Tostig, and killed all the men of his court they could come at, both English and Danish, and seized all his weapons in York, and gold and silver, and all his monies which they could find out about anywhere there; and sent for Morcar, son of Earl Ælfgar,[6] and chose him as their earl. And he went south with all the shire, and with Nottinghamshire and Derbyshire and Lincolnshire, [*continued on p. 193*]

[11] William of Malmesbury (*Vita Wulfstani*, p. 16) says they were attacked and stripped of their possessions by robbers. [12] At Canterbury, as suffragan to Archbishop Eadsige, see p. 164, note 1. [13] Nicholas II and Alexander II respectively. [14] On instructions from King Edward who was in Gloucester at the time (Florence, I, p. 221). [15] 26–8 May. [16] Presumably so regarded inasmuch as he had invaded South Wales and killed their king Gruffydd ap Rhydderch in 1055 (cf. Florence, I, p. 222). [17] *his scipes heafod and þa bone þer mid*; Florence (I, p. 222) *the head of his ship with 'ornatura'*. [18] Half-brothers of Gruffydd ap Llewelyn, whose mother, Angharad, married their father Cynfyn after the death of Llewelyn, see Table p. 301.

E 1064 [1065] *continued from previous page*
asked that they might have Morcar as their earl. And the king granted this, and sent Harold back to them, to Northampton, on the eve of the festival of Sts Simon and Jude,[1] and made known the same to them, and gave them his hand on it,[2] and renewed the law of Cnut there. And the northern men did great harm around Northampton while he went on their message, in that they both killed men and burned houses and corn, and seized all the cattle that they could come at, which was many thousands; and they seized many hundreds of men, and led them off north with them, so that the shire and the other shires which were near there were for many years the worse. And Earl Tostig, [*continued opposite*]

THE ABINGDON MANUSCRIPT (C) 1065 *continued from p. 190*

And Tostig was then at Britford[3] with the king. And then very quickly after that, there was a great meeting at Northampton, and so [also] in Oxford, on Simon and Judes' Day;[1] and Earl Harold was there, and wanted to work their reconciliation if he could, but he could not. But all his [Tostig's] earldom unanimously deserted and outlawed him, and all those with him who promoted injustice, because he robbed God first, and then despoiled of life and of land all those he had power over. And they took Morcar as their earl, and Tostig then went across the sea, and his wife with him, to the land of Baldwin, and took winter-quarters at St Omer. And King Edward came to Westminster towards midwinter,[4] and had consecrated there that minster which he himself built to the glory of God and St Peter and all God's saints; and the church consecration was on Holy Innocents' Day;[5] and he passed away on the eve of Twelfth Night,[6] and he was buried on Twelfth Night in the same minster, as it says hereafter:

[THE DEATH OF EDWARD][7]

Here King Edward, lord of the English,
sent a righteous soul to Christ,
a holy spirit into God's keeping.
Here in the world he lived for a while
in kingly splendour, skilful in counsel;
24-and-a-half[8]
in number of years, a noble ruler,
distributed riches. Æthelred's son
ruler of heroes, greatly distinguished,
ruled Welsh and Scots, and Britons too,
Angles and Saxons, combatant champions.
Cold sea waves thus encircle
all youthful men that loyally
obeyed Edward, princely king. [*continued on p. 194*]

---

[1] 28 October.   [2] MS *hand sealde*, see p. 159, note 16.   [3] A royal manor on the Avon a mile or two south of Sarum (DB, *Wiltshire*, I, 6).   [4] Florence (I, p. 224): *and after the Feast of All Saints* (1 November) *with the help of Earl Edwin expelled Tostig from England*; and despite failing health, he held court at Christmas in London *as well as he could*.

E 1064 [1065] *continued from opposite*
and his wife and all those who wanted what he wanted, went south [*continued on p. 195*]

THE WORCESTER MANUSCRIPT (D) 1065 *continued from p. 191*

until he came to Northampton; and his brother Edwin came to meet him with the men who were in his earldom; and also many Welshmen came with him. There came Earl Harold to meet them, and they charged him with a message to the king Edward, and also sent messengers with him, and asked that they might have Morcar as their earl. And the king granted this, and sent Harold back to them, to Northampton, on the eve of the festival of Sts Simon and Jude,[1] and made known the same to them, and gave them his hand on it,[2] and renewed the law of Cnut there. And the northern men[9] did great harm around Northampton while he went on their message, in that they both killed men and burned houses and corn, and seized all the cattle that they could come at, which was many thousands; and they seized many hundreds of men, and led them off north with them, so that the shire and the other shires which were near there were for many years the worse. And Earl Tostig, and his wife and all those who wanted what he wanted, went south across the sea with him to Earl Baldwin, and he received them all, and they were there all the winter. And King Edward came to Westminster towards midwinter,[4] and had consecrated there that minster which he himself built to the glory of God and St Peter and all God's saints; and the church consecration was on Holy Innocents' Day;[5] and he passed away on the eve of Twelfth Night,[6] and he was buried on Twelfth Night in the same minster, as it says hereafter:

[THE DEATH OF EDWARD][7]

Here King Edward, lord of the English,
sent a righteous soul to Christ,
a holy spirit into God's keeping.
Here in the world he lived for a while
in kingly splendour, skilful in counsel;
24 [8] in number of years,
And he in a prosperous time,[8] a noble ruler,
distributed riches. Æthelred's son
ruler of heroes, greatly distinguished,
ruled Welsh and Scots, and Britons too,
Angles and Saxons, combatant champions.
Cold sea waves thus encircle
all youthful men that loyally
obeyed Edward, princely king. [*continued on p. 195*]

---

[5] 28 December.   [6] The twelfth night (evening) of Christmas, i.e. 5 January.   [7] This part of the annal is written in traditional alliterative verse; cf. Dobbie, *Minor Poems*, pp. 25–6. It occurs only in C and D.   [8] C *xxiiii ... and healfe tid*; D correctly reads *xxiiii* but the expression *healfe tid* 'half time' is apparently misunderstood, erased and replaced by *hælo tid* 'prosperous time'.   [9] MS *þa Ryðrenan*, presumably a slip for *þa norðernan*; E reads *þa norðerne* men.

A *continued from p. 182*
  1066. Here passed away King Edward, and Earl Harold succeeded to the kingdom and held it 40 weeks and one day, and [*continued on p. 196*]

THE ABINGDON MANUSCRIPT (C) 1065 *continued from p. 192*

The blameless king was ever blithe of mood,
though long before, bereft of land,
he lived in paths of exile widely through the world,
after Cnut had overcome the race of Æthelred,
and Danes ruled the dear kingdom
of England for 28 years
in number, dispensed riches.
Afterwards came forth, noble in array,
a king good in virtues, pure and mild;
the princely Edward defended homeland,
country and nation, until the very bitter death
suddenly came and seized so dear
a prince from the earth. Angels conveyed the
righteous soul into heaven's light.
However, the wise man committed the kingdom
to a distinguished man, Harold himself,
a princely earl, who at all times
loyally obeyed his superior[1]
in words and deeds, neglecting nothing
of which the nation's king was in need.

And here also Harold became consecrated as king,[2] and he experienced little quietness in it while he ruled the kingdom.

[1066]. In this year King Harold came from York to Westminster at the Easter which was after the midwinter that the king passed away; and Easter was then on *16 April*. Then throughout all England, a sign such as men never saw before was seen in the heavens. Some men declared that it was the star *comet*, which some men call the 'haired' star;[3] and it appeared first on the eve of the *Greater Litany*,[4] that is on *24 April*, and shone thus all the week. And soon thereafter came Earl Tostig from beyond the sea into Wight, with as great a fleet as he could get, and there he was given both money and provisions; and then went from there, and did harm everywhere along the sea-coast where he could get to, until he came to Sandwich.[5] Then when King Harold, who was in London, was informed that his brother Tostig had come to Sandwich, he gathered a greater ship-army and also land-army than any king [*continued on p. 196*]

---

[1] C *hærran*, D *herran*, a word found only in poetic texts. [2] Florence (I, pp. 224–5) says that this was on the same day as Edward's funeral; that Edward had nominated Harold, *subregulus*, as his successor, that he was elected by the chief nobles of all England, and consecrated by Aldred, archbishop of York. He adds that Harold immediately began to abolish unjust laws and make good ones, was reverent towards the Church, stern with all malefactors, and laboured by land and sea for the defence of the country. [3] Halley's comet, which the Bayeux Tapestry represents as simultaneous with Harold's coronation (dramatically but inaccurately, since it could only be seen in England 24–30 April). See Wilson, *Bayeux Tapestry*, pls 31–2. For the ascription 'haired' see

E 1064 [1065] *continued from p. 193*
across the sea with him to Earl Baldwin, and he received them all, and they
were there all the winter.

1066. In this year [1065] the minster at Westminster was consecrated on
Holy Innocents' Day,[6] and the king Edward passed away [*continued on
p. 197*]

THE WORCESTER MANUSCRIPT (D) 1065 *continued from p. 193*

> The blameless king was ever blithe of mood,
> though long before, bereft of land,
> he lived in paths of exile widely through the world,
> after Cnut had overcome the race of Æthelred,
> and Danes ruled the dear kingdom
> of England for 28 years
> in number, distributed riches.
> Afterwards came forth, noble in array,
> a king good in virtues, pure and mild;
> the princely Edward defended homeland,
> country and nation, until the very bitter death
> suddenly came and seized so dear
> a prince from the earth. Angels conveyed the
> righteous soul into heaven's light.
> However, the wise man committed the kingdom
> to a distinguished man, Harold himself,
> a princely earl, who at all times
> loyally obeyed his superior[1]
> in words and deeds, neglecting nothing
> of which the nation's king was in need.

And here also Harold became consecrated as king,[2] and he experienced little
quietness in it while he ruled the kingdom.

1066. In this year King Harold came from York to Westminster at the
Easter which was after the midwinter that the king passed away; and Easter
was then on *16 April*. Then throughout all England, a sign such as men never
saw before was seen in the heavens. Some men declared that it was the star
comet, which some men call the 'haired' star;[3] and it appeared first on the eve
of the *Greater Litany*,[4] *24 April*, and shone thus all the week. And soon
thereafter came Earl Tostig from beyond the sea into Wight, with as great a
fleet as he could get, and there he was given both money and provisions.[5] And
King Harold, his brother, gathered a greater raiding ship-army and also
raiding land-army than any king here in [*continued on p. 197*]

---

p. 83, note 20.   [4] For a contemporary sermon on the Greater Litany see Swanton, *Prose*, pp.
143–9.   [5] Florence (I, p. 225) says that Tostig came from Flanders; Gaimar (5153–82) that
most of his men were Flemings, and that they landed at *Wardstane* and harried there, and went on
to Thanet where they were joined by 17 ships from Orkney. Then, having caused great damage in
Brunemue and elsewhere, they went to the Humber. After their defeat by Edwin and Morcar the
Flemings deserted.   [6] 28 December.

A 1066 *continued from p. 194*
here came William and won England; and here in this year Christ Church[1] burned, and here a *comet* appeared on *18 April*. [*continued on p. 204*]

THE ABINGDON MANUSCRIPT (C) 1066 *continued from p. 194*

in the land had ever gathered before, because he was told for certain that Earl William from Normandy, relative[2] of King Edward, wanted to come here and win this land, just as it afterwards came to pass. Then when Tostig found out that King Harold was on his way to Sandwich, he went from Sandwich, and took some of the boatmen with him, some willingly, some unwillingly; and then turned north into. . . .,[3] and there raided in Lindsey,[4] and killed many good men there. Then when Earl Edwin and Earl Morcar[5] realised that, they came there and drove him out of the land. And he then went to Scotland – and the king of Scots[6] gave him safe-conduct and helped him with provisions – and lived there all summer. Then King Harold came to Sandwich, and waited for his fleet there, because it was long before it could be gathered. And then when his fleet was gathered, he went into Wight, and lay there all the summer and the autumn; and a land-army was kept everywhere by the sea, although in the end it was to no avail. Then when it was the *Nativity of St Mary*,[7] the men's provisions were gone, and no one could hold them there any longer. Then the men were allowed to go home, and the king rode inland, and the ships were sent[8] to London, and many perished before they came there. Then when the ships came home, King Harald from Norway then came by surprise north into the Tyne with a very great raiding ship-army – and no little one: it could be. . . .[9] or more – and Earl Tostig came to him with all that he had got, just as they had earlier spoken about; and then both went with all the fleet along the Ouse up towards York.[10] Then King Harold, in the south, was informed when he came off ship, that Harald, king in Norway, and Earl Tostig were landed near York. Then he went northward, by day and night, as quickly as he could gather his army. Then before the king Harold could come there, Earl Edwin and Earl Morcar had gathered from their earldom as great a force as they could get, and fought with that raiding-army and made a great slaughter;[11] and there many of the English people were killed and drowned and driven in flight; and the Norwegians had possession of the place of slaughter. And this fight was on the *Vigil of St Matthew the Apostle*,[12] and that was Wednesday. And then after the fight [*continued opposite*]

[1] At Canterbury. [2] There is a clear difference of emphasis between C and D, although the term 'bastard', a French loan-word, was not yet the pejorative it was later to become (*Middle English Dictionary, sub* 'bastard'); cf. Ordericus (II, pp. 2–3), *Guillelmus nothus*, 'illegitimate'. [3] A space is left in the manuscript, but 'the Humber' can be restored from D. [4] Florence (I, p. 225) says: *where he burned many manors*. [5] Earls of Mercia and Northumbria respectively. [6] i.e. Malcolm III (Malcolm Canmore). [7] 8 September. [8] *man draf*, 'one drove'. [9] A space is left in the manuscript; 'three hundred ships' might be restored from D; Florence, whose readings are normally close to C, reads: *more than five hundred large ships* (I, p. 226). [10] Florence (I, p. 226) and Simeon (II, p. 180) say they landed at Riccal; Gaimar

E 1066 *continued from p. 195*

on the eve of Twelfth Night, and was buried on Twelfth Night[13] inside the newly consecrated church in Westminster. And Earl Harold succeeded to the kingdom of England just as the king granted it him – and also men chose him for it – and was blessed as king on Twelfth Night. And the same year in which he became king, he went out against William with a raiding ship-army.[14] And meanwhile Earl Tostig came into the Humber with 60 ships. Earl Edwin came with a land-army and drove him out, and the boatmen deserted him; and he went to Scotland with 12 cutters, and Harald, the king of the Norwegians,[15] met him with 300 ships, and Tostig submitted to him. And they both went into the Humber until they came to York; and Earl Morcar and Earl Edwin fought with them, and the king of the Norwegians had the victory.[11] And King Harold was informed what had happened and was done there, and he came with a great raiding-army [*continued overleaf*]

THE WORCESTER MANUSCRIPT (D) 1066 *continued from p. 195*

the land had ever done before, because he was informed that William the Bastard[2] wanted to come here and win this land, just as it afterwards came to pass. Meanwhile Earl Tostig came into the Humber with sixty ships, and Earl Edwin came with a land-army and drove him out, and the boatmen deserted him; and he went to Scotland with 12 cutters, and there Harald king of Norway[15] met him with three hundred ships,[9] and Tostig submitted to him and became his man, and they both went into the Humber until they came to York, and there Earl Edwin and Earl Morcar, his brother, fought against them, but the Northmen had the victory. Then Harold, king of the English, was informed that this had come about there – and this fight was on the *Vigil of St Matthew*.[12] Then Harold our king came upon the Northmen by surprise, and encountered them beyond York at Stamford Bridge with a great raiding-army [*continued on p. 199*]

THE ABINGDON MANUSCRIPT (C) 1066 *continued from opposite*

Harald king of Norway and Earl Tostig went into York with as great a force as seemed to them [necessary] and they were given hostages from the town,[16] and also help with provisions, and so went from there to ship, and spoke of complete peace provided that they would all go south with them and win this land. Then in the middle of this came Harold, king of the English, with all his army on the Sunday to Tadcaster[17] and there marshalled his fleet;[18] and then on Monday went right through York. And Harald, king of Norway, and Earl Tostig and their [*continued overleaf*]

(5204) says it was *at St Wilfrid's*. [11] Florence (I, p. 226) says the battle took place on the northern bank of the River Ouse, near York; Simeon (II, p. 180) and Gaimar (5209) supply the name Fulford. [12] 20 September. [13] See p. 193, note 6. [14] Found only in E, this perhaps refers to an unofficial skirmish off the south-east coast. [15] i.e. Harald Hardrada; cf. p. 199, note 9. [16] Florence (I, p. 226) says that one-hundred-and-fifty hostages were given on either side. [17] MS *Tada*, the Roman station of Calcaria on the Ouse eight miles south-west of York; cf. Smith, *The Place-Names of the West Riding of Yorkshire*, IV, pp. 76–7. [18] *lið fylcade*; it seems as if here *lið* is used synonymously with *fyrde*; these troops may well have been shipborne; cf. the Introduction p. xxxiv.

E 1066 *continued from previous page*
of English men, and met him at Stamford Bridge, and killed him and the earl Tostig and courageously overcame all that raiding-army.[1] And meanwhile Earl William [came] up at Hastings on the Feast of *St Michael*[2] and Harold came from the north, and fought with him before all his raiding-army had come; and there he fell, and his two brothers, Gyrth and Leofwine. And William conquered this land, and came to Westminster, and Archbishop Aldred consecrated him as king. And men paid him tribute, and gave hostages, and afterwards bought their lands.

And Leofric, abbot of Peterborough, was at that campaign, and there fell ill and came home, and was dead soon after that on the night of All Saints.[3] God have mercy on his soul. In his day there was complete happiness and complete prosperity in Peterborough, and he was beloved by all people, so that the king gave to St Peter and him the abbacy in Burton,[4] and that of Coventry which the earl Leofric, who was his uncle, had made earlier, and that of Crowland and that of Thorney. And he did more to enrich the minster of Peterborough in gold and in silver and in vestments and in land, as no other man ever did before him, or after [*continued opposite*]

THE ABINGDON MANUSCRIPT (C) 1066 *continued from p. 197*
division had gone from ship beyond York to Stamford Bridge, because it had been promised them for certain that hostages would be brought to meet them there from the whole shire. Then Harold, king of the English, came upon them beyond the bridge by surprise; and there they joined battle and were fighting very hard long in the day; and there Harald, king of Norway, was killed and Earl Tostig and countless people with them, both of Northmen and of English. And the Northmen[5] fled from the English. There was one of the Norwegians who withstood the English people so that they could not cross the bridge nor gain victory. Then one Englishman shot with an arrow but it was to no avail, and then another came under the bridge and stabbed him through under the mail-coat. Then Harold, king of the English, came over the bridge, and his army along with him, and there made a great slaughter of both Norwegians and Flemings; and Harold let the king's son, who was called *The Elegant*,[6] go home to Norway with all the ships.

---

[1] Florence (I, p. 226) says the battle was fought on Monday 25 September.   [2] D *Sancte Michaeles mæsse æfen*, 28 September. E *on Sancte Michaeles mæssedæg*, 29 September.   [3] MS *ælre halgan mæsse niht*; 31 October.   [4] Burton-on-Trent, see VCH, *Stafford*, III, pp. 199–213.   [5] C ends at this point at the foot of the page, the remainder of the annal being added, on a supplementary page, by a twelfth-century scribe employing an orthography which suggests that his native language was not English (Onions, 'Some early Middle-English spellings', 505–7).   [6] MS *Mundus*. D tells us it was Olaf, whom Snorri (*Heimskringla*, ed. Jonsson, p. 505) says was keen on ceremonial. Perhaps *Mundus* is a Latin rendering of his early nickname Old Norse *skrauti* 'flashy', cf. Dickins, 'The late addition to ASC 1066 C', 148–9. [7] Leofric was the nephew of Earl Leofric of Mercia and Godgifu (Lady Godiva). Hugh Candidus (p. 66) describes some of his gifts to the monastery: *the great cross which is over the altar, made of silver and gold of marvellous workmanship . . . gold and silver candlesticks, and the great frontal before the altar, all of gold and silver and precious stones, and many reliquaries, texts of the gospels, and many other things, similarly all made of gold and silver. A chasuble of purple richly adorned*

E 1066 *continued from opposite*

him.[7] Then 'Golden Borough' became 'Wretched Borough'. The monks then chose Brand the provost as abbot, because he was a very good man, and very wise, and then sent him to the ætheling Edgar[8] because the local people thought he ought to become king, and the ætheling happily agreed it for him. Then when King William heard tell of it, he became very angry, and said that the abbot had slighted him. Then good men went between them and reconciled them, because the abbot was a rather good man; then [he] gave the king 40 marks of gold in reconciliation; and then he lived for only a little while thereafter, for only three years. Afterwards there came calamity and all evil on the minster. God have mercy on it. [*continued overleaf*]

THE WORCESTER MANUSCRIPT (D) 1066 *continued from p. 197*

of English people; and there was that day a very hard fight on both sides. There were killed Harald Fine-hair[9] and Earl Tostig, and the Northmen who remained there were put to flight, and the English fiercely attacked them from behind until some of them came to ship, some drowned, and some also burnt, and thus variously perished, so that there were few survivors, and the English had possession of the place of slaughter. The king then gave safe-conduct to Olaf, the son of the king of the Norse, and to their bishop, and to the earl of Orkney,[10] and to all those who were left on the ships. And they then went up to our king,[11] and swore oaths[12] that they would always keep peace and friendship in this land; and the king let them go home with 24[13] ships. These two national fights were accomplished within five days.

Then Earl William came from Normandy into Pevensey, on the eve of the Feast of St Michael,[2] and as soon as they were fit, made a castle at Hastings market-town.[14] Then this became known to King Harold and he gathered a great raiding-army, and came against him at the grey apple-tree.[15] And William came upon him by surprise before his people were marshalled. Nevertheless the king fought very hard against him with those men who wanted to support him, and there was a great slaughter on either side. There were killed King Harold, and Earl Leofwine his brother, and Earl Gyrth his brother, and many good men. And the French had possession of the place of slaughter, just as God granted them because of the people's sins. Archbishop Aldred and the garrison in London wanted to have Prince Edgar for king, just as was his natural right;[8] and Edwin and Morcar promised him that they would fight for him, but always when it should have been furthered, [*continued overleaf*]

---

with gold and precious stones ... and many other chasubles and copes and palls and other adornments. [8] Grandson of Edmund Ironside, see Table p. 290. [9] *Recte* Harald Hardrada; Harald Fine-hair had died c. 936. Florence (I, p. 226), Simeon (II, p. 180), Gaimar (5191) and Ordericus (II, pp. 142–3) all make the same mistake. [10] Florence (I, pp. 226–7) calls him Paul, and says he had been sent off with part of the army to guard the ships. [11] Cf. p. 197, note 16. [12] Florence (I, p. 227) says they also gave hostages. [13] *xxiiii*; Florence (I, p. 227) says *xx*. [14] Its construction is illustrated in the Bayeux Tapestry (ed. Wilson, pls. 49–50). [15] This account of the battle, found solely in D, is the only contemporary English written description to survive; for Norman narratives by William of Jumièges and William of Poitiers see Douglas and Greenaway, *Documents*, pp. 228–46.

E 1067 *continued from previous page*
1067. Here the king went across the sea, and had with him hostages and
, monies, and came back the next year on the Feast of St Nicholas;[1] and that day
Christ Church in Canterbury burned down. And he bestowed every man's
land when he came back. And [1068] that summer [*continued opposite*]

THE WORCESTER MANUSCRIPT (D) 1066 *continued from previous page*
so from day to day the later the worse it got, just as it all did in the end. This
fight took place on Pope Calixtus' Day.[2] And Earl William went back again to
Hastings, and waited there to see whether he would be submitted to; but when
he realized that no-one was willing to come to him, he went inland with all of
his raiding-army which was left to him and [what] came to him afterwards
from across the sea, and raided all that region he travelled across until he came
to Berkhamsted.[3] And there came to meet him Archbishop Aldred, and Prince
Edgar, and Earl Edwin, and Earl Morcar, and all the best men from London;[4]
and they submitted from necessity when the most harm was done – and it was
great folly that it was not done thus earlier, when God would not remedy
matters because of our sins – and gave hostages and swore him oaths, and he
promised them that he would be a loyal lord to them. And yet in the middle of
this they raided all that they went across. Then on Midwinter's Day
Archbishop Aldred[5] consecrated him king in Westminster; and he gave his
hand on it[6] and on *Christ's* book, and also swore, before he [Aldred] would set
the *crown* on his head, that he would hold this nation as well as the best of any
kings before him did, if they would be loyal to him. Nevertheless he charged
men a very stiff tax, and then in the spring went across the sea to Normandy,
and took with him Archbishop Stigand, and Æthelnoth, abbot in Glastonbury, and Prince Edgar, and Earl Edwin, and Earl Morcar, and Earl
Waltheof[7] and many other good men from England.[8] And Bishop Odo[9] and
Earl William[10] were left behind here, and they built castles widely throughout
this nation, and oppressed the wretched people; and afterwards it always
grew very much worse. When God wills, may the end be good.[11]
1067. Here the king came back again to England on the Feast of St
Nicholas.[12] And that day Christ Church in Canterbury burned down. And
Bishop Wulfwig passed away, and is buried at his bishop's seat in Dorchester.
And Prince Eadric[13] and the Welsh became hostile and they attacked the
castle-men in Hereford, and did them many injuries. And here the king set a
great tax on the wretched [*continued opposite*]

---

[1] 6 December.　[2] 14 October.　[3] On the main road 25 miles north-west of London; a
borough and manor held by Harold's thegn Eadmer Atol (DB, *Hertfordshire*, 15.1). The byname
may perhaps be rendered 'the Spiteful', cf. Tengvik, *Old English Bynames*, p. 341.　[4] Florence
(I, p. 228) includes also the names of Bishop Wulfstan of Worcester and Bishop Walter of
Hereford. As to whether Edwin and Morcar submitted at Berkhamsted or later at Barking, as
French sources say, see Freeman, *Norman Conquest*, III, pp..767–8.　[5] Rather than Stigand,
explains Florence (I, p. 228), because of that prelate's uncanonical status.　[6] Cf. p. 159, note
16.　[7] Son of Siward of Northumbria, holding an earldom in the Midlands, see Scott,
'Earl Waltheof of Northumbria', 149–213.　[8] Florence (II, p. 1) includes also 'the
noble *satrap* Æthelnoth the Kentishman'.　[9] Half-brother of the Conqueror, bishop

E 1067 *continued from opposite page*
Prince Edgar went away, and Mærleswein,[14] and many men with them, and went to Scotland, and the king Malcolm received them all, and took Margaret, the prince's sister, to wife. [*continued overleaf*]

THE WORCESTER MANUSCRIPT (D) 1067 *continued from opposite page*
people, and yet nevertheless always allowed to be raided all that they went across. And then [1068] he travelled to Devonshire, and besieged Exeter stronghold for 18 days – and there a great part of his raiding-army perished. But he promised them well – and performed badly – and they gave up the stronghold to him because the thegns had betrayed them.

And that summer Prince Edgar went away, with his mother Agatha and his two sisters, Margaret and Christina, and Mærleswein and many good men with them, and came to Scotland under King Malcolm's protection and he received them all; then the king Malcolm began to desire his sister, Margaret, as wife, but he and his men opposed it for a long time, and also she herself refused,[15] and declared that she would not have him, nor any, if the Graciousness on high would grant her that with bodily heart she might please the mighty Lord with pure continence in maidenhood in this short life. The king eagerly pressed her brother until he said 'yes' to it – also he dared not otherwise, because they had come into his power. So it came to pass as provided by God – and it could not be otherwise – just as he himself says in his gospel that even one sparrow cannot fall into a snare without his providence.[16] The foreknowing Creator knew beforehand what he wanted to have done by her, because she would increase the glory of God in that land, and direct the king out of the path of error, and turn him and his people together towards a better way, and lay aside the evil customs which that nation earlier followed – just as she afterwards did. The king then received her,[17] although it was against her will; and her customs pleased him, and [he] thanked God, who so powerfully gave him such a consort, and reflected wisely, since he was very prudent, and turned himself toward God, and despised every impurity. About that the apostle Paul, teacher of all nations, declared: *The unbelieving man is saved through the believing wife,* [*continued overleaf*]

---

of Bayeux 1049–97, made earl of Kent shortly after 1066. See Gleason, *An Ecclesiastical Barony,* pp. 8–17.   [10] William fitz Osbern, son of Osbern the steward, was made earl of Hereford shortly after 1066.   [11] The word *god* is interlined, perhaps by a later hand, and the sense may originally have been: 'May the end be when God wills'.   [12] 6 December.   [13] *Eadric cild; cild* may have written in mistake for *se wilda,* 'the Wild', the cognomen given by Ordericus (II, pp. 194–5, 228–9). Florence (II, pp. 1, 7) calls him *silvaticus* ('of the woods'). A powerful landowner in Herefordshire and Shropshire, and nephew of the infamous (*pestiferi*) Eadric Streona, he refused to surrender himself to William, and in consequence his lands were frequently harried by the Hereford garrisons; in return Eadric raided Herefordshire with the aid of the Welsh kings Bleddyn and Rhiwallon (cf. annal 1063 D). Together with other untameable (*ferocibus*) Englishmen, he was reconciled with William in 1070; see generally Reynolds, 'Eadric *silvaticus* and the English resistance', pp. 102–5.   [14] Sheriff of Lincoln and an extensive landowner through England. [15] What follows is rhetorically heightened and may derive from some Life of St Margaret. [16] Apparently an allusion to Matthew, x:29.   [17] i.e. married her – in 1070.

E 1068 *continued from previous page*

1068. Here in this year King William gave Earl Robert the earldom in Northumberland. Then [1069] the local men came against him and killed him and 9 hundred men with him.[1] And the ætheling Edgar then came to York with all the Northumbrians, and the men of the market-town made peace with him. And the king William came from the south with all his army and ravaged the town, and killed many hundreds of men; and the ætheling went back to Scotland.

1069. Here Bishop Æthelric in Peterborough[2] was accused, and was sent to Westminster, and his brother, Bishop Æthelwine, was outlawed. Then between the two Feasts of *St Mary*,[3] they, that is the sons of King Swein,[4] and his brother Jarl Osbern, came from the east from Denmark with 300 ships; [*continued opposite*]

THE WORCESTER MANUSCRIPT (D) 1067 *continued from previous page*

and likewise the unbelieving wife through the believing man etc.,[5] that is in our language: 'Very often the unbelieving man is sanctified and saved through a righteous[6] wife; and likewise, the wife through a believing man'. This aforesaid queen afterwards performed many useful works in that land to the glory of God, and also throve well in the royal estate, just as was natural to her. She was sprung from a believing and noble race; her father was the ætheling Edward, son of King Edmund – Edmund Æthelred's offspring, Æthelred Edgar's offspring, Edgar Eadred's offspring and so forth in that royal family; and her mother's family goes back to the emperor Henry who had dominion over Rome.[7]

And here Gytha, mother of Harold, travelled away to the Isle of Flatholme,[8] and the wives of many good men with her, and lived there for a certain time, and so went from there across the sea to St Omer.[9]

At this Easter the king came to Winchester – and then [1068] Easter was on *23 March*. And soon after that the Lady Matilda came here to the land, and Archbishop Aldred consecrated her queen in Westminster on Whit Sunday.[10] Then when the king was informed that the people in the north had gathered together and would stand against him if he came,[11] he went to Nottingham and built a castle there, and so went to York, and there built two castles,[12] and in Lincoln, and everywhere in that region. And Jarl Gospatric and the best men went into Scotland. [*continued opposite*]

---

[1] On 28 January 1069 (Simeon, II, p. 187).   [2] See p. 187, note 17.   [3] i.e. the Assumption, 15 August, and the Nativity, 8 September.   [4] Swein Estrithson, king of Denmark.   [5] A paraphrase of 1 Corinthians, vii:14.   [6] The scribe has added the word 'believing' as an interlinear gloss.   [7] Cf. Ritchie, *The Normans in Scotland*, pp. xiii-xiv, 389–92 *et passim*.   [8] A small island in the Bristol Channel, cf. annal 918 A.   [9] In Flanders.   [10] *Hwitan Sunnan dæg*; the Chronicle normally uses the Latinate 'Pentecost'; this is the earliest recorded use of the vernacular term, which perhaps refers to the custom of wearing white garments that day.

E 1069 *continued from opposite page*
and then the earl Waltheof travelled and came – he and the ætheling Edgar and
many hundreds of men with them – and met the fleet in the Humber, and
travelled to York, and went up and won the castles, and killed many hundreds
of men, and led many treasures to the ships and had the head men in bonds,
and lay between the Ouse and Trent all the winter. And the king William went
into that shire and completely did for it. And in this same year passed away
Brand, abbot of Peterborough, on *27 November.* [*continued on p. 205*]

THE WORCESTER MANUSCRIPT (D) 1067 *continued from opposite page*

And in the middle of this [1068] Harold's sons[13] came by surprise from Ireland
into the mouth of the Avon with a raiding ship-army, and straightway raided
across all that region; then went to Bristol and wanted to break down the town
but the townspeople fought hard against them; and then when they could not
gain anything from the town, they went to the ships with what they had
plundered, and they went thus to Somerset and went up there. And Eadnoth
the staller fought with them, and was killed there, together with many good
men on either side; and those who were left there went away from there.[14]

1068. Here in this year King William gave Earl Robert the earldom over
Northumberland, but [1069] the local men surprised him inside the
stronghold at Durham, and killed him and 900 men with him. And
immediately after that the ætheling Edgar came to York with all the
Northumbrians and the men of the stronghold made peace with him. And
King William came upon them by surprise from the south with a streaming
raiding-army and put them to flight, and then killed those who could not flee –
that was several hundreds of men; and ravaged the town and made St Peter's
minster a disgrace, and also ravaged and humiliated all the others. And the
ætheling went back again to Scotland.

After these events, towards midsummer, the sons of Harold came from
Ireland with 64 ships into the mouth of the Taw,[15] and went up there
carelessly. And Earl Brian came against them by surprise with no little
company, and fought against them, and killed all the best men who were in the
fleet; and the others, with little company, fled to the ships. And Harold's sons
went back again to Ireland.

Here passed away Aldred, archbishop of York, and is buried there
[*continued overleaf*]

---

[11] Gaimar (5373–98) says that William sent a message to York by Archbishop Aldred offering
safe-conduct and confirmation of their inheritance to all those who would come to him, but when
they came he imprisoned them and gave their lands to the French.   [12] Florence (II, p. 2): *and
placed five hundred men in them.*   [13] Godwine, Edmund and Magnus says Florence (II, p. 2),
but Gaimar (5400–2) mentions only Godwine and Edmund, and with them Tostig, son of
Swein.   [14] Florence (II, p. 3) adds that, having won the victory, and having seized no little booty
in Devon and Cornwall, Harold's sons returned to Ireland.   [15] On the north coast of Devon.

A *continued from p. 196*

1070. Here Lanfranc, who was abbot in Caen, came to England, who after
, a few days became archbishop in Canterbury.[1] He was ordained on 29 *August*
in his own bishop's seat by eight of his suffragan bishops; the others who were
not there explained by messengers and by letter why they could not be there. In
that year Thomas, who was chosen as bishop for York, came to Canterbury in
order that he be ordained according to ancient custom. Then when Lanfranc
demanded confirmation of his obedience [*continued on p. 206*]

THE WORCESTER MANUSCRIPT (D) 1068 [1069] *continued from previous page*

at his bishop's seat. And he died on *Protus and Hyacinthus'* Day;[2] and he held
the arch-seat with great dignity for 10 years all but 15 weeks. Soon thereafter
three sons[3] of King Swein with 240 ships came from Denmark into the
Humber – and Jarl Osbern and Jarl Thurkil. And there came against them
Prince Edgar, and Earl Waltheof, and Mærleswein, and Earl Gospatric with
the Northumbrians, and all the people of the land, riding and marching with
an enormous raiding-army, greatly rejoicing; and thus all resolutely went to
York and broke down and demolished the castle,[4] and won countless
treasures in there, and there killed many hundreds of French men and led
many with them to ship. And before the shipmen came there, the French had
burned down the borough, and also completely ravaged and burned down the
holy minster of *St Peter*. Then when the king learnt this, he went northward
with all of his army which he could gather, and wholly ravaged and laid waste
the shire. And the fleet lay all winter in the Humber, where the king could not
come at them.[5] And the king was in York on Midwinter's Day, and in the land
thus all the winter, and came to Winchester at the same Easter [1070]. And
Bishop Æthelric, who was in Peterborough, was accused and led to
Westminster, and his brother, Bishop Æthelwine, outlawed.[6]

1071 [1070]. Here the earl Waltheof made peace with the king. And in the
following spring the king allowed all the minsters which were in England to be
raided,[7] and in this year there was a great famine. And the minster at
Peterborough was raided – that was those men whom Bishop Æthelric earlier
[*continued on p. 206*]

---

[1] For whom see generally Gibson, *Lanfranc of Bec.*   [2] 11 September – and was buried in St
Peter's church (Florence, II, p. 3). D says the Danes came soon after Aldred's death, but E says
before, while Florence ascribes his fatal sickness to grief at their arrival.   [3] Gaimar (5428)
names these as Harald, Cnut and Beorn Leriz – the last otherwise unknown, but Swein had a large
progeny. Florence (II, p. 3) mentions only Harald and Cnut. He agrees with D against E on the
number of ships.   [4] On 19 September, says Florence (II, p. 4), the Normans in charge of the
castle set fire to the houses near it to prevent the Danes from using them as material for filling the
ditch; the fire spread and burned the city and the minster. He regards the subsequent capture of the
castle by the Danes, when more than three thousand French men were killed, as divine
vengeance.   [5] Florence (II, p. 4) says William offered money to Earl Osbeorn and secretly gave
him permission to forage along the coast, on condition that he promised to go home when the
winter was over. In the famine that followed these hostilities, he says, men were reduced to
consuming the flesh of horses, dogs, cats and even human beings.   [6] See p. 209, note
10.   [7] Florence (II, pp. 4–5) says that, on the advice of William, earl of Hereford and certain
others, they searched for and seized the money which the richer English had deposited in them.

E continued from p. 203

1070. Here the earl Waltheof made peace with the king. And in the following spring the king allowed all the minsters which were in England to be raided.[6] Then in the same year King Swein came from Denmark into the Humber, and the local people came to him and made peace with him – thought that he would conquer that land.[8] Then Christian, the Danish bishop,[9] came to Ely, and Jarl Osbern and the Danish housecarls with them. And the English people from all the Fenlands came to them – thought that they would win all that land. Then the monks of Peterborough heard say that their own men, that was Hereward[10] and his band, wanted to raid the minster – that was because they had heard say that the king had given the abbacy to a French[11] abbot called Turold,[12] and that he was a very stern man and had then come into Stamford with all his French men. There was then a sacristan called Yware; he at night took all he could: that was Christ's books and chasubles and copes and robes and such little things – whatsoever he could, and straightway before dawn travelled to the abbot Turold, and told him that he sought his protection, and informed him how the outlaws were to come to Peterborough. He did that entirely on the advice of the monks. Then straightway in the morning all the outlaws came with many ships and wanted [to get] into the minster, and the monks withstood so that they could not come in. Then they laid fire to it, and burned down all the monks' buildings and all the town, except for one building. Then, by means of fire, they came in at Bolhithe Gate.[13] The monks came to meet them, asked them for peace, but they did not care about anything, went into the minster, climbed up to the holy rood, took the crown off our Lord's head – all of pure gold – then took the rest which was underneath his feet – that was all of red gold – climbed up to the steeple, brought down the altar-frontal that was hidden there – it was all of gold and of silver.[14] They took there two golden shrines,[15] and 9 silver, and they took fifteen great roods, both of gold and of silver. They took there so much gold and silver and and so many treasures in money and in clothing and in books[16] that no man can tell another – said they did it out of [*continued on p. 207*]

---

[8] For Swein's claim to the English throne, see Table p. 292.   [9] Bishop of Aarhus.   [10] Hereward 'the Wake', a Peterborough tenant dispossessed by the Normans, and a renowned guerilla leader (Swanton, *Hereward and Others*, passim).   [11] Hugh Candidus (p. 77) says correctly 'Norman', but the two words seem to be used synonously at this stage, see Clark, ' "France" and "French" in the Anglo-Saxon Chronicle", pp. 35–45.   [12] Formerly a monk at Fécamp, but then abbot of Malmesbury. William of Malmesbury (*Gesta Pontificum*, p. 420) says of the warlike abbot that William transferred him to Peterborough with the remark that, 'since he behaved like a soldier rather than a monk, he would provide him with somebody to fight' – i.e. Hereward.   [13] To the east of the abbey (Mackreth, 'Recent work on monastic Peterborough', 19, fig. 9.)   [14] Possibly that given to the abbey by Abbot Leofric, see p. 198, note 7.   [15] Perhaps also gifts of Leofric (see p. 198, note 7); Hugh Candidus' account (p. 78) suggests that that these were taken before the tower was climbed, and thus kept in the body of the church.   [16] For books as wealth, see McKittrick, *The Carolingians and the Written Word*, pp. 135–64. Leofric had given a number of richly bound books (see p. 198, note 7).

A 1070 *continued from p. 204*

with oath-swearing, he refused and said that he did not have to do it. Then the archbishop Lanfranc got very angry with him, and ordered the bishops who had come there at Archbishop Lanfranc's command to perform service, and all the monks that they should unrobe themselves. And they did so at his command. So Thomas travelled back without blessing on that occasion. Then soon after this it happened that the archbishop Lanfranc travelled to Rome, and Thomas along with him. Then when they came there, and had spoken about other things that they wanted to speak about, Thomas began his speech: how he came to Canterbury and how the archbishop asked obedience with oath-swearing from him, and he refused it. Then the archbishop Lanfranc began to explain with open reasoning that what he had demanded he had demanded by right, and confirmed the same with strong argument before the pope Alexander[1] and before all the *council* which was gathered there; and so [they] went home. After this Thomas came to Canterbury, and humbly fulfilled all that the archbishop demanded of him, and afterwards received the blessing.[2]

[The English text of manuscript A ends here][3]

THE WORCESTER MANUSCRIPT (D) 1071 [1070] *continued from p. 204*

excommunicated because they had seized there all that he owned. And the same summer that [Danish] fleet came into the Thames, and lay there two days, and afterwards held a course for Denmark.[4] And Earl Baldwin[5] passed away, and Arnulf his son succeeded to the authority. And the king of the French[6] and Earl William[7] were to be his guardians, but Robert[8] came there, and killed Arnulf his relative and the earl William, and put the king to flight and killed many thousands of his men.[9]

1072 [1071]. Here Earl Edwin and Earl Morcar[10] ran off and travelled variously in woods and in open country,[11] until Edwin was killed by his own men, and Morcar turned by ship to [*continued on p. 208*]

---

[1] Alexander II.   [2] On the relationship between the archbishops of Canterbury and York, see Stenton, *Anglo-Saxon England*, pp. 656–7, Florence (II, p. 8) adds that Thomas's plans to subject the see of Worcester were finally defeated at a council held in a place called Pedreda. For the forged documents adduced to support the Canterbury claim, see Gibson, *Lanfranc of Bec*, pp. 231–7, and Southern, 'The Canterbury Forgeries', 193–226.   [3] It is followed by an account in Latin of Lanfranc and his synods and canons, with the consecration of his successor Anselm.   [4] This was Osbeorn's fleet; Florence (II, p. 7) says King Swein had exiled his brother for accepting William's bribes earlier (see p. 204, note 5).   [5] Baldwin VI, count of Flanders.   [6] Philip I.   [7] The Conqueror's steward, and in 1067 regent in England (see Wightman, 'The palatine earldom of William fitz Osborn', pp. 16–17).   [8] Robert 'the Frisian', brother of Baldwin VI, see Ordericus, II, pp. 280–83.   [9] D *manna*, E *menn*; the battle of Cassel in Flanders (dép. Nord), was in 1071.   [10] Sons of Earl Ælfgar of Mercia: Edwin succeeding his father to Mercia, Morcar chosen by the Northumbrians in place of Tostig (see *s.a.* 1064 E, 1065 D).   [11] *feld.*

E 1070 *continued from p. 205*

loyalty to this minster. Afterwards they made for ship, and took themselves to Ely, and entrusted all the treasures there. The Danish men thought they would overcome the French men,[12] then drove away all the monks[13] – left none there, except for one monk who was called Leofwine the Long;[14] he lay sick in the infirmary. Then Abbot Turold came, and eight times twenty French men with him, all fully armed. When he came there he found everything inside and outside burned down – all but the church alone. The outlaws were all afloat then – knew that he would come there. This was done on 2 *June*. Then when the two kings, William and Swein, came to terms, the Danish men travelled out of Ely with all the afore-mentioned treasures and took them with them. Then when they came to the middle of the sea, a great storm came and scattered all the ships in which the treasures were: some travelled to Norway, some to Ireland, some to Denmark – and all that came there was only the altar-frontal, and some shrines, and some crosses and several of the other treasures; and brought to a royal manor called. . . . ,[15] and then put it all in the church.

And then afterwards, through their carelessness and through their drunkenness, on one night the church burned down and all there was in it. Thus was the minster of Peterborough burned down and ravaged. May God Almighty through his great compassion have pity on it! And thus the abbot Turold came to Peterborough, and then the monks came back and performed the service of Christ in the church, which earlier stood a full week without any kind of rite. Then when Bishop Æthelric heard tell of that, he excommunicated all the men who had done that evil deed. There was a great famine that year, and then the following summer the fleet came from the north, from the Humber, into the Thames, and lay there two days, and afterwards held a course for Denmark.[4] And Earl Baldwin[5] passed away, and Arnulf, his son, succeeded to the authority. And Earl William[7] was to be his guardian – and also the king of the French.[6] And then Earl Robert[8] came and killed his relative Arnulf and the earl, and put the king to flight, and killed many thousands of his men.[9]

1071. Here Earl Edwin and Earl Morcar[10] ran off and travelled variously in woods and in open country.[11] Then Earl Morcar turned on ship to Ely, and Earl Edwin was killed [*continued overleaf*]

---

[12] Clark (*The Peterborough Chronicle*, p. 64, note) prefers to invert the sense of this and the previous sentence: 'Thinking the Normans would catch them, they went away to Ely and there they handed all the treasure over to the Danes'.   [13] According to Hugh Candidus (p. 80) some, including Prior Æthelwold, were taken to Ely; there the Danes promised him a bishopric and gave him the keys to the treasury, whereupon, in a clandestine fashion, he stole back certain relics, including the arm of St Oswald.   [14] A Peterborough monk by the same name witnessed a pre-Conquest territorial agreement between the abbeys of Thorney and Ramsey (Harmer, *Writs*, p. 254).   [15] A space left in the manuscript; Hugh Candidus (p. 82) says merely *a certain royal manor*, and that the sacristan Yware subsequently recovered these relics.

E 1071 *continued from previous page*
treacherously by his own men. And the bishop Æthelwine[1] and Siward Bearn and many hundreds of men with them came into Ely.[2] And then when the king William learnt about that, he ordered out ship-army and land-army, and surrounded that land, and made a bridge[3] and went in – and the ship-army [was] to the seaward. And then the outlaws all came into hand:[4] that was Bishop Æthelwine and Earl Morcar and all those who were with them, except Hereward alone, and all who wanted to be with him; and he courageously led them out. And the king took ships and weapons and many monies, and dealt with the men just as he wanted; and he sent the bishop Æthelwine to Abingdon[5] and he passed away there soon the following winter.

1072. Here King William led a ship-army and land-army to Scotland, and beset that land to seaward with ships, and led his land-army in at the Forth,[6] and there he found nothing he was the better for. And the king Malcolm came and made peace with the king William[7] and gave hostages[8] and was his man; and the king turned home with all his army. And the bishop Æthelric passed away;[9] he was ordained bishop for York but it was taken from him unjustly,[10] and he was given the bishopric in Durham, and he had it as long as he wanted, [*continued opposite*]

Ely, and there came Bishop Æthelwine[1] and Siward Bearn and many hundreds of men with them.[2] But then when the king William learnt about this, he ordered out a ship-army and land-army, and surrounded that land, and made a bridge[3] – and [the] ship-army [was] to the seaward. And then they all came into the king's hand:[4] that was Bishop Æthelwine and Earl Morcar and all those who were with them, except Hereward alone, and all who could flee away with him; and he courageously led them out. And the king took their ships and weapons and many monies, and seized all the men and did with them what he wanted; and he sent Bishop Æthelwine to Abingdon[5] and he passed away there.

1073 [1072.] Here King William led a ship-army and land-army to Scotland, and beset that land to seaward with ships, and himself travelled in with his land-army over the Forth,[6] and there he found nothing he was the better for. And King Malcolm came and made peace with King William,[7] and was his man, and gave him hostages,[8] and afterwards he turned home with all his army. And the bishop Æthelric passed away;[9] he was ordained bishop for York, but it was taken from him unjustly,[10] and he was given the bishopric at Durham, and [*continued opposite*]

---

[1] The outlawed bishop of Durham, see annal 1068 D, 1069 E. [2] Gaimar (5451–8) says they sailed from Scotland to the Humber where Morcar joined them; and then went on to meet the English at Upwell (a dozen miles north of Ely). [3] A causeway, which Florence (II, p. 9) says was two miles long. See generally Swanton, *Hereward and Others*. [4] i.e. surrendered. [5] i.e. to St Mary's Abbey, see *Chronicon Monasterii de Abingdon*, II, pp. 485–6. [6] The Forth representing the border between English and Scottish territory; cf. 'Lothian in England', *s.a.* 1091; Map p. 274. See also Breeze, 'The Anglo-Saxon Chronicle for 1072', 269–70. [7] Florence (II, p. 9) and Gaimar (5711) both locate the meeting at Abernethy (Perthshire); see Ritchie, *The Normans in Scotland*, pp. 29–38, 386. [8] Apparently including his oldest son, Duncan (see annal 1093).

E 1072 *continued from opposite page*
and afterwards relinquished it and travelled to Peterborough to St Peter's
minster where he conducted his life for 12 years. Then after the king William
won England, he took him from Peterborough and sent him to Westminster.[11]
And he passed away on *15 October*,[9] and he is buried there inside the minster
inside St Nicholas' side-chapel.[12]

1073. In this year King William led an English and French raiding-army
across the sea, and won the land of Maine, and the English greatly despoiled it;
they did for vineyards, burned down towns, and greatly despoiled that land,
and bent it all into William's hands, and afterwards they turned home to
England.

1074. In this year King William went across the sea to Normandy,
[continued overleaf]

THE WORCESTER MANUSCRIPT (D) 1073 [1072] *continued from opposite*

he had it as long as he wanted, and afterwards relinquished it and travelled to
Peterborough to St Peter's minster where he conducted his life for 12 years.
Then after William won England, he had him taken from Peterborough and
sent him to Westminster,[11] and he passed away there on *15 October*,[9] and is
buried there inside St Nicholas' side-chapel.[12]

1074 [1073]. In this year King William led an English and French raiding-
army across the sea and won the land of Maine, and the English greatly
despoiled it; they did for vineyards, burned down towns, and greatly
despoiled that land, and bent all that land into William's hands, and
afterwards they turned home.

1075 [1074]. In this year King William went across the sea to Normandy,
and on the Feast of St Grimbald[13] Prince Edgar came from the land of the
Flemings into Scotland, and the king Malcolm and his[14] sister Margaret
received him with great honour. At the same time Philip, the king of France,
sent a letter to him and ordered him to come to him, and he would give him the
castle at Montreuil[15] so that afterwards he could daily do ill-turns to those not
his friends. Well, then the king Malcolm and his sister Margaret gave him and
all his men great gifts and many treasures in furs covered with purple cloth,
and in pelisses of marten-fur, and miniver-fur and ermine-fur and in purple
cloth, and in golden and in silver vessels, and led him and all his sailors out of
his domain with great honour. But on the journey it turned out badly for them
when they were out at sea, in that very rough weather came on them, and the
raging sea and the strong wind cast them on that land so that all their ships
broke up, and they themselves came to land with difficulty, and well-nigh all
their treasure *[continued overleaf]*

---

[9] Hugh Candidus (p. 74) says that he wished to be buried in the fetters of his imprisonment as a
mark of martyrdom.   [10] Æthelric was only ever bishop of Durham. The assumption probably
comes from a misreading of annal 1041 D, taking his ordination *to Eoferwic* to mean 'for' rather
than 'at' York. Perhaps the chronicler is thinking of his expulsion by the clerks of Durham in 1056
(q.v.); he was imprisoned on the charge of robbing the church there (Simeon, I, pp.
91–2).   [11] Florence (II, p. 10) says: *into custody at Westminster*.   [12] *porticus*, see p. 44, note
10.   [13] 8 July.   [14] i.e. Edgar's sister (Malcolm's wife).   [15] Dép. Pas-de-Calais.

E 1074 *continued from previous page*
and Prince Edgar came from Scotland to Normandy, and the king revoked the outlawry on him and all his men; and he was in the king's court and took such rights as the king granted him.[1]

1075. In this year King William gave the daughter[2] of William fitz Osbern in marriage to Earl Ralph;[3] and the same Ralph was Breton on his mother's side, and his father was English – called Ralph, and was born in Norfolk. Then the king gave his [Ralph's] son the earldom in Norfolk and Suffolk. He then led that woman to Norwich.[4]

That bride-ale there was death to men.[5]

Earl Roger[6] was there, and Earl Waltheof, and bishops and abbots, and there planned that they would put the king out of [*continued opposite*]

WORCESTER MANUSCRIPT (D) 1075 [1074] *continued from previous page*

was lost. And also some of his men were captured by the French men, but he himself and those of his fittest men travelled back again to Scotland, some pitiably walking on foot, and some wretchedly riding. Then the king Malcolm advised him that he send to King William across the sea, and ask for his protection, and so also he did, and the king granted him that and sent for him. And the king Malcolm and his sister again gave him and all his men countless treasures, and very honourably sent him out of their domain again. And the sheriff of York came to meet them at Durham, and travelled all the way with them, and had them found food and fodder at each castle they came to, until they came across the sea to the king. And the king William then received him with great honour, and he was then there in his court and took such privileges as he decreed for him.[1]

1076 [1075]. In this year King William gave the daughter[2] of William fitz Osbern in marriage to Earl Ralph;[3] and the same Ralph was Breton on his mother's side, and Ralph his father was English and was born in Norfolk. And therefore the king gave his [Ralph's] son the earldom there, and Suffolk also. He then led that woman to Norwich.[4]

That bride-ale there was the death of many men.[5]

Earl Roger[6] was there, and Earl Waltheof, and bishops and abbots, [*continued opposite*]

---

[1] Edgar seems to have lived on for fifty years.   [2] Emma.   [3] Ralph 'Guader', son of Edward the Confessor's steward Ralph the Staller, was now earl of Norfolk and Suffolk, and lord of Gaël in Brittany (*The Complete Peerage*, IX, pp. 571–4). Ralph the Staller may have been termed 'English' because he was born in England (Clarke, *The English Nobility under Edward the Confessor*, p. 44). Ralph 'Guader' fought on William's side at Hastings; see generally, Freeman, *Norman Conquest*, III, 751–4; IV – V, *passim*.   [4] Florence (II, p. 10) says that Roger gave his sister to Ralph against the king's will, and that the marriage was at Exning in Cambridgeshire (now Suffolk).   [5] The Old English takes the form of a rhythmic, internally-rhyming epigram.   [6] Roger of Breteuil, earl of Hereford, son of William fitz Osbern by his first wife, and therefore a brother of the bride.

E 1075 *continued from opposite*
the kingship of England. And it soon became known to the king in Normandy, how it was planned.[7] It was Earl Roger and Earl Ralph who were the foremost in the foolish plan, and they seduced the Bretons to them, and sent east to Denmark[8] for a raiding ship-army to support them. And Roger travelled west to his earldom[9] and gathered his people to the king's detriment, but he was hindered.[10] And Ralph, also, in his earldom wanted to go forward with his people, but the castle-men which were in England, and also the local people, came against him and acted so that he did nothing[11] but went to ship at Norwich. And his wife was inside the castle, and held it until she was granted safe-conduct, and then she and all her men who wanted to go with her travelled out of England. And the king afterwards came to England and seized his relative, Earl Roger, and secured him. And he took Earl Waltheof also.

And soon after that 200 ships came from the east from Denmark, and there were on board two head men, King Swein's son Cnut, and Earl Hákon, and they dared not join battle with King William [*continued overleaf*]

THE WORCESTER MANUSCRIPT (D) 1076 [1075] *continued from opposite*

and there planned that they would drive their royal lord from his kingdom. And this soon became known to the king in Normandy.[7] Earl Ralph and Earl Roger were principals in this foolish plan, and they seduced the Bretons to them, and sent also to Denmark for a raiding ship-army to support them.[8] And Roger travelled west to his earldom[9] and gathered his people to the king's detriment, as he thought, but it turned out to their own great harm. Ralph, also, wanted to go forward with his earldom, but the castle-men which were in England, and also the local people, came against them and hindered them in everything so that they did nothing,[11] but he was glad to flee away to the ships. And his wife was inside the castle, and held it until she was granted safe-conduct, and then she and all her men who wanted to go with her travelled out of England. And the king afterwards came to England and seized his relative, Earl Roger, and set him in prison. And Earl Waltheof travelled across the sea, and confessed, and asked forgiveness and offered treasures. But the king made light of it until he came to England – and then had him taken afterwards.

And soon after this two hundred ships came from Denmark;[8] the head men there were King Swein's son Cnut, and Earl Hákon, and dared not join battle with King William, but [*continued overleaf*]

---

[7] Florence (II, p. 10) says that Waltheof, having been coerced into joining the plot, confessed to Lanfranc, and on his advice went to the king in Normandy. Ordericus (II, pp. 320–21) says he was accused on the deposition of his wife Judith, niece of the Conqueror.   [8] An appeal to Swein, son of Cnut, who thought that he also might have a claim to England (Ordericus, II, pp. 224–7). See also annals 1070, 1085, 1087.   [9] Hereford.   [10] Florence (II, p. 11) says that Roger was prevented from coming back across the Severn by Wulfstan bishop of Worcester, Æthelwig abbot of Evesham, Urse d'Abetôt sherrif of Worcester and Walter de Lacy.   [11] Florence (II, p. 11) says that Ralph encamped near Cambridge but, confronted by an Anglo-Norman army of Odo bishop of Bayeux and Geoffrey bishop of Coutances, fled to his castle at Norwich, and from there to Brittany.

E 1075 *continued from previous page*
but held on across the sea to Flanders.

And the Lady Edith passed away in Winchester 7 days before Christmas, and the king had her brought to Westminster with great honour, and laid her with King Edward, her lord.

And he was at Westminster that midwinter, and there all the Bretons who were at the bride-ale at Norwich were done for:[1]

> Some were blinded and some driven from the land.
> Thus were traitors to William laid low.[2]

1076. In this year passed away Swein, king in Denmark; and Harald, his son, succeeded to the kingdom.

And the king gave Westminster to Abbot Vitalis, who was earlier [*continued opposite*]

THE WORCESTER MANUSCRIPT (D) 1076 [1075] *continued from previous page*

travelled to York and broke into St Peter's minster, and there took much property, and so went away; but all who were in that plan perished – that was Earl Hákon's son, and many others with him.

And the Lady Edith, who was King Edward's consort, passed away in Winchester seven days before Christmas, and the king had her brought to Westminster with great honour, and laid her with King Edward, her lord.

And the king was at Westminster that midwinter; there all the Bretons who were at the bride-feast at Norwich were condemned:[1]

> Some were blinded and some exiled from the land,
> and some were reduced to ignominy.
> Thus were traitors to the king laid low.[2]

1077 [1076]. In this year passed away Swein, king in Denmark; and Harald, his son, succeeded to his kingdom. Here King William gave the abbacy at Westminster to Abbot Vitalis, who was earlier a monk at Bernay. And here Earl Waltheof was beheaded in Winchester on the Feast of St Petronella;[3] and his body was led to Crowland,[4] and there he is buried. And King William went across the sea [*continued opposite*]

---

[1] E *fordyde*, D *fordemde*, cf. Waverly Annals (p. 193) *judicati sunt*, 'were judged'.   [2] The Old English lines form a rhythmic epigram, the version in D with some rhyme.   [3] 31 May. Florence (II, p. 12) and Ordericus (II, pp. 320–23) deprecate this execution; for Waltheof's later reputation as a saint, see Swanton, *Hereward and Others*; here in E the name Waltheof is rubricated as if for the obit of a martyr.   [4] Hallowed ground, the burial-place of St Guthlac, to which Waltheof was a benefactor in life, and where, in death, he was said to perform posthumous miracles (Ordericus, II, pp. 344–51).   [5] Earl Ralph's castle in Brittany, dép. Ille-et-Vilaine (Florence, II, p. 12).   [6] Philip I of France.

E 1076 *continued from opposite*
abbot in Bernay; and Earl Waltheof was beheaded in Winchester,[3] and his body was led to Crowland.[4]

And the king went across the sea, and led his army to Brittany, and besieged the castle of Dôl,[5] and the Bretons held it until the king[6] came from the land of France; and William went from there and lost there both men and horses, and many of his treasures.

1077. Here in this year the king of the French and William, king of England, were reconciled, but it held only a little while.

And in this year, one day before the *Assumption of St Mary*,[7] London burned down, more so than it ever was before since it was founded.

And in this year [1078] Æthelwig, abbot in Evesham,[8] passed away on *16 February*. And Bishop Hereman[9] also passed away on *20 February*.

1079. In this year King Malcolm came from Scotland into England between the two Feasts of Mary[10] with a great army, which raided the land of the Northumbrians as far as the Tyne, [*continued overleaf*]

THE WORCESTER MANUSCRIPT (D) 1077 [1077] *continued from opposite*

and led his army to Brittany, and besieged the castle at Dôl,[5] but the Bretons held it until the king[6] came from the kingdom of France; and the king William went from there and lost there both men and horses, and countless treasures.

1078 [1077]. Here the moon was eclipsed three nights before Candlemas.[11] And Æthelwig, the abbot in Evesham,[8] wise in matters of the world, passed away on the Feast of *St Juliana*;[12] and Walter was set as abbot in his place. And Bishop Hereman,[9] who was bishop in Berkshire and in Wiltshire and in Dorset, passed away. And here King Malcolm captured Mæl-slæhta's[13] mother. . . .[14] and all his best men, and all his treasures and his cattle, and he himself escaped with difficulty. . . .[15] And here was the dry summer, and wild-fire came on many shires and burned down many villages, and also many towns burned down.

1079. Here Robert,[16] the son of King William, ran from his father to his uncle Robert in Flanders,[17] because his father [*continued overleaf*]

---

[7] 14 August.   [8] See generally Darlington, 'Æthelwig, abbot of Evesham', 1–22, 177–98; VCH, *Worcester*, II, pp. 112–27.   [9] See p. 164, note 3.   [10] i.e. the Assumption (15 August) and the Nativity (8 September).   [11] 30 January.   [12] 16 February.   [13] *Recte* Mael-snechtan; the son of Macbeth's stepson Lulach, king of Moray, he died in 1085 (*Annals of Ulster*, II, pp. 38–9); for the background to this power-struggle, see Skene, *Celtic Scotland*, I, pp. 410–11, 426–7.   [14] Nearly a line left blank in the manuscript.   [15] Six lines left blank in the manuscript.   [16] For whom see David, *Robert Curthose, Duke of Normandy*.   [17] Robert of Flanders was brother of Maud, wife of William the Conqueror.

E 1079 *continued from previous page*
and killed many hundreds of men, and led home much money and treasure, and men in captivity. And the same year the king William fought against his son Robert outside Normandy, near a castle called Gerberoy.[1] And the king William was wounded there, and his horse which he sat on killed.[2] And his son William was also wounded there, and many men killed.

1080. In this year Walcher, the bishop in Durham, was killed at a meeting, and a hundred men with him, French and Flemish; and he himself was born in Lotharingia.[3] The Northumbrians did this in the month of May.[4]

1081. In this year the king led an army into Wales, and there freed many hundreds of men.

1082. Here the king seized Bishop Odo;[5] and here there was a great famine.

1083. In this year the discord arose in Glastonbury between the abbot Thurstan and his monks. First it came from the abbot's lack of wisdom in that he misgoverned his monks in many things.[6] And the monks complained, lovingly, to him about it, and asked him that he would rule them justly and love them, and they would be loyal and obedient to him. But the abbot wanted nothing of it, but treated them badly, and threatened them with worse. One day the abbot strode into *chapter* and spoke against the [*continued opposite*]

THE WORCESTER MANUSCRIPT (D) 1079 *continued from previous page*

would not let him govern his earldom in Normandy which he himself and also the king Philip with his consent had given him; and the best who were in the land had sworn him oaths and taken him as lord. Here Robert fought with his father, and wounded him in the hand; and his horse was shot under him;[2] and he who brought up another for him was straightway shot with a cross-bow – that was Toki, son of Wigod;[7] and many were killed there, and also captured; and Robert turned back to the land of the Flemings. We do not want, though, to write more here of the harm which he [did] his father. . . .[8]

1080 [1130].[9] Here Angus[10] was killed by the raiding-army of the Scots, and there was a great slaughter with him. There God's justice was visited in his death, because he was all forsworn.

---

[1] Dép. Oise; an important castle on the Vexin frontier which Florence (II, p. 13) says King Philip had given him (i.e. Robert).   [2] According to Florence (II, p. 13), William was wounded in the arm; but recognising his father's voice, Robert gave him his own horse to escape on.   [3] A cleric from Liège (Simeon, II, p. 195), hence the Flemish element in his retinue.   [4] On 14 May in a church at Gateshead according to Florence (II, pp. 13–16) and Simeon (I, pp. 116–17), who provide full circumstantial accounts of the murder. After the admired Waltheof's execution, Walcher had been made earl of Durham.   [5] Taking him by surprise in the Isle of Wight as he was preparing to embark for Normandy (Ordericus, IV, pp. 40–45), William declaring that he was arresting not the bishop but his vice-regent.   [6] Among other foolish things, says Florence (II, p. 16–17) this monk from Caen despised the traditional chant and attempted to compel the conservative Glastonbury community to adopt the chant of one William of Fécamp.   [7] Perhaps Wigod of Wallingford, cup-bearer and perhaps relative of the Confessor, an influential landowner and apparently favourable to the Conqueror (Freeman, *Norman Conquest*, III, p. 76; IV, pp. 45–6, 731–4).   [8] Here half a leaf of the manuscript has been cut away.   [9] MS (D) ends with this annal, entered fifty years too early, presumably as a result of mistaking *mcxxx* for *mlxxx*. Its handwriting and orthography suggest that the scribe's native language was not English (cf. p. 198, note 5).   [10] Earl of Moray, nephew of Mæl-snechtan (see annal 1078 D), who was in rebellion against King David.

E 1083 *continued from opposite*
monks and wanted to ill treat them, and sent for laymen[11] and they came into the *chapter* fully armed upon the monks. And then the monks were very afraid of them, and did not know what they should do, but scattered. Some ran into the church[12] and locked the doors against them; and they went after them into the minster[12] and wanted to drag them out since they dare not go out. But a pitiful thing happened there that day, in that the French men broke into the choir and pelted the altar where the monks were; and some of the knights went up to the upper floor[13] and shot arrows downwards towards the sanctuary, so that many arrows stuck in the rood which stood above the altar. And the wretched monks lay around the altar, and some crept under, and earnestly called on God, praying for his mercy when they could get no mercy from men. What more can we say, but that they shot fiercely, and the others broke down the doors there, and went in and did some of the monks to death, and wounded many in there, so that the blood came down from the altar onto the steps, and from the steps to the floor.[14] There were three done to death, and eighteen wounded.[15]

And in this same year passed away Matilda, King William's queen, on the day after the Feast of All Saints.[16]

And in this same year after midwinter the king had [1084] a great and heavy tax ordered over all England – that was seventy-two pence for every hide.

1084. Here in this year passed away Wulfwold, abbot in Chertsey, on *19 April*.

1085. In this year men declared, and said for a fact, that Cnut, king of Denmark, son of King Swein, set out in this direction, and wanted to win this land with the support of Earl Robert of Flanders, because Cnut had [married] Robert's daughter. When William, king of England, learnt about this – he was then staying in Normandy because he owned both England and Normandy – he travelled into England with a greater raiding-army of mounted men and infantry from the kingdom of France and from Brittany as had ever sought out this country before – such that men wondered [*continued overleaf, and thereafter without interruption*]

---

[11] *læwede mannum*, 'lay' as distinct to clerics – apparently his French men-at-arms. [12] *cyrice. . . . mynster*, a differentiation perhaps denoting the distinction between the adjoining *vetusta ecclesia* and *major ecclesia* at Glastonbury (Taylor, *Architecture*, III, p. 985, fig. 726); the men-at-arms sought to get into the latter through the former. [13] Probably a timber gallery at the west end of the nave, or perhaps a chamber above a side-aisle (cf. Taylor, *Architecture*, III, pp. 1017–19). [14] William of Malmesbury (*History of Glastonbury*, pp. 158–9) says the blood flowed from the wounded crucifix. [15] Florence (II, p. 17) says that two monks were killed and fourteen wounded – and even some of the soldiers were injured, since the monks defended themselves with stools and candlesticks; after a judicial enquiry, the king sent the abbot back to Normandy, and most of the monks were dispersed into the custody of other abbeys; Thurstan bought back the abbacy from William Rufus for £500, but spent his time on church estates and ended his life in misery far from Glastonbury itself, as he well deserved. Ordericus Vitalis (II, pp. 270–71) remarks that many similar episodes could be related, but since these make mournful reading, he will pass on to more cheerful things. [16] 2 November.

E 1085 *continued from previous page*
how this land could feed all that raiding-army. But the king had the raiding-army distributed through all this land to his men,[1] and they fed the raiding-army, each according to the proportion of his land. And men had great labour that year, and the king had the land near the sea laid waste, so that if his enemies landed they would have nothing on which to seize so quickly. But then when the king learned for a fact that his enemies were hindered and could not set out on their expedition, he let some of the raiding-army travel to their own land, and some he kept in this land over winter.

Then at midwinter the king was at Gloucester with his council, and held his court there for 5 days; and afterwards the archbishop and ordained men had a synod for three days. There Maurice[2] was chosen as bishop in London, and William[3] for Norfolk, and Robert[4] for Cheshire: they were all the king's clerics.

After this the king had great thought and very deep conversation with his council about this land, how it was occupied, or with which men. Then he sent his men all over England into every shire and had them ascertain how many hundreds of hides there were in the shire, or what land and livestock the king himself had in the land, or what dues he ought to have in 12 months from the shire. Also he had it recorded how much land his archbishops had, and his diocesan bishops, and his abbots and his earls, and – though I tell it at too great length – what or how much each man had who was occupying land here in England, in land or in livestock, and how much money it was worth. He had it investigated so very narrowly that there was not one single hide, not one yard of land, not even (it is shameful to tell – but it seemed no shame to him to do it) one ox, not one cow, not one pig was left out, that was not set down in his record.[5] And all the records were brought to him afterwards.[6]

1085 [1086]. Here the king wore his *crown* and held his court in Winchester for the Easter, and travelled so that he was at Westminster for the Pentecost and there dubbed his son

---

[1] Florence (II, p. 18) specifies: *bishops, abbots, earls* (comes), *barons, sheriffs* (vicecomes), *and king's officers.*   [2] A former royal chancellor and friend of Ranulf Flambard; after the fire in London (*s.a.* 1086, p. 218) he embarked on a grand rebuilding of St Paul's.   [3] William de Beaufrai, nominated bishop of Elmham on Christmas Day 1085.   [4] Robert de Limesey was nominated to a bishopric of Chester on Christmas Day 1085 and consecrated 1086, but transferred his seat to Coventry in 1102.   [5] Cross-checked by investigators who did not know the area and were themselves unknown, according to a note by Robert Losinga (Stevenson, 'A contemporary description', 74; transl. Douglas and Greenaway, *Documents*, p. 912).   [6] An early twelfth-century Worcester annalist says: *And the king ordered that all should be written in one volume, and that the volume should be placed in his treasury at Winchester, and kept there* (Liebermann, *Anglo-normannische Geschichtsquellen*, pp. 21–2; transl. Douglas and Greenaway, *Documents*, p. 914). The 'Domesday' survey is conveniently edited by J. Morris *et al.*, Chichester, 1975–92.

Henry a 'rider'.[7] Afterwards he travelled about so that he came to Salisbury for Lammas,[8] and his council came to him there and all the men occupying land who were of any account[9] over all England,[10] whichever man's men they were, and all submitted to him and were his men, and swore him loyal oaths that they would be loyal to him against all other men.[11] From there he travelled into Wight because he wanted to go into Normandy,[12] and did so afterwards. First, however, he did as he was accustomed – obtained much money from his men where he might have any claim, whether with justice or otherwise. Afterwards he travelled into Normandy, and the ætheling Edgar, King Edward's relative, then turned from him because he had no great honour from him:[13] but may the Almighty God give him honour in the future. And Christina, the ætheling's sister, retired into the minster at Romsey[14] and received holy repose.

And this same year was a very heavy year, and a very laborious and sorrowful year in England, in pestilence among cattle; and corn and crops were left standing and [there was] such great misfortune with the weather as cannot easily be conceived; there was such great thundering and lightning that it killed many men; and it always got worse and worse for men. May God Almighty remedy it when it be his will!

1086 [1087]. One thousand and eighty-seven years after the birth-time of our Lord Jesus Christ, in the twenty-first year that William ruled and governed England, as God granted him, occurred a very heavy and pestiferous year in this land. Such a disease came on men that very nearly every other man had the worst illness – that is the fever, and that so severely that many men died from the illness. Afterwards, through the great bad weather which came as we already told, there came a very great famine over all England, so that many hundreds of men died wretched deaths through the famine. Alas! how wretched and how pitiful

---

[7] The word *ridere* (cf. Old French *chevalier*, 'horseman') seems to be used synonymously with 'knight', see p. 225, note 16. The sense of the Anglo-Saxon word *cniht* was primarily 'young man', cf. p. 220, note 1. This seems to be the earliest textual reference to 'knighthood' in England. The origins of the verb 'to dub' are unclear.   [8] 1 August.   [9] *þe ahtes wæron*; cf. Stenton, *The First Century of English Feudalism*, pp. 112–14.   [10] Cf. note 1; here Florence (II, p. 19), specifies: *archbishops, bishops, abbots, earls* (comes) *barons, sheriffs* (vicecomes) *with their knights*.   [11] See Cronne, 'The Salisbury oath', pp. 248–52; Stenton, *The First Century of English Feudalism*, pp. 112–14; and Holt, '1086', pp. 41–64.   [12] The Isle of Wight seems to have been a convenient staging-post, see p. 214, note 5.   [13] Florence (II, p. 19) says that, with the king's permission, he went with two hundred knights to Apulia (the Norman colony in southern Italy).   [14] See p. 118, note 2.

a time it was then! Then the miserable men lay well-nigh driven to death, and afterwards came the sharp famine and did for them completely.

Who cannot pity such a time? Or who is so hard-hearted that he cannot weep for such misfortune? But such things happen because of the people's sins, in that they will not love God and righteousness. Just so it was then in those days, that little righteousness was in this land with any man, except with monks alone – there where they behaved well. The king and the principal men greatly loved, and over-greatly, greed in gold and in silver, and did not care how sinfully it was got as long as it came to them. The king granted his land on such hard terms, the hardest he could.[1] Then a second came and offered more than the other earlier gave, and the king let it go to the man who offered him more. Then a third came and offered yet more, and the king let it go into the hands of the man who offered him most of all, and did not care how very sinfully the reeves got it from wretched men, nor how many unlawful things they did; but the greater the talk about just law, the more unlawful things were done. They levied unjust tolls and they did many other unjust things which are difficult to relate.[2]

Also, in the same year, before autumn, the holy minster of St Paul, the bishop's seat in London, burned down, and many other minsters and the largest part – and the finest – of all the town. So also, at the same time, well-nigh every major market-town in all England burned down. Alas! a pitiful and tearful time it was that year, which brought forth so many misfortunes.

Also, in the same year, before the *Assumption of St Mary*,[3] King William went from Normandy into France[4] with an army, and raided against his own lord, Philip the king, and killed a great part of his men, and burned down the town of Mantes[5] and all the holy minsters which were inside the town. And two holy men who served God living in an anchorite's cell were burned to death there.[6]

This thus done, the king William turned back to Normandy. He did a pitiful thing, and more pitiful happened to him. How more pitiful? He became ill and that afflicted him severely.

[1] For the custom of 'farming out' manors, and the high proportion of royal manors 'at farm', see Lennard, *Rural England 1086–1135*, pp. 105–75 (especially pp. 123–4, 143–9). [2] Cf. Morris, 'The office of sheriff in the early Norman period', 145–75, (*The Medieval English Sheriff*, pp. 41–74). [3] 15 August. [4] This is the first use of the word *France*, undeclined; previously *Franca-land, -rice* etc., cf. Clark, ' "France" and "French" in the Anglo-Saxon Chronicle', 37–8, 42. [5] Capital of the Vexin (dép. Seine-et-Oise), see Map p. 282. [6] Ordericus (IV, pp. 78–81) says a great number of men died in the flames at Mantes, and on his deathbed William tried to make restitution by restoring the burned churches. [7] This section is emphatically homiletic, and the writer's vehement insistence on the transience of earthly fortune more that of orator than annalist. [8] 9 September.

What can I say![7] The sharp death which spares neither powerful men nor lowly – it seized him. He died in Normandy on the day immediately after the *Nativity of St Mary,*[8] and was buried in Caen at St Stephen's minster; he had built it earlier and afterwards endowed [it] in many various ways.[9]

Alas! how false and unstable is the prosperity of this world.[10] He who was earlier a powerful king, and lord of many a land, he had nothing of any land but a seven-foot measure; and he who was at times clothed with gold and with jewels, he lay then covered over with earth.

He left behind him three sons. The eldest was called Robert, who was earl in Normandy after him. The second was called William, who wore the royal crown in England after him. The third was called Henry, to whom the father bequeathed untold treasures.

If anyone wishes to know what sort of man he was, or what honour he had, or of how many lands he was lord, then we will write about him just as we who have looked upon him and at one time lived in his court, perceived him.[11] The king William, about whom we speak, was a very wise man, and very powerful, and more worshipful and stronger than any of his predecessors were. He was kind to those good men who loved God, and stern beyond all measure to those men who opposed his[12] will. In the same place where God granted him that he might conquer England he raised a famous minster,[13] and set monks there and endowed it well. In his days the famous minster in Canterbury was built,[14] and also many others over all England. Also this land was greatly filled with monks, and they lived their life according to the rule of St Benedict, and Christendom was such in his day that every man who wanted to, followed what pertained to his order.[15]

Also he was very worshipful. He wore his royal crown[16] three times each year, as often as he was in England.[17] At Easter he wore it in Winchester, at Pentecost in Westminster, at midwinter in Gloucester; and there were then with him

---

[9] St-Etienne, founded as a penance for his irregular marriage to Matilda of Flanders (William of Malmesbury, *Gesta Regum,* II p. 327).   [10] Ordericus, who is no less exclamatory, gives the fullest account of William, describing how the chamber was robbed by his attendants, the corpse left almost naked on the floor, and funeral arrangements left to a country knight called Herluin, moved by natural goodness (IV, pp. 80–105).   [11] Another early account of William's death is added in some redactions of the *Gesta Normannorum Ducum* of William of Jumièges, ed. E. van Houts, II, pp. 184–95, transl. Douglas and Greenaway, *Documents,* pp. 303–4.   [12] Nicely ambiguous; it is unclear whether it is God's will or William's to which the chronicler refers.   [13] See *The Chronicle of Battle Abbey,* pp. 36–7, 42–5.   [14] Or rather, rebuilt, since Lanfranc was merely replacing Anglo-Saxon structures; cf. Gem, 'The significance of the 11th-century rebuilding of Christ Church', pp. 1–19.   [15] Cf. the *Waverly Annals* (p. 197): *Christendom was so exalted in his time, that each man knew what pertained to his order.*   [16] *his cyne-helm.*   [17] For these ceremonial crown-wearings, see Richardson, 'The coronation in medieval England', 126–31.

all the powerful men over all England: archbishops and diocesan bishops, abbots and earls, thegns and knights.[1] He was also a very stern man, and violent, so that no one dared do anything against his will. He had earls in his bonds who went against his will; bishops he put out of their bishoprics and abbots out of their abbacies – and thegns into prison; and finally he did not spare his own brother, called Odo. He was a powerful bishop in Normandy – his bishop's seat was in Bayeux – and he was the foremost man next to the king. And he had an earldom in England,[2] and when the king was in Normandy he was master in this land. And him he put in prison. Among other things, the good order he made in this land is not to be forgotten, so that a man who was of any account could travel over his kingdom with his bosom full of gold, unmolested;[3] and no man dare kill another man, however great a wrong he might have done the other. And if any common man had sex with a woman against her will, he immediately lost the limbs with which he played.[4]

He ruled over England, and by his astuteness it was so surveyed that there was not one hide of land in England that he did not know who had it or what it was worth, and afterwards set down in his record.[5] Wales[6] was in his control and he built castles there[7] and entirely controlled that race of men. So also Scotland he made subject to him by his great strength.[8] Normandy, that land was his by right of birth, and he ruled over the earldom which is called Maine.[9] And if he could have lived two years more he would have won Ireland by his shrewdness and without any weapon. Assuredly in his time men had great toil and very many insults.[10]

[KING WILLIAM][11]

He had castles built
and wretched men oppressed.
The king was so very stark
and seized from his subject men many a mark

[1] The use of the word *cniht* here is the earliest certain example of its use to denote rank; those who committed the outrage at Peterborough (*s.a.* 1083) were perhaps not knights in the technical sense; see generally Stenton, *First Century of English Feudalism*, pp. 132–3; Gillingham, 'Thegns and knights in eleventh-century England', 137–9.   [2] He had been made earl of Kent shortly after the Conquest, cf. annal 1087 (p. 223).   [3] For this proverbial index of law-and-order compare Bede speaking of the 'Golden Age' of Edwin of Northumbria: *a woman might travel with her new-born babe from coast to coast unmolested* (*HE*, II, 16).   [4] Cf. Robertson, *Laws*, pp. 262–3; previously, under for example the laws of Alfred (Attenborough, *Laws*, pp. 70–71), the offence of rape required merely monetary compensation.   [5] Domesday Book, see above, p. 216.   [6] *Brytland*, probably Wales rather than Brittany here, inasmuch as the chronicler lists British before Continental provinces.   [7] Cf. RCHM, *Glamorgan*, III (1a), *The Early Castles.* [8] See annal 1072 E, (*s.a.* 1073 D).   [9] See annal 1073 E (*s.a.* 1074 D).   [10] Ordericus (IV, pp. 80-81) opens William's lengthy death-bed statement with the words: *I was brought up to arms from childhood, and am deeply stained with all the blood I have shed.*

of gold, and more hundreds of pounds of silver
that he took by weight, and with great injustice
from his land's nation with little need.
He was fallen into avarice,
and he loved greediness above all.
He set up great game-preserves,[12] and he laid down laws for them,
that whosoever killed hart or hind
he was to be blinded.
He forbade [hunting] the harts, so also the boars;
he loved the stags so very much,
as if he were their father;
also he decreed for the hares that they might go free.
His powerful men lamented it, and the wretched men complained of it
but he was so severe that he did not care about the emnity of all of them;
but they must wholly follow the king's will
if they wanted to live or have land –
land or property or his good favour.
Alas, woe, that any man should be so proud,
raise up and reckon himself over all men.
May the Almighty God shew mercy to his soul
and grant him forgiveness of his sins.

We have written these things about him, both the good and the evil, that good men may take after the goodness and wholly flee[13] the evil, and go on the path that leads us to the kingdom of heaven.[14]

We can write of many things which happened in the same year. Thus it was in Denmark that the Danish, who were earlier reckoned the most faithfull of all peoples, were turned to the greatest faithlessness and to the greatest treachery which could ever happen. They chose and submitted to King Cnut and swore him oaths, and afterwards basely killed him inside a church.[15] Also it happened in Spain that the heathen men went and raided against the Christian men, and bent much of it to their control; but the king of the Christians, who was called Alfonso,[16] he

---

[11] This part of the annal, marked by poetic rhetoric and opening and closing with rhyming couplets is best set out as a poem; see Whiting, 'The Rime of King William', pp. 89–96. [12] *deorfrið*, 'beast-woodlands' (cf. Smith, *English Place-Name Elements*, I, pp. 131, 190). For an estimate of the new set-aside lands see Darby, *Domesday England*, pp. 195–207 *et passim*. [13] MS *forleon*, perhaps for *forfleon* 'flee from' or, less likely, *forlætan* 'abandon'. [14] A conventional motivation, cf. the perorations with which both Bede and Ordericus open their histories. [15] There is a Life of this Danish protomartyr by Æthelnoth, an English monk at Odensee (*Scriptores Rerum Danicarum*, III, pp. 325–90). [16] Alfonso VI of Leon and Castile, 1030–109.

sent everywhere into each land, and begged for support; and support came to him from each land which was Christian, and travelled and killed and drove away all that heathen people, and won their land through God's support.[1]

Also, in this same land [England] in the same year, passed away many powerful men: Stigand, bishop of Chichester,[2] and the abbot of St Augustine's, and the abbot of Bath and that of Pershore,[3] and then the lord of them all, William king of England, of whom we earlier spoke before. After his death his son, called William just like the father, succeeded to the kingdom[4] and was blessed as king in Westminster by Archbishop Lanfranc, three days before the Feast of Michaelmas;[5] and all the men in England submitted to him and swore him oaths. This thus done, the king travelled to Winchester and inspected the jewel-house and the treasures which his father gathered earlier; it was impossible for any man to say how much was gathered there in gold and in silver and in vessels and in purple cloth and in gems and in many other precious things which are difficult to recount.[6] The king then did as his father commanded him before he was dead: for his father's soul he distributed these treasures to each minster which was within England, to some minsters 10 marks of gold, to some 6, and to each country church[7] 60 pence; and into each shire was sent a hundred pounds in money to be distributed to poor men for his soul. And before he passed away, he commanded that all those who were under his control in confinement should be released.[8] And the king was in London that midwinter.

1087 [1088]. In this year this land was very stirred up and filled with great treachery, so that the most powerful French men who were within this land wanted to betray their lord the king, and wanted to have as king his brother Robert who was earl in Normandy. In this plan were first Bishop Odo, Bishop Geoffrey,[9] and William, bishop in Durham.[10] The king did so well by the bishop[11] that all England acted according to his plan and just as he wanted; and he thought to do by him just like Judas Iscariot did by our Lord. And Earl Roger[12] was also in that foolish plan, and

---

[1] This comment is somewhat *passé*; Alfonso's anti-Moor campaign had peaked in 1085, after which he was systematically defeated.　　[2] Not to be confused with Archbishop Stigand of Canterbury. Stigand, bishop of Selsey, had transferred his seat to Chichester in 1075.　　[3] Florence (II, pp. 19–20) supplies the names, respectively: Scolland, Ælfsige and Thurstan. [4] Bringing with him from Normandy Wulnoth and Morcar; but as soon as they arrived he placed them in confinement at Winchester (Florence, II, p. 20).　　[5] 26 September.　　[6] Florence (II, p. 21) lists: *crosses, altars, shrines, books, candlesticks, sacred vessels, pipes and various ornaments, received in exchange for jewels, gold, silver and precious stones, to be divided among the major churches and monasteries.*　　[7] *cyrcean uppeland*; Florence (II, p. 21) says: *each of the churches in his towns or manors.*　　[8] Florence (II, p. 21) specifies: Odo, bishop of Bayeux, Earl Morcar, Earl Roger, Siward Bearn, and Wulfnoth, brother of King Harold and says that Robert released Ulf son of King Harold, and Duncan son of King Malcolm, knighting them first.　　[9] Bishop of Coutances (Normandy); he had fought at Hastings and became an exceptionally large landowner in England, see Le Patourel, 'Geoffrey of Montbray', 129–61.

very many people with them – all French men; and this foolish plan[13] was planned in the spring. Then as soon as it came to the Easter, they travelled and raided and burned and laid waste the king's home-farms, and they did for the lands of all those men who were in the king's service. And each of them travelled to his castle and manned and provisioned it as best they could. Bishop Geoffrey and Robert of Mowbray[14] travelled to Bristol, and raided, and brought the plunder to the castle; and afterwards they went out from the castle and raided Bath and all the land thereabout,[15] and they laid waste all Berkeley.[16] And those men who were the chief in Hereford, and all the shire forth with them, and the men of Shropshire with a great people from Wales[17] came and raided and burned in Worcestershire, on until they came to the market-town itself, and wanted to burn the market-town, and rob the minster, and get their hands on the king's castle. Seeing these things, the reverend bishop Wulfstan became very troubled in his mind, because the castle was entrusted to him to hold; however, the men of his court went out with a few men from the castle, and through God's mercy and through the bishop's merits, killed and captured five hundred men, and put all the others to flight. The bishop of Durham did what harm he could everywhere in the north. One of them was called Roger, who ran away into the castle at Norwich,[18] and still did worst of all over all the land. Hugh also was one who did not improve anything, neither in Leicestershire nor in Northampton.[19] The bishop Odo, with whom the business[20] originated, travelled into Kent to his earldom and greatly did for it, and wholly laid waste the king's land and the archbishop's, and brought all the goods into his castle in Rochester.

Then when the king perceived all these things, and what treachery they did against him, he became greatly troubled in his mind, then sent for English men and announced his need to them, and begged their support, and promised them the best law there ever was in this land; and forbade every unjust tax, and granted men their woods and coursing[21] – but it did not last long. But nevertheless the English men came to the support of the king their lord; they travelled towards

---

[10] Succeeding Walcher, replacing secular canons by monks, and building much of the cathedral as we know it, Offler, 'William of St Calais, first Norman bishop of Durham', 258–79. [11] i.e. this bishop, the bishop of Durham. [12] Roger of Montgómery (dép. Calvados), earl of Shrewsbury, see Mason, 'Roger de Montgomery and his sons', 1–28. [13] On the events of this annal see Poole, *From Domesday Book to Magna Carta*, pp. 100ff. [14] *Rodbeard a Mundbræg* (Montbrai). [15] Florence (II, p. 24) says that at length they reached and besieged (unsuccessfully) Ilchester, south Somerset. [16] A royal estate in Gloucestershire, raided by William of Eu, says Florence (II, p. 24). [17] Florence (II, p. 24) says it was a large army of English, Normans and Welsh, led by Bernard de Newmarch, Roger de Lacy and Ralph de Mortimer, with the men of Earl Roger of Shrewsbury. [18] Roger Bigot, earl of Norfolk and a large landowner there (DB, *Norfolk, passim*). [19] Hugh of Grandmesnil (dép. Calvados), castellan of Leicester, was an important landowner in the area (DB, *Leicestershire, passim*). [20] MS *cyng* 'king', apparently in error for *þing* 'thing, matter'. [21] *slætinge*; hunting or baiting with dogs.

Rochester[1] and wanted to get the bishop Odo – thought that if they had him who was earlier head in the foolish plan, they could the better get all the others. They came then to the castle at Tonbridge;[2] inside the castle were Bishop Odo's knights and many others who wanted to hold with him against the king. But the English men travelled and attacked the castle, and the men who were in there made peace with the king. The king with his raiding-army travelled towards Rochester, and supposed that the bishop was in there, but it became known to the king that the bishop had journied to the castle at Pevensey;[3] and the king with his raiding-army travelled after, and besieged the castle around with a very great raiding-army for fully six weeks.

In the middle of this, Robert, the earl of Normandy, the king's brother, gathered a very great company, and thought to win England with the support of those men in this land who were against the king; and he sent some of his men to this land, and would come afterwards himself. But the English men who guarded the sea captured some of the men and killed and drowned more than anyone knew how to reckon.

Afterwards their food ran short inside the castle; then they begged safe-conduct, and gave it up to the king. And the bishop swore that he would go out of England, and not come to this land any more unless the king sent for him, and that he would give up the castle in Rochester. Just so, the bishop travelled and was to give up the castle [of Rochester] and the king sent his men with him. Then the men who were in the castle rose, and seized the bishop and the king's men and put them in confinement. Within the castle were very good knights: Eustace the young,[4] and three sons of Earl Roger,[5] and all the best-born men who were in this land or in Normandy.

Then when the king realised these things, he travelled after them with the raiding-army that he had there, and sent over all England, and commanded that every man who was not a scoundrel[6] should come to him, French and English, from town and from country.[7] A great company then came to him, and he went [to] Rochester and besieged the castle, until they who were in it made peace and gave up the castle. The bishop Odo with the men who were inside the castle

---

[1] Which Odo had put into the charge of Eustace, count of Boulogne and Robert of Bellême (Florence, II, p. 22).   [2] Fifteen miles south of Rochester, and commanded by Gilbert, son of Richard (Florence, II, p. 23).   [3] On the Sussex coast and belonging to his brother Robert, count of Mortain (Florence, II, p. 23).   [4] Eustace III, count of Boulogne, son of the Eustace involved in the incident at Dover (*s.a.* 1052 D, 1048 E); see generally Round, 'The counts of Boulogne as English lords', 147–80.   [5] Roger of Montgomery's sons Hugh and Roger and Robert of Bellême.   [6] MS *unniðing*; William of Malmesbury (p. 362) says: *unless any wanted to be under the name 'Niðing', which means 'worthless'.* Cf. p. 171, note 17.   [7] MS *of porte and of uppelande.*   [8] Odo would join the First Crusade with his brother Robert Curthose in 1096 (q.v.), but died on the way at Palermo, where a splendid tomb was erected for him (Ordericus, IV, pp. 118–19).

travelled across the sea,[8] and the bishop thus relinquished the honour[9] which he had in this land. The king afterwards sent a raiding-army to Durham and had the castle besieged; and the bishop made peace and gave up the castle, and relinquished his bishopric and travelled to Normandy. Also many French men relinquished their lands and travelled across the sea; and the king gave their lands to the men who were loyal to him.

1089. In this year the reverend father and comfort of monks,[10] Archbishop Lanfranc, departed from this life, but we are confident that he has gone to the heavenly kingdom. Moreover a great earth-tremor happened all over England on 11 *August*;[11] and it was a very late year for corn and for crops of every kind, so that many men reaped their corn about Martinmas[12] and even later.

1090. *Thirteenth Indiction.*[13] These things thus done, just as we earlier said above about the king and about his brother and about his men, the king was deliberating how he could take vengeance on his brother Robert, distress him most, and win Normandy from him. However, by his astuteness, or by treasure, he got the castle at St Valéry,[14] and the harbour; and so also he got that at Aumale[15] and set his knights[16] in it; and they did harm in the land by raiding and by burning. After this he got more castles in the land and lodged his riders[16] in them.

When Robert the earl of Normandy realised that his sworn men had failed him and given up their castles to his detriment,[17] he sent to his lord, Philip, king of the French, and he came to Normandy with a great raiding-army. And the king and the earl with a vast army besieged the castle in which the king of England's men were. The king William of England sent to Philip, king of the French, and he, either for love of him, or for his great treasure, abandoned his man the earl Robert and his land, and travelled back to France and thus let them be. And in the middle of these things this land was greatly done for by unjust taxation and by many other misfortunes.

1091. In this year [1090][18] the king William held his court at

---

[9] *wurðscipe.*   [10] For Lanfranc's zealous support of monasticism see Eadmer, *Recent Events,* pp. 19–20.   [11] Florence (II, p. 26): *on Saturday about the third hour of the day.*   [12] 11 November.   [13] i.e. the thirteenth year of the fifty-first indiction reckoned from AD 312, cf. Cheney, *Handbook of Dates,* pp. 2–3; Poole, *Medieval Reckonings of Time,* pp. 29–31.   [14] Florence (II, p. 26): *the castle of Walter de St Valéry* (dép. Seine Maritime). [15] Florence (II, p. 26): *the castle of Odo d'Aumale* (dép. Seine Maritime).   [16] MS *sette his cnihtas . . . his rideras gelogode;* 'rider' is the term used by the chronicler when William the Conqueror dubs his younger son knight in 1085 (pp. 216–17).   [17] MS *him to hearme.* [18] Here the chronicler begins his year at Christmas, as in most of the annals which follow.

Christmas in Westminster; and after that, at Candlemas[1] he travelled, to his brother's discomfiture,[2] out of England into Normandy. While he was there, their reconciliation came about on the condition that the earl handed over to him Fécamp and the earldom of Eu[3] and Cherbourg. And in addition to that, the king's men were to be unmolested in the castles which they had earlier got from the earl against his will. And in return the king promised him to make Maine obedient, which their father won earlier, and which had then turned against the earl; and [promised him] all that his father had over there, except what he had granted to the king, and that all those who in England earlier lost their land in the earl's cause should have it again by this pact – and the earl just as much in England as was laid down in their covenants. And if the earl pass away without son by lawful wedlock, the king was to be heir of all Normandy; by this same covenant if the king die, the earl was to be heir of all England. This covenant was sworn by 12 of the best of the king's side, and 12 of the earl's – though it did not last for long.[4]

In with this pact the ætheling Edgar became deprived of lands – of those which the earl had handed over to him earlier – and went out of Normandy to Scotland, to the king his brother-in-law, and to his sister.

While the king William was out of England, the king Malcolm travelled from Scotland here into England[5] and raided across a great part of it, until the good men who looked after this land sent an army against him and turned him back. Then when King William heard of this in Normandy, he prepared for his passage and came to England,[6] and his brother the earl Robert with him, and immediately ordered his army to be called out, both the ship-army and land-army; but before he came to Scotland, four days before Michaelmas, almost all the ship-army wretchedly perished. And the king and his brother travelled with the land-army, but when the king Malcolm heard that it was intended to seek him out with an army, he went with his army out of Scotland into Lothian in England[7] and waited there. Then when the king William approached with his army,

---

[1] 2 February.   [2] *unþearfe* literally 'un-need'; Henry of Huntingdon (p. 215) says he was taking revenge *for the injury his brother had done him*.   [3] Florence (II, p. 27) says: *the earldom of Eu, the monastery of Fécamp, the abbey situated on Mont St Michel, and Cherbourg*.   [4] Florence (II, p. 27) says that, meanwhile, the king's brother Henry seized Mont St Michel (cf. note 3), with the aid of some of the monks.   [5] Florence (II, p. 28): *in May*.   [6] Florence (loc. cit.): *in August*.   [7] Lothian was the area south of the Forth, racially Anglian; 'Scotland' began north of the Forth and Edinburgh ('Edwin's fort'); cf. annal 1072 E (*s.a.* 1973 D). See generally Andersón, 'Lothian and the early Scottish kings', 98–112.   [8] See annal 1072 E (*s.a.* 1073 D).   [9] According to Florence (II, p. 28), William was to restore twelve English *vills* that Malcolm had held under the Conqueror, and pay Malcolm twelve marks of gold a year.   [10] MS *Cardeol*. Florence (II, p. 30) says the town was called in British *Cairleu* and in Latin *Lugubalia*; cf. Armstrong, *The Place-Names of Cumberland*, I, pp. 40–42.

Earl Robert and the ætheling Edgar went between and thus made a reconciliation between those kings, so that the king Malcolm came to our king and became his man, in all such obedience as he earlier did his father,[8] and affirmed it with an oath; and the king William promised him, in land and in all things, that which he had formerly had under his father.[9]

In this reconciliation the ætheling Edgar also became reconciled with the king; and then the kings parted in great reconciliation – but it did not last long. And the earl Robert lived here with the king well-nigh until Christmas, and during that found little faith in their covenants; and two days before that festival took ship in Wight and went into Normandy, and the ætheling Edgar with him.

1092. In this year the king William travelled north to Carlisle[10] with a very great army, and restored the town[11] and raised the castle, and drove out Dolfin[12] who earlier ruled the land there, and set the castle with his men, and afterwards returned south here, and sent very many peasants[13] there with women and with livestock to live there to till that land.[14]

1093. In this year in the spring the king William became so very ill in Gloucester[15] that he was everywhere declared dead; and in his affliction he promised many vows to God: to lead his own life righteously, and to grant peace and protection to God's minsters and never more again to sell them for money, and to have all just laws in his nation.[16] And the archbishopric in Canterbury, which earlier stood in his own hand, he committed to Anselm[17] who had been abbot of Bec, and to Robert his chancellor that bishopric in Lincoln,[18] and granted land to many monasteries – but he afterwards withdrew that when he was better, and relinquished all the good laws which he earlier promised us.[19]

Then after this [the] king of Scotland sent and asked for the covenants which were promised him;[20] and the king William summoned him to Gloucester, and sent him hostages to Scotland and later the ætheling Edgar, and then afterwards men to meet him who brought him to the king with great honour.[21] But then when he

---

[11] Which according to Florence (II, p. 30) had remained deserted ever since destruction by the Danes two hundred years before.   [12] Son of Gospatric (the Conqueror's earl of Northumbria) apparently ruling Cumbria under the overlordship of Malcolm (Simeon, II, p. 199; but see Kappelle, *The Norman Conquest of the North*, pp. 151–2).   [13] MS *eyrlisces*, apparently in error for *cyrlisces*; the *Annals of Waverly* (p. 202) speak of *many villeins*.   [14] For these events see generally Ritchie, *The Normans in Scotland*, pp. 52–66, and Armstrong, *The Place-Names of Cumberland*, I, pp. xxxi–xxxiii.   [15] Florence (II, p. 30) says *he was stricken seriously ill in the royal manor called Alveston, and hastened to the city of Gloucester, and lay there all through Lent*.   [16] Cf. Ordericus, IV, pp. 1176–7.   [17] For Anselm, nominated 6 March, consecrated 4 December, see Eadmer's *Life of St Anselm*, and Southern and Schmitt, ed., *Memorials of St Anselm*.   [18] Robert Bloet, nominated in March 1093; for the office of 'chancellor', see Harmer, *Writs*, pp. 58–61.   [19] Florence (II, p. 31) records a raid on Brecknock castle during Easter week by the Welsh king Rhys, and his death there, from which day, he says, kings ceased to reign in Wales.   [20] By the treaty of Abernethy, see p. 208, note 7.   [21] On St Bartholomew's Day (24 August), says Florence, II, p. 31.

came to the king, he could be entitled neither to speech with our king nor to the covenants which were earlier promised him;[1] and therefore they parted with great discord, and the king Malcolm returned home to Scotland. But quickly, after he came home, he gathered his army, and travelled into England, raiding with greater folly than behoved him, and then Robert[2] the earl of the Northumbrians with his men, by surprise trapped and killed him. Morel of Bamburgh, who was the earl's steward and King Malcolm's godfather,[3] killed him.[4] With him was also killed his son Edward, who would have been king after him if he had lived. Then when the good queen Margaret heard this – her dearest lord and son thus betrayed – she became anguished in mind to the point of death and went to church with her priests, and received her rites and prayed to God that she might give up her spirit.[5] And then the Scots chose Malcolm's brother Donald[6] as king, and drove out all the English who were with the king Malcolm earlier. Then when Duncan, King Malcolm's son, heard all this had happened thus – he was in the court of King William as his father had earlier given him as a hostage to our king's father, and remained here thus – he came to the king and gave such pledges as the king wanted to have from him, and thus with his consent went to Scotland with such support of English and of French as he could get, and deprived his relative Donald of the kingdom, and was received as king. But some of the Scots afterwards gathered, and killed well-nigh all his men, and he himself escaped with a few. Afterwards they became reconciled on condition that he never again lodged English men or French men in that land.

1094. Here [1093] the king William held his court at Christmas at Gloucester, and there came to him ambassadors from his brother, Robert of Normandy, who announced that his brother wholly renounced the peace and covenant, unless the king would fulfil all that they had earlier drawn up in the convenant; and upon that, called him forsworn and faithless unless he held to those covenants, or travelled there and cleared himself where the convenant was earlier drawn up and also sworn.

[1] Florence (II, p. 31) ascribes this to William's excessive pride and pomp, and because he wished to compel Malcolm to render obedience to him in the English court, but Malcolm would do this only within the borders of his own kingdom, as kings of Scotland had been accustomed to do in the past, and by the judgement of the leading men of both kingdoms; see generally Ritchie, *The Normans in Scotland*, pp. 59–60, 385–8. [2] Robert of Mowbray. [3] *godsib*, 'gossip', one having some kind of spiritual relationship to another (a baptized child or its parents), by acting as sponsor at baptism. [4] Florence (II, p. 31) dates this to St Brice's Day (13 November) but does not mention Morel. Gaimar (6105–17) says both Morel and one Geoffrey Engulevant ('the Belcher') were responsible, and locates the killing at Alnwick (a dozen miles south of Bamburgh). [5] Florence (II, p. 32) says that she died within three days. [6] Donald Bán, son of Duncan I. [7] 2 February. [8] Although Florence (II, p. 33) says that Losinga ('the Flatterer') was a nickname recently acquired for good reason, it seems to have been a genuine surname, borne by his father; cf. Tengvik, *Old English Bynames*, p. 349. He was formerly prior of Fécamp and was now abbot of Ramsey; see generally Barlow, *William Rufus*, p. 180; Goulburn and Symonds, *The Life . . . of Bishop Herbert de Losinga*.

Then at the Candlemas[7] the king travelled to Hastings, and while he waited there for the weather, he had the minster at Battle consecrated, and deprived Herbert Losinga,[8] bishop of Thetford, of his staff;[9] and after that, in mid-Lent, he went across the sea into Normandy. After he came there, he and his brother the earl Robert declared that they should come together in peace – and did so, and could not be agreed. Afterwards they came together again with the same men who earlier made that treaty and also swore the oaths, and attributed all the breach to the king; but he would not assent to that, nor also hold to the covenant, and therefore they turned away with great discord.

And afterwards the king won the castle at Bures[10] and seized the earl's men in it and sent some of them here to this land. In return, the earl with the support of the king of France won the castle at Argentan,[11] and in it seized Roger of Poitou[12] and seven hundred of the king's knights with him; and afterwards that at Le Houlme,[13] and each of them regularly burned the other's settlements, and also captured men.

Then the king sent here to the land and ordered 20 thousands of English men to be called out to support him in Normandy; but when they came to the sea they were ordered to turn back and, for the king's profit, to give the money they had taken – that was, each man half a pound. And they did so.[14]

And after this, the earl in Normandy,[15] with the king of France and with all those who they could gather, travelled towards Eu, where the king William was inside, and thought to besiege him inside, and thus went until they came to Longueville.[16] There the king of France was turned back through intrigue, and so afterwards the whole campaign dispersed. Here, during this, the king William sent for his brother Henry who was in the castle at Domfront,[17] but because he could not travel through Normandy in peace he sent ships for him and Hugh earl of Chester;[18] but then when they should have gone towards Eu where the king was, they went to England and came up at Southampton on the eve of the Feast of All Saints,[19] and stayed here afterwards, and at Christmas were in London.

---

[9] i.e. his pastoral staff or crosier, as sign of office. [10] Dép. Seine Maritime, see Map p. 282. [11] Dép. Orne; captured without bloodshed on the very first day of the siege according to Florence (II, p. 34). [12] A son of Roger of Montgomery, he had extensive estates in England, but had married a Poitevan heiress, hence his name here (Ordericus, IV, pp. 302–3; Mason, 'Roger de Montgomery and his sons', 14–5). [13] Dép. Orne; where according to Florence (II, p. 35) William Peveril and eight hundred defenders surrendered to Robert. [14] Florence (II, p. 35) says the king commanded Ranulf Passeflambard to take the money and send the soldiers home. [15] i.e. Robert Curthose. [16] Both castles in dép. Seine Maritime. [17] Dép. Orne. [18] Son of Richard Goz, viscount of Avranches, he had become earl of Chester about 1071; Ordericus (II, pp. 260–63) speaks of him as violent, and gross in his habits, staggering around under a mountain of fat. [19] 31 October.

Also in this same year the Welsh men[1] gathered themselves and began hostilities with the French who were in Wales or in the neighbourhood and earlier deprived them of lands, and broke down many fortresses and castles[2] and killed the men. And after their company grew, they divided themselves into more. Hugh, earl of Shropshire,[3] fought with one of these divisions and put them to flight. But nevertheless during all that year the others did not leave off doing all the evil they could.

Also in this year the Scots trapped and killed Duncan, their king, and afterwards for a second time[4] took Donald,[5] his paternal uncle, as their king, through whose instruction and instigation he was betrayed to death.

1095. In this year [1094] the king William was at Wissant[6] for the first four days of Christmas; and after the fourth day went here to the land[7] and came up at Dover. And Henry the king's brother dwelt here in the land until spring, [1095] and then, in loyalty to the king against their brother Earl Robert, went across the sea to Normandy with great treasures and frequently warred against the earl and did him great harm both in land and in men.

And then at Easter the king held his court in Winchester, and the earl Robert of Northumbria would not come to court; and therefore the king became very stirred up against him, and sent to him and sternly commanded that, if he wanted to be entitled to security, to come to court at Pentecost. In this year Easter was on 25 *March*. And then after Easter on the eve of the Feast of St Ambrose, that is 4 *April*,[8] well-nigh all over this land and well-nigh all the night, manifold stars were seen to fall from heaven, not by ones or twos, but so thickly that nobody could reckon it. After that, at Pentecost the king was in Windsor, and all his council with him, except the earl of Northumbria,[9] because the king would neither give him hostages nor grant upon pledges that he could come and go with safe-conduct.[10]

And the king therefore summoned his army and went to Northumbria against the earl,

---

[1] Florence (II, p. 25): *first the North Welsh, then the West Welsh and South Welsh.*   [2] *castles which were established in West Wales, and burned many vills and seized booty in Cheshire, Shropshire and Herefordshire; and put to death many of the English and Normans; they also destroyed the castle on the Isle of Anglesey* (Florence, loc. cit.)   [3] Who had succeeded to the earldom on the death of his father, Roger of Montgomery, on 27 July.   [4] See annal 1093.   [5] Donald Bán, see p. 228, note 6.   [6] An embarkation-point in Pas-de-Calais; cf. Grierson, 'The relations between England and Flanders', 80–81.   [7] Florence (II, p. 35) says that William returned to England on 29 December 1094 in order to fight the Welsh and straightway led an army into Wales, where he lost many men and horses.   [8] It is the Feast that is 4 April and the Eve therefore 3 April.   [9] Robert of Mowbray.

and immediately he came there he conquered many, and well-nigh all the best men of the earl's court inside one fortress,[11] and put them in captivity, and besieged the castle at Tynemouth until he conquered it, and in there the earl's brother and all those who were with him, and afterwards travelled to Bamburgh, and besieged the earl in there. But then, when the king saw that he could not conquer it, he then ordered a castle to be made in front of Bamburgh, and called it in his language *Malveisin*, that is in English 'Bad Neighbour',[12] and set it strongly with his men and afterwards went southward. Then immediately after the king had gone south, the earl travelled out one night from Bamburgh towards Tynemouth;[13] but those who were in the new castle became aware of it and went after him, and fought against and wounded and afterwards captured him;[14] and of those who were with him, some killed, some took alive.

In the middle of this it became known to the king that the Welsh men had broken down a certain castle in Wales called Montgomery,[15] and killed Earl Hugh's men who had to hold it. And therefore he ordered another army to be quickly called out, and after Michaelmas travelled into Wales. And his army split and went all through that land, until on All Saints'[16] the army all came together to Snowdon; but the Welsh always went on ahead into the mountains and moors so that they could not be come at. And then the king turned homewards because he saw that he could do no more there that winter.

Then when the king came back, he then ordered Robert the earl of Northumbria[10] to be seized and led to Bamburgh, and both eyes put out unless those who were inside would give up the castle. His wife and Morel, who was his steward and also his relative, held it.[17] Through this, the castle was then given up; and Morel was then in the king's court, and through him there were revealed many, both ordained and also lay, who were disloyal to the king in their plan, some of whom the king ordered to be brought into captivity before that season;[18] and afterwards to be announced, very peremptorily, over all this land, that all those who held land from the king, insofar as

[10] Florence (II, p. 38) says that Robert, together with William of Eu and many others, wanted to kill William and make his nephew Stephen d'Aumale king.   [11] Florence (II, p. 38) speaks of it as a small castle (*munitiuncula*) taken during the two months the king was besieging Tynemouth. This might have been what is now 'Newcastle', eight miles west, founded in 1080 by Robert Curthose (Simeon, II, p. 211).   [12] What was presumably a siege-work seems to have been incorporated into the later medieval castle complex. For similar nicknames given to siege-works (e.g. *Malassis* 'Ill-sited') see Ordericus, VI, pp. 186–7.   [13] Perhaps the castle, but Florence (II, p. 38) says the monastery of St Oswin.   [14] Having been wounded in the leg on the sixth day of the siege, he took refuge in a church but was brought out (Florence, loc. cit.).   [15] Now Hen Domen 'Old Mound', in Powys, commanding a crossing of the Severn (see Higham and Barker, *Timber Castles*, pp. 326–47). The name Montgomery derives from a Norman estate of the earls of Shrewsbury (Lloyd, *Anglo-Norman Families*, pp. 68–9).   [16] 1 November.   [17] Cf. Ordericus, IV, pp. 278–85. His wife was Matilda of Laigle (dép. Orne), niece of Hugh earl of Chester.   [18] *ær þære tide*; the *Waverly Annals* (p. 205) say *before Christmas*, which would have been the time of the next court.

they wanted to be entitled to security, that they should be at court at the season. And the king ordered the earl Robert led to Windsor, and held inside the castle there.

Also in this same year, towards Easter, the pope's envoy came here to the land; that was Bishop Walter, a man of very good life from the city of Albano; and on Pentecost, on behalf of the pope Urban,[1] he gave the archbishop Anselm his pallium, and he received it at his arch-seat in Canterbury. And the bishop Walter stayed here in the land for long in the year afterwards, and afterwards the Rome-tax[2] was sent by him – as had not been done earlier for many years.

This same year also there was very unseasonable weather; and therefore all the earth-crops ripened all too moderately throughout all this land.

1096. In this year [1095] the king William held his court at Christmas in Windsor, and William, bishop of Durham, passed away there on New Year's Day. And on the *octave of the Epiphany*,[3] the king and all his councillors were in Salisbury. There Geoffrey Bainard[4] accused William of Eu, the king's relative, of being treacherous to the king,[5] and fought him about it and overcame him in combat.[6] And after he was overcome, the king ordered his eyes to be put out, and afterwards castrated. And his steward called William,[7] who was the son of his mother's sister, the king ordered to be hanged on a cross.[8] There also Odo earl of Champagne, the king's in-law,[9] and many others were deprived of land, and some led to London and there mutilated.

This year also, at Easter, there was a very great stir throughout all this nation and in many other nations through Urban, who was called pope although he had nothing of the seat in Rome.[10] And countless people, with women and children, set out because they wanted to war against heathen nations.[11] Through this journey, the king and his brother Earl Robert became reconciled, in that the king went across the sea and redeemed all Normandy from him for money,[12] by which they were then reconciled; and afterwards the earl travelled, and with him the earl of Flanders and he of Boulogne,[13] and also many other head men. And the earl Robert and those who travelled with him stayed in Apulia for the winter; but of the people who went by Hungary, many thousands perished miserably there and on the way,

---

[1] Urban II, see note 10. [2] MS *Rom gesceot*; cf. The Institutes of Cnut: *St Peter's pence, which the English call 'Romescot'*, or The Laws of Edward the Confessor: *St Peter's pence, which is called in English 'Romescot'* (Lieberman, *Gesetze* I, pp. 293, 634). [3] i.e. the eighth day, 13 January. [4] Possibly sheriff of York in the time of the Conqueror; see Robinson, *Gilbert Crispin*, p. 38; Douglas, *Domesday Monachorum*, p. 60, note 9. [5] Florence (II, pp. 38–9) says that William was involved in the Mowbray plot (see pp. 222–3); and Ordericus (IV, pp. 284–5) adds that Hugh earl of Chester had no love for him, since William had married his sister and then neglected her, having three children by a concubine. [6] For the Norman judicial duel, see Robertson, *Laws*, pp. 232–3. [7] William de Alderi (Florence, II, p. 39). [8] MS *on rode ahon*. The sense of *rod* seems inescapable; the same words are used of the death of William of Norwich (*s.a.* 1137, p. 265); but Florence (loc. cit.) and William of Malmesbury (p. 372), say merely *hanged*. [9] MS *aðum*; normally 'son-in-law' or 'brother-in-law', but here 'uncle-by-marriage'; Odo had married the Conqueror's niece Adelaide, and was the father of Stephen of Aumale, whom the plotters wished to make king. [10] Earlier, Rufus had refused to recognise either Urban II or the anti-pope Clement II, but Urban had sent the pallium for Anselm in 1095 (q.v.).

and many, pitiful and hunger-bitten, dragged home again against winter.

This was a very heavy year throughout all the English race, both through manifold taxes and also through a very grievous famine which very much afflicted this country in the year. Also in this year, the head men who held this land regularly sent an army into Wales, and greatly afflicted many a man with that; but there was no success in that, but the destruction of men and waste of money.[14]

1097. Here in this year [1096] the king William was in Normandy at Christmas, and then towards Easter went here to this land, because he thought to hold his court in Winchester; but he was hindered by bad weather until Easter eve, so that he came up first at Aurundel, and therefore held his court at Windsor.

And after that he travelled into Wales with a great raiding-army, and through some of the Welsh who came to him and were his guides, went deeply through that land with his army, and stayed there from midsummer well-nigh until August, and lost much there in men and in horses and also in many other things. Then afterwards the Welsh men turned against their king, and chose many leaders from among themselves; one of them was called Cadwgan, who was the finest of them; he was the son of King Gruffydd's brother.[15] But then when the king saw that he could achieve nothing of his purpose there, he went back into this land, and quickly after that he had castles made along the borders.

Then after[16] Michaelmas, on 4 *October*, a strange star appeared, shining in the evening and soon going to rest. It was seen in the south-west, and the ray that stood from it shining south-east seemed to be very long, and appeared in this way well-nigh all the week.[17] Many men considered it was a *comet*.

Soon after this, Anselm the archbishop of Canterbury got leave from the king – though the king was unwilling, so it was considered – and went across the sea[18] because it seemed to him that in this nation little was done according to justice and according to his direction. And following that, after[16] Martinmas,[19] the king went across the sea into Normandy; but while he waited on the weather[20] his court did much greater[21] harm within the shires where they lay

---

[11] See generally Duncalf and Runciman, 'The First Crusade', p. 253ff.; and for the *wifan and cildan*, Porges, 'The clergy, the poor, and the non-combatants on the First Crusade', 1–23.   [12] According to Florence (II, p. 40), ten thousand marks of silver were raised by Rufus to support Robert of Normandy on the Crusade (mortgaging Normandy as security), in pursuit of which sum *bishops, abbots and abbesses broke up the gold and silver ornaments of their churches, the earls, barons and sheriffs despoiled their knights and villeins*.   [13] Respectively Robert II of Flanders and Eustace III of Boulogne.   [14] Cf. Lloyd, *A History of Wales*, p. 400ff.   [15] i.e. Bleddyn, half-brother of Gruffydd ap Llewelyn, see annal 1063 D and Table p. 301.   [16] *uppon*; for this usage, twice in this annal, see p. 239, note 9.   [17] Florence (II, p. 41) says it appeared for fifteen days from 29 September, and that some people said they saw a sign like a burning cross in the sky.   [18] Having failed to detain Anselm by argument, William exiled him, cf. Eadmer, pp. 82–92, 123–5. He stayed abroad until recalled by Henry in 1100 (q.v.).   [19] 11 November; Florence (II, p. 41) says it was about St Andrew's Day, 30 November.   [20] i.e. waiting for a favourable wind (or perhaps for gales to pass).   [21] Literally 'the most'.

than a court or raiding-army[1] ever ought to do in a land at peace.[2] This was a very heavy year in all things, and over-laborious in bad weather both when tilling should be done and again when the produce [should be] gathered in, and in excessive taxes that never ceased. Also many shires, whose work pertained to London were badly afflicted through the wall which they constructed around the Tower, and through the bridge which was well-nigh washed away, and through work on the king's hall which was constructed at Westminster;[3] and many a man was afflicted with that.

Also in this same year, soon after Michaelmas, the ætheling Edgar with the king's support travelled into Scotland with an army, and won that land with a fierce fight and drove out the king Donald,[4] and there he set as king (in allegiance to the king William) his relative Edgar who was son of King Malcolm and the queen Margaret, and afterwards went back into England.

1098. In this year [1097] at Christmas the king William was in Normandy; and Walchelin, bishop in Winchester, and Baldwin, abbot in St Edmunds, both passed away during this season.[5] And in this year also Turold, abbot of Peterborough, passed away. Also in the summer of this year, in Berkshire at Finchampstead, a pool welled up blood,[6] as many trustworthy men said who must have seen it. And Earl Hugh[7] was killed in Anglesey by foreign vikings,[8] and his brother Robert[9] became his heir, just as he acquired it of the king.[10] Before Michaelmas the heaven appeared as if it were burning well-nigh all the night. This was a very laborious year through manifold excessive taxes and through great rains which did not cease all the year; well-nigh all produce on marsh-land perished.

1099. Here [1098] the king William was in Normandy at midwinter, and at Easter came to the land here, and at Pentecost held his court for the first time in his new building at Westminster; and there gave the bishopric in Durham to Ranulf[11] his chaplain who

---

[1] MS *hired oððe here*.   [2] i.e. a land with which one is at peace, a friendly country. For the depredations characteristic of William's entourage, see Eadmer (*Recent Events*, pp. 205–6); and Henry's, below *s.a.* 1104.   [3] For the Tower of London and Westminster Hall, see Brown, *The King's Works*, I, pp. 29–32, 45–7.   [4] Donald Bán.   [5] i.e. Christmas, Baldwin on 29 December and Walchelin on 3 January.   [6] Cf. Griffiths, 'Early references to waterbloom in British lakes', 15–16. This well was destroyed by road-widening at the beginning of the twentieth century.   [7] Earl of Shrewsbury, see p. 230, note 3.   [8] MS *ut-wikingan*. Anglesey belonged to Magnus Bareleg, king of Norway, the son of Olaf the Peaceful, grandson of Harald Hardrada. Florence (II, pp. 41–2) says that Hugh earl of Chester, together with Hugh earl of Shrewsbury, invaded Anglesey, killing many of the inhabitants, blinding others, having first cut off their hands and feet and testicles. Hugh of Shrewsbury was killed on the shore by an arrow fired by Magnus himself, so it was rumoured.   [9] Robert de Bellême, elder brother of Hugh, see White, 'The first house of Bellême', 67–99; Mason, 'Roger de Montgomery and his sons', 24–6.   [10] Meaning either: with the consent of the king, or under the same conditions as his brother had it from the king.   [11] Nicknamed Flambard 'Torch-bearer', because of his habit of issuing commands as though on the king's behalf (Ordericus, IV, pp. 170–73); for an alternative view, cf. Simeon, I, pp. 139–41; see generally Southern, 'Ranulf Flambard and the early Anglo-Norman administration', 95–128.

earlier conducted and supervised all his meetings all over England; and soon after that [the king] went across the sea, and drove the earl Helias out of Maine,[12] and afterwards set it in his control; and so at Michaelmas came back here to the land. Also this year, on the Feast of St Martin[13] the tide rose so strongly and did so much damage as no-one remembered it ever did before; and there was a *new moon* on the same day. And Osmund, bishop of Salisbury, passed away during Advent.[14]

1100. In this year [1099] the king William held his court at Christmas in Gloucester, and at Easter in Winchester, and at Pentecost in Westminster.

And at Pentecost at a certain village in Berkshire[15] blood was seen to well up from the earth,[16] as many said who must have seen it. And after that, on the morning after Lammas Day,[17] the king William was shot with an arrow in hunting[18] by a man of his,[19] and afterwards brought to Winchester and buried in the bishopric[20] the thirteenth year after he succeeded to the kingdom.

He was very strong and violent over his land and his men and with all his neighbours, and very terrible. And through the advice of evil men, who were always agreeable to him, and through his own avarice, he was always harrassing this nation with raiding and with excessive taxes, because in his days every justice fell and there rose up every injustice before God and before the world. He humiliated God's church; and in his days, when the elders fell[21] in bishoprics and abbacies he either granted them all in return for money, or held in his own hand and put out at rent, because he wanted to be the heir of every man, ordained and lay.[22] And thus on the day that he fell, he had in his own hand the archbishopric in Canterbury and the bishopric in Winchester and that in Salisbury and eleven abbacies, all put out at rent. And although I prolong it further, all that was customary in this land in his time – all that was hateful to God and to just men. And therefore he was hated by well-nigh all his nation, and abhorrent to God, just as his end showed, because

---

[12] Elias de La Flèche, count of Maine.   [13] 11 November; but Florence (II, p. 44) says it was on 3 November.   [14] 3 December; subsequently canonised, cf. Jones, *The Register of S. Osmund*, II, pp. xxi-xxxvii.   [15] Presumably Finchampstead, where the same phenomenon was reported in 1098 and 1103.   [16] Florence (II, pp. 45–6): *blood flowed from a spring for three days, and the devil frequently appeared in the woods in a horrible form to many Normans, and spoke with them much concerning the king, and Ranulf* (Flambard) *and some others. Nor is it to be wondered at, for in their time law was almost silenced, and money reigned supreme in all appeals to justice,* etc.   [17] 2 August.   [18] Florence specifies: *in the New Forest, which in the English language is called* (the Forest) *of the Jutes* (cf. annal 449); a church had formerly stood in the place where the king fell, but was destroyed in the Conqueror's time to make way for game! (II, pp. 44–5).   [19] Florence (II, p. 45) specifies: *an arrow aimed carelessly by a certain Frenchman, Walter, surnamed Tirel.* See generally Ordericus (V, pp. 288–95), Hollister, 'The strange death of William Rufus', 687–53, and Barlow, *William Rufus*, pp. 408–32.   [20] Presumably in the minster rather than in the area generally. For the controversy surrounding his burial, see Barlow, op. cit., pp. 429–32.   [21] MS *ealdras . . . feollan*; i.e. when bishops or abbots died or resigned.   [22] For Rufus's despoliation of the church see Ordericus (IV, pp. 174–9) and Hollister, 'William Rufus, Henry I, and the Anglo-Norman Church', 119–40.

he departed in the midst of his injustice without repentance and any reparation.

He was killed on the Thursday and buried the next morning. And after he was buried those councillors who were near at hand chose his brother Henry as king. And straightway he gave the bishopric in Winchester to William Gifford[1] and afterwards went to London, and on the Sunday after that, before the altar in Westminster, promised to God and all the people to put down all the injustices which there were during his brother's time, and to hold the best laws which had stood in any king's day before him.[2] And then after that Maurice the bishop of London consecrated him as king, and all in this land submitted to him and swore oaths and became his men.

And soon after that, by the advice of those who were around him, the king had Ranulf bishop of Durham seized and brought into the Tower in London and held there.[3] Then before Michaelmas Anselm the archbishop of Canterbury came here to the land,[4] just as the king Henry sent for him, on the advice of his councillors, because he had gone out of this land because of the great injustice which the king William did him.[5]

And then soon after this the king took as his wife Maud, daughter of King Malcolm of Scotland and the good queen Margaret, King Edward's relative, of the rightful royal family of England. And on the Feast of St Martin[6] she was given to him in Westminster with great honour, and the archbishop Anselm married her to him and afterwards consecrated her queen.[7] And soon after this Thomas the archbishop of York passed away.[8]

Also in this same year, in autumn, the earl Robert and the earl Robert of Flanders and Eustace earl of Boulogne came home from Jerusalem into Normandy.[9] And as soon as the earl Robert came into Normandy, he was joyfully received by all the people, except for the castles which were set with the king Henry's men, against which he had many a tussle and contest.

1101. Here in this year [1100] the king Henry held his court at Christmas in Westminster, and at Easter in Winchester.

---

[1] Dean of the Rouen chapter, a chaplain to William I and chancellor to William Rufus. This prompt act signalled a reversal of his predecessor's policy of despoiling vacant sees. But contrary to Gregorian regulations, the king personally invested the new bishop with symbols of office (Matthew Paris, *Historia Anglorum*, I, p. 181), and in consequence his consecration was delayed until 11 August 1107. For the so-called 'investiture controversy', see p. 238, note 6; and for Gifford's role, see Williams, *The Norman Anonymous*, pp. 90–94.   [2] Florence (II, p. 47) and Henry I's coronation charter (Robertson, *Laws*, pp. 282–3) specify the laws of Edward the Confessor.   [3] He was arrested on 15 August, accused, says Anselm (*PL*, CLIX, 202) of failing to pass on taxes he had collected on behalf of the king.   [4] Arriving on 23 September (Eadmer, p. 124).   [5] See p. 233, note 18.   [6] 11 November.   [7] In fact the ceremony could only take place after an ecclesiastical council at Lambeth accepted her denial of the rumour that she was in fact a nun (Eadmer, pp. 127–31).   [8] 18 November 1100.   [9] Florence (II, p. 47): *with the wife* (Sibylla) *whom he had married in Sicily* – a Norman colony.

And then soon after that the head men here in the land became at odds with the king, both through their own great faithlessness and also because the earl Robert of Normandy set out with hostility here to the land. And then the king sent his ships out to sea to the damage and hindrance of his brother, but some of them afterwards failed at need, and turned away from the king and submitted to the earl Robert. Then at midsummer the king travelled out to Pevensey with all his army against his brother, and waited for him there. But in the middle of this the earl Robert came in at Portsmouth 12 days before Lammas;[10] and the king came against him with all his army. But the head men went between them, and reconciled the brothers[11] on the condition that the king relinquish all that he held within Normandy by force against the earl, and that all those in England who earlier lost their land through the earl should have it again, and also Earl Eustace[12] all his father's land here in the land, and that each year the earl Robert should have three thousand marks of silver from England; and whichever of the brothers survived the other should be heir to all of England and of Normandy, unless the deceased had an heir in lawful wedlock.[13] And then 12 of the highest from either side affirmed this by oath. And afterwards the earl stayed in the land until after Michaelmas; and during the time the earl stayed here in the land his men always did great harm as they travelled.

Also this year at Candlemas[14] the bishop Ranulf escaped by night out of the Tower in London where he was in captivity,[15] and went to Normandy; it was mostly his doing and instigation that this year the earl Robert sought out this land with hostility.

1102. In this year [1101] at the Nativity the king Henry was in Westminster, and at Easter in Winchester.

And soon after that, discord arose between the king and the earl Robert de Bellême, who had the earldom in Shrewsbury here in the land which his father Earl Roger possessed earlier, and great authority besides, both on this side of the sea and beyond. And the king travelled and besieged the castle at Arundel,[16] but when he could not win it so quickly he had castles made in front of it and there set them with his men; and afterwards travelled with all his army to Bridgnorth,[17] and

---

[10] i.e. on 20 July. Florence (II, p. 49) says he marched to Winchester and camped in a convenient place there.   [11] The 'Treaty of Alton', see David, *Robert Curthose*, pp. 131–6.   [12] Eustace III of Boulogne.   [13] Both were already married and soon had sons: William 'Adelinus' of England, William 'Clito' of Normandy. In 1102, Eustace married Mary, sister-in-law of Henry I, and their only child became Stephen's queen; see Table p. 297.   [14] 2 February 1101. This is an afterthought. Florence (II, p. 48) puts the events in proper sequence: Ranulf escaping in February and Robert invading the following July.   [15] Ordericus (V, pp. 312–13) gives a graphic account of the portly bishop ripping his ungloved hands on the rope by which he let himself down; then finding the rope too short, and having to drop to the ground; then escaping by boat with his mother, a one-eyed witch crudely cursed by the sailors with rude gestures.   [16] Belonging to Robert of Bellême. For the possible identification of one of Henry's siege-works, see Curwen, 'Rackham bank and earthwork', 168–86.   [17] Shropshire; Florence (II, p. 49) remembers its association with Æthelflæd (cf. annal 912 C).

stayed there until he had the castle, and deprived the earl Robert of land, and seized all that he had in England; and so the earl departed across the sea, and the army afterwards turned home.[1]

Then, after that, at Michaelmas the king was at Westminster, and all the head men in this land, ordained and lay; and the archbishop Anselm held a synod of ordained men, and there they set down many decrees which pertain to Christendom;[2] and there many, both French and English, lost their staffs[3] and authority which they acquired with injustice, or lived in with iniquity.

And in this same year in Pentecost week there came thieves, some from Auvergne[4] some from France and some from Flanders, and broke into the minster of Peterborough, and in there took much of value in gold and in silver, that was: crosses and chalices and candlesticks.

1103. Here in this year [1102] the king Henry was at Westminster at midwinter; and soon after that the bishop William Gifford travelled out of this land, because he did not want to receive his ordination, against the law, from the archbishop Gerard of York.[5] And then at the Easter the king held his court in Winchester; and after that the archbishop Anselm travelled from Canterbury to Rome, just as he and the king agreed.[6]

Also in this year the earl Robert of Normandy came to speak with the king here in the land; and before he travelled from here he gave up the three thousand marks which the king Henry, by covenant, had to give him each year.[7]

Also in this year, at Finchampstead in Berkshire, blood from the earth was seen.[8] This was a very disastrous year here in the land because of manifold taxes and because of pestilence among cattle and the ruin of crops, both in corn and also in all tree-crops. Also after[9] the morning of the Feast of St Lawrence, the wind here in the land did such great harm to all the crops as no-one remembered it ever did before.

In this same year passed away Matthias, abbot of Peterborough, who lived no longer than one year after he was abbot. After Michaelmas on 21 *October* he was received as abbot with a procession, and on the same day the next year he died in Gloucester and was buried there.

Ordericus (VI, pp. 30–31) alludes to a ballad reflecting popular sentiment at Robert's expulsion: *'Rejoice King Henry, give thanks to the Lord God, for you have begun to rule freely now that you have conquered Robert de Bellême and driven him out of your kingdom'*.   [2] The main topics were lay investiture (see note 6) and clerical marriage, cf. Eadmer, pp. 125–6, 129–30, 149–52, and Brooke, 'Gregorian reform in action: clerical marriage in England', 1–21, 187–8.   [3] i.e. the pastoral staffs, carried as a symbol of authority by both bishops and abbots. Among those deposed were Richard of Ely and Edwin of Ramsey.   [4] *Aluearnie*; Hugh Candidus (p. 87) says Alemannia, i.e. Germany.   [5] Gerard continued to resist Canterbury's claim to primacy, cf. Hugh the Chanter, pp. 20–25.   [6] Florence (II, p. 52) summarises the issue thus: *A great dissension arose between King Henry and Archbishop Anselm, the archbishop refusing to consent to the giving of investitures by the king, and to consecrate or communicate with those to whom the king had already given churches, because the apostolic pope had forbidden this; wherefore the king commanded Gerard, the archbishop of York, to consecrate the bishops to whom he had given investitures.* Anselm's previous journey to Rome had resulted in the forfeiture of Canterbury revenues to the king (see annal 1097); he now took with him William, bishop-elect of Winchester, and the abbots deposed from their abbeys (see note 3), while the king sent William Warelwast, later bishop of Exeter, to represent his own interests (Eadmer, pp. 156–95).

1104. Here in this year [1103] at Christmas the king Henry held his court at Westminster, and at Easter in Winchester, and at Pentecost again in Westminster.

In this year the first day of Pentecost was on 5 June, and on the Tuesday after that at midday there appeared four circles around the sun, white in colour, and each intertwined under the other as if they were plaited. All who saw it marvelled because they did not remember anything like it ever before.

After this, the earl Robert of Normandy and Robert de Bellême, whom the king Henry had earlier deprived of land and driven out of England, were reconciled. And through their reconciliation[10] the king of England and the earl of Normandy became at odds. And the king sent his people across the sea into Normandy, and the head men there in the land received them and, in betrayal of their lord the earl, lodged them in their castles, from where they caused the earl many troubles in raiding and in burning. Also this year William earl of Mortain[11] went away from the land into Normandy; but after he was gone he worked against the king, for which the king deprived him of everything and confiscated the land which he had here in the land.[12]

It is not easy to describe the miseries which this land was suffering at this time through various and manifold injustices and taxes which never left off or lessened.[13] And always wherever the king went, there was, because of his court, wholesale raiding upon his miserable people, and with that very often burnings and slaughter of men.

> All this was to gall God
> And to harrass this wretched nation.[14]

1105. In this year [1104] at the Nativity the king Henry held his court at Windsor; and after that, in the spring, he went across the sea into Normandy against his brother Earl Robert. And while he stayed there he won from his brother Caen and Bayeux[15] and almost all the castles, and the head men there in the land became subject to him.[16] And later, in the autumn, he came back again here to the land. And afterwards what he had won in Normandy remained in peace and obedient to him, except those who lived anywhere near the earl William of Mortain, whom he [the earl]

[7] See annal 1101. [8] Also reported in 1098 and 1100. [9] MS *uppon* (cf. p. 233, note 16). The *Waverly Annals* (p. 210) say *the first day after* (i.e. 11 August) a date agreed by Florence (II, p. 53). [10] Cf. Ordericus, VI, pp. 56–9. [11] Son of the Conqueror's half-brother Robert, he was earl of Cornwall and one of the greatest landowners in England (see Table, p. 298). [12] For William's rebellion and alliance with his uncle Robert de Bellême, see Ordericus, VI, pp. 58–9; William of Malmesbury, *Gesta Regum*, II, pp. 473–4. [13] The tax-collectors took paltry pieces of furniture and even the doors from houses says Eadmer, *Recent Events*, pp. 183–4. [14] The Old English lines form a rhyming couplet. [15] Florence (II, p. 54) says the king burned Bayeux and the church of St Mary there, and Caen surrendered for fear of the same treatment. [16] Florence (II, p. 54) says: *nearly all the Norman nobles snatched the gold and silver which the king had brought with him from England, and surrendered to him their castles and fortified cities and towns.*

frequently belaboured as much as he could because of his loss of land here in the land. Then before Christmas Robert de Bellême came here to this land to the king.

This was a very disastrous year here in the land through the ruin of the crops, and through the manifold taxes which never left off before the king went across – and then while he was there, and again after he came back.

1106. Here in this year at the Nativity [1105] the king was in Westminster and held his court there; and at that season Robert de Bellême went away from the king in discord, out of this land into Normandy.

Then after this, before spring, the king was at Northampton, and the earl Robert his brother came to him from Normandy; and because the king would not give him back what he had taken from him in Normandy they parted in discord and the earl immediately travelled back across the sea again.

In the first week of Lent, on the Friday, 16 February, an unusual star appeared in the evening, and for a long period after that[1] was seen shining for a while each evening. The star appeared in the south-west; it seemed to be small and dark, but the light that stood from it was very bright and seemed like an enormous beam shining north-east; and one evening it was seen as if the beam were forking in the opposite direction, towards the star.[2] Some said that they saw more unknown stars at this time, but we cannot write about it more clearly because we did not see it ourselves. On the night before the morning of *The Lord's Supper*,[3] that is the Thursday before Easter, two moons were seen in the heavens before day, one to the east and the other to the west, both full; and the same day the moon was 14 days old.[4]

At Easter the king was at Bath, and at Pentecost at Salisbury, because he did not want to hold a court on his setting out across the sea. After that, before August the king travelled across the sea into Normandy, and almost all who were there in the land submitted themselves to his will,[5] except for Robert de Bellême and the earl of Mortain and a few other head men who still held with the earl of Normandy. And therefore the king afterwards went with an army and besieged a certain castle of the earl of Mortain, called Tinchebray.[6]

---

[1] Florence (II, p. 54) says it shone for twenty-five days.   [2] i.e. the light of the tail of the comet seemed to be streaming towards, instead of from, the nucleus (cf. *Anglo-Saxon Dictionary*, Supplement, sub *ongeanweardes*).   [3] Maundy Thursday was 21 March that year.   [4] MS *wæs se mona xiiiiᵃ*.   [5] Again the principal men of Normandy *came running after the king's gold and silver and delivered up to him the townships, castles and cities* (Eadmer, p. 176), cf. p. 239, note 16.   [6] Dép. Orne.   [7] 28 September.   [8] This was the decisive battle for control of Normandy, see generally David, *Robert Curthose*, pp. 245–8; Davis, 'A contemporary account of the Battle of Tinchebrai', (1909), 728–32, (1910), 295–6; Douglas and Greenaway, *Documents*, pp. 329–30.

While the king was besieging the castle, the earl Robert of Normandy came against the king with his army on the eve of Michaelmas,[7] and with him Robert de Bellême, William earl of Mortain, and all those who agreed with them; but the strength and the victory were the king's.[8] There the earl of Normandy was seized,[9] and the earl of Mortain, and Robert d'Estouteville,[10] and afterwards sent to England and brought into captivity. Robert de Bellême was put to flight there, and William Crispin[11] captured and many along with him. The ætheling Edgar, who a little earlier had gone over from the king to the earl, was also seized there, whom the king afterwards let go unmolested. Afterwards the king conquered all that was in Normandy, and set it under his will and control.

Also this year there were very heavy and continual conflicts between the emperor of Saxony and his son; during these conflicts the father passed away, and the son succeeded to the authority.[12]

1107. In this year at Christmas [1106] the king Henry was in Normandy and arranged and set that land under his control, and after that in spring came here to the land, and at Easter held his court in Windsor, and at Pentecost in Westminster; and afterwards, at the beginning of August, was again at Westminster, and there gave and arranged for those bishoprics and abbacies in England or in Normandy which were without head or shepherd. There were so many that there was nobody who remembered so many being given together ever before.[13]

And at this same time, among those others who received abbacies, Ernulf, who was prior in Canterbury earlier, succeeded to the abbacy in Peterborough. This was exactly some 7 years since the king Henry succeeded to the kingship, and it was the forty-first year since the French took control of this land. Many said that they saw various signs in the moon this year, and its light waxing and waning contrary to nature.

This year passed away Maurice bishop in London, and Robert abbot in Bury St Edmunds, and Richard abbot in Ely.[14] Also this year passed away Edgar, the king in Scotland, on *13 January*,[15] and Alexander his brother succeeded to the kingdom, as the king Henry granted him.[16]

---

[9] He would spend the remainder of his life as a prisoner, dying at Cardiff and taken for burial to Gloucester, where William ensured that a light was kept burning before his tomb; the wooden figural monument survives; see generally David, *Robert Curthose*, pp. 177–89, 245–8.   [10] Etoutteville-sur-Mer, dép. Seine Maritime (Lloyd, *Anglo-Norman Families*, p. 40).   [11] Brother of the abbot of Westminster (see p. 247, note 20).   [12] A further phase of the Investiture Contest in Germany. Henry IV was deposed in favour of Henry V on 31 December 1105 and died on 7 August 1106; see generally Haverkamp, *Medieval Germany*, pp. 126–8.   [13] Florence (II, pp. 55–6) says that Anselm was absent from the first of these meetings, but present at the second. This effectively marked the end of the investiture dispute.   [14] Respectively on 26 September, 16 September and 16 June. In 1109, after a two-year vacancy, Ely was transformed into a bishopric, dividing the see of Lincoln (Eadmer, pp. 208–9).   [15] MS *idus Janr*; Florence, II, p. 55, says *viii idus* (6 January) and Simeon, II, p. 238, *vi idus* (8 January).   [16] Alexander was married to one of Henry's illegitimate daughters, to whom he seems to have been temperamentally and physically unsuited (William of Malmesbury, *Gesta Regum*, II, p. 476).

1108. Here in this year at the Nativity [1107] the king Henry was in Westminster, and at Easter in Winchester, and at Pentecost back in Westminster, and after that, before August, he travelled into Normandy.

And Philip the king of France passed away on 5 *August*,[1] and his son Louis[2] succeeded to the kingdom, and afterwards there arose many conflicts between the king of France and that of England while he stayed in Normandy.

Also in this year the archbishop Gerard of York passed away[3] before Pentecost, and afterwards Thomas[4] was set for it.

1109. Here in this year at Christmas [1108] and at Easter the king Henry was in Normandy, and before Pentecost[5] came here to the land and held his court in Westminster. There the covenants were completed and the oaths sworn to give his daughter to the emperor.[6]

This year there were very many thunderstorms, and those very terrifying. And the archbishop Anselm of Canterbury passed away the day of 22 *March*;[7] and the first day of Easter was on the *Greater Litany*.[8]

1110. In this year the king Henry held his court at Christmas [1109] at Westminster; and at Easter he was at Marlborough.[9] And at Pentecost he held his court for the first time in the New Windsor.[10]

This year, before spring, the king sent his daughter across the sea with manifold treasures, and gave her to the emperor. On the fifth night in the month of May the moon appeared in the evening shining brightly, and afterwards its light waned little by little so that as soon as it was night it was so wholly quenched that neither light nor circle nor anything of it at all was seen; and remained thus well-nigh until day, and afterwards appeared full and shining brightly; that same day it was a fortnight old. All that night the sky was very clear and the stars over all the heaven shining very brightly. And tree-crops were badly seized by frost that night. After that, in the month of June,[11] a star appeared in the north-east, and its ray stood out in front of it to the south-west, and was seen thus for many nights; and later on in the night, after it climbed higher, it was seen going away to the north-west.

---

[1] *Recte* 29 July.   [2] See generally, Suger, *The Deeds of Louis the Fat*.   [3] 21 May.
[4] Provost of Beverley, son of Samson, bishop of Worcester, and nephew of Archbishop Thomas II of York, see Hugh the Chanter, pp. 24–55.   [5] Florence (II, p. 59) says *about Rogation*.   [6] For the eight-year-old Matilda's marriage to Henry V, see Chibnall, *The Empress Matilda*, pp. 22–6; Leyser, 'England and the Empire in the early twelfth century', 61–70.   [7] *Recte* 21 April, the scribe writing *xi kal Apr* for *xi kal Maii*.   [8] 25 April; see p. 195, note 4.   [9] A castle in Wiltshire, see VCH, *Wiltshire*, XII, pp. 165–8.   [10] The present site, still properly 'New Windsor' as distinct from the Confessor's and Conqueror's 'Old Windsor' (Kingsbury), for which see Hope-Taylor, 'Old Windsor', 183–5.   [11] Florence (II, p. 60) says that this *stella cometa* appeared on 8 June and was visible for three weeks.   [12] Son of William de Briouze (dép. Orne), a significant landowner (DB, *Sussex*, 13); cf. Lloyd, *Anglo-Norman Families*, p. 20.   [13] See Lloyd, *Anglo-Norman Families*, p. 56.

This year Philip de Braose[12] and William Malet[13] and William Bainard[14] were deprived of land.

Also this year passed away Earl Helias who held Maine from the king Henry and on knee;[15] and after his passing, the earl of Anjou[16] succeeded and held it against the king.

This was a very disastrous year here in the land through the tax which the king took for his daughter's gift,[17] and through bad weather by which the earth-crops were badly damaged, and tree-crops all well-nigh ruined all over this land.

This year work first started on the new minster in Chertsey.[18]

1111. In this year the king Henry did not wear his *crown* at Christmas [1110], nor at Easter, nor at Pentecost; and in August he travelled across the sea into Normandy because of the enmity which some on the borders of France had towards him, and mostly because of the earl of Anjou who held Maine against him.[19] After he came there they made many big raids,[20] burnings and ravagings between them.

In this year the earl Robert of Flanders passed away[21] and his son Baldwin[22] succeeded thereto.

This year the winter was very long and heavy and severe, and through that the earth-crops were badly damaged, and there occurred the greatest pestilence among cattle that anyone could remember.

1112. All this year the king Henry stayed in Normandy because of the enmity he had with France and with the earl of Anjou who held Maine against him. And while he was there he deprived of land and drove out of Normandy the earl of Evreux[23] and William Crispin, and gave Philip de Braose back land of which he was earlier deprived. And he had Robert de Bellême siezed and put in prison.[24]

This was a very good year and very productive in woods and fields, but it was very heavy and sorrowful through an immense pestilence among men.

1113. Here in this year the king Henry was in Normandy at the Nativity [1112] and at Easter and at Pentecost, and after that [*continued overleaf*]

A FRAGMENT (H) 1113

1113. . . . so that they could hardly speak. And after that [*continued overleaf*]

---

[14] For whose family, see p. 232, note 4.   [15] MS *oncweow* presumably for *on cneow*, i.e. metaphorically in allegiance to the king. Elias de La Flèche had been expelled from Maine by William II in 1099 (q.v.).   [16] Fulk V, son-in-law of Helias.   [17] i.e. as a bridal gift or dowry.   [18] Put in hand by Abbot Hugh, a physician and nephew of King Stephen; not a new foundation so presumably a new church building, VCH, *Surrey*, I, pp. 55–64.   [19] Cf. Ordericus, VI, pp. 176–83; William of Malmesbury, *Gesta Regum*, II, pp. 480–81.   [20] MS *unrada*, here and in 1116 E (p. 246); perhaps 'ill-advised things', but in view of the context probably an example of the intensive prefix *un-*.   [21] Thrown and trampled by horses during a battle at Meaux on 4 or 5 October (Ordericus, VI, pp. 160–63).   [22] Baldwin VII.   [23] William, together with Helwise, his generally-disliked wife, were exiled to Anjou, but restored the following year (Ordericus, VI, pp. 148–9, 180–81).   [24] MS *in prisune don*; the first recorded use of this French word in an English text, cf. p. 264, note 3; Robert was confined: *in Cherbourg in the month of October* says Florence (II, p. 66).

E continued from previous page
in summer he sent Robert de Bellême here to the land into the castle at Wareham,[1] and himself came here to the land soon after that.

1114. In this year the king Henry held his court at the Nativity [1113] at Windsor, and he did not hold court again this year.

And at midsummer he travelled with an army into Wales, and the Welsh came and made peace with the king; and he had castles constructed in there.[2] And after that, in September, he went across the sea into Normandy.

This year, towards the end of May, a strange star was seen shining with long rays for many nights. Also in this same year one day[3] there was so great an ebb-tide everywhere as no-one remembered before, and such that men travelled across the Thames to the east of the bridge in London by riding and walking.[4] This year there were very great winds in the month of October, but immeasurably great on the night of *the octave of St Martin,*[5] and it was evident everywhere in woods and villages.

Also in this year the king gave the archbishopric in Canterbury to Ralph who was earlier bishop in Rochester;[6] and [*continued opposite*]

A FRAGMENT (H) 1113 *continued from previous page*

Peter abbot in Gloucester[7] departed on the day of *17 July*, and the king set thereto William, who was a monk in the same minster, on the day of *5 October*.

[1114]. In this year the king Henry was in Windsor at midwinter [1113], and there wore his crown, and there gave the bishopric in Worcester to Theobald[8] his clerk. Also he gave the abbacy in Ramsey to Rainald [who] was a monk in Caen; also he gave the abbacy in York to Richard [who] was a monk in the same minster; also he gave the abbacy at Thorney to Robert [who] was a monk at St Evroul; also he gave the earldom in Northamptonshire to David,[9] [who] was the queen's brother. After that, Thomas the archbishop in York departed on the day of *17 February*;[10] after that he gave the abbacy at Cerne[11] to William [who] was a monk at Caen. [*continued opposite*]

Florence (II, p. 66): *in strictest confinement*; where he probably remained till his death (Ordericus, VI, p. 179, note 3). [2] See generally Carr, 'Anglo-Welsh relations, 1066–1282', p. 123. [3] Florence (II, p. 67) says this was 10 October, *from midnight to midnight*. [4] Florence (loc. cit.): *between the bridge and the royal tower . . . the water scarcely reaching to their knees*; the same lack of water was reported at Yarmouth, while in the Medway there was insufficient water to keep even the smallest vessels afloat. [5] 18 November. [6] Ralph d'Escures was elected at Windsor on 26 April; the scribe of H has read *vi kal Mar* for *vi kal Maii*. He was appointed to Rochester in 1108 having fled from his abbacy at Séez during the uncertainty in Normandy *c.* 1103 (Ordericus, IV, pp. 168–71; VI, pp. 46–9). [7] Whose 'gentle devotion' gave Gloucester a remarkable Romanesque candlestick, subsequently looted and sent to Le Mans, but now in the Victoria & Albert Museum (Oman, *The Gloucester Candlestick*). [8] *Recte* Theowulf. [9] David I, king of Scotland. [10] Hugh the Chanter (pp. 54–5), presumably drawing on York archives, says 19 February. [11] Cerne Abbas, Dorset, see generally VCH, *Dorset*, II, pp. 53–8.

E 1114 *continued from opposite page*

Thomas the archbishop in York passed away, and Thurstan succeeded to it; he was earlier the king's chaplain.[12]

At the same time the king travelled towards the sea and wanted to cross, but the weather hindered him. Meanwhile he sent his writ to Ernulf, abbot of Peterborough, and commanded him to come to him with the greatest haste, because he wanted to speak with him privately. Then when he came to him, he pressed the bishopric of Rochester on him[13] – and the archbishops and bishops and the nobility[14] that was in England went along with the king. And he long resisted, but it was to no avail; and then the king ordered the archbishop that he should lead him to Canterbury and bless him as bishop whether he wanted or not.[15] This was done in the village they call Bourne;[16] that was the day of the 15 September. Then when the monks of Peterborough heard tell of that, they were as sorry as they had ever been before, because he was a very good and gentle man and did much good inside [*continued overleaf*]

A FRAGMENT (H) 1114 *continued from opposite page*

Then at Easter he was at Thorpe[17] near Northampton. After that he gave the archbishopric in Canterbury to Ralph who was bishop in Rochester, and he succeeded to it on the day of 24 *February*.[6] Then after that the abbot Nigel in Burton[18] died on the day of 3 *May*. After that, on the day of 5 *May*, Chichester burned down, and the minster there as well.

Then at Pentecost the king was at St Albans. After that, at midsummer, he travelled with his army into Wales and made castles in there;[2] and the Welsh kings came to him and became his men and swore him loyal oaths.

After that he came to Winchester and there gave the archbishopric in York to Thurstan his clerk;[12] and the abbacy at St Edmunds he gave to Albold [who] was a monk in Bec, on the day of 16 *August*. After that, on the day of the *Exaltation of the Holy Cross*,[19] he gave the abbacy in Muchelney[20] to Ealdwulf [who] was a monk in the same minster. Also he gave the abbacy in Burton[18] to Geoffrey who was a monk in the Old Minster.[21] On the same occasion, the archbishop Ralph gave the bishopric in Rochester . . .

---

[12] Elected at Winchester 15 August, but reviving the question of primacy with Canterbury and not consecrated until 1119. See generally Hugh the Chanter, pp. 56ff., and Nicholl, *Thurstan, Archbishop of York (1114–1140)*. [13] It was probably Ernulf who initiated the important compilation of laws and charters known as the *Textus Roffensis* (II, p. 18). [14] MS *dugeð*. [15] MS *wold he, nolde he*. [16] Where Henry was waiting for a favourable breeze to sail cross the sea (Hugh Candidus, p. 96). This was probably Westbourne, a manor belonging to Roger, Earl of Arundel, close to Chichester Harbour but on the edge of the New Forest convenient for hunting (DB, *Sussex*, 11.30). [17] i.e. Kingsthorpe, a royal manor adjacent to Northampton (DB, *Northamptonshire*, 1.18). [18] See p. 198, note 4. [19] 14 September, commemorating the recovery of cross relics from the Persians in 628, cf. Swanton, *Dream of the Rood*, pp. 44–5. [20] Cf. VCH, *Somerset*, II, pp. 103–7. [21] Winchester, see above, p. 26, note 8.

E 1114 *continued from previous page*
and outside while he lived there. May God Almighty dwell with him always!

Then soon after that, through the desire of the archbishop of Canterbury, the king gave the abbacy[1] to a monk of Séez who was called John; and soon after that the king and the archbishop of Canterbury sent him to Rome for the archbishop's pallium, and with him one a monk who is[2] called Warner, and the archdeacon John[3] the archbishop's nephew; and they succeeded well there.[4] This was done on the day of *21 September* in the village which they call Rowner;[5] and the same day the king went on ship in Portsmouth.

1115. Here the king Henry was in Normandy at the Nativity [1114] and while he was there he brought it about that all the head men in Normandy performed homage and loyal oaths to William, his son whom he had by his queen. And after that he came here into the land in the month of July.

This year the winter was so severe with snow and with frost that no man then alive remembered one more severe; and through that there was an immense pestilence among cattle.

In this year the pope Paschal sent the pallium here to the land to Ralph, archbishop in Canterbury, and he received it with great honour at his arch-seat in Canterbury.[6] Abbot Anselm[7] who was nephew of Archbishop Anselm and the abbot John of Peterborough brought it from Rome.

1116. In this year the king Henry was at St Albans at the Nativity [1115] and there had the minster consecrated[8] – and at Easter [he was] in Odiham.[9] And also this year there was a very heavy winter, and severe and long, for the cattle and for everything. And immediately after Easter the king travelled across the sea into Normandy; and there were many big raids[10] and plunderings and castles seized between France and Normandy. Mostly this hostility was because the king Henry helped his nephew the earl Theobald de Blois[11] who was then at war against his lord, Louis the king of France.[12]

This was a very laborious year and calamitous for the earth-crops through the immense rains that came just before August and were still very oppressive and troublesome when Candlemas[13] came. Also

---

[1] Of Peterborough, cf. Hugh Candidus (p. 97).   [2] 'was' interlined, presumably after the monk's death.   [3] In fact John only became archdeacon after his return (Eadmer, *Historia Novorum*, p. 231).   [4] For this negotiation, see Eadmer, *Historia Novorum*, pp. 226–9; and cf. annal 1119.   [5] A manor in Hampshire belonging to the king's chamberlain William Maudit, convenient both for embarkation and for hunting in the New Forest.   [6] Florence (II, p. 68) dates this 27 June.   [7] Abbot of St Saba in Rome, who had helped the English envoys (Eadmer, *Historia Novorum*, p. 228); in his uncle's day he had studied at Canterbury under Ernulf. In 1121 he became abbot of Bury St Edmunds. See generally *The Letters of Osbert of Clare*, ed. Williamson, pp. 191–200; Davis, 'The monks of St. Edmund', 236–9.   [8] Work on the building seems to have been completed *c.* 1088 and the delay in consecration is unexplained; see generally *Gesta Abbatum Sancti Albani*, I, pp. 70–71. VCH, *Hertford*, II, 483–4; RCHM, *Hertfordshire*, p. 177.   [9] A royal manor (DB, *Hampshire*, 1.1).   [10] See also annal 1111.   [11] Theobald IV, count of Blois and Chartres, son of Adela, sister of Henry I, and elder brother of the future King Stephen.

this year was so barren of mast[14] that none was heard tell of in all this land nor also in Wales. Also this year this land and the nation were regularly sorely oppressed through the taxes which the king took within boroughs and without.[15]

In this same year all the minster of Peterborough burned, and all the buildings except the chapter-house and the dormitory; and besides, the most part of the town also all burned.[16] All this happened on a Friday; that was 4 *August*.

1117. All this year the king Henry stayed in Normandy because of the hostility of the king of France and his other neighbours. And then in the summer the king of France and the earl of Flanders with him came into Normandy with an army, and stayed in there for one night, and in the morning travelled back without a battle. And Normandy was very oppressed both through taxes and through the army which the king Henry had gathered against them. Also this nation [England] became severely oppressed through the same – through manifold taxes.

This year also, on the night of *1 December*, there were immense storms,[17] with thunder, and lightning, and rain and hail. And on the night of *11 December* for much of the night[18] the moon became as if it were all bloody, and afterwards eclipsed. Also on the night of *16 December* the heaven was seen very red, as if it were fire. And on *the octave of St John the Evangelist*[19] there was the great earth-trembling in Lombardy, from which many minsters, towers and houses fell, and did great harm to men. This was a very calamitous year for corn through the rains which did not leave off well-nigh all year.

And the abbot Gilbert of Westminster[20] passed away on *6 December*; and Faricius[21] abbot of Abingdon on *23 February*. And in this same year . . .[22]

1118. Here the king Henry stayed all this year in Normandy because of the war with the king of France and the earl of Anjou and the earl of Flanders. And the earl of Flanders was wounded in Normandy and, wounded thus, went into Flanders.[23] Through the hostility of these the king became very troubled and lost much,

---

[12] Cf. Suger, *The Deeds of Louis the Fat*, pp. 111–18; Louis was assisting the exiled William 'Clito' to recover his father's dukedom of Normandy (Ordericus, VI, pp. 184–5). [13] 2 February. [14] *mæsten*: the fruit of beech, oak and other forest trees which was of vital importance as pannage (pig-fodder), see Lennard, *Rural England*, pp. 14–5, 252–60. [15] For this formula, see Harmer, *Writs*, pp. 428–9. [16] Hugh Candidus (pp. 97–8) says that also were saved: *the privy and the new refectory, in which the monks had only eaten for three days, the poor having been previously fed there.* He goes on to account for the fire's origin: *when a certain sergeant of the bakehouse was making a fire and it did not light at once, he said in a temper: 'Come Devil, blow the fire!', and the fire burst out at once and reached the roof, and ran through all the outbuildings as far as the town; and thus was fulfilled the prophecy of Bishop Æthelric, that the church should be destroyed by fire.* [17] MS *wædera*. [18] MS *lange nihtes*; cf. Gradon, review of Garmonsway, *Chronicle*, 99. [19] The eighth day beginning with the Feast on 27 December, i.e. 3 January. [20] See Robinson, *Gilbert Crispin*; and Southern, 'St Anselm and Gilbert Crispin', 78–115. [21] A celebrated Italian physician, previously cellarer of Malmesbury, cf. *Chronicon de Abingdon*, II, pp. 44, 285–6 *et passim*. [22] The annal was never completed, and a line-and-a-half remains blank; perhaps it was intended to note the refounding of Peterborough as in Hugh Candidus p. 98. [23] He was wounded in fighting either at Bures (Ordericus, VI, pp. 190–91) or Eu (Suger, *Deeds of Louis*, p. 116) in September, and retired to Aumale, where he died the following June.

both in money and also in land; and his own men troubled him most, who frequently deserted and betrayed him and turned over to his enemies, and gave up their castles to them to the king's harm and betrayal. England paid dear for all this through manifold taxes which did not leave off all this year.

In this year one evening in the week of the Ephiphany there was very great lightning, and after that immense thunder-claps.

And the queen Maud passed away in Westminster on the day of *1 May*, and was buried there.[1] And the earl Robert of Meulan[2] also passed away this year.

Also in this year, on the Feast of St Thomas,[3] there was so very immense a great wind that no-one then alive remembered one greater; and it was seen everywhere in houses and also in trees.

This year also passed away the pope Paschal, and John of Gaeta whose other name was Gelasius succeeded to the papacy.[4]

1119. All this year the king Henry stayed in Normandy, and was regularly very troubled through the war with the king of France and also his own men who had turned away from him with treachery, until the two kings with their people joined battle in Normandy.[5] There the king of France was put to flight and all his best men seized. And afterwards many of King Henry's men who were earlier against him with their castles, submitted to him and came to terms; and some of the castles he seized by force.

This year William, son of King Henry and the queen Maud, travelled into Normandy to his father, and there the earl of Anjou's daughter[6] was given to him and wedded as wife.[7]

On the eve of Michaelmas[8] there was a great earth-trembling here in the land in certain places, though most severe in Gloucestershire and in Worcestershire.

In this same year the pope Gelasius[4] passed away on this side of the mountains, and was buried in Cluny.[9] And after him the archbishop of Vienne was chosen as pope, who took the name Calixtus;[10] afterwards on the Feast of *St Luke the Evangelist*[11] he came into France to Rheims and there held a *council*;[12] and the archbishop Thurstan

---

[1] William of Malmesbury (*Gesta Regum*, II, pp. 493–5) says the queen had lived in in some state at Westminster and had an interest in church music.   [2] Count of Meulan in the French Vexin and earl of Leicester, he had fought at Hastings half a century earlier and became one of Henry I's most valued councillors (Eadmer, *Recent Events*, pp. 204–5; William of Malmesbury, *Gesta Regum*, II, pp. 482–3).   [3] 21 December.   [4] In defiance of the Emperor, Gelasius II was elected on 24 January, and consecrated 10 March, whereupon the emperor appointed Gregory VIII, termed anti-pope (Ordericus, VI, pp. 184–5).   [5] The Battle of Brémule (dép. Eure), 2 August 1119, fought for control of the Vexin, a buffer-region between Normandy and France; see generally Le Patourel *The Norman Empire*, pp. 82–4 and Map p. 282.   [6] Maud.   [7] Cf. Ordericus, VI, pp. 224–5; William of Malmesbury, *Gesta Regum*, pp. 482, 495.   [8] 28 September.   [9] Gelasius had crossed the Alps (cf. annal 1129) to ask for French help against the Emperor Henry V and his new anti-pope Gregory VIII. Cluny in Burgundy was the mother-house of an influential reformed Benedictine monastic order.   [10] The aristocratic Guy of Burgundy (Calixtus II), cf. Ordericus, VI, pp. 208–11.   [11] 18 October.   [12] Cf. Ordericus, VI, pp. 252–77; Simeon, II, pp. 254–7.   [13] Hugh the Chanter, p. 73–4; Ordericus, VI, pp. 252–3; William of Malmesbury, *Gesta Pontificum*, pp. 264–5.

of York travelled to it; and because he had received his ordination from the pope against the law and against the arch-seat in Canterbury and against the king's will, the king forbade him any return passage to England;[13] and thus he lost[14] his archbishopric and went towards Rome with the pope.

Also in this year the earl Baldwin[15] of Flanders passed away from the wounds which he received in Normandy; and after him Charles, his father's sister's son, succeeded to the authority; he was son of Cnut, the holy king of Denmark.[16]

1120. This year the king of England and that of France became reconciled;[17] and after their reconciliation all the king Henry's own men inside Normandy and the earl of Flanders and that of Ponthieu[18] came to terms with him. Then after this the king Henry disposed his castles and his land in Normandy according to his wishes, and so went to the land here before Advent.

And on the journey the king's two sons William and Richard were drowned – and Richard earl of Chester and Ottuel his brother, and very many of the king's court: stewards, and chamberlains, and cup-bearers, and various officials, and countless very distinguished people along with them.[19] To their friends the death of these was a double grief: one that they lost this life so suddenly, the other that few of their bodies were found anywhere afterwards.

This year the light came to *the Sepulchre of the Lord* in Jerusalem twice: once at Easter and another time on *the Assumption of St Mary*,[20] just as the faithful said who came from there.[21]

And the archbishop Thurstan of York came to terms with the king through the pope, and came here to the land and received his bishopric, although it was very displeasing to the archbishop of Canterbury.[22]

1121. Here the king Henry was in Brampton[23] at Christmas [1120]; and after that, in Windsor before Candlemas[24] Adeliza who was daughter of the commander[25] of Louvain was given him as wife, and afterwards consecrated as queen.

And the moon eclipsed on the eve of *5 April*, and was a *14* [-day] *moon.*

---

[14] MS *þærnode*; perhaps an otherwise unrecorded Old English verb *þear(f)nian,* cf. *Middle English Dictionary,* sub *tharnan* (c).   [15] Baldwin VII, see p. 247, note 23.   [16] See annal 1086, p. 221.   [17] Louis now recognised the young William 'Adelinus' (later drowned in the White Ship disaster) as duke of Normandy. (Hugh the Chanter, p. 97; Simeon, II, p. 258).   [18] Charles of Flanders and William I of Ponthieu.   [19] Ordericus Vitalis gives a good circumstantial account (VI, pp. 294–330) of the wreck of the White Ship on the night of 25–6 November, which he attributes to drunken captain and crew. There was on board he says: *too great a crowd of wild and headstrong young men,* only two surviving out of some three hundred. The future King Stephen had been on board but, observing the situation, disembarked.   [20] 15 August.   [21] A supernatural lighting of the lamps in the Holy Sepulchre; cf. *Peregrinationes Tres,* p. 152; perhaps a regular event, since a candle so lit was among relics given to Exeter by Athelstan (Swanton, *Prose,* p. 21).   [22] See p. 245, note 12, and Hugh the Chanter, pp. 89–104, Eadmer, *Historia Novorum,* pp. 258–9.   [23] A royal manor adjoining Huntingdon (DB, *Huntingdonshire,* 1.8).   [24] As the king had been a widower for a long time, Ralph, archbishop of Canterbury, urged marriage so that he should no longer lead an improper life; Adèla was chosen by a council meeting at London on 6 January, they were married on 29 January and the queen consecrated and crowned the next day (Florence, II, pp. 75–6).   [25] MS *heretoga*; at this stage the sense 'war-leader' has shifted in the direction of a territorial status; cf. The Laws of Edward the Confessor: *the leader of a province which among the English are called 'heretoches'* (Liebermann, *Gesetze,* I, p. 656). In the late Peterborough addition s.a. 656 (p. 32) the rank is listed between earl and thegn.

And at Easter the king was at Berkeley, and after that at Pentecost he held a great court in Westminster; and later in the summer went into Wales with an army. And the Welsh came to meet him, and they came to terms with him according to the king's wishes.

This year the earl of Anjou came to his land from Jerusalem,[1] and afterwards sent here to the land and had fetched his daughter who was earlier given as wife to the king's son William.[2]

And on the night of *Christmas Eve*[3] there was a very great wind over all this land, and that was evident in many things.

1122. In this year the king Henry was in Norwich at Christmas [1121] and at *Easter* he was in Northampton.

In the preceding spring the town of Gloucester burned down.[4] Then when the monks were singing their mass and the deacon had begun the gospel 'As Jesus passed by'[5] the fire came in the upper part of the steeple and burned down all the minster and all the treasures which were inside there except for a few books and three chasubles; that was on the day of *8 March*.

And after that, the Tuesday after Palm Sunday[6] there was a very great wind on that day, *22 March*;[7] after that many signs came far and wide in England, and many illusions were seen and heard. And the night of *25 July* there was a very great earthquake over all Somersetshire and in Gloucestershire. Afterwards on the day of *8 September*, that was on the Feast of St Mary,[8] there occured a great wind from 9 a.m. in the morning[9] of the day until dark night.

This same year Ralph the archbishop of Canterbury passed away; that was on the day of *20 October*. After that there were many ship-men on sea and on water, and [who] said that they saw in the north-east a great and broad fire near the earth, and it grew in length up to the sky; and the sky opened on four sides and fought against it as if it would quench it, and then the fire grew no more up to the heavens. They saw that fire at the break of day, and it[10] lasted until it was light over all; that was on the day of *7 December*.

---

[1] Fulk V had gone there on a pilgrimage two years earlier (1120), cf. Runciman, *Crusades*, II, pp. 177–233; Ordericus, VI, pp. 308–11.   [2] And now widowed as a result of William's death in the loss of the White Ship, see p. 249, note 19.   [3] *Vigilia Natalis Domini.*   [4] On 9 March says Florence (II, p. 77).   [5] i.e. John ix, the gospel-reading for the Wednesday in the fourth week of Lent, that year 8 March.   [6] The Sunday before Easter, commemorating Christ's entry into Jerusalem when palm branches were waved by the populace (John, xii:13)   [7] *Recte* 21 March.   [8] i.e. The Nativity of St Mary.   [9] MS *þa undern dæies*; see p. 16, note 7.   [10] Presumably an aurora borealis; cf. annal 1131.

1123. In this year the king Henry was at Dunstable[11] at Christmas-time[12] [1122] and the earl's envoys came from Anjou to him there;[13] and from there he travelled to Woodstock,[14] and his bishops and all his court with him. Then it happened on a Wednesday, that was on *10 January*, that the king was riding in his deer-park, the bishop Roger of Salisbury[15] on one side of him and the bishop Robert Bloet of Lincoln on the other side of him; and [they] rode there talking. Then the bishop of Lincoln sank down and said to the king: 'Lord king, I am dying'. And the king got down from his horse and caught him in his arms, and had him carried home to his lodging; and he was soon dead. And he was conveyed to Lincoln with great honour and buried in front of St Mary's altar; and the bishop of Chester [who] was called Robert Pecceth[16] buried him.

Then immediately after that the king sent his writs over all England and asked all his bishops and his abbots and his thegns[17] that they should come to his council-meeting, to Gloucester, to join him on Candlemas Day;[18] and they did so. Then when they were all gathered, the king asked them that they should choose an archbishop for Canterbury for themselves,[19] whomsoever they wanted, and he would give them his consent to it. Then the bishops spoke between themselves and said that they did not want ever again to have a man from monastic orders as archbishop over them, but all went together to the king and desired that they might chose as archbishop a man from the secular clergy, whomsoever they wanted; and the king gave them his consent to it. This was all done through the bishop of Salisbury, and through the bishop of Lincoln before his death, because they never liked monastic rule, but were always against monks and their rule. And the prior and the monks of Canterbury and all the others who were men in monastic orders withstood it fully two days, but it was to no avail because the bishop of Salisbury was strong and ruled all England, and was against it with all his power and ability. Then they chose a clerk[20] [who] was called William of Corbeil[21] – he was

---

[11] A new-town planted c. 1119 (Beresford, *New Towns of the Middle Ages*, p. 394) where c. 1132 the king would found an Augustinian priory (VCH, *Bedfordshire*, III, pp. 350, 355–6). It was the site of an early twelfth-century school and the location of the earliest recorded miracle play in England (*Gesta Abbatum Monasterii Sancti Albani*, I, p. 73). [12] MS *Cristes-tide*. [13] To negotiate the return of his daughter's dowry (see note 2 and p. 249, note 19). [14] A royal manor in Oxfordshire, where Henry kept an exotic menagerie (William of Malmesbury, *Gesta Regum*, II, p. 485). [15] Henry's chief minister, see West, *Justiciarship in England*, pp. 16–19. [16] The origin of this surname seems unknown; Eadmer (*Historia Novorum*, pp. 290–91) says he had formerly been in charge of the royal bread and wine. [17] At this stage Old English *þegn* seems to have broadened its use to refer to the king's secular lords in general. [18] 2 February. [19] Cf. Hugh the Chanter, pp. 108–11; William of Malmesbury, *Gesta Pontificum*, p. 146, note 4; Bethell, 'English Black Monks and episcopal elections in the 1120s', 673–98. [20] i.e. one of the (secular) clergy. [21] See Bethell, 'William of Corbeil and the Canterbury York dispute', 145–59.

a canon from a minster called Cicc[1] – and brought him before the king, and the king gave him the archbishopric, and all the bishops accepted him. The monks and earls and almost all the thegns who were there opposed him.

At the same time the envoys of the earl[2] went away from the king with discord – did not account for anything of his gift.[3]

At the same time there came a certain legate from Rome [who] was called Henry;[4] he was abbot of the minster of St Jean d'Angély, and he came about the Rome-tax.[5] And he told the king that it was against the law that a clerk should be set over monks; and even so, in their chapter they had earlier chosen an archbishop according to the law.[6] But because of [his] love for the bishop of Salisbury the king would not reverse it. Then immediately after that the archbishop travelled to Canterbury and was received there, although it was against their will, and was immediately blessed as bishop there[7] by the bishop of London,[8] and the bishop Ernulf of Rochester, and the bishop William Gifford of Winchester, and the bishop Bernard of Wales,[9] and the bishop Roger of Salisbury. Then soon, in the spring, the archbishop travelled to Rome for his pallium; and with him travelled the bishop Bernard of Wales, and Sigefrith[10] abbot of Glastonbury, and Anselm abbot of St Edmunds,[11] and John archdeacon of Canterbury, and Gifford [who] was the king's court clerk.

At the same time the archbishop Thurstan of York travelled to Rome at the pope's command, and came there three days[12] before the archbishop of Canterbury came and was there received with great honour. Then the archbishop of Canterbury came, and was there a whole week before he could get to have talk with the pope; that was because the pope was given to understand that he had received the archbishopric in opposition to the monks of the minster, and against the law. But what overcame Rome was what overcomes all the world, that is gold and silver. And the pope relented and gave him his pallium; and the archbishop swore (by St Peter's head and St Paul's[13]) submission to him in all those things which the pope laid on him, and then [the pope] sent him home with his blessing.

Then while the archbishop was out of the land, the king gave the bishopric of Bath to the queen's chancellor who was called Godfrey; he was born at Louvain. That was on the day of *the Annunciation to St Mary*[14] at Woodstock. Then soon after that the king travelled to Winchester and

---

[1] i.e. St Osyth, the former name being replaced from the later twelfth century by that of its most famous dévot (see Reaney, *The Place-Names of Essex*, pp. 347–8).   [2] Fulk of Anjou.
[3] Count Fulk's *sandermen* had come to claim back the dowry which he had paid for his, now-widowed, daughter (cf. p. 248, note 7), but which Henry refused to return (Simeon, II, p. 267).   [4] Henry of Poitou, see Clark, 'This ecclesiastical adventurer', 548–60. See also annals 1127–8, 1130–32.   [5] Rome scot; cf. p. 232, note 2.   [6] i.e. canonically.   [7] Thurstan's suggestion that he should perform the ceremony having been rejected (Hugh the Chanter, pp. 109–11).   [8] Richard of Belmeis (Beaumais–sur-Dive, dép. Calvados), see Lloyd, *Anglo-Norman Families*, pp. 13–14.   [9] Bishop of St David's.   [10] Brother of Ralph, archbishop of Canterbury; he was made bishop of Chichester in 1125.   [11] See p. 246, note 7.   [12] Hugh the Chanter (p. 111) says it was a week before.

was there all Easter-time, and then while he was there he gave the bishopric of Lincoln to a certain clerk [who] was called Alexander;[15] he was the nephew of the bishop of Salisbury;[16] this he did all for love of this bishop.

Then the king travelled from there to Portsmouth and lay there all over Pentecost week. Then as soon as he had a wind, he travelled over into Normandy, and then entrusted all England into the care and control of the bishop Roger of Salisbury. Then the king was in Normandy all the year, and then great hostility grew between him and his thegns, so that Waleran[17] the earl of Meulan, and Almaric,[18] and Hugh of Montfort,[19] and William of Roumare,[20] and many others turned from him and held their castles against him.[21] And the king held out strongly against them; and this same year he won from Waleran his castle of Pont Audemer,[22] and Montfort from Hugh; and afterwards he always succeeded the better the longer he went on.

This same year, before the bishop of Lincoln came to his bishopric, almost the whole town of Lincoln burned down,[23] and a countless host of people, men and women, burned to death, and such great damage was done there that no-one could describe it to another. That was the day of *19 May*.

1124. All this year the king Henry was in Normandy; that was because of the great hostilities that he had with the king Louis of France and with the earl of Anjou, and most of all with his own men.

Then on the day of *the Annunciation to St Mary*[24] it happened that the earl Waleran of Meulan travelled from one of his castles called Beaumont close to another castle of his, Vatteville.[25] With him travelled Almaric the steward of the king of France, Hugh son of Gervase[26] and Hugh of Montfort and many other good knights.[27] Then the king's knights from all the castles that were round about came against them and fought with them and put them to flight,[28] and seized the earl Waleran, and Hugh son of Gervase, and Hugh of Montfort, and twenty-five other knights, and brought them to the king. And the king had the earl Waleran and Hugh son of Gervase put in captivity in the castle in Rouen, and he sent Hugh of Montfort to England

---

[13] Presumably on relics, unless *hevod*, 'head', is written in mistake for *wevod*, 'altar'.   [14] 25 March.   [15] Alexander 'the magnificent', to whom Henry of Huntingdon dedicated his *Historia Anglorum* and Geoffrey of Monmouth his *Prophecies of Merlin*.   [16] Roger, bishop of Salisbury 1107–39.   [17] Son of Robert of Beaumont, count of Meulan and earl of Leicester; see White, 'The career of Waleran, count of Meulan and earl of Worcester', 19–48.   [18] Almaric of Montfort-l'Amaury, father-in-law of Waleran.   [19] Hugh of Montfort-sur-Risle, brother-in-law of Waleran.   [20] Half-brother of Ranulf, earl of Chester (see annal 1140); he was later earl of Lincoln, cf. *Complete Peerage*, VII p. 667ff.   [21] Hoping to make William 'Clito' duke of Normandy (Ordericus, VI, pp. 332–5).   [22] Dép. Eure; for the siege see Ordericus, VI, pp. 336–7, 340–43.   [23] *Margan Annals*, p. 11 (s.a. 1122); cf. Hill, *Medieval Lincoln*, p. 173.   [24] 25 March.   [25] They are a dozen miles apart, on the Risle and Seine respectively, see Map p. 282.   [26] Brother-in-law of Waleran, see White, 'The career of Waleran', 24, note 4.   [27] MS *cnihte*, the term seems now to have shifted from its Old English sense of 'young man, youth' to the more specific Middle English one of status, cf. *Middle English Dictionary, sub* 'knight' 1 (a) and 4.   [28] At Bourgthéroulde (dép. Eure), Ordericus, VI, pp. 348–51.

and had him placed in vicious bonds[1] in the castle in Gloucester, and of the others he sent as many as he thought north and south into captivity in his castles. Then afterwards the king travelled and won all the earl Waleran's castles in Normandy and all the others which his adversaries held against him.

All this hostility was because of the son of Earl Robert of Normandy, called William.[2] The same William had taken to wife the younger daughter of Fulk earl of Anjou; and therefore the king of France and all the earls and all the powerful men held with him, and said that the king held his brother Robert in captivity wrongfully, and put to flight his son William out of Normandy unjustly.

This same year in England there were many failures in grain and in all crops,[3] so that between Christmas and Candlemas the seed-wheat for an acre, that is two baskets of seed,[4] sold at six shillings, and that of barley, that is three baskets of seed, at six shillings, and the seed-oats for an acre, that is four baskets of seed, at four shillings. That was because the grain was scarce and the penny was so bad that the man who had a pound at a market could not buy twelve penn'orth with it.

In this same year passed away the blessed Bishop Ernulf of Rochester who was abbot in Peterborough earlier; that was on the day of *15 March*. And after that on the day of *23 April* the king Alexander of Scotland passed away, and David[5] his brother who was earl in Northamptonshire succeeded to the kingdom and had both together: the kingdom in Scotland and the earldom in England. And on the day of *14 December* passed away the pope in Rome who was called Calixtus;[6] and Honorius[7] succeeded to the papacy.

This same year, after the Feast of St Andrew[8] before Christmas Ralph Basset[9] and the king's thegns held a council at Hundehoh[10] in Leicestershire, and there hanged many more thieves than ever were before, that was in a little while forty-four men in all; and despoiled six men of their eyes and of their stones.[11] Numbers of honest men said that many were despoiled with great injustice there; but our Lord God Almighty who

---

[1] MS *on ifele bendas*; cf. the Old French expression 'durance vile'.   [2] See p. 247, note 12.   [3] Simeon (II, p. 275) describes the subsequent famine and high mortality.   [4] MS *sædleap*, a term still widely in use in the nineteenth century, see Wright, *English Dialect Dictionary*, V, p. 315, *sub* 'seed-lip'.   [5] David I, king of Scotland 1124–53, see Ritchie, *The Normans in Scotland*, pp. 125–30 *et passim*.   [6] Calixtus II; 'in Rome', i.e. specifically not the anti-pope.   [7] Honorius II.   [8] 30 November.   [9] A prominent member of the king's court acting as itinerant justiciar (Stenton, *Justice*, pp. 60–62).   [10] Perhaps Hundehaug in Cossington, Leicester, cf. Cox, 'Leicestershire moot-sites', 14–15.   [11] i.e. testicles, euphemistically.   [12] Perhaps a liturgical echo: *God . . . from whom no secrets are hid*, cf. *The Leofric Missal*, p. 177.   [13] For Henry I's decree concerning the coinage, see Robertson, *Laws*, pp. 284–5.   [14] See generally Hollister, 'Royal acts of mutilation', 330–40 (*Monarchy, Magnates*, pp. 291–301).

sees and knows all secrets,[12] he sees that the wretched people are oppressed with every injustice: first they are robbed of their goods, and afterwards they are killed. It was a very heavy year. The man who had any property was robbed of it by severe taxes and by severe courts; he who had none died of starvation.

1125. In this year before Christmas [1124] the king Henry sent from Normandy to England and commanded that all the moneyers who were in England should be deprived of their limbs, that was the right hand of each of them and their stones below;[13] that was because the man who had a pound could not buy a penn'orth at a market. And the bishop Roger of Salisbury sent over all England and commanded them all that they should come to Winchester at Christmas. Then when they came there they were seized one by one, and each deprived of the right hand and the stones below.[14] All this was done inside the twelve nights;[15] and it was all very proper because they had done for all the land with their great fraud,[16] which they all paid for.

In this year the pope sent a cardinal from Rome to this land [who] was called John of Crema. He came first to the king in Normandy, and the king received him with great honour and afterwards commended him to the archbishop William of Canterbury, and he led him to Canterbury, and there he was received with great honour and with a great *procession*, and he sang the high mass on Easter Day at Christ's altar; and afterwards he travelled over all England to all the bishoprics and abbacies which were in this land, and everywhere he was received with honour, and all gave him great and splendid gifts. And afterwards, on *the Nativity of St Mary* in September[17] he held his *council* in London[18] for three full days, with archbishops, and with diocesan bishops, and abbots, and clerics and lay;[19] and there commanded those same laws which Archbishop Anselm had earlier decreed, and many more, though it was of little avail. And from there he went across the sea soon after Michaelmas, and thus to Rome[20] – and the archbishop William of Canterbury, and the archbishop Thurstan of York, and the bishop Alexander of Lincoln, and John the bishop of Lothian,[21] and the abbot Geoffrey of St Albans[22] – and were received there by the pope Honorius[23] with great honour, and were there all the winter.[24]

In this same year on the Feast of St Lawrence[25] there occurred so great a flood

---

[15] i.e. between Christmas and Epiphany, finishing with Twelfth Night.   [16] *mid here micele fals.* In the Laws of Canute (Robertson, *Laws*, pp. 178–9), the word *fals* is used with the meaning 'bad money or 'adulteration'. In Æthelred's (Robertson, pp. 74–5), a forger is called *falsarius*.   [17] 8 September.   [18] At Westinster, cf. *Councils and Synods*, pp. 733–41.   [19] MS *and lǣred and lawed*, 'learned and lewd', a frequent rhetorical collocation.   [20] Where he seems to have been reprimanded as a result of scandal involving his dealings with a prostitute while in England, cf. *Councils and Synods*, p. 732, and Henry of Huntingdon, p. 246.   [21] i.e. of Glasgow, a see recently restored by King David I, cf. Ritchie, *The Normans in Scotland*, pp. 151–3.   [22] A patron of anchorites, including Christina of Markyate (*Gesta Abbatum Sancti Albani*, I, 72–105).   [23] Honorius II.   [24] In yet another attempt to settle the primacy dispute.   [25] 10 August.

that many villages and men were drowned, and bridges broken down, and corn and pasture wholly destroyed, and famine and disease among men and among cattle; and there occurred greater unseasonableness for all crops than for many years before.

And this same year on *14 October* the abbot John of Peterborough passed away.

1126. All this year the king Henry was in Normandy right up to after harvest; then he came to this land between *the Nativity of St Mary* and Michaelmas.[1] With him came the queen[2] and his daughter whom he had earlier given as wife to the emperor Henry of Lorraine.[3] And he brought with him the earl Waleran and Hugh son of Gervase; and he sent the earl to Bridgnorth in captivity, and afterwards he sent him from there to Wallingford, and Hugh to Windsor, and had him put in strict confinement.[4]

And then after Michaelmas came David, the king of Scots, from Scotland here to the land; and the king Henry received him with great honour, and he then stayed the whole year in this land.

In this same year the king had his brother Robert taken from the bishop Roger of Salisbury, and committed him to his son Robert earl of Gloucester,[5] and had him led to Bristol and there put in the castle.[6] That was all done through the advice of his daughter and through her uncle, David[7] the king of Scots.

1127. This year the king Henry held his court at Christmas [1126] in Windsor.[8] David the king of Scots was there, and all the head [men], clerical and lay,[9] that were in England; and there he had archbishops, and bishops, and abbots, and earls, and all those thegns who were there, swear England and Normandy after his day into the hand of his daughter Æthelic,[10] who was earlier wife of the emperor of Saxony;[3] and afterwards sent her to Normandy (and with her travelled her brother Robert, earl of Gloucester, and Brian,[11] son of the earl Alan Fergant), and had her wedded to the son of the earl of Anjou, [who] was called Geoffrey Martel.[12] Despite the fact that it offended all the French and English, the king did it in order to have peace from the

---

[1] i.e. between 8 and 29 September; on the 11th, says Simeon (II, p. 281).   [2] Adela.
[3] Now widowed, since Henry V had died the previous year, see generally Chibnall, *The Empress Matilda*.   [4] MS *on harde bande*; cf. p. 254, note 1.   [5] The oldest, but illegitimate, son of Henry (*Complete Peerage*, V, p. 683) to whom William of Malmesbury dedicated his *Historia Novella* (p. 1); cf. Patterson, 'William of Malmesbury's Robert of Gloucester', 983–97.   [6] He remained in confinement, dying in Cardiff in 1134, see p. 241, note 9.   [7] Brother-in-law of Henry I who married his sister Maud, see Table, p. 297.   [8] The continuator of Florence (II, p. 84) says that on this occasion the archbishop of York wanted to take an equal part with the archbishop of Canterbury in crowning the king, but that general opinion insisted that he should play no part in it.   [9] MS *læred and læwed*, cf. p. 255, note 19.   [10] i.e. Adeliza, the ex-empress Matilda, see note 3. See generally William of Malmesbury, *Historia Novella*, pp. 4–5.   [11] A cousin, see Table p. 299.   [12] Geoffrey 'Plantaganet', see Table p. 299.

earl of Anjou, and in order to have help against William[13] his nephew.

In the spring-time[14] this same year the earl Charles of Flanders[15] was killed by his own men in a certain church where he lay before the altar and prayed to God during the mass.[16] And the king of France brought William the son of the earl of Normandy, and gave him the earldom, and the local people accepted him. This same William had earlier taken to wife the daughter of the earl of Anjou,[17] but they were afterwards divorced for consanguinity. That was all through the king Henry of England. Afterwards he took to wife the sister of the wife of the king of France,[18] and therefore the king gave him the earldom of Flanders.

This same year he gave the abbacy of Peterborough to an abbot [who] was called Henry of Poitou.[19] He had his abbacy of St Jean d'Angély in hand, and all the archbishops and bishops said that it was against the law, and that he could not have two abbacies in hand; but the same Henry gave the king to understand that he had left his abbacy because of the great hostility that was in that land, and he did that through the advice and leave of the pope of Rome and of the abbot of Cluny,[20] and because he was legate about the Rome-tax.[21] But despite that it was just not so; but he wanted to have both in hand – and had so, for as long as it was God's will. While in his clerk's orders he was bishop in Soissons; afterwards he became a monk in Cluny, and later became prior in the same minster; and later he became prior in Savigny.[22] After that, because he was relative[23] of the king of England and of the earl of Poitou, the earl gave him the abbacy of St Jean d'Angély. Afterwards through his great tricks he then got hold of the archbishopric of Besançon, and then had it in hand for three days; then he lost it, justly, because earlier he had got hold of it unjustly. Then afterwards he got hold of the bishopric of Saintes, which was five miles[24] from his abbacy; he had that in hand well-nigh a week; the abbot of Cluny got him out from there, just as he earlier did from Besançon. Then it occurred to him that, if he could get firmly rooted in England, he could

---

[13] William 'Clito'.   [14] *bone lenten tide*; perhaps, in view of the circumstances of this incident, 'the time of Lent'; Ordericus (VI, pp. 370–71) says it was 1 March.   [15] Son of Canute, king of Denmark.   [16] For a good contemporary account by a palace notary, see Galbert of Bruges, *The Murder of Charles the Good, Count of Flanders.*   [17] Maud, daughter of Fulk V of Anjou. She later became a nun at Fontevrault, and subsequently abbess.   [18] Joan, daughter of Rainier of Montferrat. She was half-sister to Adelaide of Savoy, wife of Louis VI of France.   [19] See p. 252, note 4. Much of the following account of Abbot Henry is paralleled in the Chronicle of Hugh Candidus (pp. 99–104).   [20] The mother-house of St-Jean d'Angély.   [21] Hugh Candidus (p. 100): *And because he would never be quiet, he got the office of collecting the Rome-tax in England, so that by this means he might gain an abbacy.*   [22] Either Savigny-le-Vieux, dép. Manche, or Cluniac Souvigny, dép. Allier.   [23] Our knowledge of this complex web of relationships is only partial, cf. Clark, *The Peterborough Chronicle*, p. 101, note 35.   [24] In fact three times as far; the error probably results from equating English miles with Continental leagues.

get all his own way; then besought the king, and said to him that he was an old man and a broken-down man, and that he could not endure the great injustices and the great hostilities there were in their land; and then, personally and by means of all his well-known friends, begged for the abbacy of Peterborough. And the king granted it to him because he was his relative, and because he had been a principal in swearing the oath and witnessing when the son of the earl of Normandy and the daughter of the earl of Anjou were divorced for consanguinity. Thus wretchedly the abbacy was given, between Christmas and Candlemas at London; and so he travelled with the king to Winchester, and from there he came to Peterborough, and there he stayed exactly as drones do in a hive. All that the bees carry in, drones devour and carry off; and so did he. All that he could take, inside or outside, from clergy and lay, he sent across the sea, and did nothing good there nor left nothing good there.

Let it not be thought remarkable, the truth of what we say, because it was fully known over all the land, that immediately after he came there (that was the Sunday when they sing *Awake, why sleepest thou, O Lord?*[1]) then soon afterwards many men saw and heard many huntsmen hunting.[2] The huntsmen were black and huge and loathesome, and their hounds all black and wide-eyed and loathesome, and they rode on black horses and on black billy-goats.[3] This was seen in the very deer-park of the town of Peterborough, and in all the woods there were from that same town to Stamford; and the monks heard the horns blow that they blew in the night. Honest men who kept watch in the night said that it seemed to them there might well have been about twenty or thirty horn-blowers. This was seen and heard from when he came there, all that Lenten-tide right up to Easter. This was his entrance: of his exit we cannot yet say. May God provide!

1128. All this year the king Henry was in Normandy because of the hostility that was between him and his nephew the earl of Flanders.[4] But the earl became wounded by a young man in a battle,[5] and thus wounded went to the minster of St Bertin,[6] and straightway became a monk there, and afterwards lived for five days, and then he died and was buried there. God have mercy on his soul! That was on the day of 27 *July*.

---

[1] Psalm xliii, 23ff., the introit appointed for mass on the second Sunday before Lent (6 February that year).   [2] Hugh Candidus (p. 101) gives a similar account of the 'Wild Hunt': *In the very year in which he* (Henry) *came to the abbey, marvellous portents were seen and heard at night during the whole of Lent, throughout the woodland and plains, from the monastery as far as Stamford; for there appeared, as it were, hunters with horns and hounds, all being jet black, their horses and their hounds as well, and some rode, as it were, on goats and had great eyes and there were twenty or thirty together. And this is no false tale, for many men of faithful report both saw them and heard the horns.* Ordericus (IV, pp. 236–47) tells of a similar incident in Normandy in 1091. For other parallels see Flasdieck, 'Harlekin', (1937) 225–338, (1942) 56–69.   [3] Horned beasts, anciently associated with Woden (cf. Swanton, 'Finglesham Man', 313–15), were now closely associated with the Devil.

This same year passed away the bishop Ranulf Passeflambard[7] of Durham, and was buried there on *5 September*.

And this same year the afore-mentioned Abbot Henry travelled home to Poitou to his own minster, by leave of the king. He gave the king to understand that he would relinquish that minster and that land and stay with him there in England and in the minster of Peterborough, but despite that it was not so. He did it because he wanted, through his great wiles, to stay there, were it twelve months or more, and come back afterwards. God Almighty have pity on that unhappy place!

This same year Hugh of the Temple[8] came from Jerusalem to the king in Normandy; and the king received him with great honour, and gave him great treasures in gold and in silver; and afterwards he sent him to England, and there he was received by all good men, and all gave him treasures – and in Scotland likewise – and by him sent much wealth, all in gold and in silver, to Jerusalem. And he summoned people out to Jerusalem; and then there went, with him and after him, as great a number of people as ever did before since the first expedition[9] which was in Pope Urban's day,[10] though little came of it. He said that a great battle was set between the Christians and the heathen; then when they came there, it was nothing but lies; thus all the people became wretchedly afflicted.

1129. In this year the king sent to England for the earl Waleran[11] and for Hugh son of Gervase[12] and they gave hostages for them there. And Hugh travelled home to France to his own lands, and Waleran remained with the king, and the king gave him all his lands, except for his castle only. Afterwards in the autumn the king came to England, and the earl came with him and they then became as good friends as they were earlier enemies.

Then soon, by the king's advice and by his leave, the archbishop William of Canterbury sent over all England and summoned bishops and abbots and archdeacons and all the priors, monks and canons that were in all the cells in England, and to all those who had to care for and look after Christendom, that they should all come to London at Michaelmas, and should there speak of all God's dues.[13] Then when they came there, the meeting began

---

[4] William 'Clito'.   [5] Fatally wounded in the siege of Aalst in Flanders (Ordericus, VI, pp. 374–9).   [6] At St Omer, dép. Pas-de-Calais.   [7] Normally simply Flambard (see p. 234, note 11); the reason for this alternative is unclear; for his death, see Simeon, I, pp. 140–41.   [8] Hugh de Payns (dép. Aube), one of the founders and Grand Master of the Order of Knights Templar, for whom see generally Barber, *The New Knighthood*, *passim*.   [9] i.e. the first Crusade, see annal 1096.   [10] Urban II.   [11] Count of Meulan.   [12] For whom see p. 253, note 26.   [13] MS *Godes rihtes*; cf. Robertson, *Laws*, references cited p. 393; Harmer, *Writs*, p. 487.

on Monday and continued right on till the Friday. When it all came out, it turned out to be all about archdeacons' wives and priests' wives – that they should relinquish them by the Feast of St Andrew[1] and anyone who would not do so was to forgo his church and his house and his home,[2] and never more have any further claim to them. This was commanded by the archbishop William of Canterbury and all the diocesan bishops who were then in England; and the king gave them all leave to travel home, and so they travelled home. And all the decrees were of no avail – all kept their wives by leave of the king, just as they did before.

In the same year the bishop William Gifford of Winchester passed away and was buried there on 25 *January*. And after Michaelmas the king Henry gave the bishopric to his nephew the abbot Henry of Glastonbury,[3] and he was consecrated as bishop by the archbishop William of Canterbury on the day of 17 *November*.

This same year passed away Pope Honorius.[4] Before he was well dead two popes were chosen there. The one was called Peter; he was a monk of Cluny and born from the most powerful men of Rome,[5] and with him held those from Rome and the duke of Sicily.[6] The other was called Gregory;[7] he was a clerk and was put to flight out of Rome by the other pope and his relatives; with him held the emperor of Saxony[8] and the king of France[9] and the king Henry of England, and all those this side of the mountains.[10] Now occured such great heresy in Christendom as there ever was before. May Christ establish counsel for his miserable people!

This same year, on the eve of the Feast of St Nicholas,[11] a little before day, there was a great earthquake.

1130. This year the minster of Canterbury was consecrated by the archbishop William on the day of 4 *May*.[12] There were there the bishops: John of Rochester, Gilbert 'Universalis'[13] of London, Henry of Winchester, Alexander of Lincoln, Roger of Salisbury, Simon of Worcester, Roger of Coventry, Godfrey of Bath, Everard of Norwich, Sigefrith of Chichester, Bernard of St David's, Audoen of Evreux[14] from Normandy, John of Séez.[15]

---

[1] 30 November.   [2] i.e. home-farm or glebe.   [3] Henry of Blois, brother of the future King Stephen; he held abbacy and bishopric in plurality until his death in 1171; see generally Knowles, *Monastic Order*, pp. 286–93.   [4] Honorius II.   [5] Peter de Pierleoni, descended from a family of Jewish moneylenders, now anti-pope taking the name Anacletus II; see generally Stroll, *The Jewish Pope*.   [6] The Norman Roger II, brother-in-law of Anacletus (note 5).   [7] Who took the name Innocent II.   [8] Lothair II.   [9] Louis VI.   [10] i.e. the Alps; cf. annal 1119.   [11] St Nicholas' Day was 6 December.   [12] In the presence of the king and queen, King David of Scotland and all the bishops of England says Gervase, I, p. 96; II, p. 383.   [13] Probably so-called because of his remarkable range of knowledge, see Smalley, 'Gilbert Universalis', (1935) 235–62, (1936) 24–60.   [14] Brother of Thurstan, archbishop of York, see Hugh the Chanter, p. 123.   [15] Abbot of Peterborough (cf. annal 1114, p. 246).

On the fourth day after that, the king Henry was in Rochester, and the borough almost burned down; and the archbishop William consecrated St Andrew's minster,[16] the afore-mentioned bishops with him. And at harvest the king Henry travelled across the sea into Normandy.

This same year the abbot Henry of Angély[17] came to Peterborough after Easter and said that he had wholly relinquished the minster [of Angély]. After him, with the king's leave, the abbot called Peter of Cluny came to England[18] and was received with great honour everywhere wheresoever he came. He came to Peterborough and there the abbot Henry promised him that he would get him the minster of Peterborough so that it would be subject to Cluny. But as it says in the proverb: 'Hedge abides that fields divides'.[19] May God Almighty destroy evil plans! And soon after that the abbot of Cluny travelled home to his [own] country.

1131. This year after Christmas [1130], on Sunday night[20] at the first sleep,[21] the heaven on the north side was all as if it were a burning fire, so that all who saw it were more afraid than they ever were before; that was on *11 January*. This same year there was as great a pestilence among livestock as anyone remembered before over the whole of England; that was among cattle and among pigs so that in the village where ten or twelve ploughs were going not one remained there, and the man that had two or three hundred pigs had not one left. After that the hens died, then the meat and the cheese and the butter were short. May God improve it when it is His will!

And the king Henry came home to England before harvest after the earlier Feast of St Peter.[22]

This same year before Easter the abbot Henry went across the sea to Normandy from Peterborough, and there spoke with the king and told him that the abbot of Cluny had commanded him that he should come to him and hand over to him the abbacy of Angély; and afterwards, by his leave, he would come home. So he travelled home to his own minster,[23] and stayed there right up to midsummer day; and the next day after the Feast of St John[24] the monks chose an abbot from themselves, and brought him into church with *procession*, sang the *Te Deum Laudamus*,[25] rang the bells, set him in the abbot's seat and did him all such obedience

---

[16] The continuator of Florence (II, p. 92) says that the fire was on 7 May, and that the 'new church' of St Andrew's, (i.e. Rochester Cathedral), was consecrated the following day, Ascension Day.   [17] See annal 1123.   [18] See *The Letters of Peter the Venerable*, I, p. 150; II, pp. 131, 259.   [19] MS *hæge sitteð þa aceres dæleth*; this does not correspond with any saying in extant collections of Old English proverbs.   [20] MS *Moneniht*, the eve of Monday. In 1131 the first Sunday after the days of Christmas was 11 January.   [21] This probably refers to the period between the services of nocturns and matins.   [22] 29 June.   [23] i.e. Angély.   [24] i.e. 25 June, the Nativity of St John being 24 June.   [25] *We praise thee O God*, a hymn commonly used at matins but specially suited to occasions of celebration.

as they should do their abbot; and the earl[1] and all the head men and the monks of the minster put Henry, the other abbot, to flight out of the minster. They had to, from necessity; they had never experienced one good day in five-and-twenty years. Here all his great cunning failed him; now he need creep into his great bag [of tricks], into every corner [to see] if there were at least one dodgy trick so that he might deceive Christ and all Christian people yet once more. Then he travelled into Cluny, and there he was held so that he could not go east nor west.[2] The abbot of Cluny said that they had lost the minster of St Jean [d'Angély] through him and through his great stupidity. Then he knew no better remedy for himself but to promise them and swear oaths on relics that, if he could reach England, he would get them the minster of Peterborough, so that he should set there a prior from Cluny, and sacristan and treasurer and wardrobe-keeper, and he would commit to them everything that was inside and outside the minster. Thus he travelled into France[3] and stayed there all that year. May Christ take measures for the wretched monks of Peterborough and for that wretched place! Now they need the help of Christ and of all Christian people.

1132. This year King Henry came to this land. Then came Abbot Henry, and accused the monks of Peterborough to the king because he wished to subject that minster to Cluny, so that the king was well-nigh lured[4] and sent for the monks. And through God's mercy and through the bishop of Salisbury and the bishop of Lincoln and the other powerful men who were there, the king then knew that he acted with treachery. Then when he could do nothing more, he wished that his nephew[5] should be abbot in Peterborough; but Christ did not want it. It was not very long after that that the king sent for him, and made him give up the abbacy of Peterborough and go out of the land; and the king gave the abbacy to a prior of St Neot's [who] was called Martin. He came into the minster with great honour on the Feast of St Peter.[6]

1135. In this year, at the Lammas,[7] the king Henry went across the sea, and the next day, while he lay asleep on ship, the day darkened

---

[1] Of Aquitaine.   [2] Hugh Candidus (p. 102) says: *He was not permitted to go out or to come in until by his craft and cunning he had hoodwinked them.*   [3] Cluny being in Burgundy.   [4] In fact King Henry was already friendly towards the Cluniacs, Knowles, *Monastic Order*, pp. 280–82.   [5] Hugh Candidus (p. 103) supplies the name Gerard.   [6] 20 June.   [7] 1 August.   [8] In fact the king's journey and the eclipse took place in 1133 (William of Malmesbury, *Gesta Regum*, II, pp. 535–56; Simeon, II, pp. 285, 295–6); the dramatic but anachronistic juxtaposition of eclipse with the death of the king is not dissimilar to the Bayeux Tapestry treatment of comet and Conquest (see p. 194, note 3).   [9] i.e. 2 December.   [10] MS *þa þestre sona*; metaphorically, cf. Ker, 'Some notes on the Peterborough Chronicle', 136–7. For such dark days following Henry I's death, see *Gesta Stephani*, pp. 2–5.   [11] The illegitimate Robert of Gloucester, see annal 1126.   [12] In the chancel of Henry's own large Cluniac foundation on the Thames (VCH, *Berkshire*, II, pp. 62–73), a building decorated to the highest contemporary standards (Zarneki, *English Romanesque Art*, pp. 167–71).   [13] See generally Southern, 'The place of Henry I in English history', 127–69. For this formula cf. p. 220, note 3.

over all lands, and the sun became as if it were a three-night-old moon – and stars around it at midday. Men became very astonished and terrified, and said that something important would come after this; so it did, because that very year it happened the king died in Normandy[8] the next day after the Feast of St Andrew.[9] Then this land immediately grew dark[10] because every man who could immediately robbed another. Then his son[11] and his friends took and brought his body to England, and buried it at Reading.[12] He was a good man and was held in great awe. In his time no man dared do wrong against another; he made peace for man and beast; no man dared say anything but good to whoever carried their load of gold and silver.[13]

In the middle of this his nephew Stephen de Blois[14] had come to England, and came to London, and the London people received him and sent for the archbishop William Corbeil and consecrated him as king on midwinter's day.[15] In this king's time it was all strife and evil and robbery because the powerful men who were traitors immediately rose against him [1136]; first of all Baldwin de Redvers,[16] and held Exeter against him; and the king besieged it, and afterwards Baldwin came to terms. Then the others took[17] and held their castles against him; and David, king of Scotland, took to warring upon him; then, notwithstanding, their envoys travelled between them and they came together and were reconciled, though it was to little avail.

1137. This year the king Stephen went across the sea to Normandy, and was received there because they imagined that he would be just like the uncle was, and because he still[18] had his treasury; but he distributed and scattered it stupidly.[19] King Henry had gathered a great amount [in] gold and silver – and no good was done with it for his soul.[20]

When the king Stephen came to England he held his council[21] at Oxford, and there he seized the bishop Roger of Salisbury and his nephews[22] Alexander bishop of Lincoln and the chancellor Roger, and put all in prison until they gave up their castles. Then when the traitors realised that Stephen was a mild man, gentle and good, and imposed no penalty,[23] they committed every enormity.[24] They had done him homage and sworn oaths, but they held to no pledge.

---

[14] Cf. generally, Davis, *King Stephen, 1135–1154.* [15] Like Stephen himself, one of those who had sworn loyalty to Matilda in 1127 (q.v.). [16] i.e. Reviers (dép. Calvados); Baldwin became earl of Devon before midsummer 1141 (*Complete Peerage*, IV, pp. 311–12). For the siege see *Gesta Stephani*, p. 30ff., and for the siege-works see Exeter Archaeology, *Danes Castle, Exeter 1992.* [17] Here the verb is probably to be taken in the same idiomatic sense as in the next sentence, cf. Sisam, 'Notes on Middle English texts', 385. [18] MS *hadde get*; or perhaps 'had got' (Henry's treasure). [19] Much of it went to St Denis in Paris, and part made into an extraordinarily bejewelled crucifix, see Panofsky, *Abbot Suger*, pp. 58–9, 180–83. [20] William of Malmesbury (*Historia Novella*, p. 17) says that Henry I's treasury taken over by Stephen amounted to nearly £100,000. [21] MS *macod he his gadering.* The Council of Oxford, June, 1139. [22] A euphemism in the case of Roger the chancellor, who was son of Roger of Salisbury, cf. Ordericus, VI, pp. 530–31, or more ironically William of Malmesbury, *Historia Novella*, p. 27. See generally, Lowe, 'Never say *nefa* again', 27–35. [23] MS *na justise ne dide*; cf. Dickins, 'The Peterborough annal for 1137', 342. [24] MS *þa diden hi alle wunder.*

They were all forsworn and their pledges lost because every powerful man made his castles and held them against him, and filled the land full of castles. They greatly oppressed the wretched men of the land with castle-work;[1] then when the castles were made, they filled them with devils and evil men. Then both by night and by day they seized those men whom they imagined had any wealth, common men[2] and women, and put them in prison[3] to get their gold and silver, and tortured them with unspeakable tortures,[4] for no martyrs were ever tortured as they were. They hung them up by the feet and smoked them with foul smoke. They hung them by the thumbs, or by the head, and hung mail-coats on their feet. They put knotted strings round their heads and twisted till it went to the brains. They put them in dungeons where there were adders and snakes and toads, and destroyed them thus. Some they put into a 'crucet-hus',[5] that is, into a chest that was short and narrow and shallow, and put sharp stones in there and crushed the man in there, so that he had all the limbs broken. In many of the castles was a 'lof and grin',[6] that were chains such that two or three men had enough to do to carry one. It was made thus: it is fastened to a beam, and a sharp iron put around the man's throat and his neck so that he could not move in any direction, neither sit nor lie nor sleep, but carry all that iron. Many thousands they destroyed with hunger.

I do not know nor can I tell all the horrors nor all the tortures that they did to wretched men in this land. And it lasted the 19 years while Stephen was king,[7] and it always grew worse and worse. They laid a tax upon the villages time and again, and called it *tenserie*.[8] Then when the wretched men had no more to give, they robbed and burned all the villages, so that you could well go a whole day's journey and never find anyone occupying a village or land tilled. Then corn was dear, and flesh and cheese and butter, because there was none in the land. Wretched men starved with hunger; some who were once powerful men went on alms; some fled out of the land. Never before was there more wretchedness in the land, nor ever did heathen men worse than they did. Too many times[9] they spared neither church nor churchyard,[10] but took everything of value that

---

[1] A type of forced labour condemned by Pope Eugenius III writing in 23 July 1147 (*Chronicon Monasterii de Abingdon*, II, p. 200).   [2] *carlmen*; cf. p. 220, annal 1086.   [3] MS *diden heom in prisun; in prisun* interlined as an afterthought (for the punctuation see Ker, 'Some notes on the Peterborough Chronicle', 137–8). The use of the French word 'prison', rather than the previous 'bonds' (cf. p. 254, note 1; p. 256, note 4) seems appropriate to the alien *castles*.   [4] See Ker, 'Some notes on the Peterborough Chronicle', 137–8.   [5] Latin *cruciatus* with a suffix made by 'popular etymology', see Gerritson, 'A ghost-word: crucet-hus', 300–1. Simeon (I, pp. 153–4) describes similar atrocities.   [6] Another unusual term, hence the annalist's explanation, cf. Dickins, 'The Peterborough Annal for 1137', 342; Magoun, 'Two lexicographical notes', 411–12; Emerson, 'The crux in the Peterborough Chronicle', 170–72.   [7] These words indicate that the annal was not written before Stephen's death in 1154.   [8] i.e. 'protection money'; Old French *tenser*, 'to protect', cf. Round, *Geoffrey de Mandeville*, pp. 215, 414–16.   [9] MS *oversithon*; cf. Sisam, 'Notes on Middle English texts', 385–6.   [10] Cf. the looting of Cambridge churches by Geoffrey de Mandeville (*Gesta Stephani*, pp. 164–5), or Urse d'Abetôt's building a castle which encroached on the monks' cemetery at Worcester, for which he was roundly cursed by Bishop Aldred: 'If you're called Urse, you have God's curse!' (William of Malmesbury, *Gesta Pontificum*, p. 253).

was in it, and afterwards burned the church and everything together. They did not spare the land of bishops nor of abbots nor of priests, but robbed monks and clerks; and every man who was the stronger[11] [robbed] another. If two or three men came riding to a village, all the villagers[12] fled because of them – imagined that they were robbers. The bishops and the clergy always cursed them but that was nothing to them, because they were all accursed and forsworn and lost.

Wherever men tilled, the earth bore no corn because the land was all done for by such doings; and they said openly that Christ and His saints slept.[13] Such things, and more than we know how to tell, we suffered 19 years for our sins.

In all this evil time, Abbot Martin held his abbacy for 20 and a half years and 8 days with great energy, and provided everything necessary for the monks and the guests, and held great alms-givings[14] in the house; and nevertheless worked on the church and set lands and revenues for it, and endowed it well, and had it roofed,[15] and brought them into the new minster with great honour on the Feast of St Peter;[16] that was *in the year 1140 from the incarnation of the Lord, 23 from the burning of the place.*[17] And he went to Rome and was well received there by the pope Eugenius and there got privileges, one for all the lands of the abbacy and another for the lands that pertain to the sacrist;[18] and if he could have lived longer he meant to do the same for the treasurer.[19] And he got back lands which powerful men held by force. From William Maudit who held the castle of Rockingham he won Cottingham and Easton; and from Hugh de Vatteville he won Irthlingborough and Stanwick and 60 shillings each year from Aldwinkle. And he made many monks and planted a vineyard[20] and made many buildings, and altered the town better than it was before,[21] and was a good monk and a good man, and therefore God and good men loved him.

Now we wish to tell some part of what happened in King Stephen's time.[22] In his time the Jews of Norwich bought a Christian child before Easter, and tortured him with all the same tortures with which our Lord was tortured, and on Good Friday[23] hanged him on a cross for love of our Lord, and afterwards buried him – imagined that it would be concealed, but our Lord showed that he was a holy martyr, and the monks took him and buried him reverently in the minster, and

---

[11] MS *over-myhte*, cf. Dickins, loc. cit. in note 6. [12] MS *tun. . . . tunscipe.* [13] It is unclear whether this saying should be assigned to those suffering or those perpetrating evil. [14] MS *carited*; but *caritas* has the further sense of 'monastic allowance or measure of food or drink', and also the technical one of 'commemoration feasts' at the anniversaries of benefactors. [15] As usual, building had begun at the east end; only the choir of the church was complete at this date, the tower and transepts being added by Martin's successor (Hugh Candidus, p. 130; VCH, *Northamptonshire*, II, pp. 432–3. [16] 29 June. [17] See above, *s.a.* 1116. [18] The two documents are given in full by Hugh Candidus (pp. 109–19). [19] MS *horderwycan*, normally the office of treasurer, but variously used; Hugh Candidus (pp. 122–3) says *cellarer and chamberlain*. [20] MS *winiærd*; part of the Peterborough precinct is still called The Vineyard (VCH, *Northamptonshire*, II, p. 448). [21] Hugh Candidus (p. 122) says he altered the position of the monastery gateway, the market, quay and *vill.* [22] Stephen reigned 1135–54. [23] MS *lang fridæi*; 'long Friday', perhaps so called from the length of fasts and services.

through our Lord he performs wonderful and manifold miracles; and he is called St William.[1]

1138. In this year David king of Scotland came to this land with an immense army and wanted to win this land. And there came against him William earl of Aumale to whom the king had entrusted York, and other steadfast men with a few men, and fought with them and put the king to flight at the Standard[2] and killed a very great number of his company.

1140 [1139]. In this year the king Stephen wanted to take Robert earl of Gloucester, the son of King Henry, but he could not because he became aware of it.[3]

[1140]. After that, in the spring, the sun and the day darkened about noon-time in the day when men were eating, so that men lit candles to eat by; and that was 20 *March*, and men were very astonished.

[1136]. After that William archbishop of Canterbury passed away, and [1139] the king made Theobald, who was abbot in Bec, archbishop.[4]

[1140]. After that there grew a very great war between the king and Ranulf earl of Chester;[5] not because he did not give him all that he could ask him, as he did all others, but always the more he gave them, the worse they were to him. The earl held Lincoln against the king, and deprived him of all that he ought to have. And the king went there and besieged him and his brother William of Roumare[6] in the castle; and the earl stole out and travelled for Robert earl of Gloucester, and brought him there with a great army [1141] and on Candlemas Day[7] they fought hard against their lord and seized him because his men betrayed him and fled, and led him to Bristol and put [him] in prison and in fetters[8] there. Then the whole of England was more disturbed than it ever was before, and every evil was in the land.

[1139]. After that came the daughter of King Henry, who had been empress in Germany and was now countess in Anjou, and came to London; [1141] and the London people wanted to seize her, and she fled and lost a great deal there.[9]

[1141]. After that, the bishop of Winchester, Henry the brother of King Stephen, spoke with Earl Robert and with the empress and swore them oaths that he would never more hold with the king his brother, and cursed all the men who held with him, and told them that he would give up Winchester to them, and had them come there. Then when they were in there, the king's queen came with all her forces

---

[1] This is the earliest known accusation of ritual murder brought against the Jewish community, cf. Roth, 'The Feast of Purim', 520–26. See generally Thomas of Monmouth, *The Life and Miracles of St William*; Anderson, *A Saint at Stake*. [2] The battle of the Standard, fought near Northallerton, 22 August, was so called because it was fought around a mast to which there were attached banners of Sts Peter, John of Beverley and Wilfrid of Ripon (Aelred, *Relatio de Standardo*; Richard of Hexham, pp. 162–3, transl. Douglas and Greenaway, *Documents*, p. 346). For the background to the invasion see Green, 'Anglo-Scottish relations, 1066–1174', pp. 53–72. [3] Robert had formally renounced his allegiance in 1138 (William of Malmesbury, *Historia Novella*, pp. 22–3; *Gesta Stephani*, pp. 116–17). [4] See generally Saltman, *Theobald, Archbishop of Canterbury*. [5] See generally Alexander, *Ranulf of Chester*. [6] Earl of Lincoln, see p. 253. [7] 2 February. [8] Cf. *Gesta Stephani*, pp. 114–15. [9] For the events between her landing at Arundel, Sussex, in September 1139, and flight from London to Oxford in June 1141, see *Gesta Stephani*, pp. 86–127; Chibnall, *The Empress Matilda*, pp. 80–105.

and besieged them[10] so that there was great hunger in there. Then when they could endure it no longer, they stole out and fled, and those outside became aware of it and followed them and seized Robert earl of Gloucester and led him to Rochester and put him in prison there. And the empress fled into a minster.[11] Then the wise men travelled between and reconciled the king's friends and the earl's friends, so that the king should be let out of prison [in exchange] for the earl, and the earl for the king; and they did so.[12]

[1142]. Then after that, the king and Earl Ranulf[13] were reconciled at Stamford and swore oaths and affirmed pledges that neither of them should betray the other; and it availed nothing, because [1146] the king, through wicked advice, afterwards seized him in Northampton[14] and put him in prison; and soon after, on worse advice, he let him out on condition that he swore on relics and found hostages [as assurance] that he should give up all his castles. Some he gave up, and some he did not give; and then did worse here than he should.[15]

Then England was very divided: some held with the king and some with the empress, because then when the king was in prison the earls and the powerful men imagined that he would never come out again, and were reconciled with the empress and brought her into Oxford [1141] and gave her the town. Then when the king got out he heard tell of it and took his army and [1142] besieged her in the tower;[16] and in the night she was let down from the tower with ropes and stole out, and she fled and went on foot to Wallingford.[17]

[1147]. After that she travelled across the sea,[18] and [1141–4] those of Normandy all turned away from the king and to the earl of Anjou,[19] some of their own will, and some against their will, because he besieged them until they gave up their castles; and they had no help from the king.

[1140]. Then Eustace the king's son travelled to France and took to wife the sister of the king of France[20] and thought to get Normandy through that, but he had little success, and with just cause, because he was an evil man,[21] because wheresoever he came he did more evil than good; he robbed the lands and laid great taxes on them. He brought his wife to England and put her in the castle in Canterbury.[22]

---

[10] August–September 1141, *Gesta Stephani*, pp. 130–31. Queen Matilda, *a woman of subtlety . . . forgetting the weakness of her sex and woman's softness*, had previously played a part in raising London against the Empress, *Gesta Stephani*, pp. 122–7.   [11] Perhaps Wherwell, eight miles north of Winchester (cf. *Gesta Stephani*, pp. 130–33), but see Chibnall, *The Empress Matilda*, p. 114.   [12] Stephen was released from Bristol on 1 November 1141.   [13] Earl of Chester.   [14] Or possibly Southampton: MS *Hamtun*.   [15] English understatement; for Ranulf's rampage after his release, see *Gesta Stephani*, pp. 198–201.   [16] 26 September–December, 1142, and burnt the town (William of Malmesbury, *Historia Novella*, pp. 74, 76–7; *Gesta Stephani*, pp. 140–43).   [17] A dozen miles down the Thames, where the castle was held by Matilda's cousin, Brian, son of Alan Fergant (cf. annal 1127, p. 256).   [18] December 1142.   [19] Geoffrey of Anjou finally won Normandy in 1144.   [20] February 1140.   [21] The *Gesta Stephani* (pp. 208–9) represents Eustace as a paragon of knighthood but (pp. 222–3) a ruthless soldier.   [22] MS *þe caste . . . tebyri*.

She was a good woman but she had little happiness with him, and Christ did not wish that he should rule long, and he [1153] and his mother [1152] both died.[1]

[1151]. And the earl of Anjou died[2] and his son Henry took on the authority.[3] And [1152] the queen of France separated from the king, and she came to the young earl Henry and he took her to wife, and all Poitou with her.[4] Then [1153] he travelled into England with a great army, and won castles, and the king travelled against him with a much greater army; and nevertheless they did not fight, but the archbishop and the wise men travelled between them and made that pact that the king should be lord and king while he lived, and after his day Henry would be king, and he should hold him as father, and he him as son, and peace and reconciliation should be between them and in all England.[5] This and the other conditions that they made, the king and the earl and the bishops and the earls[6] and all powerful men swore to hold. Then the earl was received with great honour at Winchester and at London, and all did him homage and swore to hold the peace; and soon it became a very good peace, such as there never was before. Then the king was stronger than he ever was before; and the earl travelled across the sea,[7] and all the people loved him because he did good justice and made peace.

1154. In this year the king Stephen died[8] and was buried where his wife and his son[9] were buried at Faversham, the minster that they made.[10] When the king died the earl was beyond the sea, and no man dared do other than good because of great awe of him. Then when he came to England, he was received with great honour and was blessed as king in London on the Sunday before midwinter day,[11] and there held a great court.

Then the very day that Martin abbot of Peterborough should have gone there [to court] he fell sick, and he died *on 2 January*, and within the day[12] the monks chose another from themselves who is called William de Vatteville, a good clerk[13] and good man, and well loved by the king and by all good men. And [they] buried the abbot solemnly in the morning[14] and immediately the chosen abbot and the monks with him travelled to Oxford to the king, and he gave him that abbacy, and he made his way immediately to Lincoln and was there blessed as abbot before he came home, and was afterwards received with great

---

[1] Eustace in August, 1153, and his mother, Matilda of Boulogne, in May 1152. [2] 7 September 1151. [3] i.e. the Duchy of Normandy; this was the future Henry II of England. [4] Eleanor of Aquitaine was separated from Louis VII in March, 1152, and married to Henry the following May. [5] The Treaty of Winchester, November 1153, Douglas and Greenaway, *Documents*, pp. 436–9, and cf. Henry of Huntingdon, p. 289. [6] This is presumably the English earls, as distinct from the young Earl Henry spoken of earlier (MS: *te eorl . . . and te eorles*). [7] Before Easter 1154. [8] 25 October 1154. [9] i.e. Matilda of Boulogne and Eustace. [10] A Cluniac priory founded by Stephen in 1148 and in which Matilda displayed particular interest, cf. VCH, *Kent*, II, pp. 137–8. [11] 19 December 1154. [12] *innen dæis*, see Einarsson, 'Two Scandinavisms in the Peterborough Chronicle', 20.

honour at Peterborough with a great procession; and so likewise was he at Ramsey and at Thorney and at Crowland[15] and Spalding and at St Albans, and went home[16] and is now abbot, and has made a fine beginning. *Christ grant that he may end thus!*[17]

[Manuscript E ends here][18]

[13] As William was a monk, *clerc* cannot here denote any secular order (cf. annal 963 E), but rather his learned ·character, cf. *Middle English Dictionary*, *sub* clerk 2(a). [14] MS: *on . . . en byrieden*; Hugh Candidus (p. 124): *a few days later*. [15] The end of the manuscript is mutilated and some readings partly conjecture. [16] Reading *for ham*; MS *Forham* suggests a further place-name concluding the list of religious houses, but none is convincingly identified. [17] In fact Abbot William was eventually deposed in 1175 after being arraigned by Robert the archdeacon – unjustly according to Hugh Candidus (pp. 131–2): *He would have done better had he not been impeded by great misfortunes, and interferences which he endured at times from traitors inside his household, but more often from men of substance outside.* [18] In the bottom right hand corner of the folio, the scribe compressing his hand-writing and abbreviating words in order to get in all that he has to say.

MAPS

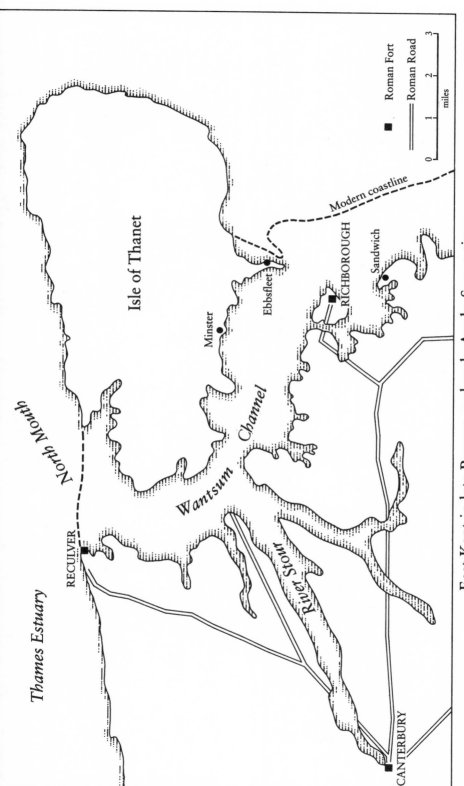

Thames Estuary

North Mouth

RECULVER

Isle of Thanet

Minster

Ebbsfleet

Wantsum Channel

RICHBOROUGH

Sandwich

River Stour

CANTERBURY

Modern coastline

■ Roman Fort

Roman Road

miles

0   1   2   3

East Kent in late Roman and early Anglo-Saxon times

Districts in Anglo-Saxon times

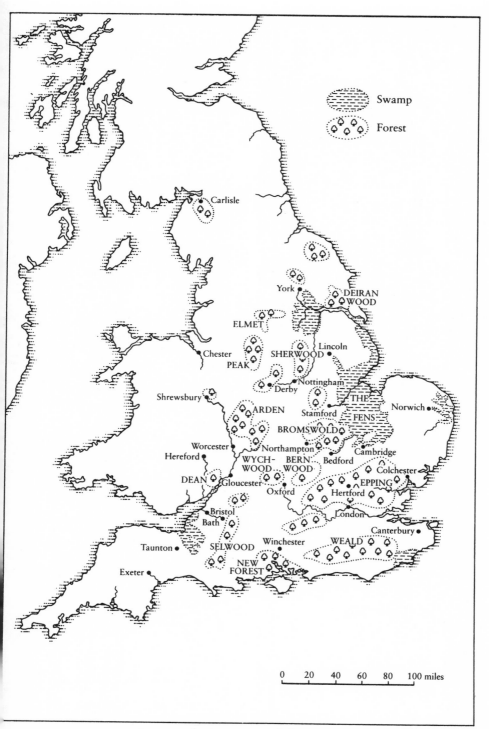

Swamp

Forest

Carlisle

York

DEIRAN WOOD

ELMET

Chester

Lincoln

SHERWOOD

PEAK

Nottingham

Derby

Shrewsbury

ARDEN

Stamford

THE FENS

Norwich

BROMSWOLD

Worcester

Northampton

Cambridge

Hereford

WYCH-WOOD

BERN-WOOD

Bedford

Colchester

DEAN

Gloucester

Oxford

EPPING

Hertford

Bristol

London

Canterbury

Bath

Taunton

SELWOOD

Winchester

WEALD

Exeter

NEW FOREST

0 20 40 60 80 100 miles

Areas of swamp and forest

Bishoprics *circa* 800

DURHAM

YORK

LICHFIELD

HEREFORD

WORCESTER

DORCHESTER

ELMHAM

RAMSBURY

LONDON

WELLS

WINCHESTER

ROCH-
ESTER

CANTER-
BURY

SHERBORNE

SELSEY

CORNWALL
& DEVON

0   20   40   60   80   100 miles

Bishoprics *circa* 1040

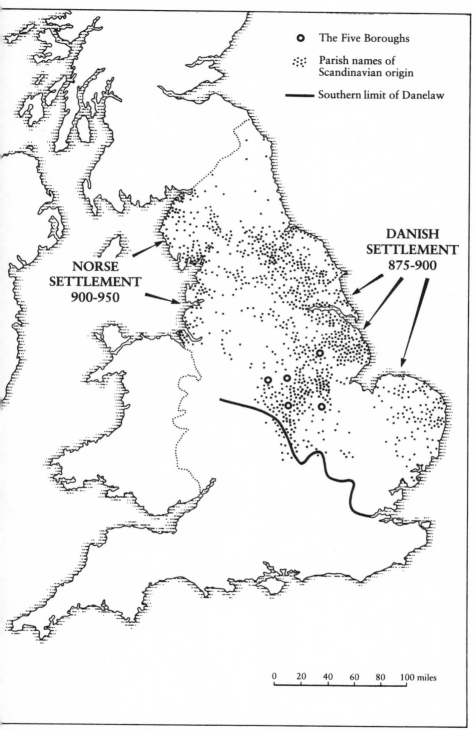

The Five Boroughs

Parish names of
Scandinavian origin

Southern limit of Danelaw

DANISH
SETTLEMENT
875-900

NORSE
SETTLEMENT
900-950

0   20   40   60   80   100 miles

Scandinavian settlement in England

Territorial jurisdiction *circa* 1045

Territorial jurisdiction on the eve of the Conquest

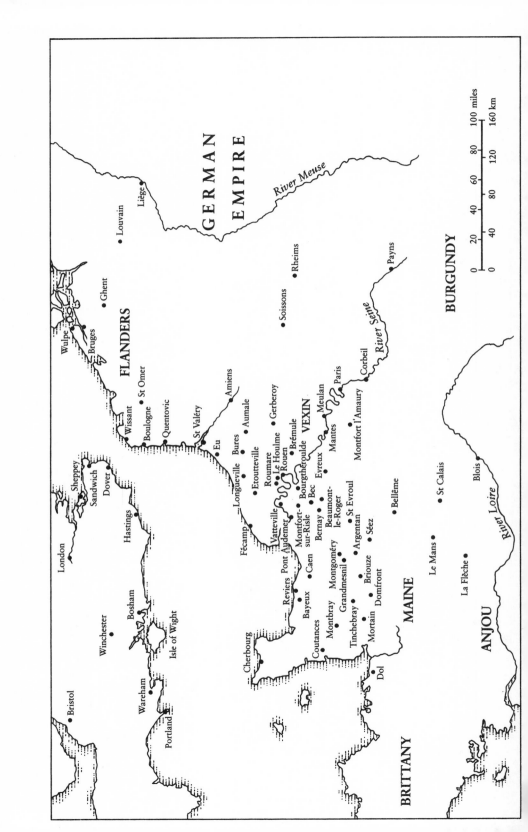

GENEALOGICAL TABLES

Descendants of Æthelberht of Kent

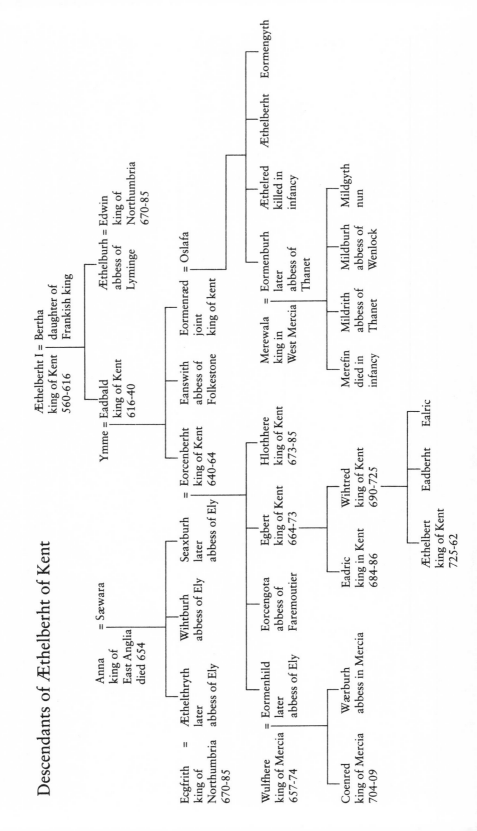

Descendants of Yffe of Deira

Yffe
├── Ælfric
│   └── Osric, king of Deira 632-33
│   └── Oswine, king of Deira killed 651
└── Ælle, king of Deira 560-88
    ├── son or daughter
    │   └── Hereric = Breguswith, killed c. 613
    │   ├── Hereswith = Æthelric of East Anglia
    │   │   ├── Ealdwulf, king of East Anglia 663-713
    │   │   └── Ælfwold, king of East Anglia died 749
    │   └── Hilda, abbes of Whitby
    └── Acha = Æthelfrith, king of Northumbria (see p. 286)
        ├── Osfrith, killed 632
        │   └── Yffe, died in childhood
        ├── Eadfrith, killed 633-641
        ├── Edwin, king of Northumbria 616-33
        │   └── (1) Cwenburh, daughter of Ceorl, king of Mercia
        │   └── = (2) Æthelburh, daughter of Æthelberht, king of Kent (see p. 284)
        │   ├── Æthelhun, died in infancy
        │   ├── Æthelthryth, died in infancy
        │   └── Uscfrea, died in childhood
        └── Oswy, king of Northumbria (see p. 286) = Eanflæd

Descendants of Ida, king of Bernicia

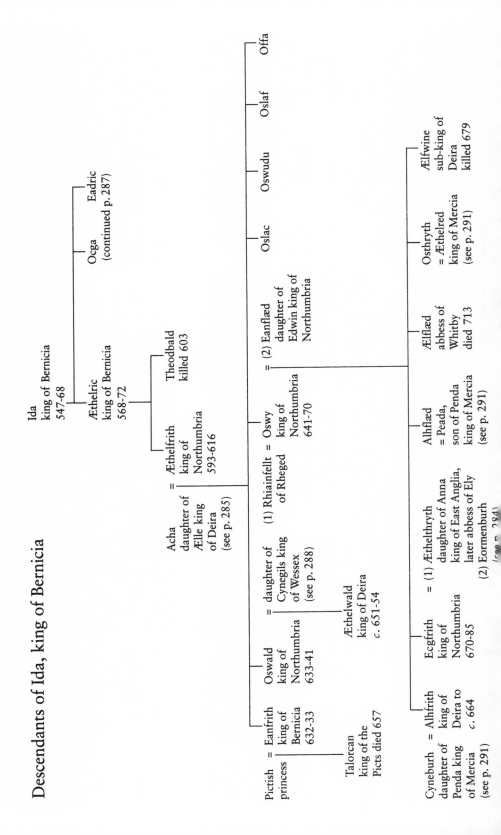

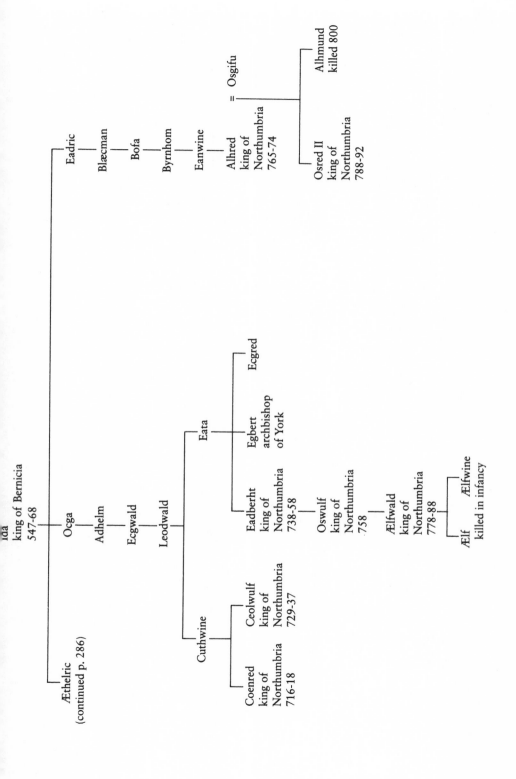

Ida
king of Bernicia
547-68

Æthelric
(continued p. 286)

Eadric

Ocga

Adhelm

Ecgwald

Leodwald

Blæcman

Bofa

Byrnhom

Eanwine

Alhred
king of Northumbria
765-74

= Osgifu

Cuthwine

Eata

Coenred
king of
Northumbria
716-18

Ceolwulf
king of
Northumbria
729-37

Eadberht
king of
Northumbria
738-58

Egbert
archbishop
of York

Ecgred

Oswulf
king of
Northumbria
758

Ælfwald
king of
Northumbria
778-88

Ælf

Ælfwine
killed in infancy

Osred II
king of
Northumbria
788-92

Alhmund
killed 800

Descendants of Cerdic, king of Wessex

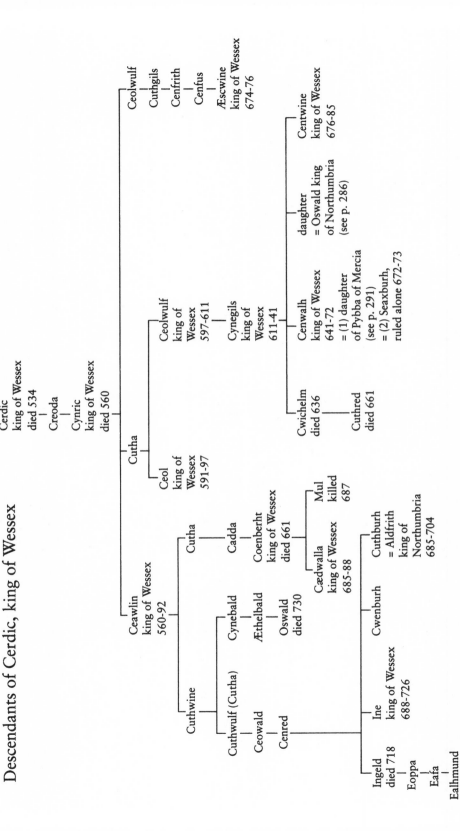

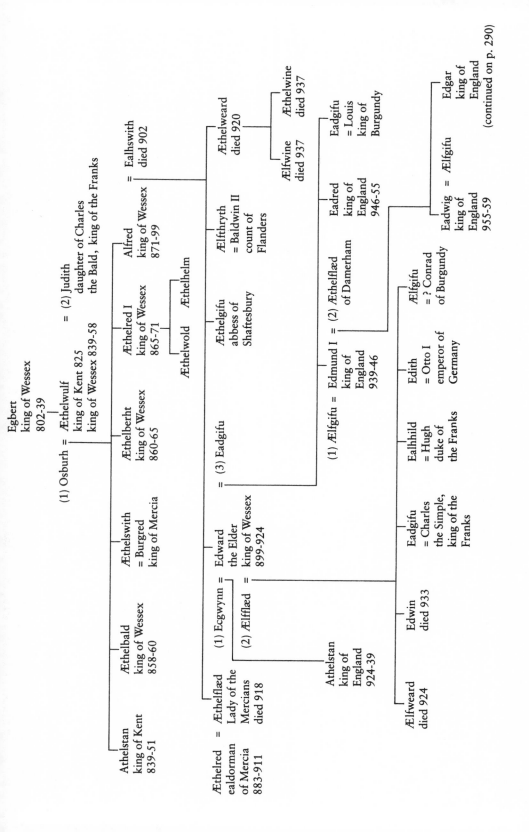

Egbert
king of Wessex
802-39

(1) Osburh = Æthelwulf = (2) Judith
king of Kent 825   daughter of Charles
king of Wessex 839-58   the Bald, king of the Franks

Athelstan   Æthelbald   Æthelswith   Æthelberht   Æthelred I   Alfred   = Ealhswith
king of Kent   king of Wessex = Burgred   king of Wessex king of Wessex   king of Wessex   died 902
839-51   858-60   king of Mercia   860-65   865-71   871-99

Æthelred = Æthelflæd   Edward   = (3) Eadgifu   Æthelwold   Æthelflæth   Æthelweard
ealdorman Lady of the   the Elder   = Baldwin II   died 920
of Mercia Mercians   king of Wessex   Æthelhelm   count of
883-911   died 918   899-924   Flanders
           (1) Ecgwynn =
           (2) Æthelflæd =   Æthelgifu   Ælfwine   Æthelwine
                                                            abbess of   died 937   died 937
                                                            Shaftesbury

Athelstan   (1) Ælfgifu = Edmund I = (2) Æthelflæd   Eadgifu
king of England   king of England of Damerham   = Louis
924-39   939-46   king of Burgundy

Ælfweard   Edwin   Eadgifu   Ealhhild   Edith   Ælfgifu   Eadred   Eadwig = Ælfgifu   Edgar
died 924   died 933 = Charles   = Hugh duke of = Otto I   = ? Conrad   king of England king of England   king of England
                    the Simple,   the Franks   emperor of   of Burgundy   946-55   955-59
                    king of the   Germany
                    Franks

(continued on p. 290)

Descendants of Edgar, king of England

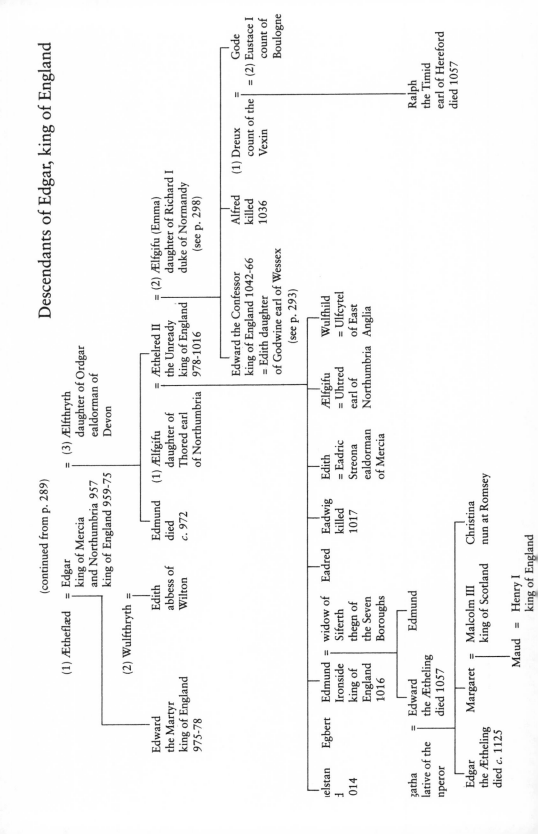

(continued from p. 289)

(1) Ætheflæd = Edgar king of Mercia and Northumbria 957 king of England 959-75 = (3) Ælfthryth daughter of Ordgar ealdorman of Devon

(2) Wulfthryth =

Edith abbess of Wilton

Edward the Martyr king of England 975-78

(1) Ælfgifu daughter of Thored earl of Northumbria = Æthelred II the Unready king of England 978-1016 = (2) Ælfgifu (Emma) daughter of Richard I duke of Normandy (see p. 298)

Edmund died c. 972

Edward the Confessor king of England 1042-66 = Edith daughter of Godwine earl of Wessex (see p. 293)

Alfred killed 1036

Gode = Eustace I count of Boulogne

(1) Dreux count of the Vexin = = (2)

Ralph the Timid earl of Hereford died 1057

Æthelstan d 1014

Egbert

Edmund Ironside king of England 1016 = widow of Siferth thegn of the Seven Boroughs

Eadred

Eadwig killed 1017

Edith = Eadric Streona ealdorman of Mercia

Ælfgifu = Uhtred earl of Northumbria

Wulfhild = Ulfcytel of East Anglia

Agatha relative of the Emperor = Edward the Ætheling died 1057

Edmund

Christina nun at Romsey

Margaret = Malcolm III king of Scotland

Edgar the Ætheling died c. 1125

Maud = Henry I king of England

Descendants of Pybba of Mercia

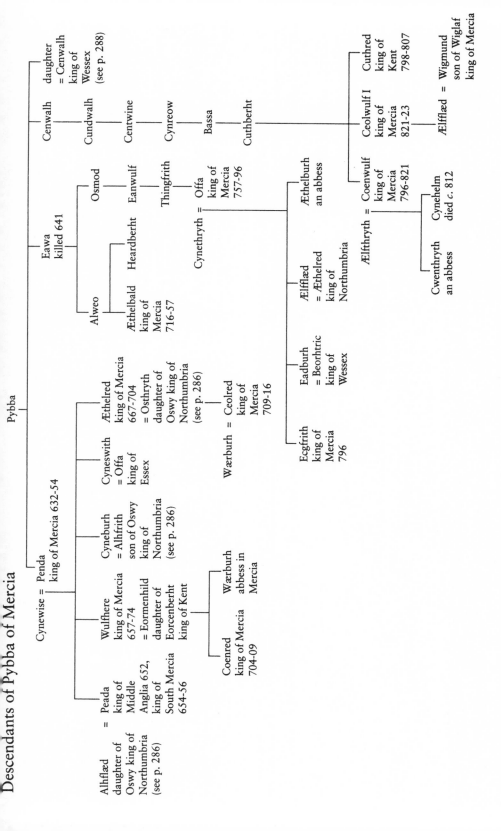

Relationships of Emma (Ælfgifu)

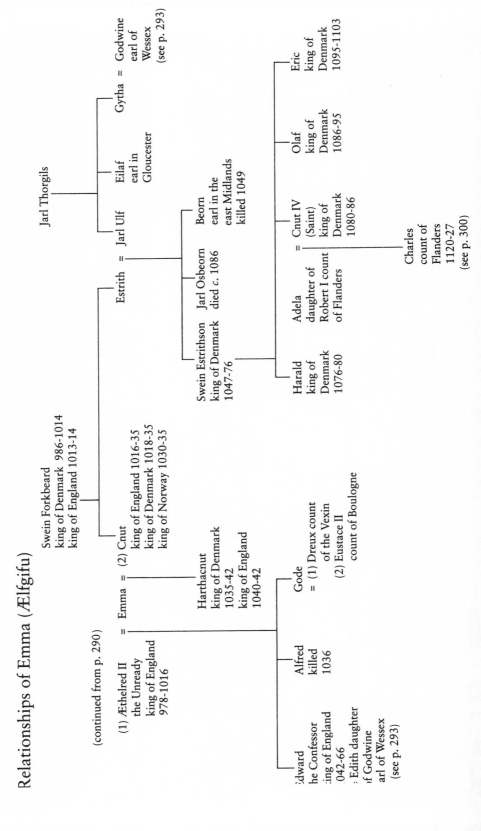

(continued from p. 290)

Jarl Thorgils

(1) Æthelred II the Unready king of England 978-1016 = Emma = (2) Cnut king of England 1016-35 king of Denmark 1018-35 king of Norway 1030-35

Estrith = Jarl Ulf

Jarl Ulf | Eilaf earl in Gloucester | Gytha = Godwine earl of Wessex (see p. 293)

dward he Confessor ing of England 042-66 : Edith daughter of Godwine arl of Wessex (see p. 293)

Alfred killed 1036

Harthacnut king of Denmark 1035-42 king of England 1040-42

Gode = (1) Dreux count of the Vexin (2) Eustace II count of Boulogne

Beorn earl in the east Midlands killed 1049

Jarl Osbeorn died c. 1086

Swein Estrithson king of Denmark 1047-76

Harald king of Denmark 1076-80

Adela daughter of Robert I count of Flanders = Cnut IV (Saint) king of Denmark 1080-86

Olaf king of Denmark 1086-95

Eric king of Denmark 1095-1103

Charles count of Flanders 1120-27 (see p. 300)

Descendants of Godwine, earl of Wessex

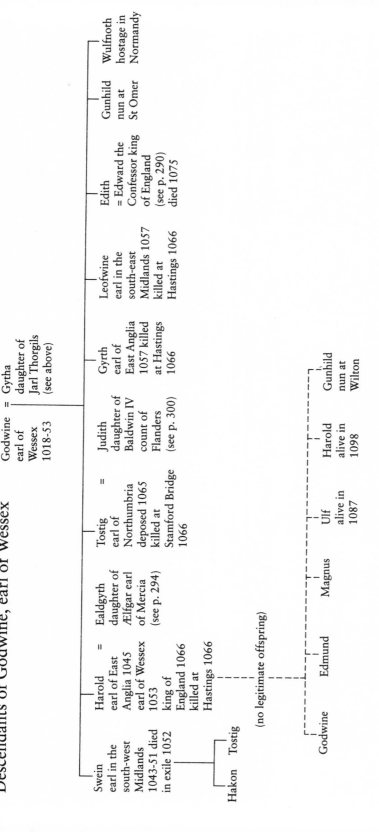

Godwine earl of Wessex 1018–53 = Gytha daughter of Jarl Thorgils (see above)

Swein earl in the south-west Midlands 1043–51 died in exile 1052

Harold earl of East Anglia 1045 earl of Wessex 1053 king of England 1066 killed at Hastings 1066 = **Ealdgyth** daughter of Ælfgar earl of Mercia (see p. 294)

Tostig earl of Northumbria deposed 1065 killed at Stamford Bridge 1066 = **Judith** daughter of Baldwin IV count of Flanders (see p. 300)

Gyrth earl of East Anglia 1057 killed at Hastings 1066

Leofwine earl in the south-east Midlands 1057 killed at Hastings 1066

Edith = Edward the Confessor king of England (see p. 290) died 1075

Gunhild nun at St Omer

Wulfnoth hostage in Normandy

Hakon   Tostig

(no legitimate offspring)

Godwine   Edmund   Magnus   Ulf alive in 1087   Harold alive in 1098   Gunhild nun at Wilton

Family of Leofric and Godiva of Mercia

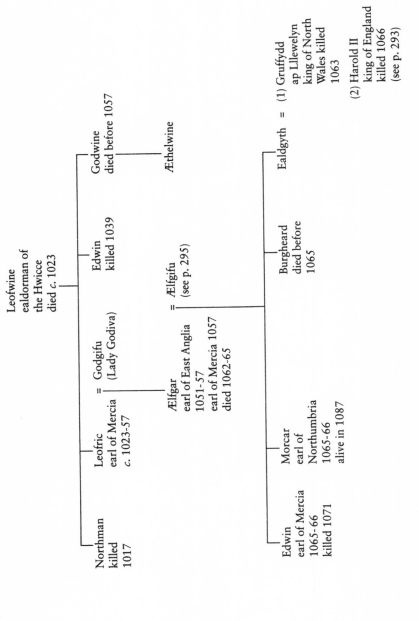

Leofwine
ealdorman of
the Hwicce
died *c.* 1023

Northman
killed
1017

Leofric
earl of Mercia
c. 1023-57

= Godgifu
(Lady Godiva)

Edwin
killed 1039

Godwine
died before 1057

Æthelwine

Ælfgar
earl of East Anglia
1051-57
earl of Mercia 1057
died 1062-65

= Ælfgifu
(see p. 295)

Edwin
earl of Mercia
1065-66
killed 1071

Morcar
earl of
Northumbria
1065-66
alive in 1087

Burgheard
died before
1065

Ealdgyth = (1) Gruffydd
ap Lllewelyn
king of North
Wales killed
1063

(2) Harold II
king of England
killed 1066
(see p. 293)

The family of Wulfrun (Mercian Lady)

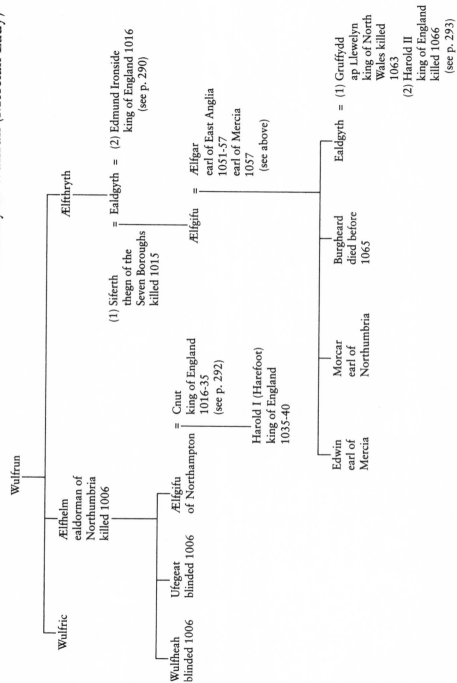

Wulfrun

Wulfric

Ælfhelm
ealdorman of
Northumbria
killed 1006

Ælfthryth

Wulfheah
blinded 1006

Ufegeat
blinded 1006

Ælfgifu
of Northampton
= Cnut
king of England
1016-35
(see p. 292)

Harold I (Harefoot)
king of England
1035-40

Ælfgifu

Ealdgyth = (1) Siferth
thegn of the
Seven Boroughs
killed 1015

(2) Edmund Ironside
king of England 1016
(see p. 290)

=

Ælfgar
earl of East Anglia
1051-57
earl of Mercia
1057
(see above)

Edwin
earl of
Mercia

Morcar
earl of
Northumbria

Burgheard
died before
1065

Ealdgyth = (1) Gruffydd
ap Llewelyn
king of North
Wales killed
1063

(2) Harold II
king of England
killed 1066
(see p. 293)

Descendants of Waltheof, earl of Northumbria

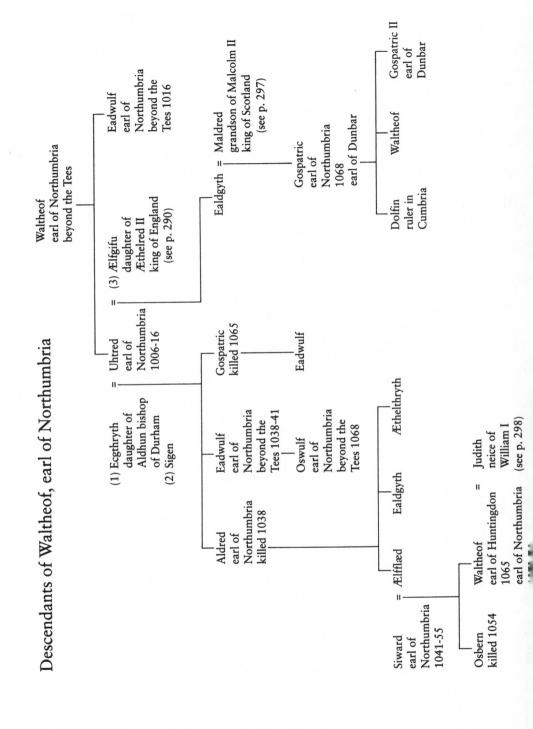

Waltheof
earl of Northumbria
beyond the Tees

Uhtred
earl of
Northumbria
1006-16

= (1) Ecgthryth
daughter of
Aldhun bishop
of Durham
(2) Sigen

= (3) Ælfgifu
daughter of
Æthelred II
king of England
(see p. 290)

Eadwulf
earl of
Northumbria
beyond the
Tees 1016

Aldred
earl of
Northumbria
killed 1038

Eadwulf
earl of
Northumbria
beyond the
Tees 1038-41

Gospatric
killed 1065

Eadwulf

Oswulf
earl of
Northumbria
beyond the
Tees 1068

Ealdgyth = Maldred
grandson of Malcolm II
king of Scotland
(see p. 297)

Gospatric
earl of
Northumbria
1068
earl of Dunbar

Dolfin
ruler in
Cumbria

Waltheof

Gospatric II
earl of
Dunbar

Siward
earl of
Northumbria
1041-55

= Ælfflæd   Ealdgyth   Æthelthryth

Osbern
killed 1054

Waltheof
earl of Huntingdon
1065
earl of Northumbria

= Judith
neice of
William I
(see p. 298)

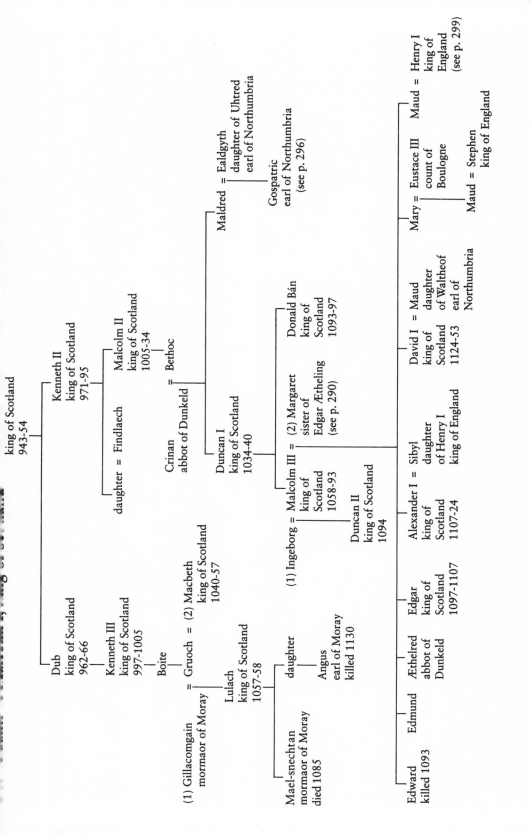

Malcolm I
king of Scotland
943-54

Dub
king of Scotland
962-66

Kenneth II
king of Scotland
971-95

Kenneth III
king of Scotland
997-1005

Boite

Malcolm II
king of Scotland
1005-34

= Bethoc

daughter = Findlaech

Crinan
abbot of Dunkeld

Gruoch = (2) Macbeth
king of Scotland
1040-57

(1) Gillacomgain
mormaor of Moray

Maldred = Ealdgyth
daughter of Uhtred
earl of Northumbria

Gospatric
earl of Northumbria
(see p. 296)

Duncan I
king of Scotland
1034-40

Lulach
king of Scotland
1057-58

Mael-snechtan
mormaor of Moray
died 1085

daughter

Angus
earl of Moray
killed 1130

(1) Ingeborg = Malcolm III = (2) Margaret
king of   sister of
Scotland   Edgar Ætheling
1058-93   (see p. 290)

Duncan II
king of Scotland
1094

Donald Bán
king of
Scotland
1093-97

Edward
killed 1093

Edmund

Æthelred
abbot of
Dunkeld

Edgar
king of Scotland
1097-1107

Alexander I = Sibyl
king of   daughter
Scotland   of Henry I
1107-24   king of England

David I = Maud
king of   daughter
Scotland   of Waltheof
1124-53   earl of
           Northumbria

Mary = Eustace III
count of
Boulogne

Maud = Henry I
king of England
(see p. 299)

Maud = Stephen
king of England

Descendants of Richard, duke of Normandy

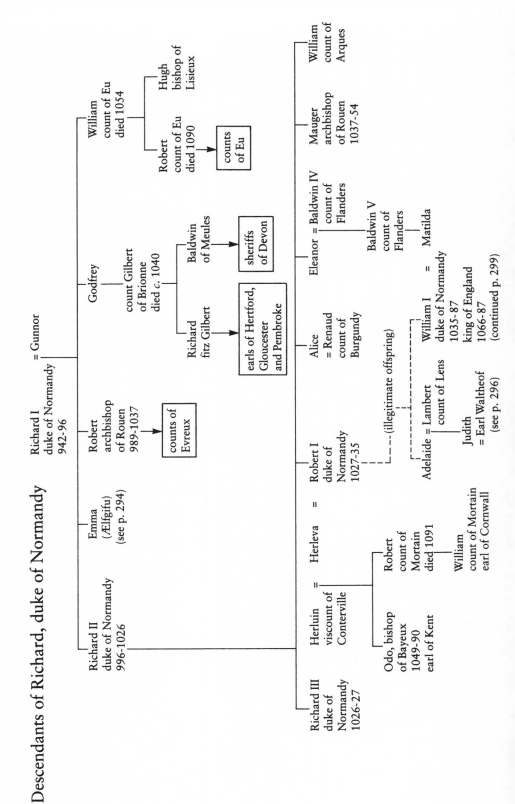

Descendants of William I (the Conqueror)

(continued from p. 298)

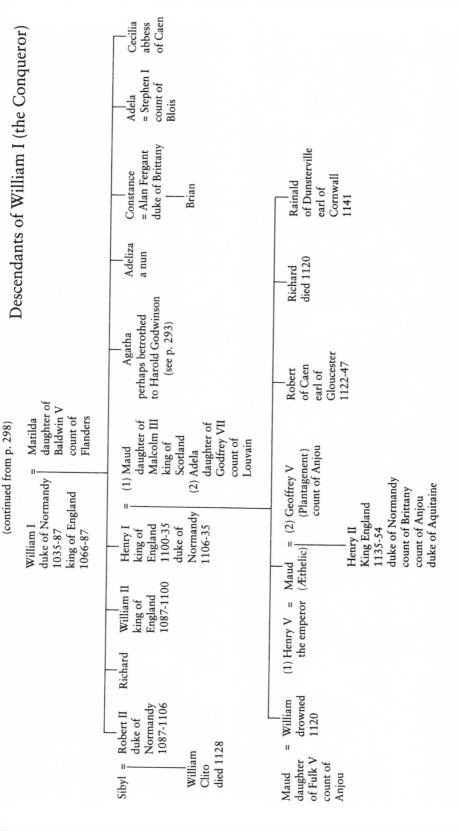

William I
duke of Normandy
1035-87
king of England
1066-87

= Matilda
daughter of
Baldwin V
count of
Flanders

Sibyl =

Robert II
duke of
Normandy
1087-1106

Richard

William II
king of
England
1087-1100

Henry I
king of
England
1100-35
duke of
Normandy
1106-35

=

(1) Maud
daughter of
Malcolm III
king of
Scotland

(2) Adela
daughter of
Godfrey VII
count of
Louvain

Agatha
perhaps betrothed
to Harold Godwinson
(see p. 293)

Adeliza
a nun

Constance
= Alan Fergant
duke of Brittany

Adela
= Stephen I
count of
Blois

Cecilia
abbess
of Caen

William
Clito
died 1128

Brian

Maud
daughter
of Fulk V
count of
Anjou

=

William
drowned
1120

(1) Henry V
the emperor

=

Maud
(Æthelic)

=

(2) Geoffrey V
(Plantagenet)
count of Anjou

Robert
of Caen
earl of
Gloucester
1122-47

Richard
died 1120

Rainald
of Dunsterville
earl of
Cornwall
1141

Henry II
King England
1135-54
duke of Normandy
count of Brittany
count of Anjou
duke of Aquitaine

Descendants of Baldwin IV count of Flanders

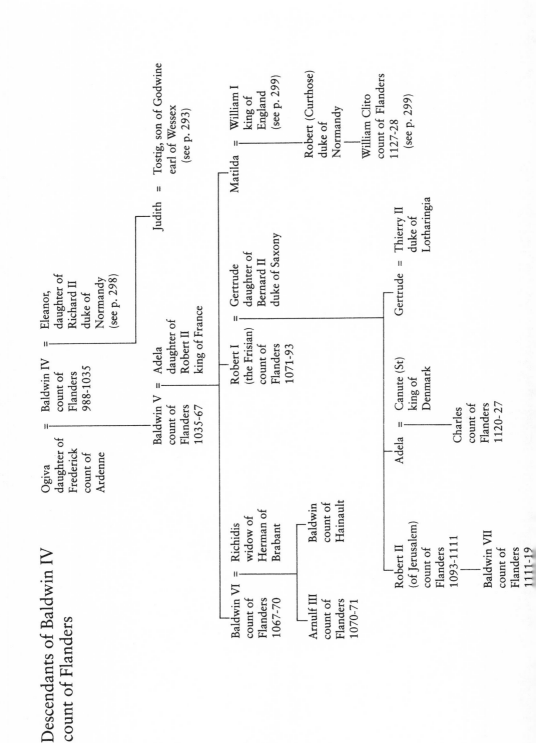

Ogiva daughter of Frederick count of Ardenne = Baldwin IV count of Flanders 988-1035 = Eleanor, daughter of Richard II duke of Normandy (see p. 298)

Judith = Tostig, son of Godwine earl of Wessex (see p. 293)

Baldwin V count of Flanders 1035-67 = Adela daughter of Robert II king of France

Robert I (the Frisian) count of Flanders 1071-93 = Gertrude daughter of Bernard II duke of Saxony

Matilda = William I king of England (see p. 299)

Robert (Curthose) duke of Normandy

William Clito count of Flanders 1127-28 (see p. 299)

Gertrude = Thierry II duke of Lotharingia

Baldwin VI count of Flanders 1067-70 = Richidis widow of Herman of Brabant

Baldwin count of Hainault

Arnulf III count of Flanders 1070-71

Adela = Canute (St) king of Denmark

Charles count of Flanders 1120-27

Robert II (of Jerusalem) count of Flanders 1093-1111

Baldwin VII count of Flanders 1111-19

Descendants of Rhodri ap Merfyn, king of Gwynedd

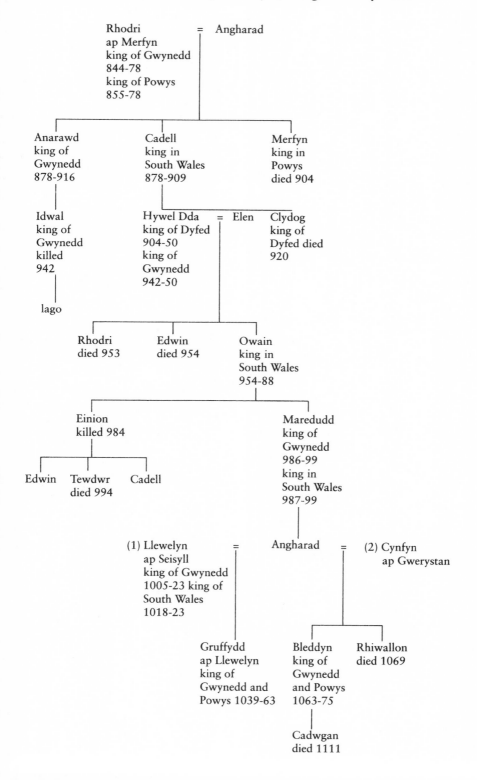

BIBLIOGRAPHY

This is confined to references used in footnotes. For MSS and editions see the Introduction.

Abels, R. P., *Lordship and Military Obligation in Anglo-Saxon England* (London, 1988).

Ælfric, ed. B. Thorpe, *The Homilies of the Anglo-Saxon Church* (London, 1844–6).

Aelred (Ailred) of Rievaulx, 'Relatio de Standardo', in *Chronicles of the reigns of Stephen, Henry II and Richard I*, ed. R. Howlett, Rolls Series LXXXII (London, 1886), III, pp. 181–99.

—— *Vita S. Edwardi Regis et Confessoris*, *Patrologia Latina* CXCV, cols. 737–90.

Æthelnoth of Odensee, *Life of Cnut*, ed. J. Langebek, *et al.*, *Scriptores Rerum Danicarum* (Copenhagen 1772–1878), III, pp. 325–90.

Æthelweard, *Chronicle*, ed. A. Campbell (London, 1962).

Alcuin, *Letters*, ed. E. Duemmler, *Monumenta Germaniae Historica, Epistolae Karolini Aevi* (Berlin, 1895), II, pp. 1–481.

—— *The Bishops, Kings, and Saints of York*, ed. P. Godman (Oxford, 1982).

Aldhelm, *Opera*, ed. R. Ehwald, *Monumenta Germaniae Historica, Auctorum Antiquissimi* XV (Berlin, 1919).

Alexander, J. W., *Ranulf of Chester, a Relic of Conquest* (Athens, Georgia, 1983).

Amory, F., 'The viking Hasting in Franco-Scandinavian legend', in *Saints, Scholars and Heroes: Studies in Medieval Culture in Honour of Charles W. Jones*, ed. M. H. King and W. M. Stevens (Collegeville, Minnesota, 1979), II, pp. 265–86.

Anderson, A. O., *Scottish Annals from English Chroniclers AD 500 to 1286* (London, 1908).

Anderson, M. D., *A Saint at Stake: the strange death of William of Norwich, 1144* (London, 1964).

Andersón, M. O., 'Lothian and the early Scottish kings', *Scottish Historical Review* XXXIX (1960), 98–112.

—— *Kings and Kingship in Early Scotland* (Edinburgh, 1973).

Andressohn, J. C., *The Ancestry and Life of Godfrey of Bouillon* (Bloomington, Indiana, 1947).

An Anglo-Saxon Dictionary, ed. J. Bosworth and T. N. Toller (London, 1898, 1922); enlarged addenda and corrigenda by A. Campbell (Oxford, 1972).

Annales Cambriae, ed. J. Williams ab Ithel, Rolls Series XX (London, 1860).

Annals of Lindisfarne, ed. G. H. Pertz, *Monumenta Germaniae Historica*, *Scriptores* XIX (Hannover, 1866), pp. 502–7.

Annals of St-Bertin, ed. J. L. Nelson (Manchester, 1991).

Annals of St Neots, ed. Dumville and M. Lapidge, *The Anglo-Saxon Chronicle: A Collaborative Edition*, 17 (Cambridge, 1984).

Annals of St-Vaast, ed. B. de Simson, *Monumenta Germaniae Historica*, *Scriptores Rerum Germanicarum in usum scholarim, separatim editi*, XII (Hannover, 1909).

Annals of Ulster, ed. W. M. Hennessy and B. MacCarthy (Dublin, 1887–1901).

Amstrong A. M. *et al.*, *The Place-Names of Cumberland*, English Place-Name Society XX-XXII (Cambridge, 1950–52).

Ashdown, M., 'The single combat in certain cycles of English and Scandinavian traditional romance', *Modern Language Review* XVII (1922), 113–30.

—— *English and Norse Document relating to the Reign of Ethelred the Unready* (Cambridge, 1930).

Asser, Life of King Alfred, ed. W. H. Stevenson, new impression (Oxford, 1959); translated by S. Keynes and M. Lapidge in *Alfred the Great: Asser's Life of King Alfred and other Contemporary Sources* (Harmondsworth, 1983), pp. 65–110.

Attenborough, F. L., ed., *The Laws of the Earliest English Kings* (Cambridge, 1922).

Bannerman, J., *Studies in the History of Dalriada* (Edinburgh, 1974).

Barber, M., *The New Knighthood: a History of the Order of the Temple* (Cambridge, 1994).

Barlow, F., ed., *The Life of King Edward who rests at Westminster, attributed to a monk of St Bertin* (London, 1962), 2nd edn (Oxford, 1992).

—— *The English Church 1000–1066, A Constitutional History* (London, 1963).

—— 'A view of Archbishop Lanfranc', *Journal of Ecclesiastical History* XVI (1965), 163–77.

—— *et al.*, *Leofric of Exeter* (Exeter, 1972).

—— *William Rufus* (London, 1983).

Barraclough, G., 'The Anglo-Saxon writ', *History* XXXIX (1954), 193–215.

Barrow, G. W. S., *The Anglo-Norman Era in Scottish History* (Oxford, 1980).

Bassett, S. R., 'A probable Mercian royal mausoleum at Winchcombe, Gloucestershire', *Antiquaries Journal* LXV (1985), 82–100.

—— ed., *The Origins of Anglo-Saxon Kingdoms* (Leicester, 1989).

—— 'Anglo-Saxon Shrewsbury and its churches', *Midland History* XVI (1991), 1–23.

Bately, J. M., 'Lexical evidence for the authorship of the prose psalms in the Paris Psalter', *Anglo-Saxon England* X (1982), 69–95.

—— *The Anglo-Saxon Chronicle: Texts and Textual Relationships* (Reading, 1991).

—— 'The Anglo-Saxon Chronicle', in *The Battle of Maldon*, ed. D. Scragg (Oxford, 1991), pp. 37–50.

Battiscombe, C. F., *The Relics of St Cuthbert* (Durham, 1956).

Beaven, M. L. R., 'The regnal dates of Alfred, Edward the Elder, and Athelstan', *English Historical Review* XXXII (1917), 517–31.

—— 'The beginning of the year in the Alfredian Chronicle (866–87)', *English Historical Review* XXXII (1918), 328–42.

Bede, *Ecclesiastical History of the English People*, ed. B. Colgrave and R. A. B. Mynors (Oxford, 1969). (Cited by book and chapter.) *The Old English Version of Bede's Ecclesiastical History*, ed. Miller, Early English Text Society, Old Series XCV-XCVI, CX-CXI (London, 1890–98).

—— *De Temporum Ratione, Patrologia Latina* XC, 293–578.

—— *De Tonitruis, Patrologia Latina* XC, 609–14.

—— *Vita Sanctorum Abbatum Monasterii in Wiramutha et Girvum, Patrologia Latina* XCIV, 711–30.

Beeler, J. H., 'Castles and strategy in Norman and early Angevin England', *Speculum* XXXI (1956), 581–601.

Beowulf and its Analogues, ed. G. N. Garmonsway and J. Simpson (London, 1968).

Beresford, M., *New Towns of the Middle Ages: Town plantation in England, Wales and Gascony* (London, 1967).

Bethell, D. L., 'William of Corbeil and the Canterbury York dispute', *Journal of Ecclesiastical History* XIX (1968), 145–59.

—— 'English Black Monks and episcopal elections in the 1120s', *English Historical Review* LXXXVI (1969), 673–98.

Biddle, M. ed., *Winchester in the Early Middle Ages* (Oxford, 1976).

—— 'Seasonal festivals and residence: Winchester, Westminster and Gloucester in the tenth to twelfth centuries', *Anglo-Norman Studies* VIII (1985), pp. 51–72.

Biddle, M. and Kjølbye-Biddle, B., 'Repton 1985', *Bulletin of the Council for British Archaeology Churches Committee* XXII (1985), 1–5.

Binns, A., 'The ships of the vikings, were they "viking ships"?', in *Proceedings of the Eighth Viking Congress*, ed. H. Bekker-Nielsen *et al.* (Odense, 1981), pp. 287–94.

—— 'The navigation of viking ships round the British Isles in Old English and Old Norse sources', *Proceedings of The Fifth Viking Congress*, ed. B. Niclasen (Tórshavn, 1968), pp. 103–17.

Blackburn, M. A. S., ed., *Anglo-Saxon Monetary History* (Leicester, 1986).

Blair, J., 'From minster to parish church' in *Minsters and Parish Churches: the local church in transition, 950–1200*, ed. J. Blair (Oxford, 1988), pp. 1–20.

—— 'Minster churches in the landscape', in *Anglo-Saxon Settlements*, ed. D. Hooke (Oxford, 1988), pp. 35–58.

Blair, P. H., 'The Moore Memoranda on Northumbrian History', in *The Early Cultures of North-West Europe*, ed. C. Fox and B. Dickins (Cambridge, 1950), pp. 245–57.

—— 'The Bernicians and their northern frontier', in *Studies in Early British History*, ed., N. K. Chadwick (Cambridge, 1954), pp. 137–72.

Bradley, S. A. J., ed., *Anglo-Saxon Poetry* (London, 1982).

Brandon, P., 'The South Saxon Andredesweald', in *The South Saxons*, ed. P. Brandon (Chichester, 1978), pp. 138–59.

Breeze, A., 'The Anglo-Saxon Chronicle for 1072 and the fords of Frew, Scotland', *Notes and Queries*, CCXXXVII (1992), 269–70.

Brooke, C. N. L., 'Gregorian reform in action: clerical marriage in England, 1050–1200', *Cambridge Historical Journal* XII (1956), 1–21, 187–8.

Brooks, N., *The Early History of the Church of Canterbury: Christ Church from 597–1066* (Leicester, 1984).

—— 'The creation and early structure of the kingdom of Kent', in *The Origins of Anglo-Saxon Kingdoms*, ed. S. Bassett (Leicester, 1989), pp. 55–74.

Brown, R. A. *et al.*, The History of the King's Works, I-II, *The Middle Ages* (London, 1963).

Brown, R. A., *Origins of English Feudalism* (London, 1973).

Bruce-Mitford, R., *The Sutton Hoo Ship Burial* (London, 1975–83).

Byrhtferth, *Manual*, ed. S. J. Crawford, Early English Text Society, Original Series CLXXVII (London, 1929)

Byrne, F. J., *Irish Kings and High Kings* (London, 1973).

Caesar, *The Gallic War*, ed. H. J. Edwards (London, 1917).

Campbell, A., ed., *The Battle of Brunanburh* (London, 1938).

—— ed., *Charters of Rochester* (London, 1973).

Campbell, J., 'Observations on English government from the tenth century to the twelfth century', *Transactions of the Royal Historical Society*, 5th Series XXV (1975), 39–54.

—— 'Some agents and agencies of the late Anglo-Saxon state', in *Domesday Studies*, ed. J. C. Holt (Woodbridge, 1987), pp. 201–18.

Campbell, M. W., 'Queen Emma and Ælfgifu of Northampton: Canute the Great's women', *Mediaeval Scandinavia* IV (1971), 66–79.

—— 'Note sur les déplacements de Tostig Godwinson en 1066', *Annales de Normandie* XXII (1972), 3–9.

The Canterbury Psalter, ed. M. R. James (London, 1935).

Carr, A. D., 'Anglo-Welsh relations, 1066–1282', in *England and her Neighbours, 1066–1453*, ed. M. Jones and M. Vale (London, 1989), pp. 121–38.

Cartularium Saxonicum, ed. W. de G. Birch (London, 1885–99).

Cartulary of the Monastery of St Frideswide at Oxford, The, ed. S. R. Wigram (Oxford, 1895–6).

Chadwick, H. M., *Studies on Anglo-Saxon Institutions* (Cambridge, 1905).

—— *The Origin of the English Nation* (Cambridge, 1907).

Chadwick H. M. and Chadwick, N. K., 'Vortigern', in N. K. Chadwick, ed., *Studies in Early British History* (Cambridge, 1954), pp. 21–46.

Chadwick, N. K., ed., *Studies in Early British History* (Cambridge, 1954).

—— ed., *Celt and Saxon: Studies in the Early British Border* (Cambridge, 1963)

—— 'The Battle of Chester: a study of sources', in N. K. Chadwick, ed., *Celt and Saxon: Studies in the Early British Border* (Cambridge, 1963), pp. 167–85.

Chaney, W. A., *The Cult of Kingship in Anglo-Saxon England: the Transition from Paganism to Christianity* (Manchester, 1970).

Chaplais, P., 'The royal Anglo-Saxon "chancery" of the tenth century revisited', in H. Mayr-Harting and R. I. Moore, ed., *Studies in Medieval History presented to R. H. C. Davis* (London, 1985), pp. 41–51.

Charles-Edwards, T. M., 'Palladius, Prosper, and Leo the Great: mission and primatial authority', in D. N. Dumville *et al.*, *Saint Patrick, AD 493–1993* (Woodbridge, 1993), pp. 1–12.

Cheney, C. R., *Handbook of Dates for Students of English History*, revd edn (London, 1981).

Chibnall, M., *The Empress Matilda, Queen Consort, Queen Mother and Lady of the English* (Oxford, 1991).

Chronicle of Battle Abbey, ed. E. Searle (Oxford, 1980).

Chronicon Monasterii de Abingdon, ed. J. Stevenson, Rolls Series II (London, 1858).

Chronicon Abbatiae Rameseiensis, ed. W. D. Macray, Rolls Series LXXXIII (London, 1886).

Clanchy, M. T., *From Memory to Written Record: England 1066–1307*, 2nd edn (Oxford, 1993).

Clapham, J. H., 'The horsing of the Danes', *English Historical Review* XXV (1910), 287–93.

Clark, C. 'Notes on MS. Laud Misc. 636', *Medium Ævum* XXIII (1954), 71–5.

—— ' "France" and "French" in the Anglo-Saxon Chronicle', *Leeds Studies in English*, New Series III (1969), 35–45.

—— 'This ecclesiastical adventurer: Henry of Saint-Jean d'Angély', *English Historical Review* LXXXIV (1969), 548–60.

—— 'The narrative mode of The Anglo-Saxon Chronicle before the Conquest', in *England before the Conquest: Studies presented to Dorothy Whitelock*, ed. P. Clemoes and K. Hughes (Cambridge, 1971), pp. 215–35.

Clarke, P. A., *The English Nobility under Edward the Confessor* (Oxford, 1994).

Cleasby, R. (revd G. Vigfusson), *An Icelandic-English Dictionary*, 2nd edn with a supplement by W. A. Craigie (Oxford, 1957).

Codex Lindisfarnensis, ed. T. D. Kendrick *et al.* (Oltun and Lausanne, 1956–60).

The Complete Peerage, ed. V. Gibbs *et al.*, revd H. A. Doubleday and H. de Walden (London, 1910–40).

Cooper, J., *The Last Four Anglo-Saxon Archbishops of York* (York, 1970).

Coulson, C., 'The castles of the Anarchy', in E. King, ed., *The Anarchy of King Stephen's Reign* (Oxford, 1994), pp. 67–92.

Councils and Synods, with other documents relating to the English Church, ed. D. Whitelock *et al.* (Oxford, 1981).

Cox, B. H., 'Leicestershire moot-sites: the place-name evidence', *Transactions of the Leicestershire Archaeological and Historical Society* XLVII (1971–2), 14–21.

Cramp, R. J., *Corpus of Anglo-Saxon Sculpture in England* (Oxford, 1984 in progress).

Cronne, H. A., 'The Salisbury oath', *History* XIX (1934–5), 248–52.

Crouch, D., *The Beaumont Twins: the Roots and Branches of Power in the Twelfth Century* (Cambridge, 1986).

Crumlin-Pederson, O., 'The vikings and the Hanseatic merchants', in *A History of Seafaring based on Underwater Archaeology*, ed. G. F. Bass (London, 1972), pp. 181–204.

—— 'Viking shipbuilding and Seamanship', in *Proceedings of the Eighth Viking Congress*, ed. H. Bekker-Nielsen *et al.* (Odense, 1981), pp. 271–86.

Crummy, P., *Aspects of Anglo-Saxon and Norman Colchester* (London, 1981).

Cunliffe, B., *Excavations at Porchester Castle*, II, *Saxon* (London, 1976).

Curwen, E., 'Rackham bank and earthwork', *Sussex Archaeological Collections* LXXIII (1932), 168–86.

Dales, D., *Dunstan, Saint and Statesman* (Cambridge, 1988).

Dalton, P., *Conquest, Anarchy and Lordship: Yorkshire 1066–1154* (Cambridge, 1994).

Darby, H. C., *Domesday England* (Cambridge, 1977).

Darlington, R. R., 'Æthelwig, abbot of Evesham', *English Historical Review* XLVIII (1933), 1–22, 177–98.

Darlington, R. R. and McGurk, P., 'The Chronicon ex Chronicis of Florence of Worcester and its uses of sources for English history before 1066', *Anglo-Norman Studies* V (1982), 185–96.

David, C. W., *David Curthose, Duke of Normandy* (Cambridge, Mass., 1920).

Davis, C. R., 'Cultural assimilation in the Anglo-Saxon royal genealogies', *Anglo-Saxon England* XXI (1992), 23–36.

Davis, H. W. C., 'A contemporary account of the Battle of Tinchebrai', *English Historical Review* XXIV (1909), 728–32; XXV (1910), 295–6.

Davis, R. H. C., 'The monks of St Edmund 1021–1148', *History* XL (1955), 236–9.

—— *King Stephen, 1135–1154* (London, 1967).

—— 'Alfred and Guthrum's frontier', *English Historical Review* XCVII (1982), 803–10.

DB, *Domesday Book*, gen. ed. J. Morris (Chichester, 1975–92). (Cited by section.)

Deanesly, M., *Augustine of Canterbury* (London, 1964).

Demidoff, L., 'The death of Sven Forkbeard – in reality and later tradition', *Mediaeval Scandinavia* XI (1978–9), 30–47.

Dickins, B., 'The Peterborough annal for 1137', *Review of English Studies* II (1926), 341–3.

—— 'The day of Byrhtnoth's death and other obits from a twelfth-century Ely kalendar', *Leeds Studies in English* VI (1937), 14–24.

—— 'The day of the Battle of Æthelingadene', *Leeds Studies in English* VI (1937), 25–7.

—— 'The Cult of S. Olave in the British Isles', *Saga-book of the Viking Society* XII (1937–45), 53–80.

—— 'The late addition to ASC 1066 C', *Proceedings of the Leeds Philosophical and Literary Society* V (1940), 148–9.

Dickinson, W. C., *Scotland from the Earliest Times to 1603* (Edinburgh, 1961).

Dobbie, E. v. K., ed., *The Anglo-Saxon Minor Poems* (New York, 1942).

Dodgson, J. M., *The Place-Names of Cheshire*, English Place-Name Society XLIV-LIV (Cambridge, 1970–81).

Dolley, R. H. M., 'A new Anglo-Saxon mint – Medeshamstede', *The British Numismatic Journal* XXVII (1952–4), 263–5.

—— 'The so-called piedforts of Alfred the Great', *The Numismatic Chronicle*, 6th Series XIV (1954), 76–92.

Domesday Book, ed. J. Morris *et al.* (Chichester, 1975–92). (Cited by section.)

Douglas, D. C. ed., *The Domesday Monachorum of Christ Church Canterbury* (London, 1944).

—— 'Edward the Confessor, Duke William of Normandy, and the English succession', *English Historical Review* LXVIII (1953), 526–45.

Douglas, D. C. and Greenaway, G. W., eds, *English Historical Documents 1042–1189*, 2nd edn (London, 1981).

Driscoll, S. T. and Nieke, M. R., eds, *Power and Politics in Early Medieval Britain and Ireland* (Edinburgh, 1988).

Dumville, D. N., 'Kingship, genealogies and regnal lists', in *Early Medieval Kingship*, ed. P. H. Sawyer and I. N. Wood (Leeds, 1977), pp. 72–104.

—— 'The ætheling: a study in Anglo-Saxon constitutional history', *Anglo-Saxon England* VIII (1979), 1–33.

—— 'The West Saxon genealogical regnal list: manuscripts and texts', *Anglia* CIV (1986), 1–32.

—— 'The West Saxon genealogical regnal list and the chronology of early Wessex', *Peritia* IV (1985), 21–66.

—— ' "Acta Palladii" preserved in Patrician hagiography', in *Saint Patrick*, ed. D. N. Dumville (Woodbridge, 1993), pp. 65–84.

—— *Wessex and England from Alfred to Edgar* (Woodbridge, 1992).

Duncalf, F. and Runciman, S., 'The First Crusade', in K. M. Setton, ed., *A History of the Crusades*, 2nd edn (Madison, Wisconsin, 1969–89), I, pp. 253–341.

Duncan, A. A. M., *Scotland: the Making of the Kingdom* (Edinburgh, 1975).

Eadmer, *Historia Novorum in Anglia*, ed. M. Rule, Rolls Series LXXXI (London, 1884); books i-iv translated by G. Bosanquet as *History of Recent Events in England* (London, 1964).

—— *The Life of St Anselm, Archbishop of Canterbury*, ed. R. W. Southern (London, 1962).

—— *Life of Oswald*, ed. J. Raine, *The Historians of York and its Archbishops*, Rolls Series LXXI (London, 1879–94), II, pp. 1–59.

Eagles, B., 'Lindsey', in *The Origins of Anglo-Saxon Kingdoms*, ed. S. Bassett (Leicester, 1989), pp. 202–12.

Eddius Stephanus, *The Life of Bishop Wilfrid*, ed. B. Colgrave (Cambridge, 1927) (reprinted 1985).

Egils Saga, ed. C. Fell (London, 1975). (Cited by chapter.)

Einarsson, S., 'Two Scandinavisms in the Peterborough Chronicle', *Journal of English and Germanic Philology* XXXVII (1938), 18–20.

Ekwall, E., *The Place-Names of Lancashire* (Manchester, 1922).

Emerson, O. F., 'The crux in the Peterborough Chronicle', *Modern Language Notes* XLI (1926), 170–72.

Encomium Emmae Reginae, ed. A. Campbell, Camden 3rd Series LXXII (London, 1949).

Exeter Archaeology, *South-West Water: Danes Castle, Exeter 1992* (Exeter, forthcoming)

Eyrbyggja Saga, transl. H. Pälsson and P. Edwards, revd edn (Harmondsworth, 1989).

Farmer, D. H., *The Oxford Dictionary of Saints* (Oxford, 1978).

Faulkes, A., 'Descent from the gods,' *Mediaeval Scandinavia* XI (1978–9), 92–125.

Faull, M. L., 'The semantic development of Old English *wealh*', *Leeds Studies in English*, New Series VIII (1975), 20–44.

Finberg, H. R. P., *Tavistock Abbey: a Study in the Social and Economic History of Devon* (Cambridge, 1951).

—— *Early Charters of the West Midlands*, 2nd edn (Leicester, 1972).

Finegan, J., *Handbook of Biblical Chronology: principles of time reckoning in the ancient world* (Princeton, NJ, 1964).

Fisher, D. J. V., 'The anti-monastic reaction in the reign of Edward the Martyr', *Cambridge Historical Journal* X (1950–52), 254–70.

Flasdieck, H. M., 'Harlekin. Germanischer Mythos in romanischer Wandlung', *Anglia* LXI (1937), 225–340; LXVI (1942), 59–69.

Fleming, R., *Kings and Lords in Conquest England* (Cambridge, 1991).

Florence, *Chronicon ex Chronicis*, ed. B. Thorpe (London, 1848–9), transl. J. Stevenson, *The Church Historians of England* (London, 1853–68), II.

Flower, R., 'Laurence Nowell and the discovery of England in Tudor times', *Proceedings of the British Academy* XXI (1936), 47–73.

Freeman, E. A., *The History of the Norman Conquest of England, its Causes and its Results* (Oxford, 1867).

Fryde, E. B. *et al.*, ed., *Handbook of British Chronology*, 3rd edn (London, 1986).

Gaimar, G., *L'Estoire des Engleis*, ed. A. Bell (Oxford, 1960).

Galbert of Bruges, *The Murder of Charles the Good, Count of Flanders*, ed. J. B. Ross (New York, 1960).

Gelling, M., *The Place-Names of Oxfordshire*, English Place-Name Society XXXIII-XXXIV (Cambridge, 1953–4).

—— *The Place-Names of Berkshire*, English Place-Name Society XLIX-LI (Cambridge, 1973–6).

Gelling, M. and Foxall H. D. G., *The Place-Names of Shropshire*, English Place-Name Society LXII-LXIII (Nottingham, 1990).

Gem, R., 'The significance of the 11th-century rebuilding of Christ Church and St Augustine's, Canterbury, in the development of Romanesque architecture', in *Medieval Art and Architecture at Canterbury before 1220*, ed. N. Coldstream and P. Draper (London, 1982), pp. 1–19.

Gerritson, J., 'A ghost-word: crucet-hus', *English Studies* XLII (1961), 300–1.

Gervase of Canterbury, *Historical Works*, ed. W. Stubbs, Rolls Series LXXIII (London, 1879–80).

Gesta Abbatum Monasterii Sancti Albani, ed. H. T. Riley, Rolls Series XXVIII, 4 (London, 1867–9).

Gesta Stephani, ed. K. R. Potter, 2nd edn (Oxford, 1976).

Gibson, M., *Lanfranc of Bec* (Oxford, 1978).

Gillingham, J., 'Thegns and knights in eleventh-century England: Who was then the gentleman?', *Transactions of the Royal Historical Society*, 6th Series V (1995), 129–53.

Gleason, S. E., *An Ecclesiastical Barony of the Middle Ages: the Bishopric of Bayeaux, 1066–1204* (Cambridge, Mass., 1936).

Glover, R., 'English warfare in 1066', *English Historical Review* LXVII (1952), 1–18.

Godfrey, J., *The Church in Anglo-Saxon England* (Cambridge, 1962).

Goulburn E. M. and Symonds, H., *The Life, Letters, and Sermons of Bishop Herbert de Losinga* (Oxford, 1878).

Gover, J. E. B. *et al.*, *The Place-Names of Devon*, English Place-Name Society VIII-IX (Cambridge, 1931–2).

—— *The Place-Names of Northamptonshire*, English Place-Name Society X (Cambridge, 1933).

—— *The Place-Names of Hertfordshire*, English Place-Name Society XV (Cambridge, 1938).

—— *The Place-Names of Wiltshire*, English Place-Name Society XVI (Cambridge, 1939).

—— *The Place-Names of Middlesex*, English Place-Name Society XVIII (Cambridge, 1942).

Gradon, P., review of *The Anglo-Saxon Chronicle*, ed. G. N. Garmonsway, *Medium Ævum* XXV (1956), 98–102.

Green, J., 'The sheriffs of William the Conqueror', *Anglo-Norman Studies* V (1982), 129–45.

—— 'Anglo-Scottish relations, 1066–1174', in *England and her Neighbours, 1066–1453*, ed. M. Jones and M. Vale (London, 1989), pp. 53–72.

Gregory I ('the Great'), *Dialogues*, ed. A. de Vogüé, transl. A. Antin (Paris, 1978–80); Old English translation ascribed to Bishop Wærferth of Worcester, ed. H. Hecht, *Dialogue Gregors des Grossen* (Leipzig, 1900).

—— *King Alfred's West-Saxon Version of Gregory's Cura Pastoralis*, ed. H. Sweet, Early English Text Society, Original Series XLV, L (London, 1871).

The Earliest Life of Gregory the Great, ed. B. Colgrave (Lawrence, Kansas, 1968).

Grierson, P., 'A visit of Earl Harold to Flanders in 1056', *English Historical Review* LI (1936), 90–97.

—— 'The relations between England and Flanders before the Norman Conquest', *Transactions of the Royal Historical Society*, 4th Series XXIII (1941), 71–112; reprinted in *Essays in Medieval History*, ed. R. W. Southern (London, 1968), pp. 61–92.

Griffiths, B. M., 'Early references to waterbloom in British lakes', *Proceedings of The Linnean Society of London* CLI (1938–9), 12–19.

Haddan, A. W. and Stubbs, W., eds, *Councils and Ecclesiastical Documents relating to Great Britain and Ireland* (Oxford, 1869–71).

Hardy, T. D., *Descriptive Catalogue of Materials relating to the History of Great Britain and Ireland*, Rolls Series XXVI (London, 1862).

Harmer, F. E., *Select English Historical Documents of the Ninth and Tenth Centuries* (Cambridge, 1914).

—— *Anglo-Saxon Writs* (Manchester, 1952).

Harrison, K., *The Framework of Anglo-Saxon History* (Cambridge, 1976).

Hart, C. R., *The Early Charters of Eastern England* (Leicester, 1966).

—— 'Athelstan "Half King" and his family', *Anglo-Saxon England* II (1973), 115–44; reprinted in *The Danelaw* (London, 1992), pp. 569–604.

—— *The Early Charters of Northern England and the North Midlands* (Leicester, 1975).

—— 'The ealdordom of Essex', in *An Essex Tribute: Essays presented to Frederick G. Emmison*, ed. K. Neale (Chelmsford, 1987), pp. 57–84; reprinted in *The Danelaw* (London, 1992), pp. 115–40.

Haslam, J., ed., *Anglo-Saxon Towns in Southern England* (Chichester, 1984).

Hassall J. M. and Hill, D., 'Pont del'Arche: Frankish influence on the West Saxon burh?', *Archaeological Journal* CXXVII (1970), 188–95.

Haverkamp, A., *Medieval Germany 1056–1273*, 2nd edn (Oxford, 1992).

Hawkes, C. F. C. 'The Jutes of Kent', in *Dark Age Britain*, ed. D. B. Harden (London, 1956), pp. 91–111.

Henry, Archdeacon of Huntingdon, *History of the English*, ed. T. Arnold, Rolls Series LXXIV (London, 1879).

Higham, N. J., *An English Empire: Bede and the Early Anglo-Saxon Kings* (Manchester, 1995).

Higham, R. and Barber, P., *Timber Castles* (London, 1992).

Hill, D., 'The Burghal Hidage – Lyng', *Proceedings of the Somerset Archaeological and Natural History Society* CXI (1967), 64–6.

—— *Ethelred the Unready: Papers from the Millenary Conference* (Oxford, 1978).

—— *An Atlas of Anglo-Saxon England* (Oxford, 1981).

Hill, J. W. F., *Medieval Lincoln* (Cambridge, 1948).

Hill, T. D., 'The myth of the Ark-born son of Noe and the West-Saxon royal genealogical tables', *Harvard Theological Review* LXXX (1987), 379–83.

Historia et Cartularium Monasterii Sancti Petri Gloucestri, ed. W. H. Hart, Rolls Series XXXIII (London, 1863–5).

Historians of the Church of York and its Archbishops, ed. J. Raine, Rolls Series LXXI (London, 1879–94).

Ho Pen Yoke, 'Ancient and Medieval observations of comets and novae in Chinese sources', *Vistas in Astronomy* V (1962), 127–225.

Hollister, C. W., *Anglo-Saxon Military Institutions on the Eve of the Norman Conquest* (Oxford, 1962).

—— 'The strange death of William Rufus', *Speculum* XLVIII (1973), 687–53.

—— 'Royal acts of mutilation: the case against Henry I', *Albion* X (1978), 330–40; reprinted in *Monarchy, Magnates and Institutions in the Anglo-Norman World* (London, 1986), pp. 291–301.

—— 'William Rufus, Henry I, and the Anglo-Norman Church', *Peritia* VI-VII (1987–8), 119–40.

Holt, J. C., '1086', in *Domesday Studies*, ed. J. C. Holt (Woodbridge, 1987), pp. 41–64.

Hooke, D., *The Anglo-Saxon Landscape: the Kingdom of the Hwicce* (Manchester, 1985).

Hooper, N., 'The housecarls in England in the eleventh century', *Anglo-Norman Studies* VII (1984), 161–76.

Hope, W. St J., 'Recent discoveries in the abbey church of St Austin at Canterbury', *Archaeologia* LXVI (1914–15), 377–400.

Hope-Taylor, B., 'Old Windsor', in D. M. Wilson and J. G. Hurst, eds, 'Medieval Britain in 1957', *Medieval Archaeology* II (1959), 183–213 (183–5).

Horden P., 'Disease, dragons and saints: the management of epidemics in the Dark Ages', in T. Ranger and P. Slack, eds, *Epidemics and Ideas: Essays on the historical perception of Pestilence* (Cambridge, 1992), pp. 45–76.

Horsman, V. *et al.*, Aspects of Saxo-Norman London (London, 1988–92).

Hoskins, W. G., *The Westward Expansion of Wessex* (Leicester, 1960).

Hoskins W. G. and Finberg, H. P. R., *Devonshire Studies* (London, 1952).

Howorth, H. H., 'The Anglo-Saxon Chronicle, its origin and history', *Archaeological Journal* LXV (1908), 141–204; LXVI (1909), 105–44.

Hugh Candidus, *The Chronicle of a Monk of Peterborough*, ed. W. T. Mellows (Oxford, 1949).

Hugh the Chanter, *The History of the Church of York, 1066–1127,* ed. C. Johnson, revd M. Brett *et al.* (Oxford, 1990).

Hughes, M. W., 'Grimsditch and Cuthwulf's expedition to the Chilterns in AD 571', *Antiquity* V (1931), 291–314.

Hunt, J., 'Piety, prestige or politics? The house of Leofric and the foundation and patronage of Coventry priory', in G. Demidowicz, *Coventry's First Cathedral* (Stamford, 1994), pp. 97–117.

Isaacs, N. D., 'The death of Edgar (and others)', *American Notes and Queries* IV (1965), 52–5; reprinted in *Structural Principles in Old English Poetry* (Knoxville, Tenn., 1968), pp. 89–93.

Isidore, *Etymologiarum sive Originum*, ed. W. M. Lindsay (Oxford, 1911). (Cited by book and chapter.)

James, M. R., 'Two Lives of St Ethelbert, King and Martyr', *English Historical Review* XXXII (1917), 214–44.

John of Peterborough, *Chronicle*, ed. J. A. Giles (London, 1845).

John, E., 'The world of Abbot Ælfric', in *Ideal and Reality in Frankish and Anglo-Saxon Society*, ed. P. Wormald *et al.* (Oxford, 1983), pp. 300–16.

Jones, C. W., *Saints' Lives and Chronicles in Early England* (Ithaca, NY., 1947).

Jones, W. H. R., ed., *The Register of S. Osmund*, Rolls Series LXXVIII (London, 1883–4).

Jost, K., 'Wulfstan und die angelsächsische Chronik', *Anglia* LXVII (1923), 105–23.

Kapelle, W. E., *The Norman Conquest of the North: the Region and its Transformation, 1000–1135* (London, 1979).

Kelly, S. E., ed., *Charters of Shaftesbury Abbey* (Oxford, 1995).

Kemble, J. M., ed., *Codex Diplomaticus Aevi Saxonici* (London, 1839–48).

Ker, N. R., 'Some notes on the Peterborough Chronicle', *Medium Ævum* III (1934), 136–8.

—— *Catalogue of Manuscripts containing Anglo-Saxon*, 2nd edn (Oxford, 1990).

Kershaw, N., *Anglo-Saxon and Norse Poems* (Cambridge, 1922).

Keynes, S., 'The æthelings in Normandy', *Anglo-Norman Studies* XIII (1991), 173–206.

Keyser, J. R. and Munch, P. A., *Norges Gamle Love indtil 1837* (Christiania, 1846–95).

King, E., *Peterborough Abbey 1086–1310, a Study in the Land Market* (Cambridge, 1973).

—— ed., *The Anarchy of King Stephen's Reign* (Oxford, 1994).

Kirby, D. P. 'Strathclyde and Cumbria: a survey of historical development to 1092', *Transactions of The Cumberland and Westmorland Antiquarian and Archaeological Society* NS LXII (1962), 77–94.

—— *The Earliest English Kings* (London, 1991).

Knowles, D., *et al.*, *The Heads of Religious Houses, England and Wales, 940–1216* (Cambridge, 1972).

Kökeritz, H., *The Place-Names of the Isle of Wight* (Uppsala, 1940).

Lanfranc, *The Letters of Lanfranc, Archbishop of Canterbury*, ed. H. Clover and M. Gibson (Oxford, 1979).

Larson, L. M., *The King's Household in England before the Norman Conquest* (Madison, Wisconsin, 1904).

Lawson, M. K., 'The collection of Danegeld and Heregeld in the reigns of Aethelred II and Cnut', *English Historical Review* XCIX (1984), 721–38.

Le Patourel, J. H., 'Geoffrey of Montbray, bishop of Coutances, 1049–1093', *English Historical Review* LIX (1944), 129–61.

—— *The Norman Empire* (Oxford, 1976).

Lebecq, S., 'On the use of the word "Frisian" in the 6th-10th centuries written sources: some interpretations', in *Maritime Celts, Frisians and Saxons*, ed. S. McGrail (London, 1990), pp. 85–90.

Leechdoms, Wortcunning, and Starcraft of Early England, ed. O. Cockayne, Rolls Series XXXV (London, 1864–6).

Leeds, E. T., 'The West Saxon invasion and the Icknield Way', *History* X (1925), 97–109.

Leges Henrici Primi, ed. L. J. Downer (Oxford, 1972).

Lennard, R., *Rural England 1086–1135* (Oxford, 1959).

The Leofric Missal, ed. F. E. Warren (Oxford, 1883).

Levison, W., *England and the Continent in the Eighth Century* (Oxford, 1946).

Leyser, K., 'England and the Empire in the early twelfth century', *Transactions of the Royal Historical Society*, 5th Series X (1960), 61–83.

Liber Historiae Francorum, ed. B. Krusch, *Monumenta Germaniae Historica, Scriptores Rerum Merovingicarum*, 2 (Hanover, 1888), pp. 215–328; transl. B. S. Bachrach (Lawrence, Kansas, 1973).

Liber Pontificalis, transl. R. Davis, *The Book of Pontiffs* (Liverpool, 1989).

Liber Vitae: Register and Martyrology of New Minster and Hyde Abbey, Winchester, ed. W. de G. Birch (London, 1892).

Liebermann, F., *Ungedruckte anglo-normannische Geschichtsquellen* (Strassburg, 1879).

—— *Die Gesetze der Angelsachsen* (Halle, 1903–16).

Lloyd, J. E., *A History of Wales*, 3rd edn (London, 1939).

Llywarch Hen, *The Poetry of*, ed. P. K. Ford (Berkeley, California, 1974).

Logan, F. D., *The Vikings in History*, 2nd edn (London, 1991).

Lowe, K. A., 'Never say *nefa* again: problems of translation in Old English charters', *Neuphilologische Mitteilungen* XCIV (1993), 27–35.

Loyd, L. C., *The Origins of some Anglo-Norman Families* (Leeds, 1951).

Loyn, H. R., 'The term ealdorman in the translations prepared at the time of King Alfred', *English Historical Review* LXVIII (1953), 513–25.

—— 'Gesiths and thegns in Anglo-Saxon England from the seventh to the tenth century', *English Historical Review* LXX (1955), 529–49.

—— *The Governance of Anglo-Saxon England, 500–1087* (London, 1984).

Lund, N., 'King Edgar and the Danelaw', *Mediaeval Scandinavia* IX (1976), 181–95.

—— 'The armies of Swein Forkbeard and Cnut: *leding* or *lið*?', *Anglo-Saxon England* XV (1986), 105–18.

Lunt, W. E., *Financial Relations of the Papacy with England to 1327* (Cambridge, Mass., 1939).

Lyon, C. S. S. and Stewart, B. H. I. H., 'The Northumbrian viking coins in the Cuerdale hoard', in *Anglo-Saxon Coins*, ed. R. H. M. Dolley (London, 1961), pp. 96–121.

Mackinlay, J. B., *Saint Edmund, King and Martyr* (London, 1893).

Mackreth, D., 'Recent work on monastic Peterborough', *Durobrivae* IX (1984), 18–21.

Macquarie, A., 'The kings of Strathclyde, *c.* 400–1018', in *Medieval Scotland: Crown, Lordship and Community; Essays presented to G. W. S. Barrow*, eds, A. Grant and K. J. Stringer (Edinburgh, 1993), pp. 1–19.

Magoun, F. P., 'Two lexicographical notes', *Modern Language Notes* XL (1925) 408–12.

—— 'Cynewulf, Cyneheard, and Osric', *Anglia* LVII (1933), 361–76.

—— 'Aldhelm's diocese of Sherborne *bewestan wuda*', *Harvard Theological Review* XXXII (1939), 103–14.

—— 'King Alfred's naval and beach battle with the Danes in 896', *Modern Language Review* XXXVII (1942), 409–14.

—— 'An English pilgrim-diary of the year 990', *Mediaeval Studies* II (1940), 231–52.

—— 'The Rome of two northern pilgrims: Archbishop Sigeric of Canterbury and Abbot Nikolás of Munkathverá', *Harvard Theological Review* XXXIII (1940), 267–89.

—— 'The Domitian Bilingual of the Old-English Annals: Notes on the F-text', *Modern Language Quarterly* VI (1945), 371–80.

—— 'On the Old-Germanic altar- or oath-ring (Stallahringr)', *Acta Philologica Scandinavica* XX (1947–9), 277–93.

Mansi, J. D. *et al.*, *Sacrorum Conciliarum nova, et amplissima collectio* (Florence, Leipzig etc., 1759–1962).

Margan Annals, ed. H. R. Luard, in *Annales Monastici*, Rolls Series XXXVI (London, 1864–9), I, pp. 1–40.

Mason, J. F. A., 'Roger de Montgomery and his sons (1067–1102)', *Transactions of the Royal Historical Society*, 5th Series XI (1963), 1–28.

Matthew, D., *The Norman Monasteries and their English Possessions* (Oxford, 1962).

Matthew Paris, *Historia Anglorum*, ed. R. Madden, Rolls Series XLIV (London, 1866–9).

Mawer, A., 'The Redemption of the Five Boroughs', *English Historical Review* XXXVIII (1923), 551–7.

Mawer, A. and Stenton, F. M., *The Place-Names of Buckinghamshire*, English Place-Name Society II (Cambridge, 1925).

—— *The Place-Names of Bedfordshire and Huntingdonshire*, English Place-Name Society III (Cambridge, 1926).

—— *The Place-Names of Sussex*, English Place-Name Society VI-VII (Cambridge, 1929–30).

Maxfield, V., ed., *The Saxon Shore: a Handbook* (Exeter, 1989).

McDougal, I., 'Serious entertainments: an examination of a peculiar type of Viking atrocity', *Anglo-Saxon England* XXII (1993), 201–25.

McGrail, S., ed., *Maritime Celts, Frisians and Saxons* (London, 1990).

McKitterick, R., *The Frankish Kingdoms under the Carolingians, 751–987* (London, 1983).

—— *The Carolingians and the Written Word* (Cambridge, 1989).

Middle English Dictionary, ed. H. Kurath *et al.* (Ann Arbor, Michigan, 1954 in progress).

Miller, E. *The Abbey and Bishopric of Ely* (Cambridge, 1951).

Mills, A. D., *The Place-Names of Dorset*, English Place-Name Society LII-III (Nottingham, 1977–80).

Moisl, H., 'Anglo-Saxon royal genealogies and Germanic oral tradition', *Journal of Medieval History* VII (1981), 215–48.

Monumenta Germaniae Historica, Epistolae Merowingici et Karolini Aevi, ed. E. Duemmler (Berlin, 1895–9).

Moore, W. J., *The Saxon Pilgrims to Rome and the Schola Saxonum* (Fribourg, 1937).

Morris, M., *Medieval Manchester* (Manchester, 1983).

Morris, W. A. 'The office of sheriff in the early Norman period', *English Historical Review* XXXIII (1918), 145–75; reprinted as 'The baronial shrievality, 1066–1100' in *The Medieval English Sheriff to 1300* (Manchester, 1927), pp. 41–74.

Myres, J. N. L., *The English Settlements* (Oxford, 1986).

Needham, G. I., *Ælfric: Lives of Three English Saints* (Exeter, 1976).

Nelson, J. L., 'The problem of King Alfred's royal anointing', *Journal of Ecclesiastical History* XVIII (1967), 145–63.

—— 'Inauguration rituals', in *Early Medieval Kingship*, ed. P. H. Sawyer and I. N. Wood (Leeds, 1977), pp. 50–71.

Nennius, *British History and The Welsh Annals*, ed. J. Morris (London, 1980).

Nicholl, D., *Thurstan, Archbishop of York (1114–1140)* (York, 1964).

Nightingale, P., 'The origin of the Court of Hustings and Danish influence on London's development into a capital city', *English Historical Review* CII (1987), 559–78.

North, J. J., *English Hammered Coinage*, 2nd edn (London, 1979–80).

O'Donovan, M. A., ed., *Charters of Sherborne* (Oxford, 1988).

Offler, H. S., 'William of St Calais, first Norman bishop of Durham', *Transactions of the Architectural and Archaeological Society of Durham and Northumberland* X (1950), 258–79.

The Old English Martyrology, ed. G. Herzfeld, Early English Text Society, Original Series CXVI (London, 1900).

Oleson, T. J., 'Edward the Confessor's promise of the throne to Duke William of Normandy', *English Historical Review* LXXII (1957), 221–8.

Oman, C., *The Gloucester Candlestick* (London, 1958).

Onions, C. T. 'Some early Middle-English spellings', *Modern Language Review* IV (1908–9), 505–7.

Ordericus Vitalis, *The Ecclesiastical History of Orderic Vitalis*, ed. M. Chibnall (Oxford, 1969–80).

—— *The Gesta Normannorum Ducum of William of Jumièges, Orderic Vitalis and Robert of Torigni*, ed. E. M. C. van Houts (Oxford, 1992–5).

Origines Islandicae, ed. G. Vigfusson and F. Y. Powell (Oxford, 1905).

Orosius, *The Old English Orosius*, ed. J. Bately, Early English Text Society, Supplementary Series VI (London, 1980).

Osbern of Canterbury, *Life of St Alphege, Patrologia Latina* CXLIX, cols. 371–94.

Parkes, M. B., 'The palaeography of the Parker manuscript of the Chronicle, laws and Sedulius, and historiography at Winchester in the late ninth and tenth centuries', *Anglo-Saxon England* V (1976), 149–71.

Patterson, R. B., 'William of Malmesbury's Robert of Gloucester: a reevaluation of the Historia Novella', *American Historical Review* LXX (1964–5), 983–97.

Pearson, M. P. *et al.*, 'Three men and a boat: Sutton Hoo and the East Saxon kingdom', *Anglo-Saxon England* XXII (1993), 27–50.

Peregrinationes Tres: Saewulf, John of Würzburg, Theodericus, ed. R. B. C. Huygens (Tournhout, 1994).

Peter the Venerable, *Letters*, ed. G. Constable (Cambridge, Mass., 1967).

Pickering, F. P., *The Calendar Pages of Medieval Service Books* (Reading, 1980).

PL, Patrologia Cursus Completus, Series Latina, ed. J. P. Migne (Paris, 1878–90).

Pliny, *Natural History*, ed. H. Rackham (London, 1938).

Poole, R. L., 'The beginning of the year in the Anglo-Saxon Chronicles', *English Historical Review* XVI (1901), 719–21.

—— *Medieval Reckonings of Time* (London, 1918).

—— *Studies in Chronology and History* (Oxford, 1934).

Porges, W., 'The clergy, the poor, and the non-combatants on the First Crusade', *Speculum* XXI (1946), 1–23.

Pretty, K., 'Defining the Magonsæte', in *The Origins of Anglo-Saxon Kingdoms*, ed. S. Bassett (Leicester, 1989), pp. 171–83.

Priscianus, *Institutiones Grammaticae*, ed. M. Hertz, in H. Keil, *Grammatici Latini* (Leipzig, 1855–1923), II-III.

Procopius, *History of the Wars*, ed. H. B. Dewing (London, 1916).

Rahtz, P., *The Saxon and Medieval Palaces at Cheddar, Excavations 1960–62* (Oxford, 1979).

Ralph de Diceto, *The Historical Works of Master Ralph de Diceto*, ed. W. Stubbs, Rolls Series LXVIII (London, 1876).

Ramsay, N. *et al.*, ed., *St Dunstan, His Life, Times and Cult* (Woodbridge, 1992).

RCHM, Royal Commission on Historic Monuments (England), (Wales), formerly Royal Commission on Ancient and Historic Monuments; issuing county inventories, in progress.

RCHM, 'Wareham west walls', *Medieval Archaeology* III (1959), 120–38.

Reaney, P. H., *The Place-Names of Essex*, English Place-Name Society XII (Cambridge, 1935).

—— *The Place-Names of Cambridgeshire and The Isle of Ely*, English Place-Name Society XIX (Cambridge, 1943).

Reynolds, S., 'Eadric silvaticus and the English resistance', *Bulletin of the Institute of Historical Research* LIV (1981), 102–5.

Richard of Hexham, *De Gestis Regis Stephani* in *Chronicles of the Reigns of*

Stephen, Henry II and Richard I, ed. R. Howlett, Rolls Series LXXXII (London 1884–9), III, pp. 139–78.

Richardson, H. G., 'The coronation in medieval England: the evolution of the office and the oath', *Traditio* XVI (1960), 111–202.

Ridyard, S. J., *The Royal Saints of Anglo-Saxon England: a Study of West Saxon and East Anglian Cults* (Cambridge, 1988).

Ritchie, R. L. G., *The Normans in Scotland* (Edinburgh, 1954).

Robertson, A. J., *The Laws of the Kings of England from Edmund to Henry I* (Cambridge, 1925).

Robinson, J. A., *Gilbert Crispin, Abbot of Westminster: a study of the Abbey under Norman Rule* (Cambridge, 1911).

Roger of Wendover, *Chronica, sive Flores Historiarum*, ed. H. O. Coxe (London, 1841–2).

Rollason, D. W., *The Mildrith Legend: a Study in Early Medieval Hagiography in England* (Leicester, 1982).

—— *Saints and Relics in Anglo-Saxon England* (Oxford, 1989).

Roth, C., 'The Feast of Purim and the origins of the blood accusation', *Speculum* VIII (1933), 520–26.

Round, J. H., *Geoffrey de Mandeville: a Study of the Anarchy* (London, 1892).

—— 'The counts of Boulogne as English lords', *Studies in Peerage and Family History* (1901), 147–80.

Rumble, A., ' "Hrepingas" reconsidered', in *Mercian Studies*, ed. A. Dornier (Leicester, 1977), pp. 169–72.

—— ed., *The Reign of Cnut: King of England, Denmark and Norway* (Leicester, 1994).

Runciman, S., *A History of the Crusades* (Cambridge, 1951–4).

Russell, J. C., 'The earlier medieval plague in the British Isles', *Viator* VII (1976), 65–78.

Ryan, J. S., 'Othin in England', *Folklore* LXXIV (1963), 460–80.

Saga of the Jomsvikings, ed. N. F. Blake (London, 1962).

Saltman, A., *Theobald, Archbishop of Canterbury* (London, 1956).

Salway, P., *Roman Britain* (Oxford, 1981).

Sawyer, B. and P., *Medieval Scandinavia from Conversion to Reformation, c. 800–1500* (London, 1993).

Sawyer, P. H., *Anglo-Saxon Charters: An Annotated List and Bibliography* (London, 1968).

—— ed., *Charters of Burton Abbey* (London, 1979).

Sawyer, P. *et al.*, 'The royal tun in pre-Conquest England', in *Ideal and Reality in Frankish and Anglo-Saxon Society*, ed. P. Wormald *et al.* (Oxford, 1983), pp. 273–99.

Saxo Grammaticus, *Gesta Danorum*, ed. M. C. Gertz, *Scriptores Historiae Danicae Minores, Medii Ævi* (Copenhagen, 1917–20), I, pp. 195–439.

Scott, F. S., 'Earl Waltheof of Northumbria', *Archaeologia Aeliana*, 4th Series XXX (1952), 149–215.

Scragg, D. G., ed., *The Battle of Maldon* (Manchester, 1981).

—— ed., *The Battle of Maldon* (Oxford, 1991).

Searle, W. G., *Onomasticon Anglo-Saxiconicum: a List of Anglo-Saxon Proper Names from the time of Beda to that of King John* (Cambridge, 1897).

Shippey, T. A., 'A missing army: some doubts about the Alfredian Chronicle', *In Geardagum* IV (1982), 41–55.

Shoesmith, R., *Hereford City Excavations, II: Excavations on and close to the Defences* (London, 1982).

Simeon (Symeon) of Durham, *Opera Omnia*, ed. T. Arnold, Rolls Series LXXV (London, 1882–5).

Sisam, C., 'Notes on Middle English texts', *Review of English Studies* New Series XIII (1962), 385–90.

Sisam, K., 'MSS. Bodley 340 and 342: Ælfric's Catholic Homilies', *Review of English Studies* VII (1931), 7–22.

—— 'Anglo-Saxon royal genealogies', *Proceedings of the British Academy* XXXIX (1953), 287–348;

Smalley, B., 'Gilbert Universalis, bishop of London (1128–34), and the problem of the "Glossa Ordinaria" ', *Recherches de Théologie Ancienne et Médiévale* VII (1935), 235–62; VIII (1936), 24–60.

Smith, A., 'Lucius of Britain: alleged king and church founder', *Folklore* XC (1979), 29–36.

Smith, A. H., 'The site of the Battle of Brunanburh', *London Mediæval Studies* I (1937), 56–9.

—— *The Place-Names of the East Riding of Yorkshire and York*, English Place-Name Society XIV (Cambridge, 1937).

—— *English Place-Name Elements*, English Place-Name Society XXV-XXVI (Cambridge, 1956).

—— *The Place-Names of the West Riding of Yorkshire*, English Place-Name Society XXXI-XXVII (Cambridge, 1961–3).

—— *The Place-Names of Gloucestershire*, English Place-Name Society XXXVIII-XLI (Cambridge, 1964–5).

—— 'The Hwicce', in *Medieval and Linguistic Studies in Honor of Francis Peabody Magoun, Jr.*, ed. J. B. Bessinger and R. P. Creed (London, 1965), pp. 56–65.

Smyth, A. P., *Scandinavian Kings in the British Isles 850–880* (Oxford, 1977).

—— *Warlords and Holy Men, Scotland AD 80–1000* (London, 1984).

—— *Scandinavian York and Dublin* (Dublin, 1987).

—— *King Alfred the Great* (Oxford, 1995).

Snorri Sturluson, *Heimskringla*, ed. F. Jónsson (Copenhagen, 1900–1); transl. S. Laing, revd J. Simpson, *Heimskringla: the Olaf Sagas* (London, 1964).

Song of Roland, transl. H. S. Robertson (London, 1972).

Southern, R. W., 'Rannulf Flambard and the early Anglo-Norman administration', *Transactions of the Royal Historical Society*, 4th Series XVI (1933), 95–128.

—— 'St Anselm and Gilbert Crispin, abbot of Westminster', *Mediaeval and Renaissance Studies* III, 78–115.

—— 'The Canterbury Forgeries', *English Historical Review* LXXIII (1958), 193–226.

—— 'The place of Henry I in English history', *Proceedings of the British Academy* XLVIII (1962), 127–69.

Southern R. W. and Schmitt, F. S., eds, *Memorials of St Anselm* (London, 1969).

Sprockel, C., *The Language of the Parker Chronicle* (The Hague, 1965).

Spurrell, F. C. J., 'Hæsten's camps at Shoebury and Benfleet, Essex,' *Essex Naturalist* IV (1890), 150–57.

Stafford, P. A., 'The "farm of one night" and the organisation of King Edward's estates in Domesday', *Economic History Review*, 2nd Series XXXIII (1980), 491–502.

—— *Unification and Conquest: a Political and Social History of England in the Tenth and Eleventh Centuries* (London, 1989).

Stancliffe, C., 'Kings who opted out', in *Ideal and Reality in Frankish and Anglo-Saxon Society*, ed. P. Wormald *et al.* (Oxford, 1983), pp. 155–76.

—— 'Where was Oswald killed?', in *Oswald: Northumbrian King to European Saint*, ed. C. Stancliffe and E. Cambridge (Stamford, 1995), pp. 84–96.

Stenton, D. M., 'Roger of Salisbury, Regni Angliae Procurator', *English Historical Review* XXXIX (1924), 79–80.

—— *English Justice between the Norman Conquest and the Great Charter, 1066–1215* (London, 1965).

Stenton, F. M., 'Æthelweard's account of the last years of King Alfred's reign', *English Historical Review* XXIV (1909), 79–84; reprinted in *Preparatory to Anglo-Saxon England*, pp. 8–13.

—— 'The Danes at Thorney Island in 893', *English Historical Review* XXVII (1912), 512–13; reprinted in *Preparatory to Anglo-Saxon England*, pp. 14–15.

—— 'The south-western element in the Old English Chronicle', in *Essays in Medieval History presented to Thomas Frederick Tout* (Manchester,

1925), pp. 15–24; reprinted in *Preparatory to Anglo-Saxon England*, pp. 106–15.

—— 'Lindsey and its kings', in *Essays in History presented to Reginald Lane Poole,* ed. H. W. C. Davies (Oxford, 1927), pp. 136–50; reprinted in *Preparatory to Anglo-Saxon England*, pp. 127–35.

—— 'Medeshamstede and its colonies', in *Historical Essays in Honour of James Tait,* ed. J. G. Edwards *et al.* (Manchester, 1933), pp. 313–26; reprinted in *Preparatory to Anglo-Saxon England*, pp. 179–92.

—— 'The historical bearing of place-name studies: the English occupation of southern Britain', *Transactions of the Royal Historical Society*, 4th Series XXII (1940), 1–22; reprinted in *Preparatory to Anglo-Saxon England*, pp. 266–80.

—— *The Latin Charters of the Anglo Saxon Period* (Oxford, 1955).

—— *The First Century of English Feudalism, 1066–1166,* 2nd edn (Oxford, 1961).

—— *Preparatory to Anglo-Saxon England, being the collected papers of Frank Merry Stenton,* ed. D. M. Stenton (Oxford, 1970).

—— *Anglo-Saxon England,* 3rd edn (Oxford, 1971).

Stevenson, F. S., 'St Botolph (Botwulf) and Iken', *Proceedings of the Suffolk Institute of Archaeology* XVIII (1924), 29–52.

Stevenson, W. H., 'A contemporary description of the Domesday survey', *English Historical Review* XXII (1907), 72–84.

Stroll, M., *The Jewish Pope* (Leiden, 1978).

Suger, *Abbot Suger on the Abbey Church of St-Denis and its Art Treasures,* ed. E. Panofsky, 2nd edn (Princeton, New Jersey, 1979).

—— *The Deeds of Louis the Fat,* ed. R. Cusimano and J. Moorhead (Washington DC, 1992).

Swanton, M. J., 'Finglesham Man; a documentary post-script', *Antiquity* XLVIII (1974), 313–15.

—— 'A fragmentary life of St Mildred and other Kentish royal saints', *Archaeologia Cantiana* XCI (1976), 15–27.

—— *Crisis and Development in Germanic Society 700–800* (Göppingen, 1982).

—— *English Literature Before Chaucer* (London, 1987).

—— *Anglo-Saxon Prose,* 2nd edn (London, 1993).

—— *The Dream of the Rood,* revd edn (Exeter, 1996).

—— *Hereward and Others* (London, forthcoming).

Sweet, H., 'Some of the sources of the Anglo-Saxon Chronicle', *Englische Studien* II (1879), 310–12.

Sweet, H., ed., *The Oldest English Texts,* Early English Text Society, Original Series LXXXIII (London, 1885).

Tacitus, *Agricola*, ed. M. Hutton, revd R. M. Ogilvie (London, 1970).

——— *Germania,* ed. M. Hutton, revd E. H. Warmington (London, 1970).

Taylor, H. M., 'Repton reconsidered: a study in structural criticism', in *England before the Conquest: Studies in primary sources presented to Dorothy Whitelock*, ed. P. Clemoes and K. Hughes (Cambridge, 1971), pp. 351–89.

Taylor, H. M. and J., *Anglo-Saxon Architecture* (Cambridge, 1965–78).

Tengvik, G., *Old English Bynames* (Uppsala, 1938).

Textus Roffensis, ed. P. Sawyer, Early English Manuscripts in Facsimile I, VII, XI (Copenhagen, 1957–62).

Thacker, A. T., 'Some terms for noblemen in Anglo-Saxon England *c.* 650–900', *Anglo-Saxon Studies in Archaeology and History* II (1981), 201–36.

——— 'Membra disjecta', in *Oswald: Northumbrian King to European Saint*, ed. C. Stancliffe and E. Cambridge (Stamford, 1995), pp. 97–127.

Theodericus, *De Locis Sanctis*, in R. B. C. Huygens, ed., *Peregrinationes Tres* (Tournhout, 1994), pp. 143–97.

Thomas of Monmouth, *The Life and Miracles of St William of Norwich*, ed. A. Jessopp and M. R. James (Cambridge, 1896).

Tolkien, J. R. R., *Finn and Hengest: the Fragment and the Episode*, ed. A. Bliss (London, 1982).

Towers, T. H., 'Thematic unity in the story of Cynewulf and Cyneheard', *Journal of English and Germanic Philology* LXII (1963), 310–16.

Vanderkindere, L., 'L'abbé Womar de Saint-Pierre de Gand', *Bulletin de la Commission Royale d'Histoire de Belgique* 5th Series VIII (1898), 296–304.

Vaughan, R., 'The chronology of the Parker Chronicle, 890–970', *English Historical Review* LXIX (1954), 59–66.

VCH, The Victoria County History (London, 1900, in progress).

Wainwright, F.T., 'The chronology of the Mercian Register', *English Historical Review* LX (1945), 385–92.

——— 'Cledemutha', *English Historical Review* LXV (1950), 203–12.

——— 'The submission to Edward the Elder', *History* New Series XXVII (1952), 114–30; reprinted in *Scandinavian England* (Chichester, 1975), pp. 325–44.

——— *The Problem of the Picts* (London, 1955).

——— 'Æthelflæd Lady of the Mercians', in *The Anglo-Saxons: Studies in some aspects of their history and Culture, presented to Bruce Dickins*, ed. P. Clemoes (London, 1959), pp. 53–69; reprinted in *Scandinavian England* (Chichester, 1975), pp. 305–24, and in *New Readings on Women in Old*

English Literature, ed. H. Damico and A. H. Olsen (Bloomington, Indiana, 1990), pp. 44–55.

Wallenberg, J. K., *Kentish Place-Names: a Topographical and Etymological Study of the Place-Name Material in Kentish Charters dated before the Conquest* (Uppsala, 1931).

Ward, S. W. *et al.*, Excavations at Chester: Saxon Occupation within the Roman Fortress (Chester, 1994).

Waterhouse, R., 'The theme and structure of 755 Anglo-Saxon Chronicle', *Neuphilologische Mitteilungen* LXX (1969), 630–40.

Waverly Annals, ed., H. R. Luard, in *Annales Monastici*, Rolls Series XXXVI (2) (London, 1864–9), II, pp. 127–411.

West, F., *The Justiciarship in England, 1066–1232* (Cambridge, 1966).

Wheeler, G. H., 'Gildas de Excidio Britanniae, Chapter 26', *English Historical Review* XLI (1926), 497–503.

Whitbread, L., 'Æthelweard and the Anglo-Saxon Chronicle', *English Historical Review* LXXIV (1959), 577–89.

White, G. H., 'The career of Waleran, count of Meulan and earl of Worcester (1104–1166)', *Transactions of the Royal Historical Society*, 4th Series XVII (1934), 19–48.

—— 'The first house of Bellême', *Transactions of the Royal Historical Society*, 4th Series XXII (1940), 67–99.

White, S. D., 'Kingship and lordship in early medieval England: the story of Cynewulf and Cyneheard', *Viator* XX (1989), 1–18.

Whitelock, D., 'A note on the career of Wulfstan the homilist', *English Historical Review* LII (1937), 460–66.

—— 'Scandinavian Personal Names in the Liber Vitae of Thorney Abbey', *Saga-Book of the Viking Society* XII (1937–45), 127–53.

—— 'Archbishop Wulfstan, homilist and statesman', *Transactions of the Royal Historical Society*, 4th Series XXIV (1942), 42–60.

—— 'Wulfstan and the laws of Cnut', *English Historical Review* LXIII (1948), 433–52.

—— 'The interpretation of The Seafarer', in *The Early Cultures of North-West Europe (H. M. Chadwick Memorial Studies)*, ed. C. Fox and B. Dickins (Cambridge, 1950), pp. 261–72.

—— 'The dealings of the kings of England with Northumbria in the tenth and eleventh centuries', in *The Anglo-Saxons: Studies in some aspects of their History and Culture, presented to Bruce Dickins*, ed. P. Clemoes (London, 1959), pp. 76–9.

—— 'Wulfstan at York', in *Medieval and Linguistic Studies in honor of Francis Peabody Magoun*, ed. J. B. Bessinger and R. P. Creed (London, 1965), pp. 214–31.

—— 'The prose of Alfred's reign', in *Continuations and Beginnings*, ed. E. G. Stanley (London, 1966), pp. 96–7.

—— 'The pre-Viking age church in East Anglia', *Anglo-Saxon England* I (1972), 1–22.

—— ed., *English Historical Documents c. 500–1042*, 2nd edn (London, 1979).

—— *History, Law and Literature in Tenth to Eleventh Century England* (London, 1981); collected essays, reprinted photolithographically retaining original pagination.

Whiting B. J., 'The Rime of King William', in *Philologica: The Malone Anniversary Studies*, ed. T. A. Kirby and H. B. Woolf (Baltimore, 1949), pp. 89–96.

Wightman, W. E., 'The palatine earldom of William fitz Osborn in Gloucestershire and Worcestershire (1066–1071)', *English Historical Review* LXXVII (1962), 6–17.

—— *The Lacy Family in England and Normandy, 1066–1194* (Oxford, 1966).

William of Jumièges, *Gesta Normannorum Ducum*, ed. E. M. C. van Houts (Oxford, 1992–5).

William of Malmesbury, *The Early History of Glastonbury*, ed. J. Scott (Woodbridge, 1981).

—— *De Gestis Pontificum Anglorum*, ed. N. E. S. A. Hamilton, Rolls Series LII (London, 1870).

—— *De Gestis Regum Anglorum*, ed. W. Stubbs, Rolls Series XC (London, 1887–9); transl, J. A. Giles, *William of Malmesbury, Chronicle of the Kings of England* (London, 1876).

—— *The Historia Novella*, ed. K. R. Potter (London, 1955).

—— *Vita Wulfstani*, ed. R. R. Darlington, Camden, 3rd Series XL (1928); transl. J. H. F. Peile, *Life of St Wulfstan, bishop of Worcester* (Oxford, 1934).

Williams, A., '*Princeps Merciorum gentis*: the family, career and connections of Ælfhere, ealdorman of Mercia, 956–983', *Anglo-Saxon England* X (1982), 143–72.

Williams, A. *et al.*, *A Biographical Dictionary of Dark Age Britain: England, Scotland and Wales c. 500–1050* (London, 1991).

Williams, G. H., *The Norman Anonymous of 1100 AD* (Cambridge, Mass., 1951).

Williams, J. H. *et al.*, *Middle Saxon Palaces at Northampton* (Northampton, 1985).

Williamson, E. W., ed., *The Letters of Osbert of Clare* (Oxford, 1929).

Wilson, D. M., *Anglo-Saxon Ornamental Metalwork 700–1100 in the British Museum* (London, 1964).

—— *The Bayeux Tapstry* (London, 1985).

Wormald, F., *English Kalendars before AD 1100*, Henry Bradshaw Society LXXII (London, 1934).

Wormald, P., 'The uses of literacy in Anglo-Saxon England and its neighbours', *Transactions of the Royal Historical Society*, 5th Series XXVII (1977), 95–1114.

—— 'Bede, the Bretwalds and the origins of the gens Anglorum', in *Ideal and Reality in Frankish and Anglo-Saxon Society*, ed. P. Wormald *et al.* (Oxford, 1983), pp. 99–129.

—— 'Engla Lond: the making of an allegiance', *The Journal of Historical Sociology* VII (1994), 1–24.

Wrenn, C. L., 'A saga of the Anglo-Saxons', *History* XXV (1940), 208–15.

Wright, C. E., *The Cultivation of Saga in Anglo-Saxon England* (Edinburgh, 1939).

Wright, J., *The English Dialect Dictionary* (London, 1898–1905).

Wulfstan, *Life of St Æthelwold*, ed. M. Lapidge and M. Winterbottom (Oxford, 1991).

Yorke, B. A. E., 'The vocabulary of Anglo-Saxon overlordship', *Anglo-Saxon Studies in Archaeology and History* II (1981), 171–200.

—— 'The foundation of the Old Minster and the state of Winchester in the seventh and eighth centuries', *Proceedings of the Hampshire Field Club & Archaeological Society* XXXVIII (1982), 75–84.

—— 'Joint kingship in Kent *c.* 560 to 785', *Archaeologia Cantiana* XCIX (1983), 1–19.

—— ed., *Bishop Æthelwold, his Career and Influence* (Woodbridge, 1988).

—— 'The Jutes of Hampshire and Wight and the origins of Wessex', in *The Origins of Anglo-Saxon Kingdoms*, ed. S. Bassett (Leicester, 1989), pp. 84–96.

Young, C. J., *Excavations at Carisbrooke Castle* (London, forthcoming).

Young, C. R., *The Royal Forests of Medieval England* (Leicester, 1979).

Zarneki, G. *et al.*, English Romanesque Art, *1066–1200* (London, 1984).

INDEX

Entries are strictly alphabetical; thus Ælfgar, bishop, precedes, Ælfgar, ealdorman, etc. Æ is treated as Ae. References are to [unadjusted] dates and MSS, with page numbers added where the annal is particularly lengthy. County names and divisions are the traditional ones.

925 A F, 943 A, 955 A, 957 D, 958 A, 963 E, 977 C, 978 E, 988
Dunwich (Suffolk), 798 F; bishops of, see also Ælfhun, Tidfrith
Durham, 1056 D, 1068 D, 1072, 1075 D, 1087 (p. 225); bishops of, see also Æthelric, Æthelwine, Ranulf, Walcher, William
Dyfed (South Wales), 918 A
Dykes, The (Cambridgeshire), 905 A (p. 94, note 1)
Dyrham (Gloucestershire), 577

Eadbald, bishop of London, 794
Eadbald, king of Kent, 616, 633 E, 639 E, 640 A, 694 A
Eadberht, ealdorman, 656 E (p. 32)
Eadberht, ealdorman, 819
Eadberht, king of Kent, 725, 748
Eadberht, king of Northumbria, son of Eata, 737 E, 738, 757 E, 768
Eadberht, Præn, king of Kent, 794, 796
Eadburh, daughter of Offa king of Mercia, wife of Beorhtric king of Wessex, 787, 836 A
Eadgyfu, abbess of Leominster, 1046 C
Eadhed, bishop of Lindsey, 678 E
Eadhelm, abbot, 952 D (p. 113, note 12)
Eadnoth I, bishop of Dorchester, 1012, 1016
Eadnoth II, bishop of Dorchester, 1046 E (p. 171), 1049 C (p. 171), 1050 D (p. 170)
Eadnoth, the staller, 1067 D (p. 203)
Eadred, king of England, 946, 947 D, 948 D, 952 D, 954 D, 955, 956 B C, 971 B, 1067 D (p. 202)
Eadred (for Cuthred), 648 E (p. 28, note 1)
Eadric (?'the Wild'), prince, 1067 D (p. 201, note 13)
Eadric Streona, ealdorman of Mercia, 1007, 1009, 1012, 1015, 1016, 1017
Eadsige, archbishop of Canterbury, 1038 E, 1040 A, 1042 E, 1043 C E, 1044 C, 1046-7 E, 1048 C, 1050 A C, 1051 D
Eadsige, king's reeve, 1001 A
Eadulf's Ness (The Naze, Essex), 1049 C, 1050 D (p. 169, note 12), 1052 E (p. 181)
Eadwig, king of England, 955, 958 D, 959

Eadwig, son of Æthelred II, 1017
Eadwig, 'the ceorls' king', 1017 D E (p. 154, note 6)
Eadwig, thegn, brother of Æfic, 1010
Eadwold, king's thegn, 905
Eadwold, son of Acca, 905
Eadwulf of Bamburgh, 924 A, 926 D
Eadwulf, earl of Northumbria, 1041 C
Eadwulf, king's thegn in Sussex, 897
Eafa the West Saxon, Pref. A, 855
Ealdberht, West Saxon ætheling, 722, 725
Ealdberht, see also Aldberht
Ealdgyth, widow of Siferth, 1015 E
Ealdred, see also Aldred
Ealdwine, bishop of Lichfield, 731 E
Ealdwulf, abbot of Peterborough, bishop of Worcester, archbishop of York, 963 E, 992 E F, 1002 E
Ealdwulf, son of Bosa, Northumbrian high-reeve, 778 E
Ealhheard, bishop of Dorchester, 897
Ealhhere, Kentish ealdorman, 851, 852 E, 853
Ealhhun, bishop of Worcester, 852 E
Ealhmund, bishop of Hexham, 766 E, 780
Ealhmund, king in Kent, father of Egbert king of Wessex, Pref. A, 784 A F, 855 A
Ealhmund, Peterborough signatory, 656 E (p. 32)
Ealhstan, bishop of Sherborne, 823, 845, 867
Ealhswith, wife of King Alfred, 902 C, 903, 905 A D
Eamont (Westmorland), 926 D
Eanbald I, archbishop of York, 779, 780, 791, 795, 796 E
Eanbald II, archbishop of York, 796 E, 797 E
Eanberht, bishop of Hexham, 806 E
Eanflæd, daughter of Edwin, king of Northumbria, 626
Eanfrith, king of Bernicia, 617 E, 634 E
Eanwulf, ealdorman of Somerset, 845 (p. 64, note 6)
Eanwulf, grandfather of Offa king of Mercia, 755 A (p. 50)
Eardwulf, king of Northumbria, 795, 806 E

Æthelwold, Nun; bishops of, see also Selsey; ealdorman of, see also Edwin
Swæfdæg, ancestor of Ælle, 560 A
Swæfheard, king of Kent, 692 E (p. 41, note 10)
Swanage (Dorset), 877
Sweden, 1025 E
Swein, earl, son of Earl Godwine, 1045 E, 1046 C E, 1047–8 E, 1049 C, 1050 C D, 1051 C, 1052 C D
Swein Estrithson, king of Denmark, 1046 D, 1048 D, 1068 D, 1069–70 E, 1075 E, 1076 D E, 1077 E, 1085
Swein Forkbeard, king of Denmark, 994 E F, 1003–4 E F, 1013–14 E
Swifneh, see also Suibhne
Swineshead (Lincolnshire), 675 E, 777 E
Swithin, St, bishop of Winchester, 861 F
Swithwulf, bishop of Rochester, 897 A
Syria, 47

Tadcaster (Yorkshire), 1066 C (p. 197)
Tætwa, ancestor of Æthelwulf, 855 A
Tamar river (Cornwall, Devon), 997 E
Tamworth (Staffordshire), 913 C D, 918 C, 922 A, 925 D, 943 D
Tanshelf (Yorkshire), 947 D
Tatwine, archbishop of Canterbury, 731, 734, 995 F
Taunton (Somerset), 722
Tavistock (Devon), 997 E
Taw river (Devon), 1068 D
Teignton, see also Kingsteignton
Telesphorus, pope, 134 E
Tempsford (Bedfordshire), 921 A, 1010 E
Tettenhall (Staffordshire), 909 D, 910 C
Thame (Oxfordshire), 971 C
Thames river, 60 BC, 823, 851 E, 871, 879, 892 E, 893–94 A, 905, 999 E, 1006 E, 1009–10 E, 1013 E, 1016, 1023 D, 1036 E, 1048 E (p. 174), 1052 E, 1070 E, 1114 E
Thanet (Isle of, district of East Kent), 851 (p. 64, note 7), 865, 969 E, 980 C, 1046 E
Thelwall (Cheshire), 923 A
Theobald, abbot of Le Bec, archbishop of Canterbury, 1140 (p. 266)
Theobald, brother of King Æthelfrith of Northumbria, 603 E

Theobald, count of Blois and Chartres, nephew of Henry I, 1116
Theobald (for Theowulf), bishop of Worcester, 1114 H
Theodore, archbishop of Canterbury, 656 E (p. 33), 668, 670, 675 E, 680, 685 E, 690, 995 F p. 130)
Theodosius the Younger, Roman emperor, 423
Thetford (Norfolk), 870, 952 D, 1004, 1010; bishops of, see also Herbert Losinga, William
Thingfrith, father of Offa king of Mercia, 755 (p. 50)
Thomas I, archbishop of York, 1070 A, 1100
Thomas II, archbishop of York, 1108, 1114 E H
Thomas, St, apostle, 883 E
Thored, earl of Northumbria, 992 E
Thored, son of Gunnar, 966 E
Thorney (Cambridgeshire), 656 E (p. 31), 1049 C, 1050 D, 1066 E (p. 198), 1114 H, 1154; abbots of, see also Oswig, Robert
Thorney Island (Sussex), 1052 D (pp. 175–6)
Thorpe (Northamptonshire), 1114 H
Throckenholt (Cambridgeshire), Peterborough estate, 656 E (p. 30)
Thunor, 640 A
Thurcytel, abbot of Bedford, 971 C
Thurcytel, jarl of Bedford, 915 D, 918 A, 920 A
Thurcytel ('Mare's Head'), 1010 E (p. 140, note 7)
Thurcytel, son of Nafena, 1016 D E (pp. 148–9)
Thurferth, hold, 911 B C (p. 97, note 14)
Thurferth, jarl, 921 A (p. 102)
Thurkil, 1039 C
Thurkil, jarl in East Anglia, 1009 E (p. 139, notes 10, 12), 1012 E (p. 143, note 16), 1017, 1020 D, 1021, 1023 C
Thurkil, Danish jarl, 1068 D
Thurstan, abbot of Glastonbury, 1083 E
Thurstan, abbot of Pershore, 1087 (p. 222, note 3)
Thurstan, archbishop of York, 1114 E H, 1119–20, 1123, 1125
Tibba, St, 963 E (p. 117)
Tiberius, Roman emperor, 16

ACKNOWLEDGEMENTS

The editor and publishers wish to thank the following for permission to use the illustrations.

The British Museum and Sheffield City Museum, Frontispiece; The British Museum, Plates 1, 5–12; Durham Cathedral Dean and Chapter, Plate 13; English Heritage, Plate 2; Stuart Blaylock, Exeter Archaeology, Plate 18; Royal Commission on Historical Monuments (England), Plates 15, 17; Suffolk County Council Archaeological Unit, Plate 3; T. Middlemass, University of Durham, © the Department of Archaeology, Plate 4; Victoria & Albert Museum, Plate 14; York Castle Museum, Plate 16.